# Dictionary of Literary Biography

## Dictionary of Literary Biography Documentary Series

# Dictionary of Literary Biography Yearbooks

1980 edited by Karen L. Rood, Jean W. Ross, and Richard Ziegfeld (1981)

1981 edited by Karen L. Rood, Jean W. Ross, and Richard Ziegfeld (1982)

1982 edited by Richard Ziegfeld; associate editors: Jean W. Ross and Lynne C. Zeigler (1983)

1983 edited by Mary Bruccoli and Jean W. Ross; associate editor Richard Ziegfeld (1984)

1984 edited by Jean W. Ross (1985)

1985 edited by Jean W. Ross (1986)

1986 edited by J. M. Brook (1987)

1987 edited by J. M. Brook (1988)

1988 edited by J. M. Brook (1989)

1989 edited by J. M. Brook (1990)

1990 edited by James W. Hipp (1991)

1991 edited by James W. Hipp (1992)

1992 edited by James W. Hipp (1993)

1993 edited by James W. Hipp, contributing editor George Garrett (1994)

1994 edited by James W. Hipp, contributing editor George Garrett (1995)

1995 edited by James W. Hipp, contributing editor George Garrett (1996)

1996 edited by Samuel W. Bruce and L. Kay Webster, contributing editor George Garrett (1997)

1997 edited by Matthew J. Bruccoli and George Garrett, with the assistance of L. Kay Webster (1998)

1998 edited by Matthew J. Bruccoli, contributing editor George Garrett, with the assistance of D. W. Thomas (1999)

1999 edited by Matthew J. Bruccoli, contributing editor George Garrett, with the assistance of D. W. Thomas (2000)

2000 edited by Matthew J. Bruccoli, contributing editor George Garrett, with the assistance of George Parker Anderson (2001)

2001 edited by Matthew J. Bruccoli, contributing editor George Garrett, with the assistance of George Parker Anderson (2002)

2002 edited by Matthew J. Bruccoli and George Garrett; George Parker Anderson, Assistant Editor (2003)

# Concise Series

**Concise Dictionary of American Literary Biography,** 7 volumes (1988–1999): *The New Consciousness, 1941–1968; Colonization to the American Renaissance, 1640–1865; Realism, Naturalism, and Local Color, 1865–1917; The Twenties, 1917–1929; The Age of Maturity, 1929–1941; Broadening Views, 1968–1988; Supplement: Modern Writers, 1900–1998.*

**Concise Dictionary of British Literary Biography,** 8 volumes (1991–1992): *Writers of the Middle Ages and Renaissance Before 1660; Writers of the Restoration and Eighteenth Century, 1660–1789; Writers of the Romantic Period, 1789–1832; Victorian Writers, 1832–1890; Late-Victorian and Edwardian Writers, 1890–1914; Modern Writers, 1914–1945; Writers After World War II, 1945–1960; Contemporary Writers, 1960 to Present.*

**Concise Dictionary of World Literary Biography,** 4 volumes (1999–2000): *Ancient Greek and Roman Writers; German Writers; African, Caribbean, and Latin American Writers; South Slavic and Eastern European Writers.*

Dictionary of Literary Biography® • Volume Two Hundred Eighty-Six

# Castilian Writers,
# 1400–1500

Dictionary of Literary Biography® • Volume Two Hundred Eighty-Six

# Castilian Writers, 1400–1500

Edited by
Frank A. Domínguez
*University of North Carolina at Chapel Hill*
and
George D. Greenia
*College of William and Mary*

A Bruccoli Clark Layman Book

GALE®

THOMSON
GALE

Detroit • New York • San Diego • San Francisco • Cleveland • New Haven, Conn. • Waterville, Maine • London • Munich

## THOMSON
### GALE

Dictionary of Literary Biography
Volume 286: Castilian Writers, 1400–1500
Frank A. Domínguez
George D. Greenia

**Advisory Board**
John Baker
William Cagle
Patrick O'Connor
George Garrett
Trudier Harris
Alvin Kernan
Kenny J. Williams

**Editorial Directors**
Matthew J. Bruccoli and Richard Layman

© 2004 by Gale. Gale is an imprint of The Gale Group, Inc., a division of Thomson Learning, Inc.

Gale and Design™ and Thomson Learning™ are trademarks used herein under license.

*For more information, contact*
The Gale Group, Inc.
27500 Drake Rd.
Farmington Hills, MI 48331-3535
Or you can visit our Internet site at
http://www.gale.com

**LIBRARY OF CONGRESS CATALOGING-IN-PUBLICATION DATA**

Castilian writers, 1400–1500 / edited by Frank A. Domínguez and George D. Greenia.
    p. cm. — (Dictionary of literary biography ; v. 286)
"A Bruccoli Clark Layman book."
Includes bibliographical references and index.
        ISBN 0-7876-6823-0 (hardcover)
        1. Spanish literature—To 1500—Bio-bibliography—Dictionaries.
        2. Authors, Spanish—To 1500—Biography—Dictionaries.
        I. Domínguez, Frank, 1945– II. Greenia, George D. III. Gale Group.
        IV. Series.

PQ6058.C37 2003
860.9'002—dc22                                    2003014965

Printed in the United States of America
10 9 8 7 6 5 4 3 2 1

*To Charles F. Fraker for his guidance and mentoring,
and to both Charles and Doris for their friendship
and support over the years*

# Contents

# Plan of the Series

The advisory board, the editors, and the publisher of the *Dictionary of Literary Biography* are joined in endorsing Mark Twain's declaration. The literature of a nation provides an inexhaustible resource of permanent worth. Our purpose is to make literature and its creators better understood and more accessible to students and the reading public, while satisfying the needs of teachers and researchers.

To meet these requirements, *literary biography* has been construed in terms of the author's achievement. The most important thing about a writer is his writing. Accordingly, the entries in *DLB* are career biographies, tracing the development of the author's canon and the evolution of his reputation.

The purpose of *DLB* is not only to provide reliable information in a usable format but also to place the figures in the larger perspective of literary history and to offer appraisals of their accomplishments by qualified scholars.

The publication plan for *DLB* resulted from two years of preparation. The project was proposed to Bruccoli Clark by Frederick G. Ruffner, president of the Gale Research Company, in November 1975. After specimen entries were prepared and typeset, an advisory board was formed to refine the entry format and develop the series rationale. In meetings held during 1976, the publisher, series editors, and advisory board approved the scheme for a comprehensive biographical dictionary of persons who contributed to literature. Editorial work on the first volume began in January 1977, and it was published in 1978. In order to make *DLB* more than a dictionary and to compile volumes that individually have claim to status as literary history, it was decided to organize volumes by topic, period, or

genre. Each of these freestanding volumes provides a biographical-bibliographical guide and overview for a particular area of literature. We are convinced that this organization—as opposed to a single alphabet method— constitutes a valuable innovation in the presentation of reference material. The volume plan necessarily requires many decisions for the placement and treatment of authors. Certain figures will be included in separate volumes, but with different entries emphasizing the aspect of his career appropriate to each volume. Ernest Hemingway, for example, is represented in *American Writers in Paris, 1920–1939* by an entry focusing on his expatriate apprenticeship; he is also in *American Novelists, 1910–1945* with an entry surveying his entire career, as well as in *American Short-Story Writers, 1910–1945, Second Series* with an entry concentrating on his short fiction. Each volume includes a cumulative index of the subject authors and articles.

Since 1981 the series has been further augmented by the *DLB Yearbooks,* which update published entries, add new entries to keep the *DLB* current with contemporary activity, and provide articles on literary history. There have also been nineteen *DLB Documentary Series* volumes, which provide illustrations, facsimiles, and biographical and critical source materials for figures, works, or groups judged to have particular interest for students. In 1999 the *Documentary Series* was incorporated into the *DLB* volume numbering system beginning with *DLB 210: Ernest Hemingway.*

We define literature as the *intellectual commerce of a nation:* not merely as belles lettres but as that ample and complex process by which ideas are generated, shaped, and transmitted. *DLB* entries are not limited to "creative writers" but extend to other figures who in their time and in their way influenced the mind of a people. Thus the series encompasses historians, journalists, publishers, book collectors, and screenwriters. By this means readers of *DLB* may be aided to perceive literature not as cult scripture in the keeping of intellectual high priests but firmly positioned at the center of a nation's life.

*DLB* includes the major writers appropriate to each volume and those standing in the ranks behind them. Scholarly and critical counsel has been sought in deciding which minor figures to include and how full their entries should be. Wherever possible, useful references are made to figures who do not warrant separate entries.

Each *DLB* volume has an expert volume editor responsible for planning the volume, selecting the figures for inclusion, and assigning the entries. Volume editors are also responsible for preparing, where appropriate, appendices surveying the major periodicals and literary and intellectual movements for their volumes, as well as lists of further readings. Work on the series as a whole is coordinated at the Bruccoli Clark Layman editorial center in Columbia, South Carolina, where the editorial staff is responsible for accuracy and utility of the published volumes.

One feature that distinguishes *DLB* is the illustration policy–its concern with the iconography of literature. Just as an author is influenced by his surroundings, so is the reader's understanding of the author enhanced by a knowledge of his environment. Therefore *DLB* volumes include not only drawings, paintings, and photographs of authors, often depicting them at various stages in their careers, but also illustrations of their families and places where they lived. Title pages are regularly reproduced in facsimile along with dust jackets for modern authors. The dust jackets are a special feature of *DLB* because they often document better than anything else the way in which an author's work was perceived in its own time. Specimens of the writers' manuscripts and letters are included when feasible.

Samuel Johnson rightly decreed that "The chief glory of every people arises from its authors." The purpose of the *Dictionary of Literary Biography* is to compile literary history in the surest way available to us–by accurate and comprehensive treatment of the lives and work of those who contributed to it.

The *DLB* Advisory Board

# Introduction

The fifteenth century was a turbulent time in Castile. Rule of the kingdom, though ostensibly in the hands of the king, was shared with powerful noble clans, the Church, and the military Orders of Santiago, Calatrava, and Alcántara, each of which had its own agenda. Exacerbating the problem, several monarchs were placed on the throne in their minority, under the control of sometimes rapacious regents and facing interference from neighboring kingdoms. And in addition to all of these issues there loomed the question of religious orthodoxy, which became increasingly important in the latter half of the century.

The forces at work in the kingdom had their roots in the previous century. The Hundred Years' War (1337-1453) between the French and English had included a minor skirmish in Castile that ended in 1369 when Enrique de Trastámara, bastard half brother of King Pedro I, murdered the latter at Montiel, took over the throne as Enrique II with the aid of English troops, and established the Trastamaran dynasty that lasted until the early sixteenth century. To secure his reign, Enrique promoted a largely new aristocracy to positions of power. Known as "el de las Mercedes" (the Bestower of Honors) to those who benefited from his regime and as "el Fraticida" (the Fratricide) to those who were crushed by it, he began the practice of doling out parts of the royal patrimony of lands and sources of income to appease the noble faction that supported him. In the late fourteenth and fifteenth centuries the heads of these noble houses received huge estates (particularly in the south) and hereditary titles.

The multiplication in Castile of titles of nobility in the French manner stemmed from these grants of the Trastamarans, as did the flowering of independent noble courts and of a courtly culture based on a concept of chivalry that bore a French imprint. Nobles and commoners under the mid to late Trastamaran rulers—mainly Juan II, Enrique IV, and Isabel I (better known to English speakers as Isabella)—promoted the creation of vernacular texts that fused this new imprint onto traditional Castilian forms. These works included chivalric romance novels and sentimental narratives; nonfictional writings on chivalry by Diego de Valera, Alfonso de Cartagena, and, later in the century, Alfonso de Palencia; and many translations of chivalric treatises.

Enrique III, known as "el Doliente" (the Ailing), took the throne in 1390 at age eleven and died at eighteen without having presided over a court that could claim much literary attainment. He was succeeded by Juan II, who created a splendid court at which lofty poetry and witty doggerel coexisted in promiscuous abundance. Like Alfonso of Aragon, "el Magnánimo" (the Magnanimous), who ruled from 1416 to 1458 and transferred his court (if not his family) to his sumptuous acquisitions in the heart of cultured Naples, Juan made Iberian court life among the most delightfully refined—and, at times, frivolous—in Europe. Juan also proved that alliances with power could be fatal: Álvaro de Luna, constable of Castile, royal confidant, and virtual dictator of Juan's affairs of state, suffered a sudden repudiation at the whim of his easily swayed sovereign that led to his summary execution in 1454. Despite its trappings of legal procedure and the approval of Luna's enemies, the execution shocked the nation and made it more wary and cynical.

Two literary figures tower over the rest in the reign of Juan II. Juan de Mena introduced a new verse form, *arte mayor,* for the vernacular epic in his *Laberinto de Fortuna* (Labyrinth of Fortune, 1444), while Íñigo López de Mendoza, Marqués de Santillana, was the first writer of sonnets in the Castilian language. Of the two innovations, only the sonnet survived to be practiced in later centuries—though often without knowledge of Santillana's contributions to the form. Though now best known for his *serranillas* (pastoral songs), rather than for his sonnets, and for the *Comedieta de Ponza* (Little Comedy of Ponza, circa 1436), Santillana also wrote several works attacking Luna. In *Doctrinal de privados* (Rule Book for Privy Councillors, after 1453), for example, Luna repents of his covetousness and pride before he climbs to the execution block. Mena, on the other hand, dedicated part of *Laberinto de Fortuna* to praise of the constable, who is the exemplary victor over Fortune in the poem.

The lives of important people who lived under the Trastamaran kings shaped the work of Fernán Pérez de Guzmán, Santillana's uncle and the great-grandfather of the poet Garcilaso de la Vega. His acquaintance with their antics and personality traits is reflected in his *Coplas de vicios e virtudes* (Verses on Vices and Virtues, before 1452) and in the biographies of his *Loores de claros varones de España* (Praises of the Famous Men of Spain, before 1452). Another important author, Enrique de Villena, prepared the way for philological humanism to enter Castile and wrote commentaries that promoted the reading of the classics in translation.

Enrique IV, who ruled from 1454 to 1474, suffered even more than his predecessor from the cajoling of competing factions of "advisers" and also from his own taste for the exotic. If not homosexual, Enrique was, at least, emotionally susceptible to handsome male companions (most damningly, in the eyes of his subjects, Moorish ones) and disinclined to consort with his bride, Juana de Portugal–or so his successors, Isabel and Fernando (Ferdinand), had him painted by the historians they commissioned to chronicle his reign.

Rumor had it that a favorite of Enrique's court, Beltrán de la Cueva, flaunted his power over the royal family by impregnating the queen in his monarch's stead. A daughter was born and given her mother's name, Juana, but gossips called her "la Beltraneja" (Beltrán's daughter) both to underscore her suspected illegitimacy and to insinuate that the true right of succession belonged to Enrique's half sister, Isabel. The conflicts that characterized the reigns of the three last Trastamaran monarchs are remembered in the *Coplas por la muerte de su padre* (Stanzas upon the Death of His Father, circa 1476–1479) of Gómez Manrique's nephew, Jorge Manrique.

Isabel boldly arranged her own marriage to Crown Prince Fernando of Aragon, whom she had never met, without seeking Enrique's approval or even informing him of her plans. In 1469, in an episode that one might find in the adventuresome chivalric novels popular at the time, she slipped away from the house arrest in Segovia ordered by Enrique and, with the help of the poet Gómez Manrique, met Fernando in Valladolid for an impromptu but surprisingly public wedding night: shortly after the newlyweds retired to the bridal chamber, the bloodied bedsheets were brought out and unfurled before enough witnesses to insure the irreversibility of the marriage, no matter how much the king or his courtiers might protest. The fait accompli left Enrique with little choice but to recognize both her powerful new alliance and her faction's claim to the throne of Castile.

Isabel secured the throne on Enrique's death in 1474; after she won the five-year dynastic war that followed, she had her chroniclers dub him "el Impotente" (the Impotent). She and Fernando, who had in the meantime succeeded to the throne of Aragon, then launched a program of cultural coalescence that included political unification, military suppression of the Beltraneja faction and the powerful nobles who supported it, and conquest of the last remaining Muslim stronghold in Granada. The notion that racial identity was correlated with moral purity led many to question whether Spaniards of Jewish or Hispano-Arab ancestry could ever be true Christians like those of unmixed blood. That notion affected every level of society and helped generate the Inquisition, a social as well as religious and political institution that the majority of Spanish citizens supported. Isabel and Fernando sought racial and religious purification through inquisitorial pursuit of *converso* (Jewish convert to Christianity) backsliders and, finally, through the expulsion of all remaining Jews in 1492. The struggle stamped a unique character on the literary products of the era, many of which were written by descendants of *conversos* or by those who were anxious to define themselves in opposition to them.

A special group of texts from this period combines vernacular Spanish with a Moorish or Hebrew writing system–that is, they were written in Arabic or Hebrew characters by minorities who spoke Castilian but had retained their original forms of literacy. These works are known as *aljamiado* literature. A few examples of such hybrid texts exist from as early as the tenth century, but even fourteenth- and fifteenth-century *aljamiado* texts are not plentiful. They indicate the change in the relations of the people of the three faiths as the Reconquest of Spain from the Muslims pushed southward to its completion with the taking of Granada in 1492.

In Spain, as elsewhere in Europe, the fifteenth century brought forth an acceleration in the composition of literary works. This phenomenon sprang in part from an evolving courtly culture that appreciated witty and refined expression in the salon, in cultivated song lyrics, in texts for theatrical recitation at genteel gatherings, and in a sort of domestic readers' theater that spread rapidly down through the families of lesser nobles to the increasingly literate middle class. The dissemination of these texts was made possible by the complementary forces of increased lay literacy and the explosion of printed materials in Spain.

Devotional literature–doctrinal and Marian works, sermons, hagiography, exempla, and encyclopedias–flourished in this period, and great ecclesiastical centers such as the bishops' extended households and clerical circles in Santiago, Barcelona, and, above all, in Toledo under Archbishop Alfonso Carrillo, kept learning and intellectual exploration alive in the absence of a vigorous university life. With the strengthening of the universities in Iberia, learned–and frequently quite progressive–centers of ecclesiastical study grew into powerful centers of literary culture by the end of the fifteenth century. Fernando de Rojas composed the greatest work of this period, the immortal *Celestina,* around 1495, when he was in his early twenties and a student at the University of Salamanca; and Antonio de Nebrija, the foremost philologist and lexicographer of the period, taught there and at Alcalá.

The cultural elites who enjoyed and composed literary works were accustomed to reading, hearing, and writing in various dialects. Authors in the royal court centers of the major kingdoms of Iberia–Lisbon in Portugal and Barcelona in Aragon, but a dozen sites in the dominant kingdoms of Castile and León–happily used Castilian, Galician, Catalan, and Provençal, as dictated by their audiences' tastes and the genre of a given composition. The fifteenth century brought a decisive move toward favoring Castilian as the language of a unified Spain, especially under the "Catholic Monarchs" Isabel and Fernando, who ruled Castile and Aragon jointly from Isabel's accession until her death in 1504. Their patronage of the nascent printing industry helped move Spanish vernacular literature from its medieval linguistic instability to its modern unity.

All presumptions of "social unity" are, of course, modern tastes and aesthetic theories projected back in time. The rise of Spain as a fully European nation-state in the nineteenth century and the consolidation of authority in the Academia Real de la Lengua Española (Royal Academy of the Spanish Language), founded in 1713, which sought to "protect and add luster" to Castilian as the national language, helped confirm a canon of works in the by then triumphant dialect of central Spain. Most literary historians decry the efforts of the Francisco Franco dictatorship between 1939 and 1973 to suppress Galician and Catalan as regional tongues with robust literary traditions, and for no period does this silencing of history falsify the literary record more than for the Middle Ages. The scholar Keith Whinnom's warning in 1967 that in the medieval period "literature in the vernacular was literature for the illiterate" should be qualified to recognize the surging rates of lay literacy in the vernacular, especially in the fifteenth century when *cancionero* (songbook or anthology) poetry and the popular sentimental and chivalric novels achieved wide circulation.

While laymen throughout Iberia slipped in and out of the various dialects of their neighboring communities, one must also recognize the potency of Latin literature in medieval Spain. It exerted the most influence on clerical authors of the first two centuries of this period, but there are still towering clerical figures at the end of the fifteenth century, such as Palencia and Nebrija, who worked mostly in Latin. Translations of classical Latin works include Virgil's *Aeneid,* translated by Villena in 1427–1428; various treatises of Cicero, translated by Alfonso de Cartagena; and an account of the Trojan War, translated by Mena circa 1442. Interest in tales of the imagined past led to the production of chivalric romances and treatises, to the translation of the popular short romance narratives *Paris and Viana* and *Flores and Blancaflor,* and to the production of the most important romance novel in Spanish, Garci Rodríguez de Montalvo's *Amadís de Gaula* (1508).

The fifteenth century also brought the birth of a new genre in medieval Spain that was routinely produced in Castilian but had regular contributors–and, presumably, audiences–in Portuguese in the west and in Catalan in the east: the sentimental novel or sentimental romance. (These names have been called into question from the time the genre was first defined in the early 1980s. The English term *novel* makes one think of dynamic characters, whereas those in these works are static; *romance* has the disadvantage of inviting confusion with the same term in Spanish, which means either a ballad or a work written in the vernacular, rather than in Latin.) These short narratives focus on the emotional states of their mournful and frustrated lovers and often employ patches of lyric poetry to underscore their heartfelt first-person accounts. Although they share a good deal of the knightly exploits of earlier medieval fiction in the style of Arthurian and French tales and something of the moral set pieces of the exemplum tradition (short stories with decisive concluding morals), the sentimental novels of Spain's fifteenth century lean more toward stories of distressed lovers from classical antiquity, such as Ovid's *Heroides;* toward medieval Christian autobiographies, such as St. Augustine's *Confessiones* (Confessions, 397–401), Boethius's *De Consolatione Philosophiae* (The Consolation of Philosophy, circa 524), and Peter Abelard's *Historia Calamitatum Meum* (Story of My Misfortunes, circa 1133) and his letters to and from Heloïse; and, finally, toward Giovanni Boccaccio's more recent Italian contribution, *Elegia di Madonna Fiammetta* (Elegy of Milady Fiammetta, 1343–1344), in which a married woman recounts her seduction and abandonment by a man other than her husband.

Other features of the sentimental genre include the use of tenderly worded letters sent by characters to one another to tell parts of the story or to explore the characters' feelings, opposition from male figures (a disapproving king, a cruel father, or a rival in love), and a sad conclusion that sometimes includes the deaths of one or both lovers. The authors of these works set themselves apart by their obvious awareness that they are working within an evolving literary tradition: they adopt selected features from their predecessors and supply innovations of their own, such as the artful and deliberate confusions among the actual author, the fictional narrator, and the protagonist of the story—they seem to enjoy teasing their audiences with the possibility that their novels represent thinly veiled versions of their own unhappy affairs of the heart. The enormous popularity of these works was propelled in good measure by their prompt diffusion through the introduction of printing in Spain. The history of the sentimental novel stretches well into the first half of the sixteenth century with another dozen titles.

The sentimental novel is thought to have been launched around 1440 by Juan Rodríguez de Padrón's *El siervo libre de amor*. The form already shows its self-aware playfulness in Rodríguez de Padrón's title, which might mean "The Willing Servant of Love" or "The Servant Free from Love." The tale ends with a renunciation of love exacted by an allegorical figure, Syndéresis (in medieval philosophy, the innate principle in the moral consciousness), who forces the author-protagonist to reflect on his woeful state by reciting its history—thereby looping the tale back to its beginning and effecting a catharsis of negative emotions by putting their origin into words: the narrative is, thus, the protagonist's cure. Rodríguez de Padrón's sole known work was followed in short order by an imitation by Dom Pedro, constable of Portugal, who seems to have been between sixteen and twenty years old when his first, and now lost, version of the *Sátira de infelice e felice vida* (Satire of Unhappy and Happy Life) was composed in Portuguese between 1445 and 1449. Dying in his twenties on the far side of the Iberian Peninsula as the fleetingly proclaimed "king of the Catalans," Pedro did not live to see his work translated into Castilian sometime between 1450 and 1453. The next entry, the anonymous *Triste deleytación* (Sad Delight), was composed in Catalonia and survives in a unique Castilian-language manuscript dating from around 1458 to 1470. It, too, is clearly indebted to Rodríguez de Padrón's inaugural effort.

Two subsequent authors came to dominate the genre of the sentimental novel. Juan de Flores was a Castilian nobleman who was chronicler to Fernando and Isabel. His principal works are *Grisel y Mirabella* (1474–1475?), in which the protagonists debate the responsibilities of men versus women in illicit affairs, and *Grimalte y Gradisa* (1477?), which is based on Boccaccio's *Elegia di Madonna Fiammetta* but does not have a female narrator. Both novels toy with the conventions of the separation of the real world from the world of fictional events. *Grisel y Mirabella* introduces a legendary figure from the Trojan War who debates a real-life poet from Flores's circle; the poet announces his antifeminist views, only to be physically ripped apart by the infuriated ladies in the audience. In *Grimalte y Gradisa* a young

damsel demands that her suitor come up with a tale even more plaintive than *Elegia di Madonna Fiammetta*. The second author of central importance, Diego de San Pedro, is significant, above all, for his masterpiece *Cárcel de amor* (Prison of Love, 1492), which became a landmark in the genre, a best-seller, and the starting point for a continuation by Nicolás Núñez four years later. In this delicate and highly stylized novel Leriano is the prisoner of love, suffering for the beautiful but indifferent Laureola. Among the allegorical characters who populate the work, such as Reason, Memory, and Will, a mysterious "Auctor" (author), who may be San Pedro himself, is the courier of their love letters and written speeches, which are transcribed in full. Leriano commits himself to intervene on behalf of his beloved in everything from siege warfare to personal combat, but she still disdains him; he dies of self-imposed hunger, his last taste of life occurring, in a scene reminiscent of the Last Supper, when he drinks from a cup containing the dissolved remnants of their shredded correspondence. The greatest success story of the genre, the *Cárcel de amor* went through more than twenty-five printings in Spain and some twenty translations abroad, earned the scorn of the Inquisition, and had a marked impact on *Celestina* in its own decade and on Miguel de Cervantes Saavedra's *El ingenioso hidalgo Don Quijote de la Mancha* (1605, 1615) more than a century later.

Travel literature in the modern sense began in the fifteenth century with two important narratives that do not involve religious pilgrimages. The *Embajada a Tamorlán* (Embassy to Tamerlane) records Ruy González Clavijo's travels to and from Samarqand via Constantinople, Trebizond, and Tehran between 1403 and 1406. *Andanças e viajes de Pero Tafur por diversas partes del mundo avidos* (Travels and Voyages Undertaken by Pero Tafur through Diverse Parts of the World) relates the nobleman Pero Tafur's travels from Sanlúcar de Barrameda to Italy, Switzerland, France, Germany, Rhodes, Cyprus, Egypt, and Judea. These travel narratives show that Castile was increasing its firsthand geographical knowledge and slowly opening to the larger world.

Among the poetic currents of the fifteenth century in Spain, two strands, one broadly popular and the other courtly, stand out for their abundant productivity, artistic accomplishment, and enduring presence on the Spanish literary scene—in the case of the popular form, well into the twentieth century both within Spain and in communities of Spaniards around the globe. This form comprises the vast corpus of *romances,* ballads that originated much earlier in the Middle Ages; the oldest derive from oral epic poems of the twelfth and thirteenth centuries. The courtly current is recorded in more than seven hundred *cancioneros;* the bulk of this poetic production created during the Trastamaran dynasty appears in the pages of these works. The contents of all the *cancioneros* have been catalogued by Brian Dutton and Jineen Krogstad in the seven-volume *El cancionero castellano del siglo XV: 1360–1520* (The Castilian Songbook of the Fifteenth Century: 1360–1520, 1990–1991). Three of these works stand out for their comprehensiveness: the *Cancionero de Baena* reflects the tastes of the court of Juan II, the *Cancionero de Estúñiga* that of the Trastamaran courts of Alfonso V and Ferrante I in Naples, and the printed *Cancionero general recopilado por Hernando del Castillo* (1511) that of the court of Isabel I.

The genteel posturing of the sentimental lyrics collected in the *cancioneros* was mocked by a rollicking, subversive, underground "poetry of protest," much of which was probably written by some of the same poets. It includes such witty and mercilessly naughty works as the *Coplas de la panadera* (Stanzas of the Baker Girl), which mocks noble participation in the Battle of Olmedo in 1445; the *Coplas del Provincial* (Stanzas of the Provincial, 1465–1466); and the rippingly obscene *Carajicomedia* (Cockeyed Comedy, 1502–1503?). Many works in this parodic genre were undoubtedly destroyed by censors.

Except for the occasional text preserved mostly by accident, works by women are rare in this period. Two women authors are included in this volume. Teresa de Cartagena was born into a powerful family of Jewish heritage in Burgos and fell deaf in early adulthood; undeterred by male resistance to a woman discoursing authoritatively on religious topics, she composed an account of the spiritual benefits of her suffering. Florencia Pinar composed four poems that are included in the *Cancionero general*. Other women writers may also be represented in the *cancioneros,* but their compositions are hard to distinguish from those by male contemporaries who routinely feigned women's voices and mouthed stereotypes that men liked to hear.

The end of the fifteenth century marks the transition to early-modern literature in Spain. The 1499 publication of the first edition of the masterpiece of the age, Rojas's dialogue novel *Comedia de Calixto y Melibea,* was followed in 1502 by an expanded and definitive version, the *Tragicomedia de Calixto y Melibea.* Both versions are now popularly subsumed under the title *Celestina.* The literary type of the go-between—or, more darkly, "panderess" or "madam," in Spanish variously called *medianera, alcahueta,* and, because of this work, *celestina*—is brought to her height in world literature in the person of Celestina. A retired prostitute and a notorious bawd, Celestina is also something of a witch, although scholars continue to debate whether she is a real sorceress or merely pantomimes white and black magic practices to pander to her clients' expectations and to bolster her self-confidence. Like Alfonso Martínez de Toledo's *Arcipreste de Talavera* (Archpriest of Talavera, 1438) and many sentimental novels, the work is presented as an exemplary moral lesson. The scions of two noble families are infatuated with each other: Calisto falls first, and most superficially, for Melibea and is led by his corrupt servant Sempronio to the services of the industrious *alcahueta* Celestina. Aided by the two remaining sex workers in her diminished retinue, ensconced in a wretched riverside shack near the tanneries, Celestina deftly plies her new client, confirms her hold on her longstanding customer Sempronio, and undermines the innocent loyalty of Calisto's young page, Pármeno. The old bawd excites the greed of her servant-class protégés, who murder her for denying them a share of Calisto's payments to her; they are immediately caught and summarily executed. That night, at his beloved's invitation, Calisto breaches Melibea's garden wall with a ladder, takes possession of that "que, tomado, no será en tu mano bolver" (which, once taken, is not in your power to restore)—her virginity—and, dashing off in a gesture of stupid bravado, falls to his death from his ladder. Melibea summons her father to listen to her bitter confession, then takes her own life by leaping from a tower. The bitingly dark tale, full of ironic foreshadowing, announces itself as a warning to the lovesick, who, overpowered by their disordered appetite, call their mistresses their god, and against "alcahuetas y malos y lisonjeros sirvientes" (go-betweens and wicked and flattering servants). But critics have consistently seen more-universal admonitions about the hollowness of desire and even of life itself—a sense of hopelessness about the human condition. Rojas came from a *converso* family, and the Inquisition had forced his grandfather to perform public penance for lapsing into Jewish ways; after earning a law degree from the University of Salamanca, Rojas successfully defended his father-in-law before another Inquisition tribunal. Many scholars have seen the apparent pessimism of *Celestina* as a reflection of the persecution that the "New Christians" faced from the "Old Christian" majority. Others have read the story as a lament for the loss of feudal and familial loyalties of the old order amid a new age's shifting alliances of convenience and cynical traffic in love of any sort. Still others consider the work a criticism of the self-indulgent immorality literature can induce in weak and sentimental readers.

*Celestina* is far from a misogynist tract; the most complex and subtle figures in the work are the women, and the most transparently foolish are the men. While he seems to have written nothing else for the rest of his life, Rojas succeeded remarkably in creating the fully realized psyches and voices of Calisto, the young swain in love with his own melancholy and desire; Melibea, a maiden desperate for an affair but shrewd enough to collaborate in her own seduction; Calisto's servant Pármeno, a boy caught between his childish affection for unworthy older-brother figures—Calisto and the older servant, Sempronio—and his inability to resist the sexual and mercenary provocations of the unworthy mother figure Celestina; Pleberio, the aged father of Melibea, who looks back over his life and realizes that it has been materially successful but ultimately useless; his wife, Alisa, a presumptuous and neglectful high-society mother who fails to perceive her daughter's maturation and sexual needs; the prostitute cousins Alicia and Areúsa, determined to forge their own destinies; and Celestina herself, a whore nostalgic about a past filled with sex, fame, and blissful drunkenness, skilled in the black arts and even more skilled in the manipulation of the latent vices of all humankind. A tour de force of psychological realism, plausible motivation, and tightly woven plot, *Celestina* in many ways creates the paradigm for the modern novel.

Many of the genres and trends of the fifteenth century continued to flourish in the sixteenth. Although the ballad tradition emerged in a growing stream in the fifteenth century, most of the extant examples of the earliest compositions were produced in the 1500s—often as cheap broadsheets sold for pennies at country fairs; later they were collected in anthologies. Italianate influences in courtly poetry, introduced by Santillana, emerged in the sixteenth century in the works of Juan Boscán and Garcilaso de la Vega. The sentimental romance was perpetuated into the first half of the 1500s, although it was displaced by new tastes for pastoral and byzantine novels and in the seventeenth century by Cervantes's Italianate *Novelas ejemplares* (Exemplary Stories, 1613). Chivalric novels of knightly adventure were published with decreased frequency after the abdication of Carlos V in 1554 but continued to be read up to the time of *Don Quijote*. And the incomparable *Celestina* spun off many earnest sequels, but those continuations never rose above riding the coattails of Spain's first modern best-seller. The tastes of the sixteenth century matured and internationalized but still retained profound echoes of Iberia's late medieval heritage.

Each entry in *Dictionary of Literary Biography* volume 286: *Castilian Writers, 1400–1500* includes a bibliography of important manuscripts, editions, and English translations of works by the subject, or in the genre, dealt with in the entry. (More-comprehensive bibliographical information is available at the Philo-Biblon website: http://sunsite.berkeley.edu/Philobiblon/phhm.html.) A biographical sketch of the author, in which each work is discussed in the context in the life of the author in which it was written, is followed by a bibliography of secondary sources selected for their utility to the nonspecialist.

—*Frank A. Domínguez and George D. Greenia*

## Acknowledgments

This book was produced by Bruccoli Clark Layman, Inc. Bland Lawson and Philip B. Dematteis were the in-house editors; they were assisted by Charles Brower.

Production manager is Philip B. Dematteis.

Administrative support was provided by Ann M. Cheschi and Carol A. Cheschi.

Accountant is Ann-Marie Holland.

Copyediting supervisor is Sally R. Evans. The copyediting staff includes Phyllis A. Avant, Caryl Brown, Leah M. Cutsinger, Melissa D. Hinton, Philip I. Jones, Rebecca Mayo, and Nancy E. Smith.

Editorial associates are Jessica Goudeau, Michael S. Martin, Catherine M. Polit, Joshua M. Robinson, and William Mathes Straney.

In-house prevetting is by Nicole A. La Rocque.

Permissions editor and database manager is Amber L. Coker.

Layout and graphics supervisor is Janet E. Hill. The graphics staff includes Zoe R. Cook and Sydney E. Hammock.

Office manager is Kathy Lawler Merlette.

Photography supervisor is Paul Talbot. Photography editor is Scott Nemzek.

Digital photographic copy work was performed by Joseph M. Bruccoli.

Systems manager is Donald Kevin Starling.

Typesetting supervisor is Kathleen M. Flanagan. The typesetting staff includes Patricia Marie Flanagan, Mark J. McEwan, and Pamela D. Norton.

Walter W. Ross did library research. He was assisted by Jo Cottingham and the following librarians at the Thomas Cooper Library of the University of South Carolina: circulation department head Tucker Taylor; reference department head Virginia W. Weathers; reference department staff Laurel Baker, Marilee Birchfield, Kate Boyd, Paul Cammarata, Joshua Garris, Gary Geer, Tom Marcil, Rose Marshall, and Sharon Verba; interlibrary loan department head Marna Hostetler; and interlibrary loan staff Bill Fetty, Nelson Rivera, and Cedric Rose.

Dictionary of Literary Biography® • Volume Two Hundred Eighty-Six

# Castilian Writers, 1400–1500

# Dictionary of Literary Biography

# Alfonso de Cartagena

*(circa 1384 – 22 July 1456)*

Noel Fallows
*University of Georgia*

WORKS: *Memoriale Virtutum* (1422)

**Manuscripts:** Madrid, Biblioteca Nacional, 9178, 9212; El Escorial, Biblioteca de San Lorenzo de El Escorial, Q-II-9; Burgos, Biblioteca de la Catedral, 117.

*Declinationes contra novam translationem Ethicorum cum Leonardo Aretino* (1427)

**Manuscript:** Krakjów, Jagiellonska Library, 3245.

**Standard edition:** Alexander Birkenmaier, "Der Streit des Alonso von Cartagena mit Leonardo Bruni Aretino," *Beiträge zur Geschichte der Philosophie des Mittelalters,* 20, no. 5 (1922): 129–236.

*Expositio super legum Gallus* (1434)

**Manuscript:** One incomplete manuscript is extant, Burgos, Biblioteca de la Catedral, 11.

*Propositio super altercatione praeminentia sedium inter oratores regum Castellae et Angliae in concilio Basiliense/Discurso sobre la precedencia del Rey Católico sobre el de Inglaterra en el Concilio de Basilea* (1434)

**Manuscripts:** Text in Latin: Burgos, Archivo de la Catedral, 11; Madrid, Biblioteca Nacional, 9262; Salamanca, Biblioteca Universitaria, 81; Vatican City, Biblioteca Apostolica Vaticana, 4150, 4151. Text in Castilian: El Escorial, Biblioteca de San Lorenzo de El Escorial, h-II-22; London, British Library, Egerton 337, Egerton 2081-1; Madrid, Biblioteca Nacional, 1091, 2347, 4236, 8631, 9256, 9262, 11379, 18657, 18720, 19006; Madrid, Real Academia de la Historia, 12-21-2-21; New York, Hispanic Society of America, B2572; Salamanca, Biblioteca Universitaria, 2198; Simancas, Archivo General de Simancas, Estado: España K-1900; Valladolid, Biblioteca Universitaria, 326, 334. The standard edition is based on a collation of the extant manuscripts.

**Standard edition:** *Edición crítica del discurso de Alfonso de Cartagena "Propositio super altercatione praeminentia sedium inter oratores regum Castellae et Angliae in concilio Basiliense": Versiones en latín y castellano,* edited by María Victoria Echevarría Gaztelumendi (Madrid: Editorial de la Universidad Complutense de Madrid, 1992).

*Sermo habitus in concilio Basiliensis per Alphonsum decanum Compostellanum oratorem serenissimi regis Castelle in solempnitate sancti Thome de Aquino; Sermo quem fecit reuerendus pater Alfonsus electus Burgensis in sacro Concilio Basiliensis in festo Omnium Sanctorum* (1435)

**Manuscript:** Vatican City, Biblioteca Apostolica Vaticana, 232.

*Allegationes super conquesta Insularum Canariae contra portugalenses* (1437)

**Manuscripts:** El Escorial, Biblioteca de San Lorenzo de El Escorial, a-IV-14; Madrid, Biblioteca Nacional, 11341, 12087, 19006, Res. 35; Madrid, Real Academia de la Historia, 9-3965; Simancas, Archivo General de Simancas, Estado: Francia K-1711, P. R. 21-14; Vatican City, Biblioteca Apostolica Vaticana, 4151. The standard edition is based on a collation of the extant manuscripts and includes a translation of the text into modern Spanish.

**Standard edition:** *Diplomacia y humanismo en el siglo XV: Edición crítica, traducción y notas de las "Allegationes super conquesta Insularum Canariae contra portugalenses" de Alfonso de Cartagena,* edited by Tomás González Rolán, Fremiot Hernández González, and Pilar Saquero Suárez-Somonte (Madrid: UNED, 1994).

*Epistula directa ad inclitum et magnificum virum Dominum Petrum Fernandi de Velasco comitem de Haro et dominum antique domus de Salas, serenissime ac invitissime domini* (ca. 1440)

**Manuscript:** Madrid, Biblioteca Nacional, 9208.

**Standard edition:** *Un tratado de Alonso de Cartagena sobre la educación y los estudios literarios,* edited by Jeremy N. H. Lawrance (Barcelona: Universidad Autónoma de Barcelona, 1979).

*Duodenarium* (1442)

**Manuscripts:** Burgos, Biblioteca de la Catedral, 42 (complete text); El Escorial, Biblioteca de San Lorenzo de El Escorial, f-III-17 (about two-thirds of text).

*De questionibus hortolanis* (ca. 1443–1447)

**Manuscripts:** Madrid, Biblioteca Nacional, 13252; Salamanca, Biblioteca Universitaria, 2619; Vatican City, Biblioteca Apostolica Vaticana, 4881.

**Standard edition:** María Morrás, "Una cuestión disputada: viejas y nuevas formas en el siglo XV. A propósito de un opúsculo inédito de Rodrigo Sánchez de Arévalo y Alfonso de Cartagena," *Atalaya,* 7 (1996): 63–102.

*Respuesta a la Qüestión fecha por el Marqués de Santillana* (1444)

**Manuscripts:** El Escorial, Biblioteca de San Lorenzo de El Escorial, h-II-22; Madrid, Biblioteca Nacional, 3666, 4236, 6609, 7099, 13127, Res. 35; Madrid, Real Academia de la Historia, 9-1029, 9-1049. The standard edition is based on a collation of the extant manuscripts.

**Standard edition:** Angel Gómez Moreno, "La *Qüestión* del Marqués de Santillana a Don Alfonso de Cartagena," *El Crotalón,* 2 (1985): 335–363; reprinted in Iñigo López de Mendoza, marqués de Santillana, *Obras completas,* edited by Moreno and Maximilian P. A. M. Kerkhof (Barcelona: Planeta, 1988), pp. 414–434.

*Doctrinal de los caballeros* (ca. 1444)

**Manuscripts:** El Escorial, Biblioteca de San Lorenzo de El Escorial, h-III-4; Madrid, Biblioteca del Museo Lázaro Galdiano, 474; Madrid, Biblioteca de Palacio, 1305, 2906; Madrid, Real Academia de la Historia, 9-712; Madrid, Biblioteca Nacional, 27, 6607, 6609, 10107, 12743, 12796, 18061; New York, Hispanic Society of America, B2704; Oxford, Bodleian Library, 597; Salamanca, Biblioteca Universitaria, 1767; Seville, Biblioteca Colombina, 7-5-29. The standard edition is based on the first published edition, which was copied directly from Cartagena's autograph manuscript, now lost.

**First publication:** *Doctrinal de los caballeros* (Burgos: Fadrique de Basilea, 1487).

**Standard editions:** Noel Fallows, *The Chivalric Vision of Alfonso de Cartagena: Study and Edition of the Doctrinal de los caualleros* (Newark, Del.: Juan de la Cuesta, 1995); Alonso de Cartagena, *Doctrinal de los cavalleros,* edited by José María Viña Liste (Santiago de Compostela: Universidade de Santiago de Compostela, 1995).

*Defensorium Unitatis Christianae* (1449)

**Manuscripts:** Madrid, Biblioteca Nacional, 442; Salamanca, Biblioteca Universitaria, 2070. The standard edition is based on a collation of the two manuscripts.

**Standard edition:** *Defensorium Unitatis Christianae,* edited by Manuel Alonso (Madrid: Consejo Superior de Investigaciones Científicas, Instituto Arias Montano, 1943).

**Edition in Spanish:** *Alonso de Cartagena y el "Defensorium Unitatis Christianae" (Introducción histórica, traducción y notas),* translated by Guillermo Verdín-Díaz (Oviedo: Universidad de Oviedo, 1992).

*Pastoral sobre las reliquias de santa Juliana* (1453)

**Manuscript:** Santander, Colegiata de Santillana del Mar, 66.

**Standard edition:** *Pastoral sobre las reliquias de santa Juliana,* in *Colección diplomática: Documentos en pergamino que hubo en la Real Ex-Colegiata de Santillana,* 2 volumes, edited by Mateo Escagedo Salmón (Santander: Dueso, 1926), I: 368–380.

*Oracional de Fernán Pérez* (1454)

**Manuscripts:** El Escorial, Biblioteca de San Lorenzo de El Escorial, Y-III-86; Madrid, Biblioteca Nacional, 64, 9156; Paris, Bibliothèque Nationale, Esp. 47; Salamanca, Biblioteca Universitaria, 1720; Santander, Biblioteca de Menéndez Pelayo, 160. The standard edition follows Santander, Biblioteca de Menéndez Pelayo, 160.

**Early edition:** *Oracional de Fernán Pérez* (Murcia: Luis Gabriel Ariño y Lope de la Roca, 1487).

**Standard edition:** *El Oracional de Alonso de Cartagena: Edición crítica,* edited by Silvia González-Quevedo Alonso (Valencia: Albatros, 1983).

*Anacephaleosis (Liber genealogiae regum Hispaniae)* (1454–1456)

**Manuscripts:** Cambridge, Mass., Houghton Library, Typ-162; Fermo, Biblioteca Comunale, 77; Madrid, Archivo Histórico Nacional, 938b; Madrid, Biblioteca Nacional, 7432, Res. 35, Vit. 19-2.

**Standard editions:** *Liber genealogiae regum Hispaniae/El libro de la genealogía de los reyes de España,* with facsimile, edited and translated by Bonifacio Palacios Martín (Madrid: Biblioteca Nacional, 1995); Yolanda Espinosa Fernández, *La Anacephaleosis de Alfonso de Cartagena. Edición, traducción, estudio,* 3 volumes (Madrid: Editorial de la Universidad Complutense, 1989).

*Apologia super psalmum Judica me Deus/Apología sobre el salmo Judica me Deus* (undated; ca. mid fifteenth century)

　　**Manuscripts:** Text in Latin: El Escorial, Biblioteca de San Lorenzo de El Escorial, 0-II-3; Madrid, Biblioteca Nacional, Vit. 18-3; Toledo, Archivo de la Catedral, 14-25. Text in Castilian: El Escorial, Biblioteca de San Lorenzo de El Escorial, a-IV-7, h-II-22; Salamanca, Biblioteca Universitaria, 1720; Santander, Biblioteca Menéndez y Pelayo, 160.

　　**Early edition:** *Apología sobre el salmo Judica me Deus,* in *Oracional de Fernán Pérez* (1487).

　　**Standard edition:** *Apología sobre el salmo Judica me Deus,* in *Antología de la literatura espiritual española: Edad Media,* 4 volumes, edited by Pedro Sainz Rodríguez (Madrid: Universidad Pontificia de Salamanca/Fundación Universitaria Española, 1980), I: 618–630.

*Glosa al Tratado de San Juan Crisóstomo* (undated; mid fifteenth century)

　　**Manuscripts:** El Escorial, Biblioteca de San Lorenzo de El Escorial, a-IV-7, d-IV-5, h-II-18, h-II-22; Madrid, Biblioteca de Palacio, II-651, 1450; Salamanca, Biblioteca Universitaria, 1720, 2198; Santander, Biblioteca Menéndez y Pelayo, 160. The standard edition is based on El Escorial, Biblioteca de San Lorenzo de El Escorial, h-II-22.

　　**Standard edition:** *Glosa al Tratado de San Juan Crisóstomo,* in *Fortuna y Providencia en la literatura castellana del siglo XV,* edited by Juan de Dios Mendoza Negrillo, Anejos del Boletín de la Real Academia Española, no. 27 (Madrid: Real Academia Española, 1973), pp. 439–448.

TRANSLATIONS: Cicero, *La Rethórica de M. Tulio Cicerón,* translated by Cartagena (ca. 1421–1433)

　　**Manuscript:** El Escorial, Biblioteca de San Lorenzo de El Escorial, T-II-12.

　　**Standard edition:** *La Rethórica de M. Tulio Cicerón,* edited by Rosalba Mascagna, Romanica Neapolitana, no. 2 (Naples: Liguori, 1969).

Cicero, *Libro de Tulio, De Senetute; Libro de Tulio, De los Ofiçios,* translated by Cartagena (1422)

　　**Manuscripts:** El Escorial, Biblioteca de San Lorenzo de El Escorial, M-II-5; London, British Library, Harl. 4796; Madrid, Biblioteca Bartolomé March, 20-4-1; Madrid, Biblioteca Nacional, 7815; Madrid, Biblioteca de Palacio, 1785. The standard edition is based on the most complete manuscript, Madrid, Biblioteca Nacional, 7815.

　　**Standard edition:** *Libros de Tulio: De Senetute; De los ofiçios,* edited by María Morrás (Alcalá de

Henares: Universidad de Alcalá de Henares, 1996).

Giovanni Boccaccio, *Caída de prínçipes,* translated by Pero López de Ayala and Cartagena (1422)

　　**Manuscripts:** Cambridge, Mass., Houghton Library, fMS. Span 67; El Escorial, Biblioteca de San Lorenzo de El Escorial, e-III-7, L-II-14; Madrid, Biblioteca Nacional, 955, 7799, 12733, 13248; Madrid, Biblioteca de Palacio, II-100; New York, Hispanic Society of America, B1196; Vienna, Österreichische Nationalbibliothek, 6030.

　　**First publication:** *Caída de prínçipes* (Seville: Meinardo Ungut & Estanislao Polono, 1495).

　　**Standard edition:** *Text and Concordance of Giovanni Boccaccio's De casibus virorum illustrium, Translated by Pero López de Ayala,* edited by Eric Naylor (Madison, Wis.: Hispanic Seminary of Medieval Studies, 1994).

Cicero, *Por Marçello,* translated by Cartagena (ca. 1422–1427)

　　**Manuscripts:** Madrid, Biblioteca Nacional, Res. 27, 9132; El Escorial, Biblioteca de San Lorenzo de El Escorial, M-II-5; London, British Library, Harl. 4796.

Seneca, *Obras de Séneca,* translated by Cartagena (ca. 1430–1434)

　　**Manuscripts:** Thirty-three manuscripts have survived, the most complete of which is El Escorial, Biblioteca de San Lorenzo de El Escorial, N-ij-6.

　　**Standard editions:** Ramón Fernández Pousa, *Libro que fizo Séneca a su amigo Galión contra las adversidades de la fortuna: Versión inédita de Alonso de Cartagena según el MS 607 de la Biblioteca Universitaria de Salamanca* (El Escorial: Ediciones Escorial, 1943); Tomás González Rolán and Pilar Saquero Suárez-Somonte, "El *Epitoma Rei Militaris* de Flavio Vegecio traducido al castellano en el siglo XV: Edición de los *Dichos de Séneca en el acto de caballería* de Alfonso de Cartagena," *Miscelánea Medieval Murciana,* 14 (1987–1988): 101–150.

Quintus Curtius, *Dichos de Quinto Curçio,* translated by Cartagena (ca. 1430–1434)

　　**Manuscript:** In *Obras de Séneca,* translated by Cartagena, El Escorial, Biblioteca de San Lorenzo de El Escorial, T-III-4.

　　**Standard edition:** Gerald L. Boarino, "Los *Dichos de Quinto Curçio:* Traducción atribuída a D. Alfonso de Cartagena," *Bulletin Hispanique,* 70 (1968): 431–436.

Alfonso de Cartagena, sometimes also known as Alonso de Cartagena, was born circa 1384, the second

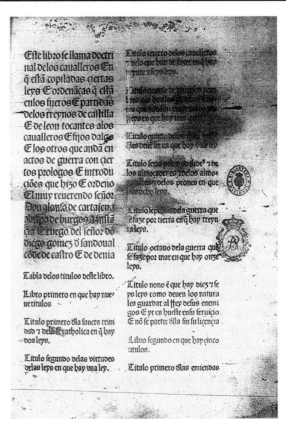

*Title page and first page from Alfonso de Cartagena's treatise on the art of war and military science (1487),*
*written circa 1444 (Biblioteca Nacional, Madrid)*

son of Selomo ha-Levi (circa 1352–1435). Selomo and his family converted to Christianity on 21 July 1390, at which time he adopted the name Pablo de Santa María, and his second son was baptized Alfonso García de Santa María. Twelve years later, in 1402, Pablo became bishop of Cartagena, and by 1415 he was appointed bishop of Burgos. Alfonso García de Santa María was thus the son of one of the most successful and prosperous *conversos* (converts) in Castile. Although it was not until 1441 that Alfonso officially adopted the surname Cartagena, most modern critics, especially Hispanists, refer to him in general as Alfonso de Cartagena.

Cartagena benefited from a privileged education. As a child he attended the cathedral school in Cartagena, and between the years 1400 and 1410 he was enrolled as a student at the University of Salamanca, where he excelled at civil and canon law. Upon graduation he entered the clergy and rose rapidly through the ranks. His first appointment was as dean of Santiago in 1415 or 1416, a post that he seems to have regarded with a certain amount of fondness, as in his will he bequeathed two hundred florins to the chapter of Santiago. By 1420 he was serving as dean of Segovia. He also enjoyed the favor of King Juan II at the Castilian court, where he served as a respected royal adviser from 1419. Operating

as a politician as well as a theologian, Cartagena was never far removed from the political intrigue that fueled the dynastic disputes of fifteenth-century Castile.

Unlike his father, Cartagena was a peripatetic prelate whose career was characterized as much by extensive travel as by literary productivity. His first diplomatic missions were to the neighboring state of Portugal. He visited the court of King João I on several occasions between 1421 and 1431. The purpose of these missions was to finalize and ratify a peace treaty between Castile and Portugal that had been stipulated in truces agreed upon in 1411. As Abdón Salazar observes in his 1976 study of Cartagena's diplomatic missions to Portugal, Castile had good reasons to postpone signing a treaty with Portugal because of Castilian claims to the Canary Islands, which were strategically important for the purposes of Atlantic seaborne exploration. The political tension between Castile and Portugal resulted in four diplomatic missions, from December 1421 to December 1422; January to April 1423; December 1424 to April 1425; and September to December 1427. Cartagena's position as royal adviser meant that he had to spend up to six consecutive months per year at the Castilian court, so he was obliged to interrupt a complicated peace process and return to Castile each year. In

1425, for example, it is known that he was present at the swearing in of Crown Prince Enrique (subsequently King Enrique IV of Castile) in the city of Valladolid. Doubtless as a consequence of these interruptions, the peace treaty of Medina del Campo was not actually signed until 30 October 1431, and even then Portugal and Castile were to squabble over Atlantic colonial possessions for many years to come.

While politically frustrating, the years that frame Cartagena's visits to Portugal were certainly fruitful from a literary point of view. While in Portugal he came into contact with the eldest son of the Portuguese king, Duarte of Avis (1390–1438), to whom he addressed two of his early works. Perhaps Cartagena's first work is his translation of Cicero's *De inventione* as *La Rethórica de M. Tulio Cicerón* (The Rhetoric of M. Tullius Cicero, circa 1421–1433), which he dedicated to Prince Duarte. In early 1422 Cartagena also translated Cicero's *De Senectute* and, later that same year, *De officiis,* both addressed to Juan Alfonso de Zamora, royal secretary of Juan II, who accompanied Cartagena to Portugal. Between 1422 and 1427 Cartagena also translated Cicero's *Pro M. Marcello Oratio* (Speech in Defense of Marcus Marcellus) as *Por Marçello.* These translations of Cicero were the first of many such translations of classical works. Indeed, at least one critic, Nicholas G. Round, determines a clear trajectory of stylistic sophistication between Cartagena's early translations of Cicero and those of Seneca that he produced later in his career.

Probably in the summer of 1422 Cartagena wrote the *Memoriale Virtutum* (Register of Virtues), his second book addressed to Prince Duarte. As the title suggests, the *Memoriale Virtutum* is a treatise on virtue, following Aristotle's *Nicomachean Ethics,* with a view to outlining the principles of effective governance and kingship. The enduring impact of this early work can be judged by the fact that the *Memoriale Virtutum* was translated into Castilian in 1474, after Cartagena's death, and a copy was presented to Queen Isabella the Catholic after she ascended the throne of Castile. By the end of September 1422 Cartagena had also put the finishing touches to a translation of Giovanni Boccaccio's *De casibus virorum illustrium* (On the Fall of Illustrious Men) that had been begun by Pero López de Ayala. The complex codicological history of this translation has been studied by Eric W. Naylor, who concludes that there are two distinct versions that correspond to two branches of manuscripts: those that were translated in their entirety by López de Ayala; and a separate branch of codices that, early in the fifteenth century, either accidentally came apart or were deliberately disassembled. It was probably one of these incomplete copies that fell into the hands of Cartagena's colleague Zamora, thereby prompting him to request that Cartagena undertake his own translation of the missing text. In both branches the work bears the title *Caída de príncipes* (The Fall of Princes).

In 1431, four years after concluding the negotiations with Portugal, Cartagena accompanied Juan II to Christian-occupied Córdoba to negotiate settlements with the Muslims of the kingdom of Granada. Cartagena returned to Castile and did not leave again until the year 1434. During this period Juan II took advantage of Cartagena's presence at court to commission several translations and paraphrases of the works of Seneca the Younger (including works erroneously attributed to Seneca). They were collected together in codices that usually bear the generic title *Obras de Séneca* (Works of Seneca). Cartagena's translations of Seneca's genuine works are *Libro de la providençia de Dios* (On God's Providence), from *De Providentia; Libro de la clemençia* (On Clemency), from *De Clementia; Libro de la providençia divina* (On Divine Providence), from *De Constantia sapientis; Libro de las siete artes liberales* (On the Seven Liberal Arts), from *Epistula 88 ad Lucilium;* and *Libro de la vida bienaventurada* (On the Blessed Life), a translation of both *De Vita beata* and *De Otio.* Cartagena's translations of works erroneously attributed to Seneca are *Copilaçión de algunos dichos de Séneca* (Compendium of Maxims by Seneca) and *Título de la amistanza o del amigo* (Treatise on Friendship), both paraphrases of different sections of Lucas Manelli's *Tabulatio et Expositio Senecae; Libro contra las adversidades de la fortuna* (Against the Adversities of Fortune), in fact a translation of *Formulae vitae honestae,* by St. Martin of Braga; *Libro de las declamaciones* (The Book of Declamations), a translation of Seneca the Elder's *Declamationes; Libro de los amonestamientos y doctrinas* (On Advice and Doctrines), a translation of a compendium of genuine and spurious Senecan treatises titled *De legalibus institutis;* and *Tratado de la guerra* (Treatise on Warfare), also known as *Dichos de Séneca en el acto de la caballería* (Seneca's Maxims on Chivalric Deeds).

*Tratado de la guerra,* referred to as such in the most complete manuscript version of the text, is a partial translation of the *Epitoma Rei Militaris* (Epitome of Military Science) by Publius Flavius Vegetius Renatus. The authorship of this translation in particular is a matter of debate, for some scholars are surprised that a man as erudite as Cartagena would confuse authors as far apart stylistically, intellectually, and chronologically as Seneca and Vegetius. It is worth noting, however, that in a later work, *Doctrinal de los caballeros* (Catechism of Knighthood, circa 1444), Cartagena's consummate treatise on the art of war and military science, Vegetius's name appears only once, in a law copied directly from the medieval legal code *Siete Partidas* (Seven Divisions). Furthermore, in his prologue to the second book of the *Doctrinal de los caballeros,* Cartagena attributes a maxim to Seneca, apparently without realizing that it is in fact from the works of Vegetius. That is to say, Cartagena had indeed read selections of Vegetius's *Epitoma Rei Militaris,* but he mistakenly attributed the work to Seneca. There is another surprising mistake of this sort in the *Doctrinal de los caballeros,* in which, despite his intimate knowledge of the text, Cartagena repeatedly attributes the *Fuero Real* (Royal Law-Code) to Alfonso VI instead of Alfonso X. This evidence, along with the fact that all of the surviving manuscript copies of *Tratado de la guerra* are included in volumes that feature other Castilian translations of Seneca that are undoubtedly by Cartagena, suggests that Cartagena is indeed the author of the *Tratado de la guerra,* even though he erroneously attributes the work to Seneca. All that remains to be said, in the words of the *Tratado de la guerra,* is that "muchas veses entre los que saben acaesçe algund error" (often those who are knowledgeable make mistakes).

Another translation, *Dichos de Quinto Curçio* (The Sayings of Quintus Curtius, circa 1430–1434), is a unique text in that it appears as an appendix in just one of the fifteenth-century manuscripts of *Obras de Séneca.* The *Dichos* constitute a translation of sayings taken from Quintus Curtius Rufus's *Historiae Alexandri Magni* (History of Alexander the Great). Once again, the question of authorship of the translation is an issue. Several scholars have studied the letters that Cartagena exchanged with the Italian humanist Pier Candido Decembrio, in particular Antonio Bravo García, James Hankins, Pilar Saquero Suárez-Somonte, Tomás González Rolán, and Vittorio Zaccaria. They concur that although Decembrio did without a doubt translate the *Historiae Alexandri Magni,* neither Cartagena nor Decembrio alludes in their correspondence to the *Dichos de Quinto Curçio* or to the Latin original from which it is drawn. Likewise, there are no direct references to the *Dichos de Quinto Curçio* or the *Historiae Alexandri Magni* in other works by Cartagena. What can be stated with certainty is that the *Dichos de Quinto Curçio* were associated with Cartagena as early as the fifteenth century, for the only surviving manuscript copy is bound in a volume of translations undertaken by Cartagena, all written in the same hand.

From 1434 to 1439 Cartagena was again involved in the world of international politics. He was dispatched along with other Castilian delegates to the Council of Basel (1431–1449). Passing through Aragon and Catalonia, the group of Castilian representatives headed for Avignon en route for Basel. On 19 July 1434, while in Avignon, Cartagena participated in a rhetorical exercise, *Expositio super legum Gallus* (Exposition on Gallic Law), which involved the explication of an obscure and complex point of civil law, specifically the law titled "De postumis instituendis vel exheredandis" (Concerning the Confirmation or the Disenfranchisement of Heirs). The exposition survives in one incomplete manuscript that

has yet to be made available in a modern edition. It is known from a contemporary chronicle written by Cartagena's uncle, Alvar García de Santa María, and perhaps not without some exaggeration, that this law had supposedly never been understood so clearly until Cartagena presented his exposition of it, nor until that moment had those present heard anyone speak so eloquently about legal matters in general. After the presentation it is said that Cartagena invited his audience to dine with him, a seemingly minor detail that nonetheless provides a glimpse of a warm and congenial personality despite the often dry subject matter of his literary works.

At the Council of Basel, Cartagena delivered two sermons and, much more importantly, two seminal speeches that set the tone for the political agenda that he pursued throughout his career. The speeches are *Propositio super altercatione praeminentia sedium inter oratores regum Castellae et Angliae in concilio Basiliense* (Proposition Concerning the Prominent Dispute about Seating between the Orators of the Kings of Castile and England at the Council of Basel, 1434), and *Allegationes super conquesta Insularum Canariae contra portugalenses* (Allegations against the Portuguese concerning the Conquest of the Canary Islands, 1437). Cartagena subsequently translated the first speech into Castilian at the request of Juan de Silva, his colleague at the council. In both speeches religious doctrine serves as a point of departure, which Cartagena then buttresses with laws and statutes from the *Siete Partidas* and other medieval law codes. As a representative of Castile at the Council of Basel he states that war against "infidels" is entirely justifiable if it means extending the frontiers of Christendom and, by implication, of Castile. In an effort to contain the often vainglorious and contentious Castilian nobility, he expounds a theory of civil nobility, following Bartolus of Sassoferrato (1314–1357), according to which the monarch's power is absolute and the nobles are subordinate to him. With the political and imperial interests of Castile firmly in mind, Cartagena framed both of the speeches at Basel within the rhetorical parameters of etymological, genealogical, and historical definition. In the speech on the preeminence of the king of Castile, for example, Cartagena traces the lineage of the Castilian monarchy as far back as Hercules, a rhetorical thrust that the English delegates ultimately could not riposte, as they lost the debate.

The Portuguese claim to the Canary Islands was tenuous at best in that the Portuguese simply proposed to conquer the islands in the name of Christendom. The Castilians, argued Cartagena, were not only just as capable of conquering islands in the name of the Catholic faith, but they could also lay claim to the Canaries for legal reasons since these islands were formerly a part of the Visigothic empire, of which the Castilian monarchs were the legal successors. The Canary Islands therefore

Page from the Siete Partidas (Seven Divisions), the Castilian legal code composed during the reign of Alfonso X (1252–1284) that was one of the sources for the laws compiled by Cartagena in Doctrinal de los caballeros, from a manuscript in the Arquivo Distrital de Braga ( from José de Azevedo Ferreira, "Fragmentos das Partidas de Alfonso X reencontrados em Bragg," Cahiers de Linguistique Hispanique Medievale, nos. 18–19 [1993–1994]; Lauinger Library, Georgetown University) already belonged to Castile. The success of the speech can be gauged by the fact that in 1436 Pope Eugene IV issued a papal bull conceding the islands to Castile, largely on the basis of Cartagena's intervention at Basel. Cartagena had, once again, acquitted himself well.

At Basel, Cartagena established contact with Italian humanists such as Aeneas Silvius Piccolomini, Francesco Pizolpasso, Poggio Bracciolini, and Decembrio. In the context of Italian humanistic thought Cartagena had composed the *Declinationes contra novam translationem Ethicorum* (Arguments against the New Translation of the Ethics, 1427) in Salamanca, a text that was not actually circulated until 1436, at the Council of Basel. The *Declinationes* constitutes a debate with Leonardo Aretino Bruni on the art of translation, specifically Bruni's 1418 translation of Aristotle's *Nicomachean Ethics.* Cartagena had known of Bruni's translation at least since the 1420s, when, during his missions to the Portuguese court, he met students who had attended the University of Bologna.

Primarily on the basis of his translations of Cicero and Seneca, as well as his interactions and correspondence with Italian humanists, Cartagena is often considered a pivotal figure in the literary and cultural transition between the Middle Ages and the Renaissance in the Iberian Peninsula. Until recently, however, Cartagena has also been the victim of a curious paradox, for while he is perceived by some as belonging to a group of Castilian scholars who paved the way for the diffusion of humanistic thought in the Iberian Peninsula, he is just as often perceived by others as an ardent defender of medieval Scholasticism. The paradox is addressed in various studies by Jeremy N. H. Lawrance and in a 1995 article by María Morrás. Morrás notes that until the mid 1990s many of Cartagena's works were not widely available, and scholars often had to content themselves with the relatively few texts that were accessible in modern editions. Now that almost the entire corpus of Cartagena's works is available to scholars, it is possible to form a more balanced view of what were previously considered contradictory positions. Morrás sensibly resolves the paradox by focusing on the diverse content and contexts of individual works. She makes a case for Cartagena's private persona, evinced especially in his correspondence with the Italian humanists—that is, with those he considered his peers—and his public persona, evinced in his (primarily didactic) works addressed to the nobility of Castile and Portugal. Morrás argues persuasively that, depending in large part on the intended audience, for Cartagena the *studia scolaticis* and the *studia humanitatis* are complementary as opposed to mutually exclusive.

Although Cartagena openly confesses in his correspondence with Bruni that he does not know Greek, he is sometimes cited as the Castilian translator of Aristotle's *Nicomachean Ethics.* This conjecture is refuted by Peter Russell and Anthony R. D. Pagden, who confirm in their own studies on the diffusion of Aristotle's moral philosophy in the Iberian Peninsula that it is likely that the *Nicomachean Ethics* was first translated into Castilian by Nuño de Guzmán, not Cartagena.

On 10 October 1435, while he was still in Basel, Cartagena was appointed bishop of Burgos. As such, he was in charge of one of the most important episcopal sees in the Iberian Peninsula, and he was certainly one of the most powerful prelates in Castile. Between 1438 and 1439 Cartagena was in Breslau, where he once again played the role of diplomat and peacemaker, reconciling the emperor Albert of Bohemia and King Casimir of Poland by dint of his rhetorical dexterity and the skillful orchestration of a marital alliance between one of Albert's daughters and the Polish king. It is known that Cartagena also visited Prague and Nuremburg before returning once more to Basel en route for Castile. Instead of traveling to these two cities, Cartagena could just as easily have headed for Italy. Surprisingly, however, despite his connections with Italian humanists, there is no firm documentary evidence to prove that he ever actually set foot in Italy. By 1440 Cartagena was dispatched to Navarre to accompany Blanche of Navarre to Castile so that she could marry Crown Prince Enrique. During this visit Cartagena also seized the opportunity to ratify peace treaties between Navarre and the kingdom of Castile. The wedding between Blanche and Enrique, attended by the bishop of Burgos, took place in Valladolid on 15 September 1440.

Cartagena's intellect was in high demand almost immediately upon his return to Castile, when various members of the nobility commissioned a series of short works. He composed an epistolary narrative in Latin titled *Epistula directa ad inclitum et magnificum virum Dominum Petrum Fernandi de Velasco comitem de Haro et dominum antique domus de Salas, serenissime ac invitissime domini* (Letter addressed to the Illustrious and Magnificent Man, Master Pedro Fernández de Velasco, Count of Haro and Lord of the Ancient House of Salas, Most Serene and Unconquered Knight, circa 1440). The epistle is essentially a pedagogical treatise in which Cartagena advises the count of Haro that because of the lessons to be learned from history, the events depicted in chronicles are to be praised as "perutiles" (extremely useful). He is quick to add that the chronicles form a stark contrast with popular chivalric fiction, in particular the tales of Tristan, Lancelot, and Amadís, whose adventures are dismissed as "nullius utilitatis" (of no use).

In the same year that he wrote the epistle to Pedro Fernández de Velasco, Cartagena participated in a debate with one of his pupils, Rodrigo Sánchez de Arévalo. The *questio,* that is, the issue under debate, was whether sight or hearing is the superior sense. Cartagena defended hearing (significantly, his niece Teresa de Cartagena was hearing impaired), while Sánchez de Arévalo argued in favor of sight. The debate, which constituted an exercise in the rhetorical art of declamation, was subsequently summarized in a treatise titled *De questionibus hortolanis* (The Garden Debate, circa 1443–1447). As in many of his other works, Cartagena complements classical allusions with sundry personal anecdotes. Indeed, in her 1996 edition of the text Morrás draws attention to the fact that *De questionibus hortolanis* is one of the few works written by Cartagena that underscores his wry sense of humor as well as his vast erudition. In this sense the debate confirms Alvar García de Santa María's description of the congenial atmosphere that he witnessed in Avignon when Cartagena explicated the *Expositio super legum Gallus.*

Along similar lines to his epistle to Fernández de Velasco, Cartagena composed the *Duodenarium* (Twelve Questions) between January and July 1442. This text survives in just two manuscripts, one of which is incomplete. It has yet to be made available in a modern edition, but the extant manuscripts have been studied in detail by Gerard Breslin. Written in Latin, the *Duodenarium* is Cartagena's reply to four of a total of twelve questions put to him by Fernán Pérez de Guzmán. Unlike the epistle to the count of Haro, Cartagena does not dwell in the *Duodenarium* on what constitutes suitable reading material; rather, he merely expresses admiration for Pérez de Guzmán's assiduity and his thirst for knowledge, despite Pérez de Guzmán's busy schedule and his deep commitment to court politics. In the *Duodenarium* Cartagena returns to a familiar theme that could be called a leitmotiv in his work; namely, the importance of bringing the Reconquest to a speedy conclusion by presenting a unified Christian front against the Muslim kingdom of Granada.

The *Respuesta a la Qüestión fecha por el Marqués de Santillana* (Response to the Question Formulated by the Marquis of Santillana) is yet another epistle. Dated 17 March 1444, it was written in Castilian and addressed to the marqués de Santillana, Pérez de Guzmán's nephew. The epistle is a testament to Cartagena's genuine interest in knighthood. In it he responds to a query submitted to him by the marqués de Santillana concerning a passage in Bruni's *De Militia* (On War), originally composed in 1421. Although Cartagena admits that he has not had the opportunity to read Bruni's treatise, he nonetheless is able to answer Santillana's question, which concerns the nature of an oath of fealty taken by Cato before a battle. Shortly after writing his reply to Santillana, Cartagena revealed the full extent of his knowledge of military matters in the *Doctrinal de los caballeros.* Indeed, in one of the extant manuscripts of the *Doc-*

*trinal de los caballeros* the marqués's *Qüestión* and Cartagena's reply precede the text as a seemingly pertinent preamble.

Many military treatises were written or translated in fifteenth-century Castile. Among the most influential were the two Castilian translations of Honoré Bouvet's *Arbre des batailles* (Tree of Battles, circa 1380s), one composed by Antón de Zorita in about 1441, the other possibly composed by Diego de Valera around 1445. Other fifteenth-century treatises include the *Tratado de la perfección del triunfo militar* (Treatise on the Perfection of Military Triumph, circa 1459), by Alfonso de Palencia, and the *Tratado de las armas* (Treatise on Arms, circa 1462–1465), by Diego de Valera. It is in the context of this rich tradition that Cartagena composed the *Doctrinal de los caballeros.* The book, written around 1444, is one of Cartagena's most widely diffused works. Sixteen fifteenth- century manuscripts survive, and at least two editions were published in the same century.

The *Doctrinal de los caballeros* is a compendium of laws and statutes copied literally from earlier law codes, especially the *Siete Partidas* and the *Fuero Real,* both composed during the reign (1252–1284) of Alfonso X, and the *Ordenamiento de Alcalá* (Legislation of Alcalá), promulgated in 1348, during the reign of Alfonso XI. Cartagena states in the prologue to book 1 that he has copied most of the text, and he always indicates the exact provenance of the laws he copies. The *Doctrinal de los caballeros* is divided into four books, each of which is in turn divided into titles and laws. Only the prologues to each of the four books, the introductions to each title, and the conclusion of the work constitute Cartagena's own writing, a fact that has confused at least one modern editor of the *Doctrinal de los caballeros.* The prologues underscore the scope of the author's erudition, for they reveal not only Cartagena's command of Castilian laws pertaining to knights, nobles, and their vassals but also his familiarity with the *Corpus Iuris Civilis* (Corpus of Civil Law), the *Corpus Iuris Canonici* (Corpus of Canon Law), the Bible, Aristotle's *Nicomachean Ethics,* the works of Cicero, Lucan, Seneca, Valerius Maximus, Augustine, St. Isidore, St. Jerome, St. Thomas Aquinas, and a host of other classical and contemporary authors and texts.

In the *Doctrinal de los caballeros* Cartagena returns to the issues that he had addressed in his speeches at the Council of Basel some ten years earlier. The text was dedicated originally to Diego Gómez de Sandoval, although another manuscript tradition exists with a dedicatory paragraph to Gómez de Sandoval's archenemy, the royal favorite Alvaro de Luna. The conflict in dedicatory paragraphs is not entirely incomprehensible. As early as 1439 the city of Burgos declared its allegiance to King Juan II of Castile and, by implication, to Luna. As bishop of Burgos, Cartagena openly supported this deci-

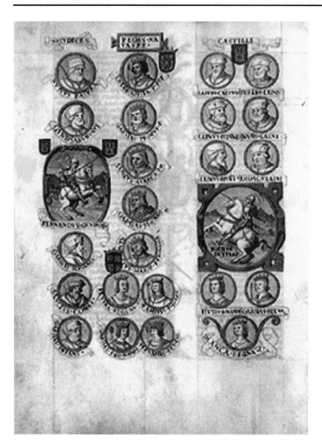

*Page from Cartagena's last work,* Anacephaleosis
*(1454–1456), on the genealogy of Spanish royalty
(Biblioteca Nacional, Madrid)*

sion. On the other hand, as Round has shown in his 1986 biography of Luna, Cartagena's relationship with the royal favorite was never as straightforward as the city's declaration suggests. Many of Cartagena's works stress unity and fraternity, and it seems clear that he saw himself as he was seen by others, as a peacemaker. Despite his public rhetoric, however, his true political allegiances were ambiguous, doubtless deliberately and necessarily so, in the turbulent political climate that characterized the reign of Juan II.

Both Gómez de Sandoval and Luna were typical members of the knightly caste in fifteenth-century Castile in the sense that they embraced political intrigue and a life of violence and rapine. In the *Doctrinal de los caballeros* Cartagena makes just-war theory relevant to ordinary knights, outlining what constitutes appropriate action, how it may be taken, and by whom, with a view to diverting knights' attention away from dynastic disputes and civil wars. The just war in this case is the Reconquest of Granada. In his 1985 study of the spread of lay literacy in fifteenth-century Castile, Lawrance observes that the very *dispositio,* the thematic arrangement of works such as the *Doctrinal de los caballeros,* indi-

cates that these books were meant to be picked up and read. By extension, it could be said that while in several works Cartagena advocates violence against the enemies of Christendom, he just as often urges the Castilian nobility to read and acquire knowledge, and it is certainly true that most careers at court during the reigns of Juan II and his successor, Enrique IV, were made or broken by dint of intrigue and negotiation as opposed to physical prowess.

The years 1445 to 1450 were perhaps the most turbulent ones of the reign of Juan II, and Cartagena apparently composed only one work at this time precisely because of his involvement in Castilian politics. The strategically important city of Burgos was preparing for imminent war with Navarre and Aragon, the cause of which was being promoted in Castile by the noble opponents of Juan II. Civil unrest reached a peak in 1449, when riots erupted in Toledo. Cartagena composed the *Defensorium Unitatis Christianae* (In Defense of Christian Unity) that same year. Although this text is generally discussed in the context of the 1449 riots, during which "Old" Christians viciously attacked *conversos* and ransacked their property (events placed in historical context by Albert Sicroff), opinions about its meaning and purpose vary. In Gregory B. Kaplan's analysis, the treatise was a response to the riots in particular and the plight of the *conversos* in general. In the *Defensorium Unitatis Christianae,* as well as the speech at the Council of Basel, Cartagena articulates what Kaplan calls the "*converso* voice." According to this theory, Cartagena, in the guise of advocating for monarchical reform and national unity, in reality presents a passionate argument on behalf of the plight of the *conversos.* This argument is based, for example, on assertions that true virtue and honor are indissolubly linked to character as opposed to lineage. In his 1993 study of the *Defensorium Unitatis Christianae* Lawrance places emphasis instead on the sincerity of Cartagena's Christian convictions. Lawrance essentially argues that since there is no evidence in the treatise of moral disaffection or rancor against those who persecuted *conversos,* it is difficult to identify characteristics that constitute a specific *converso* voice or attitude. These differences in critical opinion point to the fact that Cartagena was not only a cautious *converso* but also a consummate diplomat whose true position on the political issues of the day is often not clearly discernible.

Between 1450 and 1454 Cartagena was involved with his colleague Fernández de Velasco in the disciplinary reforms of the monastery of Oña. The series of devotional works he produced at this time reflects a period of relative calm in Cartagena's life. In 1453 he took the time to embark on a tour of the northern part of his diocese. In the town of Santillana he transferred the relics of St. Juliana from a chapel in the church to a place of honor next to the high altar. In a 16 September 1453 pastoral letter, *Pastoral sobre las reliquias de santa Juliana* (Pastoral on the Relics of St. Juliana), Cartagena announced this change to members of the diocese. The letter also constitutes a general propagandistic defense of the ancient custom of worshiping saints' relics. A year later, in 1454, he composed the *Oracional de Fernán Pérez*, a book on the benefits of prayer. Like the *Duodenarium*, it is directed to Pérez de Guzmán, but unlike the *Duodenarium*, the text is written in Castilian. An exegetical work, *Apología sobre el salmo Judica me Deus* (Apology on the Psalm "Judge Me Lord"), is affiliated with the *Oracional de Fernán Pérez* in that it appears at the end of the 1487 edition of that text. *Apología sobre el salmo Judica me Deus* is a line-by-line exegesis of Ps. 42: 1–5. The same edition of the *Oracional de Fernán Pérez*, in the pages following the *Apología sobre el salmo Judica me Deus*, also includes a brief moral treatise in the form of a commentary on St. John Chrysostom's *Quod nemo laeditur nisi a seipso* (That No One Is Harmed if Not by Himself). Cartagena's *Glosa al Tratado de San Juan Crisóstomo* (Gloss on the Treatise of Saint John Chrysostom) concerns the nature of divine providence versus free will.

The rhetorical parameters of the speeches Cartagena delivered at the Council of Basel are developed further in the *Anacephaleosis* (Genealogical Treatise, 1454–1456), his last work. Like the *Memoriale Virtutum*, this book was also translated into Castilian after his death, with the title *El libro de la genealogía de los reyes de España* (Book on the Genealogy of the Kings of Spain). Robert Brian Tate observes that the *Anacephaleosis* is based primarily on Cartagena's interpretation of Rodrigo Jiménez de Rada's thirteenth-century *Historia de rebus Hispaniae* (History of Spain). The observation is significant in that it underscores Cartagena's disapproval of fictional romances as recommended reading, an opinion he expresses most emphatically in the epistle to Fernández de Velasco. The *Anacephaleosis* can be categorized as genealogical literature, the point of which is to establish the identity of a particular individual or of a nation. Cartagena traces the royal lineage from Athanaric to Enrique IV, thereby confirming the Gothic (and therefore Christian) heritage of a man who was all too often accused of being a crypto-Muslim, as well as confirming his legitimate claim to the throne of Castile. On the basis of Cartagena's speeches delivered at the Council of Basel and the *Anacephaleosis*, the critic José Antonio Maravall describes him as one of the first authors in Spanish history who actively promoted what could be called a nationalistic agenda.

Alfonso de Cartagena died at Villasandino, on the way back to Burgos from a pilgrimage to Santiago de Compostela, on 22 July 1456, just two years after the death of Juan II and the coronation of Enrique IV.

Cartagena was buried in the Chapel of the Visitation, a chapel that he founded in Burgos Cathedral. While he lived long enough to see Enrique IV become king of Castile, he was spared the disappointment of witnessing Enrique's failures as a monarch. The political and nationalistic unity for which he yearned came to pass only after Queen Isabella ascended the throne of Castile upon her brother Enrique's death, cemented a strategically brilliant marital alliance with Ferdinand II of Aragon, and forged ruthlessly ahead with the Reconquest. From a literary perspective Cartagena's career constitutes a paradox characteristic of his epoch, which stands at the threshold of the Middle Ages and the Renaissance in Spain, for his works reveal a man of vast erudition and artistic talent who nonetheless wrote almost exclusively because of the prompting of others. Perhaps because he wrote at the request of those around him, there is no uniform voice—*converso*, humanistic, scholastic, or otherwise—in Cartagena's works, which, taken as a whole, attest to the complexity of his character, his ambitions, and the age in which he lived. The most important modern biographies of Cartagena are the sections dedicated to his life and works in the pioneering studies of Luciano Serrano and Francisco Cantera Burgos. Cartagena's literary and political career are the subject of an extensive and well-documented 2002 study by Luis Fernández Gallardo. In 1991 Morrás published an indispensable bibliographical guide to Cartagena's literary production. Morrás's study is particularly useful because she lists manuscript copies and early printed versions of Cartagena's works, as well as modern editions and a comprehensive list of secondary sources.

**Biography:**

Luis Fernández Gallardo, *Alonso de Cartagena: Una biografía política en la Castilla del siglo XV* (Madrid: Junta de Castilla y León, 2002).

**References:**

Antonio Bravo García, "Sobre las traducciones de Plutarco y de Quinto Curcio Rufo hechas por Pier Candido Decembrio y su fortuna en España," *Cuadernos de Filología Clásica*, 12 (1977): 143–185;

Gerard Breslin, "The *Duodenarium* of Alonso de Cartagena: A Brief Report on the Manuscript and Contents," *La corónica*, 18, no. 1 (1989): 90–102;

Carlos Cabrera, "Cartagena, traductor de Séneca: Aproximación al estudio del manuscrito escurialense N-ij-6," *Studia Zamorensia*, 8 (1987): 7–25;

Mar Campos Souto, "Aproximación a las fuentes y al uso de autoridades en el *Memorial de virtudes* de Alonso de Cartagena," in *Proceedings of the Eighth Colloquium*, edited by Andrew M. Beresford and Alan Deyermond, Papers of the Medieval Hispanic Research Seminar, no. 5 (London: Department of Hispanic Studies, Queen Mary and Westfield College, 1997), pp. 39–47;

Campos Souto, "Notas para una edición del *Memorial de virtudes*," in *Actas del I Congreso de Jóvenes Filólogos (A Coruña, 25–28 de septiembre de 1996): Edición y anotación de textos*, 2 volumes, edited by Carmen Parrilla García and others (A Coruña: Universidade de A Coruña, 1999), I: 153–162;

Francisco Cantera Burgos, *Alvar García de Santa María y su familia de conversos: Historia de la Judería de Burgos y de sus conversos más egregios* (Madrid: Instituto Arias Montano, 1952);

James Hankins, *Plato in the Italian Renaissance*, 2 volumes (Leiden & New York: Brill, 1990);

Arturo Hernansanz Serrano, "Hacia una edición del *Memoriale Virtutum* de Alfonso de Cartagena," *Cuadernos de Filología Clásica: Estudios Latinos*, 6 (1993): 177–193;

Olga Tudorica Impey, "Alfonso de Cartagena, traductor de Séneca y precursor del humanismo español," *Prohemio*, 3 (1972): 473–494;

Gregory B. Kaplan, "Toward the Establishment of a Christian Identity: The *conversos* and Early Castilian Humanism," *La corónica*, 25, no. 1 (1996): 53–68;

Jeremy N. H. Lawrance, "Alfonso de Cartagena y los conversos," in *Actas del primer congreso anglo-hispano*, volume 2: *Literatura*, edited by Deyermond and Ralph Penny (Madrid: Castalia, 1993), pp. 103–120;

Lawrance, "La autoridad de la letra: un aspecto de la lucha entre humanistas y escolásticos en la Castilla del siglo XV," *Atalaya*, 2 (1991): 85–107;

Lawrance, "Humanism in the Iberian Peninsula," in *The Impact of Humanism in Western Europe*, edited by Anthony Goodman and Angus MacKay (London: Longman, 1990), pp. 220–258;

Lawrance, "The Spread of Lay Literacy in Late Medieval Castile," *Bulletin of Hispanic Studies*, 62 (1985): 79–94;

José Antonio Maravall, *El concepto de España en la Edad Media*, second edition (Madrid: Instituto de Estudios Políticos, 1964);

Matías Martínez Burgos, "Don Alonso de Cartagena, Obispo de Burgos: Su testamento," *Revista de Archivos, Bibliotecas y Museos*, 63 (1957): 81–110;

María Morrás, "Repertorio de obras, MSS y documentos de Alfonso de Cartagena (ca. 1384–1456)," *Boletín Bibliográfico de la Asociación Hispánica de Literatura Medieval*, 5 (1991): 213–248;

Morrás, "*Sic et non:* En torno a Alfonso de Cartagena y los *studia humanitatis*," *Euphrosyne*, 23 (1995): 333–346;

Eric W. Naylor, "Pero López de Ayala's translation of Boccaccio's *De Casibus*," in *Hispanic Studies in Honor of Alan D. Deyermond: A North American Tribute*, edited by John S. Miletich (Madison, Wis.: Hispanic Seminary of Medieval Studies, 1986), pp. 205–216;

Anthony R. D. Pagden, "The Diffusion of Aristotle's Moral Philosophy in Spain, ca. 1400–ca. 1600," *Traditio*, 31 (1975): 287–313;

Nicholas G. Round, *The Greatest Man Uncrowned: A Study of the Fall of Don Alvaro de Luna* (London: Tamesis, 1986);

Round, "'Perdóneme Séneca': The Translational Practices of Alonso de Cartagena," *Bulletin of Hispanic Studies*, 75 (1998): 17–29;

Peter Russell and Pagden, "Nueva luz sobre una versión de la *Etica a Nicómaco*," in *Homenaje a Guillermo Guastavino: Miscelánea de estudios en el año de su jubilación como Director de la Biblioteca Nacional* (Madrid: Asociación Nacional de Bibliotecarios, Archiveros y Arqueólogos, 1974), pp. 125–148;

Abdón Salazar, "El impacto humanístico de las misiones diplomáticas de Alonso de Cartagena en la Corte de Portugal entre medievo y renacimiento (1421–31)," in *Medieval Hispanic Studies Presented to Rita Hamilton*, edited by Deyermond (London: Tamesis, 1976), pp. 215–226;

Pilar Saquero Suárez-Somonte and Tomás González Rolán, "Actitudes renacentistas en Castilla durante el siglo XV: La correspondencia entre Alfonso de Cartagena y Pier Candido Decembrio," *Cuadernos de Filología Clásica: Estudios Latinos*, 1 (1991): 195–232;

Luciano Serrano, *Los conversos, D. Pablo de Santa María y D. Alfonso de Cartagena, obispos de Burgos, gobernantes, diplomáticos y escritores* (Madrid: Consejo superior de investigaciones científicas, 1942);

Albert Sicroff, *Los estatutos de limpieza de sangre: Controversias entre los siglos XV y XVII*, translated by Mauro Armiño (Madrid: Taurus, 1985);

Robert Brian Tate, "La *Anacephaleosis* de Alfonso García de Santa María, Obispo de Burgos, 1435–1456," in *Ensayos sobre la historiografía peninsular del siglo XV* (Madrid: Gredos, 1970), pp. 55–73;

Vittorio Zaccaria, "Pier Candido Decembrio traduttore della *Republica* di Platone," *Italia medioevale e umanistica*, 2 (1959): 176–206.

# Teresa de Cartagena

## (1425? – ?)

### Dayle Seidenspinner-Núñez
#### *University of Notre Dame*

WORKS: *Arboleda de los enfermos* and *Admiraçión operum Dey* (second half of the fifteenth century)

**Manuscript:** Escorial MS III.h.24 (dated 1481).

**Edition:** *Arboleda de los enfermos y Admiraçión operum Dey,* edited by Lewis Joseph Hutton, Anejos del Boletín de la Real Academia Española, no. 16 (Madrid: Real Academia Española, 1967).

**Edition in English:** "Grove of the Infirm" and "Wonder at the Works of God," translated by Dayle Seidenspinner-Núñez, in *The Writings of Teresa de Cartagena* (Cambridge & Rochester, N.Y.: D. S. Brewer, 1998).

Despite St. Paul's injunction proscribing women's speech (1 Tim. 2:12) and the virtual male monopoly on medieval texts and literary practice, several works were written by women in fifteenth-century Spain: the *Memorias* (Memories, circa 1410) of Leonor López de Córdoba; the *Devocionario* (Prayer Book, circa 1470) of Constanza de Castilla; *Vita Christi* (The Life of Christ, 1497), by Isabel de Villena (1430–1490); some *cancioneros* (songbook or anthology of poetry) by Florencia Pinar, María Sarmiento, and Mayor Arias; and *Arboleda de los enfermos* (translated as "Grove of the Infirm," 1998) and *Admiraçión operum Dey* (translated as "Wonder at the Works of God," 1998), by Teresa de Cartagena. The last two works, which were composed sometime after 1450 and survive in a unique manuscript, have attracted increased critical and scholarly commentary. *Arboleda de los enfermos* was written first; the theme of the work is the spiritual benefit of affliction–specifically of deafness, which had been a source of anguish to Cartagena for twenty years. She wrote *Admiraçión operum Dey* to counter the *admiraçión* (incredulity) of critics who accused her of plagiarizing male authors in *Arboleda de los enfermos* and contended that a woman–particularly a handicapped woman–had nothing of value to teach.

Cartagena's writings merit critical attention on several counts. First, they are important documents of the intellectual and social landscape of fifteenth-century Spain, for both Cartagena's family and her texts were deeply rooted in the literary culture of her time. Second, *Arboleda de los enfermos* is an excellent example of the consolatory treatises cultivated widely in the fifteenth century and is the only extant one written from a woman's perspective. Third, throughout the 1400s in Spain pro- versus antifeminist debates were waged in *cancionero* poetry, moralist commentary, and sentimental romances by male clerics, poets, and writers of fiction; *Admiraçión operum Dey* represents the only authentic female voice in this controversy. Fourth, Cartagena's work is of interest in the overall context of women writers in medieval Europe; in Hispanic literature she is the spiritual precursor of both St. Teresa de Ávila in the sixteenth century and Sor Juana Inés de la Cruz in the seventeenth century in combining devotional writing with an autobiographical focus and a defense against male detractors. Finally, *Arboleda de los enfermos* and *Admiraçión operum Dey* are compelling records of personal suffering and religious experience that represent a unique example of marginalized discourse. Cartagena was thrice marginalized as an author: by her gender, her deafness, and her status as a *conversa* (converted Jew)–her family had converted to Christianity in the late fourteenth century–and she wrote at a time when anti-Jewish and anti-*converso* riots were common. The worst of these events–the Toledan Rebellion of 1449–occurred not long before the composition of *Arboleda de los enfermos.*

Teresa de Cartagena belonged to the most influential and powerful *converso* family in late-medieval Spain. Throughout the fifteenth and sixteenth centuries the Cartagena–Santa María clan was pivotal in Spain's political, religious, economic, and literary cultures. Her grandfather, Rabbi Šelomó ha-Levi, had converted to Christianity, along with his children and brothers, in 1390 or 1391 and had been baptized Pablo de Santa María. Santa María had advanced rapidly within the ranks of both church and state, becoming bishop of Cartagena in 1402 and of Burgos in 1412 and serving as royal chancellor of Castile in the courts of Enrique III and Juan II and as tutor of the latter during his minority. Author of exegetical and theological tracts and historical works, Santa María also composed an extended poem, *Siete edades del mundo* (Seven Ages of the World, circa 1416–1418; published, 1516), a compendium of universal and national history for the instruction of Castile's future monarch. His brother, Álvar García de Santa María, was an influential political figure and royal scribe, secretary, and chronicler of the court of Juan II. Pablo de Santa María's oldest son, Gonzalo García de Santa María, was a professor at the University of Salamanca, bishop of Plasencia, and a diplomatic and ecclesiastical ambassador for the Castilian court. His second son, Alonso de Cartagena, was bishop of Palencia before succeeding his father as bishop of Burgos; judge of the Royal Tribunal of Juan II; and Castile's representative at the Council of Basel. A leading humanist of his day, he was also the author of twenty-six works of law, history, and moral philosophy. The third son, Pedro de Cartagena, was a city official of Burgos, a knight in the court of Juan II, and counselor to Enrique IV and the Catholic Monarchs, Fernando and Isabel (Ferdinand and Isabella).

Teresa's affiliation with the Cartagena family was not definitively established until 1952, when Francisco Cantera Burgos found her mentioned in the will of Alonso de Cartagena, dated July 1453. She is listed as a daughter of Pedro de Cartagena and María de Sarabia and identified as a nun. This will is the only known historical document that refers to her. Cantera Burgos could not find dates of birth or death for any of the Cartagena women; they are only mentioned in documents pertaining to marriage, or primogeniture–in which Teresa, as a nun, is, of course, absent. The little else that is known about her has been culled from scattered details in her manuscript and from what is known about her family. Her name and her deafness are revealed in the introductory rubrics to *Arboleda de los enfermos,* "el qual conpuso Teresa de Cartajena seyendo apasyonada de graues dolençias, especialmente auiendo el sentido del oýr perdido del todo" (which Teresa de Cartagena composed, being afflicted with grave ailments, in particular, having completely lost her sense of hearing). The rubrics to *Admiraçión operum Dey* identify her as a nun: "Aquí comiença vn breue tractado el qual co[n]uinientemente se puede llamar Admiraçión operum Dey. Conpúsole Teresa de Cartajena, religosa de la horden de . . . a petiçión e ruego de la Señora Doña Juana de Mendoça, muger del Señor Gomes Manrique" (Here begins a brief treatise that can be fittingly called the *Wonder at the Works of God.* Teresa de Cartagena, a nun of the Order of . . . , composed it at the petition and request of Lady Juana de Mendoza, wife of Lord Gómez Manrique). Although the name of her religious order was omitted by the copyist, most scholars believe

that she was a Franciscan and lived in the monastery of Santa Clara in Burgos or in a convent in Toledo. Cartagena says that she has been deaf for twenty years and is in constant poor health; that prior to her deafness she studied at the University of Salamanca; and that after her deafness she spent much time alone, reading her books and meditating.

Cartagena was probably born about 1425 and grew up in the family home on Calle de Cantarranas la Menor, a center of social, political, and cultural activity in Burgos and a frequent stopover for visiting national and international dignitaries. In the Cartagena tradition, she and her siblings must have received excellent educations, and they would have had available the resources of the various family libraries. In all likelihood she was tutored at home and then sent to Salamanca to study in a convent as the daughter of a wealthy noble family. Her privileged position as a Cartagena must have provided an exceptional foundation in religion and moral philosophy that she later expanded and deepened with her own solitary readings.

In her discussion of human vanity in *Arboleda de los enfermos* Cartagena mentions her chronic sickliness in her *pueriçia o moçedat* (childhood), its continuation throughout her *adolesçençia* (adolescence), and her greatly increased suffering–presumably the onset of her deafness–in her *jouentut* (youth or prime). In the medieval period human ages were conventionally divided into groups of seven years: in the four-age scheme that Cartagena uses, *pueritia* lasts from birth to age fourteen, *adolescentia* from fourteen to twenty-eight, *iuventus* from twenty-eight to forty-nine, and *senectus* or *vejez* (old age) designates everything afterward; in the six-age system *infantia* lasts for seven years, *pueritia* from seven to fourteen, *adolescentia* from fourteen to twenty-eight, *iuventus* from twenty-eight to forty-nine, *senectus* from forty-nine to seventy, and *senium* (senility) covers all ages thereafter. *Iuventus,* or *jouentut,* denotes the same age range in both schemes. The precision and consistency of Cartagena's terminology and her probable knowledge of her grandfather's *Siete edades del mundo,* which reflects the same conventions, suggest that Teresa assigned the conventional numerical value to *jouentut.* In this case, she would have succumbed to deafness between her late twenties and her late forties–much later than traditionally assumed. Since she states that she is writing *Arboleda de los enfermos* after twenty years of deafness, its date of composition may be as late as between 1473–1481, the latter date provided by the copyist of the manuscript, Pero López del Trigo.

In the prologue to *Arboleda de los enfermos* Teresa addresses a *virtuosa señora* (virtuous lady) who presumably requested the composition of the work. This person is commonly thought to be Mendoza, who is explicitly identified as the addressee of *Admiración operum Dey*. This inscribed reader fulfills two rhetorical functions: it takes responsibility away from Cartagena as a writer, since she can be seen as acceding to a request rather than initiating the act of writing; and the designation of an accessible and receptive female addressee facilitates communication to a more general audience. She allegorizes her grief and confusion as she is cut off from the world and enveloped in silence and sadness, carried off to an island named "Opprobrium hominum et abiecio plebis" (The Scorn of Mankind and Outcast of the People). She enumerates her purpose for writing the treatise: to combat idleness, to share her experience with others so they may learn from it, and to give praise and thanks to God. The prologue concludes with Ps. 31:9, one of the biblical verses the treatise will gloss: "With bit and bridle bind fast their jaws, who come not near unto thee."

Cartagena presents her deafness as a well-deserved punishment inflicted by a stern, authoritative, but loving God to cut her off from the distracting noises of a world to which she was resolutely attached. While her suffering is painful on a physical or material plane, from a spiritual perspective it imposes a "blessed solitude" that isolates her from dangerous sins and from things that are inimical to body and soul. The other spiritual benefit of her deafness is silence: Cartagena interprets her lack of hearing as a divine prohibition of speaking as well, and she refuses worldly conversations and visits. Cloistered by her deafness, she turns inward, rechanneling her desires from the worldly to the spiritual; shut off from the noises and conversations of the world and enveloped in silence, she listens instead to the *las bozes de la santa dotrina que la Escritura nos ensena* (voices of holy doctrine that Scriptures teach us). One of the primary sources for her discussion of the benefits derived from deafness is the *Libro de las consolaciones de la vida humana* (Book of Consolations for Human Life, published in 1884), by Pedro de Luna, who became Benedict XIII, an antipope who was elected by French cardinals in 1394 and remained in office until 1417.

*Arboleda de los enfermos* is presented as the result of a prolonged dialogue between Cartagena and the books she has read. For her the act of reading is as profoundly autobiographical as that of writing. While *Arboleda de los enfermos* is ostensibly a gloss of Ps. 31:9, Ps. 44:10 ("Listen, O daughter, and behold, and incline thy ear: forget thy people and the house of thy father"), and 2 Cor. 12:9 ("Gladly therefore will I glory in my infirmities, that the virtue of Christ may dwell in me"), these verses, in fact, serve to gloss and inform her spiritual autobiography, marking the divine infliction of her deafness, her separation from her family, and her final celebration of the spiritual benefits of her affliction. In

*Front cover for the English translation (1998) of Teresa de Cartagena's two works (Bruccoli Clark Layman Archives)*

the process, she constructs herself largely through literary analogues, generally through male biblical figures and voices: David, Job, the blind man on the road to Jericho, Lazarus, and, ultimately, Christ. She portrays herself as a faithful sinner so beloved and chosen by God that he inflicts suffering to draw her closer to him, to protect her from the dangers of this world, and, thus, to prepare her for salvation.

The second half of *Arboleda de los enfermos* is a lengthy discussion of *Paçiençia* (Patience), who presides as abbess over the convent of afflictions. Cartagena explains that the etymology of *paçiençia–paz* (suffering) and *çiençia* (wisdom or knowledge)–indicates that patience means to suffer with prudence. She speaks of the three purposes of affliction (to test, to correct, and to condemn) and the two degrees of patience (tolerating misfortunes, and recognizing these as a blessing for spiritual profit) and offers an extended exegesis of the New

Testament parable of the five talents to demonstrate the economy of deriving spiritual profit from affliction. She expatiates on the use of afflictions to combat the seven deadly sins: suffering turns pride into humility, avarice into generosity, envy into charity, gluttony into abstinence, lust into chastity, wrath into docility, and sloth into labor. Afflictions also cure the six roots of pride: lineage, well-proportioned body, youth and beauty, eloquence and intellect, worldly dignities and honors, and abundance of riches. She interprets Job as an exemplar of patience and concludes by defining the kind of virtue Patience is: Patience's dwelling is built on the foundation of the four cardinal virtues of prudence, temperance, fortitude, and justice; and its stairway leads to the three theological virtues of hope, faith, and charity, which, in turn, guide the sufferer to God.

*Arboleda de los enfermos* has been read as a work of autoconsolation, as an attempt to overcome the isolation imposed by Cartagena's deafness, as a sermon, and as an example of women's self-writing. Her awareness of her anomaly as a woman writer is manifested in a variety of her literary strategies, such as the self-deprecating and gendered humility formulas ("la baxeza e grosería de mi mugeril yngenio" [the lowliness and grossness of my womanly mind]) she uses both to disarm potentially hostile readers and to capture their goodwill, her appropriation of male authorities and voices to support her statements, and the use of the implied female reader—the *virtuosa señora*—to justify her writing and facilitate its reception.

The ultimate failure of these strategies is recorded in the prologue to *Admiración operum Dey,* where Cartagena recounts the antagonistic reception of *Arboleda de los enfermos* by *los prudentes varones* (the prudent male readers) who rejected a woman's access to writing and disputed Cartagena's authorship of her own autobiographical and devotional text. Addressing Mendoza, Cartagena states that her reason for writing *Admiración operum Dey* is that some people have marveled at her authorship of *Arboleda de los enfermos;* while she acknowledges that this reaction is a personal insult to her, she claims to be writing for the more important reason that these doubts offend God and call into question the nature and extent of his mercy. She distinguishes between two types of wonder: wonder mixed with devotion and faith that praises and venerates God, because, in marveling at his blessings, one admires his omnipotence, wisdom, and goodness; and wonder mixed with incredulity that offends God, because it gives more importance to the thing that inspires wonder than to the greatness of its divine source. Miracles are designated as such purely by convention: all of God's creation is equally full of wonder; people marvel at some things more than others

because the former are uncommon. Thus, one marvels at a woman writing a treatise because writing is not customary for women. Men have written for so long that writing seems natural for a man and unnatural for a woman; that is, custom has been mistaken for nature. But God made men and women different so that they might complement and help each other and secure the preservation of the human race, not so that one sex might have greater advantage or excellence. As the basis of her defense, then, Cartagena is arguing for the social, rather than the divine, construction of gender: the horizontal differences with which God invested the sexes have been transformed into vertical hierarchies of superiority and inferiority.

In introducing the socially constructed inferiority of women, Cartagena calls into question other cultural conventions, as well. While literature and learning have traditionally been transmitted from male to male, it is certainly within God's power to grant to women whatever preeminences he gives to men. The biblical example of Judith and Holofernes illustrates her point: if God can overcome a woman's inherent physical weakness and endow her with the strength and courage to slay a formidable enemy such as Holofernes, surely he can illuminate the understanding and intelligence of a woman and inspire her to write.

All blessings derive from God—both blessings of nature or fortune such as bravery, beauty, intelligence, and riches, which are often mistakenly ascribed to the person who possesses them rather than to God, and blessings of grace, which are great and extraordinary, surpassing those of nature and fortune, and are attributable only to the superabundance of God's mercy. Male writing is an example of the blessings of nature and fortune, while women's writing is a blessing of grace. Cartagena strategically insists on the inscrutability of such grace-laden blessings and admonishes her detractors that to doubt her authorship of *Arboleda de los enfermos* is to question God's capacity for grace and mercy. She affirms her first work as a product of her experience and of God's teaching, not of plagiarized male sources.

In defending her earlier work the anxieties and timidity characteristic of *Arboleda de los enfermos* are replaced by an assertiveness that is evident from the beginning of *Admiración operum Dey.* Gone are the pretext of the requested work, the oblique self-dramatization through literary analogues, and the use of a figurative landscape to explore herself. Cartagena takes responsibility for her writing and directly positions herself in her text. In the process, the narrative structure of her defense becomes more complex than that of her first work: in *Arboleda de los enfermos* the confessional autobiography is directed primarily to the *virtuosa señora* and secondarily to a more general audience of which the "virtuous lady" is an extension. In *Admiraçión operum Dey* the *virtuosa señora* again serves as the primary receptor; but she is not identified with the secondary readership of Teresa's defense, those *prudentes varones* who have criticized and repudiated her earlier work. This double audience accommodates the pervasive irony that distinguishes *Admiraçión operum Dey:* while Cartagena's defense is ostensibly directed to the *virtuosa señora* who acts more as an accomplice and confidante than as a judge, rhetorical points are scored against her hostile, but absent and silenced, detractors. Not the least irony is the increasing tautology of the *prudentes varones:* the insistent repetition of the phrase *prudentes varones* while she demonstrates that their incredulity is, in fact, unwise insinuates that their prudence is culturally assigned because of their maleness, not determined by their actions.

The primary purpose of Cartagena's defense, nevertheless, is to reclaim the text her critics have denied her. In the first half of *Admiraçión operum Dey* she reaffirms her authorship by arguing its possibility—the possibility of women's writing as a blessing of grace; in the second half she reoccupies the interdicted (masculine) position of *auctor* (author), comparing her spiritually blind understanding, still bound up in worldly cares, to the parable of the blind man on the road to the worldly city of Jericho in the Gospel of Luke. Like the blind man, Cartagena's clouded understanding calls out to God to see the light, and ultimately God illuminates her understanding. *Arboleda de los enfermos* is defended as a product of this enlightened understanding that she wrote to praise God, to know God, to know herself, to deny her own will, to accept the cross of her suffering, and to follow in Christ's footsteps. Cartagena thus completes the autobiographical project that was suspended halfway through *Arboleda de los enfermos,* tracing her journey toward spiritual understanding and self-knowledge—a journey that ends in a daring *imitatio Christi* (imitation of Christ). She then examines the three powers of the soul—understanding, memory, and will—and concludes by exhorting her fellow sufferers not to permit these powers to be distracted by their physical senses or by vain material things but to apply them to seeking God, who will respond with grace and mercy.

It is not clear why López del Trigo copied what Teresa describes as a sheaf of rough drafts written in her own hand. But his manuscript of *Arboleda de los enfermos* and *Admiraçión operum Dey* provides a rare window into the world of women in fifteenth-century Spain and allows the modern reader to recover, if only in part, Cartagena's remarkable struggle—first to give meaning to her misfortune and definition to herself through writing *Arboleda de los enfermos,* and later to con-

front her detractors and defend the divine inspiration for her texts and her life and her own right to write.

**References:**

Electa Arenal and Stacey Schlau, *Untold Sisters: Hispanic Nuns in Their Own Works* (Albuquerque: University of New Mexico Press, 1989);

Denise-Renée Bargeret, "'Weak Womanly Understanding': Writers of Women from the Arcipreste de Talavera to Teresa de Cartagena," Ph.D. thesis, University of Massachusetts, Amherst, 1999;

Francisco Cantera Burgos, *Alvar García de Santa María y su familia de conversos: Historia de la judería en Burgos y de sus conversos más egregios* (Madrid: Instituto Arias Montano, 1952);

Américo Castro, *The Structure of Spanish History* (Princeton: Princeton University Press, 1954), p. 346;

Clara Esther Castro Ponce, "Teresa de Cartagena, *Arboleda de los enfermos, Admiraçion operum Dei:* edicíon crítica singular," dissertation, Brown University, 2001;

Alan Deyermond, "Las autoras medievales castellanas a la luz de las últimas investigaciones," in *Medioevo y literatura: Actas del V Congreso de la Asociación Hispánica de Literatura Medieval,* volume 1, edited by Juan Paredes (Granada: Universidad de Granada, 1995), pp. 31–52;

Deyermond, "'El convento de dolençias': The Works of Teresa de Cartagena," *Journal of Hispanic Philology,* 1 (1976–1977): 19–29;

Deyermond, "Spain's First Women Writers," in *Women in Hispanic Literature: Icons and Fallen Idols,* edited by Beth Miller (Berkeley: University of California Press, 1983), pp. 27–52;

Ottavio Di Camillo, *El humanismo castellano del siglo XV* (Valencia: Fernando Torres, 1976);

Deborah S. Ellis, "Unifying Imagery in the Works of Teresa de Cartagena: Home and the Dispossessed," *Journal of Hispanic Philology,* 17 (Fall 1992 [1995]): 43–53;

Mary Elizabeth Frieden, "Epistolarity in the Works of Teresa de Cartagena and Leonor López de Córdoba," Ph.D. thesis, University of Missouri, Columbia, 2001;

Elizabeth Teresa Howe, "Sor Teresa de Cartagena and *Entendimiento,*" *Romanische Forschungen,* 108 (1996): 133–145;

Encarnación Juárez, "The Autobiography of the Aching Body in Teresa de Cartagena's *Arboleda de los enfermos,*" in *Disability Studies: Enabling the Humanities,* edited by Sharon L. Snyder, Brenda Jo Brueggemann, and Rosemarie Garland-Thomson (New York: Modern Language Association of America, 2002), pp. 131–143;

Amy Kaminsky, *Water Lilies/Flores del Agua: An Anthology of Spanish Women Writers from the Fifteenth through the Nineteenth Century* (Minneapolis: University of Minnesota Press, 1996), pp. 37–53;

Francisco López Estrada, "Las mujeres escritoras en la Edad Media castellana," in *La condición de la mujer en la edad media: Actas del Coloquio celebrado en la Casa de Velázquez del 5 al 7 de noviembre de 1984,* edited by Yves-René Fonquerne and Alfonso Esteban (Madrid: Editorial de la Universidad Complutense, 1986), pp. 9–38;

Pedro de Luna, "Libro de las consolaciones de la vida humana," in *Escritores en prosa anteriores al siglo XV,* edited by Pascual de Gayangos, Biblioteca de Autores Españoles, volume 51 (Madrid: Sucesores de Hernando, 1884), pp. 561–602;

Juan Marichal, *Teoría e historia del ensayismo hispánico* (Madrid: Alianza Editorial, 1984), pp. 17–35;

Carmen Marimón Llorca, *Prosistas castellanas medievales* (Alicante: Publicaciones de la Caja de Ahorros Provincial, 1990), pp. 102–140;

M. Martínez Burgos, "Don Alonso de Cartagena, Obispo de Burgos: Su testamento," *Revista de Archivos, Bibliotecas y Museos,* 63 (1957): 81–110;

Louise Mirrer, "Feminist Approaches to Medieval Spanish History and Literature," *Medieval Feminist Newsletter,* 7 (Spring 1989): 2–7;

Irene Alejandra Molina, "La *Arboleda de los enfermos* de Teresa de Cartagena: Un sermón olvidado," M.A. thesis, University of Texas at Austin, 1990;

María-Milagros Rivera Garretas, "Teresa de Cartagena: Escritura en relación," *La escritura femenina: De leer a excribir II,* edited by Ángela Muñoz Fernández (Madrid: Association Cultural Al-Mudayna, 2000), pp. 95–110;

Gregorio Rodríguez Rivas, "La *Arboleda de los enfermos* de Teresa de Cartagena, literatura ascética en el siglo XV," *Entemu* (Centro Asociado de Asturias), 3 (1991): 117–130;

Dayle Seidenspinner-Núñez, "'But I Suffer Not a Woman to Speak': Two Women Writers in Late Medieval Spain," in *Hers Ancient and Modern: Women Writing in Spain and Brazil,* edited by Catherine Davies and Jane Whetnall (London: Department of Hispanic Studies, Queen Mary and Westfield College, 1997), pp. 1–14;

Seidenspinner-Núñez, "'El solo me leyó': Gendered Hermeneutics and Subversive Poetics in *Admiración operum Dey* of Teresa de Cartagena," *Medievalia,* 15 (1993): 14–23;

Manuel Serrano y Sanz, *Apuntes para una biblioteca de escritoras españolas desde el año 1410 al 1833,* 2 volumes (Madrid: Sucesores de Rivadeneyra, 1903, 1905), I: 218–233;

Ronald E. Surtz, "Image Patterns in Teresa de Cartagena's *Arboleda de los enfermos,*" in *LA CHISPA '87: Selected Proceedings,* edited by Gilbert Paolini (New Orleans: Tulane University, 1987), pp. 297–304;

Surtz, *Writing Women in Late Medieval and Early Modern Spain: The Mothers of Saint Teresa of Avila* (Philadelphia: University of Pennsylvania Press, 1995), pp. 21–40;

Luis Miguel Vicente García, "La defensa de la mujer como intelectual en Teresa de Cartagena y Sor Juana Inés de la Cruz," *Mester,* 18 (Fall 1989): 95–103.

# Juan de Flores
## (fl. 1470 – 1500)

Lillian von der Walde Moheno
*Universidad Autónoma Metropolitana–Iztapalapa*

WORKS: *Grisel y Mirabella* (1474–1475?)

**Manuscripts:** Vatican City, Biblioteca Apostolica Vaticana MS. Vat. Lat. 6966, fols. 68r–76v, fifteenth-century fragment; Milan, Biblioteca Trivulziana MS. 940, fols. 1r–76v, sixteenth century; *Historia de Torrellas y Brianda,* Seville, Biblioteca Colombina MS. 5-3-20, fols. 69r–86r, fifteenth- or early-sixteenth-century fragment.

**First publication:** *Tractado compuesto por Johan de flores a su amiga* (Lérida?: Henrique Botel?, ca. 1490–1495), Madrid, Biblioteca Nacional, I-281; San Marino, Cal., Huntingdon Library, 87232.

**Early editions:** *La hystoria de Griesel y Mirabella con la disputa de Torrellas y Braçayda* (Seville: Juan Varela de Salamanca, 1514); *La historia de Grisel y Mirabella con la disputa de Torrellas y Braçayda* (Seville: Jacobo Cromberger, 1524); *La historia de Grisel y Mirabella con la disputa de Torrellas et Braçayda* (Toledo: Miguel de Eguía, 1526); *La historia de Grisel y Mirabella con la disputa de Torrellas y Braçayda* (Seville: Juan Cromberger, 1529); *La historia de Grisel et Mirabella con la disputa de Torrellas y Braçayda* (Seville: Juan Cromberger, 1533); *La historia de Grisel y Mirabella con la disputa de Torrellas y Braçayda* (Cuenca: Juan de Cánova, 1561; Burgos: Philippe de Junta, 1562).

**Modern editions:** *Tractado compuesto por Johan de Flores a su amiga* "Grisel y Mirabella"], in Barbara Matulka, *The Novels of Juan de Flores and Their European Diffusion* (New York: Institute of French Studies, 1931; reprinted, Geneva: Slatkine, 1974), pp. 333–370; *Tractado compuesto por Johan de flores a su amiga,* facsimile edition (Madrid: Real Academia Española, 1954); *La historia de Grisel y Mirabella,* edited by Pablo Alcázar López and José A. González Núñez, Los libros del Curioso Impertinente, Serie Clásica, no. 1 (Granada: Don Quijote, 1983).

*Triunfo de Amor* (1475–1476?)

**Manuscripts:** *Triunfo de Amor,* Madrid, Biblioteca Nacional MS. 22019, 70ff., fifteenth or early six-teenth century; *Triumpho de Amor,* Seville, Biblioteca Colombina MS. 5-3-20, fols. 27r–68r, fifteenth or early sixteenth century.

**Modern editions:** *Triunfo de Amor,* edited by Antonio Gargano (Pisa: Giardini, 1981); *Crónica incompleta de los Reyes Católicos (1476–1477?) Textos y concordancias de Biblioteca Nacional ms. 22019 y Biblioteca Colombina ms. 5-3-20. "Triunfo de Amor,"* transcripted by Juan Fernández Jiménez (Madison, Wis.: Hispanic Seminary of Medieval Studies, 1986); *Trihunfo de Amor,* transcripted by Fernández Jiménez in *Admyte II. Archivo digital de manuscritos y textos españoles* (Madrid: Micronet, 1999).

**Manuscript:** *Crónica del rey don Fernando y doña Ysabel,* Madrid, Real Academia de la Historia MS. G-20, fifteenth or early sixteenth century.

**Modern edition:** *Crónica incompleta de los Reyes Católicos (1469-1476),* edited by Julio Puyol (Madrid: Academia de la Historia, 1934).

*Grimalte y Gradisa* (1477?)

**Manuscripts:** *Comiença un breue tractado compuesto por Johan de Flores el qual por la siguiente obra mudo su nombre en grimalte,* Madrid, Biblioteca Nacional MS. 22018, 55ff. (lacks the first folio); *Cartas de Grimalte y Fromista,* Seville, Biblioteca Colombina MS. 5-3-20, fols. 90r–101v, fifteenth or early six-teenth century (fragment minus the poems but with an extended finale; this testimony probably represents Flores's original version).

**First publication:** *Comiença un breue tractado compuesto por Johan de Flores: El qual por la siguiente obra mudo su nombre en grimalte* (Lérida?: Henrique Botel?, ca. 1495).

**Modern editions:** *Comiença un breue tractado compuesto por Johan de Flores el qual por la siguiente obra mudo su nombre en Grimalte* ["Grimalte y Gradissa"], in Barbara Matulka, *The Novels of Juan de Flores and Their European Diffusion,* pp. 374–432; *Grimalte y Gradissa,* edited by Pamela Waley (London: Tamesis, 1931); *Grimalte y Gradisa,* edited by Carmen Parrilla García, Monografías da Universidade de Santiago de Compostela, no. 140 (Santiago de Compostela: Universidade de Santiago de Compostela, 1988).

**Attributions:**

*La coronación de la señora Gracisla* (1475?)

**Manuscript:** *La coronacion de la señora Gracisla,* Madrid, Biblioteca Nacional MS. 22020, fols. 1r–32r, fifteenth or early sixteenth century.

**Modern edition:** *La coronación de la señora Gracisla,* in *Dos opúsculos isabelinos: "La coronación de la señora Gracisla" y Nicolás Núñez "Cárcel de Amor,"* edited by Keith Whinnom, Exeter Hispanic Texts, 22 (Exeter: University of Exeter, 1979).

*Cartas de Iseo y Tristán*

**Manuscript:** *Carta enviada por Hiseo la Brunda a Tristan de Leonis quexandose del porque la dexo presa a su causa y se caso con Hiseo de las Blancas Manos* and *Respuesta de Tristan desculpandose de la innocente culpa que le encargan,* Madrid, Biblioteca Nacional MS. 22021, fols. 8v–12v, late fifteenth or early sixteenth century.

**Modern edition:** "Carta de Iseo y respuesta de Tristán," edited by Fernando Gómez Redondo, *Dicenda: Cuadernos de Filología Hispánica,* 7 (1987): 327–356.

Thanks to the research of Joseph J. Gwara and Carmen Parrilla García, some details have begun to emerge about Juan de Flores's life. It seems certain that Flores came from Salamanca and belonged to the lower nobility. He was probably the son of Fernando de Flores, also from Salamanca, and served the houses of Alba and of the Catholic Monarchs: Fernando (Ferdinand) of Aragón and Isabel (Isabella) of Castile. In 1475 Flores was appointed *consejero real* (royal councillor) and, almost certainly, *cronista real* (royal chronicler) the following year. His service to the Castilian royal house perhaps antedated the accession of Isabel in 1474 because a "Johan de Flores" is cited as an *escribano de la cámara del rey* (scribe of the king's chamber) in a document dated 1465. In 1478 Flores was rector of the University of Salamanca, where he probably obtained the degree of *bachiller* (bachelor) and where—though there are other hypotheses—he might have established relations with his collaborator-to-be in the writing of *Grimalte y Gradisa* (1477?), Alonso de Córdoba. Córdoba has not yet been accurately identified, although it is certain that a *bachiller* with that name was associated with the University of Salamanca during the dates of Flores's rectorship and in 1480. Gwara believes, on the testimony of several passages in the *Crónica incompleta de los Reyes Católicos* (Incomplete Chronicle of the Catholic Kings, 1476–1477?), that Flores's principal activity was that of *corregidor* (provincial governor). Both Gwara and Parrilla García point to the existence of a man with that name and position in documents in the Archive of Simancas. While Castile was Flores's principal dwelling and working place, certain lexical characteristics of his writings indicate that he might have had some connection with Aragón. Some, such as Gwara, maintain that he married Beatriz de Quiñones, but other documents suggest that he married Inés de Rivas, a noblewoman from Salamanca. Flores's dates of birth and death are unknown, but his name no longer figures after 1503 among those in the service of the royal household.

Flores's literary output possibly belongs to the decade of the 1470s, but the dating of his works is still uncertain. María Eugenia Lacarra gives the following order of production to those works that mention him as author: *Grisel y Mirabella* (1474–1475?), *Triunfo de Amor* (Triumph of Love, 1475–1476?), and *Grimalte y Gradisa.* This order has not been corroborated, though Gwara has speculated that *Triunfo de Amor* was composed between September 1475 and May 1476. The *Crónica incompleta de los Reyes Católicos,* which records events up to 1477, must have been written immediately after the *Triunfo,* as an "incomplete" project that was never concluded. The attribution of this historical work to Flores seems certain, although the matter has yet to be settled because the work has received scant attention from specialists.

Basing his conclusions on linguistic and structural comparisons, Gwara also attributes the authorship of *Cartas de Iseo y Tristán* (Letters of Yseut and Tristan)—comprising *Hiseo la Brunda a Tristán* (Yseut the Blonde to Tristan) and *Respuesta de Tristán* (Tristan's Answer)—and *La coronación de la señora Gracisla* (The Crowning of Gracisla) to Flores. These works appear in a single manuscript that also includes, among other works, *Triunfo de Amor* and *Grimalte y Gradisa.* Gwara maintains that *La coronación de la señora Gracisla* was composed in 1475 to honor the future marriage of Leonor de Acuña and Pedro Álvarez Osorio II, Marqués of Astorga, and that the work depends stylistically on *Grisel y Mirabella,* but these theories have not been corroborated. Gwara demonstrates, however, that the hypothesis that the work was composed in the first decade of the sixteenth century is no longer tenable. If all of Gwara's hypotheses prove to be true, one can conjecture the following sequence of composition: *Grisel y Mirabella, La coronación de la señora Gracisla, Triunfo de Amor, Crónica incompleta de los Reyes Católicos, Grimalte y Gradisa* (1477, initial redaction? 1478–1479, with Córdoba's collaboration?), and the two letters of Yseut and Tristan (?).

Two of Flores's works have chiefly captured the attention of critics: *Grisel y Mirabella* and *Grimalte y Gradisa.* Both belong to a genre that Marcelino Menéndez y Pelayo has called *novela sentimental* (sentimental romance), inaugurated in Spain with *Siervo libre de amor* (Free Servant of Love, circa 1440), by Juan Rodríguez de Padrón (or de la Cámara). The texts of Flores are representative of the intermediary phase of the genre, characterized, according to Regula Rohland de Langbehn, by the complex structure of the fables they include, the ironic cast of the narratives, the interweaving of different themes in the stories of frustrated or unfortunate loves, and the reduction of the allegorical element that had characterized previous stories in the genre.

In the structure of Flores's sentimental romances a similar resource is used: triplication. Each romance develops three different stories, although the stories share elements that allow the work to be considered a unit. One primary story provides the title of the work and serves as the point of departure for the other two. Curiously, the treatment it receives is brief because the central and final stories develop it further. The central story also happens to be the most extensive, and it features elements that affect the primary story and also appear in the last one. The final story recapitulates, continues, and concludes the other two, with an ending that is semantically "charged" because the events recounted are so extreme and alienating. The sentimental romances of Flores are clear examples of literary innovation in fifteenth-century Spain.

*Grisel y Mirabella* was extremely popular during the fifteenth and sixteenth centuries. It was copied and printed many times. According to Gwara, the most reliable version is the one found in manuscripts at the Biblioteca Colombina in Seville and the Biblioteca Trivulziana in Milan. The work was also translated several times in the sixteenth century. Barbara Matulka gives a nearly complete account of these monolingual, bilingual, trilingual, and quadrilingual translations. The true influence of *Grisel y Mirabella* has yet to be determined, though it can be felt in contemporary texts, such as *Cárcel de Amor* (Jail of Love, 1492), by Diego de San Pedro; *Celestina* (circa 1499–1501), attributed to Fernando de Rojas; and *Penitencia de amor* (Penitence of Love, 1514), by Pedro Manuel Ximénez de Urrea. Both the *Tragedias de amor* (Tragedies of Love, 1607), by Juan Arze Solórzano, and *La ley ejecutada* (The Executed Law, circa 1632), by Lope de Vega, recast the main story of *Grisel y Mirabella*.

*Grisel y Mirabella* is preceded by a dedicatory epistle, addressed to a supposed *amiga* (friend, beloved), in which Flores indirectly praises his work and his own worth while adhering to the precepts of courtly love. This preface partially contrasts with the narrative episodes in which males and females do not act according to the notions of courtly love.

The primary story begins with violence when the pretenders to the hand of Mirabella, the only daughter of the king of Scoçia (a mythic Scotland), kill each other. Her father, who does not want her to marry, locks her up in a remote part of the palace. Grisel manages to find it and, after defeating a knight defender, gains the love of the princess. The two enjoy their love in secret for some time, but they are finally discovered and brought to trial to satisfy a law dictating that the guiltier party in a case of love is to be killed and the other banished. Grisel and Mirabella each claim the greater fault in an effort to save the other, but the judges are unable to pass sentence on them. Lawyers are then found who will argue, not the case of Grisel and Mirabella, but which parties are guiltier in an affair of love: men or women. At this point the central story begins. It is chiefly devoted to a debate between Torrellas, the defender of men, and Braçayda, the defender of women. The judges find women to be guiltier, and Mirabella is condemned to die. Braçayda appeals the sentence, but to no avail. The queen intercedes in favor of her daughter and debates with the king on the duties of a monarch who is also a father. The king nevertheless orders the sentence to be carried out, but his order is rendered moot by Grisel, who, after talking with Mirabella, jumps into the pyre prepared for her execution. Mirabella is inconsolable without Grisel. She, too, finally commits suicide, by throwing herself into her father's lion pit. The third and last story in *Grisel y Mirabella* recounts the aftermath of these events. The queen and ladies of the court take vengeance on Torrellas, using his proposal of love for Braçayda as an excuse to capture, torture, and kill him.

The narration of events in *Grisel y Mirabella* is given to a voice that is not involved in the story and is identified as "El Auctor" (The Author). By this means, Flores follows different purposes. For example, he comments on events with a different perspective from that of the reader; in this way he can be safe from the criticism of some readers. "El Auctor" regards Mirabella's father as a "just" king. There are many elements in the story, however, that allow one to question this label. Flores also frequently employs irony and ambiguity in his narrative, as is seen in the difference between the lawyers and the lovers they represent. Each of the lovers wants to assume maximum guilt in order to spare the life of the other, while their lawyers, who do not love, argue the guilt of the other sex. The same ambiguity exists in the debate between Torrellas and Braçayda. None of their arguments seems weightier than the others, and the decision in favor of Torrellas seems to lack an objective basis, bringing into question the fallibility of institutions and social laws. *Grisel y Mirabella* is indicative of a world in crisis, characterized by the violence that afflicts the kingdom at the beginning of the story and by the fact that most men and

Tractado compuesto por Johan de flores a su amiga.

Omo en fin de mis pensamiẽtos concluyr en q̃ meior seruiros pueda mi volũtad busque en que trabaie con desseo ō mas fazer me rẽo. y no me cõtento en seruiros solo en las cosas mas ami conuenibles mas habun en aꝗllas que mas agenas q̃ mias puedo lamar. Esto porque si cõ auctoridat de sciencia de que carezco: presumia hazer cosa ami biẽ scusada: no mire que daua causa de publicar mis yerros: y q̃ el que no sabe la falta ō mi flaco juizio la sepa. Y assi sin mas determiar en ello saluo senyora que vuestro fauor puede dispensar en mi ozadia: por ser yo tanto vuestro: cõ lo qual me barree ō vuestro essuerço: sin mas temor y verguẽça puse en obra esta mal compuesta letra. Y no cure de buscar aquella gracia de hablar como por a tal caso conuenia. y si ello no sta tal que de oyr sea: vos senyora merezcays la pena de mi culpa. pues sta claro q̃ sin essuerço vuestro yo no hozara atreuer me a tan loco ensayo. que si poruentura lo que no creo: algo ō bien habra en ello: a vos que seha de dar la pena: den las gracias. pues yo desto solamente soy scriuano. q̃ por la comunicacion de vuestra casa he trabaiado por fazer alguna parte delas obras ō vuestra discreciõ:

a.i.

*Opening pages from the only known fifteenth-century edition (1495) of Juan de Flores's* Grimalte y Gradisa
*( from Barbara Matulka,* The Novels of Juan de Flores and Their European Diffusion, *1931;*
*Amelia Gayle Gorgas Library, University of Alabama)*

Omiença vn breue tractado cōpu
esto por Johan de flores: el q̃l por
la siguiēte obra mudo su nombre en
grimalte. La inuēcion del qual es
sobre la fiometa . porque algunos
delos que esto leyeren : poruentura
no habrā visto su famosa scriptura : me parecerà biē
declarar la en suma . Pues assi es que esta senyo
ra sue vna d̃las que en beldat y valer alas otras eçe
dya . y seyēdo al matrimonio lygada con compāyia a
ella muy byen conuenyble : vna delas mas bienauen
turadas en su tyempo se presumia. Mas como seā
comuna cosa los mudampētos dela fortūa: desdenya
da la verguença y pospuesta la honra muy muda
do el querer del valeroso marido con hū strāyo hom
bre lamado pāphilo fue d̃ amor presa . y en esto algū
tyempo viuyendo con plazenteros deportes passaron
syn contrario impedimyento de sus amores . Y ell cō
necessidat huuo de partir adonde era natural . el q̃l
dada su fe auctorizada con infinidas iuras dentro de
quatro meses le prometio la tornada. la qual pāphi
lo no mantuuo. De que le seguio que ella mirādo la
gran affeccion q̃ le hauia y la grādeza de honores q̃
por ell perdido hauia: y ala fyn tal paga le daua :
tomo por remedio manifestar sus males alas damas
enamoradas. porque en ello tomando exemplo: cōtra
la maldad delos hōbres se apercebyessē . y asi mysmo

a.i.

women use each other for their own ends, without human solidarity or true love–in opposition to the behavior of the main characters. At the end of the work this negative picture of a world lacking in kingly authority and peopled by women who ritualistically destroy their opposition is reaffirmed, a situation that makes it impossible to affirm Flores's "feminism," as has been attempted by some critics. The romance certainly reflects the disenchantment of the author for the conventional ideologies of his time.

*Grisel y Mirabella* employs several interesting literary tricks. It fictionalizes a contemporary poet, Torrellas, who was well known for his *Coplas de maldezir de mugeres,* or *Coplas de la calidad de las donas* (Stanzas Criticizing Women, or Stanzas on the Quality of Ladies). Flores takes advantage of Torrellas's fame as a misogynist in his characterization of the lawyer of the same name, even including a reference to his *Coplas de maldezir de mugeres.* Another intertextual game is the inclusion of Braçayda, a character from the legend of Troy, who in the Middle Ages became an autonomous figure representing the inconstancy of women. Flores also incorporates certain easily recognizable traditional topics, such as the "combat of generosity" applied to lovers and to the words identified as coming from "Otro cavallero" (Another Knight), who battles Grisel. The structure of the speeches is conditioned, as in all medieval prose, by rhetoric. Each speech is introduced by a heading and is structured according to which controlling rubric of the *inventio* (invention) predominates: narrative, argumentative, or exordial. Small speeches are frequently based on the prescriptions of the *ars dictaminis* (art of writing letters) or are close to the apostrophic style of the *planctus* (plaint).

Flores's other celebrated sentimental romance, *Grimalte y Gradisa,* though interesting, had less success than *Grisel y Mirabella* in its time. Aside from two manuscripts, there is no known version other than the first extant edition (circa 1495). It had only one translation into French, Maurice Scève's *La deplourable fin de Flamete* (The Deplorable End of Fiammeta), of which two editions are known (1535 and 1536). Nevertheless, *Grimalte y Gradisa* had considerable influence on at least two later texts: *Libro del esforçado cavallero Don Tristán de Leonís y sus grandes hechos en armas* (Book of the Hardy Knight, Don Tristan de Leonis and His Great Deeds of Arms, 1501), which Pamela Waley has proven to borrow abundantly from *Grimalte y Gradisa;* and, according to Gwara, *La quarta parte de don Clarián de Landanís (Crónica de Lidamán de Ganayl)* (The Fourth Part of Don Clarian de Landanis [Chronicle of Lidaman de Ganayl], 1528), by Jerónimo López.

It is possible to think of a merging process in *Grimalte y Gradisa* because the Biblioteca Colombina manuscript does not have the poems and the description of Fiometa's tomb that are present in the other surviving editions. Córdoba wrote these sections, according to the colophon of the first edition. On the other hand, the Biblioteca Colombina manuscript includes an extended passage in the last segment of the romance that is not found in the other two versions, an expansion that suggests a later stage in the development of the work. Incidentally, if the lines introducing the poems are deleted, each segment can be followed by the next one, which proves that neither those lines nor the following poems belonged to the original text. Córdoba's contributions are not always as successful as Flores's. For example, sometimes the poems do not match well with the framing text, or the continuity is interrupted. There are virtues too, however: the description of the tomb is interesting and well done, and the introductions to the poems seek to smooth the transition from prose to poetry with such techniques as including lexical elements that appear later in the poems and incorporating internal rhymes that prepare the reader for the poetry that follows. There are even occasions when the epigraph to a poem is arranged in the same syllabic sequence as the line that precedes it or when a rhyme is repeated once more as the prose text resumes the story line.

*Grimalte y Gradisa* is an original romance in which the destiny of the two main characters depends on the success or failure of the love between Fiometa and Pánfilo. Flores continues the story of Giovanni Boccaccio's *Fiammetta* (Fiometa in Flores's work) interwoven with fresh characters. Flores begins by telling the reader that he is changing his name for that of Grimalte and then continues with a brief summary of Boccaccio's story, but related from Fiometa's point of view. With this ruse the primary story begins. Gradisa, who read the tale of Fiometa, tells her suitor, Grimalte, that she will return his love only if he manages to reunite Fiometa with her lover, Pánfilo, who abandoned her. Grimalte is to report to Gradisa by letter all that transpires in his quest. Though he complains, Grimalte searches for Fiometa, introducing the central story. After much effort he finds the unfortunate woman, and together they seek Pánfilo. When they find him, the wayward lover reiterates his unwillingness to take up with Fiometa again, a devastating rejection that brings about her death. Grimalte buries Fiometa and challenges an unwilling Pánfilo, declaring that he (Pánfilo) deserves a worse punishment, abandonment to the brute animals. Gradisa spurns Grimalte, while saying that Pánfilo will not perform the promised penance for Fiometa's death. The third linked story concerns Pánfilo's search for Grimalte, who has taken upon himself the penance for Fiometa's death. Pánfilo and Grimalte finally reunite at the ends of the earth where, thrice a week, they undergo a special torture: in a vision they witness the terrible suffering of Fiometa, who appears accompanied by infernal beings.

The fact that the author states that he is changing his name to Grimalte already stresses the fictive element of the autobiographical form of the sentimental genre and begins a game that is carried out with the collusion of the reader, who accepts the false as true. The author/Grimalte can put the story in the hands of Fiometa, who is the writer of her own book, which is itself contained in the story of Grimalte. The narrative voice of Grimalte, in turn, is authorized by Gradisa's request that he tell her everything that comes to pass in letters. Grimalte, then, assumes ultimate responsibility for the narrative as "el autor mudado" (the twice-removed author). After the central story is told, he continues to satisfy the demands of Gradisa and keeps on writing to her. The complexity of the narrative has led some critics to associate Grimalte with Flores himself, but this association results in unsustainable perspectives. There is no true relation between the author and his character; the changing of names between the author and Grimalte forewarns readers that they are dealing with a work of fiction.

Gradisa's request carries with it another problem: the change of the receptor at the beginning of the central story (the ostensible consignee of the story is the feminine character). The narrator soon abandons the "tú" (you) that refers to Gradisa in favor of addressing the reader of the book. By this means the author makes clear to the reader that Grimalte sent the "tratado" (the book) to Gradisa when there was nothing more to say. The same method, which fades the receiving "tú" (you) into a more generalized addressee, takes place in the concluding story. Significantly, this method is applied to the entire romance, as if the author were trying to make readers understand that they are the addressees of his story.

A remarkable innovation in *Grimalte and Gradisa* is the fact that the mediation in the love relationship of the primary story is the central story transformed into an *exemplum* (example or illustrative story) for Gradisa. Grimalte, far from being a peripheral character in the second story, attains profound dramatic weight. The mediator between Fiometa and Pánfilo, he also tries to further his own interests but fails at everything. It is worth mentioning that no other sentimental work of this period has characters who are as ill treated as those of Flores. His characters are truly ridiculous antiheroes, mendicants of love, absurd and cynical hypocrites and failures. The reader is aware, again, that Flores is a disenchanted author who questions the "nuevas leyes" (new laws) of love but also considers ridiculous the laws that they replaced. He takes the side of neither men nor women, for the two sexes share some traits with each other, as illustrated in the characters of Grimalte-Fiometa and Gradisa-Pánfilo. The narrative introduces antithetical, but parallel, couples, and as in *Grisel y Mirabella*, the moral position of the author is ambiguous.

Flores's *Triunfo de Amor* was seemingly less well known in his time than his sentimental romances. It does not seem to have been published, although it has survived in two manuscript versions that are derived from a common autograph, now lost. The work is interesting because of the unusual treatment of the theme of love and because the plot invites a sociopolitical reading.

*Triunfo de Amor* begins in an apparently conventional manner: the work, or "tratado," is sent to some "enamoradas dueñas" (ladies in love) by means of a letter from the author. Surprisingly, Flores uses this trick to introduce the reader to the fiction. He begins his story by posing as a witness to the events narrated. These events, by their impossible nature, actually stress the opposite–that the work is a literary artifact. At the allegorical level, however, the events are true. The allegorical technique Flores employs allows him to treat matters that were often discussed during the second half of the fifteenth century: the essence of love, monarchy, treason, justice and the legal process, inconstancy, the nature of men and women, social disorder, and so forth, themes common to other works by Flores.

*Triunfo de Amor* begins with a rebellion against Cupid by dead lovers, who finally take him to a court of law. There follows an extensive debate between Medea and the god, in which Cupid is defeated and condemned to death. Love chooses his own manner of death: he will burn himself in the flames of people in love. Because love is now lacking on Earth, where all that remains is enmity and evil, the men and women of the world decide to defend Love against the dead lovers. The dead lovers are defeated, and, in victory, Cupid shows himself to be as magnanimous toward the winners as he is toward the vanquished, as the world is filled with love. (He is magnanimous toward all except the author, as the narrator indicates.) The surfeit of love in the world eventually proves tiresome, however, and many want to abandon the court of Love. Men no longer desire to serve women and ask the god to reverse the roles of the genders, allowing men to be the objects of service instead. The last episode of the work turns the world upside down. Women have the power to choose and to serve men, while men have the anguish of awaiting the service of women. Completing the circle, the "tratado" warns the

*Title pages for the 1524 and 1529 Seville editions of Flores's* Grisel y Mirabella *(1474–1475?) (from Barbara Matulka,*
The Novels of Juan de Flores and Their European Diffusion, *1931;*
*Amelia Gayle Gorgas Library, University of Alabama)*

addressees—more concretely, the ladies of Spain—about this new law of Love.

*Triunfo de Amor* is a work of great merit. The complexities of the narrative style underscore the strange events leading to the narrator's perplexity. Readers share in the feeling of a supernatural world. Oppositions underscore the characters' lack of conformity with the events that take place and with the disorder of the world they inhabit. The living and the dead oppose each other; when that opposition is resolved, it gives way to a restless male-and-female antinomy. An important point in the construction of the narrative is the association of two different and fictitious planes. On the one hand is the supposed reality of the addressees of the work—and gallant lovers who wish to read it; on the other hand is the supposed reality of the story the narrator tells. Lastly, there is much humor associated with the stories, particularly in the last episode. Flores's humorous mood is similar in all his works: the reader smiles but is disconcerted; the object he gibes at should make him cry. Perhaps the greatest virtue of the *Triunfo de Amor* is the abundance of themes in the story, including some of the major ideological questions that

were of concern to Spanish society in the difficult decade of the 1470s.

There is little doubt that Flores wrote the so-called *Crónica incompleta de los Reyes Católicos,* an unfinished work. Its merit lies more in the treatment of events from an ideological and literary point of view than in the accuracy of its historiography—some significant events are not mentioned, and there is no strict chronological sequence. Nevertheless, the work documents the political life, customs, and preoccupations of the late fifteenth century, as well as Flores's interesting commentaries, throughout the fifty-six chapters. Finally, the novelistic style makes it attractive to contemporary readers and an important source for literary critics.

The *Cartas de Iseo y Tristán* has also been attributed to Flores. Gwara makes the same case for *La coronación de la señora Gracisla,* which, from a formal and thematic perspective, is a minor work. Gwara thinks it is a text dedicated to a young girl. In a strict sense, he says, this romance could be the first known example of literature written for children. Inexplicably, no research has been done to dissociate the text from historical fact. *La coronación de la señora Gracisla* gives an account of a "world" beauty contest, in which the beautiful and "very Castilian" Gracisla defeats the French Berilda. Though it is not an ambitious romance, it has interesting aspects. For example, it includes the initial and final letters, alien to the events, that partly work as a device of verisimilitude, and many of the long poems might have been read as a courtly divertissement. Gwara advances the possibility of its being staged with puppets.

**References:**

Antony van Beysterveldt, "Revisión de los debates feministas del siglo XV y las novelas de Juan de Flores," *Hispania,* 64 (1981): 1–13;

Marina Scordilis Brownlee, "The Counterfeit Muse: Ovid, Boccaccio, Juan de Flores," in *Discourses of Authority in Medieval and Renaissance Literature,* edited by Kevin Brownlee and Walter Stephens (Hanover, N.H.: University Press of New England, 1989), pp. 109–127, 270–274;

Scordilis Brownlee, "Language and Incest in *Grisel y Mirabella,*" *Romantic Review,* 79 (1988): 107–128;

Jorge Checa, "*Grisel y Mirabella* de Juan de Flores: rebeldía y violencia como síntomas de crisis," *Revista Canadiense de Estudios Hispánicos,* 12, no. 3 (1988): 369–382;

Alan D. Deyermond, "Las innovaciones narrativas en el reinado de los Reyes Católicos," *Revista de Literatura Medieval,* 6 (1994): 93–105;

Deyermond, *Tradiciones y puntos de vista en la ficción sentimental,* Publicaciones Medievalia, no. 5 (Mexico: Universidad Nacional Autónoma de México, 1993), pp. 35–42;

Juan Fernández Jiménez, "Visión social moderna en la obra de Juan de Flores," *Anuario Medieval,* 1 (1989): 96–106;

Patricia E. Grieve, *Desire and Death in the Spanish Sentimental Romance, 1440–1450* (Newark, Del.: Juan de la Cuesta, 1987);

Grieve, "Juan de Flores' Other Work: Technique and Genre of *Triumpho de Amor,*" *Journal of Hispanic Philology,* 5 (1980–1981): 25–40;

Joseph J. Gwara, "Another Work by Juan de Flores: *La coronación de la señora Gracisla,*" in *Studies on the Spanish Sentimental Romance, 1440–1550: Redefining a Genre,* edited by Gwara and E. Michael Gerli (London: Tamesis, 1997), pp. 75–111;

Gwara, "The Date of Juan de Flores' *Triunfo de Amor,*" *La corónica,* 16, no. 2 (1987–1988): 93–96;

Gwara, "The Identity of Juan de Flores: The Evidence of the *Crónica incompleta de los Reyes Católicos,*" *Journal of Hispanic Philology,* 11 (1987 [1988]): 103–130, 205–222;

Gwara, "A New Epithalamial Allegory by Juan de Flores: *La coronación de la señora Gracisla* (1475)," *Revista de Estudios Hispánicos* (U.S.A.), 30 (1996): 227–257;

Gwara, "A Reconsideration of the English Sources of *La coronación de la señora Gracisla,*" *Medievalia* (Mexico), 28 (1988): 1–27;

Gwara and Diane M. Wright, "A New Manuscript of Juan de Flores' *Grisel y Mirabella:* Biblioteca Apostolica Vaticana, Vat. Lat. MS 6966, ff. 68r.–76v.," *Bulletin of Hispanic Studies,* 77 (2000): 503–526;

Louise M. Haywood, "Gradissa: A Fictional Reader in/ of a Male Author's Text," *Medium Aevum,* 64, no. 1 (1995): 85–99;

María Eugenia Lacarra, "Juan de Flores y la ficción sentimental," in *Actas del IX Congreso de la Asociación Internacional de Hispanistas,* 2 volumes, edited by Sebastian Neumeister (Frankfurt am Main: Vervuert, 1989), I: 223–233;

Lacarra, "Sobre la cuestión de la autobiografía en la ficción sentimental," in *Actas del I Congreso de la Asociación Hispánica de Literatura Medieval,* edited by Vicente Beltrán (Barcelona: PPU, 1988), pp. 359–368;

Barbara Matulka, *The Novels of Juan de Flores and Their European Diffusion: A Study in Comparative Literature* (New York: Institute of French Studies, 1931; reprinted, Geneva: Slatkine, 1974);

Marcelino Menéndez y Pelayo, *Orígenes de la novela,* volume 1: *Introducción: Tratado histórico sobre la primitiva novela española,* Nueva Biblioteca de Autores Españoles, no. 1 (Madrid: Bailly-Baillière e hijos, 1905);

Antonio Cortijo Ocaña, *La evolución genérica de la ficción sentimiental de los siglos XV y SVI,* Serie A: Monografías, no. 184 (London: Tamesis, 2001);

Carmen Parrilla García, "Un cronista olvidado: Juan de Flores, autor de la *Crónica incompleta de los Reyes Católicos,*" in *The Age of the Catholic Monarchs, 1474–1516: Literary Studies in Memory of Keith Whinnom,* edited by Deyermond and Ian Macpherson (Liverpool: Liverpool University Press, 1989), pp. 123–133;

Parrilla García, "La *Derrota de Amor* de Juan de Flores," in *Studies on the Spanish Sentimental Romance, 1440–1550,* pp. 111–124;

Parrilla García, "Una versión inédita de *Grimalte y Gradisa* en la Biblioteca Colombina," in *Actas del I Congreso de la Asociación Hispánica de Literatura Medieval,* pp. 509–514;

Ascensión Rivas Hernández, "Juegos de ficción y realidad en el *Breve tractado de Grimalte y Gradissa,*" in *Humanismo y literatura en tiempos de Juan del Encina,* edited by Javier Guijarro Ceballos, Acta Salmanticensia: Estudios Filológicos, no. 271 (Salamanca:

Ediciones Universidad de Salamanca, 1999), pp. 423–430;

Mercedes Roffé, *La cuestión del género en Grisel y Mirabella de Juan de Flores* (Newark, Del.: Juan de la Cuesta, 1996);

Regula Rohland de Langbehn, "Un mundo al revés: la mujer en las obras de ficción de Juan de Flores," in *Studies on the Spanish Sentimental Romance, 1440–1550*, pp. 125–143;

Rohland de Langbehn, *La unidad genérica de la novela sentimental española de los siglos XV y XVI*, Papers of the Medieval Hispanic Research Seminar, no. 17 (London: Department of Hispanic Studies, Queen Mary and Westfield College, 1999);

Lillian von der Walde Moheno, *Amor e ilegalidad: Grisel y Mirabella, de Juan de Flores*, Publicaciones de *Medievalia*, no. 12, Serie de Estudios de Lingüística y Literatura, no. 34 (Mexico: Universidad Nacional Autónoma de México/Colegio de México, 1996);

von der Walde Moheno, "De ejemplos y consejos en *Grimalte y Gradisa*," *La corónica*, 29, no. 1 (2000): 111–121;

von der Walde Moheno, "La estructura retórica de la ficción sentimental," in *Discursos y representaciones en la Edad Media: Actas de las VI Jornadas Medievales*, edited by Concepción Company, Aurelio González, and von der Walde Moheno, Publicaciones de *Medievalia*, no. 22 (Mexico: Universidad Nacional Autónoma de México/Colegio de México, 1999), pp. 101–108;

von der Walde Moheno, "La ficción sentimental," *Medievalia* (Mexico), 25 (1997): 1–25;

von der Walde Moheno, "*Grisel y Mirabella*, de Juan de Flores: Fuente desapercibida en la obra de Fernando de Rojas," in *Actas del XIII Congreso de la Asociación Internacional de Hispanistas*, edited by Florencio Sevilla and Carlos Alvar, volume 1: *Medieval, Siglos de Oro* (Madrid: Asociación Internacional de Hispanistas/Castalia/Fundación Duques de Soria, 2000), pp. 249–255;

von der Walde Moheno, "El 'marco' de *Triunfo de Amor*, de Juan de Flores," *Lemir*, 7 (2003) <http://parnaseo.uv.es/Lemir/Revista/Revista7/Triunfo Amor.htm>;

von der Walde Moheno, "Notas sobre el estilo de Juan de Flores," in *Varia lingüística y literaria: 50 años del CELL*, volume 1: *Literatura: De la Edad Media al siglo XVIII*, edited by Marta Elena Venier and Alejandro Arteaga (Mexico: Colegio de México, 1997), pp. 103–114;

Pamela Waley, "*Cárcel de Amor* and *Grisel y Mirabella*: A Question of Priority," *Bulletin of Hispanic Studies*, 50 (1973): 340–356;

Waley, "Fiammetta and Pánfilo Continued," *Italian Studies*, 24 (1969): 15–31;

Waley, "Love and Honour in the *novelas sentimentales* of Diego de San Pedro and Juan de Flores," *Bulletin of Hispanic Studies*, 43 (1966): 253–275;

Rina Walthaus, "Espacio y alienación en *Grimalte y Gradissa* de Juan de Flores," *Scriptura*, 13 (1997): 5–18;

Barbara F. Weissberger, "Authority Figures in *Siervo libre de amor* and *Grisel y Mirabella*," *Revista de Estudios Hispánicos* (Puerto Rico), 9 (1982 [1984]): 255–262;

Weissberger, "Authors, Characters, and Readers in *Grimalte y Gradissa*," in *Creation and Re-creation: Experiments in Literary Form in Early Modern Spain—Studies in Honor of Stephen Gilman*, edited by Ronald E. Surtz and Nora Weinerth (Newark, Del.: Juan de la Cuesta, 1983), pp. 61–76;

Weissberger, "Role-reversal and Festivity in the Romances of Juan de Flores," *Journal of Hispanic Philology*, 13 (1989): 197–213;

Wright, "Readers, Writers, and Lovers in *Grimalte y Gradissa*," in *The Court and Cultural Diversity: Selected Papers from the Eighth Triennial Congress of the International Courtly Literature Society*, edited by Evelyn Mullally and John Thompson (Cambridge: D. S. Brewer, 1997), pp. 229–237.

# Juan de Lucena

## (circa 1430 – 1501)

Lucia Binotti
*University of North Carolina, Chapel Hill*

WORKS: *Dialogo de vita beata* (1463)

**Manuscripts:** This work is preserved in three manuscripts: Madrid, Biblioteca Nacional MS. 6728; Madrid, Real Academia Española MS. 158; and Madrid, Real Biblioteca II–1520, discovered in 1989.

**First publication:** *Dialogo de vita beata* (Zamora: Antonio de Centenera, 1483).

**Standard editions:** "Dialogo de vita beata," in *Opúsculos literarios de los siglos XIV a XVI,* edited by A. Paz y Mélia (Madrid: Sociedad de Bibliófilos Españoles, 1892), pp. 103–205; "Dialogo de vita beata," in *Testi spagnoli del secolo XV°,* edited by G. M. Bertini and R. Radicati di Marmorito (Turin: Gheroni, 1950), pp. 97–182.

*Epistola exhortatoria a las letras* (early 1480s)

**Manuscript:** Seville, Biblioteca Colombina 5–3–20–olim R–113.

**First publication:** "Epistola exhortatoria a las letras," in *Opúsculos literarios de los siglos XIV a XVI,* edited by A. Paz y Mélia (Madrid: Sociedad de Bibliófilos Españoles, 1892), pp. 206–243.

**Standard edition:** Lucia Binotti, "La *Epístola exhortatoria a las letras* de Juan de Lucena: Humanismo y educación en la Castilla del siglo XV. Edición y comentario," *Corónica,* 28 (2000): 51–80.

*Tratado de los galardones* (1482–1492)

**Manuscript:** Madrid, Biblioteca Nacional R–125.

**First publication and standard edition:** Rafael Lapesa, "Sobre Juan de Lucena: Escritos suyos mal conocidos o inéditos," in his *De la Edad Media a nuestros días: Estudios de historia literaria* (Madrid: Gredos, 1967), pp. 123–137.

Juan de Lucena is mainly known for his *Dialogo de vita beata* (Dialogue on the Happiness of Life), which he wrote in Italy before 1463. Considered a minor author until the 1980s, Lucena has attracted increasing scholarly attention since then. He occupies an intriguing position in the literary landscape of late-medieval Castile that complicates the task of classifying his works: are they the products of a medieval author trying to bring humanism to Spain or attempts by a Jewish convert to Christianity to prove his orthodoxy? *Dialogo de vita beata* was one of the works that introduced the Ciceronian dialogue to Spain; the ideas expressed in it developed into commonplaces in the Spanish Renaissance. The renewed interest in Lucena has also brought attention to his minor works, most prominently the *Epistola exhortatoria a las letras* (Epistle Encouraging the Study of Letters, early 1480s), a short treatise in letter form encouraging the Spanish nobility to study Latin.

Little was known about the life of the author until Jerónimo de Miguel's extensive archival research led to new discoveries and brought order to the puzzling information that was known at that point. His results will soon be published in a new critical edition of *Dialogo de vita beata.*

Lucena was born in Soria around 1430 to Juan Ramírez de Lucena and Catalina Ramírez, both of whom were *conversos* (Jews who had converted to Christianity). He began his studies in Burgo de Osma's capitular *studium* (school) and subsequently moved to Burgos to study under Alfonso de Cartagena, the bishop of the town. In 1458, probably owing to Cartagena's friendship with Pope Pius II (Aeneas Silvius Piccolomini), he obtained a post at the papal court.

Lucena thus spent his formative years in Italy, which explains his familiarity with the most debated philosophical and theological issues that preoccupied contemporary Italian humanists. Reflections on these matters took the form of vitriolic exchanges between prestigious scholars of contrasting views. For example, Poggio Bracciolini's writings on the Trinity, predestination, free will, the relation between philosophy and theology, and the reevaluation of Epicureanism were framed as a ferocious attack on those of Lorenzo Valla. Concurrent with the polemic between Poggio and Valla was a less sensational controversy that had originated earlier in the court of Alfonso V. The main contenders in this secondary but equally bitter quarrel were Valla

*Part of the title page from the first publication (1483) of Juan de Lucena's* Dialogo de vita beata
*(Biblioteca Nacional, Madrid)*

and Bartolomeo Facio. These two controversies had repercussions in humanist circles in the years that followed. Lucena caught the literary and ethical dimensions of the controversies, but instead of participating directly in the dispute he chose to translate into Spanish and rework Facio's *De vitae felicitate* (On the Happiness of Life, 1448), a treatise in dialogue form intended to refute Valla's *De vero bono* (On the True Good, 1432).

Valla had stated in *De vero bono,* a revised version of his *De voluptate* (On Pleasure, 1431), that before the Christian revelation human beings considered "utilitas rerum et experientiae delectatio" (the utility of objects and the pleasure of experience) as sufficient for worldly happiness. Valla's position was misunderstood as a defense of Epicureanism, and Facio attacked him on this basis in *De vitae felicitate.* Facio maintained that happiness cannot be attained in this world; it is, therefore, the fate of humanity to aspire to happiness in the spiritual world after death. Facio's work was one of the most popular humanist texts to circulate in Castile, and its popularity might have led Lucena to adapt it into his *Dialogo de vita beata,* which was also widely read. According to Ottavio Di Camillo, *Dialogo de vita beata* is a continuation of the debate over Valla's Epicurean solution to the problem of humanity's ultimate good or happiness but is fashioned for a different audience.

In adapting Facio's work Lucena changes the setting to Castile and adds passages and makes structural and stylistic modifications that give the work a distinctive literary character. He replaces Facio's Italian humanists Guarino da Verona, Antonio Beccadelli (who wrote under the pseudonym Panormita), and Giovanni Lamola with Spanish interlocutors of a previous generation: Alonso de Cartagena, bishop of Burgos; Iñigo López de Mendoza, Marqués de Santillana; and Juan de Mena. The views of the Spaniards only vaguely resemble those of their Italian counterparts; in fact, they do not even reflect the actual thinking of their historical models. Lucena explains in the prologue that he "resuscite' estos Petrarcas" (resuscitated these Petrarchs) who had been dead for some time to lend the authority of their names to his treatise. He appropriates Facio's work and passes it off as his own without making the slightest reference to the original author, just as Facio had extensively reworked Antonio da Barga's *Libellus de dignitate et excellentia humanae vitae* (Little Book on the Dignity and Excellence of Human Life) in his *De vitae felicitate* without acknowledgment. Lucena adopts Facio's view that Valla's *De vero bono* is a defense of Epicurean doctrines, a reprehensible body of ideas in the minds of many Spaniards of the time. Lucena's upholding of orthodox views might have been motivated by his being a *converso* and, thus, wary of being associated

32

with any school of thought that could be judged heretical. This motivation may explain why he deemed Facio's ideas worthy of translation into Spanish.

In Facio's work the three speakers meet at the house of the grammarian and Greek scholar Guarino, the teacher of the other two. Guarino opens the conversation by claiming that happiness cannot be attained in this world. The poet Lamola, in contrast, makes the case for both the active and the contemplative life as sources of happiness. This position is contested by Guarino, after which the poet Beccadelli makes a speech against earthly pleasure. Guarino then takes the stage to describe celestial happiness as the only possible goal for human beings.

In Lucena's dialogue Cartagena expresses the ideas of Guarino. Lucena understood that the most important principle of Italian humanism was its reevaluation of the power of language: a humanistic revolution would only occur through words. Thus, after Cartagena finishes his opening statement, Santillana praises his eloquence, thereby crediting the Castilian language with a rhetorical excellence parallel to that enjoyed by Latin in humanistic circles.

Lamola is split into two characters: Mena defends the active life as a source of happiness, and Santillana, also a poet, defends the contemplative life. Both are answered by Cartagena. Then Lucena himself appears, taking the place of Beccadelli in Facio's work. He makes a statement against pleasure and is asked for a verdict as to the winner of the preceding debate: a verdict that he declares himself unable to assign. Finally, like Guarino in Facio's dialogue, Cartagena concludes the work with a statement about heavenly happiness.

Lucena's inclusion of himself as a character in the dialogue, and one who performs the role of passing judgment on the ideas of three of the most respected men of letters of their time, is his most radical alteration of the structure of Facio's dialogue. Literary history, however, provides a precedent for this intrusion. Facio himself partly followed Leonardo Bruni's and Coluccio Salutati's substitution of the Ciceronian dialogue for the scholastic *disputatio*. The dialogue is an open conversation in which the characters disagree among themselves, while acknowledging the intellectual authority of one of them. This character's opinion will ultimately be accepted by everyone, but only after it has incorporated some of the contributions of the minor speakers. The clearest example of this tradition is Cicero's *De oratore* (On the Ideal Orator, 55 B.C.), the only complete manuscript of which had been discovered shortly before the composition of Facio's work. The speakers in *De oratore* are four in number, as two newcomers join the initial group of two. The appearance of a fourth character who interrupts the conversation of the other

three thus places *Dialogo de vita beata* within this newly rediscovered tradition. Other details reinforce Lucena's link to the Ciceronian dialogue. First, whereas in Facio's work the main speaker is also the host, Lucena locates the first part of his dialogue "en la sala real" (in the throne room) when the king is away; the absent host is a common feature of the Ciceronian dialogue. A second feature characteristic of the Ciceronian dialogue that Lucena copies is adapting the course of the conversation to that of daily life: in *De oratore* Crassus delivers his final speech after an interruption for a meal; in *Dialogo de vita beata* the characters move after dark to Santillana's chambers for dinner, and Cartagena delivers his final statement there. Third, while Facio's characters are scholars, Lucena's, like Cicero's, are prominent members of the political establishment who also happen to be men of letters: Cartagena was a *converso* who had served as a royal ambassador on delicate diplomatic missions; Mena was chief royal secretary for Latin letters and a member of the upwardly mobile class of newcomers who dominated Juan II's court; and Santillana was one of the most powerful aristocrats of his day. Scholarly activity was not the main occupation of the three but an entertainment for leisure time, as it had been for Cicero. As Santillana says, "quando seremos ociosos que retraídos un tanto de nuestros aferes" (we are at leisure, retreated momentarily from our ordinary businesses). Thus, the characters of both Cicero and Lucena belong to the political ruling class; they are engaged administrators who are enjoying "otium" (a restful moment) from their busy occupations. Cicero stressed the exceptional character of this leisure that comes in the midst of activity both in *De oratore* and in *Tusculanae disputationes* (Tusculan Disputations, 45 B.C.), thereby reinforcing the key political role played by his characters in the republic. That role also points to the practical application of their philosophical speculations.

Lucena returned to Spain after Pius II died in 1464. Shortly thereafter, he entered the diplomatic service of Prince Fernando (Ferdinand) of Aragon. As the prince's ambassador, he was present in 1471 when Henry VI of England and Louis XI of France signed the truce that ended the War of the Roses. That same year he conducted negotiations to renew the alliance between Fernando and Charles the Bold of Burgundy. On 12 September 1471 Lucena signed the agreement between King Enrique IV and the nobles who opposed him, which included an addendum naming Enrique's sister Isabel (Isabella) the future queen of Castile. This document has Lucena's only known autograph signature other than that on the final page of the manuscript of *Dialogo de vita beata* in the Biblioteca Nacional de Madrid; thus, paleographic examination has confirmed the identity of the author of the dialogue.

Lucena's appointment as ambassador continued under the Catholic Monarchs, Fernando and Isabel, for the next ten years. He is constantly mentioned in diplomatic documents in England or Flanders. After 1482, however, Lucena seems to have been relieved of his foreign obligations. No more secretarial documents mention him, and in *Epistola exhortatoria a las letras* he complains of an involuntary exile that is keeping him away from public affairs. From the mid 1480s onward, in fact, all records regarding Lucena concern either matters of a personal nature, mostly about his compensation as the abbot of Soria, or administrative business between the abbey chapter and the town council. These are probably the years of composition of the *Epistola exhortatoria a las letras* and *Tratado de los galardones* (Treatise on Honors), a work on heraldry.

*Epistola exhortatoria a las letras* is a short text that stresses the importance of studying *grammatica*—that is, Latin grammar—because only through knowledge of language will one attain understanding of *ciencia* (science), the supreme earthly good. The epistle seems to follow the formal guidelines recommended by the medieval *dictatores* (letter writers) for writing a letter. But it also reflects humanistic epistolary precepts, starting with the generic title Lucena gives it: *letra mensajera* (newsletter)—a label that acknowledges a distinct formal genre. Its friendly tone is reminiscent of Cicero's *Epistolae ad familiares* (Letters to His Friends) and of the many humanistic epistles that circulated in Italy at the time. Lucena emphasizes the importance of the use of the vernacular in his work, thus unambiguously identifying the audience—public servants and noblemen—he is targeting with his exhortation.

The epistle is specifically addressed to Fernán Álvarez Zapata, a royal secretary who was in charge of diplomatic relations with Portugal. The exordium, echoing a motif exploited in *Dialogo de vita beata,* opens with a consideration of two types of *otium:* that which is taken voluntarily to rest from one's daily occupations and that which one is forced to take when one is discharged from public office and sent into exile. The latter is the leisure that ultimately most benefits the community, since, when one is kept away from public life, one takes up the pen to contribute through letters what one cannot contribute through deeds. This passage echoes Cicero, as well as several humanistic Italian treatises that dealt with the distinction between the active and the contemplative life. Thus, even though the exordium follows the medieval compositional precept of starting a letter with a topic of general interest, the explicit allusion to Cicero's political troubles might be read as a reference to Lucena's own diplomatic career.

The middle section of the epistle, the *narratio,* begins with praise of Álvarez Zapeta, who, in spite of his mature age, has decided to devote an hour daily to the study of grammar. Grammar, explains Lucena, is the basis for the understanding of philosophy, which is a synonym for knowledge in general. The true philosopher is one for whom the study of letters precedes that of the other disciplines, for only through the mastery of language can one achieve an understanding of those disciplines. This viewpoint agrees with that of the early Italian humanists. Lucena abandons the medieval attribution of quasi-divine status to Latin, as if its employment necessarily brought about the truest knowledge; instead, while placing Latin on the same level as any other language, he stresses its importance as a vehicle for achieving a superior education. *Epistola exhortatoria a las letras* encapsulates the tenets on education that Lucena's mentor, Pius II, had developed in two of his best-known works: the *Ad Sigismundum Epistola* (1944, Epistle to Sigismund of Austria) and *De liberorum educatione* (On the Education of Youths), sent to Ladislaus of Bohemia in 1450. Both writers insist that a leader must be a lover of knowledge, as only those who are able to combine the study of philosophy with service in public office will benefit civic society. Both also stress the natural predisposition of human beings to study, as horses are meant to race and beasts are meant to be driven to ferocity. Lucena echoes the Pope's dictum that knowledge is the only earthly good that cannot be taken away from one and decries those who claim to possess knowledge without actually knowing anything.

As in *Dialogo de vita beata,* Lucena continually refers to situations and events that are specific to his surroundings and compares the ancients' feats to the achievements of his contemporaries. Attentive to his audience's needs, he abridges the Pope's ambitious educational program to fit the situation of the contemporary Castilian aristocracy. Thus, whereas Pius pushed Prince Ladislaus, who was already versed in Latin, to study philosophy, rhetoric, and poetry, Lucena is satisfied with the progress that his disciple is making in the study of *grammatica.* From there, he confidently declares, the rest will come. These assertions do not diminish the literary effectiveness of the epistle: Lucena is not writing for academics, nor for those who are willing to abandon their everyday chores to devote themselves to the study of letters. Rather, his is an educated audience of public servants and noblemen whose literary tastes require tailoring to the new humanistic genres imported from Italy. Their lack of knowledge of Latin notwithstanding, these readers are willing to enjoy the Ciceronian epistle and the Platonic dialogue. Furthermore, they are able to appreciate the importance of *studia humanitatis* (liberal studies), even though the vehicle of such studies, Latin, requires an unwelcome period of training.

*Tratado de los galardones* is a short work that treats the origin and ascendancy of heraldry. Like Juan Rodríguez del Padrón's *Cadira de honor* (Seat of Honor, 1439–1441), Mosén Diego de Valera's *Tractado de las armas* (A Treatise on Arms, circa 1460), Honorat Bovet's *Árbol de las batallas* (Tree of Battles, trans. circa 1430), and fragments of Cartagena's writings, the volume comprises miscellaneous reflections on courtly life, ceremonial norms, and manners. It must have been composed between 1482 and 1492, since the prologue mentions the war against Granada as a current event. No printed version of the work is known.

Lucena's involvement in Isabel's administration would account for his interest in the offices of herald and *rey de armas* (King of Arms), two important figures in the diplomatic protocol of his time. He ascribes illustrious origins to the office of herald, relating it both etymologically and mythically to the heroes of antiquity and ascribing to it functions and regulations allegedly established by Dionysus after his conquest of India and subsequently confirmed by Hercules, Alexander, Julius Caesar, and Augustus. The inventive exploitation of names and motifs of the classical world in the work displays once again Lucena's aspiration to introduce the tenets of humanism to a class of lay readers. A feature of the treatise that was central to humanist thought is the manner in which Lucena interprets the revival of antiquity. Whereas Italian humanists considered themselves the direct descendants of Roman civilization and felt an intellectual and emotional attachment to classical Rome, Spanish humanists acknowledged and respected Roman antiquity but tended to look at it more narrowly through the influence that it had on the Iberian Peninsula, admiring and imitating especially classical authors of Iberian origin such as Martial, Quintilian, and Seneca. Thus, the fascination that the classical period held for them was in great part based on the notion that the entire peninsula had been united under one monarch and one religion—an ideal that all of Castilian society shared.

The language of *Tratado de los galardones* is less Latinized than that of *Dialogo de vita beata* and even that of *Epistola exhortatoria a las letras*. Even so, one finds many instances of verbs ending sentences, some dependent infinitives, and several absolute-participle constructions. Syntactical Latinisms frame a rhetorical style rich in amplifications, enumerations, sequences of interrogative clauses, parallelisms, paradoxes, antitheses, and oxymorons.

In 1493 Lucena ceded his income from the abbey to Luis Hurtado de Mendoza, who agreed to pay him an annual pension from the rents collected by the

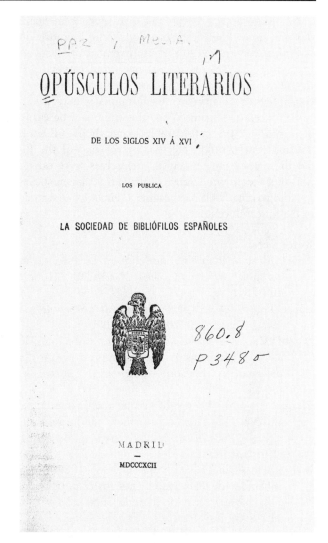

*Title page for the 1892 collection edited by A. Paz y Mélia that includes Lucena's* Dialogo de vita beata *and* Epistola exhortatoria a las letras *(Delyte W. Morris Library, Southern Illinois University at Carbondale)*

abbey. Though Lucena was probably the father of Luis de Lucena, the author of *Repetición de amores* (Repetition of Loves, circa 1496), he filed a will in 1501 that designates as his sole heir his nephew and namesake Juan Ramírez de Lucena.

As a whole, Juan de Lucena's oeuvre shows how the respect that Spanish scholars and noblemen felt for early Quattrocento Italian humanists served to make them aware of the distinct characteristics of their own national culture. Because they lived under a monarchy, for example, they felt more affinity with Italian humanists in the service of kings and princes than with those of republican Florence or Venice. A trait that Lucena shares with other Spanish humanists and that is directly related to their interpretation of classical antiquity is his understanding of rhetoric and its application to vernacular compositions. The pursuit of eloquence in Spain did not, as in Italy, lead to a flourishing literature in Latin but contributed to the improvement of Castilian literature. The preference for the vernacular over Latin has led some historians and literary critics to deny the presence of any serious humanistic activity in fifteenth-century Spain. While this claim can be easily disproved by the considerable extant body of Latin writings, one should note that by the end of the fifteenth century the humanists themselves were taking notice of the preponderance of the vernacular in speaking and writing. This use became a much-debated topic in the sixteenth century.

## References:

Ángel Alcalá, "Juan de Lucena y el pre-erasmismo español," *Revista Hispánica Moderna,* 34 (1968): 108–131;

Lucia Binotti, "Acerca de las glosas al *Diálogo de vita beata,*" *Corónica,* 29 (2001): 185–200;

Binotti, "La *Epístola exhortatoria a las letras* de Juan de Lucena: Humanismo y educación en la Castilla del siglo XV. Edición y comentario," *Corónica,* 28 (2000): 51–80;

Manuel Carrión, "Gómez Manrique y el Protonotario Lucena: Dos cartas con memoria de Jorge Manrique," *Revista de Archivos, Bibliotecas y Museos,* 81 (1978): 564–582;

Juan Carlos Conde, "El manuscrito II–1520 de la Biblioteca de Palacio: Un nuevo testimonio del *Diálogo de vita beata* de Juan de Lucena," *Corónica,* 21 (1993): 34–57;

Conde, "El manuscrito II–1520 de Palacio y la *Celestina:* Balance y estado de la cuestión," in *Cinco siglos de "Celestina": Aportaciones interpretativas,* edited by Rafael Beltrán and José Luis Canet (Valencia: University of València, 1997), pp. 161–185;

Conde, "Otro testimonio manuscrito de un villancico tradicional," *Journal of Hispanic Research,* 1 (1993): 203–206;

Conde, "El siglo XV castellano a la luz del *Diálogo de Vita Beata* de Juan de Lucena," *Dicenda,* 4 (1985): 11–34;

Carmen Crespo Tobarra, Mariano de la Campa Gutiérrez, and others, eds., *Catálogo de manuscritos de la Real Academia Española,* Anejos del *Boletín de la Real Academia Española,* no. 50 (Madrid: Real Academia Española, 1991);

Ottavio Di Camillo, *El humanismo castellano del siglo XV* (Valencia: F. Torres, 1976), pp. 255–276;

Di Camillo, "Interpretations of Humanism in Recent Spanish Renaissance Studies," *Renaissance-Quarterly,* 50, no. 4 (1997): 1190–1200;

Di Camillo, "Interpretations of the Renaissance in Spanish Historical Thought: The Last Thirty Years," *Renaissance-Quarterly,* 48, no. 2 (1995): 352–365; 49, no. 2 (1996): 360–383;

Ángel Gómez Moreno, *España y la Italia de los humanistas: Primeros ecos* (Madrid: Gredos, 1994), pp. 106, 116, 121, 142, 163, 199, 207–208;

*Inventario general de manuscritos de la Biblioteca Nacional de Madrid,* volume 11 (Madrid: Ministerio de Cultura, 1987);

Rafael Lapesa, *De la Edad Media a nuestros días: Estudios de historia literaria* (Madrid: Gredos, 1967), pp. 123–137;

Alejandro Medina Bermúdez, "El diálogo *De Vita Beata* de Juan de Lucena: Un rompecabezas histórico (I)," *Dicenda,* 15 (1997): 251–269;

Margherita Morreale, "El tratado de Juan de Lucena sobre la felicidad," *Nueva Revista de Filología Hispánica,* 9 (1955): 1–21;

Frederick John Norton, *A Descriptive Catalogue of Printing in Spain and Portugal, 1501–1520* (Cambridge: Cambridge University Press, 1978);

Gonzalo Ortiz de Montalbán and María Asunción de Mendoza Lassalle, eds., *Registro general del sello,* 12 volumes (Valladolid: Archivo General de Simancas, 1950–1974);

Antonio de la Torre and Luis Suárez Fernández, eds., *Documentos referentes a las relaciones con Portugal durante el reinado de los Reyes Católicos,* 3 volumes (Valladolid: CSIC, 1958);

Ana Vian Herrero, "El *Libro de Vita Beata* de Juan de Lucena como diálogo literario," *Bulletin Hispanique,* 93 (1991): 61–105;

María Luisa López Vidriero and José Luis Rodríguez, *Catálogo de la Real Biblioteca Tomo XI: Manuscritos,* volume 2 (Madrid: Patrimonio Nacional, 1995).

# Alfonso Fernández de Madrigal
## (El Tostado)
### *(circa 1405 – 1455)*

Carmen Parrilla
*University of La Coruña*

WORKS: *Responsio ad Dominum Palentinum super benedictione et errore Isaac* (1429–1439)

**Manuscripts:** Osma, Burgo de Osma 60, fols. 176r–179r; Cáceres, Biblioteca Provincial 08371, fols. 68v–71v.

**Modern edition:** "Un opúsculo bíblico del Tostado desconocido" [*Super benedictione et errore Isaac*], edited by Hermenegildo Zamora, *Verdad y Vida*, 31 (1973): 269–315.

*Brevis Postilla super Genesim, Exodum, Leviticum et Numeros* (1432–1435)

**Manuscripts:** Survives in two autograph manuscripts: Salamanca, Biblioteca de la Universidad de Salamanca 13; and in the *Finis Libri Numerorum et Commentarius super Deuteronomium* (1432–1453), Salamanca, Biblioteca de la Universidad de Salamanca 2504.

*Breviloquium de amore et amicitia* (1432–1436)

**Manuscripts:** Osma, Burgo de Osma 60; Cáceres, Biblioteca Provincial 08371, fols. 13r–68v.

*Breviloquio de amor y amiçiçia* (1432–1436)

**Manuscripts:** Salamanca, Biblioteca de la Universidad de Salamanca 2178, fols. 1r–74r; Madrid, Biblioteca de El Escorial h.II.15.

**Modern editions:** *Del Tostado sobre el amor*, prologue by Pedro M. Cátedra (Barcelona: Stelle dell'Orsa, 1986), pp. 71–127–comprises eight chapters corresponding to fols. 16r–20v of the *Breviloquio de amor y amiçiçia*, pp. 71–127; Carlos Heusch, ed., in his "La philosophie de l'amour dans l'Espagne su XVè siècle," Ph.D. thesis, Sorbonne Nouvelle, Paris III, 1993; *Tratados de amor en el entorno de Celestina, siglos XV–XVI*, selected and edited, with an introduction, by Cátedra (Madrid: Sociedad Estatal España Nuevo Milenio, 2001), pp. 13–30.

*De statu animarum post hanc vitam* (1432–1437)

**Manuscript:** Cáceres, Biblioteca Provincial 08371, fols. 164v–181v.

*De optima politia* (1432–1437)

**Manuscript:** Cáceres, Biblioteca Provincial 08371, fols. 153r–164v–includes an introduction that does not appear in the printed editions.

**Edition:** *Amenissimi ingenij omniuq disciplinarum laude & humanarum rerum vsu ac consilio instructissimi: diui Alphonsi epi Abulensis fructuosissima repetitio de optima politia. In qua Platonis & Socratis: alioruq; priscoru philosophantiu respublica: tanq; erronea: ac bonis moribus repugnãs excludit. Et per naturales rõnes: q legislatores: q leges & instituta: ad veram et pfectissimã politiã requirãtur: & qualiter parari postint osteditur. Et vbi: quãdo: & quo modo hoium pfectissime politizantiu pfectissima generatio haberi possit locupletissime demõstratur* (Venice: Petri Liechtenstein, 1529).

**Modern edition:** *El "De optima politia" de Alfonso de Madrigal, El Tostado: Tradución y estudio preliminar*, translated by Juan Candela Martínez (Murcia: Publicaciones de la Universidad de Murcia, 1954).

*Commentaria in primam parte Exodi et in secundam partem Exodi, in Leviticum, in primam partem Numerorum et in secundam partem Numerorum, et in Deuteronomium* (1432–1453)

**Manuscript:** Salamanca, Biblioteca de la Universidad de Salamanca 2504.

*De beata Trinitate* (1435–1437)

**Manuscripts:** Salamanca, Biblioteca de la Universidad de Salamanca 70, fols. 72r–84v; Cáceres, Biblioteca Provincial 08371, fols. 143r–152v; Madrid, Biblioteca Nacional 16, fols. 177r–185r.

*Commentarius super Genesim* (1436)

**Manuscripts:** Salamanca, Biblioteca de la Universidad de Salamanca 2511 (autograph); Cáceres, Biblioteca Provincial 08360; Madrid, Biblioteca Nacional 12247; Ávila, Cathedral of

Ávila, 7-1-B; Madrid, Archivo Histórico Nacional, Torre Longás 122.

*Commentaria in Exodum* (1436)

**Manuscripts:** Salamanca, Biblioteca de la Universidad de Salamanca 2502–2503–the first manuscript and half of the second are autographs, with marginal notes by Madrigal; Cáceres, Biblioteca Provincial 08361, 08363.

**Edition:** *Opera omnia,* second edition, volume 2 (Venice, 1527–1531).

*Commentarius in Leviticum* (1436)

**Manuscript:** Cáceres, Biblioteca Provincial 08364.

*Commentarius in Librum Numerorum* (1436)

**Manuscript:** Salamanca, Biblioteca de la Universidad de Salamanca 2500–2501–includes autograph marginal notes.

*Commentarius super Librum Josue* (1436–1438)

**Manuscripts:** Salamanca, Biblioteca de la Universidad de Salamanca 2176–2177; Toledo, Biblioteca Capitular 10-7.

*Commentaria super Iudices et Ruth* (1436–1438)

**Manuscript:** Salamanca, Biblioteca de la Universidad de Salamanca 2426 (autograph).

*Las çinco figuratas paradoxas* (1437)

**Manuscripts:** Salamanca, Biblioteca de la Universidad de Salamanca 2178, fols. 75r–232v; Madrid, Biblioteca de El Escorial a.IV.3.

**Modern edition:** *Las çinco figuratas paradoxas,* edited, with prologue and notes, by Carmen Parrilla García (Alcalá de Henares: Universidad de Alcalá de Henares, 1998).

*Liber de quinque figuratis paradoxis* (1437)

**Manuscripts:** Salamanca, Biblioteca de la Universidad de Salamanca 2695 (autograph); Madrid, Biblioteca Nacional 483.

*Commentarius super Primum Librum Regum* (1438–1440)

**Manuscripts:** Salamanca, Biblioteca de la Universidad de Salamanca 2505–2506–includes autograph notes; Toledo, Biblioteca Capitular 10–7.

*Commentarius super Secundum Librum Regum* (1438–1440)

**Manuscript:** Salamanca, Biblioteca de la Universidad de Salamanca 2507.

*Commentarius super Quartum Librum Regum* (1440)

**Manuscript:** Salamanca, Biblioteca de la Universidad de Salamanca 2508–includes autograph notes.

*Tractatus de aeternitate* (1440s)

**Manuscript:** Salamanca, Biblioteca de la Universidad de Salamanca 70, fols. 155r–184v.

*De muliere sarracena transeunte ad ritum iudaicum* (1440s)

**Manuscript:** Salamanca, Biblioteca de la Universidad de Salamanca 70, fols. 86r–111v.

*Quaestio de presciencia et predestinatione* (1440s)

**Manuscript:** Madrid, Biblioteca Nacional 16, fols. 188r–188v.

*Super Isaiae: Ecce Virgo concipiet* (1442–1446)

**Manuscripts:** Osma, Burgo de Osma 60, fols. 179r–190r; Cáceres, Biblioteca Provincial 08371, fols. 2r–12r.

*Defensorium trium conclusionum* (1443–1446)

**Manuscripts:** Madrid, Biblioteca Nacional 16, fols. 1–76; Osma, Burgo de Osma 60, fols. 10r–106r; Cáceres, Biblioteca Provincial 08371, fols. 73r–139r; Salamanca, Biblioteca de la Universidad de Salamanca 2176–2177, 2426, 2455–2460, 2500–2511.

**Editions:** *Opera omnia,* volume 9 (Venice: Gregorium de Gregoriis in aedibus Petri Liechtenstein, 1507–1508); *Eximium ac nunq[uam] satis laudatu[m] opus su[m]mi theologi et Christiani dogmatis defensoris acerrimi Alpho[n]si Thostati ep[iscop]i Abulensis a se editu[m], Defensorium triu[m] [con]clusionu[m] [con]tra emulos i[n] Romana curia disputatarum: vbi quid primum admirari debeas non facile reperies: abyssalem ibi comperies eruditionem* (Venice: Petri Liechtenstein Germani, 1531).

*Commentaria in primum partem et secundam partem Paralipomenom* (1445)

**Manuscript:** Salamanca, Biblioteca de la Universidad de Salamanca 2509–2510–includes some autograph folios, tables, and annotations.

*Respuesta del maestro de Madrigal e maestre-escuela de Salamanca* (1445)

**Manuscript:** Madrid, Biblioteca Nacional 18041, fols. 18v–19v.

*Traducción de los Chronici canones de Eusebio* (1445–1450)

**Manuscript:** Madrid, Biblioteca Nacional 10811.

*Commentaria super Matthaeum* (1446–1449)

**Manuscripts:** Salamanca, Biblioteca de la Universidad de Salamanca 2455–2460–includes autograph tables and marginal notes; Osma, Burgo de Osma 145 A–G; Cáceres, Biblioteca Pública 08365–08370; Vatican, Ottoboni lat. 44; Saragossa, Seo 11–47.

**Early edition:** *Floretum sancti Matthaei* (Seville: Pablo de Colonia y Juan de Nuremberg, 1491).

*Información y doctrina del modo de oír Missa con fruto* (1448?)

**Manuscript:** Biblioteca Lázaro Galdiano 762, fols. 207v–212v.

**Early editions:** *Información y doctrina del modo de oír Missa con fruto* (Seville: P. Von Köln, J. Pegnitzer, M. Herbst, Th. Glockner, ca. 1492); *Información y doctrina del modo de oír Missa con fruto* (Saragossa: Jorge Coci, 1503); *Información y doctrina del modo de oír Missa con fruto* (Alcalá Henares: Arnao Guillén de Brocar, 1511); *Información y doctrina del modo de oír Missa con fruto* (Valencia: Jorge Costilla, 1532).

*Comento o exposición de Eusebio de las crónicas o tiempos interpretado en vulgar* (1450–1451)

**Manuscripts:** Salamanca, Biblioteca de la Universidad de Salamanca 2479–2483 (autographs), 2485–2489; Biblioteca Nacional, 10808–10812–with the fourth part of the commentary missing, and in its place manuscript 10811, Madrigal's translation of St. Jerome's *Chronici canones,* titled *Interpretacion o traslacion del libro de las cronicas o tiempos de Eusebio Cesariense,* Madrid, Biblioteca Nacional, inserted.

**Early edition:** *Comento o exposición de Eusebio de las Crónicas* (Salamanca: Hans Giesse, 1506–1507).

*Confesional o Breve forma de confesión* (1450–1455)

**Manuscripts:** Madrid, Biblioteca Nacional 4183, fols. 1r–64v; Madrid, Biblioteca Nacional 4202, fols. 102r–130r; Madrid, Biblioteca de El Escorial a.IV.4, fols. 2r–94r, a.IV.5, fols. 1r–84v; Salamanca, Biblioteca de la Universidad de Salamanca 1756, fols. 1r–31v; New York, Biblioteca de la Hispanic Society HC397/378ª.

**Early editions:** *Confesional* (Villa Mayor de Mondoñedo, 1495); *Confesional* (Salamanca: Imprenta de Nebrija "Gramática," 1498? and 1499?); *Confesional* (Burgos: Fadrique de Basilea, 1500); *Confesional* (Burgos or Valladolid: Juan de Burgos, 1500); *Confesional* (Salamanca: Juan de Porras, 1512).

*Las diez cuestiones vulgares* (ca. 1453)

**Manuscript:** Salamanca, Biblioteca de la Universidad de Salamanca 2014.

**Early edition:** *Las diez cuestiones vulgares* (Salamanca: Hans Giesse, 1507).

**Modern editions:** "Cuestiones de filosofía moral," in *Obras escogidas de filósofos,* edited by Adolfo de Castro, Biblioteca de Autores Españoles, no. 65 (Madrid: Atlas, 1953), pp. 141–152–includes question number 7 of *Las diez cuestiones vulgares; Sobre los dioses de los gentiles,* edited by Pilar Saquero Suárez-Somonte y Tomás González Rolán (Madrid: Ediciones Clásicas, 1995)–comprises eight of *Las diez cuestiones vulgares.*

*Carta consolatoria* (1455?)

**Manuscript:** Madrid, Biblioteca Nacional 18653 (29), fols. 25r–26v.

**Modern edition:** Pedro M. Cátedra, "Una epístola consolatoria atribuída al Tostado," *Atalaya,* 3 (1993): 167–176.

*Libro que hizo en respuesta de quatro questiones que le propuso un cavallero* (1507 and 1545)

**Editions:** *Libro que hizo en respuesta de quatro questiones que le propuso un cavallero* (Salamanca: Hans

Giesse, 1507); *Libro que hizo en respuesta de quatro questiones que le propuso un cavallero* (Burgos, 1545).

**Modern edition:** "Cuestiones de filosofía moral," in *Obras escogidas de filósofos,* edited by Adolfo de Castro, Biblioteca de Autores Españoles, no. 65 (Madrid: Atlas, 1953), pp. 141–152–includes question number 4 of the *Libro que hizo en respuesta de quatro questiones que le propuso un cavallero.*

**Collection:** *Opera omnia,* 13 volumes (Venice: Gregorium de Gregoriis in aedibus Petri Liechtenstein, 1507–1531)–comprises *Commentaria in Genesim, Commentaria Paralipomenon, Paradoxae quinque,* and *Defensorium trium conclusionum;* second edition (Venice, 1527–1531)–comprises *Commentaria in Exodum, Leviticum, Numeri, Deuteronomium, Regum, in Primam Partem Matthaeum; Commentaria in Josue, in librum Iudicum, in Ruth; De optima politia; De statu animarum post hanc vitam; De beata Trinitate; Super locum Isaiae: Ecce Virgo concipiet;* and *Contra clericos concubinarios.*

Alfonso Fernández de Madrigal is well known for the vastness of his interests and the volume of his work. He wrote on theology, philosophy, and the law but is best known for his biblical commentaries and for the fact that he is one of the first authors of Latin works to become aware of the need to translate some of his works into Castilian for a noble public that could not read Latin. He was born in the village of Madrigal de las Altas Torres (Province of Ávila) in the first decade of the fifteenth century, probably around 1405.

In *Libro de los claros varones de Castilla* (1480–1486), Fernando del Pulgar describes El Tostado: "Don Alfonso, bishop of Ávila, was a man of average height, thickly built, and well proportioned. He had a large head, dominant features and a rather short neck." Scholars have never been certain of the meaning of his nickname. El Tostado ("the toasted" or "tanned") could have been the name of an ancestor or could refer to a possible darkness of his skin. In 1611 the cleric and chronicler Gil González Dávila wrote a brief biography of Madrigal, *Vida y hechos del maestro don Alonso [sic] Tostado de Madrigal, obispo de Ávila* (Life and Deeds of Alonso Tostado de Madrigal, Bishop of Ávila), in which he refers to his working-class parents as Alonso Tostado and Isabel de Ribera. The sobriquet *Tostado,* alone or tagged onto Alfonso de Madrigal, makes an early appearance in the rubrics of some of the manuscripts and early print editions of his works before the end of the fifteenth century. For example, Pedro Ximénez de Préxamo, in the 1491 Seville edition of *Floretum sancti Matthaei* (Flowers of St. Matthew), calls him "magister Alfonsus de Madrigal, scholasticus olim Salamantinus, postea vero abulensis episcopus, vulgari nostro hispano el Tostado nuncupatus" (Master Alfonsus of Madrigal, formerly a professor in Salamanca, afterward bishop of Ávila, called in our common Spanish tongue *Tostado*). This work was mined repeatedly for devotional and doctrinal texts in later years with either "Tostado" or "Madrigal" used in the headers of the passages borrowed from it. By the sixteenth century almost all the available sources were calling him "Tostado, former bishop of Ávila." "Abulense," or person of Avila, came to be a second title of identification.

According to González Dávila, though without independent documentary evidence, Madrigal did his early schooling in the Franciscan monastery in Arévalo. Pulgar adds that he continued his education in Salamanca, where he took clerical orders. As a churchman he enjoyed the customary prebends and honorary posts that generated regular income for clerics, and the documentation shows that he warded off rival claims when he had to. Other sources show that he had earned his master of arts degree by 1432, and by 1438 he was rector of the Colegio de San Bartolomé. During the second quarter of the fifteenth century and through the reign of Juan II of Castile, Madrigal was a university professor at Salamanca and a widely acclaimed ecclesiastic.

The records of the University of Salamanca in the first half of the century are too scanty to reveal Madrigal's actual program of study, so his academic training has to be inferred from hints in his own works. The colophon to the 1499? Salamanca edition of the *Confesional o Breve forma de confesión* (Confessional or Brief Form of Confession, 1450–1455) praises his meteoric transformation from student to intellectual leader of the University and Cathedral of Salamanca. Evidently, the 1430s were a period of great activity, leading to the production of many of his biblical commentaries. In *Las çinco figuratas paradoxas* (The Five Figured Paradoxes), dedicated to Queen María of Castile in 1437, El Tostado presents himself as not only a master of arts but also a graduate in theology. He must have earned a degree in theology sometime during this period, because pontifical registers show that in 1441 El Tostado referred to it during his bid for a contested chaplaincy in the diocese of Ávila. The canonical legislation of Pope Martin V stipulated that the post of *maestrescuela* (master of the schools, the chief educational authority in both academic and diocesan administrative circles) could be held only by someone with a doctorate in either civil or canon law or by a master of theology; the latter degree allowed Madrigal to receive papal confirmation of his post in 1446 and to hold it until 1454, when he became bishop of Ávila.

Madrigal's hefty corpus of work is essentially a by-product of his teaching duties at the University of Salamanca. Even those works that are ostensibly dedicated to personages not involved in academe were developed in the course of preparing for his celebrated lectures. A large portion of these works are on biblical exegesis and display the usual rigor of a good scholastic who starts from a well-informed *lectio* (reading) and moves into a thoughtful *quaestio* (interpretation of the literal sense).

Some of his works are academic *repetitiones* (that is, lectures given during public events, which were required to obtain degrees or were given once a year by a teacher on an independent theme related to the content of a course), a purely academic exercise cultivated by students and their teachers. The *repetitio* owed its structure, disposition of its content, invention, and ornament to the scholastic training conveyed through the study of the trivium. It could deal with theological, biblical, or grammatical questions; with natural or moral philosophy; or with civil or canon law. Although the *repetitiones* were highly formalized, they still owed something to the classroom performance and the teacher's demonstration of scholarship.

Other writings related to teaching and speaking are brief commentaries on a variety of themes, closely related to the *repetitiones*. They can be considered *casus* (cases) or *interpretationes* (interpretations) and often use historical references or have a juridical character. Other writings were dubbed *quaestiones,* essays for a wider public, about subjects studied at Salamanca.

One can also group under the flexible form of the *tratado* (treatise) works that are quite dissimilar in form and content. Some have a moral thrust and are dedicated to pastoral formation or canonical jurisdiction; others are historical reflections, essays on the Virgin Mary and her intervention in human affairs or on the nature of Christ, or commentaries on Aristotelian ethics or natural philosophy. Most of these works are in Latin and reflect the substance of El Tostado's academic lectures, but in the decade of the 1430s part of his production was intended for a lay public capable of receiving instruction on all sorts of matters.

Curiosity about subjects usually reserved for university study seems to have characterized the Castilian court, which began to make use of the common tongue to cultivate higher learning, as evidenced, for example, by the works of Enrique de Villena and Lope de Barrientos. The *Cancionero de Baena* (Songbook of Baena), especially compiled for the royal court around the mid fifteenth century, demonstrates how its writers delighted in poetic exchanges between theologians and scientists and how the lexicon and form of the *modo disputandi* (debate), as applied to theology and scholastic philosophy, pervaded the higher circles of the court and influenced and enlightened laypeople of all ranks. El Tostado's works constitute a program of reading for a curious yet relatively unlettered public, one that increasingly concerned the teaching clerics. Alfonso de Cartagena's *Epistula* (Epistle, 1440s), directed to the conde de Haro, delineates a self-directed study program for this public that is in accord in its general outline with what was taught at the universities, while eschewing matters better left to theologians.

El Tostado undertook the translation of some of his own works into Castilian in order to overcome the difficulties posed by Latin and wrote others in Castilian, which he later translated to Latin. This translating activity was conditioned by the level of preparation of a Castilian reading public, which determined the inclusion or exclusion of certain *quaestiones disputatae* (disputed questions), the use of different authorities, or the order of presentation of the text; but on the whole the texts reflect what was being taught at the University of Salamanca.

Through his dedication to differing language demands and limitations of his diverse readership, El Tostado ended up making some of the most important contributions to the theory and practice of translation in the fifteenth century. He considered translation a fundamental activity, for which a deep understanding of source and target languages was essential, and his comments on the propositions of St. Jerome about translation went beyond the common understanding of the time.

The first of his works are thought to be annotations of the books of the Pentateuch. They were written in the decade of the 1430s and survive in several autograph manuscripts now at the University of Salamanca library. They are the *Brevis Postilla super Genesim, Exodum, Leviticum et Numeros* (Brief Notes on Genesis, Exodus, Leviticus, and Numbers, 1432–1435) and the *Finis Libri Numerorum et Commentarius super Deuteronomium* (On the End of Numbers and a Commentary on Deuteronomy, 1432–1453). He later expanded his comments on the Pentateuch in the *Commentaria in Genesim* (Commentaries on Genesis), where he refers to himself as master of arts though he must have been close to obtaining his degree in theology, and in the *Commentaria in primam parte Exodi et in secundam partem Exodi, in Leviticum, in primam partem Numerorum et in secundam partem Numerorum, et in Deuteronomium* (Commentary on the First and Second Parts of Exodus, on Leviticus, on the First and Second Parts of Numbers, and on Deuteronomy, 1432–1433).

The *commentaria* on Genesis, Exodus, and Deuteronomy must have been written before 1437, for by this time he was writing *Las çinco figuratas paradoxas,* in which he makes reference to those works. This exegetical labor is complemented by the *Commentarius super Librum Josue* (Commentary on the Book of Joshua, 1436–1438), *Commentaria super Iudices et Ruth* (Commentary on Judges and Ruth, 1436–1438), *commentaria* on the four

books of Kings (in contemporary biblical nomenclature the First and Second Books of Samuel and the First and Second Books of Kings), and the *Commentaria in primam partem et secundam partem Paralipomenom* (Commentary on the First and Second Parts of Chronicles, 1445).

Madrigal also wrote an extensive commentary on Matthew (*Commentaria super Matthaeum,* 1446–1449), which he divided into six parts and later condensed into the *Floretum sancti Matthaei,* printed by his disciple Ximénez de Préxamo in 1491, the first of his books to be printed with movable type. El Tostado's exegesis concerns the literal interpretation of meaning in the Bible. Rarely does he venture into the more profound *sententiae* (moral sense), but along the way he does deal with natural, theological, moral, and rational questions that were common to the era, among them demoniacal possession and procreation under the influence of incubi and succubi (*Commentaria in Genesim* and *Commentaria in Exodum,* 1436), the anguish of the unbaptized (*Commentaria in Genesim*), the representation of angels or the ceremony of circumcision (*Commentaria in Exodum* and in the first book of the *Commentarius super Librum Josue*), the moral implications of homicide (*Commentaria super Iudices et Ruth*), and matrimony (*Commentaria in Genesim* and *Commentaria super Matthaeum*). Natural law, including topics such as war, treaties, and terms of engagement, is covered in studies on the Pentateuch, Chronicles, and Judges.

Madrigal probably intended to comment on all of the New and Old Testament books, but only the titles cited above have survived. It is believed that he began a commentary on Job and on the Epistle of Paul to the Hebrews, but it is doubtful that a commentary on the penitential psalms ever existed.

The "repetitions" that have survived are on theological, moral, or juridical teachings. The *repetitio* titled *De statu animarum post hanc vitam* (On the Status of Souls after Death, 1432–1437) must have been composed in the early 1430s. It begins with an exordium in which the author, as student, appears tired and dejected. He speaks to the muse Urania, who, knowing his worth, encourages him to work. The tedium and dejection that he feels comes from his excessive dedication to poetry, so Urania urges him to dedicate himself to other sorts of writing. The result is the *repetitio,* which deals with the nature and properties of the soul and its destiny after death, a subject that derives from his teaching at Salamanca. The initial *sermocinatio* (consideration) of the *repetitio* agrees with what is known about the early life of El Tostado: he recommends that students abandon poetry for more weighty matters.

After the prologue, the *repetitio* divides into two sections, each having seven conclusions. In the first he deals with the future of the soul, one of the principal concerns of Christian philosophy from the introduction of Aristotle and Latin Averroism in the thirteenth century. He evaluates and refutes ancient authorities about the transmigration of the soul and about the existence of an afterlife not in agreement with Christian orthodoxy. This section of the *repetitio* takes Aristotle's *De anima* (On the Soul, circa 350 B.C.) and *Nicomachean Ethics* and Cicero's *Tusculanae disputationes* (Tusculan Disputations, 45 B.C.) as fundamental authorities in dealing with matters concerning the knowledge accessible through the senses and knowledge accessible through the intellect. The second part of the *repetitio* deals with the consequences of attempting to reconcile pagan philosophy with Catholic doctrine, including the shopworn topic of the actual location of Hell, traditionally identified with volcanic terrains. Part of this *repetitio* was used for *Las çinco figuratas paradoxas,* which El Tostado sent to Queen María in 1437 and later translated into Latin for Juan II. *Las çinco figuratas paradoxas* abbreviates the first part of the *repetitio* by inserting Madrigal's own take on Pythagoreanism and Platonic philosophy.

The *repetitio* known as *De beata Trinitate* (The Blessed Trinity, 1435–1437) seems to date from the time El Tostado was a teacher of theology, because the colophon claims that the author has long dealt with the matter and presents him as *in theologia et artibus magistri* (a master in theology and arts). As in *De statu animarum post hanc vitam,* this *repetitio* uses the muse Urania as a model for inspiration. She is a *veneranda institutrix* (revered teacher) who stirs the writer from his slumber and calls on him to work. This *repetitio* treats the complex subject of the Trinity, but with an apologetic cast that indicates that it was meant for possible *converso* or Jewish readers. El Tostado maintains that, though there are allusions to the Trinity in the Old Testament, they do not constitute in themselves proof of its existence, and he ventures to say that, perhaps because of their propensity for idolatry, the mystery of the Trinity was not revealed to the Jews. El Tostado argues that their stubbornness and resistance to rational argument leave their only recourse a docile acceptance of the New Dispensation in which the reality of the Messiah is made explicit.

The *repetitio* known as *De optima politia* (On the Perfect State, 1432–1437) is a commentary on the political theories that Aristotle presented in his *Politics.* It considers subjects such as what is the nature of a citizen, what constitutes a city or political entity, how is the city organized, what is the status and responsibility of a citizen, and which is the best political system. Madrigal's attempts to think about political systems start from notions of the Greek city-state, merge with ideas about the "natural law" theory of scholasticism, and ultimately fit within divine precepts. By a long insertion on historical precedents in classical and biblical sources and by rejecting Plato's unmanageable idealism, El Tostado builds a more-or-less integrated vision of the justice of human laws, allowing for legal systems that offer the best fit for a given community. He comes down on the side of a democracy ruled by an elected "prince," because it seems less subject to rebellion and sedition.

Madrigal next turns to eugenics in *De optima politia.* This part of the essay seems to support the establishment of a state policy in benefit of a healthy family. After considering the importance of the father-son relationship against a background of the theory of the Ages of Man, the narrator speaks about the best time to sire the next generation: parents should not be excessively young or excessively old, and they should not engage in heavy work or dedicate themselves to idleness. As to climatic differences, temperate zones are best for the purposes of procreation. Finally, El Tostado marshals his best arguments to refute Plato's propositions about the relationship of the sexes by citing the authority of Augustine's *De bono coniugali* (On the Good of Marriage, 401) and Aristotle's *Politics.* He rejects polyandry on principle as being against nature, fostering incest, blurring the lines of descent and distinctions of caste, and destabilizing society. El Tostado is less negative on the matter of polygamy, because of the natural superiority of men over women, and assumes that men might be able to regulate access to their wives on their own.

Among Madrigal's minor works are treatises or expositions less directly tied to his teaching activities than the *repetitiones.* Two texts stand out from the rest: *Super Isaiae: Ecce Virgo concipiet* (About Isaiah: Behold a Virgin Shall Conceive, 1442–1446) and *Responsio ad Dominum Palentinum super benedictione et errore Isaac* (Answer to the Lord of Palencia about the Blessing and Error of Isaac, 1429–1439). *Super Isaiae* is a literal exposition of one of the most disputed passages in the Hebrew scriptures (Isa. 7:14) because of its centrality to the theological confrontation between Jews and Christians on the virginity of Mary. El Tostado called the *Responsio ad Dominum Palentinum super benedictione et errore Isaac* a *breviloquius* (short treatise) and dedicated it to the "Palentine lord" Gutierre Álvarez Gómez de Toledo sometime between 1429 and 1439. The question considered is Jacob tricking his father, Isaac, into giving him his blessing (and right of succession) over his slightly elder twin brother, Esau. The *Responsio ad Dominum Palentinum super benedictione et errore Isaac* therefore deals with the rights of primogeniture among the Hebrews and the implications of the incorrect blessing by a blind and old Isaac. El Tostado considers this deception a demonstration of God's untrammeled power of choice, for though Isaac wanted to bless Esau, the elder brother had already bartered his right away to

Jacob, who even enjoyed the collusion of his mother in usurping the status of chosen heir. The implication is that God acts by his own inscrutable designs and that the future is veiled even from the elect. Other brief treatises also reflect his teaching activities at the university: the *Tractatus de aeternitate* (On Eternity, 1440s), *De muliere sarracena transeunte ad ritum iudaicum* (Of Female Moslem Converts to Judaism, 1440s), and *Contra clericos concubinarios* (Against Clerics and Their Concubines) are among these, though some have questioned El Tostado's authorship of the *Contra clericos concubinarios*.

In the summer of 1443 Madrigal was sent by King Juan II of Castile to the papal court, then in residence in Siena, to handle a jurisdictional dispute with the kingdom of Aragon over a house of studies in Orihuela, a dependency of a Castilian diocese located in Aragonese territory. He framed his defense of Castilian rights before the court of cardinals in a treatise, but his doctrinal and theological competence was unexpectedly challenged by the opposition, which rebutted (and perhaps deliberately misconstrued) his arguments. Madrigal was forced to appeal to Pope Eugenius IV to validate the terms of the argument.

The Pope named a commission of three cardinals, who labeled at least five of El Tostado's key points as overstated and heretical. The cardinal Juan de Torquemada put into writing the reasons for the prison sentence. The commission held that the first two points were not heretical in themselves but dangerous and far from the common consensus because they altered the accepted date of Christ's death. Three other propositions were considered heretical because they attacked the doctrine of penance (a topic on which El Tostado had his own interpretation), the need for clerical absolution, and justification by grace, all destined to become cornerstones of the coming Reformation debate. The reproof was inconclusive. There seems to have been no formal retraction expected of Madrigal for this theological independence. Instead, he launched a self-defense in his *Defensorium trium conclusionum* (A Defense of Three Conclusions, 1443–1446), in which he furiously rejects the machinations of his colleagues abroad.

Students of Madrigal all agree that on his return from Italy in 1444–without stopping in Basel, Switzerland, where a Church council was then in session–he took refuge in the Carthusian monastery of Scala Dei in Tarragona. There he withdrew from all public contact for six months. In fact, monastic records show him being admitted as a member of the strictly cloistered religious order. According to some, King Juan II himself urged him to come out of his self-imposed exile and return to his university life in Salamanca, where he was appointed *maestrescuela* in 1446 and served in both aca-

*Tomb of Alfonso Fernández de Madrigal, sculpted by Vasco de la Zarza in 1518 at the cathedral in Avila, where Madrigal was appointed bishop in 1454 (courtesy of Frank A. Domínguez)*

demic and ecclesiastical posts until his election as bishop of Avila barely a year before his death.

The *Defensorium trium conclusionum* records the denunciation Madrigal suffered in Siena when expounding on some of his theological ideas. The work manifests his indignation at his accusers and rehearses some of his arguments on the remission of sins and the power granted to St. Peter and, through him, to the Church. Madrigal clearly envisions a power that is above that of the pope, whom he considers a mere representative of a collective. A classic "conciliarist," who endorses the collegial authority of Church councils over that of the papacy, Madrigal promotes the *potestas habitualis* (habitual power) of the bishops, who represent the congregation of the faithful, the Church, over the *potestas actualis* (actual power) of the pope. Though he did not take part in the Council of Basel, some of the ideas of the *Defensorium trium conclusionum* anticipate later thoughts about ecclesiastical versus temporal powers.

In 1437 El Tostado composed *Las çinco figuratas paradoxas,* an extensive doctrinal work on Mariology and Christology, organized as a series of propositions and replies written in Castilian. The author signals that it was written to answer Queen María of Castile's questions about some hidden metaphors concerning the Virgin as receptacle, and the representation of Christ as lion, lamb, serpent, and eagle. Each of the five metaphors is given binary and opposing explanations. The Virgin, for example, is "un vaso çerrado et non çerrado; pequeño et non pequeño; lumbroso et non lumbroso; vazío et non vazío; mas vaso limpio et non limpio" (a vessel open and closed, small and not small, bright and not bright, empty and not empty, clean and not clean). The paradoxes give rise to a lengthy exegesis based on the Bible, but with digressions based on Aristotelian physics and psychology. The methodology, however, is purely scholastic. Madrigal relies on his own commentaries on the Pentateuch and Joshua and *repetitiones* such as *De statu animarum post hanc vitam* and *De optima politia,* translating them *verbum ad verbum* (word for word) for *Las çinco figuratas paradoxas.* Each term is examined and subjected to a *disputatio,* which presents in order the objections and distinctions proper to the question. In rhetorical terms, El Tostado classifies the questions as *genus admirabile* (wondrous reflections), which because of their remarkable nature deserve to be called formal paradoxes, like the *Paradoxa stoicorum* (Paradoxes of the Stoics) of Cicero.

Madrigal first tackles the symbolic meaning of the multiple devotional titles for the Virgin Mary, which reached its highest development in the sermon books and the meditations of St. Bernard of Clairvaux and Pseudo-Bonaventure. The perpetual virginity of Mary and the doctrine of the Immaculate Conception (that Mary was conceived without the stain of original sin) are discussed along the lines of the Franciscan and Dominican debates, with the author taking a conciliatory position among the two theological factions. Christ's conception in the womb of Mary gives rise to a long scientific discussion of pregnancy that tries to reconcile Aristotelean views with contemporary medieval medical theory, including what was believed or known about embryology and the mechanics of fertilization.

The Christological character of the work is emphasized in the paradoxes that follow. The second "paradox" closely follows the arguments of Thomas Aquinas in using Christ's comparison to a lion to prove the existence of the Son of God as Incarnate Word on earth and his presence in the Eucharist. The third paradox concerns Christ's comparison to a lamb and focuses on the redemptive nature of Jesus. In this paradox he refers to the events of Christ's life and Passion in a much more emotional and pious vein and shows how Christ's ordinary human discomforts—thirst, cold, hunger—had salvific value. The fourth comparison,

Christ as serpent, takes as its starting point a commentary on chapter 21 of the Book of Numbers, in which the irresolute Israelites, on their journey to the Promised Land, are afflicted by God with venomous snakes and cured when Moses hoists up the figure of a serpent for them to gaze upon. The matter is explained from a pseudoscientific point of view as a result of certain magical or infectious powers entering through the eye when a living creature cast its gaze or breath upon them. This *aojamiento* (optics of contagion) is attributed to basilisks (who could kill with a mere glance), wolves, and menstruating females, who can all cloud the quicksilver backing of a mirror. Madrigal eventually aligns himself with the 1410 legislation of John II, who tried to outlaw various forms of superstition.

The fifth metaphor expands on the image of Christ as an eagle. This gloss relies on the properties assigned to this noble bird by classical and medieval encyclopedists. The image makes an analogy between the flight of the eagle and Christ's ascent into Heaven. The discussion then veers toward the celestial character of the resurrected human body, which leads to a consideration of the corruption of mortal bodies and original sin, the future states of the soul, and the four final dwelling places of souls that are separated from God: Hell, Purgatory, Limbo, and the relative bliss of "the bosom of Abraham," a resting place for pre-Christian souls justified by faith. Madrigal then comments on the renewal that is implied by the Resurrection and explains the symbolism of Christ, not only as eagle but also as phoenix.

In the decade of the 1430s Madrigal was also composing in Latin a work that is only known by the title of its Spanish translation, the *Breviloquio de amor y amiçiçia* (A Short Treatise on Love and Friendship, 1432–1436), dedicated to John II. The long prologue to the Spanish version reveals that the translation must have followed immediately upon the creation of the Latin work:

> Et esto por mí en stillo latino acabado, aunque tantas non fueron las fuerças commo la voluntad de servir, la vuestra real alteza a mí rescrivió que todo el latino comento en fabla vulgar tornasse. Et esto, señor, yo non entendí a mí ser mandado porque vuestra exçellente señoría en el comento dicho alguna difficultad fallasse . . . más aun queriendo aprovechar a los otros que del latino stillo non expertos, podían por el stilo vulgar exerçitar sus engenios, el dicho latino comento en romançe castellano mandó interpretar, porque si en la dicha obra algund fructo oviesse a todos fuera manifestado

> (And after I finished this in Latin, without obligation though with less aptitude than desire to be of service, your Royal Highness commanded that I translate the Latin commentary into the vulgar tongue. And this,

Lord, I did not take to be ordered by your Highness because you had difficulty in reading the commentary . . . but because you wished to enlighten others who were not so familiar with Latin to exercise their minds in the common Castilian tongue, and so, you commanded that the work be translated into Castilian romance so that whatever benefit it contained would be made available to all).

It is possible that Madrigal himself conceived the idea of reaching a new reading public through his romance translations. What is certain is that he began to channel his efforts in romance toward a public that must have had limited knowledge of Latin. He announces in the *Breviloquio de amor y amiçiçia,* however, that the translation is a new attempt at exposition, close to its original when it is possible to find a Castilian term to translate the Latin, but more creative when he is forced to expand on his text beyond the succinctness of the original Latin. In spite of this variability, he assures the monarch of the accuracy of his vernacular rendition.

The prologue also declares that the work responds to the desire of the monarch to learn the meaning of a Platonic *dictum* about friendship: "quando ovieres amigo, cumple que seas amigo del amigo del mismo, mas por esto non cumple que seas enemigo de su enemigo" (when you have a friend, you must be a friend to his friend, but it does not follow that you must be an enemy to his enemy). This bit of advice is a quotation attributed to Plato in some wisdom texts and is cited almost literally in the *Bocados de oro* (Golden Sayings, 1250–1280, an anonymous translation of Abu l Wafa' al Mubashshir ibn Fatik's *Mukhtar al Kalim wa mahasin al hilam* (1048–1049). Madrigal's treatise is not a study of Platonic philosophy, however, but an extensive reflection on books 8 and 9 of Aristotle's *Nicomachean Ethics.* The material is organized by Aristotle's definitions of affective terminology. The distinction between *amaçión* (love) and *amiçiçia* (friendship) is viewed from the perspective of the *Ethics:* "semejante la amaçión a la passión et la amiçiçia al hábito por actos engendrado" (love is similar to passion and friendship to habit engendered through repeated acts). This formulation permits El Tostado to make human love a step through which one can attain the superior goal of friendship.

Human affections show themselves as three distinct types: love of land, love of family (principally of children), and love of the flesh. The first two types of love derive from tenderness and spring naturally from reason and practicality; under the rubric of love of one's land El Tostado considers virtuous men who achieved enduring fame through extraordinary deeds done on behalf of their country. Greater attention is given to filial piety, however, a matter that concerned El Tostado more than once in his writings. He begins by saying that love between parents and children is natural and proper to the human condition and is shared by all animals. Human beings are rational; therefore, this love can sometimes lead to friendship, which will happen if parents and children establish a dialogue that is like that between friends. Such communication can only be possible when offspring become self-sufficient. The work goes into practical considerations, such as the appropriate age of marriage and the mutual duties that link parents and children. This section closes with a discussion of filial love for either father or mother, which is more amply treated in *Las çinco figuratas paradoxas,* particularly in regard to maternal love.

El Tostado dedicates eight chapters to the phenomenological characteristics of carnal love, such as the joy of sexual union itself. Although carnal love is universal throughout the animal world, it is acutely present in humans because of reason. Human sexual pleasure does not climax in copulation but through the powers of the imagination. Woven throughout the work are asides on love as a physical and psychological disturbance, such as love that is prompted by jealousy or is illicit. El Tostado's examples are taken from literary sources, and he concludes this section by alluding to the traditional cures for lovesickness, rejecting some (such as the use of prostitutes) on moral grounds and urging the avoidance of idleness and resistance to the power of memory.

The doctrine of friendship is then discussed in the second, lengthy part of the work, which expands on books 8 and 9 of the *Ethics* of Aristotle. According to El Tostado, *amiçiçia* is a habit acquired through a succession of acts, all of them perfecting the individual search for the common good. Tostado's utopian conception of a perfect society rests on Aristotle. Like Aristotle, El Tostado defends the different categories of love, which he enumerates as honesty (the best and most profitable to the individual), pleasure, and usefulness. Honest love guarantees peace, justice, and community and is praised for its benefits to friends, relatives, and even the body politic. The examination of friendship in the *Breviloquio de amor y amiçiçia* influences the use of the concept that is made in the didactic prose of the latter part of the century, particularly in the treatises on love, in sentimental fiction, and the *Celestina.*

Between 1445 and 1450 El Tostado prepared a Castilian translation of St. Jerome's *Chronici canones,* the only work that survives in an autograph manuscript. The prologue notes that Íñigo López de Mendoza, the marqués de Santillana, requested the translation, but Madrigal designed the project to leave the original historical text intact, uncluttered with explanatory insertions or commentary. From internal evidence it is known that Madrigal's gloss, known as *Comento o exposición de Eusebio de las crónicas o tiempos interpretado en vulgar* (Commentary or Exposition on Eusebius of the Chronicles or Eras Interpreted in the Vulgar Tongue), must have been started in 1450 and continued into the following year. Scholars suspect, also based on internal evidence, that the *Comento o exposición de Eusebio de las crónicas o tiempos interpretado en vulgar* was originally written in Latin before it was translated into Castilian, and that this Latin version might have been written before 1450.

St. Jerome's prologue to the *Chronici canones* comments on the concept and difficulties of translation. His translation theory, particularly in the *De optimo genere interpretandi* (The Best Way of Interpreting or Translating, circa 395), would have been known by Madrigal, who glossed and reinterpreted Jerome according to his own ideas. Madrigal explains that the translator must have a superior rhetorical knowledge of the languages and subject matter with which he works, and which he refers to as the "linaje del saber" (genealogy of knowledge). This double competency characterizes the good translator, who is *disertus* (discerning) and especially prepared to do an appropriate interpretation. El Tostado comments on the differences between a translation *verbum ad verbum* (word for word) and a translation *ad sententiam* (for meaning). He follows Jerome in distinguishing accuracy as necessary for any good translation, but El Tostado knew from experience that the ideal of syntactic equivalence could not always be attained and that faithfulness to the original text could lead to a translation that did not make sense. The translator, instead, knowing the peculiarities of each language, needs to choose the best way to translate the sense of the original text, even when this approach takes him away from the literal translation of words. This method of translating *ad sententiam* is different from interpretation and is referred to by El Tostado as "exposición o comento o glosa" (exposition, commentary, or gloss). This manner of translating is cognizant of the expressive peculiarities of each language and must be kept in mind by the translator. El Tostado pays special attention to the use of periphrasis in the amplification of verse and prose and analyzes the indispensable figures of rhetoric that must be employed by any commentary. The completion of this extensive and erudite translation, planned in five parts, was interrupted by the author's death.

The value of the *Comento o exposición de Eusebio de las crónicas o tiempos interpretado en vulgar* also lies in its encyclopedic handling of history, geography, and mythology. In his glosses El Tostado gives a Christian dress to pagan fables, employing the euhemeristic (the

presumption of a kernel of truth behind a fabulous story) and allegorical interpretations found in his source texts. He probably used Ovid, Augustine, and St. Isidore firsthand, and perhaps chapters from Alfonso's *General Estoria* and Giovanni Boccaccio's *Genealogia deorum gentilium* (Genealogy of the Pagan Gods, 1360–1375), from which many of El Tostado's citations of classical authors also probably derive.

Representative of El Tostado's work in Castilian is the genre known as *quaestiones*, brief treatises in which he expounds theological or moral issues and mythology. These *quaestiones* are less academic than his *repetitiones* and more likely to engage in speculations about theological doctrine, mythology, and morality. These qualities also make them less likely to find their way into print and, therefore, harder to trace in terms of their evolution as a genre. Toward 1453 El Tostado composed *Las diez cuestiones vulgares* (Ten Common Questions), which explores mythological and erotic matters. The questions are dedicated to mythological figures, including Apollo, Neptune, Juno, Narcissus, Venus, Diana, Minerva, and Cupid. Some of the subject matter was derived from previous works, in particular the now lost *Los Fechos de Medea* (The Deeds of Medea, before 1437) and the *Comento o exposición de Eusebio de las crónicas o tiempos interpretado en vulgar*.

Madrigal closely follows the order, names, attributes, and cultic practices (and sometimes translates the literal text) of the pagan in Boccaccio's *Genealogia deorum gentilium*. The iconographic commentary quotes many traditional interpretations, among which one can be singled out as having particular favor: astrological determinism, evident in the section dedicated to Cupid. This section consists of a brief treatment on the power worldly love has over heaven and earth, over the gods, and over humanity. According to El Tostado, this power is pernicious. It does not derive from true divine power, because Cupid's love is identified with vice and lovesickness, an illness of the soul that only encourages lust. The constable Don Pedro of Portugal must have relied on these *quaestiones* and on the *Breviloquio de amor y amiçiçia* for his *Sátira de infelice y felice vida* (Satire of an Unhappy and Happy Life, 1445–1449), while another contemporary, Luis de Lucena, in his *Repetition de amores* (Repetition on Love, 1486–1487) exploits another work mistakenly attributed to El Tostado, the *Tratado de cómo al hombre es necesario amar* (Treatise on Man's Need to Love, 1470).

The sixth question, "De las edades de nuestra vida" (On the Ages of Our Life), briefly reviews the Ages of Man, first treating the stages of the history of the world as inherited from Ovid and Virgil and echoed by El Tostado himself in his commentary on St. Jerome, *Comento o exposición de Eusebio de las crónicas o tiem-*

*pos interpretado en vulgar,* also known as the *Eusebio de los tiempos* (Eusebius on the Eras). El Tostado favors a division of the Ages of Man into six stages–infancy, childhood, adolescence, youth, maturity, and old age–following in the footsteps of Isidore of Seville. Afterward, he compares this system with those of other commentators who divide the Ages of Man into seven, five, or three periods. The commentary is based on an erudite roster of distinguished authorities.

The seventh question, "De las virtudes morales qual es más soberana" (On the Preeminent Moral Virtue), should be considered as being a "pura especulación de philosophía moral" (pure speculation on moral philosophy). After declaring the excellencies of the theological virtues, Faith, Hope, and Charity, which Madrigal sees as avatars of the virtues found in Aristotle's *Ethics,* he proclaims the preeminence of Prudence among the four cardinal virtues and tests his assertions with nine arguments that seem to undermine its status as a motor force that effectively generates the other three: Justice, Temperance, and Fortitude.

Other *questiones* explored by El Tostado in the vernacular have survived under the title *Libro que hizo en respuesta de quatro questiones que le propuso un cavallero* (Book Written in Response to Four Questions Set to Him by a Nobleman, 1507). The *cavallero* alluded to in the title was again the archbishop of Palencia, to whom El Tostado had already dedicated other works. The first question concerns why the Evangelists dealt more with the figure of John the Baptist than with the Virgin Mary, and why Luke, who dealt extensively with the affairs of the apostles, bypassed her completely. By way of response, El Tostado assembles a compendium of Old and New Testament texts that function as a defense of Holy Scripture as the Word of God and therefore true and valid, but leaves the question of the nature of the Virgin to a matter of faith, of the mystery of divine will. He is content to offer a quick and dutiful review of all of the scriptural passages that speak of Mary.

The second question treated in the *Libro que hizo en respuesta de quatro questiones que le propuso un cavallero* concerns the reasons God ordered the Hebrews to build a tabernacle with undressed stone, while the third reflects on the differences between the active life versus the contemplative life. Madrigal adopts a traditional criterion that favors the contemplative life but invites each person to choose which is best suited to his or her personal strengths. The fourth question must have held greater interest for an academic audience: which is better, moral or natural philosophy? Those who know both decide on the basis of the quality of the object analyzed and the truth value of the conclusions. According to these criteria, natural philosophy

wins. When one examines the question of which is more useful, however, moral philosophy triumphs, because while the only fruit of natural philosophy is to become wise, moral philosophy teaches people to act on that wisdom. El Tostado backs his resolution with the authority of St. Jerome's commentary on the Epistles to the Corinthians, in which St. Paul recalls a perfidious statement made against the new Christians by Greek natural philosophers.

The *Confesional o Breve forma de confesión* is a pastoral work intended to help laymen understand the sacrament of penance. Like all works of its type, the *Confesional* must have enjoyed wide circulation in manuscript copies before the first printed edition of 1495; its composition could well date back to the 1430s, especially since its author is referred to as a mere *maestro* and *bachiller.* Its organization and essential ideas concern the *remissionem peccatorum* (the remission of sins), but the text concludes by declaring itself a *formula ad rudium instructionem* (a manual for instructing the common folk) and is far removed from the aims of his *Defensorium trium conclusionum,* written years later to display his subtle mastery of theology and doctrine.

The *Confesional* begins with a review of mankind's fall into original sin in Genesis, the common inheritance of humanity. It concludes by proposing penance as the remedy for sin. In between is an exposition of the three parts of the sacrament of penance: heartfelt contrition, oral confession before a priest, and completion of the penance imposed. Practical guidelines and some cases support the explanation of these three parts. The text considers each of the seven mortal sins–pride, lust, gluttony, envy, wrath, sloth, and greed. Each sin is followed by an invitation to the penitent to engage in a comprehensive examination of conscience and a commitment to avoid sin in the future. This program of dissuasion is well suited for a pastoral work, and the sections devoted to the types of sin include concrete examples, with lust and avarice, as usual, getting the lion's share of attention. The manual ends with an examination of the sins that can be committed with the five bodily senses and a review of the formal "obras de misericordia" (works of mercy) (such as feeding the hungry and clothing the naked).

Finally, some samples of El Tostado's correspondence have survived, though one letter has been wrongly attributed to him. In a study done in the eighteenth century on the Salamancan Colegio de San Bartolomé (College of Saint Bartholomew), El Tostado is named as the author of a consolatory letter directed to a member of the House of Alba on the occasion of the death of the person's father, but the duchy of Alba was created some years after the death of El Tostado and nobody of the family Alvarez de Toledo appears to have died while he was bishop. Researchers have pointed instead to Álvaro de Estúñiga, who lost his father in 1455, as the bereaved. In any case, the letter cannot be attributed to El Tostado with certainty. Another letter tentatively ascribed to El Tostado, concerning the form in which mass is to be performed, survives in a single manuscript under the title *La siguiente información y doctrina escrivio el señor maestro e obispo de Ávila don Alfonso de Madrigal para don Alvaro de Astuñiga despues conde de Plasencia* (The Following Information and Doctrine Was Written by the Lord Master and Bishop of Ávila, Don Alfonso de Madrigal, for Don Álvaro de Estúñiga, thereafter Count of Plasencia). Still another can be found in the *Libro de las veynte cartas e quistiones* (Book of the Twenty Letters and Questions, 1445–1455) of Fernando de la Torre, which includes an answer given by El Tostado to the poet concerning a matter of conscience. De la Torre was actually acting as an intermediary for a lady who had written to him. The answer given by El Tostado seems to let slip his full awareness of the courtly game, for beneath the theme of *contemptu mundi* (contempt for the world) there seems to be a more banal game playing out between de la Torre and his female correspondent.

In 1454 Madrigal was ordained bishop of the diocese of Ávila, where he died a year later in the neighboring village of Bonilla de la Sierra. He was buried first in the central choir of the cathedral before being interred behind the main altar in a fine alabaster tomb sculpted by Vasco de la Zarza.

The influence of Alfonso de Madrigal was felt among the men of the following generation. One of the first to comment on Madrigal's literary fame was Alfonso de Palencia, who composed an artful allegorical narrative on El Tostado in a letter addressed to the aristocrat Alfonso de Velasco. The mournful tone and rhetorical styling of the narrative (in the manner of some of Madrigal's own writings) is an airy reproach to Death for leaving Spain an orphan when El Tostado died in his forties. Already legendary for his learning, he was deserving of at least another decade of life to finish the work he had begun. His passing, Palencia predicted, would bring calamities to Spain: "la muerte del eximio padre conllevará la desidia de aprender; la desidia de aprender volverá mucho más torpes y detestables las costumbres de los hombres; la vileza, que es el evidente enemigo de todos, a todos nos será hostil" (the death of this illustrious priest saps us of the will to learn, and from that collapse the habits of men will turn coarser and more detestable; everything despicable, enemy of all, will hem us in). The language is hyperbolic, but the lament is a testimony to the body of work already completed by the time of Madrigal's death.

Pulgar declared that El Tostado had composed many treatises on philosophy and theology and wrote extensively and authoritatively on sacred Scripture. Gómez Manrique has the allegorical figure of Faith say, in his *Planto de las virtudes* (Complaint of the Virtues, after 1458), that not only could the deceased El Tostado match Augustine in wisdom, but recompose the whole Bible were it to be lost. El Tostado's intelligence, penetrating analytical power, and prodigious memory have become something of a cliché in Spanish culture. Nicolás Antonio collects a whole range of panegyrics from writers who make Madrigal the equal of St. Jerome or Augustine.

Some of Pulgar's early admirers were also members of the Colegio de San Bartolomé in Salamanca–Pedro Martínez de Osma, Fernando de Roa, and Pedro Ximénez de Préxamo, who was responsible for the print edition of Tostado's *Floretum sancti Matthaei.* The work of these men differs from the work of El Tostado, however. If El Tostado was still anchored in scholastic modes of reasoning, an intellectual current in sharp decline elsewhere in Europe, his successors were early exponents of what came to be called the humanist school of Salamanca. Madrigal is a transitional figure with a prescient predilection for the work of Aquinas over Dun Scotus, and his political and judicial thought–such as his views on monarchy, his interest in the conciliar movement, and his protopsychological reflections on human emotions, natural law, and the law of nations–is more in tune with later thinkers. Despite his participation in and contributions to various currents that later became mainstream opinion, the works of El Tostado in private libraries in the sixteenth century were mainly limited to his *Floretum sancti Matthaei* and the *Confesional.* Occasionally he appears linked to the *Comento o exposición de Eusebio de las crónicas o tiempos interpretado en vulgar.* Cathedral libraries, monasteries, and convents, along with the private collections of high-ranking ecclesiastics, were the principal repositories of his *Opera omnia* (Complete Works, 1507–1508).

The first works by Madrigal to be printed were extracts from the *Commentaria super Matthaeum,* which Ximénez de Préxamo collected under the title *Floretum sancti Matthaei* in 1491. Four years later the Mondoñedo presses published the *Confesional,* and then in the first years of the sixteenth century, the *Comento o exposición de Eusebio de las crónicas o tiempos interpretado en vulgar, Las diez cuestiones vulgares,* and the *Libro que hizo en respuesta de quatro questiones que le propuso un cavallero* appeared in Salamanca. In 1503 the *Información y doctrina del modo de oír Missa con fruto* (1448?) appeared in printed form in Saragossa. Around 1506 a royal edict set the process in motion to publish El Tostado's complete works, entrusting the project to the supervision of Palacios

Rubios, Juan López de Vivero. Imprints from the presses of Gregorium de Gregoriis in Venice followed in 1507. No one is sure why it took until 1523 to print a full set of Madrigal's works, the work entrusted this time to Alonso Polo, Charles V's chaplain, and a church official from Cuenca. A second wave of Venetian imprints dates from between 1527 and 1531.

## Biography:

Gil González Dávila, *Vida y hechos del maestro don Alonso Tostado de Madrigal, obispo de Ávila* (Salamanca: Francisco Cea Tesa, 1611).

## References:

Nicolás Antonio, *Bibliotheca Hispana Vetus* (Madrid: Joaquín Ibarra, 1788), II: 255–260;

Nuria Belloso Martín, *Política y humanismo en el siglo XV: El maestro Alfonso de Madrigal, el Tostado* (Valladolid: Universidad de Valladolid / Salamanca: Caja de Ahorros y Monte de Piedad de Salamanca, 1989);

Vicente Beltrán de Heredia, "Don Alfonso Fernández de Madrigal, el Tostado. Rectificaciones históricas," in *Cartulario de la Universidad de Salamanca,* 6 volumes (Salamanca: Universidad, 1970), I: 474–499;

Beltrán de Heredia, "Edición de las obras del Tostado en Venecia bajo la dirección del maestro Alonso Polo," in *Cartulario de la Universidad de Salamanca,* I: 641–738;

Joaquín Blázquez Hernández, "Teólogos españoles del siglo XV: El Tostado. Su doctrina acerca de la justificación," *Revista Española de Teología,* 1 (1941): 211–242;

Blázquez Hernández, "El Tostado alumno graduado y profesor en la Universidad de Salamanca," in *XV Semana de Teología* (Madrid: Consejo Superior de Investigaciones Científicas, 1956), pp. 413–447;

Blázquez Hernández, "El Tostado alumno graduado y profesor en la Universidad de Salamanca: Complemento y rectificación," *Revista Española de Teología,* 32 (1972): 47–54;

J. Candela Martínez, *El "De optima politia" de Alfonso de Madrigal, el Tostado* (Murcia: Universidad de Murcia, 1954);

Tomás Carreras y Artau, "Las repeticiones salmantinas de Alfonso de Madrigal," *Revista de Filosofía,* 2 (1943): 213–236;

Jesús Luis Castillo Vegas, "El humanismo de Alfonso de Madrigal, el Tostado, y su repercusión en los maestros salmantinos del siglo XV," *Cuadernos Abulenses,* 7 (1987): 11–21;

Pedro Cátedra, *Amor y pedagogía en la edad media: Estudios de doctrina amorosa y práctica literaria* (Salamanca: Universidad de Salamanca, 1989);

Cátedra, "Un aspecto de la difusión del escrito en la Edad Media: La autotraducción al romance," *Atalaya,* 2 (1991): 67–84;

Francisco Crosas López, "Sobre los primeros mitógrafos españoles: El Tostado y Pérez de Moya," in *Actas del VI Congreso de la Asociación Hispánica de Literatura Medieval,* 2 volumes, edited by J. M. Lucía Megías (Alcalá de Henares: Universidad de Alcalá de Henares, 1997), I: 543–550;

Luisa Cuesta, "La edición de las obras del Tostado, empresa de la corona española," *Revista de Archivos, Bibliotecas y Museos,* 56 (1950): 321–334;

María Jesús Díez Garretas, *La obra literaria de Fernando de la Torre* (Valladolid: Universidad de Valladolid, 1983), pp. 127–128;

Emiliano Fernández Vallina, "Autores clásicos, mitología y siglo XV español: El ejemplo del Tostado," in *Estudios de tradición clásica y humanística: VII Jornadas de Filología Clásica de las Universidades de Castilla y León,* coordinated by Manuel Antonio Marcos Casquero (León: Universidad de León, 1993), pp. 17–28;

Fernández Vallina, "Introducción al Tostado: De su vida y de su obra," *Cuadernos Salmantinos de Filosofía,* 15 (1988): 153–177;

Fernández Vallina, "Poder y buen gobierno en Alfonso Fernández de Madrigal (El Tostado)," *Cuadernos Salmantinos de Filosofía,* 23 (1996): 255–274;

Olegario García de la Fuente, "Dos obras en castellano de Alfonso Tostado inéditas," *La Ciudad de Dios,* 168 (1955): 297–311;

David González Maeso, "Alonso de Madrigal, el Tostado, y su labor escrituraria," *Miscelánea de estudios árabes y hebraicos,* 4 (1955): 143–185;

María Isabel Hernández González, ed., *En la teoría y en la práctica de la traducción: La experiencia de los traductores castellanos a la luz de sus textos (siglos XIV–XVI)* (Salamanca: Seminario de Estudios Medievales y Renacentistas, 1998), pp. 72–105;

Carlos Heusch, "Enjeux socio-culturels des discours amoureux dans l'Espagne du XVè siècle," in *Amours et conventions littéraires en Espagne, du moyen âge au baroque* (Montpellier: Université Paul Valéry, 1996), pp. 41–61;

Ronald G. Keightley, "Alfonso de Madrigal and the *Chronici canones* of Eusebius," *Journal of Medieval and Renaissance Studies,* 7 (1977): 225–258;

Karl Kohut, "Der Beitrag der Theologie zum Literaturbegriff in der Zeit Juan II von Kastilien," *Romanische Forschungen,* 89 (1977): 183–226;

Florencio Marcos Rodríguez, "Los manuscritos de Alfonso de Madrigal conservados en la Biblioteca Universitaria de Salamanca," *Salmanticensis,* 4 (1957): 1–50;

D. W. McPheeters, "Influencias del Tostado en Salamanca a fines del siglo XV," in *Actas del VII Congreso de la Asociación Internacional de Hispanistas,* volume 2 (Rome: Bulzoni, 1982), pp. 1091–1092;

E. Martín Nieto, "Los libros deuteronómicos del Antiguo Testamento, según el Tostado, Alonso de Madrigal," *Estudios Abulenses,* 1 (1954): 56–74;

Alonso de Palencia, *Epístolas latinas,* edited by Robert B. Tate and Rafael Alemany Ferrer, Publicaciones del Seminario de Literatura Medieval y Humanística (Bellaterra, Barcelona: Universidad Autónoma, Facultad de Letras, 1982), pp. 78–100;

Fernando del Pulgar, *Claros varones de Castilla,* edited by Tate (Oxford: Clarendon Press, 1971), pp. 145–146;

Roxana Recio, "Alfonso de Madrigal (El Tostado): La traducción como teoría entre lo medieval y lo renacentista," *La corónica,* 19, no. 2 (1991): 112–131;

Recio, "El concepto de belleza de Alfonso de Madrigal (El Tostado): La problemática de la traducción literal y libre," *Livius,* 6 (1994): 59–69;

Klaus Reinhardt, "Die biblischen Autoren Spaniens bis zum Konzil von Trient," *Repertorio de historia de las ciencias eclesiásticas en España,* 5 (1976): 9–242;

Reinhardt and Horacio Santiago-Otero, *Biblioteca bíblica ibérica medieval* (Madrid: Consejo Superior de Investigaciones Científicas, 1986), pp. 64–79;

Isaías Rodríguez, "Autores espirituales españoles de la edad media," *Repertorio de historia de las ciencias eclesiásticas en España,* 1 (1967): 175–351;

Peter E. Russell, *Traducciones y traductores en la Península Ibérica, 1400–1550* (Bellaterra, Barcelona: Escuela Universitaria de Traductores e Intérpretes, Universidad Autónoma de Barcelona, 1985), pp. 26–35;

Concepción Salinas Espinosa, "Las *Cuestiones de filosofía moral* de Alfonso Fernández de Madrigal," in *Actas del IV Congreso de la Asociación Hispánica de Literatura Medieval,* volume 2 (Lisbon, 1993), pp. 295–300;

Horacio Santiago-Otero, *Manuscritos de autores medievales hispanos* (Madrid: Consejo Superior de Investigaciones Científicas, 1987), pp. 40–42;

Guillermo Serés, "Don Pedro de Portugal y el Tostado," in *Actas del III Congreso de la Asociación Hispánica de Literatura Medieval,* 2 volumes, edited by María Isabel Toro Pascua (Salamanca: Biblioteca Española del Siglo XV, Departamento de Literatura Española e Hispanoamericana, 1994), II: 975–982;

Francisco Elías Tejada, "Derivaciones éticas y políticas del aristotelismo salmantino del siglo XV (de Alfonso de Madrigal a Francisco de Vitoria)," *Miscellanea Medievalia,* 2 (1963): 707–715;

Curt Wittlin, "El oficio del traductor según Alfonso Tostado de Madrigal en su comentario al prólogo de san Jerónimo a las *Crónicas* de Eusebio," *Quaderns: Revista de traducció,* 2 (1998): 9–21.

# Gómez Manrique

## (1412? – 1490)

### Hilary W. Landwehr
*Northern Kentucky University*

WORKS: *Obras de Gómez Manrique*

**Manuscripts:** Manrique's collected poems appear in two late-fifteenth-century manuscripts: Madrid, Biblioteca del Palacio II/1250 (Vit. sala VI) and Madrid, Biblioteca Nacional MS. 7817. Both appear to have been compiled by the poet. While the Biblioteca del Palacio manuscript has more poems, the Biblioteca Nacional manuscript features compositions not found in the former. Certain of Manrique's poems were also collected in several multi-author fifteenth- and sixteenth-century *cancioneros* (songbooks or anthologies), among them the *Cancionero de Pero Guillén de Segovia* (Madrid, Biblioteca Nacional MS. 4114), which contains several poems not found in either Biblioteca del Palacio II/1250 or in Biblioteca Nacional MS. 7817, and the *Cancionero de Juan Fernandez de Ixar* (Madrid, Biblioteca Nacional MS. 2882).

**Early editions:** *Regimiento de príncipes* (Zamora: Antonio de Centenera, ca. 1482); *Cancionero general recopilado por Hernando del Castillo* (Valencia: Cristóbal Kofman, 1511)–includes Manrique's "El planto de las virtudes y poesía," "Otra suya a dos damas hermanas y muy hermosas," "Regimiento de príncipes," "Coplas para Diego Arias de Avila," "La exclamación y querella de la gobernación," "Otra obra suya suplicando al marqués de Santillana que le diese un cancionero de sus obras," and "Al maestre Francisco de Noya, maestro de Fernando, príncipe de Aragón."

**Standard editions:** *Cancionero de Gómez Manrique,* edited by D. Antonio Paz y Mélia, 2 volumes, Colección de Escritores Castellanos, nos. 36, 39 (Madrid: A. Pérez Dubrull, 1885, 1886; reprinted, with a letter by the poet and commentary by Manuel Carrión Gútiez, 1991); *Cancionero castellano del siglo XV,* edited by Raymond Foulché-Delbosc, 2 volumes, Nueva Biblioteca de Autores Españoles, nos. 19, 22 (Madrid: Bailly-Bailliere, 1912, 1915); *Poesías,* edited by Teófilo Ortega (Valencia: Tipografía Moderna,

1941); Brian Dutton, *El cancionero castellano del siglo XV, c. 1360–1520,* musical *cancioneros* edited by Jineen Krogstad, 7 volumes (Salamanca: Universidad de Salamanca, 1990–1991).

Gómez Manrique wrote more than one hundred poetic compositions. In modern times he has been recognized primarily for a single work, *Representación del nacimiento de Nuestro Señor* (Play about the Birth of Our Lord, circa 1467–1481), one of the few surviving pieces of medieval Castilian theater. During the fifteenth century, however, he was highly regarded as a poet; his lyrics were collected in several manuscript *cancioneros* and later included in *Cancionero general recopilado por Hernando del Castillo,* first published in 1511. Manrique's fellow poets admired the lofty didactic tone of his more serious poems. He was substantially influenced by the poetry of Juan de Mena and of his uncle, the marqués de Santillana. In turn, Manrique's influence is perceptible in the *Coplas a la muerte de su padre* (Stanzas upon the Death of His Father, circa 1476–1479) of his nephew Jorge Manrique.

Gómez Manrique belonged to a prominent noble family, noted as much for political and military activity as for poetic work. During much of the fifteenth century the Manriques were among the nobles siding with the infantes (princes) of Aragon, who constantly interfered with the government of their cousin King Juan II of Castile (ruled 1406–1454) and, later, with that of Juan's son King Enrique IV (ruled 1454–1474). The first mention of Manrique in historical accounts was made in 1434, when he participated in the conquest of Huéscar, snatched from the Muslim kingdom of Granada. Hernando del Pulgar notes in "El maestre don Rodrigo Manrique, conde de Paredes" (Master Rodrigo Manrique, Count of Paredes) from *Claros varones de Castilla* (Outstanding Men of Castile, 1486), that Manrique's valor in battle was rewarded by an appointment as temporary governor of the town. In 1439 Manrique participated in the Congress of Tordesillas, which attempted to resolve the continuing dispute between

*Plaque in the main stairway of the Casas Consistoriales de Toledo with* Quintillas *( five-line stanzas) by Gómez Manrique ( from Clemente Palencia Flores,* El poeta Gómez Manrique, Corregidor de Toledo, *1943; Doe Library, University of California, Berkeley)*

Juan II and his favorite adviser, Álvaro de Luna, on the one hand, and the partisans of the infantes of Aragon on the other. Manrique was wounded in battle at Arrabel in 1441, and in 1448 he cosigned a truce agreement between his brother Rodrigo, master of the Order of Santiago, and Marshall Diego Fernández de Córdoba.

As dissatisfied with the rule of Enrique IV as he had been with that of Juan II, Manrique found himself once again opposing royal authority, siding with the party of the archbishop of Toledo, Alonso Carrillo. In 1465, while serving as *corregidor* (royal governor) of Avila, Manrique participated in a symbolic dethroning of Enrique in favor of the king's half brother Prince Alfonso. After Alfonso died in 1467, Manrique changed his allegiance to Alfonso's sister, Princess Isabel (Isabella). When she decided to marry Prince Fernando (Ferdinand) of Aragon without King Enrique's consent, Manrique was the one who escorted her to the town of Valladolid, where the wedding was performed. Manrique continued in Isabel's service after she ascended to the Castilian throne in 1474, and he was appointed *corregidor* of Toledo in 1477, a position he held until his death in 1490.

It is uncertain when Manrique began his literary career because there is no indication of when most of his poems were composed. In *Morphology of Fifteenth Century Castilian Verse* (1964) Dorothy Clark describes his lines as impeccably scanned—both the octosyllables and

the longer *versos de arte mayor* (poems composed in lines of more than eight syllables), a form common in the mid fifteenth century. She notes that while Manrique continued to write late into the century, his verse forms do not reflect characteristics seen in other poets writing during the late 1400s. Since the composition of lyric verse was part of the social life of a young nobleman, it is possible that some of his poems were composed during the 1430s and 1440s, particularly the amorous and satirical verses. He composed one poem beginning "Muy alto y poderoso señor" (Most high, powerful king) upon the occasion of the birth of Prince Alfonso in 1453, which confirms that Manrique had begun writing during the reign of King Juan II, but the other poems that can be dated correspond to the reigns of Enrique IV and of the Catholic Monarchs, from their accession in 1474 until Manrique's death in 1490.

Most of Manrique's poetry consists of the courtly love lyrics, satires, occasional verse, and poetic exchanges that were commonly written in noble households. With few exceptions, these poems are found only in the compilations put together by Manrique himself. The love lyrics follow the conventions of courtly love, although the poems addressed to his wife, Juana de Mendoza, have a more personal touch. The occasional verses mark events and holidays and are usually addressed to members of Manrique's extended family and literary circle. The *preguntas y respuestas* (debate poems) are, for the most part, typical of the era in their form and content. The questions being asked tend to be ones well established in the poetic tradition, while the answers rarely propose any new conclusions. Daniela Capra has noted that Manrique's treatment of courtly love in these exchanges is often humorous or ironic, and that his other exchanges, such as those with Juan de Mazuela and Pedro de Mendoza, rise above the hackneyed norm through the incorporation of personal and historical references.

In twentieth-century literary anthologies Manrique is usually presented as the earliest medieval Castilian dramatist. He composed four works having at least some dramatic characteristics, although in only two of the cases can one be reasonably certain that they were ever staged. Two are *momos* (mummers' plays) and are designed for performance at family or court celebrations. In the one written "En nombre de las virtudes que iban momos al nacimiento de un sobrino suyo" (In the Name of the Virtues that Appeared as Mummer's Plays at the Birth of a Nephew) each stanza is a speech by an allegorical figure representing one of the cardinal or Christian virtues granting itself to the newborn. There is no introduction or conclusion and no dialogue. The second mummers' play, "Un breve tratado que hizo Gómez Manrique a mandamiento de la muy ilustre señora infanta doña Isabel para unos momos que su excelencia hizo con los fados siguientes" (A Brief Treatise that Gómez Manrique Wrote at the Order of the Most Illustrious Princess Isabel for a Mummers' Play that Her Excellency Performed with the Following Fates), was written at the behest of Princess Isabel, who, along with other ladies, assumed the guises of the Fates and recited the words on the occasion of Alfonso's fourteenth birthday, in 1467. This work is more elaborate than the first mummers' play, having an introduction and a conclusion, although once again there is no dialogue between characters. The first Fate recites a prose introduction explaining the nature and purpose of the group, and then seven ladies recite one stanza each. Isabel herself recites a longer stanza concluding the poem. The Fates wish for Alfonso to receive the secular gifts a king needs to rule well and live a good life.

Manrique's third work with dramatic characteristics is "Fechas para semana santa" (Composed for Holy Week), found only in the *Cancionero de Pero Guillén de Segovia* (circa 1480). It is part of the *planctus* tradition, in which the Virgin Mary and St. John the Baptist lament the death of Jesus. St. John goes on to speak with Mary Magdalene and engage in a brief dialogue with the Virgin.

The work for which Manrique is most often noted is his *Representación del nacimiento de Nuestro Señor*, composed between 1467 and 1481 and intended to be performed by the nuns at the convent of Calabazanos, where his sister was assistant mother superior. *Representación del nacimiento de Nuestro Señor* clearly derives from the Latin *Officium pastorum*, a shepherds' play, but, unlike Manrique's mummers' works, it is not limited to recitation by allegorical characters. The characters in *Representación del nacimiento de Nuestro Señor* display a variety of human emotions and respond to each other's utterances, even when they do not engage in true dialogue. The play opens with Joseph's speech. He is jealous and suspicious of Mary, who is about to bear a child that cannot be his. Mary, in response, prays that Joseph be enlightened, whereupon he is rebuked by an angel. After the Nativity, an angel announces Jesus' birth to the shepherds, who engage in the only real dialogue in the work as they ask each other in wonder whether they really heard an angel speak. The shepherds go to worship the newborn, and the archangels express their desire to serve Mary. At this point the physical objects associated with the mature Christ's capture and crucifixion are presented to the newborn as a foreshadowing of his eventual suffering and death. The presentation apparently causes the baby to cry; the play ends with a consoling lullaby sung by a chorus of sisters at the convent of Calabazanos.

*Representación del nacimiento de Nuestro Señor* is well grounded in medieval tradition; all of its constituent elements are found in other medieval treatments of the theme. While the play ostensibly deals with the temporal poles of Christ's life at his Nativity and Passion, the characters continually cite or allude to previous events or prophecies mentioned in the Old Testament. Alan Deyermond points out that these typological references, combined with the characters' prophecies of Christ's redemptive suffering, enable Manrique to include the entire history of human salvation, from the fall of Lucifer to the poet's own time. The Savior's birth and death are repeatedly connected as both Mary and the shepherds mention that the joy of Jesus' Nativity will turn to sorrow at his final Passion.

As in the earlier, anonymous *Auto de los Reyes Magos* (Play of the Three Kings), Manrique varies the verse forms employed. With the exception of the dialogue between the shepherds and a brief speech by a chorus of angels, both of which are based on units of three verses, the characters speak in four- or eight-line stanzas. The variations in the rhyme scheme *(abbacddc, ababcdcd )* correspond roughly to the shifts in scene. The final lullaby is written in hexasyllables. Modern studies of the play have emphasized its structure and dramatic unity. Harry Sieber makes a detailed analysis of the structural symmetry in the play, demonstrating that it follows the antiphonal structure of liturgy by alternating scenes of multiple voices with those of single characters or a group of characters speaking as one. Deyermond maintains that Manrique's linking of Old Testament prophecies to those uttered by the characters in the play and the connections established between Old and New Testament figures—such as Eve with Mary and Adam with Jesus—are techniques repeatedly employed in medieval drama and are important to the structural unity of *Representación del nacimiento de Nuestro Señor*. Deyermond also points out that the lullaby sung by the nuns, in which they declare themselves to be brides of Christ, is an example of how certain aspects of Christian life are modeled on elements from the New Testament. *Representación del nacimiento de Nuestro Señor* has not only the symmetry of the liturgy but also a temporal symmetry in which the Old Testament looks forward to Christ's life while the poet looks backward from his own time to the same pivot point.

Manrique also composed didactic poems in response to events in his political, literary, or family life. Most of these poems have been dated, at least approximately, and correspond to the reigns of Enrique IV and of the Catholic Monarchs. In these poems, unlike his courtly verse, Manrique frequently asserts that his poetic abilities are inadequate to the task he has begun. While a modest disclaimer is traditional at the begin-

*Manrique's prologue to an edition of his poem* Regimiento de príncipes *published circa 1482 (Biblioteca Nacional, Madrid; courtesy of Frank A. Domínguez)*

low poets, because they are repeatedly collected in later *cancionero* anthologies.

"Defunción del noble caballero Garcilaso de la Vega" (Death of the Noble Knight Garcilaso de la Vega), written in 1455 in *arte mayor,* is one of Manrique's earliest didactic works and appears in six *cancionero* manuscripts. It commemorates the death of a knight who fell in battle, wounded by a poisoned arrow, and heroically endured a painful end. The poem focuses on retelling the event, praising the virtues of the deceased, and presenting the grief of Garcilaso's family and fellow knights. Much of the imagery the poet employs is chosen to evoke the fearsome sounds of the event—the noisy celebration of the Muslims, as well as the screams and cries of the mourners—so that the immediate, emotional reaction to the death is preferred to the reasoned meditation on the nature of death and life commonly seen in medieval elegies. As a result, certain traditional components of the elegy, such as the *ubi sunt* (where are they now?) or images representing the transience of life, do not appear in "Defunción del noble caballero Garcilaso de la Vega." Another result of the focus of the poem is the creation of heightened contrast between the crushing grief of the family and fellow warriors on the one hand and the satisfaction with death ascribed to Enrique IV on the other, a reaction much more akin to that of the Muslim enemies. "Defunción del noble caballero Garcilaso de la Vega" therefore includes one of Manrique's earliest criticisms of his new king.

Between 1453 and 1458 Manrique wrote the poem beginning "La péñola tengo con tinta en la mano" (The pen I hold with ink in my hand) to console his sister Juana, possibly for the political reversals and the resulting economic consequences suffered by her husband, Fernando de Sandoval y Rojas, Count of Castro. Like "Defunción del noble caballero Garcilaso de la Vega," it is written in *arte mayor* and is one of Manrique's more consciously erudite works. The poet provides a prose prologue and glosses the stanzas at irregular intervals to identify the historical references he uses. The poem is organized in a focused, logical manner, with an introduction, a statement about the nature of fortune, supporting evidence from history, advice on the proper way to deal with worldly goods, and a conclusion. Human suffering is considered to be intrinsic to life in the world, where the changeable nature of fortune affects both the individual and his descendants.

Manrique much admired the work of Mena and, upon Mena's death in 1456, undertook the completion of his *Coplas de los siete pecados mortales* (Stanzas on the Seven Deadly Sins). Manrique's continuation is one of three attempted by fifteenth-century poets and was completed sometime between 1457 and 1465. The

ning of medieval poems, some scholars believe that in Manrique's case there is a genuine sense of inadequacy, perhaps owing to the poet's transition from the lighter court verse to meditations on moral themes. Yet, this is a transition common among fifteenth-century court poets, especially after experiencing reverses in their personal lives or succumbing to the general pessimism prevalent among fellow countrymen who had witnessed decades of civil unrest. Like his fellow poets, Manrique draws on a set of traditional images and historical analogies and makes extensive use of proverbs and proverb-like structures to communicate his themes. Also like his colleagues, he emphasizes the transience of the human condition, the vagaries of fortune, and the importance of good government. While Manrique displays little originality in his ideas—originality would not have been expected in that era—some of his didactic poems appear to have been highly admired by his fel-

poem is a debate between Reason and Will; the latter is presented as a seven-headed monster, with each head representing one of the mortal sins. Mena completed the treatment of pride, avarice, lust, and anger before his death. After a brief introduction, Manrique's continuation deals with the remaining sins: gluttony, envy, and sloth. He also introduces the allegorical figure of Prudence to judge the debate, prescribing remedies for each of the sins and counseling each of the three estates (clergymen, nobles, and commoners) on how they should conduct themselves. The themes emphasized are death as the inevitable equalizer of all people, the transience of worldly things, and fortune.

"Planto de las virtudes y poesía" (Lament of the Virtues and Poetry) is an elegy written on the death of the marqués de Santillana in 1458. It is accompanied in some of the *cancioneros* by a letter directed to Santillana's son, Pedro González de Mendoza, bishop of Calahorra, but both the letter and the poem appear separately as well. While Manrique mourns Santillana as a political and literary figure, he does not employ the more erudite *arte mayor* stanza, using instead a ten-line stanza of octosyllabic lines. Although the verse form is not the most erudite possible, the content follows a traditional, allegorical format. The poet begins by asking his sighs and his anger, the manifestations of his grief, to assist him in the composition of the poem. He then observes the quarrel between his feelings for Santillana and his lack of prudence and eloquence. By separating his emotions from his poetic persona, Manrique immediately places himself at a distance from his subject, as a reporter of the events about to occur. What follows is a typical dream sequence. There is a description of the renewal of springtime, in the midst of which the poet begins to feel disturbed, weeping and sighing. While seeking solitude in a monastery, he loses his way and finds himself in a terrifying valley, whose flora and fauna are contrasted with those of the traditional earthly paradise. He journeys through the valley to a fortress inhabited by eight allegorical female figures representing the seven virtues and poetry. Each woman speaks in turn, praising Santillana, mourning his loss, and placing him in the company of historical figures who exemplified the virtue she represents. Poetry speaks last, lamenting the loss of Mena and Juan Fernández de Ixar, and then commanding the poet to write about Santillana. During the ensuing argument between reluctant poet and adamant Poetry, the eulogy of the marqués as a man of letters is accomplished.

The internal discord and the persistent conflicts with Aragon that plagued Castile during the reign of Enrique IV were criticized by the king's enemies for slowing the progress of the Christian Reconquest. Manrique contributed to the criticism in two politically inspired poems. The earlier one, written under the rubric "Cuando se trataba la paz entre los señores reyes de Castilla y de Aragón y se desarinieron" (When the Kings of Castile and Aragon Were Negotiating Peace and Disagreed), is most likely a response to the breakdown of peace negotiations between Castile and Aragon that occurred in 1460. This poem appears only in Manrique's own collections of his works. "La exclamación y querella de la gobernación" (Exclamation and Complaint about Government), in contrast, was one of Manrique's most popular poems, judging by its inclusion in more than a dozen subsequent *cancionero* manuscripts and by the fact that a later gloss by Pero Díaz de Toledo also repeatedly appeared with it. Information given in Díaz de Toledo's prologue indicates that the poem was composed after 1460. It opens with a portrayal of Rome during her days of rising power and closes with the image of Rome in decadence. In between, the poet first portrays "un pueblo donde moro" (a town where I reside) as a world in which irrational behavior abounds. Then, through a series of proverbs and other statements following proverbial formulas, he draws a profusion of analogies between ineffective, irrational, or impossible behavior and the bad government he is criticizing. The number and variety of the analogies reflect the chaotic political situation in his own country and contrast that situation with the self-sacrificing behavior of the early Romans. Manrique returns to the opening theme in the penultimate stanza, in which he declares that Rome prospered while it was well ruled but fell when its rulers surrendered themselves to personal greed. The poem begins and ends with the situation in Rome, but otherwise it avoids the appearance of having a formal structure.

"Coplas para Diego Arias de Avila" (Stanzas for Diego Arias de Avila), written between 1454 and 1465, is directed to Enrique IV's accountant. The prose introduction to the poem complains of Arias's reluctance to authorize a payment from the treasury to Manrique until the poet has written a new work. Manrique modestly disclaims any talent for poetry, but he also connects his supposed poetic inadequacies to Arias's seeming inability to deliver the designated funds, thereby subverting the topos of modesty. The poet then informs Arias that if the resulting lines seem more bitter than expected, it is because Manrique has nothing left to lose except his life, which should have little value to any good person. This mingling of statements on the transitory nature of the world with sly references to the accountant's refusal to pay continues in the poem that follows the prose introduction. In its flowing rhythm and use of imagery it more closely resembles "La exclamación y querella de la gobernaión" than Manrique's earlier didactic poems. Unlike the superficially

*Undated note to Manrique from Queen Isabel I in the Archivo Municipal de Toledo (from Clemente Palencia Flores,*
*El poeta Gómez Manrique, Corregidor de Toledo, 1943; Doe Library, University of California, Berkeley)*

chaotic "La exclamación y querella de la gobernaión," however, "Coplas para Diego Arias de Avila" has a well-marked traditional structure, beginning with an invocation and a *captatio benevolentiae* (capturing of good will) and ending with a recommendation that the accountant live his life with an eye to his eternal fate rather than attaching himself to the things of this world. The poet focuses on the presentation of the theme of transience, which he reiterates throughout the poem, using such traditional images as the rapid fading of flowers and the world as the wheel of fortune. As many scholars have pointed out, in the thematic focus, use of imagery, and even the choice of *pie quebrado* (half line) verse, the poem resembles Jorge Manrique's *Coplas a la muerte de su padre* and is considered evidence of Gómez Manrique's influence on the work of his nephew.

Gómez Manrique composed "Regimiento de príncipes" (Regimen of Princes) between 1474 and 1479. It was one of several poems directed to the Catholic Monarchs by various poets, advising them on how they should rule Castile. The poem appears in five *cancionero* manuscripts, and the versions vary somewhat. While both monarchs are addressed, most of the poem is directed to King Fernando. In the prose prologue the poet states that he had intended to compose a separate poem for Queen Isabel but lacked the knowledge and the time needed to complete the task. The complaint, lack of time to write, is common in Manrique's didactic poems, particularly those composed during the last part of his career. "Regimiento de príncipes" consists of seventy-nine *coplas mixtas,* nine-line stanzas composed of four- and five-line substanzas. It begins by focusing on the dangers of *voluntad* (will) ungoverned by reason. False counselors are ruled by will, and rulers who take their advice invariably fall, as illustrated by examples presented in chronological order from biblical times through the 1369 assassination of Fernando's ancestor King Pedro the Cruel and on to the fall and death of his half brother Prince Carlos of Viana in 1461. The final example is given the most emphasis because, while history can be doubted, Prince Carlos's case occurred during Fernando's lifetime, and the king's own memory can confirm what the poet says.

Manrique then sets about giving his advice in "Regimiento de príncipes." His main recommendation is that the king read in order to acquire the wisdom to distinguish good from evil. In giving this advice, Manrique supports the common medieval belief that a good ruler must combine the force of arms with the knowledge of letters. In order to be wise, a ruler must practice and defend the Christian faith. He must learn to fear God, to place little value on the riches and power of this life, and to avoid sin. Manrique goes through the remaining Christian and the four cardinal virtues one by one, explaining how they apply to a king. In enumerating the virtues, he expands on the concepts presented in the *momos* written for Isabel to perform on Alfonso's birthday. Also like the mummers' plays, "Regimiento de príncipes" emphasizes the more pragmatic virtues. While Faith is treated in seven stanzas, Hope and Charity are covered in three and two, respectively. Prudence and Justice receive six stanzas each, while Temperance has only four. The virtue of Fortitude is undoubtedly the most important in the poet's mind, for he discusses it over the course of nine stanzas, followed by an additional six on the definition of true effort. In the virtues that he chooses to emphasize, Manrique responds to the two most common criticisms of the previous ruler, Enrique IV: that he failed to defend the faith by continuing the Christian Reconquest of the Iberian Peninsula and that he was much too weak to govern Castile properly. The portion of "Regimiento de príncipes" intended for Isabel is only one-third as long as the part directed to her husband. While Manrique does account for this situation, it must also be noted that he, like many poets writing on this topic near the start of the joint reign of the Catholic Monarchs, perceived Fernando as the stronger governing force. Manrique also uses several stanzas to praise his queen for typically feminine qualities such as beauty and gentility. He then counsels Isabel not to allow her religious devotion to take time away from her duties as a ruler, reminding her that while others can recite the prayers, she is responsible for dispensing justice and setting a good moral example. As he has already told Fernando, Manrique cautions the queen against the dangers of willfulness and urges her to follow the dictates of reason. The poet concludes by reminding both monarchs that their power is transitory and that they are obliged to rule in accordance with the will of God.

"Consolatoria para doña Juana de Mendoza" (Consolation for Juana de Mendoza) may well be Manrique's last poem. It is found in two *cancioneros*. The version in Biblioteca Nacional MS 7817 is introduced by a prose prologue, but it is missing twelve stanzas in the middle of the poetic text. The missing stanzas are found in the version in Biblioteca de Palacio II/617, a sixteenth-century compilation. Manrique states in the prologue that he wrote the poem for his wife in response to the sorrow the couple felt upon the deaths of two of their children, Luis and Catalina, within a four-month period. In a letter of condolence to Manrique, later published in Manuel Carrións article "Gómez Manrique y el protonotario Lucena" (1978), Juan de Lucena comments on the fact that Catalina's death was the latest in a series of losses in Manrique's family, beginning with his brother Rodrigo, who died in 1476, and continuing with that of his nephew Jorge and another brother, Fadrique, who both died in 1479. At the time, Manrique was *corregidor* of Toledo while his wife, as *camarera mayor* (head lady-in-waiting) to Queen Isabel, was living at court. The situation was complicated further by his wife's illness, which was serious enough that Queen Isabel summoned him to court to be with her in 1481. That Manrique was not coping well is indicated in Lucena's letter, in which the latter complains that with the loss of his daughter, Manrique has changed from a strong person who stoically accepted misfortune and even consoled others in their grief to someone weak who continues to weep over Catalina's death. In the prologue to his poem Manrique states that he composed most of "Consolatoria para doña Juana de Mendoza" during the two months after Catalina's death but was unable to complete it immediately, finding that his writing skills had deteriorated from lack of practice, a theme that is later repeated in the poem itself. Other information in the prologue and the poem itself indicates that the work was not finished until at least 1484 and perhaps as late as 1485 or 1486.

For Manrique, "Consolatoria para doña Juana de Mendoza" is an atypical didactic poem. While the poet touches on the themes of fortune and transience, he does not elaborate on them as he does in "La péñola tengo con tinta en la mano" or in "Coplas para Diego Arias de Avila." Instead, he focuses on how people are deceived into believing that earthly rewards are good and earthly suffering is evil. The consolation offered by the Catholic faith is limited to one stanza. Furthermore, Manrique draws little from his stock of traditional motifs and devices. While he handles the invocation as usual, first naming and then rejecting the classical deities in favor of the Christian God, he makes no references to classical history and employs no proverbs in the poem itself. The tone of the work is also markedly different: in his earlier elegies Manrique distances himself from the event, taking on the role of reporter or commentator, and even when he writes to console his sister on her misfortunes, he remains apart and able to expound coherently on the untrustworthy nature of the world. In this poem, however, he portrays himself immersed in grief and blaming his own sins for the tragic occurrences, conscious of the fact that the hand that now writes consoling words for his wife is, in a sense, the hand that killed her children. Manrique addresses his wife directly at several points, speaking of what she suffers and what she has lost. The deceptive nature of the world, a theme that he usually presents in the second- and third-person form of address, is expressed largely in the first-person plural, so that he remains directly involved. While many of these changes can be attributed to his need to cut back on the material in order to finish the poem, the result is a deeply personal, intimate communication between Manrique and his wife.

Twentieth-century students of *cancionero* poetry have focused much of their interest on Jorge Manrique's "Coplas a la muerte de su padre," as well as the more learned works of Mena and Santillana. Nevertheless, Gómez Manrique has received recurring attention for his *Representación del nacimiento de Nuestro Señor* and for

*Title page for the first volume of the earliest standard edition of Manrique's works (Odum Library, Valdosta State University)*

attention to Manrique's work, it remains to be seen whether his contributions will be lauded or left in relative obscurity. Scholars do agree, however, that he was a skilled didactic poet, esteemed by his colleagues, and an important mentor and model for his nephew Jorge.

**References:**

Erasmo Buceta, "Dos papeletas referentes a las *Coplas* de Jorge Manrique," *Bulletin Hispanique,* 29 (1927): 407–412;

Daniela Capra, "La renovación del diálogo en las 'Preguntas y Respuestas' de Gómez Manrique," *Romance Quarterly,* 39 (1992): 185–198;

Manuel Carrión, "Gómez Manrique y el protonotario Lucena: Dos cartas con memoria de Jorge Manrique," *Revista de Archivos, Bibliotecas y Museos,* 81 (1978): 565–582;

Dorothy Clark, *Morphology of Fifteenth Century Castilian Verse,* Duquesne Studies, Philological Series, no. 4 (Pittsburgh: Duquesne University Press, 1964);

J. P. Wickersham Crawford, *Spanish Drama before Lope de Vega,* revised edition, with bibliographical supplement by Warren T. McCready (Philadelphia: University of Pennsylvania Press, 1967);

John G. Cummins, "Pero Guillén de Segovia y el Ms. 4.114," *Hispanic Review,* 41 (1973): 6–32;

Alan Deyermond, "Historia sagrada y técnica dramática en la *Representación del Nacimiento de Nuestro Señor,* de Gómez Manrique," in *Historias y ficciones: Coloquio sobre la literatura del siglo XV,* edited by Rafael Beltrán, José Luis Canet, and Josep Sirera (Valencia: Universitat de Valencia, Departament de Filologia Espanyola, 1992), pp. 291–305;

José J. Labrador, C. Angel Zorita, and Ralph A. DiFranco, "Cuarenta y dos, no cuarenta coplas en la famosa elegía manriqueña," *Boletín de la biblioteca Menéndez Pelayo,* 61 (1985): 37–95;

Hilary W. Landwehr, "Thematic Structure and the Use of Imagery in the Didactic Poetry of Gómez Manrique," dissertation, University of North Carolina at Chapel Hill, 1986;

Rafael Lapesa, "Poesía docta y afectividad en las 'consolatorias' de Gómez Manrique," in *Estudios sobre literatura y arte dedicados al profesor Emilio Orozco Díaz,* edited by Antonio Gallego Morell, Andrés Soria, and Nicolás Marín (Granada: Universidad de Granada, 1979), II: 231–239;

Fernando Lázaro Carreter, *Teatro medieval* (Valencia: Castalia, 1958);

María Teresa Leal de Martínez, "Gómez Manrique: Su tiempo y su obra," dissertation, Universidade do Recife, 1959;

his didactic poems. In the second half of the century, scholars have come to appreciate the careful construction and the skilled employment of traditional medieval themes and images in these works, qualities that were also admired by Manrique's contemporaries. Modern scholars have also discovered that, within the narrow confines of fifteenth-century lyric, Gómez Manrique's compositions speak in an unexpectedly personal voice. In both medieval and modern times, however, the bulk of Manrique's poetry is less known. Most of these poems are found only in the poet's compilations of his own work, indicating that they had less circulation and therefore were far less popular in their day than Manrique's didactic verse. With few exceptions twentieth-century scholars have neglected them. While in recent decades there has been increasing study and reevaluation of conventional fifteenth-century genres, with some

Francisco Lluch Mora, *La huella de cuatro poetas del cancionero en las Coplas de Jorge Manrique* (Puerto Rico: Rodadero, 1964);

Francisco López Estrada, "Nueva lectura de la *Representación del Nacimiento de Nuestro Señor*, de Gómez Manrique," in *Atti del IV Colloquio della Société Internationale pour l'Etude du Théâtre Médiéval: Viterbo, 10–15 luglio 1983*, edited by Maria Chiabò, Federico Doglio, and Marina Maymone (Viterbo, Italy: Centro Studi sul Teatro Medioevale e Rinascimentale, 1984), pp. 423–446;

Juan de Mena, *Coplas de los siete pecados mortales and First Continuation*, edited by Gladys M. Rivera, Studia Humanitatis, no. 1 (Madrid: José Porrúa Turanzas, 1982);

Juan de Dios Mendoza Negrillo, *Fortuna y Providencia en la literatura del siglo XV*, Anejos del Boletín de la Real Academia Española, no. 27 (Madrid: Real Academia Española, 1973);

Helen Nader, *The Mendoza Family in the Spanish Renaissance, 1350–1550* (New Brunswick, N.J.: Rutgers University Press, 1979);

Tomás Navarro Tomás, *Métrica española: Reseña histórica y descriptiva*, sixth edition (Barcelona: Labor, 1983);

Clemente Palencia Flores, *El poeta Gómez Manrique, Corregidor de Toledo: Discurso leído el día 28 de marzo de 1943, en la recepción pública de la Real Academia de Bellas Artes y Ciencias Históricas de Toledo* (Toledo: Católica Toledana, 1943);

Mario Pinna, "Didattismo e poeticità nelle 'Coplas para el Sr. Diego Arias' di Gómez Manrique," *Annali–Sezione Romanza, Istituto Universitario Orientale* (Naples), 24, no. 1 (1982): 135–142;

Hernando del Pulgar, *Claros varones de Castilla*, edited by Jesús Domínguez Bordona (Madrid: Espasa-Calpe, 1969 [1486]);

P. Conrado Rodríguez, "El teatro religioso de Gómez Manrique," *Religión y cultura*, 27 (1934): 327–342;

Luis de Salazar y Castro, *Historia genealógica de la Casa de Lara*, 6 volumes (Bilbao: Wilsen, 1988 [1696]);

Kenneth R. Scholberg, *Introducción a la poesía de Gómez Manrique* (Madison, Wis.: Seminary of Hispanic Medieval Studies, 1984);

Scholberg, *Sátira e invectiva en la España medieval* (Madrid: Gredos, 1971);

N. D. Shergold, *A History of the Spanish Stage* (Oxford: Clarendon Press, 1967);

Harry Sieber, "Dramatic Symmetry in Gómez Manrique's *La representación del nacimiento de Nuestro Señor*," *Hispanic Review*, 33 (1965): 118–135;

Sieber, "Gómez Manrique's Last Poem: *Consolatoria para doña Juana de Mendoza*," in *Letters and Society in Fifteenth-Century Spain: Studies Presented to P. E. Russell on His Eightieth Birthday*, edited by Deyermond and Jeremy Lawrance (Llangrannog, Wales: Dolphin, 1993), pp. 153–163;

Sieber, "Narrative and Elegiac Structure in Gómez Manrique's *Defunzión del noble cavallero Garci Laso de la Vega*," in *Studies in Honor of Bruce W. Wardropper*, edited by Dian Fox, Sieber, and Robert Ter Horst (Newark, Del.: Juan de la Cuesta, 1989), pp. 279–290;

Sieber, "Sobre la fecha de muerte de Gómez Manrique," *Boletín de la Biblioteca de Menéndez Pelayo*, 59 (1983): 5–10;

Stanislav Zimic, "El teatro religioso de Gómez Manrique (1412–1491)," *Boletín de la Real Academia Española*, 57 (1977): 353–400.

# Jorge Manrique

*(circa 1440 – 24 April 1479)*

Frank A. Domínguez

*University of North Carolina at Chapel Hill*

The identification numbers assigned to the poems by Brian Dutton in *El cancionero del siglo XV, c. 1360–1520* (1990–1991) are given parenthetically.

WORKS: Minor lyrics (ca. 1460–1479)

**Manuscripts:** "Entre bien y mal doblado" (1809 Dutton)–Madrid, Biblioteca Nacional 4114, copy of *Obras de Pero Guillén y otros* (eighteenth century), 419r; Salamanca, Biblioteca Universitaria de Salamanca 2763, two manuscripts in one volume (ca. 1495 and ca. 1510), 148r; "Es amor fuerça tan fuerte" (0276 Dutton)–El Escorial, Biblioteca de San Lorenzo de El Escorial K-III-7, *Obras de Fray Iñigo de Mendoza,* 214r–215r; Oxford, All Souls College Library 189, *Siglo XVI con unos poemas del siglo XV,* 72v; "Estos y mis enojos"–London, British Library Add. 10431, *Cancionero de Rennert* (1510), 77v; "My saber no es para solo" (2965 Dutton)–Madrid, Biblioteca Nacional 4114, copy of *Obras de Pero Guillén y otros,* 351r–v; Biblioteca Nacional 7817, *Obras de Gómez Manrique* (ca. 1475), 137r; Biblioteca Nacional 1250, *Obras de Gómez Manrique,* 420–421; "No se porque me fatigo" (0666 Dutton)–Oxford, All Souls College Library 189, *Siglo XVI con unos poemas del siglo XV,* 52v; "O muy alto dios de amor" (2983 Dutton)–Madrid, Biblioteca Nacional 4114, copy of *Obras de Pero Guillén y otros,* 399r–404r; "Pues el tiempo es ya passado" (0852 Dutton)–London, British Library Add. 10431, *Cancionero de Rennert,* 46r; "Quien no estuuiere en presençia"–Modena, Biblioteca Estense a.R.8.9, *Cancionero de Modena* (ca. 1475), 22v; Madrid, Biblioteca Nacional 3777, *Obras de Badajoz* (1843), p. 122; Madrid, Biblioteca del Palacio Real 617, *Cancionero de poesías varias* (ca. 1560), 166r–v; Oxford, All Souls College Library 189, *Siglo XVI con unos poemas del siglo XV,* 31v; "Quien tanto veros desea"–Barcelona, Universitat de Barcelona 151, *Jardinet d'orats* (ca. 1488), 126r; London, British Library Add. 10431, *Cancionero de Rennert,* 106r–v.

*Portrait of Jorge Manrique in the Biblioteca Publica Provincial de Toledo (from Francisco Caravaca, "Quién fue el autor del retrato de Jorge Manrique?" Papeles de Son Armadans, 65, no. 193 [1972]: 89–99; Thomas Cooper Library, University of South Carolina)*

**Early imprints:** "Acordaos por dios señora" (6162 Dutton)–*Cancionero general de Hernando del Castillo* (Valencia: Cristóbal Kofman, 1511), 101v; *Cancionero general de Hernando del Castillo* (Valencia: Jorge Costilla, 1514), 78v; "Alla veras mis sentidos" (6151 Dutton)–*Cancionero general de Hernando del Castillo* (1511), 99r; "Cada vez que mi memoria" (6833 Dutton)–*Cancionero general de Hernando* *del Castillo* (1514), 108v; "Calle por mucho temor" (6144 Dutton)–*Cancionero general de Hernando del Castillo* (1511), 97v–98r; *Cancionero general de Hernando del Castillo* (1514), 75v; "Con dolorido cuydado" (6650 Dutton)–*Cancionero general de Hernando del Castillo* (1511), 185r; *Cancionero general de Hernando del Castillo* (1514), 162r; "Con el gran mal que me sobra" (6140 Dutton)–*Cancionero general de Hernando del Castillo* (1511), 96v–97r; *Cancionero general de Hernando del Castillo* (1514), 74v; "En una llaga mortal" (6153 Dutton)–*Cancionero general de Hernando del Castillo* (1511), 99v–100r; *Cancionero general de Hernando del Castillo* (1514), 76v–77r; "Entre bien y mal doblado" (1809 Dutton)–*Cancionero general de Hernando del Castillo* (1511), 153r; *Cancionero general de Hernando del Castillo* (1514), 134v; "Entre dos fuegos lançado" (6490 Dutton)–*Cancionero general de Hernando del Castillo* (1511), 153r; *Cancionero general de Hernando del Castillo* (1514), 134v; "Es amor fuerça tan fuerte" (0276 Dutton)–*Cancionero general de Hernando del Castillo* (1511), 98r; *Cancionero general de Hernando del Castillo* (1514), 75v; Fray Iñigo de Mendoza, *Cancionero* (Zamora?, 1483?), 87v; Ramón de Llavia, *Cancionero* (Saragossa, 1484?–1488?), 78r–78v; "Es una muerte escondida" (6302 Dutton)–*Cancionero general de Hernando del Castillo* (1511), 130r; *Cancionero general de Hernando del Castillo* (1514), 108r; "Estando triste seguro" (6148 Dutton)–*Cancionero general de Hernando del Castillo* (1511), 98v–99r; *Cancionero general de Hernando del Castillo* (1514), 76r; "Estos y mis enojos" (0933 Dutton)–*Cancionero general de Hernando del Castillo* (1511), 141r; *Cancionero general de Hernando del Castillo* (1514), 555; "Fortuna no m'amenazes" (6159 Dutton)–*Cancionero general de Hernando del Castillo* (1511), 100v–101r; *Cancionero general de Hernando del Castillo* (1514), 77v–78r; "Guay daquel que nunca atiende" (6147 Dutton)–*Cancionero general de Hernando del Castillo* (1511), 98v; "Hallo que ningun poder" (6143 Dutton)–*Cancionero general de Hernando del Castillo* (1511), 97v; *Cancionero general de Hernando del Castillo* (1514), 75v; "Hame tan bien defendido" (6152 Dutton)–*Cancionero general de Hernando del Castillo* (1511), 99r–v; *Cancionero general de Hernando del Castillo* (1514), 76r–v; "Hanme dicho que se atreue" (6788 Dutton)–*Cancionero general de Hernando del Castillo* (1511), 233v–234r; *Coplas de Juan Agraz a Juan Marmolejo* (Burgos: Basilea, 1512–1515?), 4r–4v; *Cancionero general de Hernando del Castillo* (1514), 210r; "Los fuegos que en mi encendieron" (6157 Dutton)–*Cancionero general de Hernando del Castillo* (1511), 100r–100v; *Cancionero general de Hernando del Castillo* (1514), 77r–77v; "Mi temor ha sido tal" (6160 Dutton)–*Canci-*

*onero general de Hernando del Castillo* (1511), 101r; *Cancionero general de Hernando del Castillo* (1514), 78r; "Ni beuir quiere que biua" (6161 Dutton)–*Cancionero general de Hernando del Castillo* (1511), 101r–101v; *Cancionero general de Hernando del Castillo* (1514), 78r–78v; "Ni miento ni marrepiento" (6150 Dutton)–*Cancionero general de Hernando del Castillo* (1511), 99r; "No se porque me fatigo" (0666 Dutton)–*Cancionero general de Hernando del Castillo* (1511), 125r, 203r; *Cancionero general de Hernando del Castillo* (1514), 103v; *Cancioneiro general de García de Resende* (Lisbon, 1516), 109r; "No tardes muerte que muero" (6834 Dutton)–*Cancionero general de Hernando del Castillo* (1514), 108v; "Pensando señora en vos" (6145 Dutton)–*Cancionero general de Hernando del Castillo* (1511), 98r; *Cancionero general de Hernando del Castillo* (1514), 75v; "Por vuestro gran merescer" (6835 Dutton)–*Cancionero general de Hernando del Castillo* (1514), 108v; "Porque me hiere un dolor" (6496 Dutton)–*Cancionero general de Hernando del Castillo* (1511), 154r; *Cancionero general de Hernando del Castillo* (1514), 135v; "Pues el tiempo es ya passado" (0852 Dutton)–*Cancionero general de Hernando del Castillo* (1511), 98r–98v; *Cancionero general de Hernando del Castillo* (1514), 75v–76r; "Quanto el bien temprar concierta" (6155 Dutton)–*Cancionero general de Hernando del Castillo* (1511), 100r; *Cancionero general de Hernando del Castillo* (1514), 77r; "Quanto mas pienso seruiros" (6303 Dutton)–*Cancionero general de Hernando del Castillo* (1511), 130r; "Que amador tan desdichado" (6158 Dutton)–*Cancionero general de Hernando del Castillo* (1511), 100v; *Cancionero general de Hernando del Castillo* (1514), 77v; "Quien no estuuiere en presençia" (1968 Dutton)–*Cancionero general de Hernando del Castillo* (1511), 122r; *Cancionero general de Hernando del Castillo* (1514), 101r; Juan del Encina, *Egloga de Plácida y Victoriano* (Burgos, 1518–1520?), 19r; "Quien tanto veros desea" (1090 Dutton)–*Cancionero general de Hernando del Castillo* (1511), 125r; *Cancionero general de Hernando del Castillo* (1514), 103v; "Segun el mal me siguio" (6156 Dutton)–*Cancionero general de Hernando del Castillo* (1511), 100r; *Cancionero general de Hernando del Castillo* (1514), 77r; "Señora muy acabada" (6751 Dutton)–*Cancionero general de Hernando del Castillo* (1511), 221r–221v; *Cancionero general de Hernando del Castillo* (1514), 201v–202r; *Paternoster de las mugeres* (Toledo, 1515–1520?), 2r–3r; "Siempre amar y amor seguir" (4229 Dutton)–*Cancionero general de Hernando del Castillo* (1511), 143v; *Cancionero general de Hernando del Castillo* (1514), 123r; "Ve discreto mensagero" (6141 Dutton)–*Canci-*

*onero general de Hernando del Castillo* (1511), 97r–97v; *Cancionero general de Hernando del Castillo* (1514), 75r; "Ved que congoxa la mia" (6163 Dutton)–*Cancionero general de Hernando del Castillo* (1511), 101v–102r; *Cancionero general de Hernando del Castillo* (1514), 78v–79r; "Vos cometistes traycion" (6154 Dutton)–*Cancionero general de Hernando del Castillo* (1511), 100r; "Yo calle males sufriendo" (6142 Dutton)–*Cancionero general de Hernando del Castillo* (1511), 97v; *Cancionero general de Hernando del Castillo* (1514), 75v; and "Yo soy quien libre me vi" (4166 Dutton)–*Cancionero general de Hernando del Castillo* (1511), 143v; *Cancionero general de Hernando del Castillo* (1514), 123r.

*Coplas a la muerte de su padre* (1476–1479)

**Manuscripts:** "Recuerde el alma dormida" (0277 Dutton)–London, British Library Eg. 939-Plut. 541b, *Cancionero de Egerton* (ca. 1475), 17r–20v; El Escorial, Biblioteca de San Lorenzo de El Escorial K-III-7, *Obras de Fray Iñigo de Mendoza*, 215v–225r; Harvard University, Houghton Library MS Sp. 97, *Cancionero de Oñate-Castañeda* (ca. 1485), 421v–424v; Paris, Bibliothèque Nationale Esp. 37, Baena, "O" (ca. 1445–1450), 203r–205v; Madrid, Biblioteca del Palacio Real 617, *Cancionero de poesías varias* (ca. 1560–1570), 211r–215r; Madrid, Biblioteca Nacionale 4114, copy of *Obras de Pero Guillén y otros* (eighteenth century), 407r–418r.

**Early imprints:** "Recuerde el alma dormida" (0277 Dutton)–Fray Iñigo de Mendoza, *Vita Christi fecho en coplas* (Zamora, 1482), 1r–4v; *Coplas a la muerte de su padre* (Saragossa, 1482?), 1r–4v; Mendoza, *Cancionero* (Zamora: Antonio de Centenera, ca. 1483), x1r–x4v, 67r–70v; Ramón de Llavia, *Cancionero* (Saragossa, 1484–1488?), 73r–76r; *Coplas a la muerte de su padre* (Seville: Ungut & Polono, 1494?); Mendoza, *Vita Christi fecho en coplas* (Saragossa, 1495), 109r–112r; Alonso de Cervantes, *Glosa famosísima de las Coplas de Jorge Manrique* (Lisbon: Valentim Fernandes, 1501), 3r–20r; *Coplas, con la glosa de Alonso de Cervantes* (Toledo: Hagenbach, 1505–1510?), 3r–20r; *Coplas, con la glosa de Alonso de Cervantes* (Seville: Jacobo Cromberger, 1508–1510?), a3r–c4r, 39 stanzas; *Coplas, con la glosa de Alonso de Cervantes* (Seville: Jacobo Cromberger, 1511–1512?), 3r–20r; *Coplas a la muerte de su padre* (Seville: Jacobo Cromberger, 1515?), 1r–4v; *Cancionero general* (N.p., 1535).

**Facsimile editions:** *Cancionero General* (New York: De Vinne Press, 1904; microfilm reprint, New York: Kraus, 1967); *Cancionero General*, edited by Antonio Rodríguez Moñino (Madrid: Real Academia Española, 1958); *Glosas a las Coplas de Jorge Manrique*, edited by Antonio Pérez Gómez, 6 volumes (Cieza: La fonte que mana y corre, 1961–

1963).

**Modern editions:** *Coplas que fizo Jorge Manrique por la muerte de su padre*, edited by Raymond Foulché-Delbosc (Barcelona, 1902); "Obras de Jorge Manrique," in *Cancionero Castellano del siglo XV*, edited by Foulché-Delbosc, volume 2 (Madrid: Bailly-Bailliére, 1915); *Cancionero*, edited by Augusto Cortina (Madrid: Ediciones de *La Lectura*, 1929); *Poesía*, edited by Jesús Manuel Alda Tesán (Salamanca: Anaya, 1965); *Poesía*, edited by Margarita Smerdou Altolaguirre (Madrid: Magisterio Español, 1975); *Obra completa*, edited by Miguel de Santiago (Barcelona: Ediciones 29, 1978); *Jorge Manrique*, edited by Luis Suñén (Madrid: EDAF, 1980); *Poesía*, edited by Giovanni Caravaggi (Madrid: Taurus, 1984); *Obras*, edited by Antonio Serrano de Haro (Madrid: Alhambra, 1986); *Coplas a la muerte de su padre*, edited by Carmen Díaz Castañón, third edition (Madrid: Castalia, 1988); Brian Dutton, *El cancionero del siglo XV, c. 1360–1520*, 7 volumes (Salamanca: Universidad de Salamanca, 1990–1991); *Coplas que hizo Jorge Manrique a la muerte de su padre*, edited by Vicente Beltrán (Barcelona: PPU, 1991); *Poesía*, edited by Beltrán (Barcelona: Crítica, 1993).

**Editions in English:** *Coplas de Don Jorge Manrique*, translated by Henry Wadsworth Longfellow (Boston: Allen & Ticknor, 1833); *Hispanic Anthology: Poems Translated from the Spanish by English and North American Poets*, edited by Thomas Walsh (New York: Putnam, 1920), pp. 82–105.

Jorge Manrique, Lord of Belmontejo and commander of Montizón for the Order of Santiago, is one of the three great fifteenth-century Castilian poets, along with Juan de Mena and Iñigo López de Mendoza, Marqués de Santillana. Although Manrique's poetic production was not as extensive as that of the other two, it was larger than that of most poets included in the *cancioneros* (lyric anthologies or songbooks) of the period. It consists of some forty-eight short poems and the *Coplas a la muerte de su padre* (Stanzas on the Death of His Father, 1476–1479). Yet, in terms of popularity, the *Coplas a la muerte de su padre* is by far the most enduring text of fifteenth-century Castilian letters. Not only has it been glossed and commented on from its first appearance, it has remained in print ever since and has been translated into many languages. Only one or two of the *serranillas* (songs of mountain girls) of Santillana are as popular as the *Coplas a la muerte de su padre*, although they were largely unknown until the nineteenth century.

Little is known about Manrique's early life. Facts about his father, Rodrigo Manrique, on the other hand, are plentiful. He was a prominent military leader who captured the attention of contemporary chroniclers and was included in their histories. Since *Coplas a la muerte de su padre* is about Don Rodrigo, these sources help the reader understand their setting.

Rodrigo was a son of Pero Manrique, Lord of Amusco and *adelantado* (military governor) of Castile during the reign of King Juan II. The commandery of Segura de la Sierra, which Don Rodrigo held for the Order of Santiago in the heavily fortified province of Jaén from about 1428, and Toledo, where he held the *alcaidía* (governorship) of the city castle later in life, were his principal places of residence. He was elected *treze* (one of the thirteen senior members that ruled the order) in 1440 and eventually became *maestre* (grand master) of the Order for Castile in 1474, a title he had held once before, when he contested the election of Alvaro de Luna, but which he then gave up in exchange for the title of count of Paredes.

Like all Castilian noblemen, Rodrigo Manrique led an itinerant life. Events took him north in 1440, the year traditionally given for Jorge Manrique's birth. Early in September, Pero Manrique and his sons, Diego, Rodrigo, and Gómez, were among the nobles gathered in Valladolid to celebrate the marriage of Enrique of Castile to Blanche of Navarre. Pero Manrique died in the midst of the festivities, on 21 September, leaving Don Rodrigo the town of Paredes de Nava as his inheritance, a legacy that the king confirmed the next day.

Both the marriage of Enrique and the death of Pero Manrique took place in Valladolid, so Don Rodrigo is likely to have visited nearby Paredes de Nava at this time. If, as is claimed, Jorge's birth occurred in 1440, then either Paredes de Nava or Segura de la Sierra are among the most likely places for his birth to have occurred, assuming the presence of his mother, Doña Mencía de Figueroa, a niece of the marqués de Santillana, in either place that year. Although this information is speculative, someone in an advanced state of pregnancy or who had recently given birth was unlikely to have been in attendance at the wedding.

The association with the Order of Santiago is key to understanding the political trajectory of the Manriques in general and of Jorge in particular. The Order of Santiago was originally dedicated to protecting the pilgrimage route to Santiago from Muslim attacks. This duty became less necessary in the mid thirteenth century, when the frontier moved south.

When the Reconquest reached its final phase, Christian forces ranged themselves along the northern border of Granada in heavily fortified enclaves that were originally wrested from the Muslims during the great push south by Fernando III, who reigned from 1217 to 1252. The Manrique family, in particular, occupied and defended commanderies in part of the old kingdom of Jaén that had fallen into Christian hands in 1246.

The Manriques were not motivated by simple altruism. Territory and booty were principal sources of wealth and income in medieval Castile. Like the other military orders, the Order of Santiago had received from the king vast properties in the south, which it had to secure and defend against the Muslims on behalf of the Crown. These properties were called *encomiendas* (commanderies) and the knights who held them, *comendadores* (knight commanders). Most *encomiendas* consisted of fortified castles and their dependent villages, generally located far away from cities, and vested for life on a *comendador*.

Knight commanders were answerable, in theory, only to the pope but owed immediate allegiance to his surrogate, the *maestre,* and his advisory council, the *treze.* (In practice, the principal function of this advisory council was to elect a new *maestre.*) Although not under the direct control of the king, the *encomiendas* were part of a decentralized system of defense and offense. Medieval Castile did not have a standing army but assembled a fighting force from men contributed by the king, the greater nobility, and the orders. Commanders served with a predetermined number of knights, based on the importance and value of each commandery, and were released back to their commanderies at the end of a campaign. Control of the *encomiendas* reverted to the Order for reassignment upon the death of a *comendador*.

The commanderies also had an important economic function. The bulk of the Castilian aristocracy engaged in war as a profession. It was a costly endeavor that required considerable resources. The rents of commanderies made it possible for favored second sons to engage in that profession. The Manriques were no exception.

Rodrigo Manrique was not the firstborn son of Pero Manrique. Pero's lordship of Amusco became part of the *mayorazgo* (entailed estate) of Treviño and passed to his eldest son, Diego Gómez Manrique, first Count of Treviño, who became the head of the senior branch of the line. Diego inherited the bulk of the estate. The other children of Pero Manrique, such as Rodrigo, had to fend for themselves with lesser inheritances. Pero, however, was exceptional in that he placed all of his sons in important occupations and was rich enough to establish secondary *mayorazgos* for those who were not following ecclesiastical careers. These *mayorazgos* served to establish important collateral branches of the clan.

Rodrigo Manrique's *mayorazgo* centered on the town of Paredes de Nava. Paredes de Nava, together with the income of the commandery of Segura de la Sierra and sundry civil appointments, gave him a rela-

Dezir de don jorge manrriq
por la muerte de su padre

Recuerde el alma dormida
abiue el seso y despierte
contemplando
como se passa la vida
como se viene la muerte
tan callando
quan presto se va el plazer
como despues de acordado
da dolor
como a nuestro paresçer
qual quiere tiempo passado
fue mejor

Pues si vemos lo presente
como en vn punto ses ydo
y acabado
si juzgamos sabiamente
daremos lo no venido
por passado
no se engañe nadino
pensando que a de durar
lo que espera
mas que duro lo que vio
pues que todo a de passar
por tal manera

Muestras vidas son los rios
que van adar enla mar
que es el morir
alli van los señorios
derechos ase acabar
y consumir

alli los rios caudales
alli los otros medianos
y mas chicos
alleguados son yguales
los que viué por sus manos
y los ricos

inuocaçion

Dexo las inuocaçiones
delos famosos poetas
y oradores
no curo de sus afficciones
que traen yeruas secretas
sus sabores
aaquel solo men comiendo
aquel solo inuoco yo
de verdat
que eneste mundo viuiendo
el mundo no conocio
su deydat

Este mundo es el camino
para el otro ques morada
sin pesar
pues cumple tener buen tino
para andar este camino
sin errar
partimos quando naçemos
andamos mientra viuimos
y llegamos
al tiempo que feneçemos
asi que quando morimos
descansamos

*Page from the 1482 edition of Manrique's* Coplas a la
muerte de su padre, *written 1476–1479
(Collection of Frank A. Domínguez)*

tively secure economic base from which to further his ambitions. Although he lost Paredes de Nava for a time during one of his frequent rebellions against the Crown, eventually it was restored to him, together with the title of the first count of Paredes. He never lost the commandery of Segura de la Sierra.

Rodrigo Manrique's advancement was not unusual. Many *mayorazgos* and *encomiendas* served as a springboard to new titles in mid-fifteenth-century Castile. Among Pero Manriques's sons, the first counts of Osorno and Castañeda, for example, also headed commanderies before they became counts. They all, in turn, placed some of their own sons in commanderies in Castile and León.

Rodrigo Manrique's sons and grandsons held the commanderies of Segura (Pedro, after the death of Don Rodrigo), Montizón and Chiclana (Jorge and his son, Luis), Yeste and Taivilla (the younger Rodrigo), Carri-

zosa (Enrique), and Manzanares and Villarubia (the younger Rodrigo), with the remaining serving in additional military, civil, and religious posts. Two of them served as *treze* as well.

In spite of the *mayorazgo* of Paredes and the rents of Segura, life must have been difficult for Rodrigo Manrique, because he had to rely on his own money and that of his sons to fund expensive military campaigns. Stanzas 29 and 30 of Jorge Manrique's *Coplas a la muerte de su padre* recall the trajectory of Don Rodrigo's life in general terms. They tell how he began his career in relative poverty and had to labor for every possession; how his possessions increased through battle with the Muslims but were always placed in the service of the Crown, his clan, and his religion; and how he was imbued with an intense commitment to the defense of Castile. Although Rodrigo Manrique was famous for his exploits as a warrior, and his contemporaries always mention his fortitude and his many campaigns against the Moors, the depiction of him in the *Coplas a la muerte de su padre* is one-sided, because members of the military Orders fought against Christians as often as against the Muslims. Don Rodrigo was no exception.

Conflict between the orders and the Crown was a constant fact of life. The king always sought control over the appointment of *maestres* and *comendadores* to the orders. Self-made men such as Rodrigo Manrique and his brother Gómez resisted what they saw as the constant meddling of the Crown in the affairs of the Order of Santiago, particularly when the king sought to appoint someone who had no previous ties to an Order. Such behavior was contrary to the interests of the nobles, who viewed commanderies as quasi-hereditary estates.

Often, a living commander would resign his *encomienda* in favor of a son or relative, to ensure that it remained in their clan's hands. When that was not possible because of a commander's sudden death in battle, the nobles exerted their influence to make certain that a son or a relative of the deceased knight was appointed to the *encomienda*. Although they frequently had to bow to the wishes of the king and bestow the commandery on someone else, sometimes events conspired to allow them to impose their desires. Montizón, Jorge's own commandery, is a good example.

Montizón, located in the province of Jaén about seven kilometers from Torre de Juan Abad and dominating the Guadalén River, was among the commanderies to which the Manriques felt they had a claim. It had belonged to Garcilaso de la Vega, the brother of Jorge's mother. Garcilaso had died from a poisoned-arrow wound in 1452 during an ill-fated expedition, led by King Enrique IV, to Granada. Garcilaso's relatives, including Rodrigo Manrique and the sons of the marqués de Santillana, implored the king to give Montizón to Garcilaso's son. Instead, Enrique gave the post to Nicolás Lucas, the brother of his favorite, Miguel Lucas de Iranzo, constable of Castile.

The event was significant enough to be remembered in many chronicles, among them the *Memorial de diversas hazañas* (Account of Various Deeds, circa 1482–1488) of Diego de Valera, who quotes the king as saying coldly, "Vamos a ver la fuerza que tiene la ponçoña" (Let's go see the strength of the poison). He adds that the king witnessed the death throes of the poor knight without expressing any sympathy. According to another historian, Alonso de Palencia, the king was resentful of Garcilaso's previous successes against the Muslims.

The death of Garcilaso inspired Jorge's uncle Gómez to write one of the antecedents of Jorge's *Coplas a la muerte de su padre,* "Defunción de noble caballero Garcilaso de la Vega" (Death of the Noble Knight Garcilaso de la Vega, 1455), a poem that commemorates the death of Garcilaso and its effect on the family. Montizón, however, did not remain in the possession of Nicolás Lucas for long.

Today, the castle of Montizón is one of many that command the heights of a small town. In the late 1460s, however, it was of crucial importance to Don Rodrigo and the Manrique clan. The castle was a link in the chain of fortresses that protected the Sierra de Segura and its pastures from the Muslims. Montizón also served as a buffer for the castle of Segura de la Sierra, which controlled one of the viable routes from Castile to Andalusia. In addition, it was near lands of the Order of Calatrava and the marquessate of Villena, both often at odds with Rodrigo Manrique. In order to secure his own castle, Don Rodrigo had to have Montizón and its dependencies—the commandery of Chiclana de Segura and the villages of Torre de Juan Abad and Belmontejo (which changed its name to Villamanrique in 1480)—in the hands of a Manrique family member or loyal ally.

The appointment of Nicolás Lucas as commander of Montizón must have displeased Don Rodrigo, who was one of the principal opponents of Enrique IV. The Manriques were among the nobles who were instrumental in forcing Enrique to reaffirm his half brother Alfonso's position as crown prince, rather than the king's own daughter, Juana la Beltraneja, and to surrender the direction of the Order of Santiago to the prince in 1464. Don Rodrigo also participated in a mock deposition of the king in Avila that preceded the crowning of Prince Alfonso, then eleven years old, as king of Castile in 1465. From that moment on, despite periods of apparent concord, Rodrigo openly favored Alfonso and, when the latter died suddenly in 1468, Princess Isabel (Isabella).

The death of Alfonso is remembered in one of the stanzas of *Coplas a la muerte de su padre:*

> Pues su hermano el ynocente
> que en su vida subcesor
> se llamó,
> qué corte tan excelente
> tuuo, y quánto grand señor
> que le syguió!;
> mas, como fuese mortal,
> metióle la muerte luego
> en su fragua.
> ¡O juyzio diuinal,
> quando más ardía el fuego,
> echaste agua!

> (His brother, too, whose factious zeal
> Usurped the sceptre of Castile,
> Unskilled to reign;
> What a gay, brilliant court had he,
> When all the flower of chivalry
> Was in his train!
> But he was mortal; and the breath,
> That flamed from the hot forge of Death,
> Blasted his years;
> Judgment of God! that flame by thee,
> When raging fierce and fearfully,
> Was quenched in tears!)

The original makes no reference to Alfonso's lack of skill or to his "factious zeal," though lack of skill is implied by his innocence. One of the most serious flaws of Henry Wadsworth Longfellow's 1833 translation, however, is that it makes Alfonso an active player in politics, whereas in *Coplas a la muerte de su padre* the claim is made that he called himself the successor of Enrique IV or, in one of the variant manuscript readings, that he was made a successor of the king by others and was thus a pawn. (All subsequent translations of quotations from the poem are from Longfellow's version; the source for the original text is Vicente Berám's 1991 edition. All translations of Manrique's minor lyrics are by Frank A. Domínguez.)

On 14 November 1467 one of the earliest surviving court performances in Castilian (written by Gómez Manrique) celebrated the coming of age of Alfonso. It was an important moment. Alfonso was about to leave his childhood behind and enter what the play calls "viril edad" (manhood), an age that would make him a real threat to Enrique IV. This entrance into manhood is what the play celebrates. The "play" is actually a *momo* (mummers' play) in which ladies of the court, representing the nine Fates transformed into birds by feathered costumes, prognosticate Alonso's future. Princess Isabel represented the last Fate, with a stanza that augured a bright future for Alfonso. Shortly thereafter, the prince died under suspicious circumstances while traveling to Avila with Princess Isabel. They had stopped to rest in Cardeñosa in early July. There, Alfonso ate a breaded trout and immediately, and uncharacteristically, went to bed. He did not wake up, in spite of the efforts of courtiers and physicians, and died the next day. Although he might have contracted the pulmonary form of the plague, his supporters claimed that he had been poisoned.

Earlier, in 1465, Alfonso had appointed Rodrigo Manrique constable of Castile and confirmed an annuity from state revenues to Jorge, in repayment for military service. More significantly, Alfonso had also granted the commandery of Montizón to Jorge, with the order to wrest it by force from Nicolás Lucas and the partisans of King Enrique IV.

From 1465 to 1467 Jorge Manrique and his brother Pedro attempted to regain the castle of Montizón. Pedro began the hostilities with a flanking campaign against the town of Alcaraz, during which their brother Diego was killed, but Montizón eventually capitulated. Not only did the castle's strategic location deep in Manrique territory make assistance difficult, but the troops sent by Lucas de Iranzo to relieve Montizón were routed by Día Sánchez de Benavides, an uncle of Jorge by marriage.

The documents by which Jorge Manrique swore allegiance for Montizón to Juan Pacheco, Marqués de Villena and *maestre* of Santiago, and the instrument by which he empowered one of his vassals to do so in his place, are extant: both bear Manrique's signature. Another document includes a description of the commandery made during a *visita* (periodic inspection) performed by Francisco de León, commander of the Bastimentos de León, when Alonso de Cárdenas was *maestre* of the Order of Santiago. De León partly based his comments on an older document written shortly after the fortress surrendered to Jorge Manrique. The site assessment reveals that Montizón was in good condition, except where its interior foundation had suffered in the siege. De León ordered repairs to Montizón and to Chiclana (Jorge's most frequent place of residence), which apparently was in a worse state. According to the *visitador* (inspector), Montizón was a mid-range commandery that served with five *lanzas* (each *lanza* consisted of a group of armed men), had extensive pastures and cultivated fields, and generated 220,000 *maravedíes* per year, a sum that made it one of the better commanderies of the Order of Santiago and that de León claimed was bound to grow.

The death of Prince Alfonso in 1468 caused Rodrigo Manrique to shift his allegiance to Princess Isabel. The immediate question was selecting a husband for the princess. Enrique IV wanted Isabel, his half sister, to marry Alfonso V of Portugal and even envisioned a possible marriage between the princess and the duc de Berry. Either marriage would have made her an unsuitable successor to the Castilian Crown. The rebel nobles, on the other hand, favored an alliance with Aragon.

Princess Isabel, who understood the political ramifications of a marriage alliance, agreed to marry Fernando (Ferdinand) of Aragon. Pedro and Gómez Manrique were among the people sent to receive Fernando, who traveled in disguise to Castile to deceive the forces sent by the king to prevent his coming. The marriage took place in 1469.

The nobles who favored the alliance with Aragon also consolidated their own positions through marriage. The Manriques were no exception. Rodrigo's own marriage to Elvira de Castañeda in 1469 and that of Jorge in 1470 to Guiomar de Meneses, both daughters of Pero López de Ayala, cemented the Manriques' ties with the powerful Ayala family of Toledo and indirectly favored Isabel, for the Ayalas had wavered in their support for the princess. At about this time most of Jorge's lyric poetry might have been composed.

Jorge Manrique must have begun to write about 1455 to 1460, while still in his teens. The bulk of his lyric poetry, however, was probably written between the siege of Montizón (1465–1467) and his death in 1479. It was composed in moments of relaxation with his friends in Toledo, where his father and uncle Gómez frequently resided, or at Montizón or Chiclana, where Jorge himself was supposed to reside for four months every year.

Jorge Manrique's poetry consists of accomplished pieces in the courtly-love tradition, two satires, and the *Coplas a la muerte de su padre*. If the legend surrounding the *coplas póstumas* (posthumous stanzas), said to have been found on the poet's body, is true, he may not have given the *Coplas a la muerte de su padre* its final shape when he died. Most critics, however, do not include the *coplas póstumas* in their editions of the *Coplas a la muerte de su padre*.

Manrique's poetry can be divided into three categories: long poems that treat the casuistry of love allegorically or satirize someone, such as "De don Jorge Manrique, quexándose del Dios de amor, y cómo razonan el uno con el otro" (From Don Jorge Manrique Complaining of the God of Love, and How They Debate Each Other), "A la fortuna" (To Fortune), "Otras suyas diziendo qué cosa es amor" (Other of His Stanzas Defining Love), "De la profession que hizo en la orden del amor" (Of the Vows He Took in the Order of Love), "Castillo de amor" (Castle of Love), and "Escala de amor" (Ladder of Love); shorter compositions about love, called *canciones* (songs), *esparsas* (short poems, generally of a single stanza), *preguntas y respuestas* (questions and answers), and *glosas de mote* (glosses of mottoes) that employ figures of ambiguity and repetition in their wordplay; and the *Coplas a la muerte de su padre.*

The first edition of the *Cancionero general de Hernando del Castillo* (1511) has the most complete collection of Manrique's poems, but some of the lyrics appear in other early editions and manuscripts. Brian Dutton, along with Jacqueline Steunou and Lothar Knapp, have published separate repertories that indicate where these works can be found. Dutton's appears both as an independent work (*Catálogo-índice de la poesía cancioneril del siglo XV,* 1982) and, in a version expanded with texts, in *El cancionero del siglo XV, c. 1360–1520* (1990–1991).

Many of Manrique's longer lyrics include metaphors derived from his chosen profession. "De la profession que hizo en la orden del Amor," "Castillo de amor," and "Escala de amor" draw on his experiences in the Order of Santiago and his knowledge of sieges. "De la profession que hizo en la orden del Amor" treats love as a military Order in which the knight-protagonist has taken his vows. He has spent a year as a novice, and now the order, after investing him with its habit, demands that he profess and take a vow of continence and poverty:

> Prometo de mantener
> continame*n*te pobreza
> d'alegría y de plazer;
> pero no de bie*n* querer
> ni de males ni tristeza,
> que la regla no la manda
> ni la razón no lo quiere,
> . . . q*ue* quien en tal Orden anda,
> s'alegre mientras biuiere.

(I promise to maintain poverty of happiness and pleasure continually but not of love, or sorrows, or unhappiness, for the Rule does not require it nor reason desire it . . . for a member of such an order should spend his life content).

The "rule" of this Order of Love is similar to the rule of the Order of Santiago. Knights of Santiago had to keep a copy of the Order's rule at their side at all times, learn it, and take a vow of continence that limited the times that they could have sexual relations with their wives. They also had to take vows of poverty and promise complete obedience to the Order and its *maestre.* There is a connection between a knight's submission to the will of the Order (and, by extension, to that of his father) and the subjugation of the lover to the will of the woman he loves in the poems.

In "Castillo de amor" the lover's resolve is portrayed as an impregnable castle in the service of his beloved, who also happens to be his lord:

> Hame tan bie*n* defendido,
> señora, vuestra memoria
> de muda*n*ça
> que jamás nunca ha podido
> alca*n*çar de mi victoria
> oluida*n*ça:
> porqu' estáys apoderada
> vos de toda mi firmeza
> en tal són,
> que no puede ser tomada
> a fuerça mi fortaleza
> ni a trayción.

(Your memory has prevented me from a change [of masters] so well, lady, that it has never been able to forget your victory over me: because you are the holder of all my strength so thoroughly that my fortress cannot be taken by force or treason).

The fortress has not always belonged to the lady, but memory personified led the assault that brought it into her control and ensures the lover's constancy in her service by preventing his takeover by another. The subsequent stanzas describe the emplacement and the parts of the fortress in a manner strikingly similar to Montizón's:

> La fortaleza nombrada
> está'n los altos alcores
> d'una cuesta,
> sobre vna peña tajada,
> maçiça toda de amores,
> muy bie*n* puesta,
> y tiene dos baluartes
> hazia el cabo c'a sentido
> el oluidar,
> y cerca a las otras partes,
> vn río mucho crescido,
> qu'es membrar.
> El muro tiene d'amor,
> las almenas, de lealtad. . . .

(The fortress mentioned is on the heights of a hill, on a divided rock. It is made solid with love, [and] very well arranged. It has two defenses toward one end that have felt the effects of forgetfulness, and a swollen river near the other parts that is called Remembrance. The castle walls are Love, the battlements Loyalty. . . .).

Each part of the castle is a metaphor for an aspect of the lover, who serves his lady completely and without hope.

"Escala de amor" is another poem that uses the metaphor of the castle, although it should precede the former poem because it describes a previous stage in the process of falling in love, the taking of the castle by siege:

> Estando triste, seguro
> mi voluntad reposaua,
> quando escalaron el muro
> do mi libertad estaua.
> A'scala vista subieron
> vuestra beldad y mesura,
> y tan de rezio hirieron,
> que vencieron mi cordura.

> (I was—woe is me—secure [and] my will at rest, when your beauty and comeliness scaled the wall that protected my liberty in open assault, and they struck so forcefully that they overcame my reason).

There is a description of Rodrigo Manrique's siege of Huéscar in a letter to the king (quoted in Lope Barrientos's mid-century *Refundición de la crónica del Halconero* [Remake of the Chronicle of the Master of Hawks], a work originally written by Pedro Carrillo de Huete) that describes the dangers of an assault by ladder.

"Escala de amor" is one of many poems of the period that use the siege of a castle as a metaphor for the effects of the sight of the beloved. It relies on medieval faculty psychology for part of the allegory. The poet is the castle under siege. The lady commands her troops to scale the walls. The qualities of both lover and beloved are personified in the attack. The senses are vanquished by beauty and comeliness; liberty is imprisoned; and eyes are the traitors that permit the entry of the enemy and allow steadfastness, heart, and senses to be taken. Poems such as "Escala de amor" allude to matters that Jorge Manrique knew quite well: the inadequacy of the will to effect change, the perils and suffering of campaigns, the long and costly sieges of castles, the effect of war on the fabric of buildings, and adherence to the rules of an idealized military Order.

The often arbitrary command of those in power is reflected in poems that make of the grievance a *pleito* (lawsuit). Such is the case with the overbearing or blind taskmasters in "De don Jorge Manrique quexándose del Dios de Amor" and "A la Fortuna." In "De don Jorge Manrique quexándose del Dios de Amor" Love has some of the attributes of Christ: he is the head of a *ley* (rule or religion) and, as such, is in charge of observing the strict adherence of his followers. He is called a "justo juzgador" (a just judge, a figure analogous to the spiritual head of the Order of Santiago, the prior of Santiago) who seeks out knights who do not observe the *ley,* and he brings complaints before a court of law. Of course, Love is not a "justo juzgador." According to the lover, he has not acted fairly toward a trusted vassal: he has committed a procedural error in

sentencing the lover in the latter's absence. Therefore, the lover sues Love, who then reminds him that there is another God above him who can hear his appeal. The poet, however, responds that God, too, is displeased with the lover because of his erstwhile allegiance to Love. The only remedy lies in the invalidation of the sentence Love gave:

> Más pues no fué justamente
> esa tu sentencia dada
> contra mí, por ser absente,
> agora qu'estó presente,
> revócala, pues fué errada,
> y dame plazo y traslado
> que diga de mi derecho;
> y si no fuese culpado,
> tú serás el condenado,
> yo quedaré satisfecho.

> (But that sentence was not justly pronounced against me, because I was absent. Now that I am present, revoke it, for it was ill done, and give me time to appeal to another court where I can say my piece. If I am not held to be guilty [by them], you will be condemned and I will be satisfied).

The poem continues in this vein. The poet complains about Love's disloyalty, and Love argues that it is improper for a vassal to contravene the wishes of his lord. At the conclusion of the work, Love gives in to the complaint of the lover and restores his love to him.

The *canciones, esparsas, preguntas y respuestas,* and *glosas de mote* are shorter lyrics that make intense use of figures of repetition and ambiguity to convey the emotional and psychological state of the lover. One does not find a genuine and personal expression of love in these lyrics. Rather, they are compositions in which the poet demonstrates his technical competence in using the code of courtly love.

The song "Quien no'stuviere en presencia" (Whosoever Is Not Present) deals with the same topic as the eleven-stanza "De don Jorge Manrique, quexándose del Dios de amor." Whereas the latter is a long work that uses the metaphor of a trial to say that Love wronged the poet when he judged him in absentia, "Quien no'stuviere en presencia" is a *canción,* one of the favored short lyric forms of the period that were devoted to love. Because of its brevity (twelve verses), the *canción* has to reduce the statement of the condition to its essentials. The theme, that presence is a requirement of love and absence its death, is stated in the first stanza and then expanded in the second longer stanza:

> Quien no'stuviere en presencia
> no tenga en fe confiança,
> pues son oluido y mudança

las condiciones d'ausencia.
Quie*n* quisiere ser amado
trabaje por ser presente,
que cuan presto fuere ausente,
tan presto será olvidado;
y pierda toda esperança
quie*n* no estuviere en presencia,
pues son oluido y mudança
las condiciones d'ausencia.

(Whosoever is not present should not place faith in steadfastness, for forgetfulness and change are the consequences of absence. Whosoever wishes to be loved should strive to be constantly present, for he will be forgotten as soon as he is absent: whosoever is not present should lose all his hope, forgetfulness and change are the consequences of absence).

The lyric is deceptively simple. Its brevity forces the poet to condense his thought in a few verses that associate presence with faith and remembrance, and absence with forgetfulness and change.

All of Jorge Manrique's lyrics were written in response to a particular event about which nothing is known, or in answer to, or imitation of, a poem by someone else. None of the love lyrics reflects much personal experience. The attitude toward women mirrored in these compositions derives from a poetic tradition that was centuries in the making. It conceives of a woman as being socially superior to the lover; in other words, the opposite of reality in most cases.

The power of woman is partly based on the attributes of supreme beauty. Like God's beauty, a woman's compels the will of the lover. It acts like a disease, infecting him through the eyes and taking root in the heart. Because the heart was considered to be the seat of all higher functions, including reason and will, infection was tantamount to losing control of oneself. The lover is pale, somber, listless, and powerless to act before the lady; these are the standard symptoms of lovesickness, a condition that can lead to death.

Unlike God, however, Manrique's courtly lady is unreachable. Sometimes she is unconscious of the pain she causes, but more often than not, she ignores the lover or cruelly relishes his pain. The lover is brought to the brink of death by this lack of feeling. He is a martyr of love, although his martyrdom is without sense. Martyrs die for a higher goal, lovers die for naught.

There is, however, an even more sinister side to this conception of the lady. It endows men with the qualities of fidelity and devotion that women cannot have. Women may have absolute beauty and power over men, but they are fickle by nature. Females were portrayed as deficient in reason by classical and medieval medical literature. Upper-class women were mostly housebound throughout their early lives by a concept of honor that was based on virginity and purity that could only be safeguarded by an unsullied reputation. Contact with men was limited and strictly supervised. The head of a clan also determined when and whom women were to marry. The one exception was women who formed part of the household of the queen. They had privileges and freedoms that not many other women enjoyed. As for the men, who had few opportunities to interact with most women, they fell back on traditional concepts, considering women capable of destructive behavior by their very nature. It is no wonder that they wrote of unnamed and heartless ladies, who would not—indeed, could not—reciprocate their love.

Women and men were often pawns used to secure alliances between noble houses. In 1469 Rodrigo Manrique married Elvira and arranged to have his son Jorge marry her sister, Guiomar, the next year. Elvira thus became both sister-in-law and stepmother to Jorge. Some of Jorge Manrique's poems are related to these marriages.

Although women were seldom explicitly named in the poetry of Manrique's time, their identity was occasionally revealed in acrostics or hidden in the verses of poems. Two of Manrique's compositions take advantage of this device. The first poem reveals the nature of the concealment in the rubric that accompanies it: "Otras suyas en que pone el nombre de su dama; y comiença y acaba en las letras primeras de todas las coplas y dize" (Other Stanzas by Him in Which He Mentions the Name of His Lady; and It Begins and Ends in the First Letters of all the Stanzas, and It Says). Read acrostically, the initial letter of each line in the octosyllabic octaves starts with a letter of her name; that is, all eight lines in the first stanza start with *G,* and so on. Together, they spell out GVYOMAR:

¡Guay d'aquel que nunca atiende . . . ! (I am sorry for him who never waits)
Verdadero amor y pena . . . (True love and sorrow)
Y estos males qu'e contado . . . (And these pains that I have told)
¡O, si aq*ue*stas mis passiones, . . . ! (Oh! If these my passions)
Mostrara vna triste vida . . . (I showed a sad life)
Agora q*ue* soy ya suelto, . . . (Now that I am freed)
Rauia terrible m'aquexa, . . . (A terrible rage afflicts me)

The other poem, "Otra obra suya en que puso el nombre de su esposa, y asimismo nombrados los linajes de los cuatro costados de ella, que son: Castañeda, Ayala, Silva, Meneses" (Another Work by Him in Which He Put His Wife's Name and the Names of Her Lineage on Four Sides, Which Are:

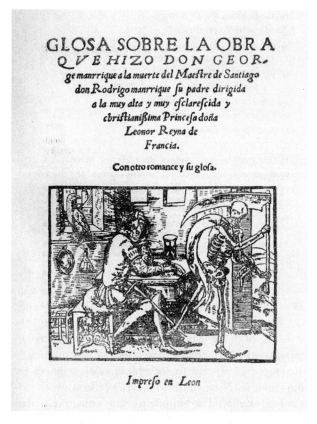

*First page of Alonso de Cervantes's gloss (1501) and title page for Jorge de Montemayor's gloss (1554) on Manrique's* Coplas
a la muerte de su padre *(from Nellie E. Sánchez Arce,* Las glosas a las Coplas de Jorge Manrique,
*1956; Thomas Cooper Library, University of South Carolina)*

Castañeda, Ayala, Silva, Meneses), similarly hides the name and lineage of his wife within the octaves, though it reveals the device in the *cabo* (ending). The first stanza reads:

> Según el mal me siGUIO
> MARauíllome de mí
> cómo assí me despedí
> q*ue* jamás no me mudó.
> Cáusame aq*ue*sta firmeza
> q*ue*, siendo de vos ausente,
> ante mí estaua presente
> contino vuestra belleza.

(Though evil sorely oppressed me, I marvel at my constancy. I tired from this constancy for, though I was absent from you, your beauty was constantly present in my mind).

Both poems stress the beauty of Guiomar, who is presented as a *belle dame sans merci* (beautiful lady without mercy), but their real import lies in the clever way in which the name of Guiomar is hidden in the verses that sing her praise. Guiomar might also have been the inspiration behind other poems that show evidence of being part of courtly games.

Manrique wrote two *motes* (mottos or poetic glosses). The first explains his own motto, *Ni miento ni m'arrepiento* (I neither lie nor repent), in a nine-line stanza that is followed by an eight-line *fin* (conclusion). The nine-line stanza extends the ambiguity of the motto in a series of antithetical anaphoric verses that begin with *ni:*

> Ni mie*n*to m'arrepiento,
> ni digo ni me desdigo,
> ni estó triste ni contento,
> ni reclamo ni consiento
> ni fío ni desconfío;
> ni bie*n* biuo ni bien muero,
> ni soy ageno ni mío,
> ni me venço ni porfío,
> ni espero ni desespero.

(I neither lie nor repent,
I neither say [anything] nor forswear myself,
I am neither sad nor happy,
I neither protest nor consent,
I neither trust nor mistrust,
I neither live well nor die well,
I neither belong to another nor to myself,

I neither conquer nor extend [my battle] in vain,
I neither hope nor despair).

The use of the negative *ni* serves to underscore the paradoxical nature of the motto; the speaker feels that he is neither fish nor fowl, but the ambiguity is dispelled by the *fin:* The motto refers to love.

The other motto is a four-line stanza with the rubric "Don Jorge Manrique sacó por cimera una añoria con sus alcaduces llenos y dixo" (Don Jorge Manrique had a waterwheel with its buckets full on top of his helmet and said). It is brief poem that could be expressed in a *letra* or *cartel* (a text that accompanied a visual image, in this case an actual waterwheel modeled on top of a helmet, and explained it): "Aquestos y mis enojos / tienen esta condicion: / que suben del coraçón / las lágrimas a los ojos" (These and my pains share this condition: They bring tears to the eyes from the heart). The poem, which appears in the *Cancionero general de Hernando del Castillo* with many other examples of *motes,* explains the significance of Jorge's jousting helmet, which had the shape of a constantly turning waterwheel. In this case, this symbol of manly power only reports the constant pain that the poet feels. "Aquestos" could only refer grammatically to "alcaduzes." They are equated to "enojos," the pains that cause the poet's tears, but are also "en ojos," the tears in his eyes.

Helmets had an important symbolic function in the Middle Ages and were often decorated during tournaments and on occasions that called for a display of power. Like the unsheathed sword, helmets served to symbolize power and manliness and were attributes of men, not of women. They were also among the most prized possessions of warriors, often distributed as prizes by kings and symbolizing, when captured, the vanquishing of an enemy. Some miniatures depict how helmets were used as part of court entertainments. MS. 2693 of the Bibliothèque Nationale of France shows a group of helmets with their accoutrements ready to be inspected by the ladies of the court. A similar event might have been the occasion of Manrique's poem. One can easily imagine that it was written on a *cartel* and placed next to the jousting helmet, or that it was sung to explain the riddle posed by the image.

The poems featuring the acrostics, together with the mottos and possibly other poems, may belong to the period of courtship immediately preceding Manrique's marriage in 1470. The marriage ceremony was divided into two parts that were often separated by considerable time. There was an early "marriage" *por palabras de futuro* (with future intention), tantamount to a betrothal, in which the participants exchanged a promise of marriage. This was followed by a later ceremony *por palabras de presente* (with immediate intention), fre-

quently before a priest, who blessed the union and celebrated a mass. Among the nobility both ceremonies were accompanied by festivities at which the poems in question could have been performed. Marriage, however, did not take the poet away from soldiering.

In December 1470 Jorge Manrique was involved in an episode similar to the taking of Montizón. Enrique IV favored the election of Juan de Valenzuela to the priorship of the Order of San Juan, to the detriment of Manrique's cousin, Alvaro de Estúñiga, son of the duke of Arévalo, who had been elected to the priorship by the Pope. Montizón was close to Consuegra, where the prior resided. When Valenzuela attempted to dispossess Alvaro, Manrique assembled a fighting force composed of his brothers and vassals. He attacked Valenzuela's forces near Toledo, routed them, and once again frustrated the plans of Enrique IV.

In 1474 Enrique IV died, and the country prepared for a war of succession between Juana, his daughter, and his half sister, Isabel. That same year Manrique also participated in the election of his father as *maestre* of the Order of Santiago for the province of Castile, an event celebrated in the *Coplas a la muerte de su padre:*

> Estas sus viejas estorias
> que con su braço pintó
> en juuentud,
> con otras nueuas vitorias
> agora las renouó
> en senetud;
> por su grand abilidad,
> por méritos y ancianía
> bien gastada,
> alcançó la dignidad
> de la grand cauallería
> del espada.

> (These are the records, half effaced,
> Which, with the hand of youth, he traced
> On history's page;
> But with fresh victories he drew
> Each fading character anew
> In his old age.
> By his unrivaled skill, by great
> And veteran service to the state,
> By worth adored,
> He stood, in his high dignity,
> The proudest knight of chivalry,
> Knight of the Sword).

Some of the principal towns of the Order of Santiago were in enemy hands. Jorge Manrique took part in his uncle Rodrigo's campaign to reduce the towns of Alcaraz, Ocaña, and Uclés to the rule of Fernando and Isabel, an event that is recounted in Fernando del Pulgar's *Claros varones de Castilla* (Noble Men of Castile, circa 1483) and in his *Cronica de los Reyes Católicos* (Chronicle of the Catholic Monarchs, 1482–1490).

The siege of Uclés was difficult. Although the town and castle belonged to the Order of Santiago, they were in the hands of partisans of the marqués de Villena and Alfonso Carrillo de Acuña, archbishop of Toledo. Rodrigo Manrique negotiated the surrender of the town, but the men in the castle resisted, knowing that they stood a good chance of being relieved by the superior forces of Villena. Rodrigo thus faced a dilemma as to whether he should stay and run the risk of being caught inside the city walls, between the castle and the relief forces that were nearing, or lift the siege. With characteristic bravado he decided not to disengage and prevailed against his foes with the help of Hurtado de Mendoza, who brought fresh reinforcements.

The two-month campaign had been so costly that Rodrigo Manrique was forced to sell some of the properties held in security for the dowry of Guiomar to pay for the siege of Uclés. Rodrigo died from cancer of the face shortly after, in his "villa de Ocaña" (town of Ocaña), also recently retaken from Villena. His will stipulated that Guiomar be repaid, but she had to sue to recover these funds after her husband, Jorge Manrique, died. The suit is interesting because it reveals that Guiomar complied with the sale of properties for fear of Rodrigo and Jorge.

Relations between Rodrigo's wife, Elvira, and Jorge seem to have been strained as well. This tension was not unusual, because interactions with stepmothers and their children were often difficult. They were made doubly so by Elvira's youth in comparison to the age of her husband, by Rodrigo's reliance on the sons of his first wife to achieve his goals, and by his long absences because of war.

The rubric of one poem, "Un combite que hizo don Jorge Manrique a su madrasta" (A Banquet that Don Jorge Manrique Held in Honor of His Stepmother), dedicates the composition to Elvira. If what the rubric says is true, the poem might have been written by Jorge between 1476 and 1479. "Un combite que hizo don Jorge Manrique a su madrasta" describes a mock banquet that the poet holds for an unnamed lady and her retainers, who enter the house to the sound of a horn. The palace in which the banquet takes place does not have a ceiling, and the floor is covered with nettles instead of fresh-smelling herbs. The seat of honor is raised high, whereas the table is sunken below it and covered with a burlap tablecloth, with underwear for napkins. The narrator, who is skimpily dressed, is the person who brings in the food. Each dish is more disgusting than the last. The meal begins with a salad of wild onions, tow, and frog heads. This is followed by

the main dishes, which are "el gallo de la Passión" (the Passion's rooster; that is, an old rooster), a hen with its chicks, two sheared rabbits, and birds in their nests, all cooked with cabbages and accompanied by rice cooked in "grassa / de un collar viejo sudado" (grease from an old collar stained with perspiration), which is meted out by the spoonful to each guest. For dessert the guests have "pasta real," a confection normally made of ground almonds and sugar, but this version is made with lye and sand and covered with soot and ashes.

It was customary to conclude an important dinner with a musical interlude. In "Un combite que hizo don Jorge Manrique a su madrasta" a lady with a *vihuela* (mandolin) enters, presumably to entertain the guests, but the description of her dress seems like a grotesque painting. She wears two shoes on one foot and a slipper on the other, socks as gloves, a slab of bacon for a headdress, a fox for earrings, a slit skirt, dried fish around her neck, and a cape of strange fashion, which has "las haldas todas delante / las nalgas todas de fuera" (the skirts all in front, the buttocks all showing). The reader does not know what she sings because the poem ends at this point, but it must not have been pleasant.

"Un combite que hizo don Jorge Manrique a su madrasta" overturns the conventions of hospitality to make fun of the lady, who is not treated like an honored person. The house in which the banquet takes place is in ruins, the dress of the participants is bizarre, the food is not fit to be eaten, and the entertainment is questionable. In addition, there is a vague sexual undertone to the whole affair that makes it quite inappropriate for a female relative, even one related by marriage. Remarkably, if the rubric is correct, the composition of "Un combite que hizo don Jorge Manrique a su madrasta" may belong to the same period as the *Coplas a la muerte de su padre*.

*Coplas a la muerte de su padre* is without question Jorge Manrique's best composition. The work is dedicated to the memory of Rodrigo Manrique, who died on 11 November 1476 in Ocaña. The poem has forty stanzas composed of twelve eight- and four-syllable lines that rhyme *abc abc def def*. Every third line is a *quebrado* (half line). The verse form, now known as the *copla manriqueña* (Manriquean stanza), is found in other lyric poetry of the period, and Jorge himself used it in some of his minor lyric poems. His fine poetic sensibility, however, must have made him realize that the alternation of long and short lines and their punctuation made the verses flexible enough to sound quite sonorous and somber or light and quick. He chose this stanza form to celebrate the life and death of his father.

*Coplas a la muerte de su padre* was set to music several times in the sixteenth century. Among these musical settings are those found in Alonso Mudarra's *Tres libros de música en cifra para vihuela* (Three Books of Music in Tablature for Mandolin, 1546), Luis Venegas de Henestrosa's *Libro de cifra nueva para tecla, harpa y vihuela* (Book of New Tablature for Keyboard, Harp and Mandolin, 1557), and Pere Albérch i Vila's *Odarum* (1561). In 1997 Víctor de Lama and Gerardo Fernández published a complete listing of the known and lost musical settings of Manrique's poem.

    *Coplas a la muerte de su padre* belongs to a long elegiac tradition, with roots in the classical elegy, which sings of the deeds and death of an individual. Manrique's most immediate sources, however, were the medieval poems about death and, above all, the deaths of prominent Castilians, particularly Gómez Manrique's "Defunción de noble caballero Garcilaso de la Vega," which also commemorates the death of a family member.

    The order of the stanzas in *Coplas a la muerte de su padre* varies in the different editions and manuscripts. For a reliable text, scholars have opted to follow one or more of the early imprints. Critics have tended to bypass the earliest imprint (1482), which has the most radical variation in the order of the stanzas, in favor of the version in the *Cancionero de Ramón de Llavia* (circa 1484–1488) or the *Cancionero general de Hernando del Castillo* of 1535. The authenticity of the stanzas that begin "Oh mundo pues que nos matas" and "Es tu comienzo lloroso," first published in Alonso de Cervantes's 1501 gloss of the poem, is questioned by some critics because they do not appear in other early editions of the work. Tradition says that these stanzas were found on the body of Jorge Manrique when he died in Santa María del Campo Rus, but most editors leave them out of the *Coplas a la muerte de su padre*. The poem appears under different titles: "*Dezir . . . ,*" "*Coplas a . . . ,*" or "*Coplas por*" la muerte de su padre. None of the manuscripts is an autograph; they all date from after Manrique's death.

    Manrique did not give the poem an overt structure. It seems to break naturally into three main sections, each consisting of several stanzas and a coda. The first section, composed of stanzas 1–24, is characterized by a sententious tone that speaks of the effect of death on all souls. It features some of the most memorable metaphors in the poem. Life is compared to a road filled with dangers and opportunities and to a river that ends in the sea. The section invokes general examples of human waywardness that one may encounter along the road leading to heaven or hell. The poem begins with a solemn warning:

> Recuerde ell alma dormida,
> abiue el seso y despierte
> contemplando

cómo se pasa la vida,
cómo se viene la muerte
tan callando.
Quánd presto se va el plazer,
cómo después de acordado
da dolor,
cómo a nuestro parescer
qualquiera tiempo pasado
fue mejor.

(O let the soul her slumbers break,
Let thought be quickened, and awake;
Awake to see
How soon this life is past and gone,
And death comes softly stealing on,
How silently!
Swiftly our pleasures glide away,
Our hearts recall the distant day
With many sighs;
The moments that are speeding fast
We heed not, but the past,–the past,
More highly prize).

    Stanzas 1–3 serve as an introduction to the poem. They tell the "sleeping" soul that it is on a forked path. Death waits at the end of both paths, but one leads to salvation, whereas the other leads to perdition. Therefore, the soul has a choice: eternal life or death. These stanzas are followed by an invocation (stanza 4) and stanzas about how estate, youth, and lineage are all treated alike by death, who is like a hunter concealed in a blind, ready to shoot the unsuspecting soul (stanzas 4–14). This section gives way to pointed examples of great Castilian men who chose wrongly and fell into the grasp of death because they did not realize the nature of the path they were on (stanzas 15–24). These stanzas are framed by a series of questions (*ubi sunt,* where are they now?) that provoke an immediate response from the reader:

¿Qué se hizo el rey don Juan? Los infantes de Aragón
¿qué se hizieron?
¿Qué fue de tanto galán?
¿Qué fue de tanta inuención
como traxieron?
Las justas y los torneos,
paramentos, bordaduras
y cimeras
¿fueron syno deuaneos?
¿Qué fueron sino verduras
de las heras?

(Where is the King, Don Juan? Where
Each royal prince and noble heir
Of Aragon ?
Where are the courtly gallantries?
The deeds of love and high emprise,
In battle done?
Tourney and joust, that charmed the eye,

And scarf, and gorgeous panoply,
And nodding plume,
What were they but a pageant scene?
What but the garlands, gay and green,
That deck the tomb?)

Rodrigo Manrique's life spanned the lives of all the people mentioned in the *ubi sunt* stanzas. Juan II, a weak king famous for the frivolity of his court, was now gone. The infantes (princes) of Aragon, who engaged in protracted wars with Castile, were finally neutralized by the early 1450s. Enrique IV, who was known for his largesse to favorites and caused much grief to the Manriques, died, it is claimed, without absolution. Prince Alfonso, who between 1465 and 1468 contested the crown of his half brother and called himself king, was dead, probably from poisoning. Luna, the favorite of Juan II, was executed by sword in Valladolid in 1453. Pacheco, *maestre* of the Order of Santiago, and his brother Pedro Girón, *maestre* of the Order of Calatrava, had suddenly died in spite of their power.

This part of the *Coplas a la muerte de su padre* follows a chronological and hierarchical order. After the kings, the infantes of Aragon, and the pretender Alfonso comes the great constable of Castile and *maestre* of the Order of Santiago under Juan II, Luna, and then Girón and Pacheco. All had their moments of glory, but, as the poem states, all ended in the clutches of doleful death. The rest of the noble orders are dealt with en masse in two stanzas that name the nobility "duques excellentes, / tantos marqueses e condes, / e varones" (excellent dukes, / so many marquesses and counts, / and barons) and the general host of the army, also divided hierarchically by flags.

Although the *ubi sunt* stanzas begin with individual examples, the named individuals join the common fate that awaits the generality of men. The section recalls one of the central metaphors of the poem:

Nuestras vidas son los ryos
que van a dar en el mar,
que es el morir;
allí van los señoríos
derechos a se acabar
y consumir.
Allí los ríos caudales,
allí los otros, medianos,
y más chicos,
allegados, son yguales
los que biuen por sus manos
y los ricos.

(Our lives are rivers, gliding free
To that unfathomed, boundless sea,
The silent grave!
Thither all earthly pomp and boast
Roll, to be swallowed up and lost
In one dark wave.

Thither the mighty torrents stray,
Thither the brook pursues its way,
And tinkling rill,
There all are equal; side by side
The poor man and the son of pride
Lie calm and still).

The second section (stanzas 25–32) introduces Rodrigo Manrique. From the first, it is obvious that he is diametrically opposed in character to the preceding figures. Jorge endows his father with all of the qualities of a proper knight. Rodrigo acts only in defense of country and family:

Aquél de buenos abrigo,
amado por virtuoso
de la gente,
el maestre don Rodrigo
Manrrique, tanto famoso
y tan valiente,
sus grandes hechos y claros
no cumple que los alabe,
pues los vieron;
ni los quiero hazer caros,
pues el mundo todo sabe
quáles fueron.

(And he, the good man's shield and shade,
To whom all hearts their homage paid,
As Virtue's son,
Roderic Manrique, he whose name
Is written on the scroll of Fame,
Spain's champion;
His signal deeds and prowess high
Demand no pompous eulogy.
Ye saw his deeds!
Why should their praise in verse be sung?
The name, that dwells on every tongue,
No minstrel needs).

This false modesty is quickly dispelled by what follows. Stanzas 27 and 28 compare Rodrigo to a series of Roman emperors and generals who each embodied a different commanding virtue. Rodrigo surpassed them because he embodied all of the virtues that had previously been divided among many. Not surprisingly, these virtues correspond to those that were supposed to guide knightly behavior in the late Middle Ages.

The third and final section of the poem is a brief play that brings onstage a personification of death (stanzas 33–39). Death's interaction with the other worthies in the poem who serve as examples is sudden and violent. It is a different matter with Rodrigo. Death comes to call at his house and invites him to drink from a cup:

. . . –Buen cauallero,
dexad el mundo engañoso
y su halago;

*vuestro* coraçón de azero
muestre su esfuerço famoso
en este trago.

(Good Cavalier, prepare
To leave this world of toil and care
   With joyful mien;
Let thy strong heart of steel this day
Put on its armor for the fray,
   The closing scene).

Longfellow's translation is unfaithful to the original because he fails to use the same metaphor that Jorge Manrique employs in this and the next stanza. The stanza compares the moment of death to a bitter drink, a common comparison derived from the Bible and used to express the difficulty of death. It is bitter because it is the final drink of the man, his final battle, and it recalls the ceremony of extreme unction. The allusion suggests Christ's words in the garden of Gethsemane, where he enjoins the Father to take the cup from him, and the Last Supper, with the injunction to drink in memory of Jesus.

Death then states how a knight achieves salvation in a stanza that has become a classic exposition of the nature of medieval society:

   –El beuir que es perdurable
no se gana con estados
   mundanales
ni con vida deleytable
en que moran los pecados
   infernales;
mas los buenos religiosos
gánanlo con oraciones
   y con lloros,
los caualleros famosos,
con trabajos y afliciones
   contra moros.

(The eternal life, beyond the sky,
Wealth cannot purchase, nor the high
   And proud estate;
The soul in dalliance laid, the spirit
Corrupt with sin, shall not inherit
   A joy so great.
But the good monk, in cloistered cell,
Shall gain it by his book and bell,
   His prayers and tears;
And the brave knight, whose arm endures
Fierce battle, and against the Moors
   His standard rears).

Like Christ, Rodrigo Manrique embraces his fate and leaves a famous name behind. His fame, although not eternal, will console those who remain. His ending, however, is also a beginning, for through extreme unction and a final declaration of faith, he achieves salvation.

Unlike the characters in the *ubi sunt* stanzas, Rodrigo dies in bed, at an advanced age, surrounded by family and servants, after having led a life of proper action:

   Asy, con tal entender,
todos sentidos humanos
   oluidados,
cercado de su muger
y de hijos y de hermanos
   y criados,
dio ell alma a quien ge la dio,
el qual la ponga en el cielo
   y en su gloria;
y aunque la vida murió,
nos dexó harto consuelo
   su memoria.

(As thus the dying warrior prayed,
Without one gathering mist or shade
   Upon his mind;
Encircled by his family,
Watched by affection's gentle eye
   So soft and kind;
His soul to Him, who gave it, rose;
God lead it to its long repose,
   Its glorious rest!
And, though the warrior's sun has set,
Its light shall linger round us yet,
   Bright, radiant, blest).

The metaphors that refer to the death of the other characters are metaphors of loss or violence. Death is a sea into which all lost souls flow. He is a hunter who awaits the unsuspecting prey in a blind, a smith who smelts souls like iron in a smithy. He is a warrior who kills knights with his lance during campaigns. These metaphors provide the context in which one has to read and interpret the panegyric to Rodrigo Manrique (stanzas 25–39) and, in particular, the *fin* (stanza 40).

The poem does not allude to the fact that two *maestres* of the Order of Santiago coexisted the year that Rodrigo Manrique died. Following Pacheco's death, Cárdenas was elected *maestre* by the province of León, and Rodrigo was elected by the province of Castile. Faced with a double election in a kingdom sundered by civil war, Isabel and Fernando decided not to favor either, although Rodrigo had the sympathy of the court and of the royal chroniclers who considered Cárdenas's claims out of place. The king and queen needed the backing of both Manrique and Cárdenas to end the civil war that afflicted Castile and to begin the final campaign against Granada. There is no doubt, however, that Rodrigo considered himself to be the legitimate *maestre,* because he had held the title before, when he had contested the election of Luna, and again, when he had been elected by the principal chapter of the order in Uclés.

*Judgment of helmets, from a late-fifteenth-century manuscript in the Bibliothèque Nationale, Paris. Decorated helmets had a highly symbolic function in medieval society; Manrique alludes to his own helmet, in the shape of a waterwheel, in the "Aquestos y mis enojos" (courtesy of Frank A. Domínguez).*

Curiously, in the *Coplas a la muerte de su padre* there is no reference to Isabel at all, and Fernando is not mentioned by name. There is only one allusion to the king, and it is not completely flattering: "Pues nuestro rey natural, / sy de las obras que obró / fue seruido, / dígalo el de Portugal / y en Castilla, quién siguió / su partido" (By the tried valor of his hand, / His monarch and his native land / Were nobly served; / Let Portugal repeat the story, / And proud Castile, who shared the glory / His arms deserved). These verses refer to the deeds performed by Rodrigo Manrique, on behalf of Fernando, against the king of Portugal, the main supporter of Juana's claim to the crown. Allied with the king of Portugal and Juana against Isabel and Fernando were the marqués de Villena and the archbishop of Toledo. Although it is not obvious in Longfellow's translation, a reader of Manrique's time would think it odd that the value of Rodrigo's service is expressed indirectly through the testimony of the main enemy, the king of Portugal,

and not directly by the king of Castile. It is also unusual that there is no mention of Isabel, although neither she nor Fernando could be mentioned in the *ubi sunt* stanzas, because they were still alive.

There may be a second allusion to the services that Rodrigo Manrique performed for the king before death enters the stage:

> Después que puso la vida
> tantas vezes por su ley
> al tablero,
> después de tan bien seruida
> la corona de su rey
> verdadero.

> (And when so oft, for weal or woe,
> His life upon the fatal throw
> Had been cast down;
> When he had served, with patriot zeal,
> Beneath the banner of Castile,
> His sovereign's crown).

Longfellow's translation makes the stanza refer exclusively to King Fernando once more, whose claim to the throne of Castile was not yet secure. It is more likely, however, that the reference is in part to God, the "true" king for whom Rodrigo Manrique had risked his life so many times on the chessboard of life ("Después de puesta la vida / tantas vezes por su ley / al tablero" [After risking his life so many times for his religion at the chessboard]), and in whose service the Order of Santiago had been created. There is a precedent for this substitution of the secular with the divine in the thirteenth-century epic *Poema de Fernán González*, in which the tenth-century Fernán González, the first count of Castile, swears vassalage to God instead of to his rightful fief lord, the king of León, and thus begins to establish the independence of Castile. In *Coplas a la muerte de su padre*, however, Jorge Manrique goes no further than to claim that his father performed true service for his religion and his "rey verdadero." The goals of the *Poema de Fernán González* and the *Coplas a la muerte de su padre* are quite different. Jorge Manrique cannot claim that his father acted independently of the kings or that Rodrigo did not owe fealty to them. Jorge can, however, imply a lack of reciprocity.

The insistence on the quality of the service of Rodrigo Manrique is introduced by the repetition of the word *después* (after). The logical question that a reader would ask is how Rodrigo was rewarded after risking his life so many times in serving his true king. Jorge Manrique's answer is twofold. If Rodrigo's service was ultimately for God, then he obtained a just reward; he was saved. If his service was for the king, there was no reward, other than that of fame.

The death of Rodrigo Manrique brought with it uncertainty and insecurity for the Manriques. Although the queen briefly tried to claim the administration of the Order of Santiago for the crown, the question of the identity of the true *maestre* of the order was resolved in Cárdenas's favor after Rodrigo's death. Later histories of the Order of Santiago, including García de Medrano's *La regla y establecimientos de la cavalleria de Santiago del Espada; con la historia del origen y principio della* (1603), clearly present Cárdenas as the legitimate successor of the thirty-ninth *maestre,* Pacheco. Rodrigo is relegated to a secondary role in these histories. Jorge Manrique's poem, however, is silent about Cárdenas and about the division of the mastership into two administrations, one for León and one for Castile. In the *Coplas a la muerte de su padre* there is only one *maestre,* Rodrigo Manrique.

The last stanza of the poem cleverly portrays a death scene that was atypical for a warrior. The number of nobles (including members of the Manrique family) who died in war was quite high. Rodrigo, on the other hand, died in bed, surrounded by his family, brothers, and *criados* (servants). Only a few individuals in those turbulent times were granted a long life by the grace of God, and fewer still kept all of their senses and strength until the end and achieved salvation. The situation of the Manrique family, however, was now quite different. They had lost the person who was essentially the head of the clan and functioned as spokesman for most of the Manriques.

The family depended on Rodrigo for protection and advancement, but his patronage reached farther. Although the death scene in the poem includes only the family, the number of people affected by Rodrigo's death would have been larger. He was a spokesman not only for immediate relatives—his wife, his sons, and their spouses—but also for the other descendants of his father, Pero Manrique; for the countless functionaries who served in administrative positions in his towns and villages; and for his allies. The term *criados* (those that were attached to his household) and the earlier *amigos* (friends and allies) therefore includes not only household servants and friends but also all those who served him in life and benefited from his protection and aid. They were the logical readers of the *Coplas a la muerte de su padre.*

Rodrigo Manrique was the principal defender of the interests of the Catholic Monarchs (Isabel and Fernando) in Andalusia. He was the main opponent in the south of the marqués de Villena, the archbishop of Toledo, and the king of Portugal, who supported Juana's bid for the crown. *Coplas a la muerte de su padre* is a clever reminder of these facts to the king and queen,

and of the debt they owed to Rodrigo's extended family and supporters.

A letter that Rodrigo Manrique sent the Catholic Monarchs from his deathbed confirms his concern for the future well-being of his family. The original text has not survived, but portions are summarized in *Cronica de Enrique IV.* The author writes that Rodrigo

> muy especialmente les rogaba que se compadeciesen de su mujer y de sus fieles criados, á quienes le apenaba dejar sin amparo ni bienes de fortuna, porque los extremados trabajos é intolerables dispendios les habían reducido á la última indigencia, de que sólo podría sacarles la liberalidad de los Reyes, á quienes servirían con la misma lealtad y sumisión que les sirvió siempre, mientras tuvo vida, el que ahora, á las puertas de la muerte, les daba los últimos consejos.

> (particularly pleaded that they take pity on his wife and his faithful servants, whom he regretted to leave without protection or the goods of fortune, because the extreme effort and intolerable expenses [of his campaigns] had reduced them to penury, from which penury only the liberality of the kings could save them; they would serve the kings with the same loyalty and submission that he always demonstrated towards them while alive, the same person who now, at the doors of death, gave them his last counsel).

The plea seems to have fallen on deaf ears. Cárdenas was elected *maestre* of the Order of Santiago for both León and Castile by the *treze* eleven months after Rodrigo's death and claimed Segura in order to secure his control over the order. No special treatment of the Manriques was forthcoming from the monarchs. The family members were not dispossessed from their *encomiendas* and offices—the clan was too powerful for that to happen, and, in any case, it was contrary to normal practice to dispossess living commanders. The assignment of new commanderies, however, was now in the hands of Cárdenas, who sought to install his supporters in vacant *encomiendas.* In the case of Jorge Manrique's son, Luis, his later appointment to the *encomienda* of Montizón was the result of the energetic efforts of his mother, Guiomar, who had to appeal to the Pope on her son's behalf. Clearly, that would not have happened if Rodrigo had still been alive.

During the last few years of his life Jorge Manrique continued to serve Fernando and Isabel in their efforts to put an end to the civil war. He also took up arms in defense of family interests in 1477, when he aided his cousin Juan de Benavides—son of Día Sánchez de Benavides, Count of Santiesteban del Puerto (who was married to an aunt of Jorge and had helped him take Montizón)—in a plan to recover Baeza from the forces of the count of Cabra. Jorge's son and daughter, Luis and Luisa Manrique, both married Benavides' children.

The count of Cabra and the *mariscal* (marshal) of Baena, his son, had been entrusted by the Catholic Monarchs with the administration of the recently captured city of Baeza. Cabra—perhaps in an effort to quell animosities among the different noble factions of the city, and perhaps as repayment for past injuries he had received from the Benavides and Manrique families—exiled Juan de Benavides and his followers from the city, hoping by this measure to avoid the civil disturbances that had plagued the city while the count was away. Together with Benavides, on 28 April at midnight, Jorge Manrique forcibly entered Baeza in search of the *mariscal,* whom they wished to capture, but did not find him. Forces quickly gathered to repel the invaders, who could not maintain their positions. Many fled, but Manrique and Benavides were among those captured.

Manrique was accused of *desacato* (disobedience) to Fernando and Isabel, a charge he vehemently denied. He posted a *cartel* (writ) in Baeza challenging anyone who wished to maintain the charge to face him in a duel. No one came forth. Although the king and queen exonerated him, the incident shows how family alliances were at times more significant than wider political considerations. It also demonstrates that Manrique had achieved sufficient renown as a warrior for the incident to be reported in the chronicles.

Near the end of his life Jorge Manrique became a captain of the Santa Hermandad de Toledo (Holy Brotherhood, or provincial constabulary, of Toledo), a new force established by the king and queen to help pacify the kingdom. In that capacity he saw his last military action in the marquessate of Villena, still not under the control of the Crown. A *memorial* (deposition or letter of request) addressed to Diego López Pacheco, second Marqués de Villena, years later by a man called Pedro de Baeza tells all that is known about the circumstances of Manrique's death.

Baeza was one of Pacheco's chief lieutenants and the man in charge of protecting Villena's lands while the latter looked for a propitious moment to capitulate to the Catholic Monarchs. In his *memorial* Baeza states that he killed Jorge Manrique in an attack against the castle of Garcimuñoz, when the poet started his incursions into the marquessate. One night, Baeza claims, he gave the poet the wound from which he later died. Baeza was also gravely wounded in the jaw. The date of Manrique's death was 24 April 1479. A century later the villagers of Garcimuñoz still remembered the event and maintained that Manrique was killed in an ambush by a lance thrust to the kidneys. According to the *Relaciones* of Felipe II (Accounts, or Census, 1575), the peo-

ple of the village of Santa María del Campo Rus, where Manrique had his encampment, could still point to a house where they claimed the poet had died. His body was taken to Uclés and laid to rest close to that of his father. Both tombs have since disappeared, but not before Luis Salazar y Castro had a chance to describe Rodrigo Manrique's tomb in his *Historia genealógica de la Casa de Lara* (1697).

Jorge Manrique's poetry represents the best of the fifteenth-century Castilian lyric in its masterful use of conventional themes, forms, and meters, and in the economy of thought that characterizes the shorter poems. Manrique's works were widely admired and imitated. The *Coplas a la muerte de su padre,* his magisterial composition, was printed often during the two centuries after his death, sometimes with the glosses of other authors. In the eighteenth century Manrique's reputation flagged in the face of changing literary taste, but he began once again to draw the attention of readers in the nineteenth century. These readers, however, followed in the footsteps of previous interpreters of the poem, who tended to favor the early stanzas, with their memorable admonitions on the transitoriness of life, over the stanzas recounting Rodrigo Manrique's accomplishments, which had been forgotten. Only later did critics realize the importance of the last section to the themes and poetic structure of the work. Far from being a poem about death, *Coplas a la muerte de su padre* is about a good life lived in the face of death. Today, Jorge Manrique's reputation rests on the entire text of the poem. The depiction of the triumph of a life of virtuous deeds over death and destruction, articulated in deceptively simple language, epitomizes Spanish aspirations and has made it an enduring part of the canon of Spanish literature.

**Bibliographies:**

Jacqueline Steunou and Lothar Knapp, *Bibliografía de los cancioneros castellanos del siglo XV y repertorio de sus géneros poéticos,* 2 volumes (Paris: Centre National de la Recherche Scientifique, 1975–1978);

Manuel Carrión Gutiéz, *Bibliografía de Jorge Manrique, 1479–1979* (Palencia: Diputación Provincial, 1979);

Brian Dutton, *El cancionero del siglo XV, c. 1360–1520,* 7 volumes (Salamanca: Universidad de Salamanca, 1990–1991).

**Biographies:**

Nicolás Antonio, "Georgius Manriquius," in *Bibliotheca Hispana Vetus,* 2 volumes (Madrid: J. Ibarra, 1788), II: 342–344;

Antonio Serrano de Haro, *Personalidad y destino de Jorge Manrique* (Madrid: Gredos, 1966).

## References:

Vicente Beltrán, "Tipología y génesis de los cancioneros: El caso de Jorge Manrique," in *Historias y ficciones: Coloquio sobre la literatura del siglo XV: Actas del Coloquio Internacional organizado por el Departament de Filologia Espanyola de la Universitat de Valencia, celebrado en Valencia los días 29, 30 y 31 de octubre de 1990,* edited by Rafael Beltrán, José L. Canet, and Josep L. Sirera, with an introduction by Evangelina Rodríguez (Valencia: Universitat de Valencia, Departament de Filologia Espanyola, 1992), pp. 167–188;

Eloy Benito Ruano, "Algunas rentas de Jorge Manrique," *Hispania* (Madrid), 25 (1965): 113–119;

Benito Ruano, "Autógrafos de Jorge Manrique," *Archivum,* 18 (1968): 107–116;

Benito Ruano, "Un episodio bélico (y un autógrafo de Jorge Manrique)," in *Estudios dedicados al profesor D. Angel Ferrari Núñez,* 2 volumes, edited by Miguel Angel Ladero Quesada, En la España medieval, no. 4 (Madrid: Universidad Complutense, 1984), I: 139–146;

Rodolfo A. Borello, "Las Coplas de Jorge Manrique: estructura y fuentes," *Cuadernos de Filología,* 1 (1967): 49–72;

Borello, "Para la historia del *ubi sunt,*" in *Lengua, Literatura, Folklore: Estudios dedicados a Rodolfo Oroz,* edited by Gastón Carrillo Herrera (Santiago: Facultad de Filosofía y Educación, Universidad de Chile, 1967), pp. 81–92;

E. Buceta, "Dos papeletas referentes a las *Coplas* de Jorge Manrique," *Bulletin Hispanique,* 29 (1927): 407–412;

Eduardo Camacho Guisado, *La elegía funeral en la poesía española* (Madrid: Gredos, 1969);

Gualterio Cangiotti, *Le Coplas di Manrique tra medioevo e umanesimo* (Bologna: Pàtron, 1964);

Francisco Caravaca, "Estudio de ocho coplas de Jorge Manrique en relación con la traducción inglesa de Longfellow," *Boletín de la Biblioteca Menéndez Pelayo,* 51 (1975): 3–90;

Caravaca, "Estudios manriqueños: Notas sobre el título *Coplas* de Jorge Manrique *a la* muerte de su padre," *Torre,* 73–74 (1971): 185–221;

Caravaca, "Notas sobre las llamadas *coplas póstumas* de Jorge Manrique," *Boletín de la Biblioteca Menéndez Pelayo,* 50 (1974): 89–135;

Caravaca, "Quién fue el autor del retrato de Jorge Manrique?" *Papeles de Son Armadans,* 65, no. 193 (1972): 89–99;

Pio Colonnello, "Honra e honrar nelle Coplas por la muerte de su padre di Jorge Manrique: Loro ambito semantico," *Annali–Sezione Romanza, Istituto Universitario Orientale* (Naples), 19 (1977): 417–434;

Gustavo Correa, "Lenguaje y ritmo en las *Coplas de Jorge Manrique a la muerte de su padre,*" *Hispania,* 63 (1980): 184–194;

Frank A. Domínguez, "Body and Soul: Jorge Manrique's *Coplas por la muerte de su padre* 13: 145–156," *Hispania,* 84 (2001): 1–10;

Domínguez, *Love and Remembrance: The Poetry of Jorge Manrique* (Lexington: University of Kentucky Press, 1989);

Domínguez, "Textos que sanan y textos que matan: la invocación en las *Coplas* de Jorge Manrique," in *Studies on Medieval Spanish Literature in Honor of Charles F. Fraker,* edited by Mercedes Vaquero and Alan Deyermond (Madison, Wis.: Hispanic Seminary of Medieval Studies, 1995), pp. 107–118;

Peter N. Dunn, "Themes and Images in the *Coplas por la muerte de su padre* of Jorge Manrique," *Medium Aevum,* 33 (1964): 169–183;

Michel Garcia, "Vivir y morir de amor en la poesía de Jorge Manrique: Intento de análisis cuantitativo," *Voces,* 2 (1991): 39–49, 134;

Stephen Gilman, "Tres retratos de la muerte en las *Coplas* de Jorge Manrique," *Nueva Revista de Filología Hispánica,* 13 (1959): 305–324;

David Hook, "An Idiosyncratic Manuscript Copy of Jorge Manrique's *Coplas por la muerte de su Padre* (Lisbon, Bibl. Nac., cod. 11353)," *Scriptorium,* 41, no. 2 (1987): 237–254;

Richard P. Kinkade, "The Historical Date of the *Coplas* and the Death of Jorge Manrique," *Speculum,* 45 (1970): 216–224;

Anna Krause, *Jorge Manrique and the Cult of Death in the Cuatrocientos* (Berkeley: University of California Press, 1937), pp. 79–176;

J. Labrador, A. Zorita, and R. A. Difranco, "Cuarenta y dos, y no cuarenta coplas en la famosa elegía manriqueña," *Boletín de la Biblioteca Menéndez Pelayo,* 61 (1985): 37–95;

Víctor de Lama and Gerardo Fernández, "Fortuna musical de las *Coplas* de Jorge Manrique en los Siglos de Oro," in *Actas del VI Congreso Internacional de la Asociación Hispánica de Literatura Medieval: Alcalá de Henares, 12–16 de septiembre de 1995,* 2 volumes, edited by José Manuel Lucía Megías (Alcalá: Servicio de publicaciones, Universidad de Alcalá de Henares, 1997), II: 867–868;

María Rosa Lida de Malkiel, "Una copla de Jorge Manrique y la tradición de Filón en la literatura española," *Revista de Filología Hispánica,* 4 (1942): 152–171;

Lida de Malkiel, *La idea de la fama en la edad media castellana* (Mexico: Fondo de Cultura Económica, 1952);

Lida de Malkiel, "Para la primera de las *Coplas de don Jorge Manrique por la muerte de su padre*," *Romance Philology,* 16 (1962): 170–173;

Derek Lomax, "Cuándo murió don Jorge Manrique?" *Revista de Filología Española,* 55 (1972): 61–62;

Francisco Márquez Villanueva, "Sobre el *Combite que hizo don Jorge Manrique a su madrastra*," in *Scripta Philologica in Honorem Juan M. Lope Blanch a los 40 años de docencia en la UNAM y a los 65 años de vida,* 3 volumes, edited by Elizabeth Luna Traill (Mexico City: Universidad Nacional Autónoma de Mexico, Instituto de Investigaciones Filológicas, 1992), III: 305–324;

Juan Martín de Nicolás Cabo, "La Mancha santiaguista según los libros de visitas (1480–1511)," in *Actas del Congreso Internacional Hispano-Portugués sobre las Ordenes Militares in la Península durante la Edad Media* (Madrid: Consejo Superior de Investigaciones Científicas, 1981), pp. 469–491;

Rosa María Montero Tejada, *Nobleza y sociedad en Castilla: El linaje Manrique, siglos XIV–XVI* (Madrid: Caja de Madrid, 1996);

Ambrosio de Morales, "Noticias históricas sacadas del Archivo de Uclés," in Francisco Valerio Cifuentes, ed., *Opúsculos castellanos de Ambrosio de Morales: Cuyos originales se conservan ineditos en la Real Biblioteca del Monasterio del Escorial* (Madrid: Benito Cano, 1793), II: 24;

Margherita Morreale, "Apuntes para el estudio de la trayectoria que desde el 'ubi sunt?' lleva hasta el 'Qué le fueron sino . . .?' de Jorge Manrique," *Thesaurus,* 30 (1975): 471–519;

Genaro Navarro, "Segura de la Sierra, lugar de nacimiento de Jorge Manrique," *Boletín del Instituto de Estudios Giennenses,* 11 (1965): 9–18;

Alonso de Palencia, *Crónica de Enrique IV,* 5 volumes, translated by D. A. Paz and Melia (Madrid: Revista de Archivos, 1908), IV: 309–320;

Ramón Paz, "Visitas a encomiendas de la provincia de Castilla en el siglo XV," in Antonio Pérez Gómez, *Miscelánea de estudios dedicado al Profesor Antonio Marín Ocete (1900–1972),* 2 volumes (Granada: University of Granada: Caja de Ahorros y Monte de Piedad de Granada, 1974), II: 877–909;

Antonio Pérez Gómez, *Glosas a la Coplas de Jorge Manrique: Noticias bibliográficas* (Cieza: La fonte que mana y corre, 1961–1963);

Julio Rodríguez Puértolas, "Jorge Manrique y la manipulación de la historia," in *Medieval and Renaissance Studies in Honour of Robert Brian Tate,* edited by Ian Michael and Richard A. Cardwell (Oxford: Dolphin, 1986), pp. 123–133;

Nicholas G. Round, "Formal Integration in Jorge Manrique's *Coplas por la muerte de su padre*," in *Readings in Spanish and Portuguese Poetry for Geoffrey Connell,* edited by Round and D. Gareth Walters (Glasgow: University of Glasgow, Department of Hispanic Studies, 1985), pp. 205–221;

Luis de Salazar y Castro, *Historia genealógica de la casa Lara,* 5 volumes (Madrid: Mateo de Llanos, 1694–1697);

Pedro Salinas, *Jorge Manrique, o tradición y originalidad* (Buenos Aires: Sudamericana, 1947);

Nellie E. Sánchez Arce, *Las glosas a las Coplas de Jorge Manrique* (Madrid: Sancha, 1956);

Luigi Sorrento, *La poesia e i problemi della poesia di Jorge Manrique* (Palermo: Palumbo, 1941).

Eusebio Julián Zarco Cuevas, ed., *Relaciones de pueblos del obispado de Cuenca,* 2 volumes (Cuenca: Imprenta del Seminario, 1927), I: 299.

# Alfonso Martínez de Toledo

*(23 January 1398? – 2 January 1468)*

Michael Agnew
*Columbia University*

WORKS: *Arcipreste de Talavera;* also known as *Corbacho* (1438)

**Manuscript:** El Escorial MS. h.III.10 (1466). The scribe is identified as Alonso de Contreras. Marcella Ciceri bases her editions on this manuscript; other modern editions rely on the early printed versions.

**First publication:** *El arcipreste de Talauera que fabla de los vicios de las malas mugeres e Complexiones de los hombres* (Seville: Meynardo Ungut & Stanislao Polono, 1498).

**Early editions:** *El arcipreste de talauera que fabla de los vicios de las malas mugeres: E complexiones de los hombres* (Toledo: Pedro Hagembach, 1500); *Arcipreste de talauera, que fabla de los vicios de las malas mugeres: E complisiones de los hombres* (Toledo: Arnao Guillén de Brocar, 1518); *Siguese un compendio breue y muy prouechoso para informacion de los que no tienen experiencia de los males y daños que causan las malas mugeres a los locos amadores: y de otras cosas annexas a este proposito. conpuesto por el bachiller Alfonso martinez de Toledo Arcipreste de Talauera. Nueuamente añadido e impresso* (Logroño: Miguel Eguia, 1529); *Arcipreste de Talauera que habla de los vicios de las malas mugereres [sic]: y complexiones de los hombres* (Seville: Andrés de Burgos, 1547).

**Modern editions:** *Arcipreste de Talavera (Corvacho o Reprobación del amor mundano),* edited by Cristóbal Pérez Pastor (Madrid: Sociedad de Bibliófilos Españoles, 1901); *El Arcipreste de Talavera, ó sea, El corbacho,* edited by Lesley Byrd Simpson (Berkeley: University of California Press, 1939); *Arcipreste de Talavera o Corbacho,* edited by Joaquín González Muela, Clásicos Castalia, no. 24 (Madrid: Castalia, 1970); *Arcipreste de Talavera,* 2 volumes, edited by Marcella Ciceri, Istituto di Filologia Romanza dell'Università di Roma: Studi, Testi e Manuali, no. 3 (Modena: S.T.E.M.-Mucchi, 1975); *Arcipreste de Talavera o Corbacho,* edited by E. Michael Gerli, Letras Hispánicas, no. 92 (Madrid: Cátedra, 1979; revised, 1998); *The Texts and Con-

cordances of the Escorial Manuscript h.III.10 of the Arcipreste de Talavera of Alfonso Martínez de Toledo,* edited by Eric W. Naylor, Spanish Series, no. 12 (Madison, Wis.: Hispanic Seminary of Medieval Studies, 1983); *Arcipreste de Talavera,* edited by Ciceri, Colección Austral, no. 95 (Madrid: Espasa-Calpe, 1990).

**Edition in English:** *Little Sermons on Sin,* translated by Lesley Byrd Simpson (Berkeley: University of California Press / London: Cambridge University Press, 1959)–omits book 4 and the epilogue.

*Atalaya de las corónicas* (begun in 1443)

**Manuscripts:** Eight manuscripts are extant, four from the fifteenth century–one a fragment–and four from the eighteenth century. The one complete modern edition is based on the British Library's fifteenth-century codex, Egerton 287.

**Editions:** *Dos escritores de la Baja Edad Media castellana: Pedro de Veragüe y el Arcipreste de Talavera, cronista real,* edited by Raúl A. del Piero, Anejos del Boletín de la Real Academia Española, no. 23 (Madrid: Real Academia Española, 1971)–includes only the first ten chapters of the *Atalaya de las corónicas; Atalaya de las corónicas,* edited by James B. Larkin, Spanish Series, no. 10 (Madison, Wis.: Hispanic Seminary of Medieval Studies, 1983).

*Vida de San Ildefonso* and *Vida de San Isidoro,* attributed to Martínez (1444); St. Ildephonsus, *De perpetua virginitate sanctae Mariae contra tres infideles,* translation attributed to Martínez (ca. 1444)

**Manuscripts:** Three manuscripts of the life of St. Ildephonsus and the tract on the Virgin Mary survive; two also include the life of St. Isidore. The modern edition of the life of St. Ildephonsus is based on the Biblioteca de Menéndez y Pelayo codex 11 and that of St. Isidore on El Escorial codex b.III.1.

**Editions:** *San Ildefonso de Toledo a través de la pluma del Arcipreste de Talavera: Estudio y edición crítica de la

*Incipit of the first publication (1498) of Alfonso Martínez de Toledo's 1438 treatise* Arcipreste de Talavera
*(Biblioteca Nacional, Madrid; courtesy of Michael Agnew)*

*Vida de San Ildefonso y de la traducción del tratado* De perpetua virginitate sanctae Mariae contra tres infideles, edited by José Madoz y Moleres, Biblioteca de Antiguos Escritores Cristianos Españoles, volume 2 (Madrid: Consejo Superior de Investigaciones Científicas, Patronato "Raimundo Lulio," Instituto "Francisco Suárez," 1943); *Vidas de San Ildefonso y San Isidoro,* edited by Madoz y Moleres, Clásicos Castellanos, no. 134 (Madrid: Espasa-Calpe, 1952).

Alfonso Martínez de Toledo's best-known work is the *Arcipreste de Talavera* (Archpriest of Talavera, 1428), also known as the *Corbacho,* a title sometimes translated as *The Whip,* though it could also be translated as *The Scourge* or, perhaps better, as *The Pizzle.* This text includes sermonizing condemnations of lust and the sins he claims that it engenders, a misogynistic diatribe, a discussion of the medical theory of humors and the influence of heavenly bodies on human physiology, and an orthodox defense of the doctrine of free will, all of which is liberally peppered with grotesque caricatures, especially of women, and titillating tales of scandal. Martínez was also the author of the *Atalaya de las corónicas* (Watchtower of the Chronicles, begun in 1443), a history of Spain from the time of the Visigothic kings that, though less familiar today than the *Arcipreste de Talavera,* might be considered his magnum opus. His authorship of hagiographies of the seventh-century ecclesiastics St. Isidore of Seville and St. Ildephonsus of Toledo and of a translation of Ildephonsus's *De perpetua virginitate sanctae Mariae contra tres infideles* (On the Perpetual Virginity of Saint Mary Directed against Three Unbelievers) has been questioned.

Martínez's jaundiced view of the world and its words in the *Arcipreste de Talavera* affects his judgment of literary genres such as chivalric romance and historiographic prose, narrative forms that, despite their apparent differences, can be equally deceiving: they "a las vezes ponen *c* por *b*" (sometimes say *x* when they should say *y*). At the beginning of the *Arcipreste de Talavera* he calls into question the truth claims of autobiography as he explicitly identifies the title of his book with his own ecclesiastical title: "Sin bautismo sea por nombre llamado *Arcipreste de Talauera,* donde quier que fuere leuado" (Unbaptized, let it be called *Archpriest of Talavera* wherever it is carried). While the text is not properly an autobiography, since no sustained narrative connects its diverse parts, it relies on the authority of a first-person narrator whom one is led to identify with the author: he claims that he was a witness to some of the scandalous tales he reports; that he, too, has been guilty of sins that he never names; and—if one accepts Martínez's authorship of the last part of the book, considered spu-

rious by some scholars—that he underwent a conversion and repented of his diatribe against women. Martínez's opening statement marks the *Arcipreste de Talavera* as a product of fallen language in a fallen world, denied even the sacrament of baptism. In constructing his biography, however, scholars customarily turn to the *Arcipreste de Talavera* for information that apparently corroborates evidence in legal documents from Martínez's lifetime.

The opening lines of the book offer one of Martínez's few apparently unambiguous indications about his life: he says that the work was "compuesto por Alfonso Martínez de Toledo, arçipreste de Talauera, en hedat suya de quarenta annos, acabado a quinze de março anno del nascimiento del nuestro salvador Ihesu Xº de mil e quatroçientos e treynta e ocho annos" (composed by Alfonso Martínez de Toledo, Archpriest of Talavera, at the age of forty years, completed on the fifteenth of March, the year of the birth of our savior Jesus Christ fourteen hundred thirty-eight). He was, then, born in 1397 or 1398, assuming that he is not merely approximating his age—or misrepresenting it, a possibility that, in a book that exposes human vanity, should not be rejected as beyond the author's capacity for irony.

Scholars generally agree that Martínez was born in Toledo. He habitually refers to himself as "de Toledo"; also, at the end of El Escorial's sixteenth-century codex b.III.1 presumably derived from Martínez's own copy, following the life of Ildephonsus, he addresses the saint: "o çibdadano del çielo enperial Ildefonso de toledo natural ruega a Ihesu Christo eternal por mi alfon aunque non tal porque nasçí pecador donde tu fueste señor" (Oh, citizen of imperial Heaven, Ildephonsus native of Toledo, pray to Jesus the eternal Christ for me, Alfonso, though not comparable to you, because I was born a sinner where you were lord). Ildephonsus was archbishop—here, therefore, referred to as "lord"—of Toledo in the seventh century. Finally, a note in a manuscript of Guido delle Colonne's *Historia destructionis Troiae* (History of the Destruction of Troy, 1287) that was once owned by Martínez says: "Ego Alfonsus Martini archipresbiter Talaverensis domini nostri regis Joannis capelanus in decretis bachalaureus ac porcionarius ecclesiae Toletanae *eadem oriundus civitate* capelanus idemque capelae regis sancti" (I, Alfonso Martínez, Archpriest of Talavera, chaplain to our lord the king Juan [II], bachelor in canon law and prebendary of the Cathedral of Toledo, hailing from that same city, and likewise chaplain of the Chapel of King Sancho).

It is not known where Martínez obtained his bachelor's degree, which he mentions in the prologue to the *Arcipreste de Talavera.* He began serving as one of

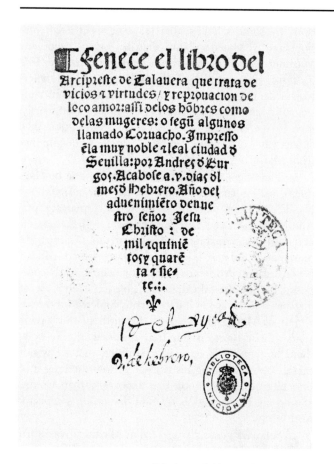

Colophon and title page from the 1547 Seville edition of the Arcipreste de Talavera
(Biblioteca Nacional, Madrid; courtesy of Michael Agnew)

twelve prebendaries in the Chapel of King Sancho in the Cathedral of Toledo in 1415, when he would have been only about seventeen; it was a significant post for someone so young, especially since it was under royal patronage. A document in the cathedral archives, signed by Martínez in 1415, indicates that he enjoyed a comfortable salary.

Martínez probably resided in the kingdom of Aragon during the two Barcelona earthquakes of 1427 and 1428, experiences he describes in the *Atalaya de las corónicas*. In the *Arcipreste de Talavera* he says that he has spent time in Tortosa, Valencia, and Barcelona; he seems to have known Barcelona well, for he refers to the refuse heap outside the city walls by its local name, *canyet*, and includes Catalan expressions for local color. In the *Atalaya de las corónicas* he claims that he witnessed earthquakes in 1420, which leads some scholars to speculate that he might have made more than one visit to Aragon and confused the later with the earlier. The earliest date that has been proposed for his first departure from Castile is 1419, and the latest date for his final return is 1430. It is likely that while

in Aragon he witnessed and perhaps participated in celebrations of Church feast days, which were notably more sumptuous in the eastern part of the Iberian Peninsula, with its vibrant tradition of liturgical theater. Late in his life Martínez helped to organize theatrical celebrations in Toledo.

One document exists pertaining to a suit Martínez filed in 1424 to obtain the post of archpriest of Talavera de la Reina, near Toledo. Another document indicates that he held the post at least as early as 1427. That document is a letter to Pope Martin V from a challenger for Martínez's post accusing Martínez of living with a woman, which would have been grounds for dismissal. In the introduction to his edition of the *Arcipreste de Talavera* E. Michael Gerli surmises that the accusation led Martínez temporarily to abandon Toledo for Aragon to avoid controversy. If this litigation was notorious, then Martínez's refusal to baptize his book and his repeated humble provisos regarding his status as a sinner would have been especially humorous for readers in the know and could have cast a highly ironic light on his vitriolic misogyny. In any case, Martínez retained his post; Gerli suggests that Martínez found it easy to defend himself owing to technical shortcomings in the petition. As archpriest, Martínez would have presided over a local ecclesiastical tribunal, governed the parish clergy under the authority of the bishop and archdeacon, and celebrated mass in the bishop's absence; all of these duties are described in the life of St. Isidore.

Erich von Richthofen claims that evidence exists that Martínez made a substantial contribution in 1427 toward the construction of the Monastery of St. Bernard; but the sixteenth-century history of Toledo he cites gives only the name "Alfonso Martínez" and mentions titles—cathedral treasurer and church warden—that no other document associates with Martínez de Toledo. According to Derek Lomax, the person referred to is probably Alfonso Martínez de Burguillos.

The thirties mark a successful period for Martínez in his ecclesiastical career. In 1430 or 1431 he obtained another benefice in the Toledo cathedral, though he soon had to defend it in litigation that, according to surviving documentation, was still unresolved in 1433. He seems to have gone to Rome in 1431 to plead his case before the Papal Curia; there he was under the protection of Juan de Casanova, cardinal of San Sixto, a former university professor in Aragon and the author of important theological works. Martínez spent two years in Rome; in 1432, while still there, he obtained an additional prebend from the Toledo cathedral, though he subsequently lost it to a rival. In December 1432 he received a prebend in the church of Santa María de Nieva in Segovia from Pope Eugenius IV. A deposition of 28 February 1433 gives his titles as archpriest of Talavera, chaplain of the Chapel of King Sancho, and prebendary of Santa María de Nieva and mentions several benefices in Toledo that he was then pursuing. His income was around 80 *libras*—a respectable sum, as Lomax observes.

Whether Martínez's Roman sojourn brought him into close contact with the humanist intelligentsia of Italy is unknown; his works reveal little, if any, humanist influence, though in Rome he would have had access to the erudition available in an important cleric's library and household. His link to the Aragonese cardinal Casanova suggests, however, that his most important intellectual influences outside of Castile may have been Catalan. Affinities between Martínez's work and that of the Franciscan preacher Francesc Eiximenis (1330–1409) have been shown, especially regarding Martínez's sympathy for Franciscanism. He might have known the Catalan translation of the works of Andreas Capellanus's late twelfth-century *De amore* (On Love), the third book of which provides the basis for the first two parts of the *Arcipreste de Talavera*, and to which he

refers frequently in that work. He might also have first encountered the writings of Giovani Boccaccio via Catalan translations.

Martínez left Italy in 1437, perhaps to disassociate himself from Casanova's conflict with the Pope when the former joined partisans of the Council of Basel; Casanova and Eugenius later reconciled. In 1434 Martínez rented property in perpetuity from the Toledo cathedral chapter for his living quarters. A document from the Cathedral archive from 1443 confirms that he continued to pay this rent regularly, as do documents from the last decade of his life. He and another cleric lost their prebends in the Chapel of King Sancho in the mid 1430s for unknown reasons, but Eugenius restored them in 1436. A document from that year refers to Martínez as King Juan II's chaplain; he refers to himself by this title in the prologue to the *Arcipreste de Talavera* and in the prologue to the *Atalaya de las corónicas* in 1443. This post and the royally funded prebend he obtained in his youth suggest that Martínez enjoyed some political prominence in Castile. Though his persistent efforts at obtaining ecclesiastical benefices might give the impression that he was a social climber, his family probably already enjoyed significant social connections. In the absence of information on his parentage, however, any judgments about his origins remain speculation—including whether he was illegitimate, as Lesley Byrd Simpson, who translated the *Arcipreste de Talavera* into English in 1959, has suggested.

Martínez reports that he completed the *Arcipreste de Talavera* on 15 March 1438. Only one manuscript survives, prepared by Alonso de Contreras in 1466 and later owned by Queen Isabel the Catholic, but the *Arcipreste de Talavera* was circulating in printed form as early as 1498. The early printed versions include significant additions, and scholars have debated whether Martínez was responsible for them. The longest and most controversial addition is the humorous concluding palinode known as the "Demanda" (Request [for forgiveness]), in which the narrator apologizes to women for having slandered them. There is some dispute over the significance of a partial date found in this epilogue. Christine J. Whitbourne argues that "año octavo a diez de setiembre" (eighth year, on the tenth of September) means 1468, and therefore the "Demanda" would not be Martínez's, since a retraction after so many years would be pointless. The "eighth year" could, however, refer to 1438; in that case, the manuscript either eliminates the epilogue or derives from an earlier version that lacks it. A reference in the "Demanda" to the narrator's old age might seem to indicate that more than a few months had passed before the composition of the epilogue; but the allegation can be taken lightly, since it is an insult spoken by an

*First page of the prologue from the only surviving manuscript for the* Arcipreste de Talavera, *copied by Alonso de Contreras in 1466. It includes Martínez de Toledo's statement that his inspiration for the work was a compendium composed by a Parisian doctor named Juan de Aussim (Copyright © Patrimonio Nacional, Madrid; courtesy of Michael Agnew).*

enraged woman who assaults the narrator physically in the nightmare recounted in the "Demanda."

Though the proper title of the work is *Arcipreste de Talavera,* the earliest surviving printed edition suggests it was "segund algunos llamado coruacho" (according to some called *Corbacho*). This title, which appears in some subsequent editions, was probably inspired by perceived affinities between the *Arcipreste de Talavera* and Boccaccio's *Corbaccio* (The Old Crow, circa 1354), especially the misogyny of the two works, though evidence that the *Corbaccio* served as a direct source for Martínez is slim at best. The alternate title was also a word in Castilian, and readers unaware of Boccaccio's text would have assumed that *corbacho* meant "pizzle-whip" or "scourge"—meanings consistent with the treatise's moralizing tone.

The title with which Martínez christens his work would seem to confer on it the authority of the pulpit. His refusal to "baptize" the book, however, points to the origin and participation of the text in a fallen world–like its author, who, as the first-person narrator, insists on his own status as a sinner. Of course, it would be preposterous to baptize a book, an inanimate object lacking free will–a faculty of the soul that preoccupies Martínez throughout the *Arcipreste de Talavera* but most explicitly in part 4. According to Christian theology, free will allows humans to choose between good and evil and, after baptism and with divine grace, to escape the corruption of a postlapsarian world. Logically, then, free will also enables the reader to choose between moral and immoral interpretations. In this light, Martínez's facetious incipit has significant implications for the interpretation of a text laden with pitfalls for unwary readers: if the author and what he writes are both symptomatic of a fallen world, how can a reader use his text as a moral guide? Martínez's first words constitute an unambiguous *caveat lector* (let the reader beware).

The prologue also appears to state its author's purpose in unambiguous terms. It reflects the influence of the medieval academic prologue, the *accessus ad auctores,* indicating the author's name and academic degree and the work's subject matter, genre ("un compendio breve" [a brief compendium]), intention, projected audience, and structure. The book is allegedly for the inexperienced, who can commit it to memory and "ponerlo en obra" (put it into practice)–a phrase whose ambiguity almost escapes notice. Unlike Juan Ruiz, archpriest of Hita, who allows that his mid-fourteenth-century *Libro de buen amor* (Book of Good Love) might serve as a lovers' guide, Martínez never proposes that the reader adopt the corrupt ways of the characters in the *Arcipreste de Talavera.* Presumably he means "put into practice the book's moral intent," but the *Arcipreste de Talavera* is

clearly testing its readers' interpretive skills. Martínez's reasons for addressing only the inexperienced also should raise a few eyebrows. The worldly-wise have no need for advice, he claims, since their knowledge already guards them from wickedness. Yet, the portraits of pertinacious sinners in his compendium suggest that knowledge of the world hardly guarantees protection from its lures.

The narrator says that he will divide his book into four parts, the first condemning *loco amor* (mad love), the second addressing the vices of women, the third describing human temperaments and their relationship to men's desires and desirability, and the fourth criticizing the attribution of events and people's characters to fate or astrological influences, which is frequently used as justification for lust. The prologue assumes the guise of a sermon, revealing the influence of *artes praedicandi* (guidebooks to preaching) that is also apparent especially in the first two parts of the *Arcipreste de Talavera.* Martínez announces his *thema* (the subject of his sermon, from scripture) by paraphrasing Matthew 22:37: "Amarás a tu Dios, tu criador e senior, sobre todas las cosas" (You will love your God, your creator and lord, above all things), an idea he will defend by exhortation and example. His tone here is apocalyptic: the Final Judgment must be near, since so many yield to the vice of *amor desordenado* (disordered love), an epidemic that leads to discord, scandal, crime, murder, and war. His readers should, therefore, flee idle conversation with the other sex and lustful, evil-speaking company. Nonetheless, he promises to give plentiful examples of such wicked speech–always, of course, to condemn it, for to speak ill of the wicked is to praise the good.

Martínez explains that his inspiration was another compendium condemning love by a certain Parisian *doctor,* that is, a holder of the highest university degree. The Contreras manuscript calls him Juan de Aussim; the name is still unidentified and is probably a scribal error. Early editions, beginning with the Toledo edition of 1500, read "Juan Gerçon": Jean de Gerson (1363–1429) was a French theologian whose writings share certain affinities with the *Arcipreste de Talavera* but who does not appear to have written such a compendium. Scholars have long recognized Martínez's debt to Andreas's twelfth-century *De amore.* The first two books of the *Arcipreste de Talavera* are clearly an *amplificatio* (expansion) of the last part of *De amore,* a palinode titled "De reprobatione amoris" (Condemnation of Love) in which Andreas rejects the earthly love he describes in the first two parts; but it is difficult to explain "Juan de Aussim" as a scribal error for "Andreas" or some variant of that name.

*Page from the manuscript for the* Arcipreste de Talavera, *showing the date on which the copy was completed and the name of the scribe, Contreras (Copyright © Patrimonio Nacional, Madrid; courtesy of Michael Agnew)*

Still, the connection between Andreas and Martínez is undeniable. The first eighteen chapters of part 1 correspond closely to the first half of "De reprobatione amoris." Above all, "mad love" displeases God; furthermore, it occasions every form of social and personal calamity: wars, murders, and offenses against one's neighbor; fear in the lover and hatred of parents, relatives, and friends; a sullied reputation; madness; dishonesty and criminality; corruption among clerics and laity alike; evil thoughts; destruction of cities; broken marriages; physical weakness; folly in the learned; and ultimate deception, for a woman's love is always false. Martínez adds to Andreas's warnings that love incites the violation of the Ten Commandments; leads to the commission of every sin and the loss of every virtue; corrupts the five senses and disturbs the three faculties of the soul—memory, understanding, and will; in short, it is the fount of all wickedness. In chapter 15 the Archpriest claims that it would be indecent to continue speaking of women's ways. Nevertheless, in chapter 24 women play the chief roles in the titillating crimes the Archpriest describes. One beautiful assassin's wickedness was so great, he claims, that even in death she wrought evil by provoking necrophilia in her executioner. He reports three other scandalous crimes that occurred in Aragon while he was there: one woman arranged her son's murder because he threatened to reveal her adultery, another castrated her husband out of jealousy, and yet another bit off her husband's tongue. Subtle readings of the Archpriest's misogyny are possible: the necrophiliac executioner is said to have suffered "*deshonra*" (dishonor), a term routinely applied to a female rape victim. Clearly, Martínez is being ironic, though the implications of his irony are open to interpretation.

Despite the alleged indecency of the subject, Martínez dedicates all of the blatantly misogynistic part 2 to a discussion of women, a discussion likewise inspired by Andreas's "De reprobatione amoris." Instead of Andreas's purely third-person description of women, however, Martínez invents long monologues spoken by female characters, vivid imitations of vulgar speech uttered by sharp-tongued caricatures intended to incite audience members' imaginations—despite having warned his audience to shun "vanas imaginaciones" (vain imaginings) and foul speech that incite wickedness and lust. He enumerates the "viçios e tachas e malas condiçiones de las malas e viçiosas mugeres, las buenas en sus virtudes aprovando" (vices and defects and evil ways of wicked and vicious women, approving of the good women in their virtues); the Archpriest will, however, say virtually nothing about the "good women" in his diatribe. To illustrate his claim that women are gossipy slanderers, he depicts spiteful

women exposing other women's concealment of their physical and moral defects, monologues that, in turn, expose the speakers' own moral shortcoming, envy. Women are greedy and covetous and fill their cabinets with jewels and cosmetics instead of devotional books. Women cannot be silenced—a charge repeated several times. Women are inconstant, yielding to others' whims like impressionable wax; yet, paradoxically, they are also manipulative, deceiving with gestures and words, a contradictory idea that exposes the Archpriest himself to the accusation of inconstancy. Women are disobedient, haughty, and so vain they will borrow others' clothing to strut about town. Women are liars, hypocrites, and given to drunkenness.

Part 2 also contains several famous narratives: four brief exemplary tales in chapter 7 tell of women whose husbands mete out unpleasant punishments for disobedience; two of whom use deception, provoking their wives' curiosity so that the women fall into traps that make them appear responsible for their own deaths, thereby tacitly revealing that men, too, are capable of deceit. Chapter 10 presents four tales of adulteresses who conceal their lovers, but the Archpriest curtails such talk lest he provide wanton women with useful advice.

Another example from part 2 is the Archpriest's claim that nuns are the most inconstant women of all, but—against his pen's wishes, he says—he will ignore them, for, confined in convents by their superiors, they lack a will of their own. Though he earlier refused to baptize an inanimate object (his book), he here grants his plume an independent will but denies it to women religious, thus calling into question the orthodoxy (or seriousness) of this preacher.

Roberto J. González Casanovas, in his 1995 study, and Catherine Brown, in her two articles on the *Arcipreste de Talavera,* both point out how the Archpriest's verbose monologue thwarts the orderly presentation of his moralizing message, and Brown in particular characterizes part 2 as verbal cross-dressing, since Martínez's narrator assumes the voices of the stereotyped women he derides. Like his vain caricatures, he seems to strut gleefully in borrowed "clothes," flaunting the same theatricality of which he accuses women. He himself seems guilty of slanderous yammering, of taking delight in speaking ill of women. If women are double-edged swords, as he claims, the narrator seems to be one, as well. For example, good words, he says at the end of part 2, are scorned nowadays, while "maldezir es gloria delectable; esto sea—quanto a mí—escusaçión, por quanto sé bien que sí dixe, que de mí ha de ser dicho" (speaking ill is sweet glory; this is my justification [for writing a book so critical], because as I have spoken I know I will be spoken of in turn). The Archpriest's

## Quarta parte

la vejez/ oy en sta dia:q̃ nr̄o señor todo lo
que hiziste/ fazes τ faras: vee τ da tiépo
E cada instante lee enel hymno dlas lau
des dala feria. v. Catad q̃ la luz se leua
ta. Enel postrimero verso/ dize. catad q̃
la atalaya esta sobre vosotros: el q̃l en
todos vuestros dias todos vr̄os fechos
cósidera/ τ catad el comiéço dla luz ha
sta la tarde q̃riédo dezir desde la virtud
fasta el vicio/o desdel bié fecho/q̃ es luz
fasta el mal hecho q̃ es tiniebla τ noche
scuridad τ tarde. Assi q̃ nr̄o señor todo
lo vee. pero espera correctió / τ emienda
a tiépo a vezes largo a vezes breue:segú
que su diuinal puidécia. Por esso dizen
muchos / o q̃ buen juez es nr̄o señor / si
no fuesse por dos cosas. La pmera que
no ay apelació de su sentécia. La segúda
que es muy vagaroso τ muy tarde faze
sus esecuciões q̃ querria el óbre/o la mu
ger: q̃ luego que otro le faze mal/o daño
q̃ luego le diesse. enesse púto la pena sin
mas tardar. Nuestro señor pues cóside
ra q̃ algúos son enel múdo q̃ avn q̃ pue
den τ poderio tiené no dá pena luego q̃
gela meresce: q̃ antes espera correctió. có
sidera τ pmite q̃l malo sea herido dl ma
lo/alas vezes en puericia/juuétud máce
bia:o vegedad. Cósidera pues q̃ barue
ro tienes: τ q̃ te has por fuerça cóel de a
feytar. Haue temor porende q̃ te no ra
pe en seco/q̃l apretar delos diétes te sera
por demas. E no digo mas: entiendelo si
querras: si no arrepétir te has. Porende
no te marauilles: si tu eres punido delos
males por ti cometidos enlos passados
tiépos/cada q̃ le a el plaze q̃ere τ por bi
en tiene. Vee tu aq̃ pues dos razões por
las q̃les no te deues marauillar: porque
los males: las muertes: las ocasiones: τ
daños viené alas vezes subitos τ arre
batados. Poréde dauid nos cóseja muy
bien. Onde dize enel penultimo psalmo.
Dios delos dioses hablo: τ llamo la tie
rra. Dize el verso: enteded bié vosotros
los q̃ oluidades a dios/q̃ alguna vez no

vos arrebate: τ no aya quié vos defien
da. en otro lugar dize enla leyenda delas
virgines enel euágelio. Velad/velad a
migos: por quáto no sabeys el dia ni la
hora q̃ nr̄o señor ha deuenir. el qual nr̄o
señor alas vezes viene : como toruillino
arrebatado τ muy adesora τ descuyda
do/porende velad amigos/ velad. Ple
ga a nr̄o señor poderoso jesu xpo: icarna
do pmogenito engendrado por la pala
bra de dios padre en aq̃l virginal viétre
dela su reuereda τ bédicta madre que a
si velemos τ nos apercibamos: τ del ene
migo sathanas nos guardemos τ delos
vicios nos corijamos: τ delos peccados
en bien nos emendemos. paq̃ quando a
quel glorioso jesu xpo : las sus diuinales
bodas quisieren recebir q̃ nos halle vela
do. E apercebidos con nuestras cande
las encendidas : que son las consciéscias
nuestras en jesu xpo: en aquella fiesta tá
marauillosa: τ en aquel cóbite tan preci
oso/ de aquellas tan sanctas τ bédictas
bodas / dela gloria de parayso para sié
pre jamas. Amen.

## El auctor faze fin ala pre
sente obra: τ demáda pdó si en algo delo
q̃ ha dicho ha enojado/o no bié dicho.

Aquellos a quien natura d
sus bienes dotó: τ amor sié
pre áso dar fauor τ gozo: q̃
oyá de su amigo mi breue
tal o q̃l epistola óderezco: a
los q̃les paz τ salud sea otorgada con a
mor de aq̃llas/ en cuyo disfauor dl todo
puesto so. hermanos en jesu xpo. Yo pues
forçado houe d ocupar mi entédimiéto é
diuersas τ muchas ymaginaciões : si me
jor me seria tal disfauor/ auiédo pseguir
lo começado continuando es pposito/o
nueuaméte buscar paz τ buena cócordia
de aq̃llas q̃ siépre matá sin cuchillo ni es
pada: τ tormentan a quien quieren sin q̃
beuan la toca. Pero si hauer q̃siere su a
mor τ querécia/ conuiene que al huego

*Final summary page from the 1498 edition of the* Arcipreste de Talavera
*(Biblioteca Nacional, Madrid; courtesy of Michael Agnew)*

ambiguity jeopardizes his intelligibility: he seems to be saying not that his "good" words will earn him others' scorn, but that he, like his characters, has engaged in *maldezir* and will, therefore, receive like treatment. The conclusion of part 2 seems to be as self-consciously ironic as the incipit.

The Archpriest promises to address men's vices in part 3, since it would be unseemly to condemn the love of women without disapproving of that of men. He proposes a fundamental difference between genders: women are reducible to general rules, but men, because of their superior intellect, resist stereotypical classification. Martínez discusses the four temperaments based on the ancient and medieval medical theory of humors derived from Galen and each temperament's corresponding zodiacal constellations: the sanguine man is a lively pleasure seeker and corresponds to Gemini, Aquarius, and Libra; the choleric is irascible and violent, corresponding to Aries, Leo, and Sagittarius; the moody phlegmatic man's signs are Cancer, Scorpio, and Pisces; the gloomy melancholic's are Taurus, Virgo, and Capricorn. Each sign influences a certain part of the body, which can thus be read for aspects of a man's character.

Every man reflects a mixture of these influences, and the Archpriest confesses that the diversity of corporeal signs is too varied for him to catalogue. To make matters worse, the same forces that produce men's physiological complexity also influence women—who are supposedly subject to general rules. The highly reductionist *Arçipreste de Talavera* thus again confronts the reader with the impossibility of reductionism, as it did in the prologue when the Archpriest asserted women's wiles were too numerous to count.

Part 3 offers further contradictions. The narrator's promised equanimity in condemning vice in both men and women proves halfhearted. Though his implied audience is now potentially female—"vean . . . qué virtudes, qué viçios tienen para amar los ombres" (let [women] contemplate what virtues and vices men have for loving)—he cannot forsake his favorite topic from part 2. Accordingly, the Archpriest criticizes the choleric man but also condemns his mistress for having incited him to attack another man who rejected her advances; he likewise criticizes the folly of women who abandon their families for the sanguine man's false love.

In this way an apparently unambiguous compendium of scientific knowledge becomes testimony to the difficulty of interpreting corporeal and heavenly signs. Constrained by such limitations, this initial, orderly exposition devolves into exemplary digressions warning about the moral defects of men so that women, presumably, can best judge how to react to them. In this way, González Casanovas argues, part 3 prepares read-

ers for the Archpriest's discussion of free will in part 4. From humoral and celestial determinism he turns to the problem of moral action, reinserting his treatise into the realm of the ethical: men's enemies are not only the Devil, the world, and women—a category Martínez substitutes for the traditional "body"—but, more important, their own "voluntad desordenada" (disordered will).

Part 4, perhaps the most problematic, demands the greatest stamina from modern readers. Some modern editions call it "Media Parte" (Middle Part) because of the manuscript abbreviation "*mjª*"—which appears, however, to be Contreras's misreading of *iiijª*, the abbreviation for "fourth." Martínez divides it into three long chapters that contrast with the manageable size of the earlier chapters. The Archpriest reaffirms with typical scholastic arguments the compatibility of free will with divine omniscience and condemns popular notions that ascribe earthly events to the influence of the stars, refining his statements in part 3. He claims that such influences are limited and that the free will of human beings and of God is the true determinant of their characters and actions. Celestial influences are physical, never moral. Attempts to read the future in the stars are vain, for though God determines their movements, his will is—the Archpriest adds in a characteristically sexist comparison—more inscrutable than that of any man's mistress. The truly pious never question God's order and accept that apparently wicked people might prosper while the seemingly good suffer, for only God can know who is truly evil or good and who merits reward.

The idea that people's true characters and piety cannot be judged leads the Archpriest to rail against men he calls *bigardos* (beghards, the masculine of Beguines, a name originally referring to members of thirteenth-century male lay brotherhoods in Low Countries, in imitation of the Beguines, but which came to mean pejoratively "heretics" or "sodomites") in what can only be termed, however anachronistically, a homophobic tirade. He maintains that these alleged archsimulators conceal the most abominable vices behind false piety, though their worst offense seems to be assuming falsified identities. He posits two types, one desiring to carry out the "acto varonil" (virile act) with other men, the other acting "como fembrezillas en sus desordenados apetitos" (like little hussies in their disordered appetites) and desiring men more powerfully than women desire them; both are signs of the Apocalypse. Amid repeated refusals to speak further of them, he returns to the beghards as if obsessed, alternately labeling them woman-haters who court young men, hypocritical backbiters who are worse than heretics, effeminates who powder their faces and speak like women (uttering, incidentally, exactly the same exclamations as the Archpriest in his own imitations of

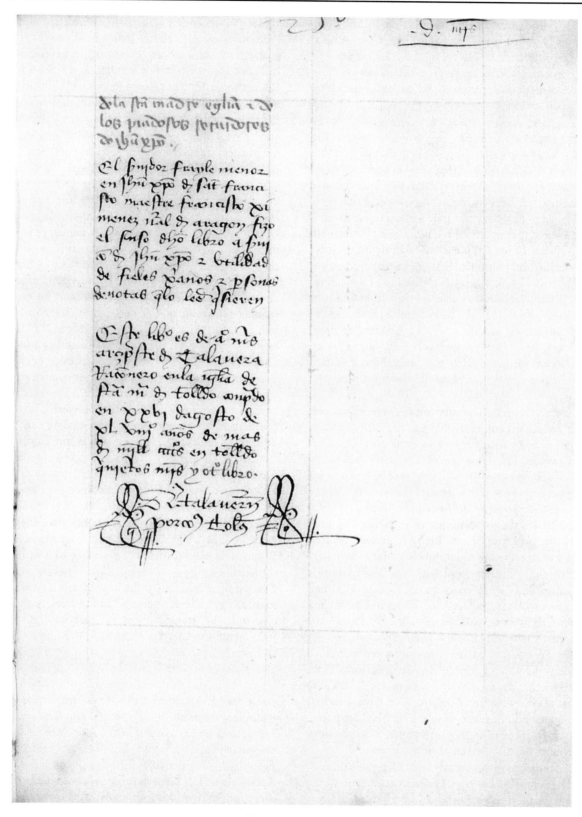

*Page from Martínez de Toledo's copy of the fourteenth-century Franciscan preacher Francesc Eiximenis's* Libro de las donas, *with a statement of ownership and Martínez de Toledo's signature (Copyright © Patrimonio Nacional, Madrid; courtesy of Michael Agnew)*

women), pursuers of beautiful women under pious pretenses, and frequenters of feminine company who despise that of men. The passage is, obviously, confused at best; the Archpriest's powers of representation seem to fail him, and it is hard to imagine what sort of men he is portraying. Furthermore, the beghards evoke his own literary persona: he condemns them above all for their inveterate simulation; yet, as Brown points out in her two essays on the *Arcipreste de Talavera,* the Archpriest himself seems guilty of the same vice when he claims to imitate authentic female voices.

Despite the general thematic austerity of part 4, the Archpriest cannot resist the temptation to relate sensationalist tales. The most emblematic is that of a sacrilegious Valencian hermit who was executed for commissioning an irreverent portrait of Christ for his private impieties. Like the beghards, the hermit poses the problem of the limits of representation—what can and cannot be licitly imitated or portrayed. The painting of a devil abusing Christ is unspeakably foul, according to the Archpriest, who nonetheless, as Brown argues, conjures up a foul image precisely by means of the unspeakability topos: at this point in the *Arcipreste de Talavera* readers schooled in the Archpriest's rhetoric no longer need racy narratives to incite their imaginations.

In chapter 2, after censuring allegorical representations of death as a skeleton and criticizing ignorant people who believe such images portray an actual animate entity with powers over humans—an error similar to believing that the stars hold power over the soul—the Archpriest appears to bring his treatise to an abrupt conclusion. Some critics regard this sudden ending as proof that he wrote part 4 in two stages, completing chapter 2 and adding chapter 3 in a later revision. This "conclusion" may be facetious, however: in chapter 3 he ignores two more promises to stop preaching, thereby ironically calling attention to his own verbosity. As if to add further confusion, having condemned the deceptiveness of allegorical representations of death, Martínez adapts an allegorical tale from Boccaccio's *De casibus virorum illustrium* (On the Fates of Famous Men, 1360) to demonstrate that Fortune (or Fate) has no power over humans. Martínez portrays the figures of Fortune and Poverty with a vividness that is lacking in Boccaccio's version, his allegorical characters echoing the speech of the caricatures of part 2. The Archpriest thus seems to complicate the representational status of the female characters of part 2, making his explicitly fictional allegorical characters here analogous to the allegedly true portraits of reality earlier in the book. Significantly, triumphant Poverty, after trampling haughty Fortune, concludes the chapter by preaching against undisciplined tongues.

In chapter 3 the Archpriest reiterates that sins proceed only from errant human will and not from celestial influences. He then ends his work by invoking the Final Judgment and urging his audience to assume responsibility for their sins, since God is omniscient and demands accountability. Imitating Andreas's conclusion, Martínez cites Matthew 25:1–13, exhorting his audience to keep their lamps lit in anticipation of the Bridegroom's arrival. As one would expect in a sermon, then, the *Arcipreste de Talavera* ultimately focuses on the audience, placing responsibility for their actions squarely on their shoulders; likewise, readers are responsible for their interpretations of the text.

Unlike the manuscript, the early printed editions do not end here but with the "Demanda." A mock epistle, the epilogue opens with a parody of St. Paul's letters: the Archpriest wishes his "hermanos en Jesucristo" (brothers in Christ) peace, health, and the love of women, an earthly love that is clearly incompatible with the "peace" that St. Paul wishes for his fellow Christians. The Archpriest asks his readers to condemn his book to the flames, a change of heart provoked by a dream in which a multitude of women drubbed him with distaffs and slippers while accusing him of hypocrisy for having once delighted in their company and now presuming to scorn love. One woman, in a scene that recalls the scuffle between Poverty and Fortune, steps on his throat, forcing out his tongue—the organ of preaching—as he gasps for air. On waking, he decides to renounce his work and beg women's forgiveness.

Ciceri insists in her two editions that the "Demanda" is apocryphal, since it contradicts the Archpriest's moralizing message; but other scholars, finding logic in the irony in the "Demanda," allow that it could be Martínez's work. Richthofen suggests that it was a sincere attempt by the author to assuage an outraged female readership. Jacob Ornstein claims that the "Demanda" is a response to Queen María's indignation at the book. Gerli, in the introduction to his edition and in his monograph, understands the epilogue to reaffirm the Archpriest's basic theses by again portraying women as domineering and vain in forcing a false retraction, even though they do so only in a dream. Marina Scordilis Brownlee, finally, views the epilogue as the last and most egregious case of programmatic self-contradiction in the work. The *Arcipreste de Talavera* thus proves to be "anti-Augustinian": portraying the author's failed conversion in its final pages, it seemingly denies redemptive readings—unlike St. Augustine's *Confessions* (written 397–401), the effectiveness of which depends on the capacity of a self-referential sermon to convert an errant reader.

In another sense, however, the *Arcipreste de Talavera* is firmly Augustinian: in insisting on the doctrine of free will, the epilogue serves as a final test of the reader's moral judgment, stating in ironic terms what Martínez repeated ad nauseam at the end of part 4. Whether or not Martínez wrote the palinode is unverifiable and, within the audience-centered logic of part 4, ultimately insignificant. Even if a shrewd contemporary wrote it, however, the "Demanda" is an integral part of the early printed editions and must be taken into consideration.

The ambiguity of the *Arcipreste de Talavera* leaves it open to several interpretations. Martínez may be a moralizing fanatic who unwittingly exposes his own contradictory reasoning in his very fanaticism. Or he may simply be a jocular figure exposing society's foibles. He may be a pragmatic physician who cures lovesickness through discourse. Or he may, like Juan Ruiz, have created an elusive author figure who does not present the opinions of the real author but exposes shortcomings in the readers, who are, according to Christian theology, sinners—like the narrator himself—who are perhaps too easily titillated by sensationalist tales even though they are couched in a moralizing sermon. If this last possibility is the case, then Martínez's treatise is quite different from the *Libro de buen amor:* while Juan Ruiz's Archpriest is openly ambiguous in his condemnation—or celebration—of earthly love, this Archpriest unambiguously denounces "disordered love."

Despite the treatise's fascinating contradictions, modern critics have until only recently skirted the thornier issues it raises, traditionally focusing instead on stylistic elements—especially the imitations of popular speech, which have led some scholars anachronistically to label the book "realist." Critics typically distinguish two registers in the *Arcipreste de Talavera:* one colloquial and the other, with its syntactic and lexical Latinisms, formal. Following Martínez's cue, however, one can delineate at least three discursive levels: speaking of illegitimate children, he says that they are "en derecho *espurios* llamados, e en romance *bastardos,* e en común bulgar de mal desir e fablar *fijos de mala puta*" (called in the language of the jurists *spurious,* in Castilian *bastards,* and in the vulgar expression of vicious speech *children of vile whores*). Martínez's tripartite division allows for an intermediate level, corresponding to his typically conversational style—neither crass, like the monologues, nor excessively formal—that is accessible to an audience without training in Latin or specialized legal and scientific knowledge.

Nonetheless, Martínez's ample use of vernacular speech probably surprised and amused contemporary readers and no doubt accounts for the continued popularity of his work in the sixteenth century. If the *Arcipreste de Talavera* was composed for a courtly audience, it would have stood out from the ornate prose in vogue during Juan II's reign. Martínez's text emphasizes orality, since it imitates preaching—especially popular sermons, with their typical rhetorical questions and exhortations addressed to an unspecified "tú" (the singular and familiar form of "you"). Also, the book was probably often read aloud to groups of listeners. Nonetheless, the Archpriest's vulgarisms seem excessive, especially given the courtly audience presumed by the opening lines of the text. An oft-cited example is the episode of the woman lamenting a lost egg:

¿Qué se fizo este huevo? ¿Quién lo tomó? ¿Quién lo levó? ¿A dó le este huevo? Aunque vedes que es blanco, quizás negro será oy este huevo. Puta, fija de puta, dime: ¿quién tomó este huevo? ¡Quién comió este huevo comida sea de mala ravia: cámaras de sangre, correncia mala le venga, amén! ¡Ay huevo mío de dos yemas, que para echar vos guardava yo! . . . ¡Ay huevo mío, qué gallo e qué gallina salieran de vos! Del gallo fiziera capón que me valiera veinte maravedises, e la gallina catorze!

(What has happened to that egg? Who took it? Who carried it off? Where is that egg? Though you'd think it was white, it's black with rotten luck today. Whore and daughter of a whore, tell me, who stole my egg? May the woman who ate that egg be eaten by rabies! May she catch a case of the bloody runs, may something nasty happen to her, amen! Oh, my double-yolked egg, I was saving you to hatch. . . . Alas, my egg, what a cock and what a hen would have hatched from you! The cock I would have made a capon worth twenty *maravedís;* the hen would have been worth fourteen!)

The speech goes on for a whole page and is followed immediately by a monologue in a similar tenor and twice as long about a lost hen. Nor is the popular speech of the monologues absent from the Archpriest's own discourse, which is peppered with proverbs and a colorful colloquial vocabulary.

Alongside this ostensibly unadorned popular style, however, Martínez incorporates formal ornaments typical of academic sermons: assonantal rhymes in his prose, hortatory exclamations, anaphora, polysyndeton, and Latinisms such as ellipsis of copula, abundant present participles, clauses ending in verbs, and *hyperbaton* (a figure of speech, using deviation from normal or logical word order to produce an effect). His treatise is a carefully fashioned rhetorical object, and his allegedly realistic portrayals of women, crafted as memorable exempla, are as highly rhetorical as the rest of the compendium. Curiously, however, as Ciceri has shown in her article on exempla in the *Arcipreste de Talavera,* his portraits often cannot logically be of a singular character or situation. For example, in the monologue

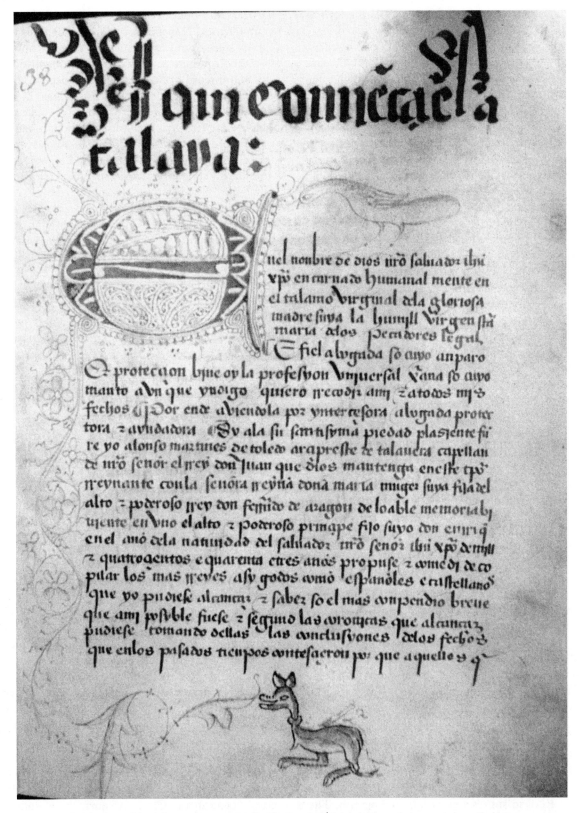

*Incipit of one of the eight extant manuscripts for Martínez de Toledo's* Atalaya de las corónicas, *the history of Spain that he began in 1443 (Madrid, Biblioteca de Palacio Real; courtesy of Michael Agnew)*

on the lost hen, the woman first describes the fowl as "la ruvia de la calça bermeja" (yellow, with red legs), then as "la de la cresta partida, çenizienta escura, cuello de parón, con la calça morada (double-crested, dark gray, with a peacock's neck and purple legs), then again as yellow, then as "gruesa como un ansarón, morisca, de los pies amarillos, crestibermeja" (fat as a goose, Moorish, with yellow feet), and, finally, as yellow for the rest of the monologue. The Archpriest seeks exhaustiveness in his stereotypes, as if to cover every contingency, to make the totalizing discourse of exemplarity seem truly total. Of course, such exhaustiveness is impossible, and the monologues prove to be exercises in excess. This procedure contradicts the principle of exemplarity, according to which one type stands for all variants: there is no need for multiple varieties of hens to be used to make the preacher's point.

The Archpriest's prolixity thus becomes a running joke. Like the thrice-delayed ending of part 4, his unheeded promises not to speak of a topic so as to avoid windiness or because of moral scruples are too frequent not to be taken as a programmatic element in the *Arcipreste de Talavera*. The Archpriest invariably reveals himself as an able and eager talker. Perhaps his most amusing promise to avoid prolixity is his avoidance in part 1, chapter 36, of reproaching clerics and nuns for fear of enmity and slander, since he who reprehends should not himself merit reprehension, and the Archpriest is not entirely safe from criticism. His shunning of prolixity here seems to reveal the same vanity he condemns in women. Furthermore, he knows how upstanding clerics provoke rulers' anger when they speak the truth, and he concludes in an ironic appeal to exemplarity that "quien en ajena cabeça castigo digno es de loor" (he who learns from another's misfortunes merits praise). Nonetheless, he unabashedly continues preaching in the following chapter, the lengthiest in part 1. Michael Solomon may be correct in holding that Martínez's description of the *Arcipreste de Talavera* as a "brief compendium" indicates that he considered it a moral breviary, like a doctor's handy vade mecum; but the designation proves ironic, given the Archpriest's penchant for long-windedness. He comes perilously close to being a caricature of a prolix preacher, whether an "academic" or a "popular" one.

The Archpriest's tendency toward verbal excess affects the ostensibly orderly structure of the text. Filling 214 manuscript pages, it is too long for one sermon; it is more like a summa of sermons, as Sara Mañero Rodicio suggests in a 1997 monograph. The text eschews the systematic organization of a compendium by including too many digressions and apparent contradictions. Brownlee points out that the *Arcipreste de Talavera* recalls Andreas's *De amore*, which promises

a systematic enunciation of its material but is similarly contradictory. Nonetheless, Martínez deploys rhetorical elements that, in principle, convey order and coherence, despite the structural and linguistic diversity and discord of the text. For instance, the opening *thema*, "You will love your God," is echoed at the end of each part (except the "Demanda"), even if, as Mañero argues, *caritas* (charity) really becomes something more like *castitas* (chastity) or *continençia* (continence) in the Archpriest's parlance. Likewise, though he is hardly a figure of constancy, the Archpriest himself, the first-person preacher-narrator, remains throughout. In "Talavera's Imagery and the Structure of the *Corbacho*" (1980) Colbert Nepaulsingh suggests that the structure of the work is more symmetrical than meets the eye: part 1 and part 4 are each about as long as parts 2 and 3 combined, making the *Arcipreste de Talavera* subtly tripartite.

Whether the text satirizes a single consistent target is as debatable as whether it successfully portrays itself as unified and coherent. The earthly "disordered love" the Archpriest condemns comprises a spectrum of phenomena, from the sin of lust to lovesickness (the medieval medical condition of *amor hereos*) to courtly love. He denounces other vices, also.

Though it does not treat courtly practices exclusively, the *Arcipreste de Talavera* conceivably represented a literary "antidote" for the "excesses" of the refined erotic poetry fashionable in Juan II's court—especially poetry sacrilegiously praising courtiers' ladies. Martínez's occasional parodies of the courtly paramour reduce the poets' aestheticized love to the same basic impulse as lust. Perhaps the Archpriest's rejection of the influence of the stars or Fortune on the soul is, in part, a response to poetic commonplaces that justify in such terms lovers' allegedly inescapable submission to their ladies. Martínez also caricatures courtly lovers in the chapter on pride in part 1 and in describing the sanguine man in part 3. Gerli suggests in his 1976 monograph *Alfonso Martínez de Toledo* (1976) that Martínez was elaborating only on book 3 of Andreas's *De amore*, since he was aware that the first two were *ars amatoria* (manual of love) and were probably more popular in courtly milieus than the "De reprobatione amoris." (The Catalan translation of Andreas's book included only the first two parts.)

The Archpriest's misogyny should also be considered in its courtly context. Despite allegedly provoking Queen María's ire, the *Arcipreste de Talavera* heralds a literary vogue in the Castilian court: the so-called pro- and antifeminist debate, a literary game that constituted a sort of rhetorical contest among male members of courtly society. That a single individual—Boccaccio—could exemplify both sides of the debate in his bitterly "antifeminist" *Corbaccio* and in his eulogistic *De claris mulieribus* (On Famous Women, circa 1362) indicates the rhetorical artificiality of the dispute. Furthermore, sexist presuppositions underlie the arguments of both "sides," with male writers determining the praise- or blameworthiness of women.

Critics such as Whitbourne and Mañero qualify the Archpriest's misogyny by claiming that he denounces only wicked women and does not spare men from criticism, but the text does not fully support such a reading: the *Arcipreste de Talavera* dwells overwhelmingly on women, typically censuring woman as a universal class; the token allusions to virtuous women and sinful men are paltry by comparison. Most modern readers would perceive the work as overbearingly misogynist. Brownlee, on the other hand, acknowledges the misogyny of the text but casts doubt on its sincerity, given the sundry contradictions in the Archpriest's arguments, making the text a clever hermeneutical test. It may be for this reason that Isabel I seems to have found the work inoffensive enough that she owned the Contreras manuscript, though one wonders how she viewed the Archpriest's claim that no woman in power is trustworthy or, for that matter, how contemporary female audiences in general might have interpreted the text. One also wonders about the ideological connotations of the *Arcipreste de Talavera* in the context of royal propaganda that masculinized Isabel so as to legitimate her authority in a system based on male succession.

Solomon's simple pragmatic explanation of the Archpriest's misogyny has important sociocultural implications: the "brief compendium," like a physician's breviary, provided a discursive antidote to lovesickness, which was perceived in Martínez's time as a real illness. Martínez's text reflects the wide contemporaneous circulation in late medieval Europe of medical treatises and preachers' arts, the former attending to corporeal health, the latter to spiritual well-being. The Archpriest argues that lust encourages the loss of both soul and body through physical debilitation from depletion of bodily humors, producing blindness, loss of taste and smell, aging, and death. Misogynist discourse should, therefore, literally cure the lover's malady by making the object of his desire repellent, and contemporary medical treatises instructed physicians to use rhetoric as one of several cures for lovesickness. Martínez's text is not, however, simply a practical medical guide. Its moral complications make the Archpriest's role as physician—and as preacher—problematic, for he commits as much verbal excess as his female caricatures, as if he is trying to "cure" with the very poison he is condemning. If the *Arcipreste de Talavera* is a curative text, it leaves the ultimate responsibility for a remedy on the readers' shoulders.

Scholars have also debated Martínez's probable sources and influences. Mañero holds that the "Juan de Aussim" mentioned in the manuscript as Martínez's primary inspiration is Gerson, as indicated in the printed editions. She finds several thematic parallels, though no textual echoes, between Gerson's writings and the *Arcipreste de Talavera*: Gerson wrote sermons against lust, a condemnation of the bawdy courtly love allegory *Roman de la rose* (Romance of the Rose), and tracts on celestial influences and predestination. Also, unlike Andreas, who had no university degree and was not from Paris, Gerson was a renowned *doctor* from that city. Furthermore, Gerson, a disciple of William of Ockham, adopted aspects of nominalist thought. Given the problematic exemplarity of the *Arcipreste de Talavera*, which concedes that universal rules cannot easily be applied to humans, the notion that Martínez espoused nominalist tenets seems compelling.

The most important source, structurally and thematically, of the *Arcipreste de Talavera* is undeniably Andreas's *De amore* (though Martínez might have believed that Gerson wrote the "De reprobatione amoris"). Many of Martínez's citations of literary, scriptural, and scientific authorities derive from Andreas, such as his reference to "Joaniçio" (Johannitius, or Hunayn ibn Ishaq, the ninth-century translator of Galen's works). Brownlee proposes a specular relationship between the two works in which the *Arcipreste de Talavera*, with the "Demanda," becomes a complete reversal of the *De amore* by first condemning love and then retracting the condemnation.

Per Nykrog suggests a similar relationship between Martínez's compendium and Juan Ruiz's *Libro de buen amor*. In one manuscript the *Libro de buen amor* ends with the sad news, conveyed by an unnamed archpriest from Talavera, that the archbishop has ruled concubinage among ecclesiastics punishable by excommunication. Nykrog suspects that the *Arcipreste de Talavera* follows this lead, becoming the "De reprobatione amoris" to Juan Ruiz's amatory guidebook. Though Martínez seems to eschew Juan Ruiz's style of irony, his references to the *Libro de buen amor*, such as calling it a treatise, may constitute another wink at the reader.

Though Martínez was probably aware of Boccaccio's *Corbaccio*—the Toledo capitular library held a Tuscan codex of the work in the early fifteenth century—no evidence exists to indicate that it directly inspired the *Arcipreste de Talavera*. Martínez does adapt the description of women's cosmetics and the allegory of Fortune and Poverty from *De casibus virorum illustrium*, expanding both significantly. He may also have been familiar with the *Decameron* (1349–1351), the first tale of which shares an important thematic connection with the *Arcipreste de Talavera* in affirming that a sinner can be the vehicle for others' salvation.

Similarities between the *Arcipreste de Talavera* and works by Eiximenis, especially regarding predestination, are probably attributable to common Patristic sources. According to Mañero, however, Martínez's citations of such sources are indirect, via the Divine Office, and reflect sound ecclesiastical training but not a theologian's meticulousness. Likewise, though his knowledge of canon law appears adequate, he cites only readily accessible juridical compendia. His allusion to the astrological treatise *Secretum secretorum* (Secret of Secrets) is similarly imprecise. His occasional citations from the *Disticha Catonis* (Distichs of Cato) provide easily digestible moral wisdom from a popular book. Thus, despite reference to a Parisian *doctor* in the prologue, Martínez's treatise is not excessively bookish, and Mañero's proposal that he had his potential audience's tastes in mind is convincing.

Scholars know little about Martínez's historical audience. Mañero posits a courtly readership–Martínez was the king's chaplain–and the text would likely have appealed to such an audience without university training. Yet, university students and scholars also probably knew the *Arcipreste de Talavera,* given the interest in the topic of love in fifteenth-century academic circles. Ciceri, noting in the introduction to her 1990 edition that most of the characters in the *Arcipreste de Talavera* are townsfolk, supposes a bourgeois readership, which was undoubtedly the case once the text became more economically accessible by circulating in print.

Better conclusions can be reached regarding the implied audience of the book, though the fictional addressees of the book are not evoked with any rigorous consistency. The prologue implies a plural male audience that is ignorant of the ways of the world. When the Archpriest begins his sermon, however, he is clearly addressing a singular experienced male lover who is on the road to perdition. Later, the addressees' gender occasionally seems ambiguous. In part 3 the Archpriest explicitly addresses women to warn them of men's vices; elsewhere, he allows for a surreptitious female audience, such as when he ceases speaking of evil women's wiles so that other women who are casually listening in might not get ideas. The "Demanda" represents the most extreme break, for its male addressees are "aquellos a quien . . . amor siempre quiso dar favor e gozo" (those to whom . . . love has always granted favor and delight). Thus, in keeping with his affirmation that general rules insufficiently describe human beings, Martínez creates multiple

implied readers, and there is, therefore, no "universal" reader in the *Arcipreste de Talavera.*

Brownlee argues that the absence of a universal reader makes the Archpriest's claims of exemplarity highly problematic, since the Augustinian principle that the text can serve as a conversion paradigm for every reader fails. In this connection, Martínez's one clearly traceable citation of Augustine is telling. At the end of part 2 he laments that the ignorant assail heaven, while the wise plunge themselves into hell, an evocation of *Confessions* 8.8.19 immediately before Augustine's conversion in the garden, a moment of doubt before his transcendental experience. In the *Arcipreste de Talavera,* however, it inspires an unexpected plea of ignorance: the Archpriest is not wise, though he has presented himself as a moral guide; but the ignorant and even the wicked can offer sound advice if their words are heeded but their actions shunned. Augustine, in contrast, hopes that his readers follow both his words and his deeds.

This passage introduces part 3, which turns to scientific learning to understand men's behavior. Predictably, such knowledge proves insufficient. Martínez seems to suggest that learning cannot guarantee morality: thus, the stories in part 1 of Virgil and Aristotle being dominated by deceiving women call into question the capacity for *letrados* (lettered men), among whom Martínez prominently includes himself, to provide moral guidance–except, perhaps, as negative examples. The reader must wonder, then, if Martínez's wisdom can be trusted.

The *Arcipreste de Talavera* characterizes all signs–whether intentionally or involuntarily produced by humans or produced by nature–as fundamentally opaque. The reader must confront the ambiguous words of adulteresses deceiving their husbands or, as Ciceri points out in her 1983 article on body language, the false tears of a woman inciting her choleric lover. The Archpriest portrays women as emblematic deceivers with a "cara con dos fazes" (two-faced countenance). Yet, the narrator himself seems two-faced, as he participates in the same ambiguous signification. Early in the work he confronts this possibility in the ambiguous statement "Non digan que non fue muger el que lo compuso este compendio." The double negative, permissible in Martínez's time, should be translated as "Let no one think that this is a woman who wrote this compendium"; but the extra *non* does suggest, "Let no one think that this is *not* a woman. . . ." It is almost impossible not to think of both mutually exclusive meanings. He creates other equivoques with the phrase *poner en prática* (put into practice); *prática* is a fifteenth-century doublet for *plática* (conversation), so that the phrase also means to put into conversation, or speak of: "porque algunas cosas pongo en prática dirán que más es avisar

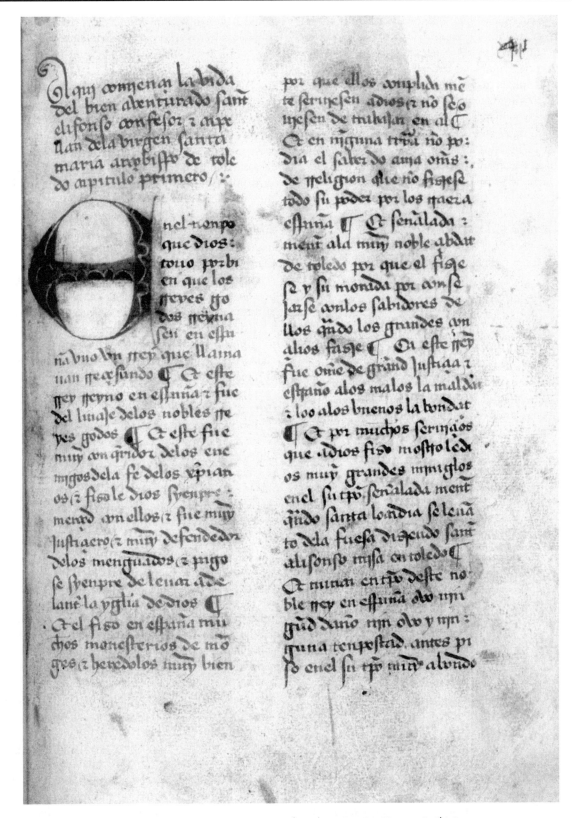

*Incipit of the* Vida de San Ildefonso *(1444), attributed to Martínez de Toledo*
*(Copyright © Patrimonio Nacional, Madrid; courtesy of Michael Agnew)*

en mal que corregir en bien" (since I speak of/put into practice certain things, people will say I advise evil rather than correct it). Such ambiguity, already encoded in the syntax and lexicon of fifteenth-century Castilian, is mirrored in his statement in part 1 that chastity is so virtuous that it can conceal other sins. If the Archpriest sounds like the flawed women of his sermon, he also implicates his readers. In a subtle rhetorical move, at the end of part 1 he makes his implied male reader a woman: introducing the topic of avaricious women, he warns, truncating a proverb that ends "entiéndeme tú, *hija*": "si algund *hombre* dello en sí algo sintiere, tome el enxemplo de 'A ti lo digo, nuera'"(if some *man* finds a little avarice in himself, let him observe the proverb, "I am speaking to you, daughter-in-law [but listen well, *daughter*]").

Only God, as Author of the universe, can evade participation in this fallen world; God likewise enjoys a perfect hermeneutic perspective as the only Reader who can see and know everything, unmediated by ambiguous language. God's perspective, Martínez warns apocalyptically at the conclusion of part 4, is that of the perfect *atalaya* (watchtower). Unlike the readers of the *Arcipreste de Talavera,* God knows every human's actions and intentions. Martínez himself adopts a similar, though more limited, narrative perspective in his historiographical work, the *Atalaya de las corónicas,* begun five years after the completion of the *Arcipreste de Talavera.*

The woefully understudied *Atalaya de las corónicas* reflects more-serious aspirations than those of the *Arcipreste de Talavera,* though Martínez characteristically incorporates entertaining elements into this work—which, like the *Arcipreste de Talavera,* he calls a "compendio breve." Juan II probably commissioned the *Atalaya de las corónicas,* though it is not addressed to him: Diego Enríquez del Castillo, the royal chaplain to Juan's son and successor, Enrique IV, was also the royal chronicler, and the ecclesiastical post may have entailed duties as royal propagandist. The *Atalaya de las corónicas* participates in the tradition known as Neogothicism, which is particularly associated with the House of Trastámara: ruling in Castile since the late fourteenth century, the Trastamaran monarchs sought self-legitimation through genealogical links to the Visigoths, who had ruled Iberia before the Moorish invasion of 711. Beginning with the first Visigoth, the *Atalaya de las corónicas* surveys the reigns of each ruler through the Castilian-Leonese dynasties to Enrique III, Juan II's father; a manuscript in the British Library includes the reign of Juan II, but Martínez probably did not write that chapter. In the prologue Martínez says that he began the *Atalaya de las corónicas* in 1443, though he does not say when—or if—he completed it. If the chapter on Juan II is his, Martínez

could have worked on it into the 1450s (Juan died in 1454). Isabel I owned one of the manuscripts.

The first word in the unusual title is typically translated as "Watchtower" but might also be rendered as "Vantage Point" or "Sentinel." The latter would mean that the *Atalaya de las corónicas,* like the *Arcipreste de Talavera,* refers to a person. The title suggests a privileged, quasi-omniscient perspective on history, or at least that of a shrewd compiler who has reduced the historiographic record to a basic, easily digestible structure. Also unusual for this period, when chronicles in the vernacular were typically anonymous, is the author's prominence in the text; Martínez marks the beginning of a trend in which chroniclers increasingly name themselves in their texts. In an opening similar to that of the *Arcipreste de Talavera* Martínez presents himself as author, and he intervenes frequently in the first person, reminding the audience that he is the compiler and is in careful control of the narrative.

Ideologically, the *Atalaya de las corónicas* responds to fifteenth-century Castilian monarchs' increasing claims to political hegemony in the Peninsula. The chronicle speaks little of other Iberian kingdoms, while frequently referring to "España" (Spain) as its subject matter. (Martínez's sources exhibit similar tendencies.) It aims to show the Castilian monarchy's antiquity and putative links to the Visigoths of Iberia's sixth and seventh centuries. The narrative is triumphalist: Pelayo, the first king of Asturias after the Moorish invasion and the supposed restorer of the Visigothic royal line, is "príncipe de la conversión de toda España e de la cristiandad della" (prince of the conversion [that is, the political and spiritual "restoration"] of all Spain and her Christian citizens), though he only ruled a small territory in the far north. Martínez describes the battle of Navas de Tolosa of 1212 in a similar vein, presenting the three Christian kings fighting the Moorish army as analogous to the Holy Trinity. The rapid review of history in the *Atalaya de las corónicas* is also providentialist, culminating implicitly in Juan II, who is named prominently in the prologue. A further ideological dimension of the *Atalaya de las corónicas* is its anti-Semitism, as in a passage alleging Jewish treachery in Toledo's fall to the Moors. One wonders how this passage might have been interpreted in the 1440s when, particularly in Toledo, there was widespread hostility toward *conversos* (Jewish converts to Christianity and their descendants).

The *Atalaya de las corónicas* appears to be a numerological composition based on the number thirty-three, Christ's age at his crucifixion. Each chapter records a single king's reign, and there is also a chapter on Muhammad, who is presented as the Devil's disciple. Pelayo, the initiator of what in historical hindsight and protonationalist propaganda became known as the

"Reconquest," is the thirty-third king in the Visigothic line in the *Atalaya de las corónicas*. He appears as a Christ figure, the redeemer of the corrupted Spain of his predecessor, King Rodrigo. Misssing from Martínez's catalogue are five early Leonese kings between Vermudo and Fruela, whom scholars suppose he inadvertently eliminated when switching sources. Martínez's erroneous list, however, makes Enrique III the thirty-second king after Pelayo and his son, Juan II, Martínez's patron, the thirty-third—a second Pelayo and a second redeemer, perhaps, for a politically troubled Castile. Significantly, Martínez does not narrate Juan's own political difficulties (if indeed he did not write the last chapter of the one manuscript that includes Juan II's reign). This arrangement suggests that Martínez did not carelessly omit material but, rather, intentionally manipulated his sources.

The structure of the chronicle is quite regular, though later chapters become progressively longer, presumably because Martínez had more source material. He consulted various chronicles that were probably accessible in the royal archives. The early chapters use the late-thirteenth-century *Estoria de España* (History of Spain), the composition of which Alfonso X (1221–1284) supervised, and possibly the *Crónica de veinte reyes* (Chronicle of Twenty Kings). For later reigns, beginning with that of Enrique I, he used material from several fourteenth-century royal chronicles; for the reigns of Pedro I to Enrique III he used those of López de Ayala. Martínez takes the greatest liberties in the early chapters, often adding direct discourse, including dialogue; he thereby enlivens the narrative and distances it from the monotonous parataxis typical of chronicles. Occasionally he elaborates an episode considerably, though the *Atalaya de las corónicas* is principally an exercise in reduction.

The division of reigns into discrete chapters in the *Atalaya de las corónicas* makes each resemble an individual exemplum. This effect is especially noticeable with Muhammad. Martínez's source, the *Estoria de España*, follows a chronological order, interrupting Muhammad's life with Peninsular and pan-European events; Martínez gathers the material on Muhammad into a story with a beginning, middle, and implicitly moralizing end. He announces this organizational principle in the prologue, where he explains that having read as many chronicles as he could uncover, he recorded each reign as a complete narrative unit so as to produce noteworthy histories in "membranças breves" (brief commemorations). His intentions are mildly didactic. First, he wishes to give pleasure: the perusal of the histories of the kingdom's ancestors is gratifying. Second, these stories can spur readers to undertake noble and chivalrous deeds.

As Fernando Gómez Redondo indicates, the *Atalaya de las corónicas* reflects, in part, the contemporaneous popularity of chivalric romance. (One might note, also, that Martínez had already blurred the lines between historiography and romance in the *Arcipreste de Talavera* by accusing both of mendacity.) Besides announcing the chivalric orientation of the *Atalaya de las corónicas* in the prologue, Martínez eliminates his sources' echoes of vernacular epic style, for example, in the legendary exploits of Charlemagne and of Fernán González, first Count of Castile, recasting these episodes in a style reminiscent of chivalric prose.

Martínez's implied audience is alluded to occasionally in the vocative as "señores" (my lords) and is noble and male. The *Atalaya de las corónicas* probably received public readings in the royal court, performances that the manageable chapter divisions would have facilitated. Martínez's innovations—dialogues, dramatic additions, injections of humor, and occasional proverbial phrases ironically applied—also make the *Atalaya de las corónicas* well suited for oral representation. Finally, the narrator's occasional asides, "commo ya oystes" (as you have already heard), suggest that Martínez intended the text to be read aloud.

With such references to previous or subsequent events, Martínez reminds his audience that he controls the narrative. He also figures prominently in the text in two episodes. In the first, after mentioning an earthquake during Athanagild's reign, he reports having experienced a tremor in Aragon to show that he is qualified to describe the phenomenon accurately. The second case provides a moment of humor: Martínez says that the Navarrese cleric who planned to rape Fernán González's future wife was an archpriest, "¡mas non el de Talavera!" (but not the one from Talavera!).

This humorous interjection shows that the *Atalaya de las corónicas* was meant to entertain, an impression that other episodes corroborate. Several stories would be worthy of the *Arcipreste de Talavera*. For example, in Martínez's rewriting of Wittiza's reign, the lecherous monarch does not pursue the wife of Fáfila, Pelayo's father; rather, in a possible echo of the biblical story of Joseph and Potiphar, the lustful queen pursues Fáfila, leading Wittiza to kill the potential adulterer. Martínez does not fail to mention details such as widespread concubinage among the clergy, whose lust was uncontrolled under Wittiza. He seems to relish relating episodes such as the thwarted rape of the future first countess of Castile by the archpriest or her swapping clothes with Fernán González so that he could escape from prison in León dressed as a woman. "La muger sabe muchas cautelas" (Woman knows many ruses), Martínez predictably concludes. Similarly theatrical is the episode in which a captain of Emperor Justinian's,

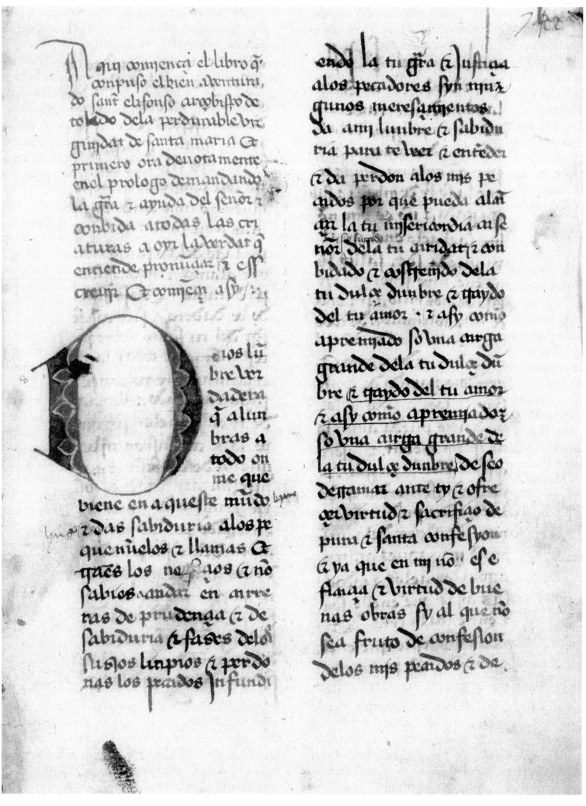

*Pages from the translation (circa 1444) of St. Ildephonsus's* De perpetua virginitate sanctae Mariae contra tres infideles, *which has been attributed to Martínez de Toledo  (Copyright © Patrimonio Nacional, Madrid; courtesy of Michael Agnew)*

el cobrimento delas mjs
peccados (z perdon delas mjs
maldades (z olujdamjento
de todos los mjs males (z
alinpiamjento de todas z
mjs suçedades por que
sueltos los lugamjentos
de todos mjs peccados alin
piado (z purificado (z jus
tificando (z santificando de
dios buena (z mjsericordio
oso juez piadoso (z reden
tor abundoso sea mostra
do alos angeles bien aven
turados (z acon pliado alos
sus coros (z ayuntado alos
sus gozos (z metido alas
sus fiestas por que sea
dios en mj (z de mj alaban
ça (z honrra (z a mj sea de
dios salud vida (z alegria
continua ment (z syenpre
verdadera mente (z syn fa
llesamjento manifiesta
(z clara mente desde aqp
ra (z en todo tpo en todo
sygto (z perdurable men
te amen z

Por ende yo indigno peccador
por mjs ppias culpas (z deme
ritos alfon mrs de talauera
in sufficient arçipreste abien
do no a Ella fenior (z deuos
yo obligado aver (z tener ala
santisyma virgin mat de açta
ynco rrupta madre de dios que
fizel presente tractado dela su
santa alabança esperan por
la cupa fecha ser tal (z el stay
de todo yo disposo yo tal (z el
deuoto con vocedri (z el por
ende supplico vnyl mente deuo
ta ment piado sa ment cono
fido (z ala su ppia madri (z al
su deuoto ylefonso glos dos
fructife por mm culpados del
yno (z pone a mj cuytado di
co sea digno de ser a torme
tado so la buenna mjsericor
dia suya no me dviese ayu
dado (z yo abogadarto del aclo
en pecial y le fonso de toledo
natural fruega a mj ppio
terial por mm il fonso con (z
no tal por (z nasa peccador
de tu fufta señor 5 vo art.
mj cresio del mj rey febrero año
fui toledo z

sent to assassinate a Visigothic king, acts like a harmless madman to deceive his victim.

A further dimension of the *Atalaya de las corónicas,* which may reflect its author's particular interests, is the attention Martínez devotes to events in Toledo–Church councils held there, its naming as the chief Hispanic see, its capture from the Moors, and so forth–and to local heroes such as St. Ildephonsus. In a second allusion to the composition of the *Atalaya de las corónicas* Martínez dates the work according to the number of years since Ildephonsus's death in 667. In short, the *Atalaya de las corónicas* reflects the same profound authorial self-awareness as the *Arcipreste de Talavera.*

Beyond the information in the prologue to the *Atalaya de las corónicas* that he was still the king's chaplain in 1443, little is known about Martínez's life during the 1440s. If he is the author of the lives of Ildephonsus and Isidore, those works can be dated based on the concluding note in codex b.III.1, housed at El Escorial, that Martínez had the works copied on 2 February 1444.

The two saints' lives and the translation of Ildephonsus's *De perpetua virginitate sanctae Mariae contra tres infideles* are traditionally attributed to Martínez by scholars. As the result of a lexical study comparing the *Arcipreste de Talavera* with the saints' lives, however, Ralph de Gorag and Lisa S. de Gorog deny Martínez's authorship of the latter. Nonetheless, the subject matters of the saints' lives, on the one hand, and that of the *Arcipreste de Talavera,* on the other hand, are radically different and call for stylistically diverse treatment–just as the overall style of the *Atalaya de las corónicas* differs markedly from that of the *Arcipreste de Talavera* because of differences in genre. Furthermore, Martínez would have been constrained by the works he was adapting–the saints' lives were based on earlier Latin versions–or translating, in the case of Ildephonsus's treatise.

Still, doubt should be cast on Martínez's authorship of these works, because the concluding note in the Escorial manuscript is ambiguous: "fize el presente tratado . . . escrevir" (I had the present treatise . . . written [or copied or composed]). This comment is hardly sufficient evidence to enable one to state categorically that Martínez wrote the works; in fact, "tratado" only refers to Ildephonsus's treatise. Even if he did not compose these texts, however, he evidently found the stories they tell and the arguments they make sufficiently congenial that he wanted his name associated with them. In addition, suggestive parallels exist between Martínez's universally acknowledged oeuvre and the three attributed works.

Martínez's onomastic link to the former archbishop of Toledo presumably contributed to his special devotion to the saint: in the manuscripts Ildephonsus's name alternately appears as "Ylefonso," "Elifonso," and "Alfonso." (That Martínez was Ildephonsus's namesake might suggest that he was born on the saint's feast day, 23 January.) As he is portrayed, Ildephonsus seems to be the virtuous counterpart of the sinful Archpriest of the *Arcipreste de Talavera:* he initially refuses the archbishopric, protesting with extreme humility that he is in no position to govern others since he is incapable of governing himself. The saint, like the Archpriest imitating women's voices, can also don a convincing disguise, a ploy he uses to flee his family while still a young man, to become a monk because he is afraid that ecclesiastical honors, which they were pressuring him to accept, will tempt him to break his vow of chastity. Ildephonsus's irreproachable motives, however, clearly contrast with the Archpriest's dubious status as an ethical model. As it is described in the saint's life, Ildephonsus's treatise on the Virgin, unlike the *Arcipreste de Talavera,* which openly participates in a morally ambiguous world, is a truly transformative text that prompts a miracle: in gratitude, the Virgin gives the archbishop a divinely fashioned chasuble.

Martínez's interest in the saint's treatise indicates his adherence to the doctrine, defended by the Franciscans, of Mary's perpetual virginity. In contrast to the way in which the *Arcipreste de Talavera* dwells on traps of the fallen world, *De perpetua virginitate sanctae Mariae* affirms Ildephonsus's belief in an eternal divine truth in which the Virgin participates, such that she transcends the contingencies of human generation, gestation, and childbirth–that is, she is exempt from their physical effects in that fallen world. Like the *Arcipreste de Talavera,* however, the treatise deals with the complexities of human discourse. The error of the three unbelievers in Mary's perpetual virginity against whom Ildephonsus directs his attack is essentially linguistic; they use language falsely in uttering heresies. He contrasts their fallen speech with the semantic integrity of the divinely inspired speech of the prophets who foretold Mary's virginity. At the same time, Ildephonsus introduces a discursive paradox: the Virgin birth is "non fablable" (ineffable); human words cannot encompass Mary's unprecedented direct link with the divine Word. Nevertheless, her perpetual virginity must be preached–made part of human discourse–as insistently as possible.

The life of St. Isidore of Seville (circa 560–636) treats matters of speech from the outset: bees leave honey in the baby Isidore's mouth, a sign of his future eloquence. He, like Martínez, writes a compendium: the encyclopedic *Etymologiae* (Etymologies), one of the Middle Ages' most frequently cited texts. Important episodes from his life also appear in the *Atalaya de las corónicas,* such as his persuading the Visigothic monarchy to abandon Arianism and the legend of his expulsion from the Iberian Peninsula of Muhammad, who, led by the Devil, had supposedly traveled to Spain to proselytize. Isidore's deeds always correspond to his words, as he practices what he preaches, something that is alien to the fallen narrative world of the *Arcipreste de Talavera.*

A problem with the two surviving manuscripts of St. Isidore's life, both of which are from the sixteenth century, is that they refer to the printing press in the final chapters. Since the printing press did not arrive in Spain until 1474, after Martínez's death, either these passages are a later scribal interpolation, or this section of the work was not written by Martínez, or Martínez was not the author of the hagiography at all. (Apropos of misattributions: Piero has shown that the sermon *Vençimiento del mundo* [Victory over the Temptations of the World], attributed to Martínez in early bibliographies, is a work from the last quarter of the century, after Martínez's death. The error arose because of a misreading of a manuscript abbreviation for the name Núñez.)

Little else is known about Martínez's activities in the 1440s. A note on a manuscript in El Escorial of Eiximenis's *Llibre de les dones* (Book of the Ladies), a misogynist work that Martínez probably read before writing the *Arcipreste de Talavera,* says: "Este libro es de Alonso Martínez, arcipreste de Talavera, racionero en la iglesia de Sta. María de Toledo, comprado en xxij dagosto de 48 años de mas mil cccc en Toledo. Quienientos marvedís, et otro libro. Alfonsus Talaverensis, porcionarius Toletanus" (This book belongs to Alonso Martínez, Archpriest of Talavera, prebendary in St. Mary's Church in Toledo, purchased on 22 August 1448 in Toledo. Five hundred *maravedís,* and another book. [Signed,] Alfonsus Talaverensis, Toledan prebendary). Cathedral records of prebendaries' salaries in 1450 indicate that Martínez was absent from Toledo until the end of the year; when he left and where he went are not known.

More-abundant documentation survives from the 1450s. Carmen Torroja Menéndez and María Rivas Palá found records in the cathedral archives of Martínez's participation in the organization of liturgical theater in Toledo; this discovery adds a dimension to his biography worthy of consideration, given his condemnation in the *Arcipreste de Talavera* of quotidian theatricality in the form of deceptive words, gestures, costumes, and actions. In 1454 Martínez received 2,500 *maravedís* for his expenses in organizing Corpus Christi celebrations. A document detailing his expenses in 1456 includes a reference to "representaciones" (theatrical performances). He was responsible for the feast of Corpus Christi again in 1457, while in 1458 he organized the "representación de los pastores" (performance of the shepherds' play) in the Christmas pageant. In 1460

the chapter compensated him for the cost of eight new pairs of wings for the "ángeles chicos" (little angels) in the Christmas play. Finally, in August 1461, coinciding with Enrique IV's stay in Toledo, Martínez was placed in charge of the performance of a play to celebrate the Assumption of the Virgin.

Torroja and Rivas's findings suggest Martínez enjoyed financial security throughout this period. In 1452 he rented a house adjacent to the property he had already rented from the chapter, presumably to expand his living quarters. Two of Martínez's servants signed the document as witnesses; one of them was apparently from the Aragonese city of Gerona and was, perhaps, hired during Martínez's sojourn in that kingdom. In 1456 Martínez paid for two prominent clerics the cathedral had invited to preach in Toledo, for which the chapter repaid him. He had to borrow money from the chapter to defend a challenge to one of his prebends in 1458; at about the same time, however, he lent money to the chapter to help repay debts it owed.

Martínez also assumed the payment of rent to the chapter for the living quarters of Mari Gómez de Herrera, whom he calls his cousin in autograph documents from 1459 and 1460; in late 1460, however, he refers to her as his niece, which is her designation in all subsequent documents. She is referred to as his inheritor in a document from 1467. Torroja and Rivas speculate that she was his former mistress; but since the only reason for casting doubt on the declared nature of her connection to Martínez is the confusion—his own, admittedly—between niece and cousin, one cannot make any firm assertions about their relationship. The identity of Fernando de Esquivel, described as Martínez's nephew in a 1462 document, also remains unknown.

Martínez seems to have been active in ecclesiastical affairs as late as 1466, when, according to documents cited by Pérez Pastor, he appeared with his colleagues in a dispute between the Hospital de la Misericordia and the twelve chaplains of the Chapel of King Sancho. Capitular documents record no receipt of salaries by him after December 1467; for that trimester Juan Sánchez collected the salary in Martínez's name. By 23 February 1468 someone else was renting his living quarters. A papal bull dated 7 March 1468 names Nicolás Fernández archpriest of Talavera; it describes Martínez's death as recent but provides no date. Martínez's tombstone in the cathedral seems to give his date of death as 2 January 1460, but the "LX" in the year is followed by a blank space; perhaps the engraver had incomplete information and left the space to be filled in later. The inscription reads: "Archpresbiter Talaveranus Toletanus Portionarius Regis Sancij Capellanus itiden Henrici 4ⁱ MCⁱCCCLX obiit die 2ⁱ Henuarius"

*Commemorative marker in the cathedral of Toledo indicating Martínez de Toledo's date of death (photograph by
E. Michael Gerli; courtesy of Michael Agnew)*

(The Archpriest of Talavera, Toledan, Prebendary [of the Chapel] of King Sancho, likewise Chaplain of Enrique IV, died 2 January 1460). The marker does not name Martínez, but a cathedral document corroborates that it is his. Two quarters of the coat of arms depicted on the tombstone correspond to the Martínez name; the other quarters represent his mother's family name with a lion rampant on an azure field. Gerli suggests in "The Burial Place and Probable Date of Death of Alfonso Martínez de Toledo" (1977) that the arms could be connected to the powerful Álvarez de Toledo family, one branch of which includes the dukes of Alva; significantly, the manuscript of the chronicle of Troy once owned by Martínez is now in the duchess of Alva's library. Such a family connection could explain Martínez's good fortune in the ecclesiastical and royal bureaucracies. The grave marker indicates that he continued as royal chaplain after Enrique IV's accession in 1454, implying that Martínez enjoyed a degree of prestige at court throughout his life; this prominence is also reflected in the fact that his coat of arms was considered sufficient identification on his tombstone. In sum, 2 January 1468 would appear to be the most likely date for his death.

The extent of Martínez's literary influence is open to debate. In traditional accounts of Spanish literary history the *Arcipreste de Talavera* is typically presented as a bridge between the *Libro de buen amor* and *La Celestina* (1499), attributed to Fernando de Rojas. These three texts are quite different from each other, and the hypothesis of a simplistic "evolutionary" linkage among them cannot withstand scrutiny. Nonetheless, important similarities, largely of a thematic nature, exist among the works. The connection of the *Arcipreste de Talavera* with Juan Ruiz is explicit; but *La Celestina* does not mention Martínez, and no passage in that work is unequivocally traceable to the *Arcipreste de Talavera*. Still, it is reasonable to suppose that the author or authors of *La Celestina* were aware of the *Arcipreste de Talavera* and, perhaps, indirectly inspired by it, especially in such passages as the misogynistic diatribe spoken by Sempronio at the beginning, Pármeno's catalogue of Celestina's cosmetics in the first *auto* (act), Areúsa's grotesque caricature of Melibea in the dinner scene in the ninth *auto,* or the frequent bestializing of the human characters. Martínez's book may have functioned as a foil for writers of "sentimental fiction," the quasi-generic designation traditionally assigned to a varied group of works in prose or mixed prose and verse that deal with the casuistry of love, the praise or blame of women, and allegorical representations of human sentiments, though only Juan Rodríguez del Padrón's *Triunfo de las donas* (Triumph of the Ladies, 1443) refers explicitly to Martínez in the prologue, and then in disparaging terms. Luis de Lucena's misogynistic *Repetición de amores* (Valedictory of Love, circa 1496), often included in this group of works, does not mention Martínez explicitly, but some passages recall the *Arcipreste de Talavera*. In the sixteenth century Juan Justiniano, in his prologue to Juan Luis Vives's *De institutione feminae Christianae* (On the Instruction of Christian Women, 1523), speaks ill of the *Arcipreste de Talavera* for criticizing women without offering them moral guidance. Finally, the playwright Juan de la Cueva, in his *El infamador* (The Defamer, 1581?), censures the Archpriest in a comic passage spoken by one of the characters. This reference indicates that the *Arcipreste de Talavera* still enjoyed significant popularity at the end of the sixteenth century, or, at least, that the work had been incorporated into the popular consciousness as the emblematic diatribe of a defamer of women. About the subsequent influence of the *Atalaya de las corónicas* practically nothing is known; it circulated in the fifteenth century, always in manuscript form, and it surely enjoyed no readership comparable to that of the *Arcipreste de Talavera*.

It is difficult to say what twenty-first-century readers will find attractive in the *Arcipreste de Talavera*. Older scholars' praise of its "realism" prove to be highly problematic, since the text has more to do with revealing the distortions of rhetoric than with providing a mimetically transparent portrait of contemporary society. Likewise, an approach to the *Arcipreste de Talavera* that views it as an objective reflection of gender relations in the fifteenth century will encounter numerous pitfalls, for the text is inextricably tied up in the subjective knots of language–as is the *Atalaya de las corónicas,* for that matter. One can say with certainty, however, that both works are eloquent testimony to the stylistically, structurally, and conceptually complex turn that vernacular prose took in fifteenth-century Castile.

## References:

Dámaso Alonso, "El Arcipreste de Talavera a medio camino entre moralista y novelista," in his *De los siglos oscuros al de oro,* Biblioteca Románica Hispánica VII: Estudios y Ensayos, no. 14 (Madrid: Gredos, 1958), pp. 125–136;

José Luis Bermejo Cabrero, "La formación jurídica del Arcipreste de Talavera," *Revista de Filología Española,* 57 (1974–1975): 111–125;

Catherine Brown, "The Archpriest's Magic Word: Representational Desire and Discursive Ascesis in the *Arcipreste de Talavera," Revista de Estudios Hispánicos,* 31 (1997): 377–401;

Brown, "Queer Representation in the *Arcipreste de Talavera,* or The *Maldezir de mugeres* is a Drag," in *Queer Iberia: Sexualities, Cultures and Crossings from the Middle Ages to the Renaissance,* edited by Josiah Blackmore and Gregory S. Hutcheson, Series Q (Durham, N.C.: Duke University Press, 1999), pp. 73–103;

Marina Scordilis Brownlee, "Hermeneutics of Reading in the *Corbacho,"* in *Medieval Texts and Contemporary Readers,* edited by Laurie A. Finke and Martin B. Schnichtman (Ithaca, N.Y.: Cornell University Press, 1987), pp. 216–233;

Marcella Ciceri, "'Arcipreste de Talavera': Il linguaggio del corpo," *Quaderni di lingue e letterature,* 8 (1983): 121–136;

Ciceri, "Gli *exempla* dell' 'Arcipreste de Talavera,'" in her *Marginalia hispanica* (Rome: Bulzoni, 1991), pp. 161–177;

Ralph de Gorog and Lisa S. de Gorog, "La atribución de las 'Vidas de San Ildefonso y San Isidoro' al Arcipreste de Talavera," *Boletín de la Real Academia Española,* 58 (1978): 169–193;

de Gorog and de Gorog, *Concordancias del "Arcipreste de Talavera,"* Biblioteca Románica Hispánica, no. 4: Textos (Madrid: Gredos, 1978);

Raúl A. Del Piero, "La *Corónica de Mahomad* del Arcipreste de Talavera," *Nueva revista de Filología Hispánica,* 14 (1960): 21–39;

Del Piero, *Dos escritores de la baja edad media castellana (Pedro de Veragüe y el Arcipreste de Talavera, cronista real),* Anejos del *Boletín de la Real Academia Española,* no. 23 (Madrid: Real Academia Española, 1971);

Del Piero, "La tradición textual de la *Atalaya de las corónicas* del Arcipreste de Talavera," *PMLA,* 81 (1966): 12–22;

Del Piero, "El *Vençimiento del mundo:* Autor, fecha, estructura," *Nueva revista de Filología Hispánica,* 15 (1961): 377–392;

Arturo Farinelli, "Note sulla fortuna del *Corbaccio* nella Spagna medievale," in *Bausteine zur romanischen Philologies: Festgabe für Adolfo Mussafia* (Halle: Niemeyer, 1905), pp. 401–460;

E. Michael Gerli, *Alfonso Martínez de Toledo,* Twayne's World Authors, no. 398 (Boston: Twayne, 1976);

Gerli, "The Burial Place and Probable Date of Death of Alfonso Martínez de Toledo," *Journal of Hispanic Philology,* 1 (1977): 231–238;

Fernando Gómez Redondo, "La materia épica en la *Atalaya de las corónicas* del Arcipreste de Talavera: El caso de Fernán González," in *Historias y ficciones: Coloquio sobre la literatura del siglo XV,* edited by Rafael Beltrán Llavador, José Luis Canet Vallés, and Josep Lluís Sirera (Valencia: Universitat de València, 1992), pp. 57–71;

Roberto J. González Casanovas, "El discurso femenino en la segunda parte del *Corbacho:* Análisis sociosemiótico del enunciado y la enunciación," in *Medioevo y literatura: Actas del V Congreso de la Asociación Hispánica de Literatura Medieval,* volume 2, edited by Juan Paredes (Granada: Universidad de Granada, 1995), pp. 433–442;

González Casanovas, "Rhetorical Strategies in the *Corbacho,* Part III: From Scholastic Logic to Homiletic Example," *La corónica,* 20, no. 1 (1991): 40–59;

Derek Lomax, "Datos biográficos sobre el Arcipreste de Talavera," in *Actas del cuarto Congreso Internacional de Hispanistas: Celebrado en Salamanca, agosto de 1971,* edited by Eugenio de Bustos Tovar (Salamanca: Asociación Internacional de Hispanistas, 1982), pp. 141–146;

Sara Mañero Rodicio, "El *Arcipreste de Talavera:* El público cortesano como elemento configurador," in *Historias y ficciones,* pp. 131–140;

Mañero Rodicio, *El Arcipreste de Talavera de Alfonso Martínez de Toledo* (Toledo: Disputación Provincial, 1997);

Colbert Nepaulsingh, "Talavera's Imagery and the Structure of the *Corbacho,*" *Revista canadiense de estudios hispánicos,* 4 (1980): 329–349;

Nepaulsingh, "Talavera's Prologue," *Romance Notes,* 16 (1975): 516–519;

Per Nykrog, "Playing Games with Fiction: *Les Quinze joyes de mariage, Il Corbaccio, El Arcipreste de Tala-*

vera," in *The Craft of Fiction: Essays in Medieval Poetics,* edited by Leigh A. Arrathoon (Rochester, Mich.: Solaris Press, 1984), pp. 423–452;

Jacob Ornstein, "La misoginia y el profeminismo en la literatura castellana," *Revista de Filología Hispánica,* 3 (1941): 219–232;

Madeleine Pardo, "Remarques sur l'*Atalaya* de l'Archiprêtre de Talavera," *Romania,* 88 (1967): 350–398;

Erich von Richthofen, "Alfonso Martínez de Toledo und sein *Arcipreste de Talavera,* ein kastilisches Prosawerk des 15. Jahrhunderts," *Zeitschrift für Romanische Philologie,* 61 (1941): 417–537;

Michael Solomon, *The Literature of Misogyny in Medieval Spain: The* Arcipreste de Talavera *and the* Spill, Cambridge Studies in Latin American and Iberian Literature, no. 10 (Cambridge: Cambridge University Press, 1997);

Carmen Torroja Menéndez and María Rivas Palá, "Arcipreste de Talavera," in their *Teatro en Toledo en el siglo XV: "Auto de la pasión" de Alonso del Campo,* Anejos del *Boletín de la Real Academia Española,* no. 35 (Madrid: Real Academia, 1977), pp. 24–34;

David Viera, "Francesc Eiximenis (1340?–1409?) y Alfonso Martínez de Toledo (1398?–1470?): Las ideas convergentes en sus obras," *Estudios franciscanos,* 76 (1975): 5–10;

Christine J. Whitbourne, *The* Arcipreste de Talavera *and the Literature of Love,* Occasional Papers in Modern Languages, no. 7 (Hull, U.K.: University of Hull, 1970).

# Juan de Mena
## (1411 – 1456)

### Philip O. Gericke
#### University of California, Riverside

**WORKS:** *Calamicleos;* also known as *La Coronación* and *La Coronación del Marqués de Santillana* (1438)

**Manuscripts:** Most of the fourteen known surviving manuscripts are fifteenth-century *cancioneros* (collections of verse) that include only the text of the poem or excerpts from it, without the poet's four prefaces and explanatory comments. Among the more significant are Madrid, Biblioteca Nacional 9985; Madrid, Academia de la Historia MS 2 (formerly 2-7-2), better known as the *Cancionero de Gallardo-San Román,* which was used by Miguel Ángel Pérez Priego as the base manuscript for his edition; and three others taken into account by Pérez Priego: Madrid, Fundación Lázaro Galdiano 208; Paris, Bibliothèque Nationale Esp. 224; and Escorial, Real Biblioteca de San Lorenzo de El Escorial N.I.13.

**First publication and early editions:** *La coronación de Juan de Mena al Marqués de Santillana* (Saragossa: Paul Hurus, between 1488 and 1498); *La Coronación* (Toulouse?: Printed by Johann Paris & Etiene Clebat?, ca. 1489); *La coronación del famoso poeta Juan de Mena: Dirigida a Íñigo López de Mendoza, Marqués de Santilla* (Seville: Printed by Stanislaw Polono, 1499); *Coronaciö copuesta por el famoso poeta Iua de Mena: Al muy illustre cauallero don Ynigo Lopez de Mendoça Marques de Santillana* (Salamanca: Printed by Haebler, 1499).

**Standard edition:** "La Coronación del Marqués de Santillana," in Mena's *Obras completas,* edited by Pérez Priego (Barcelona: Planeta, 1989), pp. 105–208.

**Editions:** *La coronación de Juan de Mena: Edición, estudio, comentario,* edited by Feliciano Delgado León (Cordova: Monte de Piedad & Caja de Ahorros de Cordova, 1978); *La coronación de Juan de Mena,* edited by María Antonia Corral (Cordova: Universidad de Cordova, 1994).

*Laberinto de Fortuna* (1444)

**Manuscripts:** Eighteen surviving manuscripts include the complete text or portions of it. The most significant are Paris, Bibliothèque Nationale Esp. 229, used by most modern editors as their base text, and Esp. 227, used by Carla de Nigris as her base. Esp. 229 has extensive marginal notes, some written in the first person and therefore probably copied from a manuscript prepared under the author's direct supervision; other less well-known manuscripts have similar notes: Barcelona, Biblioteca de Catalunya 1967; Madrid, Fundación Lázaro Galdiano 208; Seville, Biblioteca Colombina 83.6.10; and Madrid, Biblioteca de Bartolomé March 20-5-6.

**First publication and early editions:** *Laberinto de Fortuna* (Salamanca?, ca. 1481); *Comieça el labirintho* (Seville: Juan Thomas Fanario de Lumelo, 1496); *Laberinto de Fortuna,* edited by Hernán Núñez (Seville: Printed by Johannes Pegnizer & Magnus Herbst, 1499); *Laberinto de Fortuna,* edited by Francisco Sánchez de las Brozas (Salamanca: Printed by Lucas de Iunta, 1582).

**Standard edition:** *Laberinto de Fortuna,* edited by Maximiliaan P. A. M. Kerkhof, Nueva biblioteca de erudición y crítica, no. 9 (Madrid: Castalia, 1995).

**Editions:** *El laberinto de Fortuna, o, las Trescientas,* edited by José Manuel Blecua, Clásicos castellanos, no. 119 (Madrid: Espasa-Calpe, 1943); *Laberinto de Fortuna,* edited by John G. Cummins, Biblioteca Anaya, no. 90 (Salamanca: Anaya, 1968); *Laberinto de Fortuna,* edited by Louise Vasvari Fainberg (Madrid: Alhambra, 1976); *Laberinto de Fortuna,* edited by Miguel Ángel Pérez Priego (Madrid: Espasa-Calpe, 1989); *Laberinto de Fortuna y otros poemas,* edited by Carla de Nigris, preliminary study by Guillermo Serés, Biblioteca clásica, volume 14 (Barcelona: Crítica, 1994).

*Tratado de amor,* attributed to Mena (ca. 1444)

**Manuscript:** Paris, Bibliothèque Nationale Esp. 295.

**First publication:** Charles V. Aubrun, "Un traité de l'amour attribué a Juan de Mena," *Bulletin Hispanique,* 50 (1948): 333–344.

**Standard edition:** *Tratado de amor, atribuido a Juan de Mena,* edited by María Luz Gutiérrez Araus, Colección Aula magna, volume 14 (Madrid: Alcalá, 1975).

Minor poems (ca. 1444–1455)

**Manuscripts:** No single manuscript includes more than half of Mena's more than fifty shorter poems. Madrid, Academia de la Historia MS 2 (formerly 2-7-2), better known as the *Cancionero de Gallardo-San Román,* has the greatest number with sixteen. Other significant manuscripts are Modena, Biblioteca Estense alpha R.8.9 (*Cancionero de Módena*), and London, British Museum Add. 33383, known as the *Cancionero de Herberay des Essarts.*

**Early edition:** *Cancionero general recopilado por Hernando del Castillo* (Valencia: Cristóbal Kofman, 1511).

**Standard editions:** *Obra lírica,* edited by Miguel Ángel Pérez Priego (Madrid: Alhambra, 1979); *Poesie minori: Edizione critica,* edited by Carla de Nigris, Romanica neapolitana, no. 23 (Naples: Ligouri, 1988).

*Tratado sobre el título de duque* (1445)

**Manuscripts:** Madrid, Academia Española V-6-74; Copenhagen, Kongelige Library 2219 is fragmentary: only folios 1r–2v carry the text of *Tratado sobre el título de duque.*

**First publication and standard edition:** *Tratado sobre el título de duque,* edited by Louise Vasvari Fainberg (London: Tamesis, 1976).

*Memorias de algunos linages* or *Memorias genealógicas,* attributed to Mena (1448)

**Manuscript:** Madrid, Biblioteca Nacional 3390.

**First publication and standard edition:** Alfredo Carballo Picazo, "Juan de Mena: Un documento inédito y una obra atribuida," *Revista de Literatura,* 1 (1952): 269–299.

*Coplas de los pecados mortales;* also known as *Debate de la Razón contra la Voluntad* and *Disputación de vicios* (1456)

**Manuscripts:** The poem survives in nineteen manuscripts, all of which–including MS. 20-5-6 of the private library of Bartolomé March Servera (Palma de Mallorca), misleadingly titled *Poesías morales de Juan de Mena–*are *cancioneros* that also contain works of poets other than Mena. Other significant manuscripts are Madrid, Biblioteca del Palacio MS. II-1250, Gladys M. Rivera's choice as the base for her edition; Madrid, Biblioteca Nacional 7817; and Paris, Bibliothèque Nationale Esp. 510.

**First publication and early editions:** *Vita Christi y otras obras en metro de Frey Iñigo de Mendoza*

(Zamora: Printed by Antonio de Centenera, ca. 1483); *Coplas contra los pecados mortales* (Saragossa: Printed by Pablo Hurus, ca. 1488–1490); *Coplas de Fr. Iñigo de Mendoza y otros Poetas antiguos* (Burgos: Printed by Friedrich Biel, 1490–1493); *Cancionero de Hurus* (Saragossa: Printed by Pablo Hurus, 1495); *Coplas contra los pecados mortales* (Salamanca, 1500).

**Standard edition:** *Coplas de los siete pecados mortales and First Continuation,* by Mena and Gómez Manrique, edited by Gladys M. Rivera (Madrid: Porrúa Turanzas, 1982).

OTHER: [Italicus?], *Ilias latina,* translated by Mena as *Sumas de la Ylíada de Omero;* also known as *Ilíada en romance, Omero romançado,* and *Destrucción de Troya* (ca. 1442)

**Manuscripts:** Six manuscripts survive: four in the Biblioteca Nacional de Madrid, one in the Biblioteca Menéndez y Pelayo (Santander), and one in the private library of Don Bartolomé March Servera (Palma de Mallorca). Tomás González Rolán, María F. del Barrio Vega, and Antonio López Fonseca give complete descriptions in the introductory study to their *Sumas de la Ylíada de Homero* (1996). All of the manuscripts are significant except the fragmentary Biblioteca Nacional de Madrid 8600.

**First publication:** *La Ylíada de Homero en romance* (Valladolid: Arnaldo Guillén de Brocar, 1519).

**Standard edition:** *Sumas de la Ylíada de Homero,* edited by González Rolán, Barrio Vega, and López Fonseca (Madrid: Ediciones Clásicas, 1996).

Álvaro de Luna, *Libro de las virtuosas e claras mugeres,* prologue by Mena (1446)

**Manuscripts:** Four manuscripts survive, one in the Biblioteca Nacional de Madrid and three in the Biblioteca Universitaria de Salamanca. The most significant is Salamanca 2654, used by Manuel Castillo as his base for Mena's prologue.

**First publication:** *Libro de las virtuosas é claras mujeres, el qual fizo é compuso el condestable Don Álvaro de Luna, maestre de la Orden de Santiago: Dalo á luz La Sociedad de bibliófilos españoles,* edited by Marcelino Menéndez y Pelayo (Madrid: Sociedad de Bibliófilos Españoles, 1891).

**Standard edition:** *Libro de las virtuosas e claras mugeres por el condestable de Castilla Don Álvaro de Luna, maestre de la Orden de Santiago del Espada: Edición crítica,* edited by Castillo (Madrid: Menor, 1908).

A highly regarded member of the literary court of the Castilian king Juan II, Juan de Mena held royal

*Page from a manuscript in the Biblioteca Nacional, Madrid, for Juan de Mena's* La Coronación del Marqués de Santillana, *written in 1438 (from Mena's* Tratado sobre el título de duque, *edited by Louise Vasvari Fainberg, 1976; Thomas Cooper Library, University of South Carolina)*

appointments as *veinticuatro* (alderman) of Cordova, *secretario de cartas latinas* (secretary of Latin letters), and *cronista real* (royal chronicler). He was considered the outstanding poet of his time, and his works circulated widely for more than a century following his death. His influence extended into the seventeenth century, and he was not forgotten–though his works were no longer widely read–in the eighteenth. Nineteenth-century historians of literature criticized him for the Latinized syntax and lexicon characteristic of his elevated poetic style. In 1950 María Rosa Lida de Malkiel's monumental *Juan de Mena, poeta del prerrenacimiento español* (Juan de Mena, Poet of the Spanish Pre-Renaissance) refurbished his reputation and refocused scholarly attention on his works–especially his acknowledged masterpiece, *Laberinto de Fortuna* (Labyrinth of Fortune, 1444). Modern scholars consider Mena, Jorge Manrique, and Íñigo López de Mendoza (Marqués de Santillana), the three major poets of the fifteenth century.

Mena was born in Cordova in 1411. Most accounts of his lineage and formative years are based on two fifteenth-century sources: *Memorias de algunos linages* (Memories of Some Families, 1448), attributed to Mena, and Hernán Núñez's brief biographical essay in his edition of *Laberinto de Fortuna* (1499). *Memorias de algunos linages* traces the family's origins to the Valley of Mena in La Montaña, an area in northern Spain that is now part of the province of Santander; it says that they migrated to Castile in the thirteenth century, where they served King Fernando III and his successors with distinction. Núñez says that Mena was "hijo de un ciudadano de ella [Cordova] llamado según algunos dizen Pedrarias, ho[m]bre de mediano estado, y de una hermana de Rui Fernández de Peñalosa, veynte y cuatro en la dicha cibdad y señor de Almenara" (the son of a citizen of Cordova named, according to some, Pedrarias, a man of middling station, and of a sister of Rui Fernández de Peñaloza, alderman in said city and lord of Almenara). His mother's name is not recorded.

In her "La vida de Juan de Mena" (The Life of Juan de Mena, 1953) Florence Street supports a different version, offered by a seventeenth-century historian, Alonso García de Morales, according to whom Fernández de Peñalosa was the poet's paternal grandfather, not an uncle on his mother's side. Mena's father had two sons: the elder, Ruy Fernández de Peñalosa, followed in his namesake grandfather's footsteps as *veinticuatro* of Cordova. Street cites one of Mena's poems, "O rauiosas tentaciones" (Oh Rabid Temptations), as a possible reference to his own situation: "fuera yo el hijo primero / y nunca fuera el segundo" (would that I had been the first son / and that I never had been the second).

Modern scholars have suggested that Mena's immediate ancestors included *conversos* (converts to Christianity from Judaism). The thesis, based on references to the poet's lineage in the works of his contemporaries, was first proffered by Lida de Malkiel in a 1941 article. For her, the most noteworthy instance occurs in a poem by Marshal Íñigo Ortiz de Stúñiga, who links Mena to Judaism by accusing him of being an accomplice to the killing of Christ: "pues yo juro al que matastes / que no os me vayáis sin pena" (I swear to him whom you killed / that you will not get away from me without penalty). Lida de Malkiel finds this and other allusions to be compelling evidence that Mena was a *converso*, or at least the descendant of *conversos*, and Américo Castro agrees. Other scholars, however, have pointed out that Ortiz de Stúñiga's composition is not reliable as biographical evidence: it was a commonplace to call into question the lineage of one's adversary in such poetic exchanges of insults, especially when, as in this instance, personal animosity might have been involved. Scholarly consensus holds, with Street and Eugenio Asensio, that there is insufficient evidence on which to base the contention that Mena was a "New Christian."

Mena's father died shortly after Mena's birth; when his mother died a few years later, Mena and his brother were entrusted to the care of relatives. Núñez states that Mena began his university education in Salamanca at the age of twenty-three, which would represent a rather late start: the poet's considerable learning, already in evidence in his first work, would have to have been acquired in a relatively short time. A copy of his translation of the *Ilias latina* (Latin Iliad, circa 1442) is signed "dominum Johanem de mena" (Master Juan de Mena), an indication that the poet had completed the requirements for the master of arts degree–a six-year program of study. A more plausible chronology would place the beginning of Mena's university studies around 1427–1428 and their conclusion prior to his association with the royal court starting around 1434.

Núñez claims that Mena completed his education with a trip to Rome, but no evidence has been found of his attending a university or pursuing a course of study there. He was granted an ecclesiastical benefice as early as 1431 and lost his right to it upon his marriage; according to Núñez, he married a sister of one García y Lope de Vaca. No other reference to this marriage has been discovered; in his edition of Mena's *Obra lírica* (Lyrical Works, 1979) Miguel Ángel Pérez Priego contends that it took place between 1436 and 1438 and must have ended by 1442, when documents place Mena in Florence in quest of further church benefices.

Mena was acquainted with other writers in his native Cordova: he exchanged verses with Juan Agraz and Antón de Montoro and in all likelihood knew Pedro Tafur as well. His first royal appointment appears to have been as *veinticuatro* (a member of the council of twenty-four aldermen) of Cordova, probably in the mid 1430s, and his circle of literary contacts widened as he began to spend time at the royal court. One of the most significant associations formed during these years was with the future Marqués de Santillana. Mena's senior by thirteen years, López de Mendoza was one of Castile's grandees and was already respected as a poet and an avid student of the classics. In 1434–1435 Íñigo López de Mendoza occasionally hosted the royal court at his estates in Buitrago and Guadalajara, and Mena might have been a guest as part of the king's retinue; or the two could have met on one of López de Mendoza's visits to Cordova. They formed a friendship that lasted until Mena's death and that transcended the political turbulence of the time as Mena became an ardent supporter of the king's privy councillor, don Álvaro de Luna, while López de Mendoza, whose disputes with Luna dated to the 1420s, became even more rigid in his opposition to the favorite.

In 1438 López de Mendoza was military commander of the area that comprised the bishoprics of Cordova and Jaén. On 20 April forces under his command took the town of Huelma on the frontier between Christian and Muslim Spain. Although not a major victory—it was all but ignored by contemporary chroniclers and is barely remembered today—the capture of Huelma represented the first successful campaign of the Reconquest since the Battle of La Higuerela in 1431. Mena composed a poem to honor both López de Mendoza's military prowess and his intellectual accomplishments.

The work consists of fifty-one stanzas in the form of *coplas reales* (ten eight-syllable lines per stanza with the rhyme scheme *abaabccddc*). Mena provides explanatory comments in prose for each stanza and introduces the work with four preambles in ornate style. The poem is generally known as *La Coronación* (The Coronation) or *La Coronacion del Marqués de Santillana,* although the latter title is anachronistic: López de Mendoza did not receive the title of marqués until after the Battle of Olmedo in 1445. Mena himself called the work *Calamicleos,* a word of his own coinage derived from the Latin *calamitas* (calamity) and the Greek *cleos* (glory). Most scholars assign 1438 as the year of composition of the work; it was obviously completed after the taking of Huelma in April, since a reference to the battle appears in stanza 42, but how soon after the battle the poem was written cannot be determined with certainty. Stanza 43 and its commentary, though ambiguous, suggest that López de Mendoza was still in command on the frontier at the time of writing; if so, the work would have been completed no later than the end of López de Mendoza's tenure in mid 1440.

*Illuminated initial from the 1499 Seville edition of* La coronación del famoso poeta Juan de Mena: Dirigida a Íñigo Lopez de Mendoza, Marqués de Santillana *(Biblioteca Nacional, Madrid; courtesy of Frank A. Domínguez)*

The first preamble explains the title: the poem will present a vision of figures suffering eternal torment (calamity), then depict the happy state of personages being rewarded for wisdom or valor (glory). The second preamble, following the classification of writing styles as tragedy, satire, and comedy established by St. Isidore of Seville, declares that the work can be considered comedy, as it begins happily and ends well, and satire, as it reprehends vice and glorifies virtue. The third preamble attests to López de Mendoza's coronation with garlands of laurel for knowledge and of oak for valor. In the fourth preamble the author apologizes for leaving Latin quotes untranslated but promises explanations in the commentary.

The poem is an allegory in which the poet, seeking Mount Parnassus, finds himself in a wooded valley in Thessaly. Darkness overtakes him just as he reaches the edge of the River Lethe, where he encounters figures from classical legends and myths who are condemned to eternal suffering. The poet identifies each figure and describes his or her punishment: King Ninus is armless, representing his inability to take action; Jason and Ulysses burn eternally, the former for lust and the latter for duplicity and flattery; the three Harpies feast on the blood of Phineus, who is being punished for greed. The poet's journey continues until he encounters the three Furies, who are charged with inflicting punishment on those suffering. He inquires as to the reason for the unnameable tortures; Tisiphone replies that those condemned must suffer for "*mal uso*" (misuse), for which their names will be denounced throughout eternity. She urges the poet to flee the valley, to eschew the vice of laziness, and never to look back. Heeding her advice, the poet braves the dangers of the river in an oarless boat to escape the torment of the suffering souls he leaves behind. He reaches the other side of the river and falls asleep.

Awakening the following morning, the poet is tempted to look back on where he has been but, mindful of Tisiphone's warning, refrains and resumes his journey. He finally reaches the heights of Parnassus, a place of great beauty, where he sees Solomon, David, Aristotle, Homer, Lucan, Virgil, Seneca and other wise men of Cordova, Ovid, Vegetius, and Boethius. The nine Muses arrive, escorting a knight on whom everyone's attention is focused. The poet asks one of the Muses who is being so honored; she replies, "el de Mendoça es, señor de la Vega y de Buitrago" (it is de Mendoza, lord of la Vega and Buitrago). The poet fears that Lopéz de Mendoza's presence on Parnassus means that he is dead but is assured that such is not the case: the laureate lives on earth, as well as on Parnassus, and death will not be able to deprive him of the mantle he has earned. Four maidens—the cardinal virtues incarnate—emerge from among the branches and hand the honoree his crown. The poet invokes the goddess of fame to spread the word of the event and concludes with a profession of modesty, begging the reader's pardon for any inadequacies in his account.

Two points stand out in Mena's choice of exemplars. First, those who are condemned are not necessarily evildoers but are persons who have failed to do good, who through their natural endowments or stations in life had responsibilities that they did not discharge: that is, they were guilty of "misuse" of those endowments or positions. Second, those who enjoy the happiness of Parnassus are primarily men of letters—wise men and poets—although some dealt with military matters in their writings. Only David, with his slingshot, is recognized for his prowess as a warrior.

Mena's poetic vision owes far more to the Greco-Roman than to the Judeo-Christian tradition. His place of suffering is populated by figures from the ancient world; its judges are Minos, Rhadamanthus, and Aeacus; and the condemned are tormented by the Harpies and Furies, although their torments are more reminiscent of Dante's *Inferno* than of Virgil's *Aeneid*. On Parnassus, Solomon and David are outnumbered by the sages and poets who wrote in Greek and Latin. Only at the end, with the appearance of the cardinal virtues, are the two traditions brought together.

In the commentary, on the other hand, Mena places the literal meaning of the classical allusions within a Christian frame of reference and sends a clear moral message—especially in his description of the netherworld. In stanza 5, for instance, night overtakes the poet at the edge of the deep river. In the commentary he explains that the river is mortal sin and that darkness is the failure of human beings to see themselves and to recognize the error of sin. The boat without oars represents the body, which is aimless without the direction of the soul; and when the narrator rests after his flight, his repose is like that of the soul that has escaped from mortal sin.

Climbing Mount Parnassus, the narrator travels through a "selva inviolada" (inviolate forest) that, the commentary says, represents "buena e honesta sçiençia" (good and honest science). The commentary continues to explain the allusions, but now as they relate not to the struggle with sin but to the acquisition of wisdom. The forest is inhabited by "sabios prudentes" (prudent wise men)—an important distinction, since anyone may acquire knowledge without necessarily being prudent. The "gozos infinidos" (infinite joys) revealed along the way are those of knowledge, and the nine Muses become, in the commentary, the "esençiales cabsas" (essential causes) of Christian theologians: imagination, intellect, memory, science, art, study, exercise, knowledge, and virtue. The most authoritative of these causes is knowledge, and Knowledge has brought Santillana to Parnassus and dispenses lasting honor, glory, and fame to those who dwell with her. López de Mendoza is honored, continues the commentary, for his labors in the service of God and king in his battles against "desmembrando los cuerpos sarraçenos, enbiando las sus ánimas a la boca del huerco, conviene a saber del infierno" (the Saracens, whose bodies he has dismembered and whose souls he has sent to the mouth of Orcus, that is to say, to hell). His worldly seat is that of "estado e potençia e honor e riquezas e dignidades" (status and power and honor and riches and dignities), but the seat he has earned on Parnassus is the seat of "prudençia e sabiduría e buenas virtudes que guarnesçen el ánima de perfecçión" (prudence and knowledge and good virtues that outfit the soul with perfection). The branches from which the four cardinal virtues emerge represent branches of knowledge, for "de la sçiençia sale e nasçe la virtud" (virtue comes out of, and is born from, knowledge). López de Mendoza receives a crown woven of oak, says the commentary, to denote "ferocidad e valentía e esperto conosçimiento de la militar disçiplina" (ferocity, bravery, and expert knowledge of military discipline), but it is as a man of virtue that he is to be emulated. Fame must spread the word of the celebration so that future generations may overcome the obstacles to virtue, winning the crown of good repute on earth and everlasting glory with God.

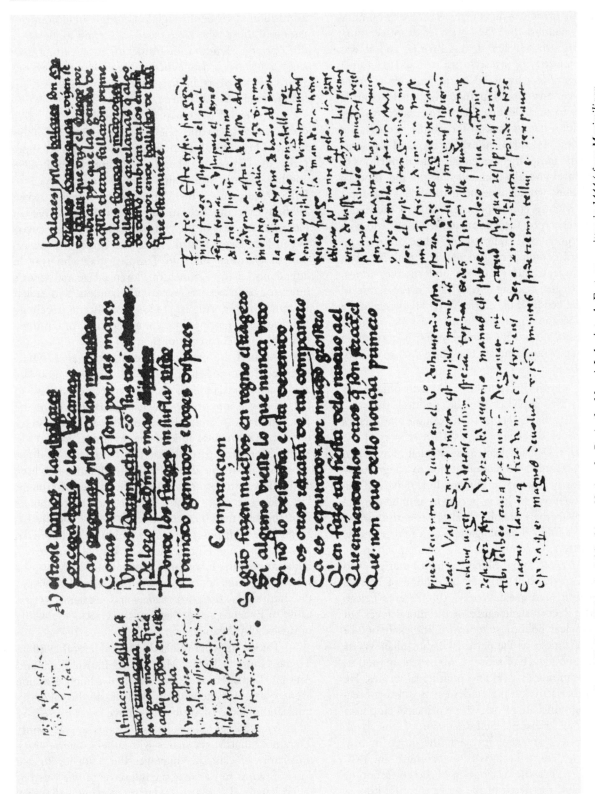

*Page from MS. Esp. 229 in the Bibliothèque Nationale, Paris, for Mena's Laberinto de Fortuna, written in 1444 (from Maximiliaan P. A. M. Kerkhof, "El MS. 229 [PN7] de la Bibliothèque Nationale de Paris: Base de las ediciones modernas del Laberinto de Fortuna de Juan de Mena," Medievalia et Humanistica, new series 14 [August 1993]; Texas Tech University Library)*

Mena's prose commentary was accorded an unfavorable evaluation by the great sixteenth-century scholar Francisco Sánchez de las Brozas, and it was severely criticized for its style as well as for rather minor errors of fact by noted literary historians of the nineteenth century. In 1939 Inez Macdonald contributed greatly to rehabilitating the commentary, situating it in a tradition dating back to the twelfth century and demonstrating its value in explicating—and in some instances emending—the poetic text. Indeed, portions of the poem are virtually unintelligible to the modern reader—as they would have been to all but the most learned of Mena's contemporaries—without the explanations furnished by the commentary. Macdonald considered the poem and commentary, taken together, an indictment of contemporary society and politics, albeit expressed in extremely cautious and discreet terms. According to her reading, Mena saw in the Battle of Huelma a reflection of the glories of La Higuerela and a prelude to continued advancement of the Reconquest, which had languished for several years, if only those charged to act would emulate Santillana's sense of duty and his valor.

Most scholars have followed Macdonald's interpretation, with emphasis on the political message, although a few have sought to reexamine the themes and purpose of the work. In his 1978 edition of the poem Feliciano Delgado León suggests that Mena's aim is neither to extol the Reconquest nor to congratulate Santillana for his victory at Huelma but, rather, to justify the coronation of a living person by uniting the real personage with the symbolic ideal of the virtuous layman who has fulfilled his obligations as a soldier and as a man of letters, in contrast to those condemned in the poem—and by extension, Mena's contemporaries—who have failed to do their duty. In his edition of Mena's *Obras completas* (Complete Works, 1989) Pérez Priego stresses the deeper significance of the moral level but still finds a clear political statement in the exaltation of López de Mendoza as the perfect knight. Julian Weiss focuses on the nature of satire as Mena understood it: as the condemning of vices and praising of virtues. He concludes that satire, in the modern sense, "was of secondary importance in a work whose principal emphasis is on a general, transcendental discussion of ethical values." The poet's journey represents the quest for true knowledge and must begin with overcoming sin. Wisdom brings with it the recognition of the perfection of eternal life and the deceit of life on earth; only knowledge remains constant and not subject to the vagaries of fortune. Virtue emanates from knowledge; Santillana, who has also made the journey described in the poem, has attained both. *La Coronación,* then, may be interpreted as an allegory of the overcoming of sin and the acquisition of virtue through knowledge. In its condemnation of those who have failed to act and in its praise of López de Mendoza for his devotion to duty, it may carry a veiled criticism aimed at Mena's contemporaries who have failed to discharge their responsibilities; but the message is subtle indeed.

No record is known to exist of López de Mendoza's reaction to the poem Mena composed in his honor. The paths of the two may have diverged temporarily as López de Mendoza became embroiled in another dispute with Luna and Mena journeyed to Italy. Documents in the Vatican archives published in 1956 by Vicente Beltrán de Heredia place Mena in Florence, the seat of the court in exile of Pope Eugene IV, in February 1442; there he was under the protection of Cardinal Juan de Torquemada, who was in attendance at the Council of Florence-Ferrara. Mena's quest for benefices was apparently fruitless, and he left Florence before August 1443—possibly on receiving notification of his appointment as secretary of Latin letters and royal chronicler of Juan II.

Around the time of his stay in Florence, Mena completed his translation of the *Ilias latina,* an abbreviated verse translation of the *Iliad* in verse ascribed to the otherwise unknown Italicus and dating from the first century A.D. In the dedication to Juan II, written in the same ornamental style as the preambles to *La Coronación,* Mena compares himself to bees who steal the substance from "melifluas flores" (mellifluous flowers), as the flowers he brings are from the garden of Homer. He offers, he says, only a sample, not the complete *Iliad;* the king may then commission the complete translation if he so disposes. He takes Guido de Columnis to task for criticizing Homer, notes by way of countervailing argument the favorable judgment of Virgil, lists the works attributed to Homer—the *Iliad,* the *Odyssey,* and the humorous *Bratachoniomachia*—and explains as the cause of Phoebus's anger against the Greeks the taking of Briseida by Agamemnon.

Taking up where Lida de Malkiel left off in 1950, Tomás González Rolán, María F. del Barrio Vega, and Antonio López Fonseca in their 1996 edition examine Mena's lexicon systematically and classify his errors in translation—some of which may have been caused by defective readings in the Latin version he was using. They note that Mena shares with other contemporary translators of classical languages the tendency to use pairs of words to translate the full sense of one word in the original. He is also given to glossing unfamiliar terms, both neologisms and familiar words imbued with new meanings. As a translator he is more conservative syntactically than he is in the ornamental style of his introduction; his lexicon is consistent with that of his other works, most notably *Laberinto de Fortuna,* as he does not hesitate to juxtapose archaic or familiar words with Latinisms, many of them of his own coinage.

Mena completed *Laberinto de Fortuna* in time to present it to Juan II in Tordesillas in February 1444. The moment could hardly have been less propitious: the king, to whom the poem is dedicated and who is addressed throughout as a sovereign among sovereigns, was being held under virtual house arrest by the princes of Aragón; Luna, the king's favorite and privy councillor, constable of Castile, and the exemplary victor over Fortune in the poem, was in exile. Clearly, the king's greatness was potential rather than actual; the achievement of national unity and the completion of the Reconquest that are recurring themes in the poem lay before him. Mena lived to see such hopes dashed, however: Luna was executed in 1453, and Juan II died the following year without having accomplished those goals.

*Laberinto de Fortuna,* also called *Las Trecientas* (The Three Hundred [Stanzas]), actually comprises 297 stanzas of *arte mayor:* that is, each stanza consists of eight twelve-syllable lines rhymed *abbaacca.* The lines are characterized by a pronounced accent pattern with a caesura at midline, predominantly *oóoóo / oóoóo.* Like *La Coronación, Laberinto de Fortuna* narrates an allegorical journey; but its structure is considerably more complex. The poet dedicates the work to the king in the opening stanza, then turns his attention to the goddess Fortune, who has the world in turmoil. He calls on her to conduct her affairs in an orderly fashion, following the example of the heavens; but he immediately corrects himself, realizing that the only order possible for Fortune is constant disorder. He asks to be shown the house where she keeps her wheel so that he may describe firsthand how she deals with people's lives.

The poet is taken up into the chariot of Bellona, goddess of war, and flown to a desert plain. He glimpses the neighboring plain through a transparent wall that surrounds it and distorts his view of what is on the other side. A thick cloud descends, blinding him; it is dissipated by a bright light, and a beautiful maiden appears. She informs him that she is the one who orders the present, disposes the future, and reveals the past, and that she is Divine Providence. Believing that he has found the true mistress of the great house, the poet asks Providence to guide him through it; she takes him to the highest point in the edifice.

Over the next twenty stanzas the poet describes the world as seen from his lofty vantage point. Finally, his guide draws his attention to three large wheels farther inside the structure: two are stationary, and one is in constant motion. Beneath them are great numbers of people, their names and fates written on their foreheads; but on one of the stationary wheels all the names are covered by a thick veil. Providence explains that the three wheels represent the past, the present, and the future; as a mortal, the poet will not be told of the future. Each wheel is made up of seven circles, each of which contains its complement of human bodies. Each circle is influenced by the Sun, the Moon, or one of the five then-known planets, and the influence of that celestial body is predominant in the lives of those who appear in the circle.

The poet contemplates each circle in order. The first, influenced by the Moon and represented by Diana, goddess of the Moon, governs hunters and those known for their chaste lives. On the wheel of the past, favored positions are occupied by figures from Greco-Roman history and mythology: Theseus, Hipermestra, Lucretia, Artemisa, Penelope, Argia, and Hercules. In the present a great queen presides; her husband, the king, is off to the left. Providence identifies her, with a reference to Spain that reflects Mena's nationalistic ideal, as "la ínclita reina d'España, muy virtuoso doña María" (the illustrious queen of Spain, the most virtuous Doña María), the wife of Juan II. Also in a high position is María, queen of Aragón and wife of Alfonso V, and slightly below the two monarchs is María Coronel, exemplary for her chastity. Juan II is exhorted to see that chastity be observed in public life and that powerful offenders be punished along with the weak. Contrary to what will be the poet's usual practice, no offenders are noted in this circle.

In the second circle, governed by Mercury, are the purveyors of wise counsel and the peacemakers. In the past Nestor, the ambassadors of Latinus, Priam, Capys, and Laocoön occupy high places; below are breakers of the peace, Simonists, and traitors: false prelates, Pandarus, Polymestor, Antenor, Aeneas, Eriphyle, and, closer to home, the traitorous Archbishop Opas and Count Julián. In the present the lowest part is full, but the poet names no names: "verdat lo permite, temor lo devieda" (truth permits it, fear forbids it). The poet concludes by excoriating the clergy for misusing the fruits of the labors of the poor and by exhorting Juan II to provide adequately for his subordinates so that greed will not impair the discharge of their duties.

The poet deals summarily with those in the highest part of the next circle, that of Venus, who are rewarded for turning vice into virtue through holy matrimony. Those below—adulterers, fornicators, practitioners of incest, and sodomites—receive more attention. Examples from the past abound: Clytemnestra and Aegisthus, Myrrha, Thereus, Macareus and Canace, Ixion, Pasiphae, and, from the more recent past, the poet Macías. No specific examples, good or bad, are given from the present. The poet inquires of Providence why otherwise prudent people are blinded by

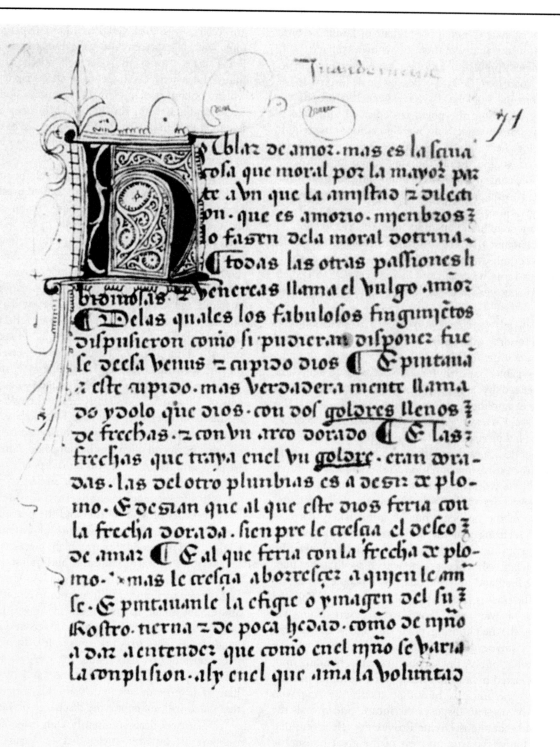

*Page from the manuscript in the Bibliothèque Nationale, Paris, for Mena's* Tratado de amor, *written circa 1444 ( from*
Tratado de amor, atribuido a Juan de Mena, *edited by María Luz Gutiérrez Araus, 1975; Doheny*
*Memorial Library, University of Southern California)*

love; she answers with a discourse on the causes and nature of true love. Addressing himself to Juan II, the poet calls on the king to punish criminal acts so that "clean, Catholic, virtuous love" will win out over the "viles actos del libidinoso fuego de Venus" (vile acts of the libidinous fire of Venus).

In the wheel of the past the upper part of the fourth circle, that of Phoebus (the Sun), holds doctors of the church, philosophers, orators, musicians, great astrologers, poets, experts in the quadrivium, and persons of knowledge. Sts. Jerome, Gregory, and Augustine are there, together with Cratus, Polemon, Empedocles, Zeno, Aristotle, Plato, and other Greek philosophers; Tubal (Jubal), the Old Testament musician, is present along with Chiron and other legendary classical musicians; the ten Sibyls are listed; and the narrator sees a large group of poets, although only Homer, Virgil, and Ennius are identified by name. In the present the only specific example is Enrique de Villena, whom the poet praises as "onra d'España e del siglo presente" (the honor of Spain and of the present age) while lamenting the condemnation of his works (by the king, according to Núñez). Those at the bottom are teachers and practitioners of the evil arts; five are mentioned, all from the past. The king's task here is to destroy the "arte malvada" (evil art) and restore the "santa prudençia" (holy prudence) by fostering the legitimate arts.

Emphasis shifts to the present as the poet contemplates the fifth circle, governed by Mars, the god of war. Praiseworthy examples from the past, dealt with in just two stanzas, include the two captains defeated by Julius Caesar in the battle for Lérida, as well as others from Roman history. In the present, Fortune has placed Juan II above all others; his seat is embellished with carvings that show the deeds of his illustrious ancestors. The king is shown in contemplation of great victories, most recently his own triumph at La Higuerela in 1431. This is Mena's "noble war": "¡O virtuosa, magnífica guerra! / En ti las querellas bolverse devían, / en ti do los nuestros muriendo bivían, / por gloria en los çielos y fama en la tierra" (Oh virtuous, magnificent war! / Quarrels should give way before you, / in whom our men, in dying, lived / in heavenly glory and in earthly fame).

The poet inveighs against civil strife with the example of the siege of Medina del Campo by the Aragonese in 1441, then lists the soldiers, both of the Reconquest and of civil war, who occupy high places on the wheel of Fortune. The first is Enrique de Guzmán, Count of Niebla, who died heroically in an assault on Gibraltar. The count is warned by the master of his fleet, who notes unfavorable omens and advises postponing the enterprise until a more favorable time.

The count, no believer in omens, sees no signs of an impending storm and orders his master to set sail: "Non los agüeros, los fechos sigamos; / pues una enpresa tan santa levamos / que más non podría ser otra ninguna, / presuma de vos e de mí la Fortuna / non que nos fuerça, mas que la forçamos" (Let us not follow omens but facts, / since we are undertaking such a holy enterprise, / more so than any other could be, / let Fortune presume of you and of me / not that she is forcing us, but rather that we are forcing her). Fortune has disposed otherwise, however: his assault repulsed, the count, who could have saved himself, returns to pick up his retreating forces and perishes along with them as his boat is swamped.

Other examples follow of valiant men who have died, some in the battles of the Reconquest, others in civil strife: Juan Pimentel, Count of Mayorga; the governor of Andalusia, Diego de Ribera; the governor of Cazorla, Rodrigo de Perea; Pedro de Narváez, son of the mayor of Antequera; the king's guardsman Juan de Merlo; Lorenzo Dávalos, chamberlain of the prince of Aragón; and Fernando de Padilla, *clavero* (keeper of the keys) of the Order of Calatrava. Providence, recounting the lament of Dávalos's mother, underscores the futility of civil discord, "donde non gana ninguno corona" (where no one earns a crown). Conspicuous by his absence is the Olympic champion of old, Milo: the circle of Mars honors fortitude, the strength born of virtue, not sheer physical prowess. So, too, should the king seek to have his kingdom governed by those who possess fortitude.

The sixth circle is governed by Jupiter. Occupying high places are those who ruled in time of peace or were noted for their devotion to civic duty, while those below are tyrants and invaders. Worthy examples from the past are Octavius, Marcus Manlius, Codrus of Athens, the Deciuses, Torquatus, the Brutuses, the Catos, and Fabricius. In the present, Juan II reigns supreme as peacemaker and giver of gifts, but the poet urges "pobres mortales" (poor mortals) not to envy the riches of kings and great lords, which are the seed of great evils, but to appreciate their own natural gifts, which kings and great lords covet. The poet extols the simple life of those who live without wealth: Amyclas had nothing to fear from Caesar. Among the many consigned to the depths, the poet names only the Dionysiuses of Syracuse, condemned for tyranny, and Ionos of Thessaly, for inventing money, the cause of so many ills. The king is called on to heal his kingdoms of this concern and inspire fear in those who serve him badly, so that justice will be upheld and made to serve the public weal uncorrupted.

The seventh circle, governed by Saturn, exalts great monarchs and persons noteworthy for their ability to mete out justice; below are those who allow evil and vice to exist and fail to punish crimes properly. The first person the poet espies is Luna, identified by Providence as he who "cavalga sobre la Fortuna / e doma su cuello con ásperas riendas" (rides on Fortune / and tames her neck with harsh reins). Luna, says the poet, is worthy of the prominent position in which the king has placed him and will always be the conqueror of Fortune. Those who thought otherwise and disassociated themselves from him may have been led astray by a practitioner of the black arts who predicted Luna's downfall; drawing on Lucan's *Pharsalia* and Ovid's *Metamorphoses,* the poet recounts the episode. The necromancer prepared a potion with which to awaken a dead person to serve as a medium. Finding a suitable corpse, she anointed it and conjured Pluto and Proserpina to send a spirit to speak through it. The spirit said that the underworld was angry with the grandees of Spain for giving respite to the infidels, thus interrupting the flow of souls to hell, and was fomenting civil strife among Castilians to ensure a supply. The spirit called on those in command to turn their wrath on the Moors and predicted that Luna would lose his power and be completely undone. The poet compares the nobles to chameleons for abandoning Luna and blames their actions on covetousness. Finding that the predictions do not materialize, the nobles returned to the sorceress, who insisted that the prophecy had been fulfilled: a statue of Luna was destroyed in Toledo. Fortune must content herself with that, since she cannot overcome the man himself. The poet, addressing Luna, notes that Fortune has remained favorable to him from that moment on.

As dawn breaks, the poet wonders whether what he has recounted was a dream or real. He inquires of Providence what is in store for the king. Providence predicts that his glory will outshine that of his illustrious predecessors, but she is silent about the details and vanishes before the poet can learn more. The poem ends with a plea to the king to make what has been prophesied come true; Providence, says the narrator, grants the king "fuerça, corage, valor e prudencia" (strength, valor, courage, and prudence) to triumph over the Moors and be glorified by his subjects.

*Laberinto de Fortuna* has an unmistakable political message: civil strife, greed, malfeasance among the powerful (laity and clergy alike), disloyalty to Luna, and the king's own tolerance of those who should be ruled with a firmer hand have placed the affairs of state in disarray. Energy must be redirected toward the great enterprise of the Reconquest, and Luna, who has had the strength, as well as the wisdom, to triumph over adverse Fortune, is the example to be emulated. The king, though praised at every turn for his virtues, is

repeatedly called on to act; the glory predicted for him is dependent on what he has yet to accomplish.

Most of what the poet encounters in his allegorical journey through the domain of Fortune is the handiwork not of Fortune but of Divine Providence. As Rafael Lapesa has shown, figures whose lives ended unhappily may occupy high places on a wheel because of their moral rectitude or valor; conversely, figures at the bottom, including such heroes of other epics as Aeneas, are there because of ethical concerns, not because their lives ended ignominiously. Human beings live, as the poet is led to believe early on, in a providential world where order, justice, and rectitude triumph over the chaos of Fortune. That providential order seems to be suspended momentarily in circle 5, however, as the count of Niebla—whose cause is just and whose valor is unquestioned—challenges Fortune and is defeated. Other noble, virtuous, and valiant men of the poet's time meet equally unhappy ends; Providence orders their place on the wheel but does not intervene to affect the course of their lives. It would appear that it is up to humans to be the makers of their own fortune; only Luna, in circle 7, is depicted as dominating the fickle goddess, and he is the one who must right the ship of state and restore providential order.

Unlike *La Coronación,* which requires the poet's extensive prose commentary to lead the reader from the literal and allegorical to the moral meaning, the moral message in *Laberinto de Fortuna* is abundantly clear. The poet excoriates those who do not live virtuously, even though he names no names in the present. The chaste, honest, and righteous are praised and accorded high places on their respective wheels. Only in circle 7 does the poet hint at another kind of virtue in the etymological sense: *virtus* (manly excellence) may be the kind of virtue that Luna possesses, and the king must follow the example of his favorite.

*Laberinto de Fortuna* has received more scholarly attention than the rest of Mena's works combined. It was edited at least fifteen times in the twentieth century, definitively by Maximiliaan P. A. M. Kerkhof in 1995. Much of Lida de Malkiel's monumental 1950 study has not been superseded, however, including her analyses of Mena's elevated poetic style, his skillful handling of his source material, and his reception. The question of classical and medieval generic antecedents and models has been more fully treated by Dorothy Clotelle Clarke.

Most scholars agree that the complementary ideals of national unity under a strong Castile and the completion of the Reconquest are the central themes of the work; there is support for the identification, first suggested by Joaquín Gimeno Casalduero in 1964, of the labyrinth in the title with the chaotic Spain of

*Page from a manuscript in the Academica Española, Madrid, for Mena's* Tratado sobre el título de duque *(1445), written on the occasion of Juan de Guzmán becoming duke of Medina Sidonia (from Mena's* Tratado sobre el título el duque, *edited by Louise Vasvari Fainberg, 1976; Thomas Cooper Library, University of South Carolina)*

Mena's day and for the view, offered by Philip O. Gericke in 1968, of Fortune as a force that has run rampant, unchecked by Providence. Several scholars have analyzed the structure of the work but have not arrived at a consensus as to how to present that structure in a manageable schema. Gimeno Casalduero proposes a division into an introduction (stanzas 1–61), the exposition of the seven circles (stanzas 62–267), and a conclusion (stanzas 268–297). Few would dispute the importance of the moral element, demonstrated by Lapesa, or of the author's political vision, emphasized by Alan D. Deyermond, as structural determinants, and there is some support for the view that the poem describes a providential order, a suspension of that order, and its restoration, although not all scholars incorporate those narrative elements into their structural schemata. Since 1985 the work has been read by Edwin J. Webber as a subtle criticism of Luna's ambition and as advocating his downfall, by Colbert I. Nepaulsingh as an apocalyptic reworking of the *Aeneid*, by James F. Burke as the description of an interior journey through the structure of the poet's own mind, by Linde M. Brocato as an attack on moral and sexual otherness, and by Gregory S. Hutcheson as an expression of New Christian disillusionment over the state of affairs in Castile.

According to Núñez, as recompense for writing *Laberinto de Fortuna* Mena was awarded the title of royal chronicler by the king, although the first surviving reference to him as such–in an exchange of poems with Pedro, Duke of Coimbra–is dated 1447–1448. His other appointment as the king's secretary of Latin letters probably dates from the same time; no documentary reference is made to it, however, until 1450.

Mena was in the most productive period of his literary life, and several works appeared in rapid succession from 1444 to 1448. The first may be *Tratado de Amor* (Treatise on Love), which is attributed to him in some manuscripts and reveals similarities in sources and treatment to the circle of Venus in *Laberinto de Fortuna*. This similarity has led most scholars to conclude that it was composed around the same time. Street, however, deems it part of Mena's juvenilia. The case for attribution to Mena was made convincingly by Lida de Malkiel in 1950 and by Street in 1952 on the basis of internal evidence.

*Tratado de Amor* lacks preliminary material such as a dedication or preamble. The author goes quickly to the matter at hand: since licit (that is, conjugal) love has attracted so little attention from poets, he will deal more extensively with illicit and insane love, listing first the causes that induce it and then those that repel it. Ovid is the primary source, but Lida de Malkiel (1950) finds translations and reminiscences of several other Latin

authors, including Virgil, Lucan, Pliny the Elder, Statius, Boethius, and the seldom-read Tibullus. She classifies the style as didactic, aspiring to the simple elegance appropriate for an essay, without violent *hyperbaton* (a transposition of usual word order) or accumulation of Latinisms.

Mena's next work seems to have been *Tratado sobre el título de duque* (Treatise on the Title of Duke), dedicated to Juan de Guzmán, Duke of Medina Sidonia and third Count of Niebla, the son of the count of Niebla commemorated in *Laberinto de Fortuna*. As Louise Vasvari Fainberg points out in her 1976 edition of the work, the dukedom was conferred on 17 February 1445; a reasonable supposition is that Mena composed the work in honor of the occasion and presented it to its dedicatee during that year. Of the ten original chapters, portions of two are lost because of a lacuna in the manuscript.

In the dedication the author notes that the title–the highest the king can bestow–is well deserved by its recipient because of his lineage and great service to the realm. The ostensible purpose of the work is to detail prerogatives and ceremonies that correspond to the title, but several chapters end with lengthy panegyrics to the new duke. The chapters deal, respectively, with the origins of the title and how it is attained; how a duke's title should derive from the name of a province or a city rather than from the name of a town or castle; the types of crowns and which are appropriate for dukes; the types of ensigns a duke may carry; the authority of dukes to hear challenges and set times and places for duels; how and when a duke may confer knighthood (the chapter is truncated); the number and kinds of officials a duke is entitled to appoint (most of the chapter is missing); the heraldic devices and the rights thereunto pertaining; and the prerogatives of ducal dignity.

Vasvari Fainberg's introduction to her edition of *Tratado sobre el título de duque* includes a comprehensive treatment of language, style, and sources, with apposite comparisons to the author's other works. She finds the style to be in the same ornamental-didactic mode as parts of *La Coronación* and the translation of the *Ilias latina* and the choice of source material and its handling to be characteristic of Mena, as well. The question of the attribution of the work to Mena appears to have been resolved.

In 1446 Luna, still constable of Castile and by then also master of the Order of Santiago, composed his *Libro de las virtuosas e claras mugeres* (Book of Virtuous and Illustrious Women). Mena contributed a prologue, using the ornate style typical of most of his prose works. He is unstinting in his praise of the constable: Luna has earned the gratitude of women for taking the time from his duties to write on their behalf, and Mena has been charged with expressing their thanks in writing. By coming to the defense of women, Luna has enhanced the glory of his own fame before posterity.

The last prose work ascribed to Mena, *Memorias de algunos linages,* appeared in 1448. The attribution to Mena appears in the only surviving manuscript, which is badly mutilated, and is otherwise unsubstantiated. Alfredo Carballo Picazo is inclined to reject Mena's authorship, as he finds the simple style inconsistent with Mena's other prose writings, but he acknowledges the possibility that it is an outline for a more developed and elaborate treatment. The work traces the origins of fourteen families, recounts their noteworthy deeds, and describes their coats of arms. The first is the Mena family: coming from the Valley of Mena, they served Castile well, says the author; they took part in the conquest of Baeza, which is reflected in their coat of arms. The author does not claim to be a member of the family. He professes to know Cardinal Juan de Cervantes, archbishop of Seville, and members of Cervantes's family, as well as two of Luna's pages whom Mena might reasonably be expected to have known. An interest in genealogy and heraldry is not central to Mena's other works, although he shows some knowledge of heraldry in *Tratado sobre el título de duque.*

During this period Mena was actively involved in the literary life of the court. He wrote many shorter poems typical of the courtly poetry of his day, some fifty of which survive. He composed love lyrics, occasional verses, and satirical pieces, and took part in exchanges with other poets. Pérez Priego (1979) has shown that eleven of his poems are datable on internal evidence to 1444–1455; the others could reasonably be assigned to this period, as well. Mena was esteemed in his own time for his satirical verses—though few of them have been preserved—and for his love poetry, but this aspect of his production has been obscured by his longer works. King Juan II is most frequently favored in his panegyrics; Luna is praised, in lines reminiscent of *Laberinto de Fortuna,* as a "firme roque, non mudable / por fortuna nin por miedo" (firm rock, not mutable / by fortune nor by fear). Other recipients of laudatory poems include the duke of Coimbra and Guzmán, Count of Niebla. In his exchanges with Santillana the mutual regard of the two men is apparent, which is remarkable in light of their political differences. In the opposite vein, Mena takes Ortiz de Stúñiga to task for his criticism of the Battle of Olmedo, calling him "capitán de la porquera" (captain of the pigsty) and accusing him of frivolousness and cowardice. Mena's humorous attack on an archpriest who sold him a mule in poor condition—"¿Quál diablo me topó / con este cabezpacido?" (What devil made me run / into this ton-

surehead?)—is viewed by scholars as part of the long tradition of anticlerical satire.

While these poems are not innovative metrically, their range of styles is broad. Like the longer poems, many combine Latinisms with rhetorical devices, mythological allusions, *hyperbaton,* obscure syntax, and obsolete usages that render them inaccessible to all but a select learned audience. Only a few, such as "El sol clarecía los montes acayos" (The Sun Dawned on the Achaean Mountains)—also known as "Claro escuro" (Chiaroscuro)—and "Ya non sufre mi cuidado" (My Worry Cannot Stand Any More), have received individual attention beyond the introductory studies and commentaries of the standard editions.

In 1449 or 1450 Mena married Marina Méndez, who may have been related to the Biedma and Sotomayor families. He had pursued litigation for, and had been granted, a benefice that he resigned because of this marriage. Neither of his two marriages produced offspring.

In 1453 Luna was executed by order of the king. Mena wrote nothing about his hero's fall from grace; in a matter of months he was granted income from properties in Cordova that had belonged to Luna. Some suspect that the grant was made to guarantee favorable treatment from the royal chronicler. It may have bought silence, as there is no evidence that Mena contributed a single word—favorable or otherwise—to the chronicle of Juan II, his official title notwithstanding. After Juan II's death in 1454, he retained his position as royal chronicler and the income from it under King Enrique IV, but he probably spent less time at court. In 1455 he celebrated Santillana's visit to Seville with a poem, "Muy alegre queda Tetis" (Thetis Is Very Glad). In May 1456 he and his wife were cosignatories in a property matter. In September of that year the royal chronicler's stipend was reassigned because of Mena's death, which resulted, according to one source, from a fall from a mule, or—more probably—from some ailment that caused a "fierce pain in his side." He was buried at Torrelaguna on lands belonging to Santillana; tradition has it that Santillana paid his funeral expenses and had a monument erected in his honor.

At his death Mena left unfinished his *Coplas de los pecados mortales* (Stanzas on the Mortal Sins). He had completed 106 stanzas, which in all likelihood constituted more than half of the poem. His contemporaries Gómez Manrique and Pero Guillén de Segovia continued the work, as did Jerónimo de Olivares some years later. The poem is in *arte menor:* each stanza consists of eight octosyllabic lines rhymed *abbaacca.* It is an allegorical poem, like *La Coronación* and *Laberinto de Fortuna,* but this time the allegory—in the tradition of Prudentius's *Psychomachia*—represents the conflict between will and

*Page from the manuscript in the Biblioteca del Palacio, Madrid, for Mena's* Coplas de los pecados mortales, *written in 1456 (from* Coplas de los siete pecados mortales and First Continuation, *edited by Gladys M. Rivera, 1982; Ralph Brown Draughton Library, Auburn University)*

reason and is devoid of classical trappings. The poet banishes the pagan muses, having invoked the Christian muse in his opening line. He reflects on life as ongoing death–"ca la muerte no es morir, / pues consiste en el bevir, / mas es fin de la carrera" (for death is not dying, / since it consists of living, / but it is the end of the road)– and he rues the time he has spent in acquiring classical knowledge and adorning his writings:

> Non se gaste más pavilo
> en saber quién fue Pegaso,
> las dos cunbres de Pernaso,
> los siete braços del Nilo,
> pues nos llegamos al filo
> y sabemos que de nos
> juzgando reçibe Dios
> más la obra qu'el estilo

> (Let no more wick be spent
> In learning who was Pegasus,
> The two peaks of Parnassus,
> The seven arms of the Nile;
> For we get to the edge,
> And we know that from us
> God in judging receives
> More the work and not the style).

Mena's palinode is not without self-deprecating humor–"mis grandes viçios defiendo / y a los agenos afeo" (I defend my own great vices / and make those of others ugly), he says of his earlier works–and he does not propose to abandon poetry altogether but merely to strip it of "lo superfluo" (what is frivolous) and "lo dañoso" (what is harmful). He then proceeds to the material at hand: Prudence is to adjudicate the conflict between Will and Reason. Will has seven faces, the seven deadly sins of Pride, Avarice, Lust, Anger, Gluttony, Envy, and Sloth. The poet is disturbed by the vision of this chimera but is reassured when Reason appears. Reason engages each sin in debate, beginning with Pride; the poem ends during Reason's reply to Anger and thus presents no conclusions, although it is safe to say that Prudence would have declared Reason the victor.

The events of 1453–1454 may well have produced a profound disillusionment in the poet, causing him to turn his attention away from worldly concerns and toward asceticism. It would be inaccurate, however, to view *Coplas de los pecados mortales* as a total reversal of everything Mena had written previously. His strong moral bent is evident in his earlier works, and the style–while clearly not the Latinized one of those works–shows that he "no desdeña los recursos adquiridos en su variada experimentación" (does not disdain the devices acquired in his varied experimentation), as Lida de Malkiel puts it in *Juan de Mena, poeta del pre-*

*rrenacimiento español. Coplas de los pecados mortales* makes restrained use of the classical simile, metaphor, and lexical borrowings.

Mena came to be regarded as the premier poet of his generation; his works received editorial treatment usually reserved for the classics, being printed with the commentary of scholars such as Núñez and Sánchez de las Brozas. He was often wrongly credited with being the first true poet in the Castilian language, and such sixteenth-century poets as Juan Boscán Almogáver, Garcilaso de la Vega, Cristóbal de Castillejo, and, most notably, Fernando de Herrera were influenced by him in varying degrees. So, too, was Luis de Góngora, possibly the greatest Spanish poet of the seventeenth century and, like Mena, a native of Cordova; reminiscences of Mena can be found in some of the most noted characteristics of Góngora's style, such as his predilection for the Latinate neologism and his violent *hyperbata*.

Over time Mena came to be looked on as a treasured relic of a distant past, to be revered but not read and certainly not imitated. In the eighteenth century his works were accorded mention in histories of literature but were not studied; in the nineteenth he was taken to task for his "unnatural" style and lexicon. The process of reevaluation begun in the twentieth century has returned *Laberinto de Fortuna*, at least, to its place among the major works of the period before 1500. Mena is regarded today, along with Santillana, as one of the poets who best represents the period of transition between the Middle Ages and the Renaissance.

## References:

Eugenio Asensio, "La peculiaridad literaria de los conversos," *Anuario de Estudios Medievales*, 4 (1967): 327–351;

Vicente Beltrán de Heredia, "Nuevos documentos inéditos sobre el poeta Juan de Mena," *Salmanticensis*, 3 (1956): 502–508;

Linde M. Brocato, "'Tened por espejo su fin': Mapping Gender and Sex in Fifteenth- and Sixteeenth-Century Spain," in *Queer Iberia: Sexualities, Cultures, and Crossings from the Middle Ages to the Renaissance*, edited by Josiah Blackmore and Gregory S. Hutcheson (Durham, N.C. & London: Duke University Press, 1999), pp. 325–365;

James F. Burke, "The Interior Journey and the Structure of Juan de Mena's *Laberinto de Fortuna*," *Revista de Estudios Hispánicos*, 22 (1988): 27–45;

Alfredo Carballo Picazo, "Juan de Mena: Un documento inédito y una obra atribuida," *Revista de Literatura*, 1 (1952): 269–299;

Américo Castro, *España en su historia* (Buenos Aires: Losada, 1948); translated by Edmund L. King as *The Stucture of Spanish History* (Princeton: Princeton

University Press, 1954), pp. 18, 490, 524, 557, 563, 564, 606, 624;

Dorothy Clotelle Clarke, *Juan de Mena's* Laberinto de Fortuna: *Classic Epic and Mester de Clerecía* (University, Miss.: Romance Monographs, 1973);

Alan D. Deyermond, "Structure and Style as Instruments of Propaganda in Juan de Mena's *Laberinto de Fortuna,*" *Proceedings of the Patristic, Medieval and Renaissance Conference,* 5 (1983): 159–167;

Ralph Di Franco, "Formalist Critics and the *Laberinto de Fortuna,*" *Hispanic Journal,* 6 (1985): 165–172;

Brian Dutton, *Catálogo-índice de la poesía cancioneril del siglo XV* (Madison, Wis.: Hispanic Seminary of Medieval Studies, 1982);

Dutton and Jineen Krogstad, *El Cancionero del siglo XV, c. 1360–1520,* 7 volumes (Salamanca: University of Salamanca, 1990–1991);

Charles Faulhaber, Ángel Gómez Moreno, Angela Moll Dexeus, and Antonio Cortijo Ocaña, *BETA (Biblioteca Electrónica de Textos Españoles)* <http://sunsite.berkeley.edu/Philobiblon/BETA/0000.html>;

María Lourdes García-Macho and Antonina Saba, *El léxico de la "Ylíada de Homero en romance" traducida por Juan de Mena* (Madrid: Universidad Nacional de Educación a Distancia, 1998);

Philip O. Gericke, "Mena's *Laberinto de Fortuna:* Apocalypse Now?" *La corónica,* 17, no. 2 (1989): 1–17;

Gericke, "The Narrative Structure of the *Laberinto de Fortuna,*" *Romance Philology,* 21 (1968): 512–522;

Joaquín Gimeno Casalduero, "Notas sobre el *Laberinto de Fortuna,*" *Modern Language Notes,* 79 (1964): 271–294;

Gregory S. Hutcheson, "Cracks in the Labyrinth: Juan de Mena, *Converso* Experience, and the Rise of the Spanish Nation," *La corónica,* 25, no. 1 (1996): 37–52;

Maximiliaan P. A. M. Kerkhof, "El MS. 229 (PN7) de la Bibliothèque Nationale de Paris: Base de las ediciones modernas del *Labertino de fortuna* de Juan de Mena," *Medievalia et Humanistica,* new series 14 (August 1993);

Rafael Lapesa, "El elemento moral en el *Laberinto* de Mena: Su influjo en la disposicion de la obra," *Hispanic Review,* 27 (1959): 257–266;

María Rosa Lida de Malkiel, *La idea de la Fama en la Edad Media castellana* (Mexico City, Madrid & Buenos Aires: Fondo de Cultura Económica, 1952), pp. 115, 168, 231, 242, 244, 252–253, 256, 276, 278–292;

Lida de Malkiel, *Juan de Mena, poeta del prerrenacimiento español,* Publicaciones de la Nueva revista de filología hispánica, no. 1 (Mexico City: Colegio de México, 1950; enlarged by Yakov Malkiel, Mexico City: Centro de Estudios Lingüísticos y Literarios, Colegio de México, 1984);

Lida de Malkiel, "Para la biografía de Juan de Mena," *Revista de Filología Hispánica,* 3 (1941): 150–154;

Inez Macdonald, "The *Coronación* of Juan de Mena: Poem and Commentary," *Hispanic Review,* 7 (1939): 125–144;

M. Muñoz Vásquez, "Aportación documental a la biografía de Juan de Mena," *Boletín de la Real Academia de Cordova,* 28 (1957): 147–165;

Colbert I. Nepaulsingh, *Towards a History of Literary Composition in Medieval Spain* (Toronto, Buffalo, N.Y. & London: University of Toronto Press, 1986), pp. 109–124;

M. A. Ortí Belmonte, "Aportaciones a la vida y obra de Juan de Mena," *Boletín de la Real Academia de Cordova,* 28 (1957): 3–88;

Florence Street, "La paternidad del *Tratado de Amor,*" *Bulletin Hispanique,* 54 (1952): 15–32;

Street, "La vida de Juan de Mena," *Bulletin Hispanique,* 55 (1953): 149–173;

Alberto Varvaro, *Premesse ad un'edizione critica delle poesie minori di Juan de Mena* (Naples: Ligouri, 1964);

Edwin J. Webber, "El enigma del *Laberinto de Fortuna,*" in *Philologica Hispaniensia in Honorem Manuel Alvar,* volume 3 (Madrid: Gredos, 1986), pp. 563–557;

Julian Weiss, "Juan de Mena's *Coronación:* Satire or *Sátira?*" *Journal of Hispanic Philology,* 6 (1982): 113–138;

Weiss, *The Poet's Art: Literary Theory in Castile c. 1400–1460,* Medium Aevum Monographs, new series 14 (Oxford: Society for the Study of Mediaeval Languages and Literature, 1900).

# Garci Rodríguez de Montalvo

*(circa 1450? – before 1505)*

William Thomas Little
*California Polytechnic State University*

BOOKS: *Los quatro libros del Virtuoso cauallero Amadís de Gaula* (Saragossa: Jorge Coci Aleman, 1508);

*Las sergas del virtuoso cauallero Esplandián hijo de Amadís de Gaula (que fueron escritas en griego por la mano de aquel gran maestro Helisabad)* (Seville?, 1510?).

**Editions:** *Los quatro libros del virtuoso cauallero Amadís de Gaula* (Rome: Antonio Martínez de Salamanca, 1519);

*Las sergas del virtuoso cauallero esplādian hijo de Amadis de Gaula* (Toledo: Juan de Villaquirán, 1521);

*Libros de caballerías: Con un discuro preliminar y un catálogo razonado,* edited by Pascual de Gayangos, Biblioteca de autores espanoles, volume 40 (Madrid: Rivadeneyra, 1857);

*Amadís de Gaula: Novela de caballerías, refundida y modernizada,* edited by Ángel Rosenblat, second edition (Buenos Aires: Editorial Losada, 1940);

*Amadís de Gaula: Selección estudio y notas,* edited by Victorino López, fifth edition (Saragossa: Editiorial Ebro, 1963);

*Amadís de Gaula,* 2 volumes, edited by Juan Manuel Cacho Blecua (Madrid: Ediciones Cátedra, 1987).

**Editions in English:** *The fifth booke of the most pleasant and delectable historie of Amadis de Gaule: Containing the first part of the most strange valiant and worthy actes of Esplandian sonne to Amadis, etc.,* translated anonymously (London: Printed by Adam Islip, sold by Hugh Jackson, 1598);

*The Fifth Book of the Most Pleasant and Delectable History of Amadis De Gaule, Containing the first Part of the most strange, valiant, and worthy Acts of Esplandian Son to Amadis De Gaule, etc.,* translated anonymously (London: Printed by Thomas Johnson for Andrew Kembe & Charles Tyus, 1664);

*Amadis of Gaul, by Vasco Lobeira (from the Spanish Version of Garciordonez de Montalvo),* 4 volumes, translated by Robert Southey (London: Printed by N. Biggs for T. N. Longman & O. Rees, 1803);

*The Queen of California: The Origin of the Name of California, with a Translation from the Sergas of Esplandian,* translated by Edward Everett Hale, Colt Press Series of California Classics, no. 4 (San Francisco: Colt Press, 1945);

*Amadis of Gaul: A Novel of Chivalry of the 14th Century Presumably First Written in Spanish, Revised and Reworked by Garci Rodriguez de Montalvo Prior to 1505; Translated from the Putative Princeps of Saragossa, 1508,* 2 volumes, translated by Edwin B. Place and Herbert C. Behm, Studies in Romance Languages, no. 11 (Lexington: University Press of Kentucky, 1974, 1975);

*The Labors of the Very Brave Knight Esplandián,* translated by William Thomas Little, Medieval and Renaissance Texts and Studies, volume 92 (Binghamton: Center for Medieval and Early Renaissance Studies, State University of New York at Binghamton, 1992).

*Amadís de Gaula* was the first prose chivalric romance of the Spanish-speaking world. The work is thought to have been first published in 1508 as *Los quatro libros del Virtuoso cauallero Amadís de Gaula* (The Four Books of the Virtuous Cavalier Amadís of Gaul); in a 1909 article Grace S. Williams mentions an unauthenticated 1496 edition, but it has never been found. The story is continued in *Las sergas del virtuoso cauallero Esplandián hijo de Amadís de Gaula (que fueron escritas en griego por la mano de aquel gran maestro Helisabad)* (The Deeds of the Virtuous Cavalier Esplandián, son of Amadís of Gaul [Which Were Written in Greek by the Hand of That Great Master Helisabad]), thought to have been written by the same author and published in 1510.

Uncertainty concerning the identity of the author of *Amadís de Gaula* has led scholars to postulate Spanish, Portuguese, and French origins for the work. As early as the fourteenth century a Portuguese chronicler claimed that the Portuguese Vasco de Lobeira was the author of *Amadís de Gaula.* This idea was revived several times by Portuguese and American scholars. In 1873 the Portuguese scholar Teófilo Braga attempted to prove Lobeira's authorship. Later (1915, 1916) he postulated a Hebrew version of *Amadís de Gaula* translated from a Portuguese original; Juan Bautista Avalle-Arce, Juan Manuel Cacho Blecua, James Donald Fogelquist, and Martín de Riquer have refuted this theory. Some scholars have claimed to detect words of Portuguese origin in the text, but Cacho Blecua has shown most of these claims to be inaccurate. Claims of a French original are even more tenuous than the Portuguese claims. Avalle-Arce concludes that the original *Amadís de Gaula* was written in the Castilian-Leonese dialect of northwestern Spain.

The author of the work is identified in the 1508 edition as Garci Rodríguez de Montalvo; a typographical error in the second known edition (1519), perpetuated in subsequent editions until the twentieth century, resulted in the name being given as Garci Gutiérrez de Montalvo (1510) or as Garci Ordóñez de Montalvo (1519). Since Montalvo died even before the 1508 edition was published, he was unable to correct the error.

In the prologue to the 1508 edition Montalvo refers to an earlier medieval version of the story in three books that he reworked into his four books, with some additions to the fourth. The earliest known mention of a literary character named Amadís is in *Regimiento de los príncipes* (On the Government of Rulers, 1344), a Spanish translation of Giles of Rome's *De regimine principum* (circa 1280), where Amadís is included along with Tristan, Zifar, Mars, and Achilles in a list of knights who are known for their prowess in combat and for their chivalric attentions to women. In the early fifteenth century there is a reference to a knightly character named Florestán de Leguizamón; Amadís's half brother in book 1 of *Amadís de Gaula* is called Florestán. "Amadís" appears in the fifteenth century as a name given to dogs, which, according to Avalle-Arce's *Amadís de Gaula: El primitivo y el de Montalvo* (*Amadís de Gaula: The Original and the Version of Montalvo*, 1990), is a sign of its popularity. Further references to Amadís in the fifteenth century can be found in the anonymous Catalan romance *Curial e Güelfa* (circa 1435–1462), in ballads. In the *Cancionero de Baena* (Songbook [Compiled by Juan Alfonso] de Baena, circa 1430) six of the fifty poets represented refer to Amadís or other characters in the original Amadís material. The earliest of these poets is Pero Ferruz, who flourished in the court of Enrique II between 1360 and 1379. Ferruz mentions the three Amadís books and describes the hero as handsome, sturdy in the face of hardships, faithful, famous, and brave. Ferruz also states that Amadís is dead; Montalvo's reworking of the tale, written more than a century later, omits mention of Amadís's death.

The most important documentary evidence of a pre-Montalvo Amadís story consists of fragments of four pages from a manuscript from about 1420, now in the Bancroft Library at the University of California at Berkeley, that support Montalvo's statement that he reworked an existing version of *Amadís de Gaula* while keeping many passages virtually intact. These fragments also demonstrate that the character of Amadís's son, Esplandián, was not invented by Montalvo. On the basis of both textual and extratextual analysis, Avalle-Arce postulates in *Amadís de Gaula: El primitivo y el de Montalvo* that the original version of *Amadís de Gaula* was most likely created during the reign of Sancho IV of Castile from 1284 to 1295. No complete version of this original text is known to be extant. The dates Avalle-Arce proposes for the first version coincide with the period that, he says, marks "los albores del cultivo de la prosa artística castellana" (the dawn of the flowering of Spanish artistic prose). The original version was probably fairly short, according to Avalle-Arce, because in that period "la prosa artística castellana no estaba lo suficientemente de sarrollada como para emprender empresas de alto vuelo" (the artistic prose narrative in Spanish was not developed enough to undertake highly ambitious projects).

The primitive text apparently ended with Esplandián killing his father, Amadís, by accident and Oriana, mother of the former and wife of the latter, committing suicide by throwing herself out a window when she hears of the tragedy. In book 5, chapter 29, of Montalvo's version, father and son fight nearly to the death without recognizing each other; in the following chapter the narrator alludes to the original tragic version but quickly adds: "Mas no fue así, que aquel gran maestro Elisabat le sanó de sus llagas" (But none of that is true, for Master Helisabad cured him of his wounds). In Montalvo's retelling Amadís must live so that he can be a witness to his son's superiority in knightly combat and so that he can join Esplandián in fighting for a cause that Montalvo posits as more noble than individual glory: a worldwide battle to save Christendom from paganism. At the end of the prologue to book 1 Montalvo says that he "corregiole de los antiguos originales que estaban corruptos" (corrected the corrupted ancient originals) of three no-longer-extant volumes dealing with Amadís; according to Avalle-Arce, these volumes correspond roughly with Montalvo's first three books. Montalvo goes on to say that he added most of the fourth book and created the fifth himself. Stylistic variations, changes in characters, new materials, sermonizing interpolations, and references to historical events and personages—especially the Reyes Católicos (Catholic Monarchs)—from the 1470s through the 1490s indicate that Montalvo took as long as two decades to compose the work.

Since book 4 ends with four significant plot elements unresolved, and since all four are resolved in book 5, one may reasonably conclude that they were present in the earlier manuscript version that Montalvo recast. Montalvo, however, made significant changes to the characters, style, values, and plot of the texts that he reworked so that all five books are the product of a late-fifteenth-century Spanish worldview.

Critics generally agree that most of book 1, some of book 2, little of book 3, and none of books 4 and 5 are the direct reworking of an earlier text. They disagree, however, about the quality of the results. For Avalle-Arce in *Amadís de Gaula: El primitivo y el de Montalvo,* "Montalvo's rare creative art and extraordinary economy of narrative techniques are admirable from any point of view." On the other hand, Edwin B. Place and Samuel Gili Gaya react negatively to Montalvo's revisionist worldview. Admitting that Arthurian chivalry was no longer a viable force in late-fifteenth-century Spanish society, Gili Gaya says in his "*Las sergas de Esplandián* como crítica de la caballería bretona" (*Las sergas de Esplandián* as a Critique of Breton Chivalry, 1947) that Montalvo undermined Breton-style knight-errantry, "al mismo tiempo que su fantasía se complace en idear una serie inacabable de descomunales lances, sin la coherencia interna que a los del *Amadís* comunicaba la personalidad del protagonista" (while his imagination was content to contrive an interminable series of monstrous episodes and battles, without the internal coherence that the protagonist's personality lent to the events in *Amadís*). In addition to the earlier Amadís sources, several other major medieval texts that have been seen as significant influences on Montalvo's five books include Guido delle Colonne's *Historia troiana* (Trojan History, circa 1285); Giovanni Boccaccio's *De casibus virorum illustrium* (The Fate of Illustrious Men, circa 1370), which Montalvo probably knew in a Spanish translation by Pero López de Ayala (*Caída de príncipes,* books 1–8 of *De casibus virorum illustrium,* circa 1393) and Juan Alfonso de Zamora (bks. 9–10 of *De casibus virorum illustrium,* circa 1422); and Francesco Petrarca's (Petrarch's) *De remediis utriusque fortunae* (On Remedies against Various Kinds of Fortune, circa 1370), of which a few Spanish translations were available. To mirror and critique the social and historical realities of his lifetime, which had encompassed the Turkish siege and capture of Christian Constantinople in 1453 and the conquest of Moorish Granada by the Catholic Monarchs in 1492, Montalvo draws inspiration from classical and Spanish myths, medieval narratives of the Trojan War, the Breton Cycle of chivalric romances, and contemporary events.

The little that is known or conjectured about Montalvo's life derives mainly from the work of two scholars: Pascual de Gayangos, who published an edition of *Amadís de Gaula* in 1857, based most of his ideas on evidence in the novel itself, while Narciso Alonso

Cortés relied on archival research in Medina del Campo and Valladolid for his 1933 article on Montalvo. According to de Gayangos and Alonso Cortés, Montalvo was probably born in the middle of the fifteenth century in Medina del Campo, a powerful and prosperous city ruled by an oligarchy of seven families. Two of the families had joined the oligarchy in 1206; one of these families descended from Martín Gutiérrez de Montalvo, eighth *Señor* (Lord) of Botalorno. Garci Rodríguez de Montalvo belonged to this family, which was known in Medina del Campo as the Pollino lineage. While Montalvo's family considered 1206 as its heroic point of origin, its actual origins can be traced to 1082, when Hernán Martínez de Montalvo accompanied King Alfonso I in taking several towns in Castile from the Muslims.

Each of Medina del Campo's ruling families elected a *regidor* (alderman) to the town council, and each *regidor* was the head of his respective family. The printer of the 1508 edition of *Amadís de Gaula* says, in a note inserted between the prologue and the beginning of book 1, that Garci Rodríguez de Montalvo had been an alderman of Medina del Campo in the 1490s. The author was, then, a powerful man; he was also wealthy, because the minimum worth required for election as *regidor* was the considerable sum of 200,000 *maravedís*. He would have had leisure to write, to travel, and to hunt, which the author says in chapter 99 of *Las sergas de Esplandián* is his favorite pastime.

Medina del Campo was the favorite residence of the Catholic Monarchs, Fernando and Isabel (Ferdinand and Isabella); Isabel felt more comfortable there than anywhere else in Spain, so court culture was readily available for Montalvo to observe. The many sermonizing asides concerning monarchs and grandees throughout Montalvo's five books make his text an anatomy of Spanish government and mores during the last half of the fifteenth century. Montalvo was knighted by Fernando and Isabel for his participation in the war with the Moorish kingdom of Granada of 1482 to 1492.

A document in the Chancellery Archive of Valladolid dated 1497 details a *pleito* (lawsuit or judicial action) against a García Rodríguez de Montalvo of Medina del Campo. Since the writer's nephew, who had the same name, also lived in Medina del Campo at that time, it is impossible to say which is the individual named in the judicial action; but the case described in the document parallels aspects of *Amadís de Gaula*. In 1496 a resident of Mojados, a village near Medina del Campo, accused his wife, Juana, of adultery, and she was jailed for a month. According to the judicial action, García Rodríguez de Montalvo and Gerónimo de Birbes took her from the jail, put her under the protection of a church, and then took her to another place. Montalvo and Birbes were found guilty of interfering with the law and condemned to exile from the jurisdictional territory of the court. Alonso Cortés maintains that the author was probably not the person named in the judicial action; but Montalvo's knightly characters repeatedly attempt rescues like the one described and get into trouble for doing so. Furthermore, the longest and most seemingly autobiographical chapter of the two works, chapter 99 of *Las sergas de Esplandián,* deals with a depression caused by the author's inability to handle his affairs as one of the narrators of the work, Urganda la Desconocida (Urganda the Unknown), says that he should. The author says that he has gone hunting near Castillejo; this town is located far from the region around Medina del Campo and could be the place of exile in which Montalvo wrote his books.

A document from another lawsuit, dated 1505, indicates that Montalvo had died before that year. A question raised in the 1505 suit is whether Montalvo's children knew that he had renounced his lineage; one of the children testifies that the reason for the renunciation was that Montalvo's relatives had refused to give a bond for one of Montalvo's servants. This concern for a servant parallels the respect with which servants are treated throughout *Amadís de Gaula* and *Las sergas de Esplandián.* Most notable in this regard is the favorable characterization of Carmela in the latter work. For example, she selflessly dedicates her life totally to serving him; while in love with him, she nevertheless supports him as he courts his future wife; and she acts as his messenger even in highly dangerous situations.

Some critics have speculated that Montalvo was a *converso* (a convert from Judaism to Christianity or a descendant of converts). Several characters in *Amadís de Gaula* and *Las sergas de Esplandián* are converts, albeit not specifically from Judaism to Christianity. Among them are Balán, who is converted from an evil giant to a good one when he joins Amadís's side in the concluding battles of book 4, and the corsair Frandalo in book 5, who converts from paganism to Christianity.

Another clue to Montalvo's possible *converso* origins is found in Ruy Páez de Ribera's *Florisando* (1510), the first sequel to Montalvo's five-part work. Book 6 of the Amadís cycle is designed as a refutation of what Páez de Ribera views as the unchristian elements in Montalvo's version of the story. Montalvo's book 5 ends with the enchantment of Amadís, his brothers, his son, and their wives by Urganda; in Páez de Ribera's sequel Urganda is defeated; the mythical Arthurian wizard, Helisabad, is replaced by a Christian monk; Amadís, who had retired as a respected elder statesman in Montalvo's version, returns as the most prominent king in Christendom; and a minor Roman character, Arquisil, defeats a clearly unchristian allegorical knight named Fortune. Toward the end of this anti-Montalvo sequel a group of monks disenchant Amadís and Esplandián by means of Christian prayers, and one monk makes a transparently anti-Semitic speech listing twenty arguments as to why God visits the sins of some on others. Finally, Páez de Ribera refers to the Inquisition as a divine tool that punished Jews for the sin of killing Christ. Páez de Ribera therefore reaffirms what he believes to be the orthodox Catholic basis of the Amadís myth, although we now know that pre-Montalvo versions of the Amadís story were even less "Christian" than Montalvo's.

Judging by his works, Montalvo had a nobleman's highly developed sense of the importance of genealogy: both *Amadís de Gaula* and *Las sergas de Esplandián* include detailed genealogies of the major characters. Given the Spanish obsession at the time with *pureza de sangre* (purity of Christian bloodlines), it may be significant that Montalvo creates the longest and most detailed genealogy in all five books for Balán, the "converted" giant. Balán is descended from Madanfabul, Amadís's archenemy, and his genealogy covers eight generations of this clan of evil antagonists. The characteristics of this genealogy tend to support speculation about Montalvo's possible *converso* heritage, because the narrative voice seems to be subtly identifying with a cohesive group of his non-Christian characters.

As with most medieval chivalric romances, it is impossible definitively to connect place-names in Montalvo's work with actual locations, especially at the beginning; toward the end, however, fictional geography tends to converge with real geography. Place descriptions also tend to become more specific and detailed—and, therefore, less mythical—the farther south the places are located. The difference between fictional and real geography appears to be related to the degree to which Montalvo was familiar with the places he is describing. Christopher Columbus's four voyages between 1492 and 1504 were slowly changing the European conception of the earth; but since the texts Montalvo used to compose books 1 through 3 were written before those voyages, much of his geography is essentially medieval. Because they are so seamlessly wedded, the real places are mythicized, and the fictional ones are concretized.

In the first paragraph of book 1 of *Amadís de Gaula* the reader is introduced to the Christian king Garínter of Pequeña Bretaña (Little Britain) and the young King Perión of Gaula. Neither Pequeña Bretaña nor Gaula is described in any way: they are mythical northern lands in the fictional landscape of early medieval European Celtic/Arthurian lore. Other fictional locales dealt with in a similar fashion in books 1 and 2 are Escocia (Scotland), Irlanda (Ireland), Denamarcha (Denmark), twenty-two named islands or groups of islands, and two key settings: King Lisuarte's Gran Bretaña (Great Britain) and the Ínsula Firme (Firm Island), Amadís's mysterious stronghold and the center of the erotic themes and plots of the work. The Ínsula Firme reminds many scholars of Mont St. Michel in Brittany, while another prominent site, the Montaña Defendida (Forbidden Mountain), resembles the Rock of Gibraltar. In book 3 the protagonist's adventures take him to Suecia (Sweden), Alemaña (Germany), and lands bordering the Roman Empire: Dacia, Romania, Greece, and Constantinople. The action expands to include the Arabian king's domain of Aráviga and islands that seem to be in the Mediterranean. Spain itself is presented in a casual manner, with no location assigned to it and no description given of it; the author apparently assumes that his readers are fully familiar with it.

Only three places in Spain can be linked to Montalvo with any degree of certainty. One is Mojados, the residence of the adulterous lady and the offended husband in the 1497 judicial action; it is not mentioned in *Amadís de Gaula* or *Las sergas de Esplandián*. Another is Alhama, a town in Andalusia to which Montalvo was sent by the Catholic Monarchs in 1482 to serve for a year as a guard on the Christian-Muslim border. The name Alhama does not appear in any of the five books of Montalvo's work, but several places have similar names or, like Alhama, are captured border towns. Three of the fictional locales he creates have a real sense of place about them. In contrast to the Celtic place-names in books 1 to 4 that might have been inspired by Alhama, these are the border towns in the kingdom of Persia: Alfarín, Galacia, and Xanthinomela. While Xanthinomela may be based on a real place in Turkey, the other two remind one of a fortified town on the border between Granada and Castile. These minor places are depicted more realistically than are places such as Gran Bretaña and Gaula that predominate in books 1 to 4 or the important historical places in book 5 such as Constantinople, Rome, Ctesiphon, and Ténedos Island.

The third place that can be linked to Montalvo is his hometown. One feels the presence of Medina del Campo throughout the narrative, but its name never appears. Montalvo would have been inspired by the castles that punctuate the Castilian landscape nearby, including La Mota, which sits prominently on a hill overlooking the town like the alcazar on the Ínsula Firme. Furthermore, he would have had firsthand knowledge of specific features of castle architecture, such as the walls that protected and completely encircled Medina del Campo until they were razed following the unsuccessful rebellion of the *Comuneros* (Spanish townspeople and local nobles who attempted to resist

*Title page for the 1508 Saragossa edition of Garci Rodríguez de Montalvo's classic chivalric romance (from Montalvo,* Amadís de Gaula: Selección estudio y notas, *edited by Victorino López, 1963; Thomas Cooper Library, University of South Carolina)*

royal authority) against Carlos I in 1522. Other aspects of Medina del Campo that may have inspired parts of Montalvo's work include its legal status as a town in the royal patrimony; its three-century history as a border market town; the presence of prominent communities of *conversos,* Jews, and Mudejars (resident Muslims); and its status as the site of an important international merchants' fair. Finally, while not a diocesan center, Medina del Campo was a seat of the tribunal of the Inquisition from 1486 until 1516. Montalvo's hometown was, then, a place where, as in his text, orthodoxy and heterodoxy could be found in equal measure.

In terms of sheer length, Montalvo's corpus is impressive, comprising some 615,000 words. The first four books include 427 named characters, and more than 150 are added in *Las sergas de Esplandián*. Books 1 through 4 constitute roughly 70 percent of the work as a whole, with book 1 accounting for about 18 percent, book 2 for 13 percent, book 3 for 16 percent, and book

4 for 23 percent; at 30 percent, then, book 5 comprises the largest part of Montalvo's overall production. Nevertheless, the pacing and complication of the plot are nearly uniform; the introduction of new characters is gradual; the characters' psychological development is subtle, if seemingly minimal; and authorial intrusions are constant, although not excessive even for modern tastes. At the most superficial level Montalvo maintains an impression of unity by relying on stock narrative phrases (such as: "La parte primera [segunda, tercera, quarta] desta gran historia vos ha contado" (as the first [second, third, fourth] part of this great short has told you); "aquello que dél en estas sus *Sergas* se scrive" (as will be told you in its *Labors*); "Cuenta la historia que" (the story relates that); "assí como lo contaremos en vn ramo desta ystoria que se llama *Las sergas de Esplandián*" (as we will tell you in a branch of this story that is called *The Labors of Esplandián*), plot units (tripartite episodes involving incremental difficulties), foreshadowing (Lisuarte's early brusqueness vis-à-vis his wife, Brisena, in book 1 foreshadows serious difficulties with his daughter Oriana in books 2 and 3) and symbolism (swords, precious stones, etc.) Occasionally, the narrator omits detailed descriptions and shortens lists, telling the reader that he is skipping these things to avoid prolixity.

One can only fully discern the unity and cohesion of the work, however, by taking into consideration what has traditionally been seen as Montalvo's weakest text—the fifth and concluding book, *Las sergas de Esplandián*. Throughout the first four books, emendations, narrative intrusions, foreshadowing, and announcements forecast the adventures in book 5. While differences exist between *Amadís de Gaula* and *Las sergas de Esplandián*—the most noteworthy being that the title character of *Las sergas de Esplandián* is more "Christian" than Amadís—Montalvo took great care to integrate the five books.

Ever since the priest at the beginning of part 1 of Miguel de Cervantes saavedra's *Don Quijote de la Mancha* (1605, 1615) burned *Las sergas de Esplandián* in an auto-da-fé of chivalric romances and books of poetry, many critics have considered the first four books a work of admirable quality and dismissed the concluding book as a separate and inferior text. Following this tradition, modern editions have typically included only the first four books. The most notable of these editions are those prepared by Cacho Blecua (1987), Avalle-Arce (1991), and the English translation by Place and Herbert C. Behm (1974, 1975). A few critics, however, disagree with this neglect of *Las sergas de Esplandián*. Avalle-Arce, in his *Amadís de Gaula: El primitivo y el de Montalvo* Avalle-Arce comes the closest of any critic to demonstrating that Montalvo sought to create an integrated opus in five books. Avalle-Arce refers to "la sutil labor de lanzadera

que efectúa Montalvo con fines de crear un inmenso *corpus* narrativo de íntima unidad entre lo que él heredó de la tradición literaria, el nuevo *Amadís . . .* y *Las sergas de Esplandián*" (the subtle shuttle work that Montalvo carried out in order to create an immense narrative *corpus* wherein he produced a close unity between what he inherited from the literary tradition, the new *Amadís . . .* and *Las sergas de Esplandián*). Fogelquist concedes that book 5 "functions adequately either as a continuation of the four Books of *Amadís* or as a separate entity." Other critics who have voiced support for the notion that the five volumes function together as an artistic whole include Cacho Blecua in 1986 and Susana Gil-Albarellos in 1999. But even Avalle-Arce, the critic most sympathetic to the view that the *Amadís de Gaula* should refer to the complete five-book composite, limits his critical edition to the first four books and characterizes *Las sergas de Esplandián* as "la primera continuación independiente first independent continuation" (the first independent continuation) of the story.

Montalvo's five books present a vast fictional panorama in which the action centers on a three-sided conflict that spans three generations: one conflict is between Amadís, prince of the kingdom of Gaula, and Lisuarte, king of Gran Bretaña, and is initiated by the unfair treatment of Amadís by Lisuarte and his allies. Another conflict pits Amadís and Lisuarte against a faction that opposes both of them, a band comprises evil knights and their allies within the realm, plus their foreign allies: evil giants, the kings of Persia and Arabia, and Queen Califía and her Amazon warriors from the pagan island of California, whose name was given to the lands on the northern Pacific coast of New Spain.

In addition to the entertaining plot, Montalvo's five books provide a manual of chivalric etiquette, a political primer for the education of late-medieval princes, and a critique of fifteenth-century Spanish culture, society, and mores. Amadís, his parents, his siblings, his son Esplandián, and his other relatives are presented as exemplars of chivalric manners but are also given individual personal traits. Amadís is renowned for knightly prowess, but he is also taciturn, sensitive, proud, loyal, and a perfectly faithful lover. His beloved, Oriana, is beautiful, also faithful, and passionate. Amadís's brother Galaor is the second most able knight in combat; at the same time, he has made a name for himself for his enjoyment of sex. The protagonist's half brother Floristán, on the contrary, is distinguished by his good manners and self-control. Balancing his portrait of chivalric etiquette, Montalvo paints a nuanced picture of the strengths and weaknesses of medieval lords. This primer for princes focuses on King Lisuarte, the central character of the work. While he is the finest of the monarchs depicted in the fictional *Amadís* world, he is brought to grief by his stubborn pride. His attempt to marry off his daughter Oriana to a king not of her choosing so as to save face as an unchallengeable monarch is the principal cause of the conflict of books 1 through 4. The narrator inserts his own moralizing views in the middle of the action to underscore his dissatisfaction with monarchs who, through their neglect of justice and pursuit of their personal agendas, do not protect the people and the peace of their kingdoms. The latter charge obtains especially at the end of book 4 when Lisuarte secretly leaves his kingdom in vain pursuit of already outmoded ideal knightly fame and is trapped and imprisoned by an adversary.

The length, episodic structure, and leisurely pace of the work combine to mask its depth and subtleties. The first four books give the impression of failing to achieve closure. In book 4, chapter 117, Amadís is victorious in his climactic war against Lisuarte, and Arcaláus the Enchanter, the most evil knight of the work and Amadís's fiercest antagonist, is taken prisoner. In chapter 125 all of the principal knights and the ladies they serve are married, and they all celebrate the peace before departing for their own lands. The work seems to have arrived at a happy denouement by the end of chapter 126; yet, six more long chapters remain. Normally, such a concluding section—even one as long as six chapters—would serve as a coda or summation. In this case, however, new adventures begin as the author continues a plot that he has projected over five books. In chapter 123 the narrator inserts a statement concerning what will happen in book 5, and Urganda arrives in her Great Serpent Caravel; the sorceress and her magico-mechanical ship will play significant roles in book 5. Furthermore, Amadís's preeminence gradually fades throughout the concluding chapters of book 4, while that of his son, Esplandián, increases. This shift from father to son is accompanied by the moving of the center of action from the mystical Celtic territories of the early books to islands and kingdoms in the central and eastern Mediterranean.

The last chapter of the fourth book of *Amadís de Gaula* includes unresolved mysteries that lead smoothly and logically to book 5. Lisuarte, behaving fully in character by recklessly hunting alone and nobly attempting to rescue a damsel who appears to be in distress, is captured and imprisoned again; and Urganda returns to preside over the final episode of the book, in which the reformed giant Balán dubs Esplandián a knight. But Esplandián has yet to win a sword that his father, Amadís, failed to win three chapters earlier; Arcaláus the Enchanter is freed and is in a vengeful frame of mind that foreshadows new adventures; and a promise to return to her that Amadís had made to

Leonorina, princess of the kingdom of Constantinople, has yet to be fulfilled.

All of these plot elements are resolved in book 5. Not fully apparent at the end of book 4, however, is Montalvo's true objective: to write a war epic to rival the ancient narratives of the Trojan War. He does so in book 5 by presenting a major modern war between the assembled forces of Christendom and those of the pagan world.

Book 1 is set in a mystical time that, anachronistically, is simultaneously pagan Celtic, early Christian, and late medieval; Amadís's birth takes place near the time of the founding of Christianity. Later, a long genealogy links the giant Balán to forebears who had lived at the time of Uther Pendragon and King Arthur in the fourth and fifth centuries. In book 5 the concluding war scenes mirror the fall of Constantinople in the fifteenth century.

As Montalvo shifts the temporal frame of the texts, he also shifts its moral frames. In books 1 through 4 the author repeatedly steps out of the story to issue moralizing statements aimed at convincing readers to live by high standards of conduct. Although these messages are compatible with Christian morality, most often they do not present specifically Christian doctrines but call for the tempered use of reason. In this sense Amadís is the paragon of medieval, but not exclusively Christian, chivalric virtues.

By contrast, the moral landscape in *Las sergas de Esplandián* is overtly Christian. Book 5 directly and indirectly praises the Catholic Monarchs' evangelizing of the Moors of Granada. In this way book 5, unlike books 1 through 4, can be categorized as a moral-didactic chivalric romance. References to Jesus Christ, the Savior, the almighty Lord, and God are much more frequent in *Las sergas de Esplandián* than in *Amadís de Gaula*. While book 5 is intended to show the superiority of Christianity to paganism—a catchall term for Islam, perhaps for Judaism, and for other non-Christian belief systems—books 1 through 4 are meant to show the superiority of Amadís and his allies, who uphold the medieval chivalric code more perfectly than do other knights. Amadís's enemies are bad not because of their religious beliefs but because they fail to adhere to the knightly code. In the first four books Montalvo posits five qualities that should exist in the perfect *caballero* (knight): virtue, *esfuerzo* (effort, zeal, or courage), reason, love, and Christian piety. In those books the first four qualities are emphasized, while the fifth is either taken for granted or not regarded as of paramount importance. The religion-centered ideology that predominated in Spain during Montalvo's lifetime, however, led him to expand the plot of the received Amadís material and conclude the work with one of the most brutal religious wars in the pages of world literature.

Given the religious passions of the age in which Montalvo lived, and the fact that he wrote his work during what has been called the last Crusade–the Spanish campaign to take Granada–all five books are surprisingly unchurched. Esplandián is much less dogmatically Roman Catholic than, for example, the hero of Joanot Martorell and Martí Joan de Galba's *Tirant lo blanc* (Tirant the White, 1490). The word *Dios* (God) is used most often as part of a greeting rather than as an invocation of divine intercession. References to Jesus Christ are rare in the first four books, though they do pepper book 5. The entire work has few clerical characters, and one of those–a bishop–is imprisoned by Amadís. There are scant references to the Virgin Mary and even fewer to characters hearing mass. There are no biblical citations in Latin or Spanish. The Trinity is passed over in silence, and one finds but two trifling references to the Church hierarchy. There are no invocations of saints or martyrs, and no cathedrals or churches are worked into the landscape– just a few hermitages whose presence serves to advance the action. Book 2 describes Apolidón as a Greek prince, lover, knight, astrologer, necromancer, and wizard who built the magnificent palaces on the Ínsula Firme and set up the enchanted tests of love and beauty that the main characters attempt to overcome; Montalvo neither Christianizes nor criticizes the character's magical practices, even though Catholic doctrine condemned them. Furthermore, the narrator rules God out as the creator of Esplandián's amazing ship, the Great Serpent Caravel, given to him by Urganda while allowing that magic, sorcery, or human ingenuity might be responsible for producing the complex machine. Also, both in his moralizing interpolations and by the example of the deeds of his characters he criticizes his hyper-religious times for not upholding the knightly virtues that are embodied in Fernando *el Católico,* whom he describes, most notably in book 5, as a model modern knight. Montalvo apparently endeavored to protect himself from Church censorship and the Inquisition by ending his prologue to book 1 with a profession of faith: "teniendo y creyendo yo firmamente todo lo que la Sancta Iglesia tiene y manda" (firmly hold to and believe in everything that the Holy Church holds to and enjoins).

The narrative structure of the five books is highly complex. The first narrative voice is that of the inferred author: the dominant voice in all of the books is that of a standard omniscient narrator. But soon the reader perceives that this narrator actually has two voices: that of the original writer and that of the redactor-scribe invented by Montalvo in the prologue to book 1. This redactor scribe, the second omniscient narrator, purports at times to be an historian whose duty is to tell the truth by attempting to suspend the reader's disbelief, even where the subject is enchantment, magic, and superhuman achievements. Another narrator speaks directly to the reader to point out that the first-level narrator is about to stop relating one episode and turn to another. Still another voice delivers the exemplary minisermons about moral topics such as pride, the fall of princes, and the vices and virtues of monarchs. In addition, characters give summations of their own actions or provide information that comes from outside previously known narrative limits. This narrative feature is most prominent in book 3 when Amadís defeats the monster Endriago.

In book 5 the narrative structure becomes even more complex. According to the prologue to book 1, which makes no claims about the provenance of the first four books, *Las sergas de Esplandián* was an ancient Greek manuscript that was nearly indecipherable; it was discovered in a tomb below a hermitage near Constantinople and brought to Spain by a Hungarian merchant (chivalric romances were frequently supposed to have been written originally in languages considered exotic by medieval Europeans, such as Greek or Arabic). That manuscript, of course, has its own Greek narrator. Helisabad, a character who is added to Amadís's entourage in book 3, chapter 72, is a cleric, an ambassador, a physician who cures the hero of the wounds he receives in his innumerable battles, and a polyglot who teaches Amadís the languages spoken in the regions where his adventures take him. Among the languages in which he is proficient is Greek. In addition to the double role he plays in books 3 and 4 as character and narrator, in book 5 he is charged with witnessing Esplandián's deeds and writing a chronicle about them in Greek–the text that is being read by the reader. (Montalvo himself implicitly takes responsibility for the Spanish although he never claims to know Greek.)

Urganda the Unknown is a lady who is served by an unnamed knight and travels widely with an entourage of damsels, dwarfs, and squires. She is also a fairy endowed with magical and prophetic powers, and she functions as a separate narrative voice, reviewing past actions and predicting future events. She provides equipment and information that control virtually all of book 5, so that the reader is led to believe that the actions of the main characters in that book are caused by her supernatural powers. In chapter 98 of book 5 Urganda establishes a dialogue with a voice identified as *el Autor* (the Author), who by this device becomes a character in the text. The reader knows that the Author is a man, because he describes himself as a knight who enjoys hunting. Urganda orders the

Author, a double for the first-level narrative voice, to cease writing until she gives him permission to continue. He admits that he is worn out and depressed, but Urganda accuses him of being a simple, unlettered man with a peasant's education who cannot manage himself or his household and derides him further by calling him clumsy and dim-witted. Content that he has been duly chastised, she allows him to resume writing and even sends her niece Julianda to act as the Author's scribe and sometimes as his muse. Paradoxically, Julianda's function, according to Urganda, is to read aloud and interpret to Helisabad the Greek text that he has been writing since the beginning of book 5. The dialogue between Urganda and the Author ends when she asks him which of the female characters is the most beautiful woman in the world. Surprisingly, he does not say that it is Oriana, Amadís's wife and Esplandián's mother; instead, he replies that Briolanja is the most beautiful. Having answered correctly, the Author disappears, leaving the narration to the omniscient narrator. (Cervantes imitated the scene in the Cueva de Montesinos episode in part 2 of *Don Quijote*.)

Throughout the work the Author claims that he is not up to the task of writing it. Yet, despite characterizing himself, through Urganda, as clumsy and dim-witted, he demonstrates that he commands a wide range of classical rhetorical devices, including *amplificatio* (artful expansions), *exempla* (moral fables), *interpretatio* (incorporated commentary), *expositio* (description), *peripeteia* (change of fortune), *anagnorisis* (recognition scenes), *artes dictaminis* (writing of epistles), and *artes arengandi* (battle speeches). Cacho Blecua points out in his edition of *Amadís de Gaula* that protestations of modesty are not unusual in medieval authors but are yet another standard rhetorical device, *excusatio propter infirmitatem,* the purpose of which is to gain the reader's sympathy by posing as ill or inept. The modesty displayed in book 5, chapters 98 and 99, however, is too protracted to be only a rhetorical show and seems to provide clues about the personality and character of the real Montalvo.

Montalvo's texts are rooted in the genre of chivalric romance, the most prominent feature of which is the linear narration of virtually unlimited episodes. Book 1 begins with a prenarrative genesis in the begetting of Amadís's mother, Elisena. Amadís is then conceived during Elisena's clandestine visit to the bedchamber of Perión, king of Gaula. Following standard mythical patterns, Amadís is born while his father is absent, and the baby is abandoned by his mother, who sets him adrift, Moses-like, in a basket that floats down a river and out to sea. This circumstance gives the young hero the name by which he is first known: "Donzel del Mar" (Squire of the Sea). Amadís discovers his real name and is knighted by his own father, Perión, who does not realize that the young knight is his son. He goes to the court of the greatest king of the time, Lisuarte of Gran Bretaña, where he enters the service of the king's wife, falls in love with Lisuarte's daughter Oriana, and battles and maims Arcaláus the Enchanter, who becomes the hero's major antagonist. He engages in armed combat with giants, evil knights, and other enemies of Gran Bretaña, many of whom he maims or kills. By means of these battles and by resisting the amorous advances of beautiful ladies such as Madasima and Briolanja, Amadís earns fame and glory and is acclaimed the greatest, most perfect knight who ever lived. Montalvo demonstrates expert narrative skill in bringing about the exaltation of his protagonist. Characters—especially Amadís's brother, Galaor, his half-brother Florestán, and his cousin Agrajes—continuously move from place to place; episodes parallel, alternate, or contrast with each other; and foreshadowing is constant by means of images, recursive episodes, prophecies, messenger damsels, authorial interventions, and letters. The psychological portraiture of the main characters, though unobtrusive at first, becomes relatively complex the deeper into the text one advances. The result of such complexity is the creation of a dynamic fictional world.

Amadís's principal characteristics are knightly prowess, fidelity, and humility. He is, of course, the paragon of virtues: handsome, athletic, durable, intelligent, generous, self-confident, self-controlled, sensitive, faithful, tolerant, and reasonable. He is also self-destructively emotional, prone to excessive weeping—crying per se is not presented as a defect in *Amadís de Gaula*—and imprudently curious. While some characters have only a few identifying traits—Galaor is amorous, Agrajes is hotheaded, Brian de Monjaste has "un sentido de humor español (a Spanish sense of humor)—others are given much more psychological depth. For example, Lisuarte is the greatest of all kings: he has enormous knightly prowess, he is charismatic and loved by most of his subjects, he governs well, and he takes pride in his sense of honor, dignity, justice, and reason. On the other hand, he has a flawed sense of self-importance, he contradicts himself, he dissembles and lies, he is suspicious and jealous, and he forces his daughter Oriana to marry against her will, even though the ethics of the fictional kingdom of Gran Bretaña and the narrator's ethics of sexual democracy and tolerance oppose this violation of his daughter's human rights. Lisuarte is depicted at the pinnacle of his power in book 1, chapter 39.

In the last four chapters of book 1 a female character appears who plays a key role in the plot and who holds special fascination for Montalvo and his narrators. Briolanja, queen of Sobradisa, is described as young and

Page from the 1519 Rome edition of Amadís de Gaula (from Amadís de Gaula: Novela de caballerías, refundida y modernizada, edited by Ángel Rosenblat, 1940; Thomas Cooper Library, University of South Carolina)

divinely beautiful. In chapter 40 Amadís begins a quest to restore her kingdom to her; she falls in love with him, but Amadís does not return her affections. The narrator gives five versions of Briolanja and Amadís's relationship: Amadís accepts Briolanja's advances; Amadís resists Briolanja with a supreme effort of fidelity to Oriana; Amadís and Briolanja have intercourse after the queen of Sobradisa imprisons him; Oriana gives her champion permission to have sex with Briolanja in order to free him; and Briolanja requires Amadís to remain in her service only until Galaor returns to her. The narrator says that the last version is the correct one, because in book 4 Briolanja will marry Galaor. The existence of so many versions of the Briolanja story illustrates both the

lucid side of Montalvo's narrative skill and the fact that other versions of the textual materials antedate Montalvo's creative effort.

The hero's dwarf returns to Gran Bretaña and erroneously tells Oriana that Amadís is in love with Briolanja. Oriana becomes destructively and vindictively jealous. In the last chapter of book 1 the narrator defends a woman's right to freedom in matters of love. The book ends with a speech by Briolanja in which she sets forth her ideals, declaring her opposition to vainglory and illusory worldliness.

Book 2 opens with a description of the fabulous enchantments installed on the Ínsula Firme by the prince-wizard Apolidón a century earlier; the fantastic nature of the island appears not to be derived from the original Amadís material but to be Montalvo's invention. The central feature of these enchantments is the tests of the Arch of Faithful Lovers: one test is reserved for a knight with more prowess than Apolidón, the other for a lady more beautiful than Apolidón's mistress.

The first half of book 2 concerns the stories of various characters who sally forth attempting to find Amadís, who has retreated alone to a wild crag known as Peña Pobre (Woeful Cliff) to pine in nearly suicidal agony over Oriana's rejection. During this period of lonely suffering he changes his name to Beltenebrós (Fair Shadows), a name that suggests his handsomeness and the shadows (*tenebrae*) of sorrow cast over his life. Others, including Lisuarte, become jealous of Beltenebrós, whose fame and glory increase while he fights to defend the king.

In the middle of the book, after an epistolary reconciliation, Amadís and Oriana are united in the magical haven of Miraflores Castle, near Vindilisora (Windsor?), the capital of Gran Bretaña, where they spend a week of amatory bliss. Their encounter is not condemned by the narrator but is justified after the fact as a secret marriage, which they reveal to no one to their near undoing. As a result of their dalliance, Oriana becomes pregnant with Esplandián. Book 2 ends with jealous courtiers causing Lisuarte to declare Amadís persona non grata in his court. The stage is now set for a war between Amadís and Lisuarte over the question of whether Madasima and her mother, Gromadaça, the lady of Mongaça castle, have the right to determine their own destiny against Lisuarte's feudal prerogatives over the castle. Also at issue is Lisuarte's intransigent defense of a hastily contrived lie that he had promised the castle to another daughter, Leonoreta.

Book 3 opens with this war and continues with Amadís leaving the Ínsula Firme and traveling through Gaul, Germany, Bohemia, Romania, and Greece to Constantinople in search of adventure. On the way he changes his name several more times: to the Cavallero del Enano (Knight of the Dwarf), Cavallero de la Verde España (Knight of the Green Sword), and Cavallero Griego (Greek Knight). Before arriving in Constantinople, he wins the most significant test in all of the first four books: on Ínsula de Diablo (Devil's Island) he defeats Endriago, a hideous monster who was the product of incest and murdered his own mother. Amadís is nearly killed in the battle but is saved by Helisabad and exceptionally, the narrator points out, by God's grace. Here Montalvo makes one of the two distinctly anti-Semitic statements in the work. Then, in order to defend his protagonist, the narrator affirms that Amadís comes from Christian ancestors but notes that not all who have such pure blood live up to the nobility of

thought and deed that they are supposed to display naturally. The other not-so-subtle anti-Semitic comment occurs in book 5, chapter 102, when the narrator says that the Catholic Monarchs "limpiaron de aquella sucia lepra, de aquella malvada herejía que en sus reinos sembrada por mucho años estaba, así de los visibles como de los invisibles" (cleaned out that dirty leprosy [a code word for Jews and/or conversos], that wicked heresy of both the visible and invisible kinds that had been sown in their realms for many years).

In a scene that is notable for its realistic detail, Esplandián is born near the beginning of book 3, which, not coincidentally, is at the midpoint of the 133 chapters into which the first four books are divided. Two chapters later, with help from a disguised Amadís, Lisuarte and his Roman allies defeat Arcaláus the Enchanter and the Arabian king. In an unusually rapid advance in the narrative chronology, just two chapters further on, Amadís and Esplandián come across each other for the second time when the boy is already four years old: they meet but do not recognize each other. At the end of the third book Lisuarte orders Oriana to appear before him, and she leaves her idyllic castle under armed guard. Lisuarte orders her to marry the emperor of Rome for the purpose of increasing his own power and prestige. He refuses to relent in the face of her distress, and Oriana is forced to board a ship of the Roman fleet. Amadís's knights attack and defeat the Romans at sea, rescuing Oriana, and all return to the safety of Ínsula Firme.

Although it is the longest of the four books of *Amadís de Gaula,* book 4 is simpler than the previous three and less medieval in character. Beginning with the prologue, the narrative changes its focus from courtly love to postmedieval Christian concerns. Avalle-Arce and Cacho Blecua note that this shift in emphasis parallels the spirit of the age in which Montalvo was writing, for in 1494 the Spanish Pope Alexander VI conferred the title of Reyes Católicos on Fernando and Isabel. The plot is a carefully constructed war story with three contending forces: Amadís and his allies, the knights of Ínsula Firme, Ireland, Gaul, Germany, Scotland, Bohemia, Constantinople, and Grasinda's and Briolanja's kingdoms; Lisuarte and the knights of Gran Bretaña who remain loyal to him, royal Irish knights, and the remnants of the Roman forces that failed to take Oriana to Rome; and an alliance of seven pagan kings assembled by Arcaláus the Enchanter, who plan to take advantage of the anticipated mutual annihilation of the first two camps. (A vestigial sign that book 4 is drawn from medieval sources is the fact that the seven pagan kings are meant to symbolize the seven deadly sins.) Consultations and preparations are carried out within the armies of Amadís and Lisuarte, and envoys are dispatched to their respective allies. By the middle of book 4 all of the contending forces are gathered for a war that Amadís would have liked to avoid by diplomatic means but that Lisuarte, manipulated by self-interested advisers and convinced that his decisions are divinely ordained, insists on waging.

The conflict begins with a typically medieval individual combat between the hero and an arrogant champion of the Roman forces. It is followed by brutal fighting between the two Christian camps, during which Amadís kills the emperor of Rome. The sermonizing narrator interrupts the action to tell the reader that, though Amadís had the means to destroy Lisuarte, he did not do so because of his love for Oriana; Lisuarte, on the other hand, encourages his forces to fight to the death, even though he knows that his side is doomed to defeat.

The hermit Nasciano reveals to Lisuarte the truth about Esplandián's birth and Amadís and Oriana's secret marriage. The king agrees to suspend the fighting to give the hermit the opportunity to negotiate peace terms. But as Lisuarte's forces are retreating, Arcaláus and the Arabian king attack and nearly defeat the remnant of his army. Amadís rushes to the rescue, saving his father-in-law and taking Arcaláus prisoner.

After protracted peace negotiations, Lisuarte gives a conciliatory speech and proclaims that Amadís and Oriana, not Leonoreta, will be the heirs to the throne of Gran Bretaña. He then has Leonoreta marry the new emperor of Rome. Lisuarte, however, remains jealous of Amadís. After several minor chivalric encounters, all of the major knights and their respective ladies celebrate public nuptials—Galaor and Briolanja, Agrajes and Olinda, Florestán and Sardamira, Grasandor and Mabilia, Galvanes and Madasima, Cuadragante and Grasinda, Bruneo de Bonamar and Melicia, and Arquisil and Leonoreta—and Oriana triumphs as the most faithful lady in the test of the Arch of Faithful Lovers on the Ínsula Firme. Urganda makes several prophecies, and all of the characters return to their homes.

The fourth section of book 4 prepares the reader for book 5. Amadís disobeys Oriana's injunction against further chivalric exploits and sallies forth to fight the pagan giant Balán, whom he defeats and converts to his cause without insisting that Balán become a Christian. Amadís then fails tests on the Enchantress Damsel's Crag that are reserved for Esplandián and falls victim to a ruse by Arcaláus's wife. At the same time, Lisuarte is captured and imprisoned in a giant's fortress on the Montaña Defendida, on the border between Constantinople and Persia. Esplandián is dubbed a knight in a ceremony presided over by Urganda, and Amadís tells his son of the promise he

had made to the daughter of the emperor of Constantinople to return her kingdom to her—a promise that Esplandián is destined to fulfill in book 5. Amadís thus passes the generational baton to his son.

*Las sergas de Esplandián* begins with Esplandián finding Lisuarte and freeing him from captivity. Lisuarte returns to Gran Bretaña and abdicates in favor of Amadís and Oriana. Amadís and Esplandián, not recognizing one another, fight a nearly fatal duel; when Esplandián wins, his triumph is greater than if he had killed Amadís, because the father remains alive to bear witness to the son's superior knightly prowess and moral character.

Throughout the first half of the book chivalric adventures reminiscent of those in books 1 through 4 alternate with preparations for a climactic war between the Christian allies of Constantinople and a vast array of pagan enemies, the most important of which are the kingdoms of Persia and of the Amazons. In the war, which fictionally reverses the fall of Constantinople to the Ottoman Turks in 1453, Lisuarte and Perión die, Amadís defeats (but does not kill) the Amazon queen Calafía in single combat, and Esplandián defeats her sister. As at the end of book 4, after the Christian victory, several marriages take place—among those who marry are Talanque, Amadís's heroic nephew, and Calafía, the queen of California—and the Christians depart for their homelands. Esplandián and Leonorina ascend the throne of Constantinople—the pinnacle of human achievement. In chapter 178 they sail to the queen's island, where "pasaron por muy extrañas cosas de grandísimas" (they underwent many amazing adventures). Urganda uses her magic powers to sink into the sea the main characters of *Amadís de Gaula* and *Las sergas de Esplandián* who had not gone to distant continents. Finally, in the last chapter (184), all the characters are frozen in time and space by Urganda.

From the prologue to book 1 until the heroes and heroines' apotheoses at the end of *Las sergas,* Montalvo presents Esplandián as both the harbinger of Christian Messianism and the eclipsing of the legacy of pagan or pre-Christian Arthurian chivalry. By focusing on the exploits of Esplandián, Montalvo envisions the reunification of the fragmented and contentious parts of Christian Europe that dominated the world he knew.

Montalvo's romance was one of the most widely read works of secular fiction in Europe during the sixteenth and seventeenth centuries. Twenty Spanish editions of *Amadís de Gaula* were published in the sixteenth century after the first in 1508, including two in 1519 and one each in 1521, 1526, 1531, 1539, 1547, 1551, 1552, 1553, 1586, and 1587. By 1650, 267 editions or reprintings had appeared in Spain. The first Spanish edition of book 5 of which mention has been found is

*Las sergas del virtuoso cauallero Esplandián hijo de Amadís de Gaula (que fueron escritas en griego por la mano de aquel gran maestro Helisabad)* (The Deeds of the Virtuous Knight Esplandián, Son of Amadís of Gaul [Which Were Written in Greek by the Hand of That Great Master Helisabad]), which was supposed to have been published in Seville in 1510. No copies of this edition are known to be extant, and some scholars doubt that it ever existed. Sixteenth-century Spanish editions of the fifth book appeared in 1519, 1521 (this edition, published in Toledo with a suitably long chivalric romance title by Juan de Villaquirán, has many typographical inaccuracies), 1523, 1525, 1526, 1542, 1549, two in 1587, and 1588.

The first four books were translated into French by Nicolas de Herberay in 1540. In 1541 they were translated into Hebrew by Yaakov di Algaba and published in Constantinople by Eliezer bar Gershom Sonsino; this translation is the first romance or novella ever to appear in Hebrew. The first four books appeared in Italian in 1546 and in German between 1569 and 1572; the work was so popular in Frankfurt am Main that the publisher, Sigmund Feyerabend, said in 1581 that he made more money from it than from works by Martin Luther. The first English translation, published anonymously in 1598, was made not from one of the Spanish editions of Montalvo's work but from Herberay's French version, which was considerably altered from the original. In the introduction to his own 1803 free translation of *Amadís de Gaula* into English, the poet Robert Southey said that Herberay "has omitted much that is curious in manners, and inserted much that is abominable in morals; he is inaccurate and obscene. There is occasionally, though but rarely, a rude and savage nakedness in the original which I have veiled. The Frenchman has always delighted to expose it; he has dilated single phrases into whole paragraphs, with that love of lewdness which is so peculiarly and characteristically the disgrace of French literature." A two-volume English translation of the first four books by Place and Behm was published in 1974 and 1975. English translations of book 5 appeared in 1598, 1664–a relatively accurate rendering–and 1992.

Montalvo's five books spawned a huge number of continuations and imitations, beginning with Páez de Ribera's "sixth book," published the same year as the putative first edition of Montalvo's fifth book. Between 1526 and 1549 nine more sequels were published in Spanish. Italian versions expanded the story to eighteen volumes, French to nineteen, and German to twenty-four. Each of the sequels added still more characters to the vast number in Montalvo's works; and instead of the unity found in Montalvo's five books, many of the sequels give the impression of being disconnected

mazes. Henry Thomas said of the popularity of the genre: "During the hundred years that followed the publication of *Amadís of Gaul,* fifty romances of chivalry appeared in Spain and Portugal. They were published at the rate of almost one per year between 1508 and 1550; to these were added nine more between 1550 and . . . 1588; and three more appeared before the publication of *Don Quixote.*"

Like modern popular fiction, chivalric novels were escapist entertainment while also mirroring the realities of the time and the values and tastes of the literate and semiliterate public. They were read by common soldiers, priests, conquistadors, kings, writers, philosophers, nobles, and saints, including, in Spain alone, by their own testimony, Spain's Holy Roman Emperor, Carlos V; the conquistadores Hernán Cortés and Bernal Díaz de Castillo; the preeminent playwright Lope de Vega; the humanist Luis Vives; and even the mystics and religious reformers Ignatius of Loyola and Teresa de Ávila. Not all readers, however, approved of these works. Among those who wanted them banned were Alonso López Pinciano, Melchor Cano, Benito Arias Montano, and, evidently, Cervantes, who parodied them so successfully in *Don Quixote* with the stated purpose of ending the popularity of chivalric romances. Nevertheless, the Spanish Inquisition, probably recognizing that the chivalric romances were allied more closely with traditional Spanish cultural values than with heterodox ones, never placed any of the works on the *Index Librorum Prohibitorum* (Index of Forbidden Books). And Cervantes's attempt "to inspire mankind with an abhorrence of the false and improbable stories recounted in books of chivalry," in the words of Tobias Smollett's 1755 translation, only succeeded in keeping the memory of the genre alive. *Amadís de Gaula* and its imitators inspired Renaissance epic poems such as Ludovico Ariosto's *Orlando Furioso* (1516) and Edmund Spenser's *The Faerie Queene* (1590–1613).

By the eighteenth century the popularity of *Amadís de Gaula* had waned considerably. According to Denis Diderot and Jean le Rond d'Alembert's *Encyclopédie* (1765), the Enlightenment banished chivalric romances from the realm of good taste: "On vint à ne plus goûter les faits inimitables d'Amadis" (One no longer relishes the inimitable deeds of Amadis). Despite the Encyclopedists' judgment, in 1779 Johann Christian Bach composed a commissioned opera in Paris titled *Amadis des Gaules.* Then, in 1857 Gayangos's edition of all five of Montalvo's books revived the popularity of the work in Spain and established an essential reference point for all subsequent *Amadís* scholarship.

*Amadís de Gaula* can be said to mark the passage from substantial medieval prose narratives based on folklore and the art of the story to the novelistic genre proper. It inspired novels in Europe and the Americas by Sir Walter Scott, Alessandro Manzoni, Stendhal (Marie Henri Bayle), Honoré de Balzac, Charles Dickens, Mark Twain, John Steinbeck, William Faulkner, Carlos Fuentes, Mario Vargas Llosa, and Gabriel García Márquez. The artistic genius of this large, important, and enduring work resides in the special conjunction of its Spanish historical context, the particular textual materials from which it was produced, and a talented but evasive writer. Garci Rodríguez de Montalvo reshaped his complex mythical materials so thoroughly that *Amadís de Gaula* and *Las sergas de Esplandián* achieved a living dialogue with their contemporary culture and beyond.

**References:**

Narciso Alonso Cortés, "Montalvo, el del *Amadís*," *Revue Hispanique,* 81 (1933): 434–442;

J. Amezcua, "La oposición de Montalvo al mundo del *Amadís de Gaula*," *Nueva Revista de Filología Hispánica,* 21 (1972): 320–337;

Juan Bautista Avalle-Arce, *Amadís de Gaula: El primitivo y el de Montalvo* (Mexico: Fondo de Cultura Económica, 1990);

Avalle-Arce, "El arco de los leales amadores en el *Amadís*," *Nueva Revista de Filología Hispánica,* 6 (1952): 149–156;

Avalle-Arce, "El nacimiento de Amadís," in *Essays on Narrative Fiction in the Iberian Peninsula in Honour of Frank Pierce,* edited by R. B. Tate (Oxford: Dolphin, 1982), pp. 15–25;

Avalle-Arce, "The Primitive Version of *Amadís de Gaula*," in *The Late Middle Ages,* edited by Peter Cocozzella, ACTA: Proceedings of SUNY Regional Conference in Medieval Studies, no. 8 (Binghamton, N.Y.: Center for Medieval and Early Renaissance Studies, State University of New York, 1984), pp. 1–22;

Sigmund J. Barber, *"Amadis de Gaule" and the German Enlightenment* (New York: Peter Lang, 1984);

Eugène Baret, *De l'Amadis de Gaule et de son influence sur les moeurs et la littérature au XVIᵉ et au XVIIᵉ siècle* (Paris: Firmin-Didot, 1873);

A. Blanco, *Esplandián; Amadís: 500 años* (Valladolid: Diputación Provincial, 1998);

Teófilo Braga, *Formaçao do* Amadis de Gaula (Porto: Imprensa Portugueza, 1873);

Braga, *Versao hebraica do* Amadís de Gaula, 2 volumes (Coimbra: Universidade do Coimbra, 1915, 1916);

Juan Manuel Cacho Blecua, *Amadís: Heroísmo mítico-cortesano* (Madrid: Cupsa/Universidad de Zaragoza, 1979);

Cacho Blecua, "El entrelazamiento en el *Amadís* y en las *Sergas de Esplandián*," in *Studia in honorem Prof. M. de Riquer,* volume 1 (Barcelona: Quaderns Crema, 1986), pp. 235–271;

Federico Francisco Curto Herrero, *Estructura de los libros españoles de caballerías en el siglo XVI* (Madrid: Fundación Juan March, 1976): 82–306;

Alan D. Deyermond, "The Lost Genre of Medieval Spanish Literature," *Hispanic Revue,* 43 (1975): 231–259;

José María Díez Borque, "Edición e ilustración de las novelas de caballerías castellanas en el siglo XVI," *Synthesis,* 8 (1981): 21–58;

Daniel Eisenberg, *Castilian Romances of Chivalry in the Sixteenth Century* (London: Grant & Cutler, 1979), pp. 129–236;

Eisenberg, *Romances of Chivalry in the Spanish Golden Age* (Newark, Del.: Juan de la Cuesta, 1982), pp. 27–130;

Eisenberg and Mari Carmen Marín Pina, *Bibliografía de los libros de caballerías castellanos* (Saragossa: Prensas Universitarias de Zaragoza, 2000), pp. 129–233;

Antonio Escamilla Cid, *Montalbo: Opúsculo para su historia* (Madrid: Comercial Malvar, 1985);

James Donald Fogelquist, *El* Amadís *y el género de la historia fingida* (Madrid: José Porrúa Turanzas, 1982);

Raymond Foulché-Delbosc, "Sergas," *Revue Hispanique,* 23 (1910): 591–593;

María Cruz García de Enterría, "Libros de caballerías y romancero," *Journal of Hispanic Philology,* 10 (1986): 103–115;

Susana Gil-Albarellos, Amadís de Gaula *y el género caballeresco en España* (Valladolid: Universidad de Valladolid, 1999);

Samuel Gili Gaya, Amadís de Gaula: *Lección profesada el día 18 de febrero de 1956 en la Cátedra Milá y Fontanals* (Barcelona: Universidad de Barcelona, Facultad de Filosofia y Letras, 1956);

Gili Gaya, "*Las sergas de Esplandián* como crítica de la caballería bretona," *Boletín de la Biblioteca de Menéndez y Pelayo,* 23 (1947): 103–111;

Eloy R. González, "Función de las profecías en el *Amadís de Gaula*," *Nueva Revista de Filología Hispánica,* 31 (1982): 282–291;

González and Jennifer T. Roberts, "Montalvo's Recantation, Revisited," *Bulletin of Hispanic Studies,* 55 (1978): 203–210;

Irving A. Leonard, *Romances of Chivalry in the Spanish Indies* (Berkeley: University of California Press, 1933), pp. 3–43;

María Rosa Lida de Malkiel, "Arthurian Literature in Spain and Portugal," in *Arthurian Literature in the Middle Ages,* edited by Roger Sherman Loomis (Oxford: Clarendon Press, 1959), pp. 406–418;

Lida de Malkiel, "El desenlace del Amadís primitivo," *Romance Philology,* 6 (1953): 283–289;

Lida de Malkiel, "Dos huellas del *Esplandián* en el *Quixote* y el *Persiles,*" *Romance Philology,* 9 (1955–1956): 156–162;

Lida de Malkiel, "La literatura artúrica en España y Portugal," in her *Estudios de literatura española y comparada* (Buenos Aires: Editorial Universitaria de Buenos Aires, 1966), pp. 134–148;

William Thomas Little, "Spain's Fantastic Vision and the Mythic Creation of California," *California Geographer,* 27 (1987): 1–38;

Zvi Malachi, *The Loving Knight: The Romance* Amadís de Gaula *and Its Hebrew Adaptation* (Petah-Tikva, Israel: Haberman Institute for Literary Research, 1982);

John J. O'Connor, *Amadis de Gaule and Its Influence on Elizabethan Literature* (New Brunswick, N.J.: Rutgers University Press, 1970);

Lilia E. F. de Orduna, ed., *Amadís de Gaula: Estudios sobre narrativa caballeresca castellana en la primera mitad del siglo XVI* (Kassel, Germany: Edition Reichenberger, 1992);

Edwin B. Place, "Montalvo's Outrageous Recantation," *Hispanic Review,* 37 (January 1969): 192–198;

Ruth Putnam and Herbert I. Priestly, *California: The Name,* University of California Publications in History, volume 4, no. 4 (Berkeley: University of California Press, 1917);

Martín de Riquer, *Los caballeros andantes españoles del siglo XV* (Madrid: Gredos, 1967), pp. 10–13, 50–51;

Riquer, *Estudios sobre el* Amadís de Gaula (Barcelona: Sirmio, 1987);

Antonio R. Rodríguez-Moñino, ed., *El primer manuscrito del* Amadís de Gaula: *Noticia bibliográfica* (Madrid: Silverio Aguirre Torre, 1957);

Harvey L. Sharrer, "Briolanja as a Name in Early Fifteenth-Century Portugal: Echo of a Reworked Portuguese *Amadis de Gaula?*" *La Corónica,* 19, no. 1 (1990): 112–118;

Sharrer, *A Critical Bibliography of Hispanic Arthurian Material* (London: Grant & Cutler, 1977);

Harry Sieber, "The Romance of Chivalry in Spain: From Rodríguez de Montalvo to Cervantes," in *Romance: Generic Transformation from Chrétien de Troyes to Cervantes,* edited by Kevin Brownlee and Marina Scordilis Brownlee (Hanover, N.H.: Published by University Press of New England for Dartmouth College, 1985), pp. 202–219;

Henry Thomas, *Spanish and Portuguese Romances of Chivalry; The Revival of the Romance of Chivalry in the Spanish Peninsula, and Its extension and Influence Abroad* (Cambridge: Cambridge University Press, 1920);

Antony Van Beysterveldt, *Amadís-Esplandián-Calisto: Historia de un linaje adulterado* (Potomac, Md.: Studia Humanitatis, 1982);

Frida Weber de Kurlat, "Estructura novelesca del *Amadís de Gaula,*" *Revista de Literaturas Modernas,* 5 (1966): 29–54;

Judith A. Whitenack, "Conversion to Christianity in the Spanish Romance of Chivalry, 1490–1524," *Journal of Hispanic Philology,* 13 (1988): 13–39;

Grace S. Williams, "The *Amadís* Question," *Revue Hispanique,* 21 (1909): 1–167.

# Antonio de Nebrija

*(1442 or 1444 – 3 July 1522)*

José Perona
*Universidad de Murcia*

WORKS: *Introductiones latinae* (1481)

**Manuscripts:** Madrid, Biblioteca Nacional I-1599; bilingual version, Madrid, Biblioteca Nacional I-1009; Saragossa, Biblioteca del Seminario de Zaragoza.

**First publication:** *Aelius Antonius lebrixeñ. Petro Mendozae. S.R.E. Cardinali hispano . . .* (Salamanca, 1481); facsimile edition, *Introductiones latinae* (Salamanca: M. Paláez del Rosal, 1981).

**Early imprints:** *Introductiones latinae* (Venice: Christophorum de Cremona, 1491); republished as *Recognitio* [Manuscript: Madrid, Biblioteca Nacional] (Salamanca, 1495).

**Edition in English:** *A Briefe Introduction to Syntax, Compendiously Shewing the True Use, Grounds, and Reason of Latin Construction; Collected for the Most Part out of Nabrissa His Spanish Copie, with the Concordance Supplyed, by I. H. Med. Doct. Together with the More Difficult Assertions, Proved by the Use of the Learned Languages* (London: G. Edmondson, 1631).

*Repetitiones* or *Relectiones* (1485–1513)

**First publications:** *De membris et partibus grammaticae* (Salamanca, 1485); *De corruptis hispanorum ignorantia quarundarum litterarum vocibus* (Salamanca, 1486); *De vi ac potestate litterarum* (Salamanca, 1503)–facsimile edition, *De vi ac potestate litterarum: Introducción, edición, traducción, notas y edición facsimilar,* edited by Antonio Quilis and Pilar Usábel (Madrid: Sociedad General Española de Librería, 1987); *De peregrinarum dictionum accentu* (Salamanca, 1506); *De etymologia dictionis* (Salamanca, 1507); *De analogia hoc est de proportione* (Salamanca, 1508); *De mensuris* (Salamanca, 1510)–facsimile edition, *De mensuris Repetición sexta sobre las medidas,* edited by Jenaro Costas Rodríguez (Salamanca: University of Salamanca, 1981); *De ponderibus* (Salamanca, 1511); *De numeris* (Salamanca, 1512); and *De accentu latino aut latinitate donato* (Salamanca, 1513).

**Modern edition:** "Antonii Nebrissensis de vi ac potestate litterarum," in *Corpus Hebraicum Nebrissense: La obra hebraica de Antonio de Nebrija,* edited by Carlos del Valle Rodríguez (Madrid: Aben Ezra Ediciones, 2000).

*Introducciones latinas, contrapuesto el romance al latín* (1488?)

**First publication:** *A la muy alta y muy esclarecida princesa doña isabel la tercera deste nombre reyna y señora natural de españa y las islas de nuestro mar. Comiençan las introduciones latinas del maestro antonio de nebrissa, contrapuesto el romance al latin por mandado de su alteza* (Salamanca, 1488?).

**Early imprint:** *Introducciones latinas, contrapuesto el romance al latín, para que con facilidad puedan aprender todos, y principalmente las religiosas, y otras mugeres dedicadas a Dios, que para este fin mando hacer S.A. la reyna católica Doña Isabel al Maestro Don Antonio de Nebrija* (Madrid: Joachin de Ibarra, 1773).

**Modern edition:** *Introducciones latinas, contrapuesto el romance al latín, c. 1488,* edited by Miguel Ángel Esparza and Vicente Calvo (Münster: Nodus, 1996).

*Differentiae* (ca. 1491)

**First publication:** *Differentiae excerptae ex Laurentio Valla, Nonio Marcello et Servio Honorato* (Venice, ca. 1491).

*Gramática de la lengua castellana* (1492)

**First publication:** *A la mui alta y assi esclarecida princesa doña Isabel la tercera deste nombre Reina y señora natural de España y las islas de nuestro mar. Comienza la gramatica que nueva mente hizo el maestro Antonio de lebrixa sobre la lengua castellana. Y pone primero el prologo. Leelo en buen ora* (Salamanca, 1492); facsimile edition, *Gramática castellana: Texto establecido sobre la ed. "princeps" de 1492,* 2 volumes, edited, with an introduction, by Pascual Galindo and Luis Ortiz (Madrid: Edición de la Junta del Centenario, 1946).

**Modern editions:** In *Gramática de la lengua castellana (Salamanca, 1492); Muestra de la istoria de las antigüedades de Espana; Reglas de orthographia en la lengua castellana,* edited by Ignacio González-Llubera (London & New York: H. Milford, Oxford University Press, 1926), pp. 1–170; notes, pp. 171–

202; *Gramática de la lengua castellana,* edited by Antonio Quilis (Madrid: Editora Nacional, 1981).

*Diccionario latino-español* (1492)

**Manuscripts:** Madrid, Biblioteca Nacional I-1269, I-1281; New York, Hispanic Society of America.

**First publication:** *Lexicon hoc est dictionarium . . .* (Salamanca, 1492); facsimile edition, *Diccionario latino-español (Salamanca, 1492),* edited by Germán Colón and Amadeu J. Soberanas (Barcelona: Puvill, 1979).

*Vocabulario español-latino* (ca. 1493–1495)

**Manuscripts:** Madrid, Biblioteca Nacional; London, British Museum.

**First publication:** *Al mui magnifico e assi ilustre señor don Juan de estuñiga . . . Comiença el prólogo del maestro Antonio de lebrixa gramatico en la interpretación de las palabras castellanas en lengua latina* (Salamanca, 1495); facsimile edition, *Vocabulario español-latino* (Madrid: Real Academia Española, 1989).

**Modern edition:** *Vocabulario de romance en latín (Sevilla, 1516),* edited by Gerald J. MacDonald (Madrid: Castalia, 1973).

*Vafre dicta philosphorum* (1496)

**Manuscript:** Madrid, Biblioteca Nacional R-1357.

**First publication:** *Vafre dicta philosphorum* (Salamanca, 1496).

**Early imprints:** *Vafre dicta philosphorum* (Salamanca, 1498); *Vafre dicta philosophorum cum glossematis* (Burgos: F. Biel, 1498–1500); *Aelii Antonii Nebrissensis Vafre dicta philosophorum* (Seville, 1498–1500?).

*In cosmographia libri introductionum* (1498)

**Manuscript:** Salamanca, Universidad de Salamanca.

**First publication:** *In cosmographia libri introductionum* (Salamanca, 1498).

**Early imprint:** *In Cosmographiae libros introductorium* (Paris: S. Colin, 1533).

**Modern edition:** *Elio Antonio de Nebrija, cosmógrafo,* Latin text with Spanish translation, edited by Virginia Bonmatí Sánchez (Lebrija: Hermandad de los Santos de Lebrija/Agrija Ediciones, 2000).

*Aurea expositio hymnorum* (1501)

**First publication:** *Aurea expositio hymnorum una cum textu* (Saragossa: J. Coci, 1508).

**Early imprints:** *Aurea expositio hymnorum una cum textu* (Logroño: A. Guillén de Brocar, 1510; Saragossa: J. Coci, 1520); *Hymnorum recognitio per Antonium Nebrissen cum aurea illorum expositione* (Granada: Sancho & Sebastián de Nebrija, 1534).

*In Aulus Persium Flaccum poetam satiricon interpretatio* (1503)

**Manuscript:** Seville, Biblioteca Colombiana; Madrid, Biblioteca del Real Monasterio de El Escorial.

**First publication:** *Aelii Antonii Nebrissensis grammatici. In A. Persium Flaccum poetam satyricum interpretatio* (Seville: J. Kroberger, 1504).

**Early imprints:** *Aelii Antonii Nebrissensis gra[m]matici. In A. Persium Flaccum poetam satyricu[m] interpretatio* (Alcalá de Henares: A. Guillén de Brocar, 1514); *Commentaria Aelii Antonii Nebrissensis grammatici, in sex A. Persii satyras* (Paris: R. Estienne, 1527); *Auli Persii Flacci Satirae, cum interpretatioe Aelii Antonii Nebrissensis grammatici atq[ue] regii historiographi* (Logroño: M. de Eguia, 1529).

*Psicomachia: Aurelii Prudentii Clementis viri consularis libelli cum commento* (1503)

**Manuscript:** Oxford, Bodleian Library.

**First publication:** *Aurelij Prudentij Clementis viri consularis libelli* (Logroño: A. Guillén de Brocar, 1512).

**Early imprints:** *Aurelii Prudentii Clementis, viri consularis opera multo quam antea castigatiora* (Antwerp: M. Keyser, 1536); *Aurelii Prudentii Clementis, Viri Consularis, opera; commentarijs a Elij Antonij Nebrissensis* (Antwerp: C. van Diest, 1546).

*Iuris civilis lexicon* (1506)

**Manuscripts:** Murcia, Biblioteca Antonio de Lebrija, Universidad de Murcia 5-B-2933; Madrid, Biblioteca Nacional R-14059, R-7687.

**First publication:** *Ad perquam reuerendum Patrem ac notabilissimum Dominum Do. Ioannem fonsecam Episcopum Pallantium ac Comitem a Pernia. Aelij Antonii Nebrissensis grammatici in iuris ciuilis lexicon Prefatio incipitur . . . Aelii Antonii Nebrissensis grammatici in quasdam ciuilis dictiones por ordinem alphabeticarum digestas in priscis autoribus noua interpretamenta incipitur* (Salamanca, 1506).

**Modern edition:** *Iuris civilis lexicon,* edited, with an introduction, by José Perona, Aelii Antonii Nebrissensis grammatici opera, no. 3 (Salamanca: Universidad de Salamanca, 2000).

*Parvum vocabularium* (1506)

**First publication:** In *Aenigmata iuris civilis* (Salamanca, 1506).

**Modern edition:** *Aelii Antonii Nebrissensis Noua Iuris Ciuiles Dictiones in ordinem alphabetarum digestae, Estudios Románicos,* special Luis Rubio issue, 2 (1987–1988): 1109–1136.

*Latina vocabula ex iure civile in Voces Hispanienses interpretata* (ca. 1506)

**First publication:** *Latina vocabula ex iure civile in Voces Hispanienses interpretata,* in *Aenigmata iuris civiles* (Salamanca, 1506)—includes *Iuris Civilis Lexicon, Ex observationibus Aelii Antonii Nebrissensis in libros iuris ciuilis, Pomponii Laeti de Romanorum magistratibus, sacerdotiis, iurisperitis, legibus ad M. Patagatum libellus, Leges quae solent citari in historiis Pomponio Laeto, Cice-*

*rones topica ad ius civile accommodata, Parvum vocabularium* [titled *Novae Iuris civilis dictiones*], and two undated, untitled texts; fascimile edition, in *Iuris Civilis Lexicon, 1506.*

**Modern edition:** *Latina vocabula ex iure civile in Voces Hispanienses interpretata,* in *Aelii Antonii Nebrissensis grammatici opera,* edited by José Perona, no. 3 (Salamanca: Universidad de Salamanca, 2000), pp. 241–257.

*De litteris graecis* (1507?)

**Manuscript:** Salamanca, Universitaria de Salamanca.

**First publication:** *Antonius ad lectorem: De litteris graecis* (Logroño, 1507?).

*Commentum ad In Janum* (1511)

**First publication:** *P. Martyris angli / mediolanensis opera. Legatio babilonica Occeani decas / Poemata / Epigrammata / Cum preuilegio* (Hispali [Seville], 1511).

**Modern edition:** *Comentario al poema In Ianum de Pedro Mártir de Anglería,* edited by Carmen Codoñer, in *Aelii Antonii Nebrissensi grammatici opera,* no. 1 (Salamanca: Universidad de Salamanca, 1992).

*Artis rhetoricae* (1515)

**Manuscript:** Madrid, Biblioteca Nacional R-1363.

**First publication:** *Artis rhetoricae compendiosa coaptatio ex Aristotele Cicerone & Quintiliano* (Alcalá de Henares: A. Guillén de Brocar, 1515).

*De litteris hebraicis* (ca. 1515)

**Manuscripts:** Madrid, Biblioteca Nacional R-1754, R-2212, R-8162.

**First publication:** *Aelij Antonij Nebrissensis de litteris hebraicis cum quibusdam annotationibus in scripturam sacram* (Alcalá de Henares: A. Guillén de Brocar, ca. 1515).

**Modern edition:** "Aelii Antonii Nebrissensis de litteris hebraicis cum quibusdam annotationibus in scripturam sacram," in *Corpus Hebraicum Nebrissense: La obra hebraica de Antonio de Nebrija,* edited by Carlos del Valle Rodriguez (Madrid: Aben Ezra Ediciones, 2000), pp. 97–159.

*Tertia quinquagena* (1516)

**Manuscripts:** Madrid, Biblioteca Nacional R-1347, R-2252, R-2699.

**First publication:** *Tertia quinquagena (Quinquaginta Sacrae Scripturae loci non vulgariter ennarrati)* (Compluti [Alcalá de Henares], 1516).

**Early imprint:** *Tertia quinquagena,* in *Latina vocabula in voces hispanienses interpretata,* II, edited by José Perona, *Cahiers de Linguistique Hispanique Médiévale,* no. 16 (1991): 189–365.

*Reglas de orthographia en la lengua castellana* (1517)

**Manuscript:** Madrid, Biblioteca Nacional R-1363.

**First publication:** *Reglas de orthographia en la lengua castellana* (Alcalá de Henares: A. Guillén de Brocar,

1517); facsimile edition, *Gramática castellana, 1492; El ortographia castellana, 1517,* edited by R. C. Alston, European linguistics, 1480–1700, no. 2 (Yorkshire: Scolar, 1969).

**Modern edition:** *Reglas de Ortographia en la lengua castellana,* edited by Ántonio Quilis (Bogotá: Instituto Caro y Cuervo, 1977).

*Lexicon earum uocum quae ad medicinalem materiam pertinent* (1518)

**First publication:** *Lexicon earum uocum quae ad medicinalem materiam pertinent* (Compluti [Alcalá de Henares], 1518).

**Modern edition:** *Lexicon earum uocum quae ad medicinalem materiam pertinet,* in *Latina vocabula in uoces hispanienses interpretata,* II, edited by José Perona, *Cahiers de Linguistique Hispanique Médiévale,* no. 16 (1991): 189–365–Nebrija's continuation of Johannes Ruellius' translation of Dioscorides' Greek original, *Pedacii Dioscorides Anazarbei de medicinali materia libri quinque. De virulentis animalibus & venenos cane rabioso, & forum notis ac remediis libri quattuor. Ioanne Ruellio Suessionensi interprete,* edited by Nebrija (Compluti [Alcalá de Henares], 1518).

*Dictionarium medicum* (1545)

**First publication:** *Dictionarium Aelii Antonii Nebrissensis iam denuo innumeris dictionibus locupletatum . . .* (Antwerp: Iohannis Steelsii, 1545).

**Modern edition:** *Dictionarium medicum: El Diccionario médico de Elio Antonio de Nebrija,* edited by Avelina Carrera de la Red, Aelii Antonii Nebrissensis grammatici opera, no. 4 (Salamanca: Universidad de Salamanca, 2001).

*Muestra de la historia de las antigüedades de España . . .* (unfinished, undated)

**Manuscript:** Salamanca, Universitaria de Salamanca.

**Modern edition:** In *Gramática de la lengua castellana (Salamanca, 1492); Muestra de la istoria de las antigüedades de Espana; Reglas de orthographia en la lengua castellana,* edited by Ignacio González-Llubera (London & New York: H. Milford, Oxford University Press, 1926), pp. 203–228.

*Annotationes in libros pandectarum* (?)

**Manuscript:** Bologna, Biblioteca del Colegio de España.

**Modern edition:** *Annotationes in libros pandectarum,* edited by Antonio García y García, translated into Spanish by Arantxa Domingo Malvadí, Aelii Antonii Nebrissensis grammatici opera, no. 2 (Salamanca: Universidad de Salamanca, 1996).

OTHER: Hernando del Pulgar, *Rerum a Ferdinando & Elisabe Hispaniarum foelicissimis Regibus gestarum Decades due;* and Luis Correa, *Belli Navariensis libri duo,* translated and edited by Nebrija (ca. 1509–1522)

**Manuscript:** Madrid, Biblioteca Nacional R-6698.

**First publication:** *Rerum a Fernando & Elisabe Hispaniarum foelicissimis Regibus gestarum Decades Duas, Necnon belli Navariensis libros duos* (Granada: Sancho Nebrija, 1545).

**Early imprints:** In *Rerum Hispanicarum scriptores aliquot, quorum nomina versa pagina indicabit* (Frankfurt: A. Wechel, 1579), pp. 1073–1234; in *Hispaniae illustratae seu rerum urbiumq[ue] Hispaniae, Lusitaniae, Aethiopiae et Indiae scriptores varij,* edited by Andreas Schott, Johann Pistorius, and Franciscus Schott (Frankfurt: C. de Marne, 1603–1608), I: 786–926.

**Modern edition in Spanish:** Correa, *Historia de la guerra de Navarra,* edited and translated by José López de Toro (Madrid, 1953).

Antonio de Nebrija was the most important grammarian and lexicographer of the Spanish Middle Ages. His chief works were published and republished many times during and after his life, making his bibliography highly complex. Although he published learned translations and wrote commentaries, Latin poetry, and histories, his fame rests upon his works on grammar and lexicography.

Antonio de Cala y Xarana was born in Nebrixa (modern Lebrija), in the province of Seville, to Juan Martínez de Cala y Hinojosa and Catalina de Xarana y Ojo, but he changed his name to reflect that of his place of origin, a practice fashionable among European humanists of his age. For this reason he is known as Elio Antonio de Nebrija.

There is some uncertainty about Nebrija's date of birth. In the prologue to the *Vocabulario español-latino* (Spanish-Latin Vocabulary, circa 1493–1495) he states that he wrote that work at age fifty-one and that he was born a year before the Battle of Olmedo (1445), which would make his birth year 1444. He then adds dates for other landmarks in his life: he left for Italy at age nineteen, stayed there for ten years, and then served Alfonso de Fonseca, archbishop of Seville, for three years. But elsewhere Nebrija writes that when Fonseca died in 1473, he, Nebrija, was thirty-one years old, which would make his birth year 1442. Traditionally, 1444 has been accepted as the year of his birth.

Other facts about Nebrija's early life also derive largely from the autobiographical comments in the prologues to his scholarly works. He was the second of five brothers and spent his early years in Nebrixa. In the prologue to the *Vocabulario español-latino* he discusses his hobbies, his early schooling in grammar and logic, and

his arrival at the University of Salamanca, where he studied with distinguished professors—among them, Apolonio in mathematics, Pascual de Aranda in natural philosophy, and Pedro de Osma in moral philosophy. One can infer from the curriculum at Salamanca that Nebrija also studied geometry, arithmetic, algebra, physics, logic, Greek, Hebrew, rhetoric, music, and especially law and theology, as evidenced by a scholarship he received from the bishopric of Seville to study in the Colegio de San Clemente o de los Españoles in Bologna, where he lodged with the "theologians."

Little is known about Nebrija's stay in Italy, except that he was exposed to the works of such scholars as Lorenzo Valla, Angelo Poliziano (Politian), Ermolao Barbaro (Hermolaus Barbarus), Francesco Filelfo, and Giulio Pomponio Leto. In the prologue to the *Vocabulario español-latino* Nebrija writes:

> Assi que en edad de diez i nueve años io fue a italia: no por la causa que otros van: o por ganar rentas de iglesia: o para traer formulas de derecho civil i canónico: o para trovar mercaderias: mas para que por la lei de la tornada despues de luengo tiempo restituiesse en la possesion de su tierra perdida los autores del latin: que estauan ia muchos años desterrados de españa

> (So at nineteen years of age, I went to Italy, not to follow the steps of others or to gain prebends from the church, or earn patents of canon or civil law, or to trade in merchandise; but, in order that upon my return I might restore Latin authors to a land lost to them, for they had been long in exile from Spain).

Valla became one of Nebrija's guides and mentors. In his *Elegantiarum linguae latinae* (Elegances of the Latin Language, 1471), Valla's objective was to recover the *puritas* (purity) of the Latin tongue. In order to achieve this goal, he remonstrated against the quality of the Latin used in law, medicine, and the study of Holy Scripture; the best-known authorities in these fields wrote in a style Valla considered barbarous. He particularly objected to the study manuals used in universities and schools, such as the *Doctrinale* (1199) of Alexander de Villa Dei, the *Graecismus* (1212) of Eberhardus of Bethun, and Johannes Marchesinus's *Mammotrectus super bibliam* (Manual of the Bible, circa 1300). These authors, censured in Valla's works, are also criticized in the prologue to Nebrija's *Diccionario latino-español* (Spanish-Latin Dictionary, 1492), where they join Juan de Pastrana and Papias as authors who were eventually shunned in Spain thanks to the efforts of Nebrija.

Valla was not alone. Lorenzo de' Medici had given another humanist, Poliziano, access to a new manuscript of the *Digestum,* or Pandects, the collection of Roman-law writings compiled at the order of the emperor Justinian and first published in 533. The result was the *prima centuria* (first hundred) of Poliziano's *Miscellanea* (1489), which included about a hundred critical glosses of Greek and Latin words and became the model followed by Nebrija in his *Iuris civilis lexicon* (Lexicon of Civil Law, 1506). Barbaro's *Castigationes Plinianae* (A Critical Revision of the Texts of Pliny, 1492–1493), the commentaries on Aristotle by Theodorus Gazes, and the fundamental works of Galen and Aulus Cornelius Celsus were also guides for Nebrija.

The humanists' debate of the 1400s affected the totality of Nebrija's work. From Italy he brought the ideals of the *renovatio* (renewal) of the Latin language. In particular, he endorsed the principles of Valla's *Elegantiarum linguae latinae,* but he also paid attention to Spanish, one of the vulgar "tongues," which had admitted Andalusian and Arab words into its lexicon. These words were now, thanks to Nebrija, to be added definitively to the Spanish word fund. Nebrija composed the first grammar of a Romance language and two bilingual dictionaries (Latin-Spanish and Spanish-Latin) that shaped the subsequent development of Spanish lexicography. Also from the example of Italian humanists came the idea of immersing himself in the history of Spain and its "antiquities," evidenced in Nebrija's unfinished, undated *Muestra de la historia de las antigüedades de España* (Account of the History of the Antiquities of Spain), a history of Spain that was translated into Latin, the international language of learned discourse, and two texts about the conquest of Navarra and Granada.

In 1470 Fonseca recalled Nebrija to Spain to oversee the education of his nephew. When Fonseca died three years later, Nebrija signed a five-year contract as lector with the University of Salamanca. In 1476 he competed for and obtained the *Cátedra de Prima de Gramática* (First Chair of Grammar). In 1481 he published his first work, the *Introductiones latinae,* which rapidly became a best-seller, going through eleven editions. In 1485 Nebrija published a second version of the *Introductiones latinae,* with a section in verse. On the basis of this edition he wrote his bilingual grammar *Introducciones latinas, contrapuesto el romance al latín* (Introduction to Latin, with Romance and Latin Contrasted, 1488?); the revised Spanish portion was published as the famous *Gramática de la lengua castellana* (Grammar of the Castilian Language) in 1492. A definitive edition of the Latin part of the bilingual grammar was published in 1495 with the title *Recognitio.* The fourth and fifth editions of the *Introductiones latinae* were published as independent volumes, but many editions of the work were published in the sixteenth century, independently or cou-

pled with other texts. After a decree issued by Philip II in 1598, *Introductiones latinae* became the sole text used at every Spanish university. In total, the number of editions of the *Introductiones latinae* exceeds one hundred.

The *Repetitiones* or *Relectiones* (1485–1513) were the inaugural lectures with which Nebrija opened each of his university courses. The name by which they are known indicates that these works are thought to reflect the content of the courses he gave, but in more elaborate form. Nebrija published each of them in the year that a particular class was given. Many of these works did not go through second editions, and some are incomplete. The most important of them is the second, *De corruptis hispanorum ignorantia quarundarum litterarum vocibus* (1486), which was the basis of the later *De vi ac potestate litterarum* (Of the Valor and Potential of Letters, 1503). The sixth, seventh, and eighth *repetitiones, De mensuris* (On Measurements, 1510), *De ponderibus* (On Coinage, 1511), and *De numeris* (On Numbers, 1512), are specialized lexicons that follow the pattern of *De Doctrina Christiana* (396–426) of Augustine, who thought that the study of vocabulary was indispensable to an understanding of the Bible. The majority of the words in these three lexicons had already appeared in the *Diccionario latino-español.*

During a long stay with the Catholic Monarchs, Fernando (Ferdinand) and Isabel (Isabella), in Salamanca, Fray Hernando de Talavera asked Nebrija for a text concerning the pilgrimage of the monarchs to Santiago de Compostela and for a translation of the *Introductiones latinae.* The request was perhaps the origin of the *Gramática de la lengua castellana.* Nebrija might have presented *Muestra de la historia de las antigüedades de España* to Queen Isabel at this time.

No doubt Nebrija was bored with his teaching assignments in Salamanca because what he had learned in Italy had little to do with his duties as a professor of grammar in Spain. The chairs of grammar were also poorly paid, and Nebrija lost his ecclesiastical income in 1487 when he married Isabel Montesino de Solís, with whom he eventually fathered seven children. When the master of the Order of Alcántara, Don Juan de Zúñiga, offered him a post, Nebrija renounced his position in Salamanca and moved to Zalamea de la Serena (Badajoz), where he resided for the next twelve years, producing the wealth of works for which he is now celebrated and devoting unparalleled attention to the Spanish language.

In the prologue to the *Vocabulario español-latino* Nebrija mentions the *Introducciones latinas, contrapuesto el romance al latín,* the *Diccionario latino-español,* and the *Gramática de la lengua castellana,* as well as other minor works that have not survived. During this period he

*Page of entries for the letter* A *from the 1492 edition of Antonio de Nebrija's* Diccionario latino-español (*from* Diccionario latino-español [Salamanca, 1492], *edited by Germán Colón and Amadeu J. Soberanas, 1979; Thomas Cooper Library, University of South Carolina*)

also published *Differentiae excerptae ex Laurentio Valla, Nonio Marcello et Servio Honorato* (Differences Taken from Lorenzo Valla, Nennius Marcellus, and Servius Honoratus, circa 1491), the *Recognitio* (the third edition of *Introductiones latinae*), *Muestra de la historia de las antigüedades de España, Vafre dicta philosphorum* (Maxims of the Philosopher Told with Wit, 1496), *In cosmographia libri introductionum* (Critical Introduction to Cosmography, 1498), and *Aurea expositio hymnorum* (Golden Commentary on Hymns, 1501). *De vi ac potestate litterarum*, the *Psicomachia: Aurelii Prudentii Clementis viri consularis libelli cum commento* (Psychomachia: The Books of Consul Aurelius Clemens Prudentius with Commentary), and *In A. Persium Flaccum poetam satiricon interpretatio* (A Commentary on the Satires of A. Persius Flaccus) all date from 1503. Toward the end of his stay in Zalamea, Nebrija received a summons from Francisco, Cardenal Jiménez de Cisneros, to form part of the committee officially formed in 1502 and charged with the task of producing the great *Biblia Políglota Complutense* (Polyglot Bible of Alcalá de Henares, 1514–1517).

What Nebrija called the *arte de hablar* (art of speaking) followed the Roman author Quintilian's concept of rhetoric. Quintilian recommended a period of apprenticeship for learning the rules of a language before passing on to the study of the authors and texts that made up the canon. Establishing these authors and texts was one of the tasks that consumed Nebrija over the span of his career.

The other great mission of Nebrija's intellectual life was the study of language. In the prologue to his *Diccionario latino-español* he argues, following Quintilian, that mastery of language requires a long apprenticeship, starting with the study of nouns and verbs, their accidental features as the parts of a sentence. Then he makes a further refinement: "Lo que toca a la materia hizo se en aquellos ocho volúmenes que escreuimos delas significaciones delos vocablos: lo que a la forma en las dichas cinco obras de grammatica que en parte estan ia publicadas & en parte se han de publicar" (What concerns the matter rests in those eight volumes that we wrote on the meaning of words; what concerns the form rests in the aforementioned five volumes on grammar, of which part are published and part are yet to be published). In other words, the content of the art of speaking is lexicography, and the form is grammar (orthography, prosody, etymology, and syntax). Though form precedes matter, matter has become a subject of itself that relies on juridical, historical, poetic, philosophic, religious, and encyclopedic texts that the form (grammar) attempts to teach. Grammar is therefore not the final objective of the *renovatio* but the coupling of Latin with the language of the people. Nebrija's final objective was to recuperate the precision and subtleties of Latin so that they could be taught and imitated.

This goal can be traced throughout Nebrija's works. In the prologue to *Introducciones latinas, contrapuesto el romance al latín* he couples the recuperation of classical Latin with the excellence of Spanish by adding a brief excursus on Iberian geography and a list of classical authors who were born in Hispania: Lucan, Seneca, Valerius Martiales, Marcus Fabius (Quintilian), and Pomponius Mela: "ninguna cosa otra nos falta sino el conocimiento dela lengua en que esta no sola mente fundada nuestra religion & republica christiana: mas avun el derecho ciuil & canonico . . . La medicina . . . el conocimiento de todas las artes que dicen de humanidad . . ." (we lack nothing but knowledge of the language on which not only our religion and Christian republic is founded, but also civil and canon law . . . medicine . . . [and] knowledge of all the arts known as the humanities . . .). This trilogy of learning–Holy Scripture, law, and medicine–can be recovered only through intimacy with Latin uncontaminated by the corrupted texts and barbarous manuals of medieval Latin and reacquired from authoritative sources.

After creating a new "manual" in his *Introductiones latinae,* Nebrija began to gather citations taken from classical orators, poets, physicians, historians, and jurists that could form the base of a truly authoritative dictionary, one that could confront the reigning vulgarities with true classical Latin and ensure the beginning of a new

appreciation of the language. That is why Nebrija insisted, under the influence of Queen Isabel, Fray Hernando de Talavera, and Juan de Zúñiga, on making Spanish the vehicle for conveying knowledge of Latin. The mediating language was no longer to be a form of school Latin but the Castilian vernacular. This notion led to a refocusing of the objectives of Nebrija, who initially thought only of renewing the study of Latin in its purest forms.

Nebrija initially dedicated himself to gathering and editing the texts of Latin and Greek philosophers written in Latin (until the creation of the new fonts used for the *Biblia Políglota Complutense,* there was no movable type in Spain that allowed printing in Greek), such as his *Vafre dicta philosphorum* and his editions of Persius and Prudentius. In *Aurea expositio hymnorum* Nebrija rewrote the hymns sung in churches. His encyclopedic *In cosmographia libri introductionum* covered natural sciences; *De vi ac potestate litterarum* and the *Recognitio* gave improved descriptions of classical phonology and the Latin writing system. The Spanish language, however, gradually acquired a more prominent role in Nebrija's work.

This new prominence was part of the reason why Nebrija's two bilingual dictionaries (Spanish-Latin and Latin-Spanish) evolved in independent editions. A bilingual dictionary had originally formed part of the *Introductiones latinae* and was reprinted in the *Recognitio.* It bifurcated into independent editions as the *Diccionario latino-español* and the *Vocabulario español-latino.* There are also dictionaries in other foreign languages that include Nebrija's Spanish corpus but are not his work. These are bilingual dictionaries in which Latin has been substituted by such languages as Catalan, French, and Italian (Sicilian). (Curiously, Nebrija did not create a monolingual Spanish-Spanish dictionary, as he did a grammar, but his corpus was the cornerstone of later Spanish dictionaries.) As a professor of Latin he knew the poverty of the education in Latin among the Spanish nobility at a time of increasing political and social engagement of Spaniards in Italy, where Latin had become a revolutionary tool of the middle class. All these concerns played a role in the writing and publication of the *Gramática de la lengua castellana.*

The use of the Spanish language as a tool for political propaganda is expressed in the dedicatory prologue of *Gramática de la lengua castellana* to Queen Isabel. Now that Spain was united and pacified under the Catholic Monarchs, the arts of peace should flourish; first and foremost among these should be the study of the native language, now subject to clear rules and assuming the prestige formerly accorded only to Latin and Greek. It should be an instrument fit to recount the deeds of the queen, a task not to be left to foreign tongues. Repeating the words of the bishop of Ávila,

148

the *Gramática de la lengua castellana* could also impose Spanish on the conquered (at this time, the Muslim population of Granada) and teach those who needed to learn Castilian (Viscayans, French, Italians, and so forth). Two months after the grammar was presented to the queen, Christopher Columbus sailed to the New World. Five centuries later, about four hundred million people were using Spanish as their first or second language.

The *Gramática de la lengua castellana* has a medieval structure. It covers orthography, or the art of writing correctly; prosody, the art of crafting poetic meter; etymology, the study of the meaning of words and parts of speech; and syntax, the study of the sequencing of words. Two novelties differentiate it from the earlier Latin and bilingual grammars of Nebrija: the description of the writing system and sounds of Spanish in book 1 and the introduction of noun and verbal paradigms in book 5. Nebrija maintains that the sounds of Spanish are indivisible and finite and tries to have each letter faithfully represent a sound. He uses the term *letra* (letter) to signify what is now meant by grapheme, *boz* (voice) to represent the spoken word, and *palabra* (word) to indicate the written word. From the point of view of the syllable, Nebrija distinguishes between *vocales* (vowels), which may be pronounced alone, and *consonantes* (consonants), which need vowels. The consonants are divided into *mudas* (mutes: *b, c, ch, d, f, g, p, ph, t, th*, consonant *i*, and the semivocalic *u*) and *semivocales* (semivowels: *l, m, n, r, s*, and *z*). The latter include some vocalic sound when compared with the mutes. By their articulation they are *bilabiales* (bilabials: *p, ph*, and *b*); *labiodentales* (labiodentals: *f* and *v*); *linguodentales* (linguodentals: *t, th*, and *d*); *linguoalveolares* (linguoalveolars, composed of palatals and linguovelars, according to Nebrija: *c, ch*, and *g*). The consonants are also classified as *no aspiradas* (unaspirated, further divided into *apretadas* [unvoiced]: *p, t*, and *c*–and *medias* [middle]: *b, d*, and *g*) and *aspiradas* (aspirated: *pt, ph*, and *ch*). Nebrija's orthography, given his insistence that every letter should represent a single sound, acquires new letters and drops others. Of the twenty-three letters of Latin, only twelve have a single sound: *a, b, d, e, f, m, o, p, r, s, t*, and *z*. The rest of the letters represent multiple sounds or are not sounded. Nebrija's system eliminates the letters *q, k*, and *y*. Four letters are allographemes of *c, l*, and *n;* they become the graphemes *ç, ll, ñ*, and *ch* with tilde.

In spite of Nebrija's growing attention to Spanish, his love of Latin literature was not forgotten. He aspired to create a three-volume "Thesaurus linguae latinae" (Treasury of the Latin Language) as an alternative to the inept late-medieval encyclopedias, such as the *Magnae derivationes* (The Greater Derivations, circa 1200) of Uguccione da Pisa, the *Glossa ordinaria* or

*Glossa magna* (Great Gloss, 1220–1250) of Franciscus Accursius, and Giovanni Balbi's *Catholicon* (Universal Manual, 1286), which were studied along with the seventh-century *Etymologiae* (Etymologies) of St. Isidore of Seville. The thesaurus was never published as such but became the foundation of Nebrija's later volumes on the Latin language, such as the *Latina vocabula ex iure civile in voces Hispanienses interpretata* (Latin Vocabulary of Civil Jurisprudence Translated into Spanish, circa 1506?) and two *repetitiones, De mensuris* and *De numeris*. Nebrija also based his bilingual dictionaries in part on the lexical entries included in the spadework for the planned thesaurus.

In the prologue to the *Diccionario latino-español* Nebrija explains his manner of defining words:

> Mas las razones & argumentos que me movieron a interpretar en una o en otra manera. Eso mesmo la declaracion de los vocablos & otras partes de la gramatica: diferimos lo para aquellos tres volumenes que destas cosas en breve tenemos de publicar. Obra grande, copiosa & de cosas diversas, fraguada de cuatrocientos mui aprouados autores. Y tenia en voluntas publicar primero aquella: sino fuera de vuestra magnifica S. Perseguido: que començasse ia a publicar alguna cosa. & no le burlasse mas con vana esperança

> (But in the principles and reasoning that led me to interpret in one or another manner, and the explanation of words and of the other parts of grammar, we differ from those three volumes that we are soon to publish. This work is large and copious, composed of many diverse things, illustrated by the works of four hundred very respected authors. And I wished to publish it [the volume on the principles and reasoning] first, except for the insistence of your magnificence, who urged me to publish something, and not put you off with vain hopes).

Two details in the prologue bear explanation. The number 3 refers to the three principal branches of study–law, medicine, and Holy Scripture–and may be a reference as well to the *Iuris civilis lexicon*, the *Tertia Quinquagena* (The Third Fifty, 1516; that is, Nebrija's third attempt at publishing a text with fifty commonplaces taken from the Bible after he ran into trouble with the censors over two previous attempts), and a medical lexicon that may or may not be Nebrija's since it was not published during his lifetime. Despite the boast that he consulted four hundred classical authorities in refining his treatise, there was nowhere near that number of respected and "approved" Latin authors whose works were available in Spain before 1500. The number must refer to the new Greek and Latin authors whose writings were added to the canon by the Italian humanists.

In the prologue to the *Diccionario latino-español* Nebrija also states that bilingual dictionaries tended to compile terms for specialized use and betrayed a certain hastiness in their organization, equipped as they were with few grammatical or etymological glosses. Nebrija's later word lists were modeled on Quintilian, who divided words into five classes: Oscan (proto-Latin), old Latin, new Latin, barbarian, and approved neologisms. Nebrija follows Quintilian's counsel on validating the place of words in the language. Old and new words receive little space in the lexicon, with reliance on the authority of the *auctores* (authors), who alone can legitimately coin neologisms. Of the approved words, Nebrija includes those that have to do with poetry and rhetoric, while rarer terms receive little attention. In the prologue Nebrija goes on to proffer a theory of syntax, as well as his views on the historical and geographical lexicography of Latin.

Nebrija knew that Latin had borrowed Greek and foreign ("barbarian") words in the past; that old and new forms of a given word might coexist for long periods; that, given the geographical extension of the Roman Empire, one could validly designate a local style as "Hispanic Latin"; and that words had specialized meanings according to their context and the authors using them. The prologue to the *Diccionario latino-español* is a sketch of a diachronic lexicography of Latin that, upon its translation, became a linguistic history and geography of the emergent Romance languages. Nebrija included many words that belong to what is today accepted as Hispanic Latin, and he gives special attention to his Andalusian roots. This focus led him to include some dialectal forms of Spanish that grated on the ears of the generation of Juan de Valdés (1491–1541), who accused him of being an Andalusian who used a hybrid form of Spanish.

In 1503 authorities at the University of Salamanca wrote to Nebrija encouraging him to enter the running for another professorial chair. He won it but did not go to Salamanca. Only after the death of Juan de Zúñiga in 1504 did Nebrija return to the city and take possession of his chair in 1505. In 1506 he delivered his third *repetitio*, *De peregrinum dictionum accentu* (On Accentual Shift), which deals with Greek and Hebrew words and their proper accentuation. In October of the same year Nebrija published the *Iuris civilis lexicon*, a technical glossary composed of six hundred *lemmas* (word stems) with their Latin definitions, citations from classical *auctores* that vouch for their authenticity, and complementary citations gathered by Tribonianus in the *Digestum* of Justinian. The *Iuris civilis lexicon* also appeared as part of a great encyclopedia titled *Aenigmata Iuris Civilis* (Obscure Points in Civil Law), which went through several editions in the six-

teenth century. This encyclopedia included other works written or edited by Nebrija: the *Magistratum romanorum nomina a Pomponio Laeto, Ejusdem Antonii Nebrissensis observationes quaedam, Ciceronis topica ad jus civile accomodata, Leges quae solent citari in Historiïs ex Pomponio Laeto, Latina vocabula ex iure civili in voces Hispanienses interpretata,* and *Parvum vocabularium.* Here and there in the *Iuris civilis lexicon* are ferocious attacks against Accursius, the prototypical speaker of wretched Latin and ignorant Greek, who only *sueña, adivina o alucina* (dreams, guesses or hallucinates). Nebrija debunks Accursius with two thousand citations from such authors as Livius Andronicus, translator of Homer's *Odyssey* into Latin; Apicius, author of *De re coquinaria* (On Cooking); Apuleius of Madaura; Aristotle; Aulus Gellius; Julius Caesar; Cato the Elder; Catullus; Celsus; Cicero; Columella; Frontinus; Galen; Horace; Julius Firmicus Maternus; Juvenal; Livy; Lucan; Licilius; Lucretius; Martial; Pomponius Mela; Naevius; Ovid; Persius; Plautus; Pliny the Elder; Quintilian; Sallust; Seneca the Younger; Silius Italicus; Strabo; Suetonius; Terence; Ptolemy; Valerius Maximus; Varro; Vergil; and Vitruvius. To these writers Nebrija adds the Church Fathers and grammarians up to the fifth century A.D. In the critical apparatus of this thesaurus on civil law he not only attacks the medieval canon of the West but also adds specific critiques of the Latin writing system, grammar, phonetics, Greek loanwords, and the meanings of both simple and technical terms.

After Nebrija completed his three lexicons (*Iuris civilis lexicon, Tertia Quinquagena,* and *De medicinali materia* [On Medicinal Compounds]), he grouped the Latin terms gathered in those works according to semantic fields (words that belonged to the house, religion, writing, drink, plants, herbs, stations, and so forth) and proceeded to give their Castilian equivalents. When he did not find one, he would give a general definition, for example, *planta, arbol,* or *yerba no conocida* (plant, tree, or unknown herb). This is where he gave "palabras castellanas a las latinas" (Spanish words for Latin terms), as he says in the prologue to *Diccionario latino-español,* or incorporated Arabic terms when a Spanish equivalent could not be found.

In 1507 Nebrija delivered his fourth *repetitio, De etymologia dictionis* (On the Etymology of Words), and, in 1508, his fifth, *De analogia hoc est de proportione* (On Analogy, or Proportion). While he was away from his academic residence and the University of Salamanca from 1508 to 1509, his academic superiors declared his chair vacant. Perhaps to console him, King Fernando named him *cronista real* (royal chronicler), but Nebrija really wanted a university chair that paid better. In October of 1509 he was examined for a professorship in rhetoric at the university and won it. In 1510 he delivered the sixth *repetitio, De mensuris,* on measures in Greek, Hebrew, and Latin; in 1511, the seventh, *De ponderibus,* on weights and their equivalents; and in 1512, the eighth, *De numeris.* The second edition of the *Diccionario latino-español* was also published in 1512, with ten thousand new terms and a glossary of Latin place-names gathered from Greek and Latin authors. In 1513 Nebrija published his ninth and final *repetitio, De accentu latino aut latinitate donato* (On the Accent in Latin), and he attempted to obtain a second chair at the University of Salamanca, that of grammar, left vacant by the death of Tizón. University officials, tired of his absences and criticisms, did not grant him the honor, and the embittered Nebrija left, never to return.

In 1514 Cisneros offered Nebrija the chair of rhetoric at the new University of Alcalá de Henares, in the province of Madrid, with the generous provision that any classroom teaching he might perform would be optional. With the patronage of Cisneros and sufficient income to insulate him from academic infighting, he completed all his remaining new work by age sixty and devoted himself thereafter to republishing earlier works. In 1516 Nebrija published the *Tertia Quinquagena,* which corrects fifty garbled Latin passages in Scripture. He did not actually publish his first attempt at these corrections, and the second attempt was kept, and perhaps destroyed, by the inquisitor general, Fray Diego de Deza, a friend of Nebrija from his school days. Like his other works, the *Tertia Quinquagena* relies on material gathered for his other dictionaries and, again, includes a list of works that are criticized for faulty interpretation–for example, Marchesinus's *Mammotrectus super bibliam,* Balbi's *Catholicon,* Accursius's *Glossa magna,* Remigius's *Interpretationes nominum hebraicorum* (The Interpretation of Hebrew Words), Nicolás de Lyra's *Postillae in vetus et novum testamentum* (Commentary on the Old and New Testament, 1322–1331), and Hugo de Saint-Cher's *Correctoria* (Corrections, 1236–1256). Even St. Jerome, the Latin translator of the Bible, is faulted for some of his translations from the Greek. To these writers and their works, Nebrija opposes the work of such Church Fathers as Augustine, Rufinus, and Gregory; Greek and Latin authors such as Pollio Vitruvius, Pliny the Elder, Galen, Plutarch, Horace, Vergil, Strabo, Varro, Aristotle, Seneca the Younger, Juvenal, Catullus, and Apuleius; and the works of such contemporaries as Valla, Poliziano, and Barbaro. Full of confidence, Nebrija suggested emendations to Scripture that were not, however, acceptable to Cisneros or Deza.

In 1517 Nebrija published his *Reglas de orthographia en la lengua castellana* (Rules of Orthography of the Spanish Language). In this work he rounds out the ideas on Castilian orthography already promulgated in the *Gramática de la lengua castellana* and *De vi ac potestate litterarum.*

In the Middle Ages one studied the works of Pliny the Elder, Galen, and Celsus on medicine. With the reawakening of the knowledge of Greek, however, *De medicinali materia,* a manual of botany by the emperor Nero's personal doctor, Dioscorides Pedanius of Anazarbos, gained decisive prominence. Both Poliziano and Jean Ruel translated it, and Nebrija claimed to have possessed both translations. In 1518 he edited Ruel's Latin translation of *De medicinali materia* and added to it a Greek-Latin-Spanish dictionary titled *In ordinem alphabeticarum nomina plantarum, metallorum aliorumque rerum quae ad medicinalem materiam pertinent* (The Names of Plants, Metals, and Other Things that Pertain to Medicinal Matters in Alphabetical Order). During his last years at Alcalá de Henares, Nebrija continued to work at improving and extending his lexical work. He died on 3 July 1522 in Alcalá de Henares.

Some of Nebrija's works were published posthumously. *Rerum a Ferdinando & Elisabe Hispaniarum foelicissimis Regibus gestarum Decades Duas, Necnon belli Navariensis libros duos* (Two Decades of Noble Deeds Performed by Their Serene Majesties Fernando and Isabel, with Two Books on the War in Navarre) was published in 1545 in Granada by his son Sancho, a printer, together with the thirteenth-century *Cronica* of Archbishop Rodrigo Jiménez de Rada. It is now universally acknowledged that the account of the war in Granada in *Rerum a Ferdinando & Elisabe* is a translation and reworking of Hernando del Pulgar's *Crónica de los Reyes Católicos* (Chronicle of the Catholic Monarchs, 1482–1490), while the account of the war in Navarre is a translation of *La Conquista del Reyno de Navarra* (The Conquest of the Kingdom of Navarra, 1513), by Luis Correa. Nebrija suppressed many negative or unfavorable aspects of his originals, increased the negative descriptions of the enemies of the Catholic Monarchs, and justified their expansionist policy as an effort to reestablish the territorial integrity of the former Hispania. He upheld the rights of the Catholic Monarchs to the conquest of territory, rights that in Italy–especially in Naples–were beginning to be contested by contemporary Italian historians. Nebrija states that the historian should be magnanimous and not re-inflict the misfortune of Philip of Macedonia or his son Alexander the Great, who failed to cultivate eloquent historians or poets who could memorialize their deeds. The dead and living historians that occur to Nebrija–Barbarus, Poliziano, Pico della Mirandola, Antonius Flaminius, and Aldus Romanus–were all Italian, but Nebrija is oddly hostile to them:

*First page of the first edition (1495) of Nebrija's* Vocabulario español-latino *(from Felix G. Olmedo,*
Nebrija, 1441–1522: Debelador de la barbarie, comentador eclesiástico, pedagogo-poeta,
*1942; William T. Young Library, University of Kentucky)*

No creo, con todo, que la objetividad de la Historia pueda confiarse con absoluta seguridad a extranjeros, y menos a los italianos, codiciosos únicamente de su prestigio. Nos envidian nuestra gloria, se enfadan porque les gobernamos, se han confabulado para despreciar a todos los extranjeros y, llamándonos bárbaros y aldeanos, nos insultan con una denominación infame . . . siempre que este pueblo transmita literatura, lo corromperá todo

(I do not believe that we can trust foreigners with the objectivity of history, much less Italians, always thirsting after their own prestige. They envy our glory, they resent the fact that we rule them, they have plotted

against all strangers and, calling us barbarians, and bumpkins, they insult us with degrading names . . . whenever this nation is in charge of transmitting learning it will corrupt everything).

It is one thing to follow Italian models when trying to revive *studia humanitatis* (humanistic studies), another to allow them to serve as models for a national history. Nebrija cites Spanish models from classical antiquity instead. He emulates such Cordoban writers as Columella, Canius (a poet from Gades, Spain), Silius Italicus, the two Senecas, and Lucan, but he claims that his authority derives from being a witness to the events he narrates: "Además, en lo que vamos a narrar o intervinimos nosotros, mientras se realizaba, o hemos recibido información de testigos presenciales; y como si adivinara que algún día tendría que realizar esta tarea, puntualmente investigaba todos los detalles, los preguntaba o los anotaba" (In addition, what we are about to narrate are events in which we took part while they were happening, or about which we received the accounts of eyewitnesses; and, as if I could intuit that I was to undertake this task someday, I promptly investigated all the circumstances, double checked them, and took notes on them). The fact is, however, that Nebrija was named royal chronicler in 1509, some years after the events in the two translated histories took place. It is much more likely that someone in the inner circle of the king or some royal secretary pointed out to Nebrija the need to translate Pulgar's and Correa's histories into Latin so that they could be read in the rest of Europe, particularly in Italy. By the time they were published by Sancho Nebrija in 1545, Charles V had inherited Milan and was enmeshed in Italian politics.

Several more of Nebrija's works were published after his death. The *Dictionarium medicum* (Dictionary of Medicine) was published in 1545 under the supervision of L. Nuñez, who revised it at will and might have falsely ascribed it to Nebrija. The *Nebrissensis biblica* (Biblical Matters by Nebrija) is a manuscript preserved in the Vatican Library that was edited by Pascual Galindo and Luis Ortiz and published in two volumes in 1944 and 1950. The *Gramática de la lengua castellana* was not republished until the eighteenth century.

Nebrija was a productive author who built on previous work and republished much of it under new titles. Subsequent publishers followed his practice even after his death, and throughout the sixteenth century his poems, letters, commentaries, and brief grammatical treatises were added to the *Introductiones latinae*. The text became complex and hard to use, so much so that a replacement was deemed necessary by some. Francisco Sánchez de las Brozas ("El Brocense") proposed that his own *Minerva, o la propiedad de la lengua latina* (Minerva, or the Properties of the Latin Language, 1563) be recognized as the manual used by University of Salamanca students instead of Nebrija's *Introductiones latinae*. University officials made a Solomonic decision: El Brocense had to teach from *el Antonio* (as Nebrija's book was known at the time), and the university would publish his *Minerva*. The *actas* (official records) of the university show, however, that El Brocense managed to give his lessons based on *Minerva* and not from his rival's text.

In 1594 a royal query was sent to the faculties at Valladolid, Salamanca, and Alcalá de Henares asking whether the universities should continue to use Nebrija's

book or compose a new grammar. The Valladolid faculty answered yes to the continued use of *Introductiones latinae* but proposed that the text be updated and published in Castilian. The Salamanca faculty was indecisive and decided to continue using Nebrija's text but add or leave out material according to what each teacher thought best. In 1598 Philip II ordered that the *Introductiones latinae* be revised, a project entrusted to the Jesuit Luis de la Cerda, and confirmed as the only grammar text that was to be taught. The University of Salamanca approved the revision in 1604, and it remained in use until 1691, when the section on prosody was further amended. The text continued to be used until 1770.

The impact of the *Introductiones latinae* was tremendous, with no new grammars or methods of instruction proposed after its 1604 revision. In the nineteenth century Miguel de Unamuno failed his examinations for a position at the University of Salamanca because he did not cling to Nebrija but opted instead for foreign exponents of new approaches to historical and comparative grammar, such as Peter Corssen, Theodor Mommsen, and Konrad Burdach. Nebrija's bilingual dictionaries went through a similar historical trajectory of a period of prestige followed by displacement by foreign innovations.

Nebrija was transformed from an author to an authority whose name guaranteed the prestige of any work, regardless of its paternity. The *Iuris civilis lexicon,* for example, was combined with a medieval dictionary titled *Vocabularius utriusque iuris* (Vocabulary of Either [Canon or Civil] Law) and with glosses borrowed from Andrea Alciato and Guillaume Budé in 14 sixteenth-century editions that were published under Nebrija's name. Some of Nebrija's Spanish-Latin bilingual lexicons were also published in combination with the work of others. Gloria Guerrero Ramos counts 93 editions of Nebrija's dictionary, but there were also what Antonio Odriozola calls "phantom" editions. Odriozola believes that while 300 editions of Nebrija's total works are undoubtedly genuine, already by the sixteenth century there were up to 176 editions that were not.

The *Gramática de la lengua castellana* was used for the purposes claimed by Nebrija in his prologue, to teach Spanish to "pueblos de peregrinas lenguas" (people of diverse tongues). Intriguingly, the first grammars of American tongues (Nahuatl, Quechua, and Chibcha) were not modeled on the *Gramática* but on the *Introductiones latinae*.

In 1992 the fifth centenary of the first edition of the *Gramática de la lengua castellana* was celebrated by conferences held in Murcia and Salamanca, the proceedings of which were published in 1994. An electronic edition of the *Obra de Nebrija* (Works of Nebrija) was also edited by the Fundación Antonio de Nebrija and published in 1992 by Virginia Bonmatí Sánchez and Gregorio Bartolomé Martínez. To these were added the important *Bibliografía Nebrisense: Las obras completas del humanista Antonio de Nebrija desde 1481 hasta nuestros días* (Bibliography of Nebrija: The Complete Works of the Humanist Antonio de Nebrija from 1481 to the Present Time, 1999), by Miguel Ángel Esparza Torres and Hans-Josef Niederehe; Carlos del Valle Rodríguez's edition of the *Corpus hebraicum nebrissense: La obra hebraica de Antonio de Nebrija* (Nebrija's Hebrew Corpus: The Hebrew Works of Antonio de Nebrija, 2000); and the edition of the *Opera Latina* (Latin Works) directed by Carmen Codoñer in Salamanca. This scholarly activity testifies to a renewed interest in the author of the *Gramática de la lengua castellana* in the context of his historical works and from an international perspective.

## Bibliographies:

Nicolás Antonio, *Bibliotheca hispana nova; sive, Hispanorum scriptorum qui ab anno MD ad MDCLXXXIV floruere notitia,* 2 volumes (Madrid: Joachin de Ibarra, 1783, 1788; reprint, Madrid: Visor Libros, 1996);

Carlo Malagola, ed., *Statuti della Università e dei Collegi dello Studio Bolognese* (Bologna: Nicola Zanichelli, 1788);

Konrad Haebler, *Bibliografía ibérica del siglo XV: Enumeración de todos los libros impresos en España y Portugal hasta el año de 1500 con notas críticas* (The Hague: M. Nijhoff, 1903);

Pedro Lemus y Rubio, "El maestro Elio Antonio de Lebrixa I," *Revue Hispanique,* 22 (1910): 459–508; 29 (1913): 13–120;

Félix Olmedo, *Nebrija, 1441–1522: Debelador de la barbarie, comentador eclesiástico, pedagogo-poeta* (Madrid: Editora Nacional, 1942);

Olmedo, *Nebrija en Salamanca, 1475–1513* (Madrid: Editora Nacional, 1944);

Antonio Odriozola, "La Caracola del bibliófilo Nebrisense o La casa a cuestas indispensable para navegar por el proceloso de sus obras," *Revista de Bibliografía Nacional,* 7 (1946): 3–112;

Frederick J. Norton, *A Descriptive Catalogue of Printing in Spain and Portugal, 1501–1520* (Cambridge & New York: Cambridge University Press, 1978); translated by Daniel Martín Arguedas as *La imprenta en España, 1501–1520,* edited and revised by Julian Martín Abad (Madrid: Ollero & Ramos, 1997);

Amadeu J. Soberanas, "Las 'Introductiones Latinae' de Nebrija en Cataluña: Guía Bibliográfica," in *Nebrija a Catalunya: Exposició commemorativa en el cinque centenari de les Introductiones Latinae,* edited by Francisco Rico and Soberanas (Barcelona: Biblioteca de Catalunya, 1981), pp. 24–68;

Virginia Bonmatí Sánchez and Gregorio Bartolomé Martínez, *Catálogo de las Obras de Antonio de Nebrija, en soporte informático* (Madrid: Fundación Antonio de Nebrija, 1992);

Margarita Becedas, "Obras de Nebrija en la Biblioteca Universitaria de Salamanca (Siglos XV–XVI)," in *Antonio de Nebrija: Edad Media y Renacimiento,* edited by Carmen Codoñer and Juan Antonio González Iglesias (Salamanca: Universidad de Salamanca, 1994), pp. 575–595;

Miguel Ángel Esparza Torres and Hans-Josef Niederehe, *Bibliografía Nebrisense: Las obras completas del humanista Antonio de Nebrija desde 1481 hasta nuestros días* (Amsterdam & Philadelphia: J. Benjamins, 1999);

Julian Martín Abad, *Post-incunables Ibéricos* (Madrid: Ollero & Ramos, 2001).

## References:

Amado Alonso, "Examen de las noticias de Nebrija sobre antigua pronunciación española," *Nueva Revista de Filología Hispánica,* 3 (1949): 1–82;

Manuel Alvar, *Nebrija y estudios sobre la Edad de Oro* (Madrid: Consejo Superior de Investigaciones Científicas, 1997);

Alvar, "Nebrija y tres gramáticas de lenguas americanas," in Nebrija, *Gramática de la lengua castellana,* edited by Alvar and Antonio Quilis, volume 3: *Estudios Nebrisenses* (Madrid: Ediciones de Cultura Hispánica, 1992), pp. 313–339;

Manuel Alvar Ezquerra, "Nebrija, autor de diccionarios," *Cuadernos de Historia Moderna,* 1, no. 3 (1992): 199–209;

Alvar Ezquerra, "Notas sobre el repertorio léxico de Andrés Gutiérrez cerezo," in *Homenaje al profesor José Fradejas Lebrero,* edited by José Romera, Ana Freire López, and Antonio Lorente Medina (Madrid: UNED, 1993), III: 785–793;

Alvar Ezquerra, "Los primeros siglos de nuestra lexicografía," in *Estudios de lexicografía diacrónica del español: V centenario del Vocabularium Ecclesiasticum de Rodrigo Fernández de Santaella,* edited by Antonia Medina Guerra (Malaga: Universidad de Malaga, 2001), pp. 137–179;

Marcel Bataillon, *Erasmo y España: Estudios sobre la historia espiritual del siglo XVI,* translated by Antonio Alatorre, second edition (Mexico: Fondo de Cultura Económica, 1966);

Carmen Codoñer, "Las gramáticas de Elio Antonio de Nebrija," in Nebrija, *Gramática de la lengua castellana,* III: 75–96;

Helmut Coing, *Handbuch der Quellen und Literatur der neueren Europaïschen Privatrechtsgeschichte,* volume 1 (Munich: Beck, 1973);

Víctor García de la Concha, ed., *Nebrija y la introducción del Renacimiento en España* (Salamanca: Universidad de Salamanca, 1983);

Armando Cotarelo, *Nebrija científico* (Madrid: Editorial Magisterio Español, 1947);

Ricardo Escavy, Miguel Hernández Terrés, and Antonio Roldán, eds., *Actas del Congreso Internacional de Historiografía Lingüística: Nebrija V centenario,* 3 volumes (Murcia: Universidad de Murcia, 1994);

Abraham Esteve Serrano, *Contribución al estudio de las ideas ortográficas en España* (Murcia: Universidad de Murcia, 1977);

Manuel Fernández Álvarez, Laureano Robles Carcedo, and Luis Enrique Rodríguez-San Pedro Bezares, eds., *La Universidad de Salamanca,* 3 volumes (Salamanca: Universidad de Salamanca, 1989–1990);

Julio Fernández Sevilla, "Un maestro preterido: Elio Antonio de Nebrija," *Thesaurus,* 29, no. 1 (1974): 1–33;

María Lourdes García Macho, *El léxico castellano de los vocabularios de Antonio de Nebrija: Concordancia lematizada,* 3 volumes (Hildesheim & New York: Olms-Weidmann, 1996);

Eugenio Garin, *La educación en Europa, 1400–1600: Problemas y programas,* translated by Elena Méndez Lloret (Barcelona: Crítica, 1987);

Garin, *Italian Humanism: Philosophy and Civic Life in the Renaissance,* translated by Peter Munz (New York: Harper & Row, 1965);

Garin, "La letteratura degli umanisti," in *Storia della Letteratura Italiana,* edited by Amilio Cecchi and Natalino Sapegno, volume 3: *Il Quattrocento e l'Ariosto* (Milan: Garzanti, 1976), pp. 1–279;

Luis Gil Fernández, *Panorama social del humanismo español (1500–1800)* (Madrid: Alhambra, 1981);

Gloria Guerrero Ramos, *El léxico en el Diccionario (1492) y en el Vocabulario (1495?) de Nebrija* (Seville: Universidad de Sevilla, 1995);

Guillermo Guitarte, "Alcance y sentido de la opiniones de Valdés sobre Nebrija," in *Estudios Filológicos y lingüísticos: Homenaje a Ángel Rosenblat en sus 70 años* (Caracas: Instituto Pedagógico, 1974), pp. 247–288;

Gregorio Hinojo Andrés, *Obras históricas de Nebrija: Estudio filológico* (Salamanca: Universidad de Salamanca, 1991);

Domenico Maffei, *Gli inizi dell'umanesimo giuridico* (Milan: Giuffré, 1956);

Felipe Maíllo Salgado, *Los arabismos del castellano en la Baja Edad Media: Consideraciones históricas y filológicas* (Salamanca: Universidad de Salamanca, 1983);

Antonio Pérez-Martín, *Proles aegidiana* (Bologna: Real Colegio de España, 1979);

José Perona, "Antonio de Nebrija y los lenguajes científicos," *Voces,* 5 (1994): 65–89;

Perona, "Elio Antonio de Nebrija, grammaticus," in Antonio de Nebrija, *Gramática de la lengua castellana,* 3 volumes, edited by Alvar and Antonio Quilis (Madrid: Ediciones de Cultura Hispánica, 1992), III: 13–74;

Hastings Rashdall, *The Universities of Europe in the Middle Ages,* revised edition, 3 volumes, edited by F. M. Powicke and A. B. Emden (Oxford: Oxford University Press, 1936);

Francisco Rico, *Nebrija frente a los bárbaros: El canon de gramáticos nefastos en las polémicas del humanismo* (Salamanca: Universidad de Salamanca, 1978);

Rico, "Un prólogo al Renacimiento español: La dedicatoria de Nebrija a las *Introducciones latinas,*" in *Seis lecciones sobre la España de los Siglos de Oro,* edited by Pedro M. Piñero Ramírez and Rogelio Reyes Cano (Seville: Universidad de Sevilla, 1981), pp. 59–84;

Ángel Sáenz-Badillos, *La filología bíblica en los primeros helenistas de Alcalá* (Navarre: Verbo Divino, 1990);

Robert B. Tate, "La historiografía del reinado de los reyes Católicos," in *Antonio de Nebrija: Edad Media y renacimiento,* edited by Codoñer and Juan Antonio González Iglesias (Salamanca: Universidad de Salamanca, 1994), pp. 17–28;

Tate, "Nebrija, historiador," in his *Ensayos sobre la historiografía peninsular del siglo XV* (Madrid: Gredos, 1970), pp. 181–211;

Tate, "The Rewriting of the Historical Past: *Hispania et Europa,*" in *L'histoire et les nouveaux publics dans l'Europe Médiévale (XIIIe–XVe siècles): Actes du colloque international organisé par la Fondation européenne de la science à la Casa de Velasquez, Madrid, 23–24 avril 1993,* edited by Jean-Philippe Genêt (Paris: Publications de La Sorbonne, 1997), pp. 241–247;

Francis Tollis, "Nebrija frente a la realidad enunciativa y grafofónica del lenguaje: a propósito de una terminología," in Nebrija, *Gramática de la lengua castellana,* III: 261–312;

Cipriano Muñoz y Manzano, Conde de la Viñaza, *Biblioteca histórica de la filología castellana,* volume 3 (Madrid: M. Tello, 1893; reprint, Madrid: Atlas, 1978).

# Alfonso de Palencia

*(21 July 1424 – 31 March 1492)*

Madeleine Pardo
*University of Paris–Nanterre*

WORKS: *Ad nobilissimum militem sapientissimumque dominum Alfonsum de Velasco in funebrem abulensis famosissime praesulis* (ca. 1455)

**Manuscript:** Madrid, Biblioteca del Noviciado 133.

**Edition and Spanish translation:** *Epístolas Latinas,* edited and translated by Rafael Alemany Ferrer and Robert Brian Tate (Barcelona: Universidad Autónoma, 1982), pp. 78–100.

*Bellum luporum cum canibus* (ca. 1456); translated by Palencia as *Batalla campal entre los lobos y los perros* (1457)

**Manuscript:** No manuscript is known to survive.

**First edition:** *La guerra & batalla campal entre los perros & los lobos avida* (Seville: Cuatro compañeros alemanes, ca. 1490).

**Editions:** "Batalla Campal de los Perros y Lobos," in *Dos tratados de Alfonso de Palencia, con un estudio biográfico y un glosario,* edited by Antonio María Fabié, Libros de Antaño, volume 5 (Madrid: Librería de los Bibliófilos Alfonso Durán, 1876), pp. 9–104; Matilde Lopez Serrano, "El incunable *Batalla campal de los perros contra los lobos,*" *Revista de Bibliografia Nacional,* 6 (1945): 249–302.

*De Perfectione Militaris Triumphi* (ca. 1458)

**Manuscripts:** Escorial, S. III. 14; Madrid, Biblioteca Nacional 10.076.

**Edition:** "De Perfectione Militaris Triumphi," in *La Perfeçión del Triunfo,* edited by Javier Durán Barceló (Salamanca: Ediciones Universidad de Salamanca, Textos Recuperados, 1995), pp. 73–128.

*La Perfeçión del Triunfo,* translated by Palencia (1459)

**First edition:** *La Perfeçión del Triunfo* (Seville: Pablo de Colonia, Juan Pegnitzer, Magno Herbt & Tomás Glockner, ca. 1490).

**Editions:** "Tratado de la perfeccion del triunfo militar," in *Dos tratados de Alfonso de Palencia, con un estudio biográfico y un glosario,* edited by Fabié, Libros de Antaño, volume 5 (Madrid: Librería de los Bibliófilos Alfonso Durán, 1876), pp. 105–167;

"Tratado de la Perfección del Triunfo Militar," in *Prosistas castellanos del siglo XV,* volume 1, edited by Mario Penna, Biblioteca de autores españoles, no. 116 (Madrid: Atlas, 1959), pp. 345–392; "La Perfeçión del Triunfo," in *La Perfeçión del Triunfo,* edited by Durán Barceló (Salamanca: Ediciones Universidad de Salamanca, Textos Recuperados, 1995), pp. 129–198.

Letters from Palencia's first stay in Seville (1453): *Nobilitatem tuam prestantissimo decoratam* (to a man named Velasco); *De laudibus Hispalis ad Reverendum Dominum archidiaconum de Carrione Alfonsi Palentini epistola; Domino Petro Lunensi Alfonsus Palentinus salutem plurimam dicit; Didaco ut fratri amantissimo, laboris ejus inpositori motorique; Alfonsus Palentinus Fernando maximi policis viro salutem plurimam dicit;* and *Alfonsus Palentinus Fernando maximi policis viro salutem plurimam dicit*

**Manuscript:** Biblioteca capitular de la catedral de Burgo de Osma 57, fols. 121v–129v.

**Edition and Spanish translation:** *Epístolas Latinas,* edited and translated by Alemany Ferrer and Tate (Barcelona: Universidad Autónoma, 1982), pp. 31–56.

*Ejusdem Alfonsi epistola ad Vespasianum librarium Florentinum* (ca. 1463)

**Manuscript:** Montserrat Monastery 882, fols. 15–15v.

**Edition and Spanish translation:** *Epístolas Latinas,* edited and translated by Alemany Ferrer and Tate (Barcelona: Universidad Autónoma, 1982), pp. 75–77.

*Sapientissimo viro patrique ornatus ac utilis cujusque doctrine magistro domino Georgio Trapesuntio Alfonsus Palentinus hispanus historiographus salutem plurimam dicit* (1465)

**Manuscripts:** Madrid, Biblioteca Nacional 7446, fols. 264r–267r; Rome, Vatican Lat. 6845, fols. 28r–31r.

**Edition and Spanish translation:** *Epístolas Latinas,* edited and translated by Alemany Ferrer and

Tate (Barcelona: Universidad Autónoma, 1982), pp. 57–63.

*De sinonymis elegantibus libri III* (1472)

**Manuscript:** Madrid, Biblioteca del Noviciado, 128.

**First edition**: *De sinonymis elegantibus libri III* (Seville: Meynardo Ungut & Stanislao Polono, 1491).

*Decem . . . libri Antiquitatem hispaniae gentis enarraueram / Auiendo yo contado en diez libros la antiguedad de la gente española* (before 1475)

**Manuscript:** No manuscript has been located. The work is cited by Palencia in the "Mençion del trabajo passado et del propósito para adelante" in his *Universal vocabulario en latin y en romance* (1488, 1490).

*Ut decem aliis et imperium romanorum in Hispania et gothorum deinde ferociam usque ad Arabicam rabiem explicarem / con proposito de explicar en otros diez el imperio de los Romanos en españa e desde ende la ferocidad de los godos fasta la rauia morisca* (before 1475)

**Manuscript:** No manuscript has been located. The work is cited by Palencia in the "Mençion del trabajo passado et del propósito para adelante" in his *Universal vocabulario en latin y en romance* (1488, 1490).

*Vel ad recuperationem amplitudinis a mauris occupate summa sit in parte obliterata in parte nonnunquam perversa [y] voluissem hoc equidem gentis nostrae detrimentum recenti cura reparare* (before 1475)

**Manuscript:** No manuscript has been located. The work is cited by Palencia in the "Mençion del trabajo passado et del propósito para adelante" in his *Universal vocabulario en latin y en romance* (1488, 1490).

*Conosçiendo [y] la suma de cómo se fue recobrando lo que los moros auían ocupado en parte sea faltosa y en parte algunas veces peruertida [y] quisiera yo con reciente cuydado reparar la quiebra de nuestra gente* (before 1475)

**Manuscript:** No manuscript has been located. The work is cited by Palencia in the "Mençion del trabajo passado et del propósito para adelante" in his *Universal vocabulario en latin y en romance* (1488, 1490).

*Vita beatissimi Ildephonsi archipresulis toletani / lavida del bienaventurado Sant alfonso arçobispo de Toledo* (ca. 1475)

**Manuscript:** No manuscript has been located. The work is cited by Palencia in the "Mençion del trabajo passado et del propósito para adelante" in his *Universal vocabulario en latin y en romance* (1488, 1490).

*Gesta Hispaniensia ex annalibus suorum dierum colligentis,* decades 1–3 (ca. 1477)

**Manuscripts:** Madrid, Real Academia de la Historia 9/6482–includes decades 1–3; decade 1: Madrid, Biblioteca Nacional 6544, 1636, 1710, 1772, 1781, 19.439 (autograph, designated M [*Matritensis*] by Tate and Jeremy Lawrance); Madrid, Real Academia de la Historia, 5335; León, Residencia Salesiana, no shelfmark (designated A [*Astutellensis*] by Tate and Lawrance); Seville, Biblioteca Arzobispal 33–156; British Library Add. 8683; decade 2: Madrid, Biblioteca Nacional 1636, 1741; Madrid, Real Academia de la Historia 9/6482; Seville, Biblioteca Arzobispal 33156; Salamanca, Biblioteca universitaria 2559; Paris, Bibliothèque Nationale new Latin acquisitions 2058; and decade 3: León, Residencia Salesiana A (*Astutellensis*); Seville, Biblioteca Arzobispal 33156; Salamanca, Biblioteca universitaria 2559; Madrid, Biblioteca Nacional 1636, 1772, 7430; Madrid, Real Academia de la Historia 9/2185, 9/6482.

**Editions**: *Gesta Hispaniensia ex annalibus suorum dierum colligentis* (Madrid: Academia de la Historia, 1835); *Gesta Hispaniensia ex annalibus suorum dierum collecta,* 2 volumes, edited and translated by Tate and Lawrance (Madrid: Real Academia de la Historia, 1998–1999).

**Edition in Spanish:** *Crónica de Enrique IV escrita en latín por Alfonso de Palencia,* 4 volumes, translated by Antonio Paz y Melia, Colección de escritores castellanos, volumes 126, 127, 130, 134 (Madrid: Tipografía de la *Revista de Archivos,* 1904–1908); and Biblioteca de Autores Españoles, Madrid, Atlas, 3 volumes, I: 1973; II and III: 1975.

*Gesta Hispaniensia ex annalibus suorum dierum colligentis,* decade 4 (circa 1480)

**Manuscript:** Madrid, Real Academia de la Historia 9/453.

**Edition and Spanish translation:** *Cuarta Década de Alonso de Palencia,* 2 volumes, edited and translated by José López de Toro, Archivo Documental Español, volume 24 (Madrid: Real Academia de la Historia, 1970).

*Canarorum in insulis fortunatis habitantium mores atque superstitiones profecto mirabiles / las costumbres e falsas religiones por çierto marauillosas de los canarios que moran en las yslas fortunadas* (ca. 1482)

**Manuscript:** No manuscript has been located. The work is cited by Palencia in the "Mençion del trabajo passado et del propósito para adelante" in his *Universal vocabulario en latin y en romance* (1488, 1490).

*Compendiolum breve, quo civitatem, oppidorum atque fluminum nomina hispanorum innotescant* (26 August 1482)

**Manuscript**: Montserrat Monastery 882, fols. 16–27v.

**Edition**: Anscari Mundó and Tate, "The *Compendiolum* of Alfonso de Palencia: A Humanist Treatise on the Geography of the Iberian Peninsula," *Journal of Medieval and Renaissance Studies,* 5 (1975): 253–278.

*Bellum adversus Granatenses* (1482–1489)

**Manuscripts**: Madrid, Biblioteca Nacional 1627; Madrid, Real Academia de la Historia, 9/2186, 9/6482; Seville, Biblioteca Arzobispal, 33–156.

**Editions in Spanish**: "Guerra de Granada," in *Crónica de Enrique IV escrita en latín por Alfonso de Palencia,* volume 5, translated by Paz y Melia, Colección de escritores castellanos, volume 138 (Madrid: Tipografía de la *Revista de Archivos,* 1909), pp. 75–240; Biblioteca de Autores Españoles, Madrid, t.III, 1975; republished as *Guerra de Granada,* preliminary study by Rafael Gerardo Peinado Santaella, Archivum, no. 66 (Granada: Universidad de Granada, 1998).

*Relación verdadera de lo acahecido en la prisión del rey chico de Granada en el Arroyo que llaman de Martín González, el dia 21,* attributed to Palencia (22 April 1483)

**Manuscript**: New York, Hispanic Society of America B 2586.

**Editions**: *Relaciones de algunos sucesos de los últimos tiempos del reino de Granada,* edited by Enrique Lafuente y Alcántara (Madrid: Sociedad de Bibliófilos Españoles, 1868), pp. 47–67; Carmen Caselles, "Alfonso de Palencia y la historiografía humanista," dissertation, City University of New York, 1991, pp. 249–274.

*De adulatoriis Salutationibus laudatio nunque epictetis opinionem, non ratione usatis / de las lisonjeras salutationes epistolares e de los adjectiuos de las loanças usadas por opinion e no por razon* (before 1488)

**Manuscript**: No manuscript has been located. The work is cited by Palencia in the "Mençion del trabajo passado et del propósito para adelante" in his *Universal vocabulario en latin y en romance* (1488, 1490).

*De vera suficientia ducum atque legatorum / de la verdadera suficiençia de los cabdillos e de los embaxadores* (before 1488)

**Manuscript**: No manuscript has been located. The work is cited by Palencia in the "Mençion del trabajo passado et del propósito para adelante" in his *Universal vocabulario en latin y en romance* (1488).

*Universal vocabulario en latin y en romance* (1488, 1490)

**Manuscripts**: León, Colegiata de San Isidoro 52 (letters *A–N*); Escorial, Monasterio f. II. 11 (letters *O–Z*)–includes "Mençion del trabajo passado et del propósito para adelante," fols. 481b–482d.

**First edition**: *Universal vocabulario en latin y en romance,* 2 volumes (Seville: Paulus de Colonia, Johannes Pegnitzer, Magno Herbst & Thomas Glockner, 1490)–includes "Mençión del trabajo passado e del propósito para adelante," volume 2, fols. 548d–549b; *Universal vocabulario en latin y en romance,* facsimile edition (Madrid: Comisión Permanente de la Asociación de Academias de la Lengua Espanola, 1967); Edition on CD-ROM: ADMYTE, 1992.

BOOK: *Epistola ad Johannem Episcopum Astoricensem De Bello Granatensi* (Seville: Meynardo Ungut & Stanislao Polono, 1492).

**Editions**: Antonio Marín Ocete, "Una obra poco conocida de Alonso de Palencia," *Anales de la Facultad de Filosofía y Letras, Universidad de Granada,* 4–5 (1929): 93–111; Carta del Historiador Alfonso de Palencia al Reverendo Padre en Cristo y muy docto señor don Juan, obispo de Astorga, in *Epístolas Latinas,* edited and translated by Rafael Alemany Ferrer and Robert Brian Tate (Barcelona: Universidad Autónoma, 1982), pp. 101–117.

TRANSLATIONS BY PALENCIA: Domenico Cavalca, *El Espejo de la Cruz* (1485)

**Manuscript**: Toledo, Catedral, armario 17, no. 17.

**First edition**: *El Espejo de la Cruz* (Seville: Antonio Martinez, 1486).

**Second edition**: *El Espejo de la Cruz* (Seville: Meynardo Ungut & Stanislao Polono, 1492).

**Modern edition**: *Espejo de la Cruz: Testo critico,* edited by Isabella Scoma (Messina: Edizioni di Nicoló, 1996).

Plutarch, *Plutarcho,* 2 volumes (Seville: Paulo de Colonia, Johannes de Nuremberg, Magno Alemanes & Thomas Alemanes, 1491).

Flavius Josephus, *Guerras de los judíos con los romanos* (Seville: Meynardo Ungut & Stanislao Polono, 1492).

Josephus, *Contra Appion Gramático* (Seville: Meynardo Ungut & Stanislao Polono, 1492).

Alfonso de Palencia is a representative figure of the beginnings of humanism in fifteenth-century Castile; his active participation in political life parallels his literary and historical output and makes him a perfect example of "civic humanism." The many diplomatic missions with which he was charged made him aware of the necessity, and the difficulty, of obtaining reliable information, while his personal curiosity made

Autograph manuscript page in the Biblioteca Nacional, Madrid, from decade 1 of Alfonso de Palencia's history of Castile from 1440 to 1477, the Gesta Hispaniensia ex annalibus suorum dierum colligentis (from Gesta Hispaniensia ex annalibus suorum dierum collecta, volume 2, edited by Robert Brian Tate and Jeremy Lawrance, 1999; Thomas Cooper Library, University of South Carolina)

him an interested participant in the intellectual life of his time. He contributed to the introduction of Italian humanist thought in Castile.

In spite of these achievements, Palencia has not been accorded the scholarly attention that he merits. Several reasons can be advanced to explain this neglect: most of his works are in Latin and in limited circulation; he belonged to the Aragonese party that favored the preeminence of King Fernando (Ferdinand) over Queen Isabel (Isabella), leading the queen to choose Hernando del Pulgar as her official chronicler; and his linguistic works have been obscured by those of Antonio de Nebrija, printed a few years later, and by the fact that Palencia was not a professor and, therefore, did not have an academic readership.

Though knowledge of Palencia's life and works has been greatly advanced by the research of Robert Brian Tate, much remains unknown or uncertain. The main sources of information are documents, letters, the prologues to his works, and the "Mençion del trabajo passado et del propósito para adelante" (List of past work and future projects) which appears at the end of the 1488 manuscript of his *Universal vocabulario en latin y en romance* (Universal Vocabulary in Latin and Romance languages) and, with variants, in the incunabulum edition of 1490. There Palencia lists the works he has written up to that time, some of which are now lost. Other important sources of information about Palencia are the many autobiographical passages in the first four "decades" of his *Gesta Hispaniensia ex annalibus suorum dierum colligentis* (circa 1477, Hispanic Facts Collected from Contemporaneous Annals). That source, however, though priceless, has to be used with care: the information is often unverifiable and is sometimes hard to believe, because the author tends to magnify his role as a participant in the events he narrates.

Alfonso Fernández Palencia was born on 21 July 1424 in Palencia. He remembers the city contemptuously in a letter written around 1455 to the archdeacon of Carrion, in which he also praises the city of Seville at great length. Julio Puyol y Alonso, Ludwig Pfändl, Juan Torres Fontes, and Americo Castro have argued that Palencia was of *converso* (Jewish convert to Christianity) ancestry, but they are forced to rely on circumstantial evidence such as his belief in omens, his superstitious credulity coupled with a critical spirit, his vehement satire of clerical and papal corruption, and his favorable opinion of *conversos* in many passages in the *Gesta Hispaniensia*. But a combination of credulity and critical spirit is found in many writers of the period, and the opinions he expresses about *conversos* in the *Gesta Hispaniensia* are not uniform but depend on the individual, community, or region with which he is dealing and on the narrative structure and discursive strategy he is

employing at a given point. One may be tempted to have recourse to the old hypothesis of *converso* origins to account for the personal tone of the *Gesta Hispaniensia* and for the way it reveals and hides aspects of the author's personality, but in the absence of proof one should seek other explanations.

Palencia was probably the son of Luis González de Palencia. A brief letter addressed to "Didaco ut fratri amantissimo" (Diego, most beloved brother) and accompanied by a since-lost description of Roman monuments, allows one to suppose that he had a brother—unless the addressee is, as Tate suggests, Diego Rodríguez de Almela. Nothing is known about his childhood.

Palencia's early education most likely took place at the cathedral school of Burgos under the direction of Bishop Alfonso de Cartagena. Cartagena represented King Juan II of Castile at the Council of Basel in the mid 1430s and later in an embassy to the king of Bohemia; his absence lasted from 1435 to 1439, during which he established relations with many humanists. Whether Palencia's initial contact with Cartagena preceded or followed the bishop's voyage is unknown. The only fact about which one can be certain is given in the first decade of the *Gesta Hispaniensia*, where Palencia says that he was seventeen when he accompanied Cartagena to a 7 May 1441 meeting at Maqueda between the envoys of Juan II and Álvaro de Luna, and terms himself a "familiar" of the bishop at that time ("eorum uni Burgensi ego in aetate annorum septem et decem famulabar"). This passage is only the second time that a date is given in the first decade and the first time that one is given in complete form, indicating that the event was especially important to Palencia. Whatever the duration of the relationship might have been, the influence exercised by Cartagena over Palencia was profound: he served as both a teacher and a model for the younger man. Cartagena probably procured for Palencia a prebend for handling diocesan affairs before the Roman Curia, a fact that is entered in the accounts of the chapter of the cathedral of Burgos in 1450.

In about 1442 Palencia began a ten-year sojourn in Italy that was of decisive importance to his education. Probably owing to a recommendation by Cartagena, he began his stay there in the service of Cardinal Joannes Bessarion, whose home was a veritable academy frequented by eminent men of letters such as Theodore Gaza, Joannes Argyropulos, Francesco Filelfo, Leonardo Bruni, Flavio Biondo, Poggio Bracciolini, and Lorenzo Valla. Before moving to Rome in 1443 Bessarion had lived in Florence, where George of Trebizond, a Greek scholar of Cretan origins, taught rhetoric beginning in the autumn of 1442. At about the same time as Bessarion was posted in Rome, Trebizond was also sent to Rome as apostolic secretary to Pope Nicolas V and as lector in the Studio Romano, a center of learning less structured and traditional than the university. Thus, Palencia may have been taught by Trebizond while he resided in the Bessarion household. Trebizond's professorial reputation was great, and his manual of rhetoric, *Rhetoricorum libri V,* had been printed for the first time in Venice in 1433–1434 (in Spain, it was first printed in Alcalá in 1511). Trebizond's ideas were not original, but he knew how to make a clear and well-reasoned synthesis of the uses of rhetoric beyond its normal function as an indispensable instrument of civic life. Following Cicero's comments in *De oratore,* he proposed a theory of the craft of historical writing, the fundamental precept of which was the need to follow a chronological and causal order. Such an approach allows the historian to respect the structure of *consilia acta eventus* (deliberations, events, consequences), while allowing for the digressions that he finds pertinent to his narrative.

That Palencia maintained contact with Trebizond is made evident by an exchange between Palencia and Trebizond. In a letter dated 1465, when Trebizond was at the court of Ferrante of Naples, Palencia recognizes his debt to his "pater optime" (master) and asks for Trebizond's opinion of Bruni's interpretation of the Aristotelian concept of the summum bonum. He also recalls his youthful years in Rome, his love of Italy, and the care lavished on him by Bessarion when he was sick.

While he was in Florence, Palencia also met Donato Acciauoli, Carlo Marsuppini, and the librarian Vespasiano da Bisticci in Florence. That he remained in contact with the latter is clear from a letter addressed to Palencia in 1463 by Acciauoli on behalf of Vespasiano; the letter concerns a shipment of books destined for the archbishop of Seville, Alfonso de Fonseca II.

In the *Gesta Hispaniensia,* where portraits and biographies of contemporaries abound, the first of Palencia's three teachers, Cartagena, is given fulsome but brief praise: "grauitate honestateque insignem uirum ac doctrina singularem" (famous for his seriousness and honesty and outstanding for his doctrine). His death in 1456, however, is not mentioned. Bessarion, by contrast, is the object of a portrait and a brief biography in which praise–"alter nostrorum temporum Plato"–is tempered with criticism of his "creuit postea in senectute tumor" (excessive ambition in old age). Of Trebizond there is no trace: he was not a prelate, noble, or ambassador and, therefore, did not exist for the purposes of history.

Bessarion left Rome in 1450 to become legate to Bologna. Palencia may have undertaken a journey to Florence at this time, but in 1453 he was back in Rome, where, as he recalls in decade 1, he heard rumors at the Vatican about the advance of the Turks on Constantinople.

Palencia returned to Spain in 1453, bringing with him from Italy an intellectual training based in the seven liberal arts. He was convinced of the power of knowledge and of the need to transmit it. The rhetoric he learned from Trebizond governed his writings throughout his life. He was trained in learned exercises and in the copying of manuscripts. He may also have brought back from humanist Italy a taste for polemic and satire, a keener view of individuals and an ability to depict them, and an enhanced consciousness of himself as an individual.

In a letter of around 1453 addressed to Pedro de Luna, illegitimate son of Álvaro de Luna, Palencia excuses himself for not writing since his return from Italy because of unspecified problems. He also says that he is sending a meditation inspired by the tragic end of Luna's father, who had recently been executed. That text has not survived, but echoes of it appear in the long account of the life and death of the elder Luna in the first decade of the *Gesta Hispaniensia.*

Another letter (1453?) is addressed to someone named Velasco–in all probability Alfonso de Velasco, brother of Pedro Fernández de Velasco, count of Haro. In it, Palencia recalls that his family has always been in the service of the Velascos. The letter indicates that on his return from Italy he was in search of a patron who could introduce him to men of letters in Seville. To Velasco he also addressed a beautiful allegorical elegy on the death of the learned bishop of Avila, Alfonso de Madrigal, known as "el Tostado" (the Toasted or Tanned One), in September 1455; it is the first known work from Palencia's pen other than personal letters. Death disrupts the peaceful life of shepherds by striking down their shepherd of souls, the bishop. One hears the first critique of the moral decadence of Spain in the depiction of the flight of virtues that follows the death of Madrigal. Whether Palencia was personally acquainted with Madrigal is unknown, but the long elegy dedicated to him makes Palencia's silence about the death of Cartagena all the more surprising.

In the summer of 1456 King Enrique IV of Castile resided in Seville during his Andalusian campaign. Probably on the recommendation of Alfonso de Velasco, Palencia was attached to the train of the archbishop of Seville, Alfonso de Fonseca I, who accompanied the king on his return to Castile. On 6 December 1456 Palencia succeeded the recently deceased Juan de Mena as *cronista y secretario de latin* (royal chronicler and secretary of Latin letters), with a daily emolument of fifteen *maravedís* for the first duty and twenty for the second. In 1458 the archbishop gave him the *refrendo* (right of countersigning) of the bulls of crusade of Pope

Calixto III. These posts were a perfect vantage point from which to watch the court. As part of the entourage of the archbishop, Palencia had access to a man who, together with Juan Pacheco, headed the *consejo real* (royal council). In his *Gesta Hispaniensia* Palencia portrays both men, especially Pacheco, in a negative light.

Palencia composed his first two Latin treatises in the form of fables and translated both into Castilian so that their lessons would be accessible to lay readers. The first is an animal fable, *Bellum luporum cum canibus* (War of the Wolves and the Dogs), in Castilian *Batalla campal de los perros contra los lobos* (The Pitched Battle of the Dogs Against the Wolves); the Latin text of the work has not been preserved. In the "despedida de la obra" (epilogue of the book) he says that he composed the work in 1457, though he does not specify whether he is referring to the Latin or the Castilian version. Since he mentions that he is soliciting the post of chronicler, which he obtained in December 1456, one can assume that the Latin text was written in 1456 and that 1457 is the date of the translation.

Palencia introduces the *Batalla campal de los perros contra los lobos* as a preliminary exercise in the manner of Homer, who was believed to have written the *Batrachomyomachia* before writing the *Iliad*. He says that he wrote the work both to exercise his pen and to give his readers a foretaste of his ability as an historian: "experimentar . . . quanto valdria mi peñola en la historial conposicion de los fechos de España" (to experience . . . how good my pen would be at the historical composition of the deeds of Spain). Throughout the narrative, which is at once serious and comic, Palencia shows his abilities as a Latinist and rhetorician. The *Batalla campal de los perros contra los lobos,* in which, in order not to be exterminated, the wolves and dogs decided to stop fighting and to live as before, denounces the incessant confrontations of the *bandos* (clans) and makes the Battle of Olmedo (1445) emblematic of such struggles. The first Andalusian campaigns of Enrique IV in 1455 and 1456 are similar examples of vain and ill-conceived struggles.

Palencia's second allegory, *De Perfectione Militaris Triumphi* (Perfection of military triumph) (circa 1458), *La Perfeçión del Triunfo* (1459) in Castilian, proposes a remedy. El Exerçiçio (Exercise) arrives from "la mas extendida España" (the so extensive Spain) and cannot find Triunfo (Triumph). La Esperiençia (Experience) advises Exerçiçio to consult her daughter, La Discreçion (Discretion), who lives in Italy. La Discreçion permits El Exerçiçio to find Gloridoneo (Glorifier), who, through Orden (Order) and Obediençia (Obedience), knows Triunfo. Orden, Obediençia, and Exerçiçio are the three pillars of *disciplina militaris* and, in a larger sense, of good government. The Latin version

of the allegory is dedicated to Alfonso Carrillo, archbishop of Toledo; the Castilian version is dedicated to Fernando de Guzmán, *comendador* (commander) of Calatrava. Alfonso V's celebration on 26 February 1443 of his conquest of Naples may have been one inspiration for the Castilian version of the work, which appeared the year after the king died. Another may have been Carrillo's assuming the leadership of the malcontents in 1457, during the Andalusian campaign. This work constitutes the first time that a relationship can be established among Palencia, Carrillo and his followers, and the Aragonese House of Trastámara.

Between 1460 and 1465 Palencia had his first important political experiences. Alfonso de Fonseca I, called *el Viejo* (the Old One), demanded that the Pope give his nephew, Alfonso de Fonseca II, known as *el Joven* (the Young One), the archbishopric of Seville when Fonseca I was transferred to Santiago de Compostela. Fonseca I thereby was able to accumulate the rents of both sees. Later he tried to make another exchange with his nephew, but Fonseca II refused to cooperate. Fonseca I then persuaded the Pope to depose his nephew from the see of Seville, but he learned that Enrique IV intended to dispossess both uncle and nephew of their positions. Fonseca II, who was a partisan of Carrillo and whom, according to the sketches in the *Gesta Hispaniensia,* Palencia seems to have liked, took refuge in Ecija. In a letter to Vespasiano da Bisticci in November or December 1463 Palencia describes the problems caused by these events, refers to his own temporary withdrawal from public affairs because "ferox mula edentulum me fecit" (a mule's kick took my teeth away), and discusses Florence and books. In decade 1 of the *Gesta Hispaniensia* he says that he aided in the reconciliation of the two Fonsecas at the monastery of Cuevas in Seville, acting as "interprete tamquam caduceatore" (both mediator and messenger). In 1464 Fonseca I ordered him to join a delegation to Rome to defend the archbishop's rights against the king.

Palencia devotes many pages of decade 1 to that mission. During his journey to Rome, he says, he learned of the death of Pius II on 15 August and the election of Pietro Barbo on 31 August. The election filled him with sadness, because he disapproved of the cardinal's character. He attended Barbo's coronation as Paul II and obtained an audience with the Pope in September. The archbishop's representatives chose him as their spokesman because he was the best Latin speaker among them.

Meanwhile, a junta of grandees led by Carrillo and Pacheco had gathered in Burgos from 26 to 28 July and had sent a manifesto to all the towns in the kingdom enumerating their accusations against Enrique IV, including the charge that the infanta Juana was not his daughter. In Rome, Palencia and the other members of his mission received a copy of the manifesto and were directed to read it to the Pope and the cardinals and defend the nobles' position. The Pope, however, refused to condemn the king; on the contrary, he agreed to forgive the *annata* (a papal tax on the first year of ecclesiastical benefits) of Prince Alfonso, on whom the king conferred the *maestrazgo* (mastership of the order) of Santiago, giving up his attempt to elect his favorite, Beltrán de la Cueva, to the office. Palencia arranges his narrative at this point to suggest that he audaciously objects to the Pope's decision. He draws a negative image of the Roman Curia, particularly of Cardinals Juan de Carvajal and Juan de Mella. According to Palencia, Roman corruption reinforces Castilian corruption, of which Enrique IV is the prime example.

Palencia was happy to be in Italy once more, but Roman decadence filled him with sadness. He decided to profit from the journey by buying and copying manuscripts, making sketches of ancient monuments, and renewing his friendship with his old teacher. In answer to a letter from Palencia, Trebizond expressed his happiness at seeing a former student whose qualities he always appreciated and who, "doctiorem ac eloquentiorum esse percepi quam existimaram . . . facundia, elegantia, facilitate vicisti opinionem meam" (with your eloquence, with your elegance, with your ease, . . . exceeded my expectations). Palencia bought two copies of Trebizond's translation from Greek to Latin of the *Thesauri de Sancta et consubstantiali Trinitate* (Treasures of the Holy Consubstantial Trinity) of Saint Cyril of Alexandria and translations of Aristotle's *De anima* (On the Soul), *Rhetorica,* and *De generatione et corruptione.*

Palencia returned to Seville at the beginning of 1465. The conflict between the nobles and the king culminated in the *farsa de Ávila* (Farce of Ávila) on 5 June 1465, when Enrique IV was deposed in effigy and his half brother was proclaimed king as Alfonso XII. Knowledge of that strange ceremony reached Seville on 8 June. On 15 June, Palencia read letters from Alfonso to the *regidores* (municipal magistrates) of Seville. His commentary secured the adherence of Don Juan de Guzmán, duque de Medina-Sidonia, to the new king.

In 1465 Palencia was secretary to García Alvarez de Toledo, Count of Alba. How long he had occupied that position is unknown; he seems to have left the service of Fonseca I at this time. As Tate says, in a sign of the confusion of the times Enrique IV conferred on Palencia the positions of *escribanía de cámara y notaría* (chamber secretary and notary) with a *quitacion* (remuneration) of 10,200 *maravedís* and ten annual *excusados* (compensations). Another benefit from Enrique came his way in September, even though Palencia was completely committed to the party of Prince Alfonso,

headed by Carrillo and Pacheco. Whether Palencia had an official post in Alfonso's household is not known, but he addressed the prince as "*rey*" (king) until Alfonso's death in 1468. In the first decade of the *Gesta Hispaniensia* he depicts himself as a confidant, counselor, and intermediary of the prince. Because, at Alfonso's request, he recommended that the Hermandad (Brotherhood, the rural police) intervene in the conflict over Cadiz that pitted the Ponce de Leóns against the Medina-Sidonias, he was threatened with death by the young heirs to the titles of both families, Enrique de Guzmán and Rodrigo Ponce de León. He owed the commutation of the sentence to exile to the goodwill of the old duke, Don Juan de Guzmán.

Palencia accompanied Prince Alfonso on the day of the second Battle of Olmedo in August 1467. In September he was made aware of the capitulation of Segovia, the favorite residence of Enrique IV. At the same time Enrique's chaplain, Diego Enríquez del Castillo, was arrested, and the chronicle of Enrique's reign that he was writing was given to Palencia for examination. Palencia judged that the text falsified events, particularly the account of the Battle of Olmedo, and the chronicler's life was spared only because of his clerical robes.

According to the prologue to the *Gesta Hispaniensia,* the distortions of Castillo were what moved Palencia to begin his own truthful account. The prologue also indicates that he has made the narrative "magna cum voluptate" (more agreeable) by writing about the glorious "antiquitatem Hispanae gentis" (antiquity of the Spanish people). The antiquity of the Spanish people is again addressed in the "Mençion del trabajo passado et del propósito para adelante," where Palencia says "Auiendo yo contado en diez libros la antiguedad de la gente española" (I wish to continue that story in ten books) that will deal with the Romans, the Visigoths, and the Moors before getting to the account of the Reconquest. No such works have been found.

The last words of the third decade indicate that it was completed in 1477. The purposeful and violent character of the first decade, which covers the years 1440 to 1468, indicates that the final redaction postdates the death of Enrique IV. The second decade covers the years 1468 to 1474 and the third 1474 to 1477. These three works are the first true example of humanist historiography in Castile. The titles, as Palencia indicates, are meant to evoke the Roman historian Livy's *Decades.* The rigorous division into books and chapters—each decade has ten books, and each book has ten chapters—respects the order of the events and is a way of shaping the complexity of a universe inhabited by more than six hundred individuals who are often described and always judged. By inserting himself into

Alfonsi Palentini Historiographi gesta hispaniēñ ex annalibus
suorum dierum colligentis prologus incipit.

# MAGNA CVM VOLVPTATE QVI

retuli iam dudum antiquitatem hispane gentis: cogor nuper scribere: que cala
mus horret: nimirumq̃ sistillus pre fœditate rerum decidat: atq̃ obscuretur mens:
quum nihil clarum offeratur: sed diu anceps fuerim inter alterutram vel omitten
di vel adeundi presentis historie considerationem. Quippe hinc susceptum honus
illinc vero premebat future dedignatio narrationis: et quod officium iusserat,
animus pariter aspernabatur./ Quid enim allicit magis scriptorem q̃ magnitudo
negotij luciddaq̃ species qualitatis? Q, si secus accidat: et nil fere aliud preter ama
ritudinem delibetur: vniverse offenduntur mentis vires: et ingenium sequitur
dispositionem voluntatis infecte iam acerbitate intoleranda materie. Verum
enim vero superadditur ad scribendum irritatio haud lenta: quum videam sub
ductos a principibus maximis assentatores pravos: qui nihilominus calamo
nituntur cum laudibus efferre infima, turpiaq̃ celare fuco: q̃ vel bo vituperanda
comprobarint vel dissimulatione texerunt./ Quod quidem perversionis genus
ipsa veritate abolendum curabo. Neq̃ eorum sentencia magnifacienda mihi est, i·
qui fœda nimium crimina dicunt, pretermittenda historicis: ne de seculo in secu
lum facinorum detestabilium memoria repat. hi profecto insipidi sint: si credunt
si credunt conferre magis ad mores, huiuscemodi pretermissionem q̃ vituperationē
malorum. Nam ex consensu dilatationem potius q̃ ex reprehensione imitatio
nem secuturam quicumq̃ non iners iudicabit. Igitur labore meo efficere conabor
vt legentibus innotescat, non defuisse cultorem veritatis quemadmodum non de
sint falsitatis auctores: quos facile ex ambagibus narrationis comprehendent./
Si henrrici regis quarti vitam differentem perlegant ad descriptione subsecuta./
Quum etiam tyrannidis diffusa pestis exemplo principis non modo in hominibus
huius regni contagionem induxerit: sed per orbem maximam subministrarit
male faciendi licentiam, ita vt a primis seculis vsq̃ hac nunquam tam ampla
creverit malorum seges. Vnde acerbius in auditorum antea criminum in tan
tam devenerit latitudinem q̃ vix videatur locus esse probitati, nisi messis hec
ipsa sit superna manu perusta. Et territi mortales libidinem perniciosam sibi
fuisse cognoscentes ad aurei seculi nitorem ac observationem sanctarum legum
glorieq̃ cupiditatem reducantur. Et apertissime sentiant: vitijs inherere deso
lationem infamem cum perpetua pugnitione: quemadmodum cum laude pre
mioq̃ eterno sit virtutibus decoris ornamentum. Deinceps ad institutum narratio
nis opus accedendum est.

*Manuscript page from the prologue to decade 1 of the* Gesta Hispaniensia *in the Biblioteca Arzobispal, Seville (from* Gesta Hispaniensia ex annalibus suorum dierum collecta, *volume 2, edited by Tate and Lawrance, 1999; Thomas Cooper Library, University of South Carolina)*

the work as a narrator able to manipulate points of view, Palencia seeks to compensate for his political frustrations by transforming history into memoirs.

The first decade ends with the death of Prince Alfonso on 5 July 1468, at age fourteen; Palencia accuses Pacheco of having him poisoned. The second decade opens with a meditation that deplores Alfonso's death and consoles the reader about the sad state of Spain; its true objective is to seek legitimization for Princess Isabel, the king's sister. Palencia, like other partisans of Alfonso, recognized Isabel as the legitimate heir of the kingdom—she was acknowledged as such by Seville on 18 July—and as a possible match for Fernando, crown prince of the Aragonese branch of the Trastámara. Isabel, however, wisely refused the title of queen, choosing instead to be crown princess. That title was recognized by Enrique IV in the Accord of Toros de Guisando on 19 September 1468. Isabel's decision to marry Fernando was a considerable risk, since she had to break her agreement not to marry without Enrique IV's consent; but an alliance was worth the breach with the king, because it gained the support of Aragon in the question of the succession to the throne of Castile. The Carrillo faction took matters into its own hands in arranging the wedding.

In his account in decade 2 of the *Gesta Hispaniensia* Palencia assigns himself an essential role as go-between in the negotiations that preceded the marriage. He says that he met with the king of Aragon, Juan II, at Tarragona, just after Bernat Margarit surrendered Girona to the French on 1 June 1469, and persuaded him, together with the nobles who surrounded him, of the great opportunity that the union brought them. Accompanied by Pedro de la Caballería, he returned to Castile, where he gave as gage for the marriage accord a necklace valued at 40,000 ducats that Fernando had redeemed from the moneylenders of Valencia and 20,000 gold florins. At this point a note of criticism of Isabel appears in the narrative: according to Palencia, the princess misused 8,000 florins in a grant to her principal favorites. Criticism of Isabel's misuse of funds to reward favored courtiers is one of the constants of the two succeeding decades and ends in an open conflict that is not resolved until the *Bellum adversus Granatenses* (The War against Granada, 1482–1489). In that work Palencia's depiction of the queen is one of perfection, although he continues to deplore the effects on her of pernicious flatterers.

In the company of one of those favorites of Isabel's, Gutierre de Cárdenas, Palencia undertook a clandestine voyage to Aragon in 1469 to bring Fernando to Castile. The trip took Palencia by seldom-traveled byways, often at night, from Valladolid to Burgo de Osma, to Saragossa, and back to Valladolid with the prince. The adventures fill the longest chapter in the decades after the one devoted to the life and death of Álvaro de Luna (decade 2, book 12, chapter 3). The story is like a mininovel with Palencia as the hero; Gutierre de Cárdenas, who was replaced by Pero Vaca on the return trip, is reduced to the role of a comical companion. The chapter is a perfect example of Palencia's historical writings. One can see the tension that existed between the politician and the historian as the writer appropriates the narrative to promote his own person.

Fernando and Isabel were married in Valladolid on 16 October 1469. At the beginning of December, Fernando entrusted Palencia with a mission to Aragon to ask his father for financial aid to pay his guard. On 20 October of the following year, at Val de Lozoya, Enrique IV declared his daughter Juana his heir, thus annulling the Accord of Toros de Guisando. The party that opposed Isabel and Fernando united around Juana and her possible marriage partners. Palencia told Carrillo that the prince and princess's sojourn to Medina de Rioseco did not offer sufficient guarantees for their safety; with Palencia's aid, the archbishop persuaded them to reside in Dueñas, where he promised to join them.

In Seville, Palencia mediated between Guzmán and the prince and princess. The mediation resulted in an accord dated 19 February 1473, which he signed "yo el cronista Alfonso de Palencia, secretario de los Prínçipes e del su consejo" (I, Alfonso de Palencia, chronicler and secretary of the Princes and member of their council). The duque de Medina-Sidonia then charged Palencia with securing the prince's support in his struggle with the marqués de Cadiz. On his way to Fernando, Palencia learned that the prince had left for Aragon to help his father. He says that his trip was, nonetheless, useful, because he succeeded in preventing Isabel from agreeing to the demands of the Mendozas, who wanted to bring her to Guadalajara. He also persuaded her not to go to Seville in place of Fernando. Learning that Fernando had rejoined Isabel in Segovia on 27 December 1473, he again prepared to solicit the prince's aid for Guzmán. According to his account, he joined Fernando and Isabel in Segovia, where, fearing danger, he was secreted by the prince in a storeroom, from which he overheard details of a conspiracy to rid the king of the prince and princess and their daughter, Isabel. Carrillo was finally convinced of the danger; Fernando and Isabel's daughter did not rejoin them in Segovia, and Fernando left the city for Turégano.

Pacheco died on 4 October 1474, and the duque de Medina-Sidonia became a candidate for the office of *maestrazgo* of Santiago that was vacated by his death. At the duke's command, Palencia began a grand tour in the company of Pedro de la Algava that took him to the palace of Rodrigo Manrique and then to Saragossa, where he caught up with Fernando. The prince sent Palencia to Castellón to take the counsel of his father on the disposition of the *maestrazgo*. On the road back to Saragossa, Palencia learned that the French had taken Elna. The event forced Palencia and the prince to modify their plans. He was in the company of the prince at Saragossa when he learned of the death of Enrique IV three days earlier, on 12 December 1474, and of Isabel's self-proclamation as queen of Castile at Segovia. This act confirmed Palencia's fears concerning Isabel's ambition.

By chance, Palencia is in the entourage of the prince and in the company of the Aragonese jurist Alfonso de la Caballería when the party makes its entrance into Castile at the opening of the third decade. The autobiographical passages become more numerous as Palencia enters his preferred role as counselor and mediator between Juan II of Aragon and Fernando and among Castile, Aragon, and Andalusia. Whatever one takes to be the truth in this partisan narrative, one cannot gainsay the author's rich political and diplomatic experience or the clarity of his analysis of events and of the principal characters involved in them.

Fernando, unsure and restless, questioned his two counselors, the jurist Caballería and the "qui multa historiarum uolumina perlegisti" (learned historian) Palencia. But Palencia could not lay his fears to rest, and, more important, he was powerless to remedy the fact that his opinions had discredited him at court.

After their return to Castile, Palencia left Segovia, where Archbishop Carrillo and Cardinal Mendoza were taking opposing sides, and went to Seville. He retained the title of *cronista,* and in 1476 Isabel sanctioned payment to him of 60,000 *maravedís* annually as "mi cronista, secretario e del mi consejo" (my chronicler, secretary, and member of my council).

In the midst of his duties, Palencia found time to compose the *De sinonymis elegantibus libri III,* which he dedicated to Alfonso de Fonseca II in 1472. This important lexicographical work, which was printed in Seville in 1491, belongs to the tradition started by St. Isidore's seventh-century *Etymologiae* (Etymologies) but partakes of a humanist erudition that evokes the method employed by Flavio Biondo in his *Romae Triumphantis Libri Decem* (1482, Ten Books of Triumphant Rome).

The struggle for power between Fernando and Isabel was apparently settled by the Concord of Segovia of 15 January 1475, which made them equals, but soon a graver danger arrived: Alfonso V of Portugal, pretender to Princess Juana's hand in marriage, entered Castile at the head of an invading army. Archbishop Carrillo accused the king and queen of ingratitude and,

together with other nobles, supported Alfonso V's claims. Palencia seems to have established a home in Seville at this time, for the duque de Medina-Sidonia had him chosen as mediator, along with Antonio Rodríguez de Lillo, in a struggle between Gómez Suárez de Figueroa, Count of Feria, and Alfonso de Cárdenas. Although the mission was aborted, Cárdenas was unmasked as a traitor. The Battle of Baltanás on 17 September 1475 gave rise to the most scurrilous rumors about Rodrigo Pimentel, Count of Benavente, who was suspected of double-dealing, but Palencia denies any responsibility for them: "auctor haberi recuso" (I refuse to be considered as the author). In 1476 Palencia, still in the company of Rodríguez de Lillo, was charged with obtaining from Gonzalo de Estúñiga, alcalde (mayor) of Palos, the freedom of the king of Gambia, who had been imprisoned during an expedition to Guinea. Fernando then directed the two men to raise the funds to send an Andalusian fleet to Guinea to counteract the ambition of the Portuguese. They financed a fleet of twenty-five light ships that was placed under the command of Carlos de Valera, the son of Diego de Valera.

An institution that was dear to Palencia, the Hermandad, established in Burgos in 1475 by Fernando and Isabel and in Madrigal in 1476 by the Cortes (Parliament), again made him a go-between. The king and queen, who wished to profit from the continuous rivalries between the duque de Medina-Sidonia and the marqués de Cadiz, found the duke's opposition to the Portuguese lukewarm and threatened to put the Andalusian forces in the hands of the marqués; but the trick backfired, and the marqués demanded to be allowed to defy the duke. Fernando and Isabel sent two negotiators, backed by the power of the Hermandad, to settle the matter; one of them was Palencia. Palencia, who was openly sympathetic to the new institution, gained the enmity of the duke. A new trip to Castile, where he had gone to give evidence on the situation in Andalusia, found him in the company of Isabel at Tordesillas in July 1476. Sick, he had to delay his return to Valladolid, where he arrived after riots in Segovia. He immediately went to Vitoria, where he met Fernando and Fernando's father, Juan II, and counseled Fernando not to go to Aragon. After the victory in Toro on 20 October 1476 and the collapse of the Portuguese faction, Palencia remained with Fernando; he may have regained his old status as counselor, for the reader finds him acting as such at Simancas, where he reminded the king of Juan II's advice about how to deal with France and the clans of Navarre.

In 1477, while at Medina del Campo, Palencia received an order from Fernando to tell the Andalusians of his intention to establish the Hermandad among them. The duque de Medina-Sidonia feigned

*Manuscript page from decade 2 of the* Gesta Hispaniensia *in the Bibliothèque Nationale, Paris ( from* Gesta Hispaniensia ex annalibus suorum dierum collecta, *volume 2, edited by Tate and Lawrance, 1999; Thomas Cooper Library, University of South Carolina)*

acquiescence, then reversed his decision in a fit of madness that only Palencia seems to have been able to calm. Fifty days later the Hermandad was established in Andalusia. At the same time, in May 1477 Isabel sent her majordomo, Pedro de Silva, to be her personal agent in Seville.

The visit of the king and queen to Seville gives Palencia a final opportunity to write an account in which he gives himself the role of counselor and to reorganize reality to give the occasion what he considers its true meaning. Isabel was the first to enter Seville on 24 July 1477. Palencia criticizes the queen for preceding Fernando in her entry into the city. Instead of recounting the celebrations organized by the Sevillians, Palencia tells the reader about the warnings that he gave the queen. Fernando entered the city on 13 September; Palencia accuses the Sevillians of receiving him badly. He continues to report on the royal journey in this critical manner until the end of 1477, when he says he finished the third decade.

The first three decades are cited in the "Mençion del trabajo passado et del propósito para adelante" of 1488: "Tres decas de nuestro tiempo" (Three decades of our time). The existence of a fourth decade, however, had already been mentioned by Nicolas Antonio in his *Bibliotheca Hispana Vetus* (1669). José Toro (1966) found an incomplete manuscript that covers the events of the years 1478 to 1480, the time that elapses between the end of the third decade and the beginning of the *Bellum adversus Granatenses,* the latter of which is cited by Palencia in the "Mençion del trabajo passado et del propósito para adelante" as "los anales de la Guerra de Granada que he aceptado escribir" (the annals of the War of Granada that I have agreed to write). The omission of reference to the fourth decade may be accounted for by the fact that he was still writing it or by the fact that it is a more "confidential" work because of its highly critical nature. It includes a reference to what seems to be Palencia's last political mission: his participation with his assistant Diego de Merlo in the preparation for the conquest of the Insulae Fortunatae (Canary Islands), an event that he describes in passing. A more expansive work on the subject–"alibi a me ipso explicatius resumptam" (explained by me elsewhere in full length)–is without doubt *Las costumbres e falsas religiones por çierto marauillosas de los canarios que moran en las yslas fortunadas* (Really Wonderful Customs and False Religions of Canarians Who Live in Fortunate Islands) that is listed in the "Mençion del trabajo passado et del propósito para adelante" but has not been located. Merlo was recompensed for his expenditures in outfitting the expedition to the Canaries, but Palencia was not. The fourth decade shows evidence of a curiosity and an openness to unknown horizons that are perhaps a sign of new times in Palencia. This decade also provides the first contemporary account of the death of the poet Jorge Manrique on 24 April 1479, as well as the first comments on his work.

The Cortes of Toledo in 1480 marked the end of Palencia's political career. One of the problems addressed by the Cortes was the question of the succession. After the birth of Prince Juan, Isabel was accused by Fernando's partisans of wishing to name her son heir to the throne in preference to her husband. Palencia was in the cathedral of Toledo in his capacity of royal chronicler for the presentation of the prince and for the swearing of fealty by the grandees. The queen tried to have Palencia's account of the event submitted to censure by a learned prelate ("alicuius docti praesulis censurae"), probably Cardinal Mendoza. This attempt of censure is the first known judgment of the decades, but it concerns the pro-Aragonese views of a counselor whom the queen had reasons to mistrust rather than the quality of the work itself. Palencia says in decade 4 that he protested, recalling his integrity and his past services, but the die was cast. In 1481 the queen chose Pulgar as official chronicler. Relations between Palencia and Pulgar were already established and seem to have remained cordial, as evidenced by two letters that have survived.

Palencia was no longer *consejero de la corona* (counselor to the crown), but Fernando renewed his payment as *cronista* in 1479. He was confirmed in that post in 1481, 1482, and 1483 and continued to receive the emolument until his death, although a reduction in the salary was made by a *declaratoria de Cortes* in 1480 that also reduced by 10,000 the 35,000 *maravedís* paid to Pulgar.

In the prologue to the *Compendiolum breve, quo civitatem, oppidorum atque fluminum nomina hispanorum innotescant* (1482, Brief Compendium in which are noted the names of Spanish Cities, Fortresses and Rivers), dedicated to Pedro de Ponte on 26 August 1482, Palencia confesses to being gravely affected by his fall from grace, to the point of considering abandoning his work: "nauseam intulit ingenio meo adeo internam" (produced internal nausea in my mind). The *Compendiolum breve, quo civitatem, oppidorum atque fluminum nomina hispanorum innotescant,* recently discovered in 1966, is the only known work that derives some of its content from Palencia's projected "antiguedad de la gente española"; it belongs to an erudite humanist current that seeks to identify Peninsular toponyms with those of ancient geographers and historians.

Palencia was concerned with his burial and with the disposition of his library. On 15 September 1480 the *cabildo* (chapter) of the cathedral of Seville was ordered to find a place for the burial of Alonso de Palencia, "cronista del rey nuestro señor," and to be ready to receive his books after his death. A place was found for him in what today is the Capilla de San Pedro; but everything has disappeared, including the books, of which there is no trace in the cathedral's library. The majority of books that belonged to Palencia are in the library of the University of Salamanca and are a legacy of the Toledan canon Alonso Ortiz, who gave the to the university at the end of the fifteenth century.

Documents show that in 1483 Palencia was living in the parish of San Llorente and acted as a witness in a contract signed by his godson, Diego de Medina, a *converso* merchant. In 1485 Palencia is called a *clérigo* (cleric) for the first time in a list of the members of the *capítulo* (chapter) of the cathedral of Seville and of the inquisitors who are exempt from paying certain important duties. His last trip was to Malaga, where he signed as a witness for a *privilegio de juro* (privilege of rent) in favor of Rodrigo de Ulloa on 10 December 1488.

Retired from civic and political life, Palencia translated at the behest of Luis de Medina, *veinticuatro* (on of the 24 municipal magistrates of Seville) of Seville, an ascetic Tuscan treatise by Domenico Cavalca, *Lo Specchio della Croce* (The Mirror of the Cross), which Fray Juan Melgarejo, prior of the monastery of San Isidoro del Campo, had brought back from Italy. The translation was finished on 21 June 1485 and printed, at the command of the prior, on 20 February 1486 as *El Espejo de la Cruz.*

Palencia then began to write the *Bellum adversus Granatenses.* In this work, which can be considered the fifth decade of the *Gesta Hispaniensia,* he follows the method he had employed in his other histories: he looks for the causes of events, multiplies the web of intrigues, gives background sketches of his characters, and places the analysis of local situations in the larger context of international politics. This time, however, there is a central theme: the war of Granada. The narrative is rigorously structured chronologically, with each "book" corresponding to a year; but the books are not divided into chapters, perhaps because of Palencia's death–the last book is hardly begun–and the autobiographical passages disappear. Although Palencia remains critical of events, the king and queen are frequent objects of praise, albeit measured praise. But at the end the voice of the author is raised once more to criticize historians who flatter their subjects.

At the command of Isabel, to whom he dedicated it, Palencia wrote the *Universal vocabulario en latin y en romance;* the work was finished in 1488 and printed in Seville in 1490–two years before Nebrija's *Dictionarium Latino-hispanicum et Hispanico-latinum.* Palencia's *Universal vocabulario en latin y en romance* is laid out in two columns: the left column is a monolingual Latin dictionary, while the one on the right comprises not always literal transla-

tions into Castilian of the terms in the left column. The Latin part depends largely on previous medieval works on language, such as that of Pappias; the novelty of the work resides in having the Latin and the translations into Castilian in parallel columns. At the end of the manuscript for the *Universal vocabulario en latin y en romance* Palencia appends the "Mençion del trabajo passado et del propósito para adelante," which is revised in the 1490 edition.

Palencia's final compositions were his translation of Plutarch's *Lives* and of two works by the Jewish historian Flavius Josephus. The two Plutarch volumes were dedicated to Rodrigo Ponce de León, Duque de Cadiz, and published in 1491. Palencia's translation of the fifty-six brief biographies was based on the 1478 edition of Giovanni Antonio Campano, which was based in turn on the Latin text established by several Italian humanists. In the prologue Palencia mentions his "extrema vejez" (advanced age) and his fear of not being able to complete the translation. In the prologues to Josephus's *Guerras de los judíos con los romanos* (Wars of the Jews against the Romans, 1492) and *Contra Appion Gramático* (Against Apion the Grammarian, 1492) Palencia addresses the queen. The texts are translated from the Latin versions of Rufino d'Aquileia; according to Javier Durán Barceló, Palencia's source is the Verona edition of 1480.

On 8 January 1492 Palencia wrote a letter to the bishop of Astorga, Juan Ruiz de Medina, in which he describes the capture of Granada; the letter is a sketch of what would have been the end of the *Bellum adversus Granatenses.* In the last years of his life Palencia took an interest in the newly invented printing press. According to a report by the prior of the Cartuja de Santa María de las Cuevas published in 1573, he retired to the monastery to prepare the *Gesta Hispaniensia* for the press. Death interrupted his work on 31 March 1492, and the manuscript remained in Santa María de las Cuevas.

A marginal note in a sixteenth-century hand to a manuscript of the *Compendio universal de las historias romanas et de otros libros . . . hecho por a. de. a.* (Universal Compendium of the History of Rome and Other Books . . . Done by A. of A.) reads "créese que fue Alonso de Avila hijo del coronista Hernando [sic] de Palencia" (It is supposed to be Alonso de Ávila, son of the chronicler Hernando [sic] de Palencia). After careful study of the work, Jean Pierre Jardin concluded that the author was probably Alfonso de Almela, brother of Diego Rodríguez de Almela. The attribution to Palencia of *Relación verdadera de lo acahecido en la prisión del rey chico de Granada en el arroyo que llaman de Martín González, el día 21, 22 de Abril del año de 1483* (True Story of What Happened in the Prison of Granada's King Chico in the Stream Called Martin Gonzalez on April 21 and 22,

Alfonsi Palentini historiographi ante narrationem annalium tertia in decade contentorum prefatio incipit feliciter.

VONIAM PARS MAXIMA superiorum annalium continet facinora nel obscura minus nel obscena: iam uidetur opereprecium prefari: quemadmodum henrico uita functo cui in re hereditario coniungitur regine helisabeth successit in regine castelle et legionis inclitus fernandus aragonum princeps. Et magis magisq́ cœperit tutiorum aduersus iuste exagitari contentio. Nam qui tyrannide freti abutebantur potentatibus, egerrime tulerant henrici mortem: cuius obnequiciam ampla malorum exaruisset seges. z perspecta spe mediocri nobilitatis atq́ populorum op̄ fines neq́ regis malorum omnium exterminium foret: pleriq́ procerum noue agitabantur curie inuestigandi ulteriorem solite iniquitatis occasionem. que multitudine oppresse flocifaceret desiderium. Videbant enim q̄ expergefacte regnicolarum mentes cuperent sibi legum uindicare fauorem. Que quidem leges diu detruse in ergastulo abiectionis si forte producent in lucem / oppressis libertatem ac oppressoribus penas ediceret. Quas obrice in uigilandum censebant iniquissimi quiq́ recentibus obstaculis. quibus laudati regis compesceretur nitor: atq́ tyrannidis in olentia perduraret. sponte ignari q̄ negetur perpetuitas facinoribus uiolentie: q̄tumq́ discriminis insit: quibus ob insitam prauitatem resistendi uirtutibus cupiditas augetur. Nec non libenter se oblitos prodiderunt tyranni sumatce multorum mirabilium que a temporibus initii connubii principum deus optimus maximus fecisset indicans maiora facturum: ut insontes a manu sontium erepti resumant uires cum uiolentorum exidio. Quam ego mirabilium gestorum narrationem letus aggredior. neluti qui post luem acerbi doloris licitam consequitur uoluptatem. z tamq́ seuissima qui fuerit iactatus in altum procella: sed iam re uectus fauorabili aura inspicati portum. z quemadmodum uidet quis gaudenter auroram ubi oppacitas tenebrarum diuturna modestissimi in gesserint occasionem errorum.

*Manuscript page from the prologue to decade 3 of the* Gesta Hispaniensia
*(Residencia Salesiana, León; courtesy of Madeleine Pardo)*

1483 ["Chico" was the king's nickname]) has not been established, in spite of an interesting argument by Carmen Caselles.

The first two decades of the *Gesta Hispaniensia* may have been the source text for the anonymous *Crónica castellana* (Castilian Chronicle, circa 1481–1482); but the latter cannot be Palencia's work, because its mistakes in interpreting Latin chronology would never have been made by him. Those decades may also have been the source for the *Memorial de diversas hazañas* (Memorial of Diverse Feats, circa 1486–1487) of Diego de Valera. The dependence of these two works on Palencia's has yet to be clarified.

The partisan historical works of Alfonso de Palencia have been the object of equally partisan judgments. Palencia's open denunciation of the evils that afflicted Spain under Enrique IV has occasioned a debate over the nature of the *Gesta Hispaniensia:* is it scandalously mendacious or courageously truthful? The debate is often carried on without knowledge of the text itself. The *Gesta Hispaniensia* captured the interest of the Real Academia de la Historia (Royal Academy of History), which attempted to edit the Latin text in 1835. The long labor of the commission gathered for that purpose resulted in the publication of only ninety-six pages of the text of the first decade and the appearance of the important diplomatic collection known as *Memorias de Enrique IV* (Memories of Enrique IV, 1913). Early scholars who studied Palencia's writings include Amador de los Ríos (1865) and Tomás Rodríguez (1888). Particularly important are a 1914 article by Antonio Paz y Melia and, above all, his translation of the three first decades and the *Bellum adversus Granatenses* (1904–1909), which are the editions from which later critics and historians such as Georges Cirot (1909, 1918), Puyol y Alonso (1921), and Mario Penna (1959) have worked. A threshold was crossed in knowledge of the historian and his texts through the many works published since 1970 by Tate. Relying on the most important recently discovered manuscripts, Tate and Jeremy Lawrance are currently producing an edition of the Latin text of the *Gesta Hispaniensia* accompanied by a translation and voluminous notes that allows one to approach the work in a rigorous fashion for the first time.

Since the 1990s researchers such as Barceló (1991, 1992), Caselles, and Madeleine Pardo have approached Alfonso de Palencia's historical works not in terms of their truthfulness or lack thereof but from the point of view of their craftsmanship. This new attention to the linguistic and literary works of the author liberates him from the limiting role of accuser of Enrique IV. The variety and number of works that he composed show the range of his curiosity and ambitions. As Tate says, Palencia wished to be "un orator

ciceroniano, profesional de las letras y hombre enciclopédico a la vez" (a Ciceronian orator, a professional writer, and an encyclopedic man at the same time).

## Bibliographies:
Nicolás Antonio, *Bibliotheca Hispana Vetus,* edited by Francisco Pérez Bayer (Turin: Bottega d'Erasmo, 1963), part 2, nos. 769–810;

Javier Durán Barceló, "Bibliografía de Alfonso de Palencia (Cuaderno bibliográfico, 12)," *Boletín Bibliográfico de la Asociación Hispánica de Literatura Medieval,* 9 (1995): 287–335.

## References:
Rafael Alemany Ferrer, "Acerca del supuesto origen converso de Alfonso de Palencia," in *Estudi General (Miscellània conmemorativa del desè aniversari del Collegi Universitari de Girona), Revista del Colegi Universitari de Girona 1.2,* 2 (1981): 35–40;

José María Balcells Doménech, "Alonso de Palencia y la epopeya burlesca," in *Actas I Congreso Nacional de Latín medieval (León, 1–4 Diciembre 1993),* edited by Maurilio Pérez González (León: Publicaciones de la Universidad León, 1995), pp. 237–243;

Carmen Caselles, "Alfonso de Palencia y la historiografía humanista," dissertation, City University of New York, 1991;

Américo Castro, *De la edad conflictiva: El drama de la Honra en Espana y en su literatura,* second enlarged and corrected edition (Madrid: Taurus, 1961);

Georges Cirot, "Les *Décades* d'Alfonso de Palencia, la *Chronique castillane de Henri* IV attribuée à Palencia et le *Memorial de diversas hazañas* de Diego de Valera," *Bulletin Hispanique,* 11 (1909): 425–442;

Javier Durán Barceló, "Alfonso de Palencia: Traductor de Flavio Josefo," in *Proyección histórica de España en sus tres culturas: Castilla y León, América y el Mediterráneo,* edited by E. Lorenzo Díaz (Valladolid: Junta de Castilla y León, 1993), pp. 27–34;

Durán Barceló, "Obra poética, retórica, lexicografía y filosofía moral de Alfonso de Palencia. Ediciones críticas del *De Perfectione militaris triumphi* y *La Perfeçión del triunfo,*" dissertation, University of Michigan, 1992;

Antonio María Fabié, *La vida y escritos de Alonso de Palencia* (Madrid: Fortanet, 1875);

Jean Pierre Jardin, "Le règne de Jean II vu depuis Murcie," *Mélanges de la Casa de Velázquez,* 30, no. 1 (1994): 207–225;

Jeremy Lawrance, "Memory and Invention in Fifteenth-Century Iberian Historiography," in *Cursos da Arrábida, A História: Entre Memória e Invenção,* edited by Pedro Cardim (Publicações Europa-América, 1998), pp. 91–128;

José López de Toro, "La Cuarta Década de Alonso de Palencia," *Boletín de la Real Academia de la Historia,* 159 (1966): 89–100;

Amador de Los Ríos, *Historia crítica de la Literatura Española,* volume 7 (Madrid: J. Rodríguez, 1865), pp. 157–165;

Anscari Mundo, "Una llietra d'Alfons de Palència a Vespasiá da Bisticci," in *Studi di bibliografia e di storia in onore di Tamaro de Marinis,* volume 3 (Verona: Stamperia Valdonega, 1964), pp. 271–281;

Madeleine Pardo, "Alfonso de Palencia, historien: Etudes sur les *Gesta Hispaniensia,*" Ph.D. thesis, University of Paris, 1999–;

Antonio Paz y Melia, *El cronista Alonso de Palencia: Su vida y sus obras; sus "Décadas" y las "Crónicas" contemporáneas; ilustraciones de las "Décadas" y notas varias* (Madrid: Hispanic Society of America, 1914);

Mario Penna, "Estudio preliminar," in *Prosistas castellanos del siglo XV,* volume 1, edited by Penna, Biblioteca de autores españoles, no. 116 (Madrid: Atlas, 1959), pp. cxxxvi–clxviii;

Ludwig Pfandl, "Uber Alfonso Fernández de Palencia," *Zeitschrift fur romanische Philologie,* 55 (1935): 340–360;

Julio Puyol y Alonso, "Los cronistas de Enrique IV," *Boletín de la Real Academia de la Historia,* 78 (1921): 399–415, 488–496; 79 (1921): 11–28, 118–144;

Real Academia de la Historia, *Memorias de Don Enrique de Castilla: Contiene la colección diplomática del mismo rey* (Madrid: Establecimento Tipografico de Fortanet, 1913);

Tomás Rodríguez, "El cronista Alfonso de Palencia," *Ciudad de Dios* (Valladolid), 15 (1888): 17–26, 77–87, 149–156, 224–229, 298–303;

Robert Brian Tate, "Alfonso de Palencia and His *Antigüedades de España,*" in *The Age of the Catholic Monarchs 1474–1516: Literary Studies in Memory of Keith Whinnom,* edited by Alan D. Deyermond and Ian MacPherson, *Bulletin of Hispanic Studies,* special issue (Liverpool: Liverpool University Press, 1989), pp. 193–196;

Tate, "Alfonso de Palencia y los preceptos de la historiografía," in *Nebrija y la introducción del Renacimiento en España: Actas de la III Academia Literaria Renacentista,* edited by Victor García de la Concha (Salamanca: Academia Literaria Renacentista, Universidad de Salamanca, 1983), pp. 37–51;

Tate, "The Civic Humanism of Alfonso de Palencia," *Nottingham Renaissance and Medieval Studies,* 23 (1979): 25–44;

Tate, "Las *Décadas* de Alfonso de Palencia: un análisis historiográfico," in *Estudios dedicados a James Leslie Brooks,* edited by J. M. Ruiz Veintemilla (Barcelona: Puvill, 1984), pp. 223–241;

Tate, *Ensayos sobre la historiografía peninsular del siglo XV,* Biblioteca Románica Hispánica, Estudios y Ensayos, no. 145 (Madrid: Gredos, 1970);

Tate, "La historiografía en el reinado de los Reyes Católicos," in *Antonio de Nebrija: Edad Media y Renacimiento,* edited by Carmen Codoñer and Juan Antonio González Iglesias, Acta Salmanticensia: Estudios Filológicos, no. 257 (Salamanca: Ediciones Universidad de Salamanca, 1994), pp. 17–28;

Tate, "Poles Apart–Two Official Historians of the Catholic Monarchs–Alfonso de Palencia and Fernando del Pulgar," in *Pensamiento medieval hispano, Homenaje a Horacio Santiago-Otero,* edited by José María Soto Rábanos (Madrid: CSIC, 1998), pp. 439–463;

Tate, "Political Allegory in Fifteenth-Century Spain: A Study of the *Batalla campal de los perros contra los lobos* by Alfonso de Palencia (1423–92)," *Journal of Hispanic Philology,* 1 (1977): 169–186;

Tate, "La sociedad castellana en la obra de Alfonso de Palencia," in *Actas del III Coloquio de Historia Medieval Andaluza: La sociedad medieval andaluza, grupos no privilegiados* (Jaén: Diputación Provincial, 1986), pp. 5–23;

Juan Torres Fontes, *Estudios sobre la "Crónica de Enrique IV" del Dr. Galíndez de Carvajal* (Murcia: CSIC, 1946).

# Fernán Pérez de Guzmán

## (circa 1377 – circa 1460)

### Derek C. Carr
#### University of British Columbia

WORKS: Miscellaneous verse before 1432

**Manuscript:** In *Cancionero de Baena* (ca. 1445–1450), Paris, Bibliothèque Nationale Esp. 37.

**First publication:** In *El Cancionero de Juan Alfonso de Baena (Siglo XV)* (Madrid: M. Rivadeneyra, 1851).

Religious and didactic verse after 1432, including *Proverbios*, *La coronación de las quatro virtudes* (both 1445–1449), *Confesión rimada*, *Coplas de vicios y virtudes*, and *Loores de los claros varones de España* (all before 1452), *Cient trinadas a loor de la Virgen María*, and various hymns and sacred songs

**Manuscripts:** The earliest copies of *Confesión rimada*, *Coplas de vicios y virtudes*, and *Loores de los claros varones de España* are in the *Cancionero del duque de Gor* (1452), Madrid, Biblioteca Bartolomé March 23-7-1. The remaining poetry is dispersed throughout various fifteenth-century manuscripts, of which the most significant are Barcelona, Monasterio de Montserrat 992 (*Cancionero catalán*, ca. 1495); Barcelona, Universitat Central 116 (*Obras de Mena y otros*); Geneva, Fondation Martin Bodmer 45 (*Cancionero del Conde de Haro*, ca. 1470); Harvard University, Houghton MS Sp 97 (*Cancionero de Oñate Castañeda*, ca. 1485); London, British Library Egerton 939 (*Cancionero de Egerton*, ca. 1475); Madrid, Real Academia de la Historia 2 MS 2 (*Cancionero de San Román*, ca. 1454); Madrid, Biblioteca Lázaro-Galdiano 30 (ca. 1490); Madrid, Biblioteca Bartolomé March 20-5-6 (*Cancionero de Barrantes*, ca. 1490) and 25-10-9 (*Obras de Fernán Pérez de Guzmán*, ca. 1480); Madrid, Biblioteca Nacional 2882 (*Cancionero de Híjar*, fifteenth–sixteenth century), 3681 (ca. 1499), 3686 (*Obras de Santillana y Pérez de Guzmán*, ca. 1460), 10047 (ca. 1460), and Vitrina 17-7 (*Cancionero de Stúñiga*, ca. 1462); New York, Hispanic Society of America B2280 (*Cancionero de Vindel*, ca. 1480) and B2489 (*Obras de Fernán Pérez de Guzmán*, ca. 1470); Paris, Bibliothèque Nationale Esp. 228 (*Cancionero castellano de París*, fifteenth cen-

tury) and Esp. 510 (*Cancionero de Salvá*, ca. 1480); Rome, Biblioteca Casanatense 1098 (*Cancionero de Roma*, ca. 1465); and Salamanca, Biblioteca Universitaria 2198 (Coplas de Fernán Pérez de Guzmán, fifteenth century).

**First publication:** In *Cancionero de Llabia* (Saragossa, n.d. [ca. 1490]); *Coplas de Fernand Pérez de Guzmán* (Seville: Menardo Ungut alemán & Lançalao polono, 1492); *Las sietecientas* (Seville: J. Cromberger, 1506)—comprises *Coplas de vicios y virtudes*, *Confesión rimada*, the *Himnos*, and *La doctrina que dieron a Sarra*.

Historical prose, including *Mar de istorias* and *Generaciones y semblanzas* (both ca. 1450–1455)

**Manuscripts:** The *Mar de istorias* is in three manuscripts in Madrid, Biblioteca Nacional 7557 (fifteenth century), 7575 (fifteenth century), and 9564 (1440–1460). The oldest copy of *Generaciones y semblanzas* is El Escorial Biblioteca de El Escorial Z-III-2 (fifteenth century); additional fifteenth-century copies are Florence, Biblioteca Nazionale Magliabecchiano XXIV, 148; and Madrid, Fundación Lázaro-Galdiano 435. Other copies are from the sixteenth and seventeenth centuries: London, British Library Egerton 301; Madrid, Biblioteca Nacional 1619 and 6156; Madrid, Biblioteca de la Real Academia de la Historia 9-496; and Santiago de Compostela, Biblioteca Xeral Universitaria 575. The *Floresta de filósofos* is in Madrid, Biblioteca Nacional 4515 (fifteenth century). The letter to Fray Gonzalo de Ocaña is in El Escorial, Biblioteca de El Escorial b.II.9 (fifteenth century); Madrid, Academia de la Historia San Millán 59 (fifteenth century); Madrid, Biblioteca Nacional 66 and 13075 (both fifteenth century); and the Castilian translation of Bernard of Chartres, *Epistola super gubernatione rei familiaris*, in El Escorial, Biblioteca de El Escorial S-II-4.

**First publications:** Letter to Alfonso de Cartagena (ca. 1453), in *Tractado que se llama el oracional de Fernand Peres por que contiene Respueste a algunas* *questiones que fizo el noble cauallero Fernan Peres de Guzman al reuerendo padre virtuoso perlado Don Alfonso de Cartajena* (Murcia: G. Loys & L. de Roca, 1487); *Generaciones y semblanzas,* in *Cronica del serenissimo rey don Juan el segundo deste nombre* (Logroño: A. Guillén de Brocar, 1517); *Floresta de philosophos,* edited by Raymond Foulché-Delbosc, *Revue Hispanique,* 11 (1904): 5–154.

**Standard editions:** Complete poetry, in *Cancionero castellano del siglo XV, c. 1360–1520,* edited by Foulché-Delbosc, Nueva biblioteca de autores españoles, no. 19 (Madrid: Bailly-Baillière, 1912), pp. 575–759; *Mar de istorias,* edited by Foulché-Delbosc, *Revue Hispanique,* 28 (1913): 442–622; letters to Gonzalo de Ocaña and Cartagena, in *Generaciones y semblanzas,* edited by Jesús Domínguez Bordona, Clásicos Castellanos (Madrid: Espasa-Calpe, 1941), pp. 209–221; *Generaciones y semblanzas,* edited by R. B. Tate (London: Tamesis, 1965); poems in *El cancionero castellano del siglo XV,* edited by Brian Dutton, 7 volumes, Biblioteca española del siglo XV, Serie maior, nos. 1–7 (Salamanca: Universidad de Salamanca, 1990–1991).

**Edition in English:** *Pen Portraits of Illustrious Castilians* (translation of *Generaciones y semblanzas*), edited and translated by Marie Gillette and Loretta Zehngut (Washington, D.C.: Catholic University of America Press, 2003).

Fernán Pérez de Guzmán was the third lord of Batres, a *villa* (small town) situated slightly to the southwest of Madrid, between Navalcarnero and Illescas. The son of Pedro Suárez de Guzmán and Elvira de Ayala, he belonged to a family related to some of the most prominent personalities in late-medieval Spain. His uncle, Pero López de Ayala, an historian, translator, and poet, was chancellor of Castile. Pérez de Guzmán was, in turn, the uncle of Íñigo López de Mendoza, Marqués de Santillana, one of the most powerful noblemen of his day and one of the finest poets in fifteenth-century Spain. Other relatives included the lyric and dramatic poet Gómez Manrique and his nephew Jorge Manrique, best known for his *Coplas a la muerte de su padre* (Verses on the Death of His Father, circa 1476–1479). Garcilaso de la Vega (1501?–1536), a major poet of the Golden Age of Spanish literature, was Pérez de Guzmán's great-grandson.

Until the early sixteenth century, Pérez de Guzmán was highly admired for his own poetry, which circulated widely in manuscript form and in early printed editions. Consisting chiefly of religious and didactic verse, it was praised by his contemporaries for its doctrinal and ethical content. Changes in literary taste led his poetry to fall out of general favor, and, until the late twentieth century, his literary reputation has rested largely on the prose work *Generaciones y semblanzas* (Lineages and Likenesses, circa 1450–1455), much appreciated for its limpid style. Since the 1980s, studies by scholars such as Marie de Menaca, Dorothy S. Severin, Fiona Maguire, Julian Weiss, Lucía Guzzi Harrison, and José Antonio Barrio Sánchez have provided a basis for a balanced global reassessment of Pérez de Guzmán's total literary output.

Pérez de Guzmán was born into a Castile recently riven by dynastic upheaval. Most of his adult life coincided with the long reign of Juan II, a period characterized by considerable political turmoil, much of it centered on disputes between the Crown and the old nobility. Factionalism was the order of the day, with armed conflicts frequently breaking out between the supporters and opponents of Álvaro de Luna, the royal favorite who dominated the Castilian political scene. The military and political interventions of the infantes Juan and Enrique of Aragon in the affairs of Castile contributed to the divided and shifting loyalties of the reign.

Pérez de Guzmán's lifetime was also a period of significant ideological change, filled with the polemics that such changes bring. The cultural developments discernible in Spain during the first half of the fifteenth century included the gradual decline of French influence and the rise of Italian influence; increasing interest in classical antiquity and the commissioning of translations of the Latin classics; among the nobility, the amassing of large personal libraries; and a general fascination with works of history. Jeremy N. H. Lawrance has referred to such phenomena as the "rise of lay literacy" and "vernacular humanism." The process was not uniform and was fraught with contradictions, but Pérez de Guzmán was an active participant.

Details of Pérez de Guzmán's life are scant and must be gleaned principally from the *Crónica de Juan II* (Chronicle of John II), by Alvar García de Santa María and others; the *Crónica del halconero de Juan II* (Chronicle of the Falconer of John II), by Pedro Carrillo de Huete; and the *Refundición de la Crónica del halconero* (Reworking of the Chronicle of the Falconer), by Lope Barrientos, all first published in 1517 and all formerly falsely attributed to Pérez de Guzmán. Autobiographical information in Pérez de Guzmán's own writings is minimal. Raymond Foulché-Delbosc suggested that Pérez de Guzmán was most likely born during the period 1377–1379 and that 1460 was probably the year of his death. Pérez de Guzmán was married to the marquesa de Avellaneda. A son, Pero Guzmán y Avellaneda, took possession of the Batres estates in 1461. There may have been an earlier marriage to Leonor de los Paños, to whom Pérez de Guzmán addressed three of his early lyrics in the *Cancionero de Baena* (Baena Songbook, circa 1445–1450) and to whom the rubrics of the manuscript refer as "su muger" (his wife). His personal library of twenty-nine volumes, though not as rich as some of his contemporaries' collections, reflects the tenor of the age, with its emphasis on works of Stoic philosophy as well as classical and Iberian historiography. More surprising are the texts that come from *converso* ( Jewish convert) circles.

The absence of solid documentation makes Pérez de Guzmán's formative years a matter of speculation. He probably received the typical upbringing of a young aristocrat. Instruction in Christian doctrine would have been an important part of his early education. (In later life, at least, he was a devout Christian, though remarkably open-minded.) He would have had training in horsemanship and the use of arms. As heir to the Batres estates, Pérez de Guzmán would have been taught by example the skills necessary for the administration of his possessions. His presence at court would have given him firsthand knowledge of the workings of government and politics, thereby laying the foundations for the subsequent reflections on governance and the state of the nation that are found in his work.

Pérez de Guzmán's literary career suggests a love of reading implanted at an early age, most likely by a household tutor, then nourished by contact with like-minded individuals in aristocratic and clerical circles. It is clear from his writings that he had been schooled in the subjects of the *trivium* (grammar, logic, and rhetoric), the first part of the medieval system of education, though there is nothing to indicate that he ever attended a university. In fact, the flourishing of lay literacy in aristocratic circles during his lifetime had little to do with the universities.

In stanza 384 of *Loores de los claros varones de España* (Praises of the Famous Men of Spain, before 1452), in the section dedicated to Benedict XIII (Cardinal Pedro de Luna, Antipope from 1394 to 1423), Pérez de Guzmán claims to have seen the Antipope face to face, "yo muy niño en Aviñón" (when I was a little child in Avignon). This encounter, according to Jesús Domínguez Bordona, must have taken place around 1394, the year in which the cardinal was "elected" pope. At that time Pérez de Guzmán would have been at least fifteen years old, which is hardly "muy niño." As he wrote the verses when he was approaching sixty, it is entirely possible that the memory of his age at the time of the encounter was no longer precise or that some rhetorical embellishment was involved.

This visit to Avignon implies a journey through Aragon and Catalonia, with perhaps a sojourn at the Aragonese court in Barcelona en route. Early experi-ence of Aragonese and Franco-Provençal culture might have made a significant impact on Pérez de Guzmán. In stanza 317 of *Loores de los claros varones de España* he states that Aragon was a nation of which "siempre fui afeccionado" (I was always fond). He was an admirer of Fernando de Antequera, co-regent of Castile during the minority of Juan II and subsequently King Fernando I of Aragon. When Pérez de Guzmán first appears in the *Crónica de Juan II,* he is acting on behalf of Aragonese interests.

Domínguez Bordona states that the earliest mention of Pérez de Guzmán in the *Crónica de Juan II* is in the entry for 1419, but his claim (repeated by others) that Pérez de Guzmán is listed among the supporters of Prince Enrique of Aragon is not borne out by the text of the chronicle. Nevertheless, Pérez de Guzmán was definitely with the prince in Ocaña in 1421. In the company of Lopez de Mendoza, archbishop of Santiago, he intervened on Enrique's behalf with Juan II of Castile in matters pertaining to the disputed ownership of the marquessate of Villena. Pérez de Guzmán's diplomatic mission was unsuccessful; Enrique was required to disband his forces and withdraw from the territory he had occupied in the marquessate.

By 1429 Pérez de Guzmán was in the service of the king of Castile. The *Refundición de la Crónica del halconero* relates that at Christmas of that year, Juan II sent him on a mission (ultimately unsuccessful) to persuade a group of Castilian nobles loyal to Enrique of Aragon to desist from their intention of abjuring fealty to the Crown of Castile and abandoning the realm. An often-repeated anecdote tells of Pérez de Guzmán's arrest in 1431 by order of Juan II over a noisy altercation. Conducted in the king's presence, in total disregard of accepted protocol, Pérez de Guzmán's quarrel was with a certain Juan de Vera concerning the reward for saving the life of Pero Meléndez Valdés at the Battle of Higueruela. The story is found in epístola 51 of the *Centón epistolario* (Epistolary Miscellany, 1499), variously attributed to Juan Antonio Vera Zúñiga y Figueroa, Conde de la Roca, to Gil González Dávila, and to Fernán Gómez de Cibdareal. This "exuberant piece of fiction," as Nicholas G. Round has described the *Centón epistolario,* is a notoriously unreliable compilation as far as historical veracity is concerned. As R. B. Tate points out, the incident is not mentioned in any other contemporary source, and the account may be entirely apocryphal.

There is ample documentation—much of it in the *semblanza* (pen portrait) of Luna—of the events of 1432, which proved to be a turning point in the life of Pérez de Guzmán. Jealous of the hold that Luna exerted over Juan II, a group of nobles, including Pérez de Guzmán and several of his relatives, moved against the royal

*Title page for a 1506 collection of some of Fernán Pérez de Guzmán's religious and didactic verse (Biblioteca Nacional, Madrid)*

*de Baena,* compiled around 1445–1450, includes fourteen pieces of Pérez de Guzmán's occasional verse that date from before his retirement to Batres. In addition to the three short lyrics (*Baena,* poems 551, 569, and 570) dedicated to Leonor, the other pieces are four poems (*Baena* 113, 119, 545, and 553) that form part of a literary exchange with Alfonso Alvarez de Villasandino. Two (*Baena* 232 and 547) are part of an exchange with the Italian-born Francisco Imperial. Two more (*Baena* 549 and 550) are *preguntas* (questions) intended to initiate an exchange with Gutierre de Toledo, archdeacon of Guadalajara, who was Pérez de Guzmán's cousin. The *respuestas* (replies) are not recorded. There is a stately reflection (*Baena* 571) on mortality, the transitoriness of life, and the vanity of fame, wealth, and worldly power that was inspired by the death in 1404 of Diego Hurtado de Mendoza, the admiral of Castile. This poem is followed by a similar reflection on the fall of princes, the inevitability of death, and the obligation of the Christian to lead a life of virtue (*Baena* 572). Perhaps incongruously, in view of the tone of the previous two poems, the final piece by Pérez de Guzmán in the *Cancionero de Baena* (573) consists of seven stanzas of extravagant praise for "su amiga" (his lady friend). Three different poets were inspired to write *respuestas* of disbelief in the existence of such a paragon of womanly perfection (*Baena* 574, 575, and 576). Pérez de Guzmán's poem was probably intended to generate such a response; the *amiga* in question might have been nothing more than a literary invention.

By and large, the casual reader of today will find little of great consequence in this early poetry, with the possible exception of *Baena* 571 and 572, in which the reflections on the human condition still have a universal appeal. The issues involved in the *preguntas y respuestas*–love, poetry, fate, wealth, age, and political satire–are couched in such a way as to make them a pretext for displays of literary virtuosity rather than serious discussion of pressing matters of personal concern. The topical allusions are now difficult or impossible to grasp, the wit and wordplay elusive and obscure, without detailed historical and philological notes to explicate it all. Yet, such verbal jousting was the stock-in-trade of much of the *cancionero* poetry of Pérez de Guzmán's time. The *pregunta y respuesta* format provided the court poets with an opportunity to demonstrate their intellectual acuity, linguistic prowess, and mastery of form and technique. A *respuesta,* for example, would be expected to follow the meter, rhyme scheme, and often the rhyme words of the *pregunta.* On such skills were the poets judged, and it is clear that Pérez de Guzmán could match wits with the best of them.

In seclusion after 1432, Pérez de Guzmán turned his back on the type of court poetry collected in the

favorite, claiming that he had deceived and bewitched the king. The attempted coup was unsuccessful and was followed on 7 February 1432 by the arrest, imprisonment, and, in some cases, banishment of most of the principals involved. Pérez de Guzmán himself was placed in the custody of Carrillo de Huete and was set free on 16 September 1432 as part of a gesture of magnanimity by Luna toward his erstwhile opponents.

After his release from custody, Pérez de Guzmán returned to Batres. He appears to have played no further role in the political life of Castile. The withdrawal from court life might have been an exile self-imposed out of sheer disgust for the politics of the day, or it might have been the result of continued suspicion of his loyalties, given his long-standing partiality to Prince Enrique of Aragon and his undisguised hatred for Luna. Absence from the center of power led Pérez de Guzmán to the cultivation of literature and learning.

Although it is impossible to establish a precise chronology for all of Pérez de Guzmán's works, a general schema has been outlined by Weiss. The *Cancionero*

*Cancionero de Baena* to dedicate himself to more-serious literature. His most significant poetic works include the *Confesión rimada* (Rhymed Confession), the *Coplas de vicios y virtudes* (Verses on Vices and Virtues), and *Loores de los claros varones de España,* all written before 1452, when the earliest surviving manuscript was produced. His *Proverbios* (Proverbs) and *La coronación de las quatro virtudes* (The Coronation of the Four Virtues) were written shortly before Santillana's *Proemio y carta al Condestable de Portugal* (Introduction and Letter to the Constable of Portugal), which belongs to the period 1445–1449. *La coronación de las quatro virtudes* can have been written no earlier than the latter part of 1445, as in it Pérez de Guzmán refers to his nephew as "el marqués" (the marquess), a title López de Mendoza acquired in August of that year.

The *Confesión rimada* follows a pattern employed by López de Ayala in his *Rimado de palacio* (Palace Verses, circa 1400) and is indebted structurally and thematically to contemporary manuals for confessors. After a brief paraphrase of the first part of the *Confiteor* (I confess) of the Latin Mass, the poet makes a close examination of conscience and then confesses, detailing the extent to which he has transgressed against the Ten Commandments. He follows a similar procedure for the Seven Deadly Sins and for his failure to practice the Seven Corporal and Spiritual Works of Mercy. He concludes with a paraphrase of the second part of the *Confiteor* in which he prays for the intercession of the Virgin Mary and all the saints for the forgiveness of his sins. The overall tone of this long poem—there are 189 eight-line stanzas—is devout and moralistic. But, as Alan D. Deyermond has observed with reference to the confessional part of López de Ayala's *Rimado de palacio,* inasmuch as the poem conforms to a conventional pattern, it is not necessary to regard it as a deeply felt personal confession. Pérez de Guzmán uses the model to indulge in general reflections on human frailty and to issue commonplace condemnations of those who live in a dissolute and profligate manner, of the self-seeking and acquisitive nobility, and of the venality of the clergy.

The *Coplas de vicios y virtudes,* dedicated to the chronicler García de Santa María, consists of 463 eight-line stanzas that make up a collection of ethical, moral, and sociopolitical observations and exhortations in which Christian thought and Senecan stoicism tend to merge. As in the case of the *Confesión rimada,* the *Coplas de vicios y virtudes* demonstrates the same fluctuation between, or attempt to meld, what Weiss has called "the private voice of the individual poet and the collective voice of received wisdom and understanding." Where the private voice is most noticeable, the reader can perhaps best appreciate the subtle irony, wry humor, and profound understanding of the duality of

human nature that Pérez de Guzmán displays here and elsewhere in his writings. In stanzas 16 and 47 he justifies his rejection of the ornate style of writing practiced by such contemporaries as Santillana, Enrique de Villena, and Juan de Mena. In stanza 60, "De gracia infusa e libre albedrío" (On Infused Grace and Free Will), Pérez de Guzmán returns to a doctrinal issue that reflects a contemporary preoccupation with the questions of free will, predestination, and salvation.

The tendentious tone of much of the *Coplas de vicios y virtudes* does not imply an absence of generosity of spirit or a failure to understand human weakness. In stanzas 77–85 Pérez de Guzmán warns against judging individuals by the actions of their youth: "Yerra quien cuyda apresçiar / por las flores los frutales" (He errs who thinks that he can judge / the fruit trees by their blossom). In stanzas 127–128 he cautions that "non está el seso en mucho fablar nin aún en mucho callar" (wisdom does not reside in endless talk, nor yet in endless silence). His perception of the reign of Juan II may well be summed up in stanzas 197–"allí los muy nobles penan / e los siervos son señores" (there the most noble suffer / and the servants are their lords)–and 436, "Del rey virtuoso e pueblo obediente" (On the Virtuous King and Obedient People), in which he observes that "nunca el pueblo obedesce / al rey que es defectuoso" (The people never obey / a king who is deficient). Stanzas 290, "De saber lo pasado" (On Knowing the Past), and 291, "De saber lo porvenir" (On Knowing the Future), encapsulate Pérez de Guzmán's ideas on the importance of history as a guide to the present and future. Stanzas 315–324, on the complementary values of the "Vida activa e contemplativa" (The Active and Contemplative Life), are followed immediately (stanzas 325–333) by a discussion, "De sciencia e cavallería" (On Learning and Knighthood). Here Pérez de Guzmán adumbrates an ideal–a harmonious combination of arms and letters–that is generally out of tune with the dominant ideology of the time but is related to the ideas of Santillana and Villena, even though they differed substantially in their concept of what constituted appropriate *sciencia.* Pérez de Guzmán might have had Villena in mind when he wrote "De saber lo porvenir," in which he inveighs against those who place their trust in false and forbidden knowledge: astrology, necromancy, the invocation of spirits and *phuntones* (phantoms), and the interpretation of sneezes and the flight of crows. He castigates Villena in similar terms in the *Generaciones y semblanzas.*

Pérez de Guzmán dedicated the 409 stanzas of the *Loores de los claros varones de España* to his nephew Fernán Gómez de Guzmán, a knight commander of the military Order of Calatrava. The poem is the fruit of Pérez de Guzmán's conviction that Spain had paid too little attention to its illustrious figures of former times: "España non caresció / de quien virtudes usase, / mas menguó e fallesció / en ella quien las notase" (Spain was not lacking / in those who demonstrated virtues, / but there waned and perished / in her those who could record them).

He begins his account in the mythical past with the three-headed Gerion, who symbolized valor, wisdom, and justice and was the guide of those who ruled well. Cases of heroic resistance to Roman domination follow (stanzas 17–30), then examples of illustrious Hispano-Romans, such as Trajan, Theodosius, Seneca the Younger, Lucan, Quintilian, and Paulus Orosius. In this section of the poem Pérez de Guzmán inserts his well-known condemnation of the "worthless eloquence" of Virgil and Ovid (stanzas 46–49) and exalts the study of history and moral philosophy.

From Roman times Pérez de Guzmán passes to the conquest of Rome by Alaric the Goth and to exemplary figures from Visigothic Spain (stanzas 61–112). Pelayo merits attention as the initiator of resistance to the Islamic conquest of the Iberian Peninsula (stanzas 113–123). The remainder of the poem deals principally with those medieval kings and queens of Castile and Aragon whom Pérez de Guzmán considers worthy of mention. He also includes the mythical Bernardo del Carpio (stanza 146), as well as Count Fernán González (stanzas 160–171) and Ruy Díaz de Vivar, "el Cid" (stanzas 217–221), all subjects of popular medieval epics. In his praise of Córdoba (stanzas 285–299), a city he compares to ancient Athens, Pérez de Guzmán also expresses admiration for non-Christian Spaniards, such as the Muslim philosopher Averroës and the Jewish medical doctor and thinker Maimonides. The poem concludes with stanzas (382–392) dedicated to Benedict XIII, Cardinal Gil de Albornoz (stanzas 393–402), and a final section on Spanish poets (stanzas 403–408).

The *Proverbios* consists of a six-stanza introduction in *octavillas* (eight-line stanzas of octosyllabic verse), followed by 102 quatrains of lapidary aphorisms. The genre was also cultivated by the marqués de Santillana and may owe its inspiration to the gnomic *Proverbios morales* (Moral Proverbs, circa 1355) by the Hispano-Jewish poet Rabbi Santob de Carrión de los Condes.

Pérez de Guzmán dedicated to Santillana his *Coronación de las quatro virtudes cardenales,* a didactic poem of sixty-six stanzas in which themes already encountered in his other works are reiterated. Justice is essential for a well-ordered civil life and is, by implication, sorely lacking in the Castile of his own day. All human activity must be informed by prudence and reinforced by its natural offshoots: assiduous study, industry, and especially *discreción,* a key concept in Pérez de Guzmán's writings. It is not "discretion" in the everyday sense of that word but

the exercise of wisdom and right judgment to determine individual or collective conduct. Although Pérez de Guzmán clearly admires physical valor, his treatment of *fortaleza* (fortitude) is concerned principally with the moral quality that resists evil, suffers persecution for the sake of justice, and withstands with equanimity the blows of fortune. *Templanza* (temperance) is the supreme virtue that rules the others, tempering rigorous justice with clemency, restraining impetuous fortitude, and investing prudence with appropriate authority, wisdom, and sobriety. Temperance holds all things in balance, prevents excess, and represents the medieval ideal of *mesura* (dignified restraint), a notion not unlike that of the Roman *gravitas.*

In the conclusion to the *Coronación de las quatro virtudes cardenales* (stanzas 62–66) Pérez de Guzmán addresses his dedicatee directly. He justifies his straightforward and "rustic" style in a series of plant metaphors. Suggesting to Santillana that Seneca the moralist was more "fruitful" with his plain prose than Virgil's *Aeneid,* with all its rhetorical ornamentation, he issues a reprimand to the marqués for allowing thorns to grow among the carnations, lilies, and greenery of his own poetry. Some commentators have taken this criticism to be an oblique condemnation of Santillana's love affairs. In the context of the poem, however, it almost certainly refers to Santillana's continued cultivation of amatory verse and, in particular, his admiration for the pagan poets and his use of pagan imagery and classical allusions in his compositions.

Pérez de Guzmán enjoyed a close friendship with the bishop of Burgos, Alfonso de Cartagena. The bishop's death in 1456 inspired Pérez de Guzmán to write a heartfelt lament, noteworthy for the personal tone of the invective against death and fortune (stanzas 6–7), the complaint on the demise of virtuous, worthwhile, and beneficent men (stanzas 8–9), and, in stanza 5, for what is almost certainly an echo of the tercets of Petrarch's Sonnet 116, the subject of a learned commentary attributed to Villena by Derek C. Carr and Weiss.

The considerable poetic output of Pérez de Guzmán also includes religious verse. There are hymns dedicated to various saints, as well as a rhymed *amplificatio* (amplification) of the prayers *Ave Maria* (Hail Mary), *Pater noster* (Our Father), and *Te Deum laudamus* (We Praise Thee, God). Of the several hymns to the Virgin Mary, the most delightful and fresh are the *Cient trinadas a loor de la Virgen María* (One Hundred Three-line Stanzas in Praise of the Virgin Mary) and the song "O María, luz del día" (O Mary, light of the day). Although the songs are conventional in content and language, the semipopular lyric form gives them an immediacy that is absent from the other hymns. In many respects they resemble the *Cantigas de loor* (Songs of Praise) among the *Cantigas de*

*Santa María* (Songs of St. Mary) compiled in the thirteenth century by King Alfonso X, "The Learned," and may reflect a familiarity with that collection. It is virtually certain that they would have had musical settings, and may well have been *contrafacta*–songs written to fit existing melodies.

Pérez de Guzmán may have been the compiler, if not the author, of the *Floresta de filósofos* (Anthology of Philosophers), a collection of aphorisms taken chiefly from Seneca the Younger. A translation of Bernard of Chartres's *Epistola super gubernatione rei familiaris* (Letter on the Administration of Household Affairs) has been attributed to Pérez de Guzmán, as well as some notes on the *Fuero viejo de Castilla* (Old Legal Code of Castile).

From a probably considerable correspondence, two finely crafted letters by Pérez de Guzmán survive. One is to Fray Gonzalo de Ocaña, prior of the convent of Santa María de la Sisla, requesting a translation of Pope St. Gregory's I *Dialogues* (593). In the other, to his close friend Cartagena, Pérez de Guzmán seeks advice on the matter of prayer. In response, the bishop of Burgos composed a treatise on the subject, *El oracional de Fernán Pérez* (1454). The *Mar de istorias* (Sea of Histories, translated circa 1433–1451) is basically a translation of Giovanni Colonna's *Mare historiarum* (circa 1340s), with interpolations from the Latin work *Planeta* (1218), by Diego García de Campos. *Mar de istorias* consists of a series of biographies of heroes from the classical past, Christian saints and scholars, and other fictional and historical personages, as well as religious and ethnic groups, such as the Albigensian heretics and the Tartars, and social organizations, such as the medieval military orders.

Pérez de Guzmán's *Generaciones y semblanzas* may have been intended as a continuation of the *Mar de historias* or as an independent work. In it he provides vivid pen portraits of thirty-four individuals who played a significant role in Spain during his long lifetime. Most of the biographical sketches were written before 1450, although the last two were added later, after the deaths of the subjects: Luna in 1453 and Juan II in 1454.

The apparent simplicity of style is deceptive. The portraits are not just casual pieces but are crafted according to a rhetorical model. Francisco López Estrada sees in them the various categories of the rhetorical *descriptio* (description). Carlos Clavería links the model to a rhetorical stereotype that can be traced back to medieval theories of physiognomy, classical historical biography deriving from Suetonius, and a framework requiring an enumeration of the vices and virtues of the subject portrayed.

Of particular interest are the portraits of Fernando I of Aragon, presented as a paragon of the prudent monarch; of the upstart commoner Ferrán Alonso de Robles, emblematic of the self-interest that governed Castile; of Juan II, the ineffectual ruler par excellence; of Luna, whose cupidity and duplicity symbolized all that was wrong with the nation; and of Villena, with whom Pérez de Guzmán shared many ideals and of whose heterodox erudition and Latinate grandiloquence he thoroughly disapproved. The passionate defense of the "new Christians" in the *semblanza* of Pablo de Santa María, a former chief rabbi, convert, and later bishop of Burgos, is remarkable in an age when such views were becoming increasingly unpopular.

Tate has described the introduction to the *Generaciones y semblanzas* as the first Castilian treatise on the nature of history and the duties of the historian. As Carr has suggested, however, Pérez de Guzmán's introduction may be a reaction to Villena's treatment of the same issue in the introduction and notes to his translation (1427–1428) of Virgil's *Aeneid*. Both Villena and Pérez de Guzmán share a concern for *fama* (fame) and for the futility of pursuing it if no adequate historical record can be kept. Both agree that the historiographer must have an excellent command of rhetoric, though their notions of good style are diametrically opposed. Pérez de Guzmán goes further than Villena in insisting that the historian should be scrupulous about the veracity of his sources (Villena was quite uncritical in this regard) and that he should await the death of the king or prince about whose reign he writes so that he can publish the truth without fear.

In his sociopolitical thinking Pérez de Guzmán shared with Villena a firm belief in the need for an educated and virtuous ruling class united under a wise, prudent, and enlightened monarch. Both authors display a great admiration for the Roman Empire, presenting it as a political model that Spain would do well to imitate. In this regard they can be seen as foreshadowing the imperial ideal that took root during the reign of Fernando II (Ferdinand) and Isabel I (Isabella) and came to fruition during the Hapsburg period. Pérez de Guzmán appeared to sense the direction in which the political trends of late-medieval Europe were moving–that is, toward the establishment of the centralized nation-state with power vested in the Crown and with the ancient privileges and prerogatives of the cities, the nobility, the church, and the military orders severely curtailed. At the same time, for other reasons, he vigorously opposed Luna, whose political aims, nevertheless, coincided in large part with his own beliefs.

Weiss has pointed to a similar ambivalence elsewhere in Pérez de Guzmán's life and works. He withdrew from public life, but he continued to maintain contact with prominent public figures and had much to say about the duties and responsibilities of those who held public office. Although he cultivated what he called a "rustic eloquence," he was at the same time a subtle manipulator of rhetorical technique, not as detached as he pretended to be from the ornate style practiced by such poets as Santillana. Pérez de Guzmán attempted to develop a universal, rather than an individual, poetic voice to provide himself with the moral authority of a latter-day prophet so that he could speak from his self-appointed isolation as the conscience of the nation. Yet, as Weiss argues, this attempt at self-effacement in favor of universality represents the concern of "someone who participated fully in the aristocratic struggle to define personal and national identities."

**References:**

Lope Barrientos, *Refundición de la Crónica del halconero,* edited by Juan de Mata Carriazo, Colección de crónicas españolas, no. 9 (Madrid: Espasa-Calpe, 1946);

José Antonio Barrio Sánchez, "Fernán Pérez de Guzmán's 'Cancionero': Edition and Study," dissertation, Universidad Nacional de Educación a Distancia, 1992;

Derek C. Carr, "A Fifteenth-Century Castilian Translation and Commentary of a Petrarchan Sonnet: Biblioteca Nacional Ms. 10186, fols. 196r–199r," *Revista Canadiense de Estudios Hispánicos,* 5 (1981): 123–143;

Carr, "Pérez de Guzmán and Villena: A Polemic on Historiography?" in *Hispanic Studies in Honor of Alan D. Deyermond: A North American Tribute,* edited by John S. Miletich (Madison, Wis.: Hispanic Seminary of Medieval Studies, 1986), pp. 57–70;

Pedro Carrillo de Huete, *Crónica del halconero de Juan II,* edited by Carriazo, Colección de crónicas españolas, no. 8 (Madrid: Espasa-Calpe, 1946);

Carlos Clavería, "Notas sobre la caracterización de la personalidad en 'Generaciones y semblanzas,'" *Anales de la Universidad de Murcia,* 10 (1951–1952): 481–526;

"Comienza la crónica del serenísimo príncipe don Juan, segundo rey deste nombre en Castilla y en Leon," in *Crónicas de los reyes de Castilla, desde don Alfonso el Sabio hasta los católicos don Fernando y dona Isabel,* edited by Cayetano Rosell, 3 volumes, Biblioteca de autores españoles, nos. 66, 68, 70 (Madrid: M. Rivadeneyra, 1875–1878; reprinted, Madrid: Atlas, 1953), II: 277–695;

Alan D. Deyermond, *La Edad Media,* translated by Luis Alonzo López, Historia de la literatura española, no. 1 (Barcelona: Ariel, 1992);

Jesús Domínguez Bordona, introduction to Pérez de Guzmán, *Generaciones y semblanzas,* edited by Domínguez Bordona, Clásicos Castellanos (Madrid: Espasa-Calpe, 1941);

Raymond Foulché-Delbosc, "Etude bibliographique sur Fernán Pérez de Guzmán," *Revue Hispanique,* 16 (1907): 26–55;

Alvar García de Santa María, *Crónica de Juan II,* Colección de documentos inéditos para la historia de España, nos. 99, 100 (Madrid: R. Marco y Viñas, 1891; reprinted, Vaduz: Kraus, 1966);

Fernán Gómez de Cibdareal, "Centón epistolario," in *Epistolario español,* volume 1, edited by Eugenio de Ochoa, Biblioteca de autores españoles, no. 13 (Madrid: M. Rivadeneyra, 1850; reprinted, Madrid: Atlas, 1945), pp. 1–36;

Lucía Guzzi Harrison, "El tema de vicio y virtud en las 'Coplas' de Fernán Pérez de Guzmán," dissertation, University of Kentucky, 1995;

Jeremy N. H. Lawrance, "On Fifteenth-Century Spanish Vernacular Humanism," in *Medieval and Renaissance Studies in Honour of Robert Brian Tate,* edited by Ian Michael and Richard A. Cadwell (Oxford: Dolphin, 1986), pp. 63–79;

Lawrance, "The Spread of Lay Literacy in Late Medieval Castile," *Bulletin of Hispanic Studies,* 62 (1985): 79–94;

Francisco López Estrada, "La retórica en las 'Generaciones y semblanzas' de Fernán Pérez de Guzmán," *Revista de Filología Española,* 30 (1946): 310–352;

Marie de Menaca, "Passé national et projet politique dans les *Loores de los claros varones de España* de Fernán Pérez de Guzmán," *Textes et Langages,* 4 (1983): 111–161;

Nicholas G. Round, "Renaissance Culture and Its Opponents in Fifteenth-Century Castile," *Modern Language Review,* 57 (1962): 204–215;

Dorothy S. Severin and Fiona Maguire, "Fernán Pérez de Guzmán's *Loores de santos:* Texts and Traditions," in *Saints and Their Authors: Studies in Medieval Hispanic Hagiography in Honor of John K. Walsh,* edited by Jane E. Connolly, Deyermond, and Brian Dutton (Madison, Wis.: Hispanic Seminary of Medieval Studies, 1990), pp. 151–168;

R. B. Tate, introduction to Pérez de Guzmán, *Generaciones y semblanzas* (London: Tamesis, 1965);

Julian Weiss, "*La affección poetal virtuosa:* Petrarch's Sonnet 116 as Poetic Manifesto for Fifteenth-Century Castile," *Modern Language Review,* 86 (1991): 70–78;

Weiss, "Fernán Pérez de Guzmán: Poet in Exile," *Speculum,* 66 (1991): 96–108;

Weiss, *The Poet's Art: Literary Theory in Castile c. 1400–60,* Medium Aevum Monographs, new series 14 (Oxford: Society for the Study of Mediaeval Languages and Literature, 1990).

# Florencia Pinar

*(fl. circa late fifteenth century)*

Gregory B. Kaplan
*University of Tennessee*

WORKS: "Canción de una dama que se dice Florencia Pinar," "Otra canción de la misma señora a unas perdices que le enbiaron bivas," "Glosa de Florencia," and "Canción de Florencia Pinar" (late fifteenth century)

**Editions:** The four poems were published in the *Cancionero general recopilado por Hernando del Castillo* (Valencia: Cristóbal Kofman, 1511), fols. 125v–126r, 144r, 185v; *Cancionero general recopilado por Hernando del Castillo (Valencia, 1511),* facsimile edition, edited by Antonio Rodríguez-Moñino (Madrid: Real Academia Española, 1958), fols. 125v–126r, 144r, 185v.

**Editions in English:** *The Defiant Muse: Hispanic Feminist Poems from the Middle Ages to the Present,* edited by Angel Flores and Kate Flores (New York: Feminist Press at the City University of New York, 1986)—includes "Destas aues su nación" (The nature of these birds) and "Ell amor ha tales mañas" (So wily are the ways of love), pp. 16–19, translated by Kate Flores; [three poems], translated by Joseph Snow, in his "The Spanish Love Poet Florencia Pinar," in *Medieval Women Writers,* edited by Katherina M. Wilson (Athens: University of Georgia Press, 1984; Manchester: Manchester University Press, 1984), pp. 320–332.

Florencia Pinar probably lived most of her life during the second half of the fifteenth century. She is known for being one of a handful of female poets whose works appear in Spanish compilations of poetry, called *cancioneros* (songbooks), of the fifteenth and early sixteenth centuries. Although Pinar's identity has yet to be established historically, she is the most significant literary figure among these female poets. As Alan D. Deyermond has observed, the Spanish "*cancioneros* include the work of only half a dozen named and two anonymous" female poets, "and all but one of these are represented by only a few lines. Pinar is the exception." In addition to being the best-known female poet of the late

Spanish Middle Ages, Pinar is also recognized among modern scholars for her skilled manipulation of *cancionero* language and for distinguishing herself from both her female and male contemporaries through her frequent recourse to uncharacteristically concrete poetic imagery.

Pinar's place and date of birth are unknown. In spite of the dearth of historical information about her, several aspects of her life may be revealed in her poetry. The fact that she could compose verse in Castilian suggests that she had some formal education, which would have been more common among women of the upper classes. Her upper-class background appears to be confirmed by a rubric to one of her poems, which refers to her as a "dama" (lady), that is, a woman of privileged socio-economic status. Another rubric calls her a "señora," a title normally used to designate a married woman. Her inclusion among the poets in the *Cancionero general* (General Songbook, 1511) may indicate that she was considered to be among the most skilled and renowned contemporary poets. She also may have been associated with the royal court at some point in her life, as were many of the male poets in the *Cancionero general*. Although no basis exists for speculation regarding the chronological order in which Pinar composed her works, their inclusion in the *Cancionero general* suggests that they were written during the second half of the fifteenth century. There are several additional poems in other late-medieval Spanish *cancioneros* that also may have been composed by her, but the fact that the poems are not attributed consistently to her in these songbooks prevents any definite conclusions regarding authorship.

There is another poet, with twelve poems in the *Cancionero general,* who shares Pinar's surname: Gerónimo Pinar. As in Pinar's case, the fact that this Gerónimo Pinar appears in the *Cancionero general* suggests that he lived during the late fifteenth century, and several scholars, including Deyermond and Barbara Fulks, have identified him as Pinar's brother. Aside from his name, nothing more is known about Gerónimo Pinar, and the fact that his proper name is not mentioned in any of the rubrics to his works has caused critical speculation regarding whether any more poems ascribed to "Pinar" might have been composed by Florencia. In some instances such speculation is not plausible since the author of several of the poems is definitely a male, as revealed by the masculine ending of the adjective *dicho* in rubrics that refer to that individual as "dicho Pinar" (the aforementioned Pinar).

In modern times Pinar has received a fair amount of critical attention. Scholars of the nineteenth and early twentieth centuries such as José Amador de los Ríos and Manuel Serrano y Sanz tended to regard her as an insignificant author. During the last decades of the twentieth century, Pinar's works were reevaluated on several occasions, and she has gained a reputation in scholarly circles for her skills as a *cancionero* love poet. In 1978, and again in 1983, Deyermond shed new light on the sexual allusions inspired by Pinar's animal imagery. A year after Deyermond's second study, Joseph Snow provided further analysis of the discourse and imagery that informs Pinar's poetry, in addition to translating three of her poems into English. Fulks, in 1990, and Roxana Recio, in 1992, offered new visions of Pinar's feminine voice and laid the foundations for alternative interpretations of the sexual imagery in her poetry.

Three of the poems composed by Pinar are *canciones* (songs), that is, lyric poems that were intended to be sung aloud. The *canción,* one of the most popular forms of Spanish *cancionero* poetry, typically consists of twelve octosyllabic lines divided into one four-line *estribillo* (refrain) and one eight-line stanza. The number of total lines can vary depending on the *estribillo,* which may comprise as little as three or as many as five lines. Regardless of its length, a *canción* may be separated into three sections. In the first the poet presents the central theme in the *estribillo.* The second section is usually the first four lines of the stanza. In these lines she elaborates on the central theme while changing the rhyme scheme. The third section of a *canción* is typically the final four lines of the stanza, and the transition between the second and third sections is indicated by a return to the original rhyme pattern. Insofar as the third section reprises the *estribillo,* the number of lines is usually equal to the number in the initial section of the poem. In the closing lines of the poem, the poet usually repeats terms or phrases from the *estribillo.* Although religious *canciones* were sometimes composed, most *canciones* are secular love poems.

Pinar's "Canción de una dama que se dice Florencia Pinar" (Song by a Lady Called Florencia Pinar) is a poem of fourteen lines. The invention of the five-line *estribillo* employed by Pinar in this poem is attributed by scholars to the *cancionero* poet Jorge Manrique. Pinar's

use of this *estribillo* might also provide a clue as to an approximate date of her birth insofar as this type of *estribillo* was a favorite of poets who were born between 1431 and 1445, as Vicente Beltrán and Keith Whinnom have indicated. The second stanza of "Canción de una dama que se dice Florencia Pinar" includes the remaining nine lines. The end rhyme is consonantal (or a complete rhyme) and follows a scheme of *abbab cdd-cabbab.* "Canción de una dama que se dice Florencia Pinar" depicts as its theme the conflicting emotions experienced by one who is in love, a topic on which *cancionero* poets often focused.

The wordplay employed by Pinar in "Canción de una dama que se dice Florencia Pinar" is also similar to those found in other contemporary poems. *Cancionero* poetry is frequently informed by images or conceits (in Spanish, *conceptos*) created by associations of semantically unrelated (and sometimes antithetical) terms and phrases, exploitations of literary figures of speech, and other types of wordplay. In "Canción de una dama que se dice Florencia Pinar" Pinar demonstrates a genuine talent for formulating conceits—a technique known as *conceptismo*—in order to communicate the theme of the poem, that love is, at one and the same time, a source of pain and pleasure.

The contrast between these two emotions is reproduced in the poem through Pinar's exploitation of the acoustic and orthographic relationships between *ay,* an interjection that expresses a lover's passionate sigh, and *hay,* the impersonal form of the verb *haber,* meaning "there is" or "there are." Since the initial consonant of *hay* is silent (although it may have been aspirated during Pinar's time), *hay* and *ay* are homonyms. Moreover, *hay* was written during Pinar's time without the initial consonant, which made it an orthographic homonym with *ay* as well. Pinar takes advantage of these similarities by using *ay* twenty times in the poem, as both an impersonal verb and an interjection. On most occasions, the meaning of the term is determined by its grammatical functions in the particular line in which it appears. For example, in the eighth line, "ay donde ay penas de amores" (a sigh!, wherever there is love's pain), the initial *ay* serves as the interjection, while the second *ay* is the verb. The following line, "muy gran bien si de él gozares" (great pleasure, if one embraces love), completes this thought by asserting that love, while it is a destructive force ( *penas*), is also the source of great enjoyment ("muy gran bien"). On other occasions, the precise meaning of *ay* is open to interpretation, which reinforces the central theme that love provides both suffering and enjoyment. An example of this ambiguity is found in the phrase "ay glorias" from line 7, which might either be translated as "a sigh! pleasures!" or as "there are pleasures."

## Las obras de pinar.

penfando ca donde yria
nunca mas trifte veria
aquié yo táto me di
y aun q̃ yo no me quetaua
del partir defefperado
en fecreto fofpiraua
por qué trifte membiaua
damoxes defamparado

¶Por do hallo fer doblados
los males de mi dolencia
pues por cafos defaftrados
dalgunos viejos pecados
hago nueua penitécia
y ala fin las cofas mias
van de mal tã en peor
q̃ con muertas alegrias
van mis entrañas vazias
damoxes q̃ no damoz

¶Van mis glias mortiguas
mis ĝtas fiépre crefciédo das
mis cuytas todas dobladas
mis fuerças muy dfmayadas
tras delas vueftras corriédo
Mas fiédo vos enemiga
dela victoria q̃ figo
quiero q̃ claro fe diga
ques ellalma muy amiga
yel coraçon enemigo

¶Voyme de llanos en fierras
voy por aguas dela mar
voyme de tierras en tierras
huyendo de vueftras guerras
con fecreto fofpirar
y pues no me fatiffaze
el quexar por donde fuere
mas me pefa q̃ me plaze
vifto q̃ nada fe haze
de quáto mi vida quiere

¶Y vos dama muy fefuda
y de difcretas efpejo
arredrados de muy cruda

quádos demádaua ayuda
vos me dauades confejo
y confte tal partir
voy penfando fi boluiere
comos tengo de dezir
q̃ por vos ya mi beuir
ni halla vida ni muere

¶Y por ques poco effoça
el qué poca agua faboga (do
digo ques bié comparado
qué cafa dellaboxado
no fe deue métar foga
y en métar q̃ vos me diftes
defabrigo por abrigo
mis plazeres tornã triftes
pues mi alma q̃ prdiftes
ni queda ni va comigo

¶Y lo q̃ comigo va
es mi fe fiépre foldada
y efta do quiera q̃ fta
minguno le prouara
q̃ jamas fueffe quebrada
Antes por tener muy firme
vos quebraftes lo foldado
por q̃ pudieffe plañirme
y entre todos maldezirme
fin ventura defdichado

¶Y pues no vale el plañir
ni maprouecha el quexar
quierome dexar morir
q̃ perderos y beuir
no fera fi no penar
Mas fi no fe cae el cielo
yo faldre defta triftoz
aun q̃ con todo recelo
q̃ fera vueftro confuelo
fin confuelo fin fauor

¶Z leno de táta amargura
quié podra partir gozofo
fi no con vna locura
del q̃ no tiene ventura

deue de fer porfiofo
y fi defto mi feñora
voy perdiédo la vigor
vueftra culpa es mi debdoz
pues con vida matadora
parto yo trifte amadoz

¶No parto de vos y fi
quedo con vos y no quedo
pero fi parto day
fiépre vo de vos anti
y a vos torno quádo quedo
y fi no eftoy fiépre alla
memorados lo paffado
defque torne fe os dira
como eftoy por vos aca
damoxes defamparado

¶Fin
¶Y entre táto beutire
con aql mal del milano
q̃ fi bolar no podre
para aqllo q̃ querre
fiépre terne el pico fano
El pico para quexarme
de vueftra grã diffauor
yel fefo para mudarme
la vida para apartarme
damoxes q̃ no damoz

### ¶Cancion de florécia pinar.

¶El lamoz ha tales mañas
q̃ quié no fe guarda dellas
fi felentra enlas entrañas
no puede falir fin ellas

¶El lamoz es vn gufano
bié mirada fu figura
es vn cáger de natura
q̃ come todo lo fano
Por fus burlas por fus fañas
del fe dan tales querellas
q̃ fi entra enlas entrañas
no puede falir fin ellas

*Folio 185v from the 1511 edition of the* Cancionero general recopilado por Hernando del Castillo, *which includes the* “Canción de Florencia Pinar” *(Real Academia Española, Madrid; courtesy of Frank A. Domínguez)*

In "Canción de una dama que se dice Florencia Pinar" Pinar's poetic persona seems to exalt the pleasures associated with being caught by love. Lines 4 and 5 of the *estribillo*–"ay vn ay con q[ue] sesquiue / quie[n] sin ay beuir so suele" (there is also a sigh with which they– / unused to life without their sighs– / can counter it)–which are almost completely repeated in the final two lines of the poem, console the afflicted lover by asserting that the perturbation caused by love can be overcome. In lines 8 through 12 the poetic persona argues that the pain felt by the anguished lover is worth being endured, even if it means placing one's life into jeopardy, because of the magnitude of the potential reward offered by love. One of the words used in line 9 in order to express this reward, *gozares* (pleasures), can convey the notion of sexual fulfillment. Similarly, the word *glorias* has been interpreted as an allusion to sexual intercourse, further strengthening the generally accepted critical opinion that the love of which Pinar writes is physical in nature.

At the same time, the path toward winning the reward of love is clouded in "Canción de una dama que se dice Florencia Pinar." As part of the wordplay on *ay* and *hay*, the poet's use of *ay* in line 4 as both a verb and an interjection helps to convey the ironic notion that the remedy for the pain caused by love is love itself. In the repetition of the *estribillo* at the end of the poem, however, the initial *ay* of line 4 is omitted in line 13, with the remaining *ay* functioning as a verb–thus reiterating that there is a remedy for the wounds inflicted by love but eliminating the inference that love is that remedy. This ambiguous tone, and the abstract nature of Pinar's imagery in this poem, differentiates "Canción de una dama que se dice Florencia Pinar" from her other two *canciones,* which focus on the perils associated with love by means of more concrete imagery.

In "Otra canción de la misma señora a unas perdizes que le embiaron bivas" (Another Song by the Same Lady for Some Partridges That Were Sent to Her Live), Pinar again casts her poetic persona in the role of the anguished lover. Like "Canción de una dama que se dice Florencia Pinar," this poem comprises a five-line *estribillo* and a nine-line stanza. The end rhyme, which is again consonantal, follows a scheme of *abaab cddcabaab.*

The *estribillo* that opens "Otra canción de la misma señora a unas perdizes que le embiaron bivas" communicates the despair felt by an individual at having surrendered her freedom to love. Although the gender of this individual is not explicitly revealed, scholars have traditionally interpreted the first-person singular pronoun *yo* in lines 4 and 13 and the first-person singular possessive pronoun *mía* in lines 5 and 14 as terms that identify the poetic persona in "Otra canción de la misma señora a unas perdizes que le embiaron bivas"

with Pinar herself. The fact that the name of the particular bird *(perdiz)* with which Pinar compares her poetic persona is a feminine noun in Spanish again suggests a feminine identity for this individual.

In the *estribillo* Pinar establishes a correspondence between the entrapped poetic persona and the confinement of the partridges, ostensibly in "en prisión" (a cage), where they traditionally were kept prior to being killed for the table. Like the caged partridges, whose confinement encumbers their joyful singing, the narrator is tormented as a captive of love. She reveals in line 5 that her cries of anguish have fallen on deaf ears and also implies that she is frustrated by this situation. The second stanza of the poem reinforces through alliteration the complaint for lost freedom. The initial consonant of *perdiz,* the Spanish word for partridge, the symbol of the poetic persona's captivity, resonates within the work through the repetition of the initial consonant *p* in several words–*perdiendo* (losing), *prisión, passión* (passion), and *prendieron* (they caught)–that express the individual's loss of happiness after succumbing to love.

The imagery with which Pinar depicts the suffering of her poetic persona in "Otra canción de la misma señora a unas perdizes que le embiaron bivas" is commonly thought to possess sexual allusions frequently found in *cancionero* love poems. Although such allusions may be explicit at times, they are more frequently expressed in an oblique manner. As such, the phrase "grave passión" (grave passion) in lines 4 and 13 may refer to emotional stress or to pain experienced during sexual intercourse, to which the term *glorias* in line 7 is also understood to allude. The partridges of the title have also been considered as euphemisms for a man's sexual conquest of a woman. Deyermond hypothesizes that Pinar selected a partridge in order to evoke its characteristics according to the medieval bestiary, which describes the bird as licentious. Medieval animal lore also describes female partridges as especially promiscuous, with the result being that they easily become pregnant. Caged partridges that lose their desire to sing after they are trapped share the predicament of the poetic persona, who experiences the same plight and unhappiness as the doomed birds. The gender of those responsible for caging the partridges is revealed by the masculine endings to an adjectival phrase found in line 9, "essos mismos" (the same).

Scholars such as José Amador de los Ríos and Deyermond have suggested that Pinar composed "Otra canción de la misma señora a unas perdizes que le embiaron bivas" in order to vent her personal emotions. For example, Deyermond asserts that Pinar evoked the bestiary depiction of the partridge in order to "identify her instincts" with uncontrollable sexual urges. In this light, the trapped condition of the partridges may be understood as a reflection of Pinar's own sense of helplessness and anguish. While such an interpretation of "Otra canción de la misma señora a unas perdizes que le embiaron bivas" is, of course, conjectural, the personal nature of several lines, namely those in the *estribillo* and line 10, "Sus nombres mi vida son" (their names [that is, predicaments] are my own), does appear to indicate an expression of suffering endured by the poet herself. Regardless of whether or not "Otra canción de la misma señora a unas perdizes que le embiaron bivas" provides a window into the poet's emotional experiences, the concrete imagery with which Pinar portrays the tribulation inflicted by love sets the poem apart from other *cancionero* works that represent the same theme in more abstract terms.

Pinar's third *canción*, "Canción de Florencia Pinar" (Song by Florencia Pinar), comprises a more traditional, four-line *estribillo* followed by a stanza of eight lines. The scheme followed by the consonantal end rhyme is *abab cddcabab*. The poem parallels Pinar's other two *canciones* in its representation of love as a pernicious force. Pinar establishes this theme in the opening stanza, in which she warns of the treachery of love. According to the *estribillo,* one must constantly be on guard against its insidiousness, a force that afflicts the lover indefinitely once that individual surrenders to passion.

As in "Otra canción de la misma señora a unas perdizes que le embiaron bivas," the imagery in "Canción de Florencia Pinar" is atypically concrete for a late-medieval *cancionero* work. The destructive influence of love is represented in line 5 by a worm, which evokes the notions of death and decay, and in lines 7–8 by a cancer that devours all that is healthy. This pessimistic vision of the effects of love is enhanced by Pinar's wordplay. The term used to describe the tricks of love, *mañas* (line 1), reverberates in the consonantal end rhyme of the *estribillo* and is repeated in the final four lines. *Mañas* rhymes with *entrañas* (entrails), the term that concludes line 3. In the final section of the poem Pinar uses *sañas* (cruelties) at the end of line 9 and links it with *entrañas* at the end of line 11. The two nouns take the reader back to *mañas.* This rhyme is complemented by others in the initial and final sections of the poem: the third-person feminine plural pronoun *ellas* in lines 2, 4, and 12 rhymes with *querellas* (complaints) in line 10, while the final *-as* syllable links the rhyme to *mañas, sañas,* and *entrañas,* thus enhancing the depiction of the tricks of love. This theme informs an additional wordplay, observed by Deyermond, that relates *entrañas* to the third person singular form of the infinitive *entrar* (to enter), the verb used in lines 3 and 11 to describe the intrusion of love into the vital organs.

In recalling the *entrañas, entra* also recalls the depths to which love afflicts the unwary lover.

Scholars commonly accept that "Canción de Florencia Pinar," like "Otra canción de la misma señora a unas perdizes que le embiaron bivas," possesses sexual overtones. Deyermond explains that *gusano* (worm) in line 5 could also refer in Old Spanish to a snake, an animal that is often employed in literature as a phallic symbol and, according to the bestiary, possesses reproductive habits that parallel the destructive powers of love.

"Canción de Florencia Pinar" is also noteworthy for establishing a poetic dialogue with a work composed by Gerónimo Pinar, her supposed (by some critics) brother. The poem in question is found immediately after "Canción de Florencia Pinar" and is preceded by the rubric "La glosa es del dicho Pinar" (The gloss is by the aforementioned Pinar). This poem marks the only occasion in which a contemporary responded in verse to one of Pinar's poems.

"La glosa es del dicho Pinar" consists of eleven stanzas of eleven lines each and a closing stanza of six lines. Various end rhymes are employed, although the scheme of the eleven-line stanzas (as in the second stanza, for example: *efeefghgghg*) remains consistent. As its rubric indicates, the poem is a *glosa* (gloss), a popular lyric form during the middle of the fifteenth century. The *glosa* was either a poetic elaboration of a popular saying (*mote*), a song (*villancico*), or a continuation of a brief lyric poem, as is the case with "La glosa es del dicho Pinar." *Glosas* were written in octosyllabic lines grouped in stanzas of varying lengths and rhyme schemes. In response to a poem, the author of a *glosa* might either replicate the stanzaic form and number of lines as the model or include key terms and phrases from that *canción.* Rather than reproducing the structure of "Canción de Florencia Pinar," the author of "Glosa del dicho Pinar" disperses words such as *mañas, entrañas,* and *gusano* and phrases such as "es un cáncer de natura" (it is a cancer by nature) throughout a much lengthier work that, like Pinar's poem, focuses on one's subjugation to the destructive power of love.

Pinar's "Glosa de Florencia" (Gloss by Florencia) participates in this trend. In this poem she transforms an ambiguous and despondent *mote,* "Mi dicha lo desconcierta" (My good fortune disturbs it), into another reflection on the frustration caused by love. The structure of the "Glosa de Florencia" is similar to her *canciones.* The poem comprises twelve octosyllabic lines, with four of these forming the *estribillo* and the remaining eight comprising a second stanza. The *mote* is included as the last line of the *estribillo* and the second stanza, and the rhyme scheme is *abab cddcabab.*

Although it would be logical to assume that the poetic persona in "Glosa de Florencia" is female, it is interesting to note that this individual is portrayed in lines 3 and 11 as a servile lover, a role typically given to representations of males in *cancionero* poetry and prose works. Regardless of the gender of the narrator, however, love again exerts a devastating influence in "Glosa de Florencia." In the *estribillo*, this figure laments through a conceit that is similar in nature to those in her *canciones* the futility of embracing love. In the initial line of the poem, "Será perderos pediros" (Asking you will mean losing you), the contrast between *perder* (to lose) and *pedir* (to ask), two similar-sounding verbs, draws attention to the frustrating situation faced by Pinar's poetic persona. Any pleasure experienced by this individual after becoming a servile lover is counteracted by the pleasure itself in lines 4 and 12, an ironic predicament that recalls the wordplay on *ay* and *hay* in "Canción de una dama que se dice Florencia Pinar." This irony is also the sense that Pinar appears to extract from the *mote*. In other words, the poetic persona's good fortune (*Mi dicha*) prevents bliss (the meaning apparently assigned to the neutral article *lo* by Pinar) from being realized (*desconcierta*): in the middle section of "Glosa de Florencia" there is a potential loss of happiness in surrendering to the pleasures of love.

Though nearly forgotten by history, Florencia Pinar is nevertheless an important literary figure. Among hundreds of writers included in late-medieval Spanish *cancioneros*, she is the only woman known to have composed a significant corpus of works. Pinar's ability to instill her works with indirect sexual allusions demonstrates her capacity for manipulating the nuances of the often formalized *cancionero* language. Although the nature of these allusions is not innovative, Pinar's use of concrete sexual imagery is rare in late-medieval Spanish lyric poetry. In a broader context Pinar's adeptness at weaving conceits into her poetic discourse and her use of poetic devices and wordplay are on a par with those of many of her male contemporaries. Like these poets, Pinar was responsible for cultivating a poetic tendency that persisted in the poetry of the Golden Age of Spanish literature in the sixteenth and seventeenth centuries. Much more than a name mentioned in the rubrics to a handful of poems, Pinar is of enduring importance to modern readers and scholars both as one of Spain's earliest female writers and as a skilled *cancionero* poet.

**References:**

José Amador de los Ríos, *Historia crítica de la literatura española,* volume 7 (Madrid: Rodriguez, 1865), pp. 257–258;

Vicente Beltrán, *La canción de amor en el otoño de la Edad Media* (Barcelona: PPU, 1988);

Peter G. Broad, "Florencia Pinar y la poética del *cancionero,*" in *La escritora hispánica: Actas de la decimotercera conferencia anual de literatura hispánicas en Indiana University of Pennsylvania,* edited by Nora Erro-Orthmann and Juan Cruz Mendizábal (Miami: Universal, 1990), pp. 26–36;

Alan D. Deyermond, "Spain's First Women Writers," in *Women in Hispanic Literature: Icons and Fallen Idols,* edited by Beth Miller (Berkeley: University of California Press, 1983), pp. 27–52;

Deyermond, "The Worm and the Partridge: Reflections on the Poetry of Florencia Pinar," *Mester,* 7 (1978): 3–8;

Barbara Fulks, "The Poet Named Florencia Pinar," *La Corónica,* 18, no. 1 (1989–1990): 33–44;

Louise Mirrer, "Género, poder y lengua en los poemas de Florencia Pinar," *Medievalia,* 19 (1995): 9–15;

Roxana Recio, "Otra dama que desaparece: La abstracción retórica en tres modelos de canción de Florencia Pinar," *Revista Canadiense de Estudios Hispánicos,* 16, no. 2 (1992): 329–339;

Manuel Serrano y Sanz, *Apuntes para una biblioteca de escritoras españolas desde el año 1401 al 1833,* volume 2 (Madrid: Sucesores de Rivadeneyra, 1905), pp. 129–130;

Keith Whinnom, *La poesía amatoria de la época de los Reyes Católicos* (Durham, U.K.: University of Durham, 1981);

Constance L. Wilkins, "Las voces de Florencia Pinar," in *III Jornadas de Literatura Espanola Medieval: Studia Hispanica Medievalia II,* edited by Rosa E. Penna and María A. Rosarossa (Buenos Aires: Facultad de Filosofía y Letras, Universidad Católica Argentina, 1992), pp. 124–130.

# Hernando del Pulgar
## (Fernando del Pulgar)
### *(circa 1436 – circa 1492)*

Joseph Abraham Levi
*Rhode Island College*

WORKS: *Letras* (1473–1484)

**Manuscript:** Santander, Biblioteca Menéndez Pelayo 78 (1485–1486) includes fifteen letters.

**First publication:** "Ferdinandi de Pulgar Epistolae ex Hispanico in Latinum idioma conversae a Juliano Magon," in Pietro Martire d' Anghiera, *Opus epistolarum Petri Martyris Anglerij Mediolanensis, Protonotarii Apostolici, Prioris Archiepiscopatus Granatensis, atque à Consiliis Rerum Indicarum Hispanicis, tanta cura excusum, ut praeter styli venustatem quoque fungi possit vice Luminis Historiae superiorum temporum: Cui accesserunt Epistolae Ferdinadi de Pulgar Coaetanei Latinae pariter atque Hispanicae cum Tractatu Hispanico de Viris Castellae Illustribus,* edited by Charles Patin (Amsterdam: Daniel Elzevir, 1670).

**Editions:** *Los claros varones de España y las treinta y dos cartas de Fernando de Pulgar* (Madrid: Printed by A. Marín, 1747); *Centón epistolario del Bachiller Gómez de Cibdareal, Generaciones y semblanzas del noble caballero Fernán Pérez de Guzmán, Claros Varones de Castilla, y Letras de Fernando de Pulgar* (Madrid: Real de la Gazeta, 1775).

**Standard editions:** "Letras," in *Epistolario español: Colección de cartas de españoles ilustres antiguos y modernos, recogida y ordenada con notas y aclaraciones históricas, criticas y biográficas,* 2 volumes, edited by Eugenio de Ochoa (Madrid: Publicidad de M. Rivadeneyra, 1850, 1870), I: 37–60; *Letras; Glosa a las Coplas de Mingo Revulgo,* edited by Jesús Domínguez Bordona (Madrid: Espasa-Calpe, 1929; revised, 1949; revised again, 1958); *Letras,* edited by Paola Elia (Pisa: Giardini, 1982); *Test and Concordance of Fernando del Pulgar, Claros varones de Castilla and Letras* [microform], edited by Michael L. Dangerfield (Madison, Wis.: Hispanic Seminary of Medieval Studies, 1986); *Letras* [computer file], edited by the Archivo digital de manuscritos y textos españoles (Madrid: Micronet, 1992).

*Crónica de los muy altos y esclarecidos reyes cathólicos don Fernando y doña Ysabel de gloriosa memoria* (1482–1490)

**Manuscript:** Madrid, Biblioteca Nacional MS. 18062.

**First publication:** *Habes in hoc volumine amice lector. Aelij Antonij Nebrissensis Rerum a Fernando [et] Elisabe Hispaniaru[m] foelicissimis regibus gestar[um] decades duas. Necno[n] belli Nauariensis libros duos. Annexa insuper Archiep[iscop]i Roderici Chronica, alijsq[ue] historijs antehac non excussis,* edited by Luis de Correra (Granada: Sancho de Nebrija, 1545);

**Editions:** *Aelii Antonii Nebrissensis Rervm A Fernando Et Elisàbe Hispaniar[um] felicissimis Regibus gestaru[m] Decades duæ, Necño belli Nauarie[n]sis libri duo. Nu[n]c secundo editi, et exactione vigilãtia ad prototypi fide[m] recogniti, & emendati. Imperiale cum Priuilegio* (Granada: Xanthus Nebrissensis, 1550); *Chrónicas de los muy altos y esclarecidos reyes católicos Don Fernando y Doña Ysabel de gloriosa memoria: Dirigida a la Católica Real Majestad del Rey don Philipe nuestro señor compvesta por el Maestro Antonio de Nebrixa, Cronista que fue de los dichos reyes Cathólicos* (Valladolid: Sebastián Martínez, 1565); *Chronica de los muy altos y esclaridos Reyes Catholicos Don Hernando y Dona Ysabel de gloriosa Memoria* (Saragossa: J. Millan, 1567); *Crónica de los señores reyes católicos don Fernando y doña Isabel de Castilla y de Aragón, escrita por su cronista Hernando del Pulgar cotexada con antiguos manuscritos y aumentada de varias ilustraciones y enmiendas* (Valencia: Printed by Benito Monfort, 1780).

**Standard editions:** *Crónicas de los reyes de Castilla, desde don Alfonso el Sabio, hasta los Católicos don Fernando y doña Isabel,* 3 volumes, edited by Cayetano Rosell, Biblioteca de autores espanoles, volumes 66, 68, and 70 (Madrid: M. Rivadeneyra, 1875–1878); *Crónica de los reyes católicos, por su secretario Fernando del Pulgar, versión inédita,* edited by Juan de Mata Carriazo (Madrid: Espasa-Calpe, 1943).

BOOKS: *Coplas de mingo reuulgo glosadas por Fernando de Pulgar* (Burgos: Fadrique de Basilea, 1485);

*Claros Varones de Castilla* (Toledo: Juan Vásquez, 1486).

**Editions**: *Claros Varones, Letras* (Saragossa: Pablo Hurus, ca. 1493);

*Claros Varones, Letras* (Seville: Stanislao Polono, 1500);

*Los claros varones despña: Hecho por Fernando del pulgar* (Saragossa, 1515);

*Coplas de Míngo Revulgo. Glosadas por Hernando de Pulgar* (Seville: Juan de León, 1545);

*Los claros varones de España* (Antwerp, 1632);

"Los claros varones de España," in Pietro Martire d' Anghiera, *Opus epistolarum Petri Martyris Anglerij Mediolanensis, Protonotarii Apostolici, Prioris Archiepiscopatus Granatensis, atque à Consiliis Rerum Indicarum Hispanicis, tanta cura excusum, ut praeter styli venustatem quoque fungi possit vice Luminis Historiae superiorum temporum: Cui accesserunt Epistolae Ferdinadi de Pulgar Coaetanei Latinae pariter atque Hispanicae cum Tractatu Hispanico de Viris Castellae Illustribus,* edited by Charles Patin (Amsterdam: Daniel Elzevir, 1670);

*Los claros varones de España y las treinta y dos cartas de Fernando de Pulgar* (Madrid: Printed by A. Marín, 1747);

*Claros varones de Castilla, y letras de Fernando de Pulgar: Consejero, secretario y coronista de los Reyes Católicos don Fernando y doña Isabel* (Madrid: Gerónimo Ortega e hijos de Ibarra, 1789);

*Los Claros varones de España: Fernando del Pulgar,* edited by Jesús Domínguez Bordona (Madrid: Espasa-Calpe, 1923; revised, 1954; revised again, 1969);

*Claros varones de Castilla: A Critical Edition,* edited by Robert Brian Tate (Oxford: Clarendon Press, 1971);

*Coplas de Mingo Revulgo, glosadas por Hernando del Pulgar,* edited by Federico Sainz de Robles (Madrid: Espasa-Calpe, 1972);

*Las Coplas de Mingo Revulgo,* edited by Vivana Brodey (Madison, Wis.: Hispanic Seminary of Medieval Studies, 1986);

*Los claros varones de España (ca. 1483): A Semi-Paleographic Edition,* edited by Joseph Abraham Levi (New York: Peter Lang, 1996).

OTHER: *La toma de Antequera: Textos de Ben al-Jatib, Fernán Pérez de Guzmán, Fernando del Pulgar, Alvár García de Santa, María y Ghillebert de Lannoy, prólogo y versión moderna del Francisco López Estrada,* edited by Francisco López Estrada (Antequera: F. Vera, 1964).

Hernando del Pulgar, also known as Fernando de Pulgar and Fernando del Pulgar, was a diplomat and humanist historian who lived during the second half of the fifteenth century. He is mainly known for two works, the *Crónica de los muy altos y esclarecidos reyes cathólicos don Fernando y doña Ysabel de gloriosa memoria* (Chronicle of the Very Powerful and Excellent Catholic Monarchs Ferdinand and Isabella of Glorious Memory, 1482–1490) and the *Claros Varones de Castilla* (Illustrious Noblemen of Castile, 1486), the latter of which is considered by many scholars to be his masterpiece. Both works show Pulgar's gratitude and dedication to King Fernando II of Aragon (who became Fernando V of Castile) and Queen Isabel I of Castile; he was especially devoted to the queen, to whom he dedicated the *Claros Varones de Castilla*. In addition, these works reflect Pulgar's accomplishments and personal involvement in the domestic and foreign politics of the time. He visited the French royal court in Paris and the Holy See on official business for the monarchs.

Pulgar was one of the most talented writers of late-medieval Spanish letters. His prose is well balanced and couched in a simple style but imbued with great eloquence. In all of his writings he expresses his opinions, which are at times pungent though always guided by truth and compassion. Almost all of his works are historical in nature.

In addition to the *Crónica de los muy altos y esclarecidos reyes cathólicos don Fernando y doña Ysabel de gloriosa memoria* and the *Claros Varones de Castilla,* Pulgar wrote the *Glosa de las Coplas de Mingo Revulgo* (Commentary on Mingo Revulgo's Couplets, 1485). The *Crónica de Enrique IV* (Chronicle of Enrique IV) and the *Historia de los Reyes Moros de Granada* (History of the Muslim Kings of Granada), also known as the *Tratado genealógico de los Reyes de Granada* (Genealogical Treatise of the Kings of Granada), are attributed to him, but no copies of these works are known to be extant. According to Antonio Nicolás, Pulgar also wrote the *Crónica del ínclito y poderoso Señor D. Henrique hijo del Señor D. Juan el II* (Chronicle of the Illustrious and Powerful King Don Enrique, Son of Lord Don Juan II). In the early twentieth century the only known manuscript of this work was owned by Gaspar Ibáñez of Segovia; previously, it had belonged to the Bibliotheca Villumbrosiana. Its whereabouts today are unknown.

Little information is available about Pulgar's private life. His name indicates that he was born in El Pulgar (The Thumb), a hamlet in the province of Toledo. Some scholars, however, point to the city of Toledo itself as his birthplace, while José Amador de los Ríos is of the opinion that he was born in Madrid. No substantial support exists for any of these claims, though Toledo seems more likely than Madrid. The dates of Pulgar's birth and death are also unknown; in all likelihood, he was born no later than 1436 and lived until about 1492 or 1493 or, according to some scholars, as late as 1500.

Hernando seems to have been a first- or second-generation *converso*. Also known as *marranos* (pigs), *anusim* (Hebrew for "the forced ones"), new Christians, and crypto-Jews, the *conversos* were Sephardim who were forced to convert to Catholicism. In Spain, Jews who had refused to convert were expelled in 1492; in Portugal, they were forced to convert in 1496–1497. Scattered and fragmentary documents in various archives in Toledo, including the records of the parish of San Vincente and the Church of Santiago in Cigales, indicate that Pulgar's father was Diego Rodríguez de Toledo, also known as Diego Rodríguez del Pulgar, an *escrivano* (notary public). During the first half of the fifteenth century most of the *escrivanos* of Toledo were *conversos*. A *converso* origin can also be inferred from Hernando de Pulgar's writings, in which he expresses his belief in individual freedom.

In both Spain and Portugal, some of those who converted were suspected of "Judaizing"—secretly practicing Judaism. Many were tried, convicted, and sentenced on such charges by the Inquisition, which was established in Spain in 1478 and in Portugal in 1536. Pulgar was never accused of Judaizing; on the contrary, he was praised by the Catholic Monarchs for his devotion to Roman Catholicism.

For wealthy Jews, conversion meant new opportunities for advancement in political and social circles, and Pulgar was raised and educated at the court of King Juan II of Castile. His acquaintances would have included clergymen, nobles, and members of royal families, and he would have received a rigorous education in Greek, Latin, and rhetoric, as well as reading the works of contemporary Spanish writers and of foreign authors such as the Italians Dante Alighieri, Francesco Petrarch, and Giovanni Boccaccio.

Juan II died in 1454 and was succeeded by his son, Enrique IV. On 22 May 1458 Pulgar was in Madrid signing documents that legalized the Cofradía del Campo de Arriaga (Brotherhood of the Country of Arriaga) in the county of Álava, which, since 1332, had been under the protection of the kingdom of Castile and Leon. In 1463, together with Diego de Ayala and Juan de Villanueva, Pulgar translated from the French King Louis XI's resolution of the disputes between Enrique IV and King Juan II of Navarre. On many occasions Pulgar interceded on Enrique IV's behalf in trying to make peace with the archbishop of Toledo, the irascible Alonso Carrillo y Acuña. In 1473, also on behalf of Enrique IV, Pulgar was in Rome on a diplomatic mission to Pope Sixtus IV. Despite Pulgar's known involvement in Enrique IV's court, no written records name him as one of the king's secretaries.

In 1474 Isabel, who had married Prince Fernando of Aragon in 1469, was crowned queen of Castile. Liv-

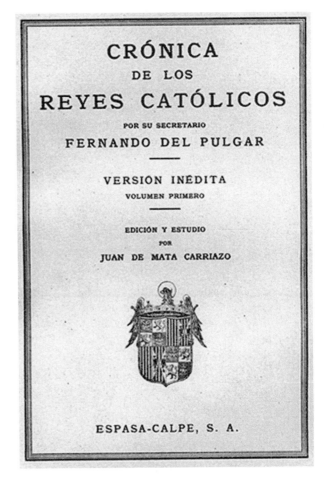

CRÓNICA
DE LOS
REYES CATÓLICOS

POR SU SECRETARIO
FERNANDO DEL PULGAR

VERSIÓN INÉDITA
VOLUMEN PRIMERO

EDICIÓN Y ESTUDIO
POR
JUAN DE MATA CARRIAZO

ESPASA-CALPE, S. A.

*Front cover for the first volume of the 1943 Madrid edition of Hernando del Pulgar's* Crónica de los muy altos y esclarecidos reyes cathólicos don Fernando y doña Ysabel de gloriosa memoria, *written between 1482 and 1490 (Walter Royal Davis Library, University of North Carolina at Chapel Hill)*

ing at court, Pulgar had the opportunity to witness first-hand the power games, intrigues, and political subterfuges of the Crown and the noble families who competed with, opposed, and even tried to overthrow the central power. An astute ruler, Isabel quelled these rivalries and created a unified state under the Castilian monarchy.

In February and again in June 1475 Pulgar traveled to Paris as the Castilian special ambassador to the court of Louis XI. On his first trip he carried the news of Enrique IV's death and Isabel's accession to the throne. His second assignment, which obliged him to remain in Paris for four months, was to plan the marriage of Charles—the newborn heir to the French throne and future King Charles VIII—to Fernando and Isabel's daughter, Princess Isabel of Castile, as well as to negotiate the restitution of the counties of Rosellón and Cerdeña to the kingdom of Aragon. On his return to Castile, the Catholic Monarchs named Pulgar councillor of state.

Sometime between 1475 and 1482 Pulgar left the court and went to one of his places of residence, either in Toledo or in Madrid, with his wife and daughter. He spent his time there reading his famous and rare books—more than eighty—coveted by many scholars of the time, and taught about fifty students who were preparing for careers in administration. During this time he wrote most of his letters. They survive in a single manuscript in the Biblioteca Menéndez Pelayo in Santander, which, however, includes only fifteen of them; the Toledo edition of 1486 brings the total to thirty-two.

The letters deal with contemporary political and military events, such as the failed marriage of Afonso V of Portugal and Princess Juana, the daughter of Enrique IV; the establishment of the Inquisition in Seville; the war against the Muslims in Granada; the sieges of Tájara and Montánchez; and the conquest of Zahara and Alhama. Most of the addressees are illustrious figures of the time, including Afonso V; Carrillo y Acuña; Fernando's uncle, Enrique Enríquez; the conde de Tendilla, Don Íñigo de Mendoça; and Queen Isabel, to whom he writes in a familiar but respectful tone. Some of the letters are full-fledged essays or treatises. A long and moving letter to his daughter, who became a nun at age twelve, and an epistle to his physician denouncing, in a lighthearted manner, the misery of old age, are moralistic-philosophical disquisitions.

In 1482 Pulgar was summoned back to court by Isabel and appointed royal historiographer. One of his letters of that year, however, indicates that he had started composing his chronicle before Isabel ordered him to move to the court: he informs the queen that he will meet her soon with a copy of the manuscript, so that she can examine it. In his capacity as royal chronicler Pulgar accompanied the monarchs to the 1485 siege of Cambil, the 1487 siege of Málaga, and the 1489 siege of Baza.

While working on his chronicle Pulgar decided to write brief biographies of some illustrious Spaniards who, for one reason or another, had not been given the attention that he thought they deserved. The result was the *Claros Varones de Castilla*. He conceived the work as a continuation of Fernán Pérez de Guzmán's *Generaciones y semblanzas* (Generations and Sketches, 1455), which ends with the reign of Juan II. *Claros Varones de Castilla* consists of brief profiles of a selected group of twenty-six noblemen from Castile and León who, Pulgar believes, are valuable examples for the politically new, yet historically ancient, Spanish people. The name of each subject, followed by his noble title, appears at the beginning of each entry, followed by the individual's family ties to the Crown and to the rest of the foreign and domestic aristocracy. Next, Pulgar provides a physical description of the person, including his customary attire. Though some of these descriptions are caricatures, most of the physical characteristics mentioned are few or vague and similar to each other, such as the often-recurring "de medianna estatura" (of medium height). The intellectual and moral characteristics of each subject are delineated and are enriched with examples of his bravery—or, in the case of a physically weak subject, of his great intellect. Unlike Pérez de Guzmán's *Generaciones y semblanzas,* which includes both virtuous and not-so-virtuous characters, the *Claros Varones de Castilla* depicts only those whose actions, in Pulgar's estimation, glorified Castile. Also, most of the subjects treated in *Claros Varones de Castilla* had descendants who were holding high office at the time Pulgar composed the work. Interspersed throughout *Claros Varones de Castilla* are references to classical and early Christian authors such as Aristotle, Seneca, Virgil, and St. Jerome, as well as to outstanding political and mythical figures of antiquity such as Publius Horacius Cocles, Caius Mucius Scaevola, Lucius Junius Brutus, Lucius Torquatus Manlius, Lucius Superbus Tarquinius, and the Etruscan king Persena.

Pulgar's *Glosa de las Coplas de Mingo Revulgo* was published around 1485 and dedicated to Pedro Fernández de Velasco, second conde de Haro and constable of Castile. It consists of enthusiastic praise of the anonymous *Coplas de Mingo Revulgo,* a poem of thirty-two nine-line stanzas probably written around 1460. Besides Pulgar himself, possible authors advanced by critics include the Franciscan friar Iñigo de Mendoza and the poets Juan de Mena and Rodrigo de Cota. (Mena and Cota are also suspected of being the author of the first part of the *Tragicomedia de Calisto y Melibea* [Tragicomedy of Callisto and Melibea, 1499], better known as the *Celestina.*)

Presented in the form of a dialogue between two shepherds, Mingo Revulgo and Gil Arrebato, the poem is a satire of the policies of Enrique IV. Mingo Revulgo attacks Enrique IV, disguised here as the shepherd Candaulo, and his protégé, Beltrán de la Cueva, for the many problems that the country is facing. Gil Arrebato, who is of noble lineage and is described as a prophet or a fortune-teller, acknowledges that some of the blame rests with Candaulo but insists that the commoners are also at fault. In his commentary Pulgar denounces the corruption and vices of the court of Enrique IV, which, together with the errors made by the monarch, almost brought the kingdom to an end.

Pulgar's chronicle of the Catholic Monarchs appears to have been completed in 1490: it halts abruptly, and with no explanation, in its account of that year. A laudatory and, at times, excessively embellished work, often inaccurate and at times fraught with affectation, it is still a decisive improvement over the traditional chronicle. Using the Roman historian Livy as a model, Pulgar presents his characters in a classically heroic way, resulting in a dramatic literary work.

The *Crónica* is divided into three books, preceded by nine preliminary chapters describing the reign of Juan II, the accession to the throne of Enrique IV, and the events preceding the marriage of Fernando and Isabel. The first book of the *Crónica* proper consists of eleven chapters, ending with the death of Enrique IV. The purpose of these first twenty chapters is to counteract the notion that Isabel had illegally usurped the throne—as, in fact, she had. The queen had summoned Pulgar from his home in 1482 and asked him to write the history for that very reason: she and Fernando knew that they could count on his loyalty and talent to legitimize their rule. The second book of the *Crónica* describes the reign of Fernando and Isabel, and the incomplete third book is devoted to the war of Granada, which did not end until 1492.

The prologue to the 1780 Valencia edition of the *Crónica de los Reyes Católicos* says that on Pulgar's death the manuscript came into the hands of Lorenzo Galíndez de Carvajal, who gave it to the humanist grammarian Antonio de Nebrija. The *Crónica* was published twice in Granada, in 1545 and 1550, in Latin by Nebrija's son Sancho, who was under the impression that his father was the author. The original Castilian version was published in 1565 in Valladolid by Nebrija's grandson, still bearing Nebrija's name as author. It was finally published under Pulgar's name in Saragossa in 1567.

Even though Hernando del Pulgar was employed by the monarchs, and his works were subject to their approval, his writings reflect his views as a *converso* in a Castile in transition from medieval to modern times. Pulgar's message is that people are essentially free and cannot be forever locked into the social status into which they were born; human equality is more important than aristocratic lineage. He believed that the monarchs he served were willing to give a voice, though limited, to people who had theretofore been reduced to silence. He was one of the most interesting characters of the reign of the Catholic Monarchs, as well as, in the eyes of some critics, the first historian of the modern era.

**Bibliographies:**

Antonio Nicolás, ed., *Bibliotheca Hispana Nova,* 2 volumes (Madrid: J. de Ibarra, 1783, 1788);

Robert Singerman, *The Jews in Spain and Portugal: A Bibliography* (New York: Garland, 1975);

José Simón Díaz, "Pulgar (Hernando de)," in *Manual de bibliografía de la literatura española,* third edition (Madrid: Gredos, 1980), p. 158;

Charles B. Faulhaber, "Pulgar, Hernando del," in his *Bibliography of Old Spanish Texts,* third edition (Madison, Wis.: Hispanic Seminary of Medieval Studies, 1985), p. 291.

**References:**

David Fintz Altabé, *Spanish and Portuguese Jewry before and after 1492* (New York: Sepher-Hermon, 1993);

José Amador de los Ríos, *Estudios históricos, políticos y literarios sobre los judíos de España* (Madrid: Díaz, 1848);

Amador de los Ríos, *Historia de los judíos de España y Portugal,* 3 volumes (Madrid: Ediciones Turner, 1984);

Juan de Mata Arroquia Carriazo, "Las arengas de pulgar," *Anales de la Universidad Hispalense,* 15 (1954): 43–74;

Yitzhak Baer, *History of the Jews in Spain,* 2 volumes, translated by Louis Schoffman (Philadelphia: Jewish Society of America, 1961, 1966);

Eloy Benito Ruano, *Los infantes de Aragón* (Madrid: Escuela de Estudios Medievales, 1952);

Benito Ruano, *Los orígenes del problema converso* (Barcelona: Ediciones El Albir, 1976);

Benito Ruano, *Toledo en el siglo XV: Vida política* (Madrid: Consejo Superior de Investigaciones Científicas, Escuela de Estudios Medievales, 1961);

Carlos Cambronero, "Cosas de antaño," *Revista Contemporánea,* 4 (1893): 59–66;

Francisco Cantera Burgos, *Alvar García de Santa María y su familia de conversos: Historia de la Judería de Burgos y de sus conversos mas egregios* (Madrid: Instituto Arias Montano, 1952);

Cantera Burgos, "Fernando del Pulgar y los conversos," *Sefarad,* 4 (1944): 295–348;

Julio Caro Baroja, *Los judíos en la España moderna e contemporánea* (Madrid: Istmo, 1978);

Francisco Cerdà y Rico, ed., *Crónica de D. Alfonso el Onceno de este nombre, de los reyes que reinaron en Castilla y en León,* volume 7 (Madrid: Antonio de Sancha, 1787);

Cerdà y Rico, ed., *Crónica del Rey D. Alonso VIII: Memórias históricas de la vida y acciones del Rey D. Alonso el Noble, octavo del nombre, recogidas por el Marqués de Mondexar,* volume 4 (Madrid: Antonio de Sancha, 1783);

Marcella Ciceri, "La tradizione manoscritta delle *Coplas de Mingo Revulgo," Quaderni di Lingue e Letterature,* 1 (1976): 191–201;

Antonio Domínguez Ortiz, *Los judeo-conversos en España y América* (Madrid: Istmo, 1988);

John Edwards, *The Jews in Christian Europe, 1400–1700* (London: Routledge, 1991);

José Fradejas Lebrero, "La patria de Fernando del Pulgar," *Epos: Revista de Filogía,* 6 (1990): 469–475;

Jocelyn Nigel Hillgarth, *The Spanish Kingdoms, 1250–1516,* 2 volumes (Oxford: Clarendon Press, 1976, 1978);

Marcelino Menéndez y Pelayo, *Historia de los heterodoxos españoles,* 3 volumes (Madrid: Librería Católica de San José, 1880–1881);

Emilio Mitre Fernández, *Judaísmo y cristianismo: Raíces de un gran conflicto histórico* (Madrid: Istmo, 1980);

Abraham Aaron Newman, *The Jews in Spain: Their Social, Political, and Cultural Life during the Middle Ages* (Philadelphia: Jewish Publication Society of America, 1942);

Joseph F. O'Callaghan, *A History of Medieval Spain* (Ithaca, N.Y.: Cornell University Press, 1983), p. 581;

María Victoria Pineda, "Las consolaciones de Fernando del Pulgar," in *Medioevo y Literatura, I–IV: Actas del V Congreso de la Asociación Hispánica de Literatura Medieval, Granada, 27 septiembre–1 octubre 1993,* edited by Juan Paredes (Granada: Universidad de Granada, 1995), pp. 65–73;

Julio Puyol y Alonso, "Los cronistas de Enrique IV: Hernando del Pulgar," *Boletín de la Real Academia de la Historia,* 79, no. 6 (1921): 126–135;

Bernard F. Reilly, *The Medieval Spains* (Cambridge: Cambridge University Press, 1993);

Martín de Riquer, Conde de Casa Dávalos, *Vida caballeresca en la España del siglo XV: Discurso leído el día 16 de mayo de 1965 en su recepción publica* (Madrid: Real Academia Española, 1965);

Julio Rodríguez-Puértolas, "Sobre el autor de las *Coplas de Mingo Revulgo,*" in *Homenaje a Rodríguez-Moñino: Estudios de erudición que le ofrecen sus amigos o discípulos hispanistas norteamericanos,* 2 volumes (Madrid: Editorial Castália, 1966), II: 131–142;

José Luis Romero, *Fernán Pérez de Guzmán y su actitud histórica* (Buenos Aires: Facultad de Filosofía y Letras, 1945);

Romero, "Sobre la biografía española del s. XV y los ideales de la vida," *Cuadernos de Historia de España,* 1–2 (1944): 115–138;

Cecil Roth, *A History of the Marranos* (Philadelphia: Jewish Publishing Society, 1947);

Cesar Silió y Cortés, *Don Álvaro de Luna y su tiempo* (Madrid: Espasa-Calpe, 1935);

Charlotte Stern, "The *Coplas de Mingo Revulgo* and the Early Spanish Drama," *Hispanic Review,* 44, no. 4 (1976): 311–332;

George Ticknor, *History of Spanish Literature,* 3 volumes (Boston: Osgood, 1872), I: 444–447;

William Thomas Walsh, *Isabel of Spain: The Last Crusader* (New York: Tudor, 1938);

Eva Maria Zuber, *Fernan Perez de Guzman und Hernando del Pulgar: Ein Beitrag zur Geschichte des literarischen Portraets in Spanien* (Basel: Satzservice PICA, 1971).

# Fernando de Rojas

(circa 1475 – 8 April 1541)

Joseph T. Snow
*Michigan State University*

WORK: *Celestina,* also known as *Comedia de Calisto y Melibea* and *Tragicomedia de Calisto y Melibea* (ca. 1495)

**Manuscript:** Madrid, Biblioteca de Palacio MS 1520, a truncated manuscript of eight folios, written in two hands, comprising the beginning of act 1. It shows revisions and may be part of a copy used by unknown printers. It became widely known only in 1990 in photographic facsimile and transcription.

**First publication:** *Comedia de Calisto y Melibea* (Burgos: Fadrique Alemán de Basilea, 1499).

**Early editions:** *Comedia de Calisto y Melibea* (Toledo: Pedro Hagembach, 1500); *Comedia de Calisto y Melibea* (Seville: Estanislao Polono, 1501); *Libro de Calixto y Melibea y dela puta vieja Celestina* (Seville, 1502); *Tragicomedia de Calisto y Melibea* (Saragossa: Jorge Coci, 1507); *Tragicomedia de Calisto y Melibea* (Seville: Jacob Cromberger, ca. 1511); *Tragicomedia de Calisto y Melibea* (Valencia: Juan Joffre, 1514); *Tragicomedia de Calisto y Melibea* (Toledo: Remón de Petras, 1526); *Tragicomedia de Calisto y Melibea* (Toledo: Juan de Ayala, 1538); *Celestina: Tragicomedia de Calisto y Melibea* (Salamanca: Mathias Gast, 1570); *Celestina: Tragicomedia de Calisto y Melibea* (Antwerp: Officina Plantiniana, 1599); *Celestina: Tragicomedia de Calisto y Melibea* (Milan: Juan Baptista Bidelo Librero, 1622).

**Standard editions:** *La Celestina: Tragicomedia de Calisto y Melibea,* 2 volumes, edited by Eugenio Krapf, introduction by Marcelino Menéndez y Pelayo (Vigo: E. Krapf, 1899, 1900); *La Celestina,* edited by Dorothy S. Severin (Madrid: Alianza, 1969); *La Celestina,* edited by Severin (Madrid: Cátedra, 1976); *Celestina: Critical Edition,* 2 volumes, edited by Miguel Marciales, Illinois Medieval Monographs, no. 1 (Urbana & Chicago: University of Illinois Press, 1985); *Comedia o Tragicomedia de Calisto y Melibea,* edited by Peter E. Russell (Madrid: Castalia, 1991); *La Celestina,* edited by F. J. Lobera and others, Biblioteca Clásica, no. 20 (Bar-

celona: Ediciones Crítica, 2000); *Celestina comentada,* edited by Louise Fothergill-Payne, Enrique Fernández Rivera, and Peter Fothergill-Payne (Salamanca: Universidad de Salamanca, 2002).

**Facsimile editions:** *Comedia de Calisto y Melibea* [facsimile of Burgos 1499 edition] (New York: De Vinne Press, 1909); *Libro de Calixto y Melibea y dela puta vieja Celestina* [facsimile of Seville 1502 edition] (Valencia: La Fonte Que Mana y Corre, 1958); *Comedia de Calisto y Melibea* [facsimile of Toledo 1500 edition] (Cologny-Geneva: Bibliotheca Bodmeriana, 1961); *Comedia de Calisto y Melibea* [facsimile of Burgos 1499 edition] (New York: Hispanic Society of America, 1970); *Tragicomedia de Calixto y Melibea* [facsimile of Valencia 1514 edition] (Madrid: Espasa-Calpe, 1975); *Edición facsimilar de La Celestina* [facsimile of Toledo 1538 edition] (Barcelona: Ediciones Antiguas, 1983); *Comedia de Calisto y Melibea,* edited by Emilio de Miguel [facsimile of Burgos 1499 edition] (Salamanca: Universidad de Salamanca, 1999); *Tragicomedia de Calisto y Melibea* [facsimile of Saragossa 1507 edition] (Toledo: Antonio Pareja, 1999); *Tragicomedia de Calisto y Melibea,* edited by Nicasio Salvador Miguel and Santiago López Ríos [facsimile of Valencia 1514 edition] (Valencia: Institució Alfons el Magnànim, 1999).

**Editions in English:** *The Spanish Bawd, Represented in Celestina: Or, The Tragicke-Comedy of Calisto and Melibea. Wherein is contained, besides the pleasantnesse and sweetenesse of the stile, many Philosophicall sentences, and profitable Instructions necessary for the younger sort: Shewing the deceits and subtilties housed in the bosomes of false servants, and Cunny-catching Bawds,* translated by James Mabbe as Don Diego Puede-Ser (London: Printed by John Beale, sold by Robert Allot, 1631); *The Celestina: A Novel in Dialogue,* translated by Lesley Byrd Simpson (Berkeley & Los Angeles: University of California Press, 1955); *Celestina: A Play in Twenty-one Acts Attributed to Fernando*

*De Rojas,* translated by Mack Hendricks Singleton (Madison: University of Wisconsin Press, 1958); *Celestina; or, The Tragi-Comedy of Calisto and Melibea,* translated by Phyllis Hartnoll (London: Dent / New York: Dutton, 1959); *The Spanish Bawd: La Celestina. Being the Tragicomedy of Calisto and Melibea,* translated by J. M. Cohen (Harmondsworth, U.K.: Penguin, 1964; New York: New York University Press, 1966); *La Celestina: Tragicomedy of Calisto and Melibea,* translated by Wallace Woolsey (New York: Las Americas, 1969).

Fernando de Rojas is generally recognized as the author, or possibly the co-author, of a single literary work popularly known as *Celestina.* The work was an immediate best-seller in Spain when it first appeared in print in 1499, and it was rapidly translated into other European languages: by 1525 close or loose versions existed in Italian, French, German, and English; by mid century the list expanded to Hebrew (now lost) and Dutch. By 1640, when the work was placed on the Index of Prohibited Books by the Roman Catholic Church for the second time, more than ninety Spanish-language editions printed in Spain, Italy, and the Netherlands existed, and it had been rendered into Latin in 1624 by the German scholar Kaspar von Barth. *Celestina* was not only translated but also adapted: its plot intrigues and boldly conceived characters inspired an anonymous popular ballad of six hundred lines around 1510, an actable eclogue in 1513, three continuations, many imitations, and a complete verse translation by Juan de Sedeño in 1540; it influenced theatrical works by major Spanish dramatists from Juan del Encina and Bartolomé de Torres Naharro through Lope de Vega to Calderón de la Barca, whose stage version of *Celestina* is now lost.

*Celestina* continues to exert a strong fascination on Spanish readers in the twenty-first century. It is consistently ranked as Spain's second masterpiece, closely shadowing Miguel de Cervantes Saavedra's *Don Quijote de la Mancha* (1605, 1616). Additionally, like *quijote* and *don juan, celestina* has become a common noun in Spanish: it denotes the traditional type of the Latin *lena* (old woman go-between, procuress, or bawd).

In comparison to other Spanish authors of the period, little is known about Rojas. A few important documents concerning him were published in 1902 by Manuel Serrano y Sanz; others were published by Rojas's descendant Fernando del Valle Lersundi in 1925 and 1929; and still others, concerning Rojas's later years in Talavera de la Reina, were published by Inés Valverde Azula in 1992. The major biographical study, Stephen Gilman's *The Spain of Fernando de Rojas* (1972), is based on the scanty historical record and on

Gilman's speculations arising largely from Rojas's belonging to a known *converso* (Jewish convert to Christianity) family.

Rojas was born in the thriving agricultural village of La Puebla de Montalbán in the province of Toledo, almost certainly in the mid 1470s. His grandfather was a Jew who was converted to Catholicism under pressure and then persecuted for secret Judaizing (continuing to practice Jewish rites). Whether the grandson of the original *converso* was a practicing Christian, as Alan D. Deyermond has posited, or a Judaizer, as others have claimed, is not known. Certainly the opening texts of *Celestina*—a letter to a friend, eleven stanzas of acrostic verses, and a prologue—and an epilogue consisting of additional stanzas by the author and by Alonso de Proaza, who corrected an early edition for publication, present a moralist's view of the work that lies between them. They exhort the reader to see the demise of the main characters—the lusting lovers, the go-between, and the two deceitful servants—as a warning to turn from the carnal "dance" of this world, to shun it, and to seek in Christ the certainty of eternal life.

The work most likely first circulated, at least in an embryonic state, as a manuscript copy within the precincts of the University of Salamanca in the mid 1490s; it was probably passed from hand to hand, commented on, and argued about by its bookish readers. In the dedicatory epistle, "El autor a un su amigo" (The Author to a Friend), first printed in the second publication of the sixteen-act *Comedia de Calisto y Melibea* in Toledo in 1500—the missing first folio of the 1499 Burgos printing would have had just enough space to include this text—the author claims to have come into possession of some anonymous *papeles* (papers) that seemed to him to have the potential to serve as a strong moral counterweight to the dangers of lovesickness that are rampant in his country and from which his correspondent suffers. He says that the desire to continue and complete the tale took firm hold on him when he read these anonymous manuscript folios, and asks his readers' indulgence if he, like his predecessor, chooses not to sign his name to the work. Since the claim that a work was written at the request, or for the benefit, of an unnamed party is a common humility topos in this period, many scholars have taken the "friend" to be a mere pretext for the "continuation" and have held that no early partial draft existed. The discovery in 1990 by Charles B. Faulhaber of eight folios from the beginning of act 1, however, provides evidence that these "anonymous papers" were not necessarily a fiction designed by an author who wished, like the supposed first author, to remain anonymous because he was unable to predict how this innovative work, with its graphic talk about sexual matters, would be received either by the general reading public or by the Inquisition's censors. In the epistolary preface the author demurs from claiming success for his effort, explaining that he is a lawyer and that imaginative literature is not his primary occupation. As if to strengthen this assertion, he claims to have devoted a scant two weeks to his completion of the novel during a vacation period when his colleagues were absent.

The epistolary preface is followed in the 1500 Toledo and 1501 Seville editions by eleven eight-line stanzas, purportedly also written by the second author, that elaborate on the idea that the young must be warned of the dire consequences to their souls if they succumb to the beguilements of the uncontrolled sensual love manifested in the sixteen acts that follow. The anonymity of the author of the preface and the verses is, however, exploded by the fact that the first letters of the lines of the verses proclaim that "el bachiller fernando de rojas acabo la comedia de calysto y melybea y fue nascido en la puebla de montalban" (the graduate Fernando de Rojas finished the Comedy of Calisto and Melibea and was born in La Puebla de Montalbán). The acrostic thus reveals the pose of anonymity as a coy teasing of the reader. Attention is called to this declaration of authorship in the verses appended to the end of the work by Proaza, a Valencian humanist working in Salamanca who prepared the text for a now-lost edition; the verses were added in the Toledo printing of the *Comedia de Calisto y Melibea* in 1500. He tells the readers that if they look at the first letters of the eleven opening strophes they will discover the name of the author, his birthplace, and his illustrious "nation." Only the name and place of origin are actually given in the acrostic verses, however. Speculation about the missing third item of information has centered on the possibility of its being an allusion to the fact that Rojas was of the "nation" of Jews; alternatively, the author's "nation" might refer to his membership in the legal profession.

The argument that the pose of anonymity was a means of hiding Rojas's identity from the Inquisition's censors thus cannot be taken seriously. On the other hand, Rojas might have allowed a friend to use his name in the acrostics, providing a shield for a still unknown and, therefore, truly anonymous author.

The introductory enigmas do not end here. In the editions of the expanded twenty-one-act *Tragicomedia de Calisto y Melibea* a new prologue was added to explain the added length and new title of the work. The question then arises as to when this prologue was written. The first extant Spanish copies of the *Tragicomedia de Calisto y Melibea* were printed by Jorge Coci in Saragossa in 1507; the third exemplar of the *Comedia de Calisto y Melibea* had been printed in 1501, so a six-year lacuna

*Title page for the earliest known extant edition (in the Bibliotheca Bodmeriana, Geneva) of Fernando de Rojas's* Celestina, *published under its original title in Toledo in 1500 by Pedro Hagembach (from* Celestinesca, *9, no. 2 [1985]; Thomas Cooper Library, University of South Carolina)*

exists in the early printing history of *Celestina*. There had been a growing demand for the work since it was first circulated, and, one gathers from the new prologue, readers wanted the central tale of misguided love to be more protracted. The colophon of the 1514 Valencia printing of the *Tragicomedia de Calisto y Melibea* states that it was based on a copy seen in Salamanca in 1500, but no further trace of this edition has been found. An edition may have been printed in Toledo by Pedro Hagembach in 1500; the colophons of several extant editions claim to have been printed in Seville in 1502, although typographical investigations have shown that none is earlier than 1510. The lack of such editions does not mean that the work was not printed in Seville or elsewhere in 1502, only that no copies of such editions have survived. Editions of the *Tragicomedia de Calisto y Melibea* must have existed before 1506: the first Italian translation was printed in Rome in January 1506, and its preface is dated 1505 by the translator, Alfonso Ordóñez, a Spaniard residing in Italy.

The prologue broaches many topics, but its thematic center is a quotation from the pre-Socratic philosopher Heraclitus: "omnia secundum litem fiunt," which is paraphrased by the author as "todas las cosas ser criadas a manera de contienda o batalla" (all things are produced as if in conflict or battle). He dedicates much space to this notion, citing many examples: storms, earthquakes, windstorms, tempestuous seas, summer and winter, birds of prey, reptiles, sea creatures, and so on. And if conflict is the norm everywhere in nature, he questions whether it should be any less so in human life from childhood to old age. This discussion leads up to his main point: readers are contentious in their understanding, for some are capable of deep reading, while others capture only surface meanings, and no ten readers of the work will agree on the import of every passage. Even the printers have intervened, he says, making his intentions less clear by editing and correcting according to their own lights, adding act summaries, and disputing the title of the work. In writing this prologue, the ostensible second author has resolved the classification of the work by rebaptizing it a 'tragicomedy.' He confesses to capitulating to readers' clamoring for an extended love affair for Calisto and Melibea, reluctantly applying his pen to the work for a second time and adding five new acts with no real hope that the new material will satisfy all readers any more than the original did. Once conflicts are set loose on this earth, he says, each new episode unchains others in a never-ending process. He insists that these new literary efforts come at the expense of his primary calling (jurisprudence is not specifically mentioned) and even of his leisure time. He adheres to the notion that he is continuing the work of a first author, identifying himself with the author of the epistolary preface who extended the work of the unknown originator of the delightful and inventive *papeles*.

The prologue reminds the reader of the author's intention, stated in the epistolary preface, to provide an antidote to the lovesickness of the young: the tragicomedy has, "de más de su agradable y dulce stilo muchas sentencias filosofales, y avisos muy necesarios para mancebos, monstrando les los engaños que están encerrados en servientes y alcahuetas" (besides its pleasant and sweet style, many philosophical maxims and warnings of vital necessity for young men, showing them the treachery practiced by servants and go-betweens). The point is repeated in a note between the prologue and the general summary of the work, placed there by the author or by the printer: "Síguese la Comedia o *Tragicomedia* de Calisto y Melibea, compuesta en reprehensión de los locos enamorados, que, vencidos en su desordenado apetito, a sus amigas llaman y dizen ser su Dios. Asi mesmo fecha en aviso de los engaños de las alcahuetas y malos y lisonjeros sirvientes" (The Following is the Comedy or Tragicomedy of Calisto

and Melibea, written to chastise love-crazed young men who, overcome by their disordered appetites, refer to their sweethearts as being their God. Also written as warning against the deceits of go-betweens and of evil and flattering servants).

What emerges from the preliminary texts is that *Celestina* was the product of a slow accretion of blocks of material, from the "papers" to the comedy and then to the tragicomedy. The preliminary materials are read today as part of a single work, but they, too, appeared over time, some in the various editions of the comedy, others, later, in the editions of the tragicomedy. These editions include new acts and an extensive catalogue of textual suppressions and additions that shape the reception of the text for later readers. The acrostic verses undergo modifications; one of the concluding stanzas is modified to stress Christian values even more; a twenty-second act appears in three Toledo editions between 1526 and 1538 and then vanishes. Printing errors creep into each edition, and the task of the corrector—the professional reader at the press in charge of guaranteeing an updated and trustworthy printed text—becomes more and more challenging. Later editions, such as the Mathias Gast edition printed in Salamanca in 1570, often seek to be more correct so as to assert their authority and increase sales. The standard title began to appear in Spanish editions when the name *Celestina* was added around 1569—it had appeared earlier in Italian and French translations—and *Tragicomedia de Calisto y Melibea* became the subtitle. Almost one hundred identified editions of the tragicomedy were printed from 1507 until it was placed on the Index of Prohibited Books by the Roman Catholic Church in 1632 and again in 1640. The final Spanish printing, by Carlos Labayen in Pamplona in 1634, was a Spanish-French dual edition that had been printed in Rouen the year before.

*Celestina* escaped the notice of the Inquisition for quite a long time, in part owing to the moralizing language in the preliminary and concluding materials. Even so, a few phrases were routinely singled out for censure and can be seen inked out in the extensive collection of copies of the work in the Spanish National Library in Madrid. These passages are principally statements in which Calisto proclaims that he worships Melibea and that she is his God. Stanzas at the end of the book confirm the didactic intent that is uppermost in the vivid presentation of Celestina's seductive world of disruptive and destructive passions. The first three octets, according to the rubrics, are by the author, who exhorts readers to turn to God to avoid the punishment of these tragic lovers, whose story has been so grippingly told, despite its calamitous—and, for the intelligent reader, instructive—consequences. He asks not to be judged as a frivolous writer, for he is, in fact, a God-fearing man. If the eroticism, lasciviousness, greed, and other sinful behaviors depicted in the work have been graphically presented, it was done to challenge readers so that they might be able to distinguish the good lessons to be had from the reprehensible behaviors so vividly modeled.

These sentiments dovetail neatly with the exposition in the prologue of how contradictory readings are the inevitable result of different kinds of readers. Some will be able to penetrate to the deeper moral frame informing the text; others will understand only parts of what happens on the surface. The entire spectrum of readers may feel well served by the text, but only those who resonate with the author's true intentions, repeated in these stanzas, will have read him accurately.

These stanzas are followed by the verses by the corrector, Proaza, who alerts the reader that he or she may possess more power than that of Orpheus, whose music could move stone (or stone-hearted folk): reading this work aloud to the young will cause those who would have indulged in senseless passion to abandon this soul-damning vice. He ends by praising the author, who has duplicated, if not surpassed, in Castilian the triumphs in Latin of Plautus and Nevius in exposing the wiles of false servants and sly women. These praises include what little information one can glean about the author from the work itself.

The historical record picks up Rojas about 1505 in La Puebla de Montalbán. In 1509 he registered as a citizen of the town of Talavera de la Reina, a few miles from his birthplace and also in the province of Toledo. He resided there for the rest of his life, occasionally serving as mayor and holding other municipal offices. His activities in Talavera de la Reina and the offices that he held, so far as they have been documented, are consonant with his having studied law. He married Leonor Álvarez de Montalbán, also of a *converso* family, and they had six children. He died on 8 April 1541. His last will and testament is a typically Christian document: after several standard phrases about his body, mind, and soul, he requests burial in Franciscan garb and disposes of his worldly possessions in a unexceptional manner. Among the books in his library, willed to his eldest son, is a single copy of an undated "libro de Calisto" (book of Calisto). The son, also named Fernando, passed this volume on to a younger brother.

An Inquisition document from a case spanning 1525–1526, when Rojas's father-in-law, Álvaro de Montalbán, was under indictment, lists his family members and describes his daughter, Leonor, as "wife of the graduate Rojas who composed Melibea." This document is the single surviving testimony from the time of the first printing of *Celestina* in 1499 to Rojas's death in

*Title page for the 1501 edition (in the Bilbliothèque Nationale, Paris) published in Seville by Estanislao Polonio ( from* Celestinesca, *9, no. 2 [1985]; Thomas Cooper Library, University of South Carolina)*

1541 that associates his name with the composition of the work. Despite the clear message of the acrostic, none of the editions carries an author's name on the title page. Documents from 1511 and after attest to the presence of the work—by title, never mentioning an author—in various private libraries. Many contemporary authors commented on it, including Feliciano de Silva, who published the first and best of the continuations, the *Segunda Celestina* (Second Celestina), in 1534, and Gaspar Gómez de Toledo, whose *Tercera parte de la tragicomedia de Celestina* (Third Part of the Tragicomedy of Celestina) was published in 1536. *Celestina,* while wildly popular and in the public eye as no other work in its day, curiously managed to elude association with Rojas's name in Spanish literary circles.

Almost no one now takes seriously the candidacies of Juan de Mena or Rodrigo de Cota as the source of the *papeles* on which Rojas claims to have stumbled. Some similarities of theme and lexicon exist with Mena's *Laberinto de la fortuna* (Labyrinth of Fortune, 1444) and Cota's *Diálogo entre el Amor y un Viejo* (Dialogue between Love and an Old Man), but they are slight and do not bear up under close scrutiny with the range of styles in the first act of *Celestina*. Nevertheless, Cota's name was attached to the published work as the "first author" well into the nineteenth century.

The texts enclosing the central fiction are still the source of the disparate opinions among scholars. The matter of authorship—how many authors there were, and how much each contributed—is still an incandescent topic. Many scholars claim that studies of the language, rhetorical style, and use of *sententiae* and proverbial refrains confirm the difference between the long first act and the twenty remaining acts. Others argue that a third author was responsible for the interpolated acts that ushered in the tragicomedy version or divide the acts differently among the supposed authors. Yet other scholars take up the notion that the framing texts are red herrings designed to deflect the attention of both general readers and Inquisition censors from the portrayal in the work of amoral behavior and force them to dwell on the proclaimed Christian intent of exposing certain vices as the source of social ills. In this view, the leading exponent of which is Emilio de Miguel Martínez, *Celestina* can have only a single author, one who is not anxious to reveal his name. In any case, if Rojas is not the author of all or most of *Celestina,* no one has yet proposed a more convincing alternative, though suggestions have ranged from various authors known to have been writing in Salamanca at the end of the fifteenth century to a group collaboration.

The earliest printed editions of the *Comedia de Calisto y Melibea* comprise sixteen acts of pure dialogue, each of which is preceded by a summary of the act that was probably added by the printer. The text does not present itself as a theatrical work to be staged but is more closely cut from the cloth of the closet drama—the humanist comedies of the fourteenth and fifteenth centuries that arrived in Spain from Italy, such as the *Poliscena* (1478) of Leonardo Aretino, which, like *Celestina,* are about arranged love affairs and the complications provided by a series of self-interested intermediaries (go-betweens, cunning servants). Like these popular comedies, the *Comedia* and the *Tragicomedia* were intended for oral readings or, as suggested in the prologue, for interpretation among small circles of friends: the main theme of unceasing conflict in the world is underscored when the author states that, dissonance being the overarching rule of reception, it is no surprise that any time ten people gather to hear the work read aloud each will understand it differently. In his concluding comments Proaza recommends that "Si amas y quieres a mucha atención / Leyendo a Calisto mouer los oyentes, / Cumple que sepas hablar entre dientes, / A vezes con gozo, esperança y passión, / A vezes ayrado con gran turbación. / Finge leyendo mil artes y modos, / Pregunta y responde por boca de todos, / Llorando y riyendo en tiempo y sazón" (If you desire and wish, while reading *Calisto,* to move your audience, you must be able to modulate your voice, now expressing joy, now hope, now passion and, at other moments, anger or a troubled mind; and while you read, imitate using a thousand small artifices: ask and answer using different voices, cry and laugh when it is called for). The practice of silent reading did not become common until later.

The action of *Celestina* begins on a high, though parodic, courtly note and then spirals downward in ever widening circles that lead to a final plaint about the chaos that rules the world and the futility of placing one's trust in worldly pleasures and rewards. While hunting with his hawk, Calisto, an attractive twenty-three-year-old of a noble family, chances upon the beautiful, sheltered, and equally wellborn twenty-year-old Melibea. Contrary to the custom in well-to-do families, she is alone in her garden, with no servant in attendance. Seizing this unexpected but welcome opportunity, Calisto declares his passion for Melibea in hyperbolic courtly rhetoric. Melibea at first responds to these overtures with prudent caution; then, recognizing in them an illicit subtext, she banishes Calisto with an angry and unambiguous rejection that is proper to her station if not to her private feelings.

Calisto seeks the counsel of his manservant Sempronio, who is purportedly seasoned in such matters. Sempronio, seeing through Calisto's courtly pretense and overblown description of Melibea, comprehends that his master really yearns to bed her, and he begins to look for ways in which he can profit from the situation. He pretends to show that women are not worthy of men in a misogynistic argument that is really designed to arouse Calisto's desire to a fever pitch. He then offers to cure his master's lovesickness with the help of an expert practitioner in the arts of love: the old, hairy-faced, and scarred procuress Celestina, who, he assures Calisto, would leap at the opportunity to help. Sempronio is the lover of Elicia, the last remaining girl in Celestina's once-prosperous bordello. Calisto's immediate acceptance of aid from the bawd confirms the true intent behind his impassioned love rhetoric.

As Sempronio pursues his embassy to Celestina's dilapidated home, another of Calisto's servants, the young Pármeno, wishing to gain parity in his master's eyes with Sempronio, warns Calisto of the true nature of this woman. As a boy Pármeno had been raised by Celestina after the death of his mother, Claudina, another of Celestina's whores. Later he had run away and spent nine years with some friars in another town. He describes Celestina's pharmaceutical potions and other semiclandestine activities and declares them all fraudulent. His severely negative portrait of Celestina is based on his experiences with her but is flamboyantly exaggerated because of his desire to please Calisto by offering sound advice and to prevent his master from falling under her corrupting influence. But his horrific descriptions of her as perfumer, seamstress, cosmetician, midwife, procuress, and witch only serve to convince Calisto that she is the perfect person to help him obtain access to, and win, Melibea.

Celestina and Sempronio have arrived at Calisto's door and overheard Pármeno's blunt assessment. Celestina realizes that she must woo Pármeno over to her side, even though she will then have to share any profit from this business three ways instead of two. Sempronio goes along with the plan, although he is no friend of the sanctimonious Pármeno.

Calisto welcomes the go-between, who lives in penury near the riverside tanneries, as effusively as he might a revered noblewoman. The greeting is wasted breath to Celestina, who wishes that he would close his mouth and open his purse. When Calisto and Sempronio leave to fetch the hundred gold coins Calisto will pay her, Celestina seizes the opportunity to introduce herself to and mollify Pármeno. In the course of the conversation she realizes who Pármeno is, and she astutely takes Pármeno down a peg by revealing that his mother, who was her teacher and friend, also practiced all the professions that Pármeno denounced in describing her to Calisto. Regaling him with tales of her experience, Celestina takes on a quasi-maternal role. Pármeno seems progressively charmed by both the sensuous and the profitable opportunities she describes to him. He weakens most when presented with a vision of Areúsa, Elicia's cousin, and her availability through Celestina.

Celestina has used her persuasive powers to bring Pármeno into confederation with herself and Sempronio; but he is even more effectively convinced to redirect his loyalties to her when, shortly after the bawd's departure, Calisto returns and demotes him to stable boy. Pármeno now personally experiences what Celestina has told him of how masters such as Calisto treat their underlings. If loyalty brings rejection, then, perhaps, disloyalty will bring him the benefits and pleasures that Celestina has promised.

Calisto's sexual longings make him impatient, and he commands Sempronio to follow the bawd and urge her to act with haste. Celestina is willing to do so, but she has some second thoughts, which she conceals from Sempronio, about this commission and its potential pitfalls for her. Melibea is the only child of Pleberio, her former neighbor, a merchant whose many businesses have prospered over the past twenty years while Celestina's have fallen on hard times. Celestina's indigence provides an economic motive for her to accept

*Title page for the longer and retitled version (in the British Library), published in Seville in 1511 by Jacob Cromberger (from* Celestinesca, *9, no. 2 [1985]; Thomas Cooper Library, University of South Carolina)*

Calisto's commission, but the fear of being caught and of the consequences, which might include a death sentence at the hands of the civil authorities, gives her pause. Moved by professional pride and a fierce desire to hurt the former neighbor whose good fortunes mock her own, Celestina reasons that she prefers offending Pleberio to angering Calisto. She minimizes her fears by calling on Plutón (the devil) in a late-night conjuration and by reading a series of positive portents on her way to Melibea's house the next day.

Celestina gains entrance to the house by offering to sell some yarn into which she has conjured Plutón's spirit. To him she attributes the serendipitous departure of Melibea's mother, Alisa, whose ailing sister has taken a sudden turn for the worse. Smugly believing that she is performing Christian charity by purchasing Celestina's yarn, Alisa leaves Celestina alone with Melibea, who is to pay for the yarn and then dismiss the old woman. In an artful conversation with Melibea, whose maid, Lucrecia, hovers fearfully in the background as a silent witness, the bawd brings a wide-ranging and flattering discussion of youth and beauty around to the main reason for her visit: Calisto. Offended by this new assault on her virtue, Melibea explodes in a fury; she reveals that she knows all too well what Celestina is and orders the bawd to leave. In truth, however, Melibea harbors a deeper interest in Calisto than her initial rejection of him would imply, and Celestina undermines her rage by inventing a toothache for Calisto.

Melibea, finding in the malady a way gracefully to repent of her anger, allows Celestina to take the girdle, or sash, that she wears around her waist and use it as a quasi-religious talisman to cure Calisto's toothache. The psychological banter of the two women in this long conversation in act 4 is regarded as one of the great triumphs of the author's considerable art of characterization. Celestina has found a coded language—that of suffering and relief—that is acceptable to her high-born quarry. Melibea takes a first crucial step away from her good breeding and family loyalty the moment she requests that Celestina return later, in secret, for a healing prayer that she intends to write out for the relief of Calisto's pain. Melibea is now collaborating with Celestina, Calisto's ambassador and voice; and even though she herself may not be aware of it on a conscious level, her maid, Lucrecia, knows full well that Melibea has promised much and will deliver even more.

Calisto is overwhelmed with Celestina's success and openly treats the sash as a fetish. Stroking and fondling the garment that has been so close to what he desires, he promises to reward the bawd's success with fine new clothing—much to the displeasure of the two servants, who chafe at the idea of indivisible profits. The confederation teeters: the servants are doubly disaffected, neither fond of Calisto nor trusting in Celestina's promises of shared booty. Always alert, Celestina is aware of these mutterings even as she greedily negotiates new rewards for herself. Followed by Pármeno as she takes her leave, Celestina solidifies her grip on him by reminiscing about the grand old times she enjoyed in the constant company of his mother, Claudina, and what deep loyalties they shared. If only the son could be like the mother!

Pármeno reminds Celestina of her promise of a girl for him just as they pass Areúsa's door. A ravishing beauty, Areúsa is of a different class of professional: she has no masters but those of her choosing. Leaving Pármeno hidden to overhear her present his case to Areúsa, Celestina counters each of the girl's excuses not to do her bidding. By stroking her to arousal as she feigns curing her menstrual pain, Celestina leads her to put aside all resistance and render immediate service to Pármeno.

Timid at first, Pármeno spends the night with Areúsa in lovemaking but feels pangs of guilt in the morning. He arranges to meet Areúsa at Celestina's house later, then speeds home to find out whether Calisto has been asking after him and to reveal to Sempronio his new status as a nonvirgin. The consolidation of the anti-Calisto confederation is now complete. While Calisto goes to the Church of the Magdalene to pray for Celestina's success, the servants go to Celestina's house for a special banquet, each with his own paramour and the table richly provisioned with food and drink purloined from Calisto's larder.

Amid the abundance of good meat and excellent wine—Celestina limits her feasting to the latter—Sempronio unwittingly ignites a furious outburst by describing Melibea as *gentil* (lovely). Elicia and Areúsa have at him with scathing denunciations of such beauty as can be purchased by women of Melibea's class, and Areúsa performs a verbal parody of the cruel language used by mistresses to belittle their female servants. Just when Celestina has succeeded in channeling these angry passions into lascivious ones, Lucrecia arrives with an urgent message from her mistress; but she momentarily forgets her errand as she gazes in wonder on the profusion of food and the lusty companionship. Her remarks move Celestina to recall nostalgically the days gone by, when there were many more girls at her table and she was much younger. Wistfully pondering her current poverty and ill fortune, she expresses premonitions of death. The others hang on her words as if spellbound, for Celestina is offering an eloquent example of what all human beings must face when old age and disappointments coincide. Celestina is never more human than in this scene. Lucrecia then recalls her purpose in coming: her mistress is in great pain and needs Celestina's ministrations. Celestina has been waiting for this news.

Act 10 opens with Melibea alone, ruing the fact that women of her class do not have the freedom to express their innermost desires as men do. She is afraid even to guess at the cause of her suffering. With practiced techniques of delay and subterfuge to weaken Melibea's resolve and good breeding, Celestina makes her beg for treatment. When Melibea confesses to herself that the cause of her suffering, Calisto, is also the prescription for its cure, she is overcome with her own daring admission and swoons. Celestina fears that she may have gone too far and that her own life could be in danger if Melibea dies. The love-struck girl recovers, however, and tells Celestina to be quiet so as not to bring the servants running and scandalize the household.

In this moment Melibea has crossed her personal Rubicon; she is a new woman and will henceforth do whatever she must to unite with Calisto and to keep their illicit relationship secret from her parents. In her exuberance she deems Celestina her mistress, faithful servant, and confidante and like Calisto recklessly places her destiny in Celestina's hands. She acknowledges that in sending Calisto her sash, she has given him possession of her body and soul. The cunning bawd promises to arrange a meeting of Melibea and Calisto at midnight.

At this point Melibea's mother returns home unexpectedly; she is suspicious on finding Celestina in her house again so soon and without her permission. Celestina and Melibea lie to explain Celestina's presence, but Alisa warns her daughter against further contact with this treacherous enemy of chastity. Melibea professes to be grateful for the warning, inaugurating her new life of intrigue and deceit and irrevocably breaking the bond of trust with, and filial duty to, her parents.

Celestina reports to the incredulous but joyful Calisto that Melibea is now more disposed to follow and obey him than her own father. He rewards her with a valuable gold chain, which demoralizes her two confederates since the prize cannot easily be divided three ways. She goes off with her payment, never thinking to share it. But the seeds of greed she has sown in Sempronio and Pármeno will soon provide her with a bitter harvest.

The two servants accompany Calisto to his interview with Melibea. To test Calisto, Melibea at first feigns coldness to him and acts as though Celestina had not completed her mission as reported. Calisto's abject misery provides Melibea the evidence she needs of his resolve and desire, and she proclaims herself his slave. Sempronio and Pármeno wait nearby with growing fears of discovery, ready to flee at the first sound of approaching footsteps. A strong door keeps the lovers apart, and their passion grows in proportion to the impossibility of indulging it. Calisto declares that he will have his servants break down the door. Melibea knows that doing so would bring discovery and ruin, and Pármeno and Sempronio want no part of such a rash act. Melibea asks about Calisto's protectors, and he describes them as brave and worthy servants—oblivious to the fact that they would betray him without a second thought. Melibea pleads with Calisto to return to her garden the next night, and he and his "bodyguards" return home.

As Calisto dozes and dreams of Melibea, Sempronio and Pármeno hasten to Celestina's house. They recapitulate for her a version of the events of the evening in which they play the heroes, and demand their share of the loot to replace the weapons that they claim were demolished in Calisto's defense. Celestina refuses, declaring that her words to them were tokens of her friendship rather than promises and telling them

*Title page for the 1514 edition (in the Biblioteca Nacional, Madrid) published in Valencia by Juan Joffre (from* Celestinesca, *9, no. 2 [1985]; Thomas Cooper Library, University of South Carolina)*

that they should claim their rewards from Calisto. Who are they, she rants, to deserve a share of the profits when she has done all the real work? Blinded to the rage that courses through them, she offers them cheap alternatives to their expected material gains, such as procuring other girls for them. A scuffle ensues, and Sempronio, egged on by Pármeno, draws his sword and stabs her; Celestina dies in the arms of Elicia. The two assassins leap from a window and land in the midst of the night patrol.

Sosia, an ignorant stable boy in Calisto's employ, gives his master an account of Sempronio and Pármeno's summary execution at dawn. When Calisto learns that they were beheaded for the murder of Celestina, his initial sense of loss is forgotten; he dismisses all three as corrupt and greedy, his egocentrism overwhelming his humanity. His single-minded purpose is to be with Melibea, and nothing will stop him now.

Calisto returns to Melibea's bower that evening. Sosia and another servant, Tristán, place a ladder against the wall of Melibea's fragrant and sensual garden, and the lovers come together in a powerful and urgent meeting of the flesh that is partly communicated to the reader through the asides of Lucrecia. Though Melibea wished to dismiss her attendant, the egotistical Calisto suggested that she remain to be a witness to his possession of Melibea. Afterward, the ravished Melibea laments that the pleasure she has experienced seems too little to compensate for the loss of her honor; but she quickly recovers from her postcoital depression and urges Calisto not to postpone his next visit.

A sudden noise comes from the street, and Calisto, in a rare show of concern for anyone other than himself, rushes unarmed to the defense of his servants. In his impetuousness he misses a step and falls to his death, his head splattered on the cobblestones below. Melibea declares that she will follow Calisto to the grave, even imitating the manner of his death.

Lucrecia runs to arouse Pleberio from his sleep. Unable to divine the cause of Melibea's distraught state, he offers to call for doctors, herbal remedies, or whatever will avail. Melibea asks only that he fetch a lute for music to soothe her pain. Once Pleberio departs, she locks herself in the house's tower, climbs to its top, and addresses her father below as though from a stage, recapitulating her duplicitous behavior and accepting the blame for betraying him and her mother and the family's good name, for allowing Celestina to conclude Calisto's immoral proposition, for the strength of her passion, for seeking solace in an illicit affair, and for Calisto's death. Bidding her father farewell and asking that her body be buried with her lover's, she commends her spirit to God and leaps to her death. Her body falls from the height in full view of her heartsick father.

Alisa enters, collapsing at the sight of her daughter's corpse. Pleberio, faced with this unimaginable loss and not knowing whether his wife has survived the shock, curses the lure of Love, the promise of Fortune, and the deceit of the World. He has been plunged suddenly into profound loneliness, his investment in ships, orchards, and the very tower of his house now all for naught as he has no heir to whom to bequeath his wealth. He remains alive but with shattered hopes, alone in "hac lachrymarum valle" (this vale of tears). These accusatory concluding words of the text pinpoint the senselessness, the lack of order and control, the relentless chaos into which the rudderless world of *Celestina* has descended. The bottom has been reached; only despair remains, for Pleberio has come face to face with a Godless world. His illusions shattered, he can see the price that has been paid for the trust that others, as well as he, have placed in the material world.

Thus ends the *Comedia de Calisto y Melibea* with act 16. The consummation of the lovers' forbidden passion in act

14 has brought swift and terrible punishment. If the first act, drawn in the likeness of the humanist comedies with their customary happy endings, did inspire a second author to try to transform the work into a tragedy, he certainly succeeded. His pessimistic vision of the world takes precedence over whatever direction the initial author had in mind. His continuation is a deeply moral tale of sin, judgment, and, finally, a terrible retribution.

According to the prologue to the tragicomedy, readers were dissatisfied with the suddenness of the final tragedies and preferred a longer love affair. This reaction motivated either the author of the first continuation–acts 2 through 16–or someone else to devise a series of interpolated acts to expand the action, deepen some of the characterizations, add a few new minor characters, and extend the lovers' trysts to a month of almost nightly encounters. The interpolated acts, commonly referred to as the "Tratado de Centurio" (Story of Centurio), first appear in the 1502 edition. The revision actually begins in act 14, in which Calisto no longer falls from the ladder. In the new finale of that act he walks home, accompanied by Sosia and Tristán. There, alone, he intones a monologue in which he first expresses anger at the municipal judge–a family friend–who summarily executed Sempronio and Pármeno; but then he imagines that the judge must have been protecting him by not allowing a trial that would have sullied his name. The matter resolved to his egotistical satisfaction, Calisto loses himself in memories of making love to Melibea.

In the new act 15, Sosia and Tristán are leaning out a window outside Calisto's chamber. Sosia identifies for Tristán the weeping woman passing along the street as Elicia, who is in search of Areúsa's house. Elicia informs Areúsa of the three deaths, which have devastated her. Areúsa, too, laments the losses; but even as she mourns, she is hatching a plan to make Melibea and Calisto pay for what their illicit affair has caused. She invites Elicia to come and live with her, but Celestina's last protégée refuses. She feels that she cannot abandon the house where she has lived so long, where she learned so much from her departed "mother," and where her clients would expect to find her. The two women then turn to the problem of getting accurate information about Calisto's schedule; Elicia suggests that it can be obtained from Sosia, and Areúsa tells Elicia to leave him to her.

The new act 16 features simultaneous scenes of Pleberio and Alisa planning the wedding of their daughter and the distraught and shamed Melibea eavesdropping with Lucrecia from an adjoining room. Two features of this act are important for characterization. The first is the absolute lack of awareness on the part of Alisa, who cannot imagine that Melibea knows anything about men and assures her husband that she knows she has reared a morally upright daughter. The second is Melibea's declaration to Lucrecia that she wishes never to marry but only and always to be near Calisto and that if her parents wish to enjoy their old age, they must let her choose how she is to spend her youth. This speech allows readers to understand the depth of Melibea's passion. Prophetically, she states that were she to lose her love, she must lose her life as well, for it is only to please him that she is truly alive.

Act 17 picks up the thread of the subplot initiated in act 15. Elicia has discovered that staying on at Celestina's house was a mistake; clients no longer come, and she is miserable. She goes to Areúsa's house to declare an end to her mourning and a return to a more pleasant existence. Sosia knocks at the door; he has been bidden by the scheming Areúsa, who hides her cousin behind a curtain to watch her charm the desired information from the stable boy. Areúsa's persuasive arts are equal to those Celestina had possessed, as if the madam's death has freed her to realize her potential.

In act 18 the two schemers hurry to the house of Centurio, a pimp with whom Areúsa had once been involved. Areúsa bribes him to go to Melibea's garden that night, find Calisto entering or leaving, and start a scuffle and even, possibly, kill Calisto. Elicia feels that a good scare would be sufficient, but Areúsa's class hatred is stronger. Centurio is a braggart but, beneath the braggadocio, as much a coward as Sempronio and Pármeno; after the women have departed, he makes plans to ask the lame Traso to take his place and only to frighten the lovers, not harm them.

The final meeting of the lovers takes place in act 19. As Calisto scales the ladder, he hears Melibea and Lucrecia conversing and decides to wait and listen. The two women evoke the sensuousness of the evening as they sing together of love and desire. Melibea, worried by Calisto's lateness, begins to imagine the things that might have delayed him. Calisto, joyful at her concern, descends into the garden. Lucrecia, also aroused, tries to embrace Calisto but is stopped by Melibea. The sexual heat increases in the lovers' coquettish exchanges and mutual declarations of passionate feeling, while outside in the street the eavesdropping Sosia declares that he could match his master's amorous prowess if given the chance. Lust has spilled over from Calisto and Melibea to their servants. After the lovers have lain together, by Lucrecia's accounting, three times, the noisy approach of Traso and his companions intrudes on their idyll. Calisto rushes out unarmed, and the fall from the ladder to his death that originally occurred in act 14 takes place. Areúsa thus gets her revenge, not as she envisioned it but by accident.

*Title page for a French translation (Bibliothèque Nationale, Paris) published in Paris in 1527 (from* Celestinesca, *9, no. 2 [1985]; Thomas Cooper Library, University of South Carolina)*

The play concludes with the rapid consequences of the original acts 15 and 16, now renumbered 20 and 21. Areúsa's dubious triumph underscores the note on which the work ends: the world is, indeed, a labyrinth of error, the "vale of tears" of Pleberio's final words. The future will be no improvement on the past; there is no escaping despair, no exit.

The year the *Comedia de Calisto y Melibea* was first published, 1499, was the twenty-fifth year of the reign of Fernando and Isabel (Ferdinand and Isabella), the *Reyes Católicos* (Catholic Monarchs) whose marriage created the political basis of modern Spain. The country they had inherited was socially fragmented, politically disunited, economically distressed, and inefficiently governed. Weak kings had ceded much of their power to noble families who would support them, and factions and feuding were commonplace. Spain had not yet completed the Reconquest of all the territories conquered by the Muslim invaders in 711, as a pocket of resistance still existed in Granada. The bloody pogroms of 1391 and earlier had put great pressure on Jews to convert to Catholicism, but Jews who thought that conversion would solve their problems were disillusioned. They were termed New Christians, and the pure-blooded Old Christians made life hard for them—especially for the prominent *conversos* who were skilled in the useful professions of medicine, law, finance, and tax collecting.

Little by little, by force and by compact, Fernando and Isabel retrieved power from the nobles and highborn prelates into whose hands it had devolved and consolidated it in the state. In the quarter century leading up to the publication of the *Comedia de Calisto y Melibea* the Catholic Monarchs obtained permission from the Vatican to inaugurate a new Spanish Inquisition in an effort to unite the country under a single religious banner. The king and queen were immensely popular, as well as powerful. The court patronized the arts, and in 1492 Antonio de Nebrija dedicated the first-ever grammar of the Spanish language to the monarchs, envisioning them in its introduction as imperial rulers. That same year the royal couple oversaw the defeat of the last Moorish king of Granada and issued an edict of expulsion of all Jews who did not accept conversion; the Inquisition, in its fervor for rooting out heresy of all manner, stayed hard on the heels of any insincere converts, or Judaizers. Also that year Christopher Columbus made the first of his four voyages to the New World; these voyages greatly expanded the social, religious, naval, and economic preeminence of Spain and gave it its first tastes of empire, world dominance, and linguistic hegemony within its expanded sphere of influence.

*Celestina* made its dramatic appearance in this atmosphere of celebration, pride, and triumph. The printing press had come to Spain only in 1474, and most of the works that came from the early presses in Valencia, Burgos, Segovia, Seville, Salamanca, and other burgeoning urban centers tended to be religious or historical texts. Nothing remotely like the *Comedia de Calisto y Melibea* had been printed in Spain. Its uncompromising and mean-spirited depiction of the upwardly mobile and expanding middle and upper-middle classes, the wealthy, the titled, the clergy, and students; its barely concealed eroticism; and its recommendation of hypocrisy as a means of surviving in a world in which public values are shallow when not totally devoid of meaning comprised an alternative view and a scathing indictment of contemporary life. It surely would have come under immediate attack from the censors had the opening and concluding texts not drawn attention to the disruptive behaviors on exhibit in the work as examples of what not to do.

The originality of *Celestina* lies in its treatment of illicit love encouraged by interested parties of the lower castes. The characters, however, are all familiar types made popular in the Roman comedy of Plautus and Terence: the ardent lover, the inaccessible and beautiful woman, the old crone *(vetula),* the procuress, and the disloyal servant *(servus fallax).* The medieval work that best exemplifies the basic Ovidian plot of *Celestina*—as well as of the fourteenth-century *Libro de buen amor* (Book of Good Love, 1330–1343)—is the twelfth-century Latin elegiac comedy *Pamphilus: De amore* (Pamphilus: On Love). *Pamphilus* is a short and unadorned work with a simple story line: boy wants girl but cannot have her; he takes Venus's advice and contracts with a go-between to procure the girl's compliance; the go-between's false assurances and beguilements earn the girl's trust; finally, the girl is seduced at her own home in a prearranged scheme hatched by the boy and the go-between. *Pamphilus,* which is extant today in several manuscripts, influenced later works throughout Europe, including *Celestina;* yet, in Rojas's hands the straightforward seduction plot becomes vastly more complicated.

*Celestina* was born in the midst of contemporary debates over the meaning of agape, *caritas,* and *concupiscentia* that are explored in Pedro M. Cátedra's *Amor y pedagogía en la Edad Media: Estudios de doctrina amorosa y práctica literaria* (Love and Pedagogy in the Middle Ages: Studies on Theories of Love and Literary Practice, 1989). Treatises on love were studied, discussed, and dissected in the university circles of Salamanca, and the ideas in them spread to the general populace and were absorbed into many popular literary works. The doctrinal issues debated in *Breviloquio de amor e amiçiçia* (Short Treatise on Love and Friendship, 1432–1436), by Alfonso Fernández de Madrigal (El Tostado); a work attributed to Juan de Mena, *Tratado de amor* (Treatise on Love, circa 1444); the *Repetición de amores* (Valedictory of Love, circa 1496) of Luis de Lucena; and the *Sentencias sobre amor* (Statements about Love), by the medical doctor and humanist thinker Francisco López de Villalobos, attained literary form not only in *Celestina* but also in amorous, devotional, and moral poetry and in chivalric and sentimental romances. In particular, the sentimental romances of Diego de San Pedro and Juan de Flores, in which the lovers do not seek to marry, prefigure many elements in *Celestina;* but they are taken to a new level by a realism that is coupled with cynicism and parody to feed the demand of the secular reading public.

The *aegritudo amoris* (extreme lovesickness) from which the male lover suffers is clinically analyzed in this corpus of treatises in its many permutations. The medical compendia of the day, such as Bernardo de Gordonio's *Lilio de medicina,* form another piece of contemporary commentary accurately reflected in *Celestina.* Treatments for Calisto's *amor hereos,* for Areúsa's "dolor de la madre" (menstrual period), and for Melibea's palpitations abound in these treatises.

The servants in *Celestina* are vain, deceitful, false to their masters, and given to rancorous murmuring. Their world is that of the humanist comedy, and it contrasts with the unreal sentimental paradise in which Calisto and Melibea have confined themselves–a fantasy world that has little chance of remaining secret for long. The underclass's resentment of their masters, their jealousies and general mistrust of each other, their bravado and cowardice, and their own carnal love interests are often parodies of those of their social betters. For example, Sempronio addresses Elicia in language the reader has heard from Calisto rhapsodizing over Melibea, and he describes Pármeno as "otro Calisto" (another Calisto) when his friend's virginity is lost with Areúsa; Sosia thinks that he could give as good an account of himself as a lover as Calisto, if he were given access to Melibea; and Areúsa makes the reader suspect that she would not mind a fling of her own with Calisto. The class boundaries blur, and the hierarchical order that ought to regulate the world is mocked–a fact that Pleberio, in another context, bemoans at the conclusion of the work as he rails against Love, Fortune, and the World. The characters who are involved in the trafficking of flesh–Claudina, Celestina, Elicia, and their clients, as well as the more independent brood of commercially available women typified by Areúsa–are an accurate reflection of the way in which the various levels of sexual congress were structured and regulated by municipal authorities in early modern Spain.

The huge debt owed to the humanist comedies by *Celestina* also manifests itself in other ways. These works were often read in university circles, where they served as texts for learning rhetoric and composition and for practicing one's Latin. Like *Celestina,* they are prose compositions divided into acts and dealing with illicit love. They place more emphasis on local color, and their scenic space and time flow more elastically, than is the case in the earlier elegiac comedies such as *Pamphilus;* asides and implicit stage directions are common; the servants carry on love affairs in the shadow of their masters and mistresses; the father often appears in scenes with the daughter; and the daughter shows a

*Page from act 20 of the 1538 edition (Biblioteca Nacional, Madrid) published in Toledo by Juan de Ayala (from* Celestinesca, *23, nos. 1–2 [1999]; Thomas Cooper Library, University of South Carolina)*

willingness to speak up for herself in the encounters with her lover. *Celestina* picks up on all of these elements and perfects them so that they lend the work a verisimilitude that is not achieved in the best of the humanist comedies, for here they are employed in an intricate concatenation of actions that lead, time and again, to tragic death, reversing the standard happy ending–usually in marriage–of the preceding Latin comedy.

Time and space in *Celestina* are fluid and immeasurable. No town is identified, and the names of streets and churches are those that appear in dozens of Spanish urban centers. Some scholars have taken great pains to make the actions in *Celestina* take place in three or five days, for they seem to follow each other in a tight sequential manner. To accomplish these neat paradigms, however, many internal allusions to time have to be discounted: the opening scene of act 1 is described in act 2 as having taken place on a vague "other day"; Calisto is said to have been suffering from his toothache for a week; Celestina claims to have spoken to Areúsa on Pármeno's behalf more than three times; Melibea tells Pleberio that "many days have passed" since Calisto declared himself to her; and so on. These passages cannot be made to go away, and they mean that in *Celestina* the reader is dealing with psychological rather than chronological time.

To account for discrepancy between the disdain for immoral behaviors and ostentatious displays in the framing texts and the lack of disclaimers in the text itself, some scholars have argued that Rojas was reacting to the unfair treatment of Jews and Judaizers; this theory has led to repeated claims of clues hidden in the text, meant to be perceived by readers who shared with him certain *converso* attitudes. Some scholars have pondered possible secret identities for the central characters: for example, that Calisto, who never offers to marry Melibea, is from the inferior caste of *conversos* who were not allowed to marry women of "serenísima sangre" (pure blood); or that Melibea, Alisa, and Pleberio are *conversos* who are eager at all costs to appear to be orthodox Catholics and strive mightily to maintain a closed family circle to protect their secret; or that Celestina, an outcast resentful of her marginal place in society, is a *conversa* with a deep hatred for successful social climbers such as Pleberio. On the other hand, Celestina and Calisto call for a priest confessor moments before they die, and Melibea offers her soul to God in a standard Christian formula as she falls to her death. None of the three has voiced concern about God before facing death, so these statements may be empty rhetoric from characters who pay no heed to a higher morality in thought or action but revert to a parroted Christian rhetoric at the last, spurred by the reality of imminent death. Alternatively, it is possible that a Catholic dogma that preaches last-minute contrition and hope of redemption, despite a life of sin, is being parodied by an author who either does not believe in that dogma or, even if he does, sees that it serves Christian hypocrites all too readily. Beyond the fictional narrative itself, one wonders whether lurking behind the self-proclaimed Christian voice of the framing texts of *Celestina* is a bitter and tormented *converso*.

Another issue that has been debated almost since the first publication of the work is whether magic plays a role in the outcome of the plot. The discussion has centered on whether the malevolent spirit summoned into Celestina's yarn is the force responsible for Alisa's need to visit her ailing sister, providing the go-between the desired private audience with Melibea, and whether it is the force responsible for reversing Melibea's initial harsh judgment of Calisto after she accepts the yarn and exchanges it for her sash. Magic is, however, invoked in many other parts of *Celestina*. In act 7 Celestina describes to Pármeno the macabre activities in which his mother, Claudina, engaged along with Celestina in cemeteries and at crossroads that earned them the censure of the authorities; both were tarred and feathered, but only Claudina was tried and found guilty of witchcraft and exposed to public disgrace in the town square. What is often called Celestina's laboratory—described by Pármeno to Calisto in exquisite detail in act 1–is a rich catalogue of magical and fetishistic ingredients for spells and charms: retorts; deer marrow; pomades made from bears, snakes, and rabbits; herbs; oils; needles; waxed threads; hairs from the chin of a goat; and so forth. Celestina draws magic circles on the road, mends maidenheads, makes and sells cosmetics from the same suspicious ingredients, and is involved in many other devious activities. The efficacy of these practices, however, is open to question. Pármeno dismisses Celestina's activities as "burla y mentira" (falsehood and trickery). Celestina herself, after obtaining Melibea's sash, thanks her diabolical ally for his intercession in this affair and for keeping his promises, but the devil does not get all the credit: Celestina attributes her achievement in part to Dame Fortune, whose favors are extended to the daring, and she credits herself, as well, for being the most skilled of the many in her profession, seeing herself as the envy of the new practitioners whose skills are not at the same level as hers. Furthermore, Alisa's sister was presumably ill before Celestina's conjuration of the previous evening; and Alisa must have been attending her regularly, since the sister's page is present and waiting to escort her. And in acts 4, 10, and 20 the point is made that Melibea was secretly smitten with Calisto from the first time she saw him, an event that predates the conjuration scene. Whether Melibea's virtuous resolve is undermined by a supernatural force, or whether, exercising her free will, she succumbs to her own inner desires remains an open question. Such considerations allow the reader to interpret Celestina's rather theatrical conjuration of the devil as an attempt to bolster her faltering confidence as she prepares mentally for this dangerous assault on Pleberio's house and honor; she voices her fears both before and after performing the rites of black magic.

Rhetoric also functions in a variety of ways in *Celestina*. Celestina is clearly an expert in manipulating and persuading others to her causes. Whenever another character proposes to her a course of action based on rational planning, good sense, or even unmitigated self-interest, Celestina is able to counter it or to bend it to her own purposes by invoking a rich store of proverbs, maxims, refrains, old saws and adages, and clichés. Such passages are evidence of the clash in Rojas's time between two ways of incorporating learning into daily life: the old knowledge handed down orally from generation to generation versus the new learning acquired through study and academic debate and through the printed word.

In *Celestina* there are readers–Melibea, Calisto, and Pleberio–and nonreaders. The behavior of the readers is influenced by what they have read, whether courtly literature such as the *De amore* (On Love, 1184–1186) of Andreas Capellanus, being perused by Calisto as the work opens; the Latin classics; or the more contemporary sentimental novels that Pleberio has recommended as edifying reading to Melibea, who mimics certain behaviors found in those emotionally overwrought stories. Pleberio is a reader of these diverse sources and uses them as guides in his life. The knowledge imparted by these texts, however, fails them all.

The nonreaders include Sempronio and Pármeno, who seem to possess rather a large amount of unexpected knowledge; Sempronio, especially, cites authors who may seem implausible for an unschooled servant to know. But classical references were much bandied about, especially in university towns such as Salamanca. One did not have to read works in the original Latin, as many had been translated; and aphorisms had been culled from the works of Seneca, Boethius, Aristotle, and Petrarch and circulated in collections of wise sayings. Clever servants can make a show of such knowledge in *Celestina* without sacrificing verisimilitude.

Respect for book learning and erudition was in the ascendancy in the latter half of the fifteenth century, offering a challenge to the influence of traditional oral wisdom. The mingling of these two sources is an important subtext throughout *Celestina*. The authority derived from experience is vividly depicted as Celestina woos various characters to do her bidding: Pármeno in acts 1 and 7, Melibea in acts 4 and 10, and Areúsa and Elicia in act 7. Time and again she evokes the carpe diem theme, deflecting every challenge to her authority by involving her verbal sparring partners in immediate pleasures. She is the arch philosopher of the hedonistic moment, and procuring pleasure is her trade. Celestina's authority and experience are a major element in her claims to be the ultimate professional; in her angry blast at Sempronio in act 12, she says: "¿Quién só yo, Sempronio? ¿Quitásteme de la putería? calla tu lengua, no amengües mis canas, que soy una vieja qual Dios me hizo, no peor que todas. . . . vivo de mi oficio, como cada qual oficial del suyo, muy limpiamente" (Who am I, Sempronio? Did you bring me out of prostitution? Hold your tongue, don't challenge my gray hairs [age, experience], I am an old woman as God has made me, no worse than others. . . . I earn my living from my own trade, as does any other person from his, and I do so honestly).

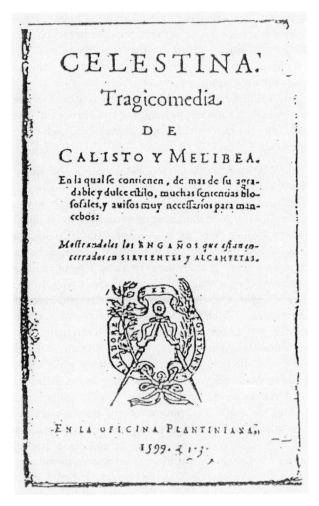

*Title page for an edition (in the private collection of Joseph T. Snow) published in Antwerp (from* Celestinesca, *9, no. 2 [1985]; Thomas Cooper Library, University of South Carolina)*

*Celestina* deals with concupiscent or Ovidian love, inconstant fortune, and hovering death. Each is an inversion of more-noble themes: love of God, the constancy of justice, and eternal life. The first two, worldly love and fortune, are pursued by all the principals. Even the aged Celestina, though no longer sexually active, still derives thrills from her occasional role as a voyeur, and Lucrecia, a secondary figure, is twice thrust into this role in the expanded twenty-one-act tragicomedy. Except for Calisto and Melibea (and her parents), every character seeks monetary advantage, and in its pursuit they abandon charitable love and inevitably move toward a swift and unredeeming death.

Self-interest, egocentrism, greed, and pleasure are the main motivators of actions in *Celestina*. The corrosive power of *cupiditas* and *concupiscentia* are resisted only briefly by Pármeno and Melibea. Each is weaned away from loyalty–Pármeno from fealty to Calisto, Melibea from her filial allegiance to her family—as honor, reputation, and honesty are bartered for ephemeral and illusory gains. But so strong are the lures of concupiscent love and of financial gain and advantage over others that nothing changes even when Celestina's life is suddenly snuffed out in act 12. Celestina is a catalyst for the release of indecent passion, not the cause of it. She promotes the outcome; but it is already latent, awaiting a practiced hand to set it free.

The destructive tendencies abroad in the world that Celestina rules are the subject of two especially eloquent speeches about moral causality. Pármeno warns Calisto in act 2: "Señor, porque perderse el otro día el neblí fue causa de tu entrada en la huerta de Melibea a le buscar, la entrada causa de la ver y hablar, la habla engendró amor, el amor parió tu pena, la pena causará perder tu cuerpo y alma y hazienda" (Sir, owing to the erratic flight of your hawk, the other day you entered the garden of Melibea seeking it; your presence there caused you to see and speak with Melibea; your conversation engendered love in you: this love engendered pain; and the pain will cause you to lose your body, your soul, and all you own). The same lesson is drawn by Pleberio in the final act: "Del mundo me quexo, porque en sí me crió, porque no me dando vida, no engendrara en él a Melibea; no nascida, no amara; no amando, cessara mi quexosa y desconsolada postrimería" (I malign the world because it gave to me life; had it not given me life, I would not have fathered Melibea; had she not been born, she would not have loved; and never having loved, my final days in this world would have not been woeful and distressing). Pleberio cannot see what lies ahead for him now any more than he could when he was born, or married, or fathered a daughter. Truly, the world is ungoverned, and people dash about blindly, heedless of those values that might console them with the promise of another life.

The reader sees that what transpires in Celestina is foreordained, supported by a mountain of ironic references to future events and to events whose causes are perceived only in retrospect. Yet the characters, despite being ignorant of the lack of order and control that guides their course of action and unwittingly blinded by their passions and desires, still act with full free will. As individuals, they uphold no eternal values, no higher moral philosophy to help them evaluate the choices they make. Calisto's meeting with Melibea is tainted by lust from the beginning, and Pleberio's reliance on worldly gain is misplaced. Rojas is suggesting that if one's decisions and deeds are not moral and responsible, they will inevitably lead to disaster. In Celestina hypocrisy reigns supreme, and no one's personal ambitions are truly fulfilled.

Calisto and the other representatives of the landed and monied classes are brought low because they have no lofty values. Calisto parodies the courtly lover; Melibea parodies the courtly lover's lady; Pleberio is a parody of the protective father who thinks that his fortune will provide the protection that his only daughter warrants; and Alisa is a parody of the mother who is easily deceived by her own daughter. The noble characters can speak in unseemly and rude language; yet, the socially humbler Pármeno and Sempronio are made fun of when they ape the hollow courtly language of their master. Lust reduces Sosia to revealing secrets that betray the master he serves. Areúsa seems to be a pushover for Celestina's guile, but she is cunningly awaiting the time when she can shine.

Celestina was condemned by some contemporaries for its erotic and immoral content and admired by others for its warnings to the young, its style, and its rhetorical excellence. In other words, readers interpreted the work in various ways then, and they still do today. The key to the contradictory appraisals of Celestina is Heraclitus's dictum, cited in Rojas's prologue, that contention and dissonance are the natural state of the universe in which humans live, thrive, and die.

Dozens of works have been based on or inspired by Celestina, and thousands of allusions have been made to it over the course of more than five centuries—a phenomenon that has acquired the sobriquet of la celestinesca (the Celestina-like, or celestinesque); but it is generally agreed that no other work rivals the original's sweeping view of human nature's dark side. The offspring of Celestina are remarkable for their variety. Less than a dozen years after the work was first published, an anonymous six-hundred-line Spanish ballad retold the story of the tragic lovers in octosyllabic verse. In 1513 Pedro Manuel Ximénez de Urrea published a stage version of Celestina; he followed it a year later with a celestinesque work, Penitencia de amor (Penitence of Love), and his Eclogue of Calisto and Melibea includes materials from the first act of Celestina. Both the ballad and the theater pieces attest and reflect the performative aspects that are implicit in the semidramatic oral readings of the original work. Even before Feliciano de Silva resuscitated Celestina in 1534 in his Segunda Celestina, many other prose works with similar love intrigues appeared. They include the 1521 trilogy of comedies Thebaida, Serafina, and Hipólita; Jaime de Huete's Comedia Tesorina of 1528; and, in the same year, Francisco Delicado's much admired Lozana andaluza (The Comely Andalusian Lass). In 1536 Gaspar Gómez de Toledo published the Tercera Parte de la tragicomedia de Celestina; in 1542 Sancho de Muñón brought out the Tragicomedia de Lisandro y Roselia llamada Elicia y por otra parte cuarta obra y tercera Celestina (Tragicomedy of Lisandro and Roselia, called Elicia, and Also the Fourth Work and Third Celestina); and in 1548 Sebastián Fernández published the *Tragedia Policiana. En la qual se tractan los muy desdichados amores de Policiano & Philomena, executados por la industria de la diabólica vieja Claudina, madre de Pármeno & maestra de Celestina* (Tragedy of Policiano. In Which We Learn of the Very Unhappy Love Affair of Policiano & Philomena Engineered by the Diabolical Old Bawd, Claudina, Mother of Pármeno and Teacher of Celestina).

Readings of the early *Celestina* texts are embedded in the *Comedia Selvagia* (1554), by Alonso de Villegas Selvago, and in Joan Rodríguez Florián's *Comedia llamada Florinea* (Comedy Called Florinea, 1554). Celestinesque prose fiction was still popular in the age of Cervantes, making its presence felt in Francisco López de Úbeda's *Libro de entretenimiento de la Pícara Justina* (Pleasing Chronicle of that Wayward Girl Justina), published in 1605–the same year as the first part of Cervantes's masterpiece, *Don Quijote*–as well as many prose fictions by the prolific Jerónimo de Salas Barbadilla, including *La hija de Celestina* (Celestina's Daughter, 1612). Throughout this period, the original *Celestina* was frequently republished.

Several theatrical texts reflect continuing familiarity with *Celestina,* from the early sixteenth century with the works of Bartolomé de Torres Naharro (*Comedia Himenea,* 1517), Lope de Rueda, and Juan de la Cueva, to the seventeenth, when Lope de Vega modeled many of his characters on figures from *Celestina*– none more closely imitative than his *El caballero de Olmedo* (The Knight of Olmedo, circa 1620), which features an intermediary, Fabia, modeled on Celestina. One of Lope's novels, *La Dorotea* (1632), also features a "Celestina" character.

Although it was not published in Spain between 1633 and 1822, *Celestina* defied efforts to repress it, and many documents attest to its having been owned and read. In 1793 the Inquisition again banned it, this time even for members of the Church's censorship panels. Once it circulated again in print, in León Amarita's handsome 1822 edition printed in Madrid, it was extolled in a wide-ranging review by the political liberal José María Blanco White from his exile in England. Since then, *Celestina* has never again been out of print. Editions of *Celestina* were published every decade of the nineteenth century after the first two; during that time, it became the revered classic it remains in the Spanish-speaking world.

After returning to print, *Celestina* once again stimulated the creation of independent works. In one of the stories in his *Escenas matritenses* (Madrid Scenes) Ramón de Mesonero Romanos depicted Celestina for the nineteenth-century reading public. This work was followed by Eugenio Hartzenbusch's 1840 novel, *Los polvos de la Madre*

*Title page for a seventeenth-century Spanish-language edition (Collection of the Hispanic Society of America, New York) published in Italy (from* Celestinesca, *9, no. 2 [1985]; Thomas Cooper Library, University of South Carolina)*

*Celestina* (The Love Powders of Mother Celestina). Francisco Goya, Cecilio Pla, and Pablo Picasso are among the well-known artists whose renderings of Celestina are reproduced in illustrated editions of the work. Operatic versions have been staged by Felipe Pedrell in Spanish in 1903, by Jerome Rosen in English in 1978, and by Maurice Ohana in French in 1988; Federico Romero wrote a *zarzuela* (light opera) version that has not been performed. The work was choreographed in 1968, 1995, and 1999.

*Celestina* has been adapted for the Spanish stage many times. Although the work has been seen by thousands of theatergoers in English, French, German, Italian, Portuguese, Swedish, Danish, Greek, Dutch, Polish, Serbo-Croatian, and Walloon, it has had a significant impact in Spanish in the Iberian Peninsula and throughout Latin America. Celestina has become a clas-

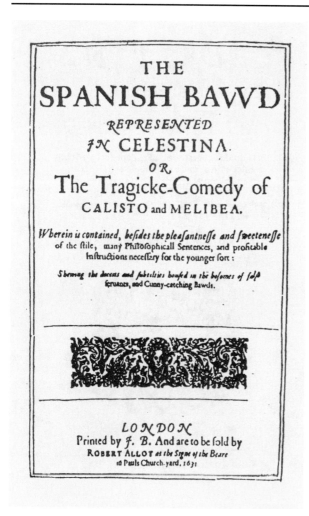

THE
SPANISH BAWD
*REPRESENTED*
*IN* CELESTINA.
OR,
The Tragicke-Comedy of
CALISTO and MELIBEA.

*Wherein is contained, besides the pleasantnesse and sweetenesse
of the stile, many Philosophicall Sentences, and profitable
Instructions necessary for the younger sort:*

*Shewing the deceits and subtilties housed in the bosomes of false
servants, and Cunny-catching Bawds.*

LONDON
Printed by *F. B.* And are to be sold by
ROBERT ALLOT at the Signe of the Beare
in Pauls Church-yard. 1631.

*Title page for the earliest-known English translation, held by the
British Library (from* Celestinesca, *10, no. 1 [1986];
Thomas Cooper Library, University of South Carolina)*

sic role for experienced actresses, some of whom played younger characters in earlier productions. In 1997 a production of *Celestina* was chosen to open Sweden's year as cultural capital of Europe.

Since 1964 *Celestina* has been filmed in Italy, in Mexico, and twice in Spain; it has been presented as a musical in London and New York; and it has been published in lavishly produced and illustrated coffee-table editions, including one with illustrations by José Segrelles and Luis Enríquez de Navarra published in Valencia in 1946 and a 1989 German translation by Fritz Vögelsang with sixty-six black-and-white Picasso illustrations published in Frankfurt am Main. The work has inspired poetry by Jorge Guillen, Manuel Mantero, and Joaquín Benito de Lucas.

Modern scholarship on *Celestina,* apart from Blanco White's 1824 review of Amarita's edition, dates only from Marcelino Menéndez y Pelayo's landmark study in the preface to the special two-volume edition prepared for the fourth centennial celebrations (1899, 1900). Since then, *Celestina* has spawned hundreds of monographs, articles, and notes; many international conferences; dozens of theses and doctoral dissertations; a scholarly journal, *Celestinesca;* websites; and even an Internet chat room. Simultaneously classic and modern, *Celestina* is well positioned to live on for another five hundred years.

**Bibliographies:**

Adrienne S. Mandel, La Celestina *Studies: A Thematic Survey and Bibliography 1824–1970* (Metuchen, N.J.: Scarecrow Press, 1971);

Joseph T. Snow, Celestina *y Fernando de Rojas: An Annotated Bibliography of World Interest 1930–1985* (Madison, Wis.: Hispanic Seminary of Medieval Studies, 1985).

**Biographies:**

Manuel Serrano y Sanz, *Noticias biográficas de Fernando de Rojas, autor de la* Celestina *y del impresor Juan de Lucena* (Madrid, 1902);

Fernando del Valle Lersundi, "Documentos referentes a Fernando de Rojas," *Revista de Filología Española,* 12 (1925): 385–396;

del Valle Lersundi, "Testamento de Fernando de Rojas, autor de *La Celestina,*" *Revista de Filología Española,* 16 (1929): 366–383;

Stephen Gilman, *The Spain of Fernando de Rojas: The Intellectual and Social Landscape of La Celestina* (Princeton: Princeton University Press, 1972);

Inés Valverde Azula, "Documentos referentes a Fernando de Rojas," *Celestinesca,* 16 (1992): 81–102.

**References:**

Candido Ayllón, *La perspectiva irónica de Fernando de Rojas* (Madrid: Porrúa, 1984);

Emilio Barón Palma, "Pármeno: La liberación del ser auténtico," *Cuadernos Hispanoamericanos,* 106 (1976): 383–400;

Marcel Bataillon, La Célestine *selon Fernando de Rojas* (Paris: Didier, 1961);

Rafael Beltrán Llavador and José Luis Canet, eds., *Cinco siglos de* Celestina: *Aportaciones interpretativas* (Valencia: Universitat de Valencia, 1997);

Erna R. Berndt-Kelley, *Amor, muerte y fortuna en* La Celestina (Madrid: Gredos, 1963);

Berndt-Kelley, "Peripecias de un título: En torno al nombre de la obra de Fernando de Rojas," *Celestinesca,* 9 (1985): 3–46;

Patrizia Botta, "La magia en *La Celestina,*" *Dicenda,* 12 (1994): 37–67;

James F. Burke, *Vision, the Gaze and the Function of the Senses in* Celestina (University Park: Pennsylvania State University Press, 2000);

José Luis Canet Vallés, *De la comedia humanística al teatro representable* (Valencia & Seville: UNED/Universidad de Sevilla/Universitat de Valencia, 1993);

Ricardo Castells, *Fernando de Rojas and the Renaissance Vision: Phantasm, Melancholy and Didacticism in* Celestina (University Park: Pennsylvania State University Press, 2000);

Américo Castro, La Celestina *como contienda literaria: Castas y casticismo* (Madrid: Revista de Occidente, 1965);

F. Castro Guisasola, *Observaciones sobre las fuentes literarias de* La Celestina (Madrid: CSIC, 1973);

Pedro M. Cátedra, *Amor y pedagogía en la Edad Media: Estudios de doctrina amorosa y práctica literaria* (Salamanca: Universidad de Salamanca, 1989);

Cátedra, ed., *Tratados de amor en el entorno de* Celestina: *Siglos XV–XVI* (Madrid: Sociedad Estatal España Nuevo Milenio, 2001);

Ivy A. Corfis and Joseph T. Snow, eds., *Fernando de Rojas and* Celestina: *Approaching the Fifth Centenary. Proceedings of an International Conference in Commemoration of the 450th Anniversary of the Death of Fernando de Rojas, Purdue University, West Lafayette, Indiana, 21–24 November 1991* (Madison, Wis.: Hispanic Seminary of Medieval Studies, 1993);

Manuel da Costa Fontes, "*Celestina's* 'hilado' and Related Symbols," *Celestinesca*, 8 (1984): 3–13;

Manuel Criado de Val, ed., La Celestina *y su contorno social: Actas del I Congreso Internacional sobre* La Celestina (Barcelona: Hispam, 1977);

Alan D. Deyermond, "Fernando de Rojas from 1499 to 1502: Born-Again Christian?" *Celestinesca*, 25 (2001): 5–22;

Deyermond, "*Hilado–cordón–cadena:* Symbolic Equivalence in *Celestina*," *Celestinesca*, 1 (1977): 6–12;

Deyermond, *The Petrarchan Sources of* La Celestina (London: Oxford University Press, 1961);

Deyermond, "Pleberio's Lost Investment: The Worldly Perspective of *Celestina* Act 21," *Modern Language Notes*, 105 (1990): 169–179;

Deyermond, "A Postscript," *Celestinesca*, 2 (1978): 25–30;

Deyermond, "The Text-Book Mishandled: Andreas Capellanus and the Opening Scene of 'La Celestina,'" *Neophilologus*, 41 (1961): 218–221;

Ottavio Di Camillo, "Etica humanística y libertinaje," in *Humanismo y literatura en tiempos de Juan del Encina*, edited by Javier Guijarro Ceballos (Salamanca: Ediciones Universidad de Salamanca, 1999), pp. 69–82;

Di Camillo, "La péñola, la imprenta y la doladera: Tres formas de cultura humanística en la Carta 'El autor a un su amigo' de la *Celestina*," in *Silva: Studia philologica in honorem Isaías Lerner*, edited by Isabel Lozano-Renieblas and Juan Carlos Mercado (Madrid: Castalia, 2001), pp. 111–126;

Peter Dunn, *Fernando de Rojas* (New York & Boston: Twayne, 1975);

Charles B. Faulhaber, "*Celestina* de Palacio: Madrid, Biblioteca de Palacio, MS 1520," *Celestinesca*, 14 (1990): 3–39;

Faulhaber, "*Celestina* de Palacio: Rojas's Holograph Manuscript," *Celestinesca*, 15 (1991): 3–52;

Louise Fothergill-Payne, "*Celestina* as a Funny Book: A Bakhtinian Reading," *Celestinesca*, 17 (1993): 29–51;

Fothergill-Payne, *Seneca and Celestina* (Cambridge: Cambridge University Press, 1988);

Miguel Garci-Gómez, *Calisto: Soñador y altañero* (Kassel: Reichenberger, 1994);

Otis Handy, "The Rhetorical and Psychological Defloration of Melibea," *Celestinesca*, 7 (1983): 17–27;

Pierre Heugas, *La Célestine et sa descendance directe* (Bourdeaux: Editions Bière, 1973);

David Hook, "The Genesis of the *Auto de Traso*," *Journal of Hispanic Philology*, 3 (1978–1979): 107–120;

Gustavo Illades Aguiar, La Celestina *en el taller salmantino* (Mexico City: UNAM, 1999);

Víctor Infantes, "Los libros 'traydos y viejos y algunos rotos' que tuvo el bachiller Fernando de Rojas, nombrado autor de la obra llamada *Celestina*," *Bulletin Hispanique*, 100 (1998): 7–51;

Joseph R. Jones, "*The Play of Poliscena*, Composed by Leonardo Aretino (English Translation of the 1478 Text)," *Celestinesca*, 10 (1986): 45–67;

Theodore L. Kassier, "*Cancionero* Poetry and the *Celestina*: From Metaphor to Reality," *Hispanófila*, 56 (1976): 1–28;

María Eugenia Lacarra Lanz, *Cómo leer* La Celestina (Madrid: Júcar, 1990);

Lacarra Lanz, "La parodia de la ficción sentimental en *Celestina*," *Celestinesca*, 13 (1989): 11–29;

María Rosa Lida de Malkiel, *La originalidad artística de* La Celestina (Buenos Aires: EUDEBA, 1970);

Lida de Malkiel, *Two Spanish Masterpieces: The* Book of Good Love *and the* Celestina (Urbana: University of Illinois Press, 1961);

Santiago López-Ríos, ed., *Estudios sobre la* Celestina (Madrid: Istmo, 2001);

José A. Maravall, *El mundo social de* La Celestina (Madrid: Gredos, 1976);

Miguel Marciales, *Celestina: Estudio crítico* (Urbana: University of Illinois Press, 1985);

Francisco Márquez Villanueva, *Orígenes y sociología del tema celestinesco* (Barcelona: Anthropos, 1993);

June H. Martin, *Love's Fools: Aucassin, Troilus, Calisto and the Parody of the Courtly Lover* (London: Tamesis, 1972);

D. W. McPheeters, *El humanista español Alonso de Proaza* (Valencia: Castalia, 1961);

McPheeters, "Melibea and the New Learning," in *Historical and Literary Perspectives: Essays in Honor of Albert Douglas Menut* (Lawrence, Kans.: Coronado Press, 1973), pp. 65–81;

Marcelino Menéndez y Pelayo, *La Celestina* (Buenos Aires: Espasa-Calpe, 1947);

I. Michael and D. Pattison, eds., *Context, Meaning and Reception of* Celestina: *A Fifth Centenary Symposium*, special issue of *Bulletin of Hispanic Studies* (Glasgow), 78 (2001);

Emilio de Miguel Martínez, La Celestina *de Rojas* (Madrid: Gredos, 1996);

Germán Orduna, "Auto–Comedia–Tragicomedia–Celestina: Perspectivas críticas de un proceso literario de creación y recepción literaria," *Celestinesca*, 12 (1988): 3–8;

Orduna, "El original manuscrito de la *Comedia* de Fernando de Rojas: Una conjetura," *Celestinesca*, 23 (1999): 3–10;

Eloísa Palafox, "De plumas, plumíferos y otros seres alados: Trayectoria y enigmas de una metáfora polifacética de la *Celestina*," *Celestinesca*, 23 (1999): 43–60;

Miguel Ángel Pérez Priego, "*La Celestina* y el teatro del siglo XVI," *Epos*, 7 (1991): 291–311;

Pérez Priego, *Cuatro comedias celestinescas* (Valencia & Seville: UNED, 1993);

Jerry R. Rank, "The Uses of 'Dios' and the Concept of God in *La Celestina*," *Revista Canadiense de Estudios Hispánicos*, 5 (1980–1981): 75–91;

Leyla Rouhi, *Mediation and Love: A Study of the European Go-Between in Key European and Near-Eastern Texts* (Amsterdam: Brill, 1999);

Rouhi, "'. . . y otros treynta officios': The Definition of a Medieval Woman's Work in *Celestina*," *Celestinesca*, 22 (1998): 21–31;

Peter E. Russell, *Temas de* La Celestina *y otros estudios: Del* Cid *al* Quijote (Barcelona: Ariel, 1978);

Nicasio Salvador Miguel, "La autoría de *La Celestina* y la fama de Rojas," *Epos*, 7 (1991): 275–290;

Salvador Miguel, "El presunto judaísmo de la *Celestina*," in *The Age of the Catholic Monarchs, 1474–1516: Literary Studies in Memory of Keith Whinnom*, edited by Alan D. Deyermond and Ian Richard MacPherson (Liverpool: Liverpool University Press, 1989), pp. 162–177;

Emma Scoles, "Il testo della *Celestina* nell'edizione Salamanca 1570," *Studi Romanzi*, 36 (1975): 7–124;

Dorothy S. Severin, "Aristotle's *Ethics* and *Celestina*," *La corónica*, 10 (1981–1982): 54–58;

Severin, "The Author's Intention from *Comedia* to *Tragicomedia de Calisto y Melibea*," *Celestinesca*, 5 (1981): 1–5;

Severin, *Memory in* La Celestina (London: Tamesis, 1970);

George A. Shipley, "Authority and Experience in *La Celestina*," *Bulletin of Hispanic Studies*, 62 (1985): 95–111;

Joseph T. Snow, "The Sexual Landscape of *Celestina*: Some Observations," in *Golden Age Studies in Memory of Daniel L. Heiple*, special issue of *Calíope*, 6, nos. 1–2 (2000): 149–166;

Snow, "Two Melibeas," in *"Nunca fue pena mayor": Estudios de literatura española en homenaje a Brian Dutton*, edited by Ana Menéndez Collera and Victoriano López Roncero (Cuenca: Universidad de Castilla La Mancha, 1996), pp. 655–662;

James Stamm, *La estructura de* La Celestina: *Una lectura analítica* (Salamanca: Universidad de Salamanca, 1988);

Catherine Swietlicki, "Rojas' View of Women: A Reanalysis of *La Celestina*," *Hispanófila*, 85 (1985): 1–13;

Gregorio Torres Nebrera, ed., Celestina: *Recepción y herencia de un mito literario* (Cáceres: Universidad de Extremadura, 2001);

Bruce W. Wardropper, "Pleberio's Lament for Melibea and the Medieval Elegiac Tradition," *Modern Language Notes*, 89 (1964): 140–152;

Keith Whinnom, "The Form of *Celestina*: Dramatic Antecedents," *Celestinesca*, 17 (1993): 129–146;

Whinnom, "Interpreting *La Celestina*: The Motives and Personality of Fernando de Rojas," in *Mediaeval and Renaissance Studies on Spain and Portugal in Honor of P. E. Russell*, edited by F. W. Holcroft and others (Oxford: Society for the Study of Mediaeval Languages and Literature, 1981), pp. 53–68.

# Rodrigo Sánchez de Arévalo

*(1404 – 4 October 1470)*

Nancy F. Marino
*Michigan State University*

WORKS: *Dialogus de remediis schismatis* (1440)

**Manuscript:** Vatican City, Biblioteca Apostolica Vaticana cod. Vat. Lat. 4002.

*De questionibus hortolanis* (ca. 1443–1447)

**Manuscripts:** Vatican City, Biblioteca Apostolica Vaticana cod. Vat. Lat. 4881, fols. 160ff; University of Salamanca cod. 2-c-4-181, fols. 72ff.

*Contra tres propositiones Concilii Basiliensis* (ca. 1447–1448)

**Manuscripts:** Vatican City, Biblioteca Apostolica Vaticana cod. Vat. Lat. 4154, fols. 1–27; cod. Vat. Lat. 4167, fols. 121–174; Padua, Biblioteca Capitularia cod. A. 45 R 2, fols. 24–52.

*De arte, disciplina, et modo alendi et erudiendi filios, pueros, et iuvenes* (1453)

**Manuscripts:** Vatican City, Biblioteca Apostolica Vaticana cod. Vat. Lat. 4881, fols. 154–159; University of Salamanca cod. 2-c-4-181, fols. 63–72.

**First publication:** "A Fifteenth-Century Treatise on Education by Bishop Rodericus Zamorensis," edited by Haywood Keniston, *Bulletin Hispanique,* 32 (1930): 204–217.

*Suma de la política* (ca. 1454–1455)

**Manuscript:** Madrid, Biblioteca Nacional MS. 1221, fols. 1ff.

**Standard edition:** *Suma de la política,* edited by Juan Beneyto Pérez, Publicaciones del Seminario de Historia de las Doctrinas Políticas, no. 2 (Madrid: Instituto Francisco de Vitoria, 1944).

*Verjel de los príncipes* (ca. 1456–1457)

**Standard edition:** *Verjel de los príncipes,* edited by Francisco R. de Uhagón (Madrid: Tello, 1900).

*Tractatus de expedientia, utilitate, et congruentia congregationis concilii generalis* (ca. 1460–1461)

**Manuscript:** University of Salamanca cod. 2-c-4-181, fols. 26–41.

*Epistola sive tractatus ad quemdam venerandum religiosum Cartusiensem* (ca. 1461–1464)

**Manuscripts:** Vatican City, Biblioteca Apostolica Vaticana cod. Vat. Lat. 3899, fols. 37ff; cod. Vat. Lat. 4881, fols. 169–173; University of Salamanca cod. 2-c-4-181, fols. 42–50.

*Brevis tractatus an mysterium Trinitatis probari possit naturali et humana ratione* (1462?)

**Manuscripts:** Vatican City, Biblioteca Apostolica Vaticana cod. Vat. Lat. 4881, fols. 174–178; University of Salamanca cod. 2-c-4-181, fols. 50ff.

*Libellus de situ et descriptione Hispaniae* (1463)

**Manuscripts:** Milan, Biblioteca Ambrosiana cod. Lat. D. 144, fols. 1–16; Padua, Biblioteca Capitularia cod. A. 45 R 2, fols. 14ff.

*Commentum Constitutionis Pientine contra peridum Turchum* (1464?)

**Manuscript:** Library of the Cathedral of Tarazona MS. 14.

*Tractatus de appellatione a sententia Romani Pontificis non informati ad seipsum bene informatum* (ca. 1464–1465)

**Manuscripts:** Vatican City, Biblioteca Apostolica Vaticana cod. Vat. Lat. 4167, fols. 177–195; cod. Barb. Lat. 1487, fols. 77–88; cod. Barb. Lat. 3716, fols. 2ff; University of Salamanca cod. 2-c-4-181, fols. 1–26.

*Libellus de libera et irrefregabili auctoritae Romani Pontificis* (ca. 1464–1467)

**Manuscripts:** Milan, Biblioteca Ambrosiana, cod. Lat. D. 144, fols. 39–53; Padua, Biblioteca Capitularia cod. A. 45 R 2, fols. 14–23.

*De castellanis et custodibus arcium* (1465?)

**Manuscripts:** Vatican City, Biblioteca Apostolica Vaticana cod. Vat. Lat. 4881, fols. 116–133; Rome, Boncampagni Archive cod. K. 29, fols. 6ff.

*An sine peccato fideles licite fugiant a locis ubi saevit pestis* (ca. 1465–1466)

**Manuscripts:** Vatican City, Biblioteca Apostolica Vaticana cod. Vat. Lat. 4881, fols. 1ff; Milan, Biblioteca Ambrosiana cod. Lat. D. 144, fols. 18–34; Padua, Biblioteca Capitularia cod. A. 45 R 2, fols. 1ff.

*Defensorium ecclesiae et status ecclesiastici* (1466)

**Manuscripts:** Vatican City, Biblioteca Apostolica Vaticana cod. Vat. Lat. 4106, fols. 1–348; Venice,

Marciana Library cod. 4, chart. A. 264. I. 208; Library of the Cathedral of Tarazona MS. 9.

*Libellus de paupertate Christi et apostolorum* (1466)

**Manuscripts:** Vatican City, Biblioteca Apostolica Vaticana cod. Vat. Lat. 969, fols. 1ff; Library of the University of Bologna MS. 1239.

*Commentum et apparatus super bulla privationis et depositionis georgii regis Bohemiae* (1467)

**Manuscripts:** Vatican City, Biblioteca Apostolica Vaticana cod. Vat. Lat. 11.505; Venice, Marciana Library cod. Marc. Z-L. CXCIV-B, fols. 1–122.

*Liber de monarchia orbis et de differentia cuiusvis humani principatus tam imperialis quam regalis et de antiquitae et iustitia utriusque* (1467)

**Manuscripts:** Vatican City, Biblioteca Apostolica Vaticana cod. Vat. Lat. 4881 fols. 1–48; Barb. Lat. 1589, fols. 1–46; University of Salamanca cod. I, 1552.

**First publication:** *Liber de monarchia orbis et de differentia cuiusvis humani principatus tam imperialis quam regalis et de antiquitae et iustitia utriusque* (Rome: Francisco de Fontecha, 1521).

*Clypeus monarchiae ecclesiae* (1468)

**Manuscripts:** Vatican City, Biblioteca Apostolica Vaticana cod. Vat. Lat. 4881, fols. 49ff; Barb. Lat. 1590.

*Disputatio de pace et bello* (1468)

**Manuscripts:** Vatican City, Biblioteca Apostolica Vaticana cod. Vat. Lat. 4881, fols. 134ff; Venice, Biblioteca Marciana cod. Marc. Lat. XI, 103, fols. 1ff; Florence, Biblioteca Laurentiana MSS. Gaddiani, cod. XX, fols. 1ff; Cambridge, Corpus Christi College MS. 166, fols. 1ff.

**Early edition:** *Cremonensium monumenta Romae extantia* (Rome: Vairani, 1778).

*De regno dividendo et quando primogenitura sit licita* (1468)

**Manuscript:** Vatican City, Biblioteca Apostolica Vaticana cod. Vat. Lat. 4881, fols. 97–117.

*Speculum vitae humanae* (1468)

**Early edition:** *Speculum vitae humanae* (Rome: Sweynheym & Pannart, 1468).

*Liber de sceleribus et infeliciatae perfidi Turchi ac de spurcitia et feditate gentis et secte sue* (ca. 1468–1469)

**Manuscripts:** Vatican City, Biblioteca Apostolica Vaticana cod. Vat. Lat. 971, fols. 1–122, and 972, fols. 1–102.

*De remediis afflictae ecclesiae militantis* (1469)

**Manuscripts:** Vatican City, Biblioteca Apostolica Vaticana cod. Vat. Lat. 6425, fols. 1ff; cod. Barb. Lat. 1487, fols. 107ff; Venice, Biblioteca Marciana cod. Z, LXC, fols. 1ff; Florence, Biblioteca Laurentiana MSS. Gaddiani, cod. 80, fols. 1ff.

*De septem questionibus circa convocationem et congregationem generalis synodi* (1470)

**Manuscript:** Vatican City, Biblioteca Apostolica Vaticana cod. Barb. Lat. 1487, fols. 89–105.

*Epistola lugubris et moesta simul et consolatoria de infelice expugnatione insulae Euboyae dictae Nigropontis* (1470)

**Manuscript:** Vatican City, Biblioteca Apostolica Vaticana cod. Vat. Lat. 5869, fols. 95ff.

**Early edition:** *Incipit epistola lugubris et moesta simul et consolatoria de infelice expugnatione insulae Euboyae dictae Nigropontis* (Rome: Ulrich Hahn, 1470).

*Historia Hispanica* (1470)

**Early edition:** *Compendiosa historia Hispanica* (Rome: Ulrich Hahn, 1470).

Rodrigo Sánchez de Arévalo, learned bishop of Oviedo, Zamora, and Palencia, secretary to Castilian kings, trusted diplomat, and author of several theological, political, and theological tracts, was born in 1404, probably in Santa María de la Nieva, Segovia. After first studying in the Dominican convent in his hometown, at the age of fourteen Sánchez de Arévalo was sent to the University of Salamanca to study law. While there is no direct documentation of the ten or so years he spent there, through his own works it is known that he was granted the degrees of bachelor of law, of theology, and of arts, and doctor of both theology and law. Sánchez de Arévalo referred to himself as "professor of both laws" (human and divine), but the title of professor was probably synonymous with that of doctor, and it is possible that he never actually lectured at Salamanca or anywhere else.

After his studies Sánchez de Arévalo decided on an ecclesiastical career instead of a life in law, the path that many of his family members had chosen before him and that he was expected to follow. His first position in the church, unspecified in the records, was at the cathedral of Burgos. Probably in this city he became acquainted with Alfonso de Cartagena, the future bishop of Burgos, who was a diplomat and adviser to King Juan II of Castile. Cartagena apparently introduced Sánchez de Arévalo to the Castilian court, where Sánchez de Arévalo joined an intellectual circle highly esteemed by the king and was a frequent participant in its discussions. Because of his impressive erudition, in 1433 Sánchez de Arévalo was made a member of the Castilian delegation to the Council of Basel, which had begun in 1431. This trip was to be the first of several journeys abroad that kept Sánchez de Arévalo absent from Castile for most of his career.

The proceedings of the Council of Basel were lengthy and arduous, since many of the participants sought reform of the church through the weakening of papal authority. The Castilian faction, which included Cartagena, was propapal, and Sánchez de Arévalo himself emerged from the dispute as a strong voice in favor of absolute papal authority. For the first six years of his involvement in the Council he attended debates and held minor positions, learning diplomacy and protocol. During this time Sánchez de Arévalo's reputation and credibility must have grown, because in April 1439 he was elected to the Committee of Twelve by the Commission for General Affairs of the Church. This committee had the responsibility of accepting or rejecting all petitions and proposals before assigning them to other bodies for consideration, and it was therefore most influential in the workings of the Council. This appointment came at a crucial time in the proceedings, since scarcely one month later the council participants were planning to depose the Pope. When it became clear that there could be no compromise solution to avoid this radical decision, the Castilian delegation withdrew from the proceedings and left Basel.

Sánchez de Arévalo returned to Castile, and in recognition for his dedicated mission to the Council he was named both canon of the cathedral of Burgos and royal chaplain. Cartagena had returned to Burgos as well and began to rely on his protégé to help arbitrate disagreements in the bishopric. The year was 1440, and Sánchez de Arévalo, at age thirty-six, was no longer a novice but a seasoned diplomat and theologian whose exposure to the ecclesiastical issues of the Council informed his opinions. He was clearly a valued member of the court. In documents dating from the same year, Sánchez de Arévalo is mentioned as Juan II's secretary and as a member of the *audiencia,* the judicial branch of the Castilian government. He was also about to embark on another diplomatic mission for the king.

Juan II's new diplomatic assignment for Sánchez de Arévalo required him to visit the rulers of Europe who either had allied themselves with the schismatic Council of Basel or had attempted to remain neutral. Apparently setting out from Burgos in the summer of 1440, Sánchez de Arévalo first visited Vienna. There he formally addressed King Frederick III in an oration that expressed the views of the Castilian king, and he also participated in debates with other churchmen concerning the issue of neutrality. From Vienna, Sánchez de Arévalo traveled to France, where he met with King Charles VII to speak of the same concerns. Although he probably returned to Castile after these two missions, Sánchez de Arévalo was soon dispatched once again to visit Eugene IV, the Pope who had been deposed and then exiled to Florence. From there Sánchez de Arévalo apparently went to Naples to confer with King Alfonso V of Aragón, then north to urge the duke of Milan to support the beleaguered Pope Eugene. Some of the orations that he delivered during this journey have been preserved in archives, and Juan

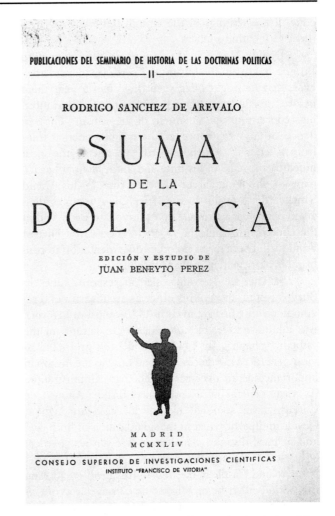

PUBLICACIONES DEL SEMINARIO DE HISTORIA DE LAS DOCTRINAS POLITICAS
— II —

RODRIGO SANCHEZ DE AREVALO

SUMA

DE LA

POLITICA

EDICIÓN Y ESTUDIO DE
JUAN BENEYTO PEREZ

MADRID
MCMXLIV

CONSEJO SUPERIOR DE INVESTIGACIONES CIENTIFICAS
INSTITUTO "FRANCISCO DE VITORIA"

*Title page for the standard edition of Rodrigo Sánchez de Arévalo's first work in Spanish, written circa 1454–1455 (Library of Congress)*

María Laboa has catalogued these orations in *Rodrigo Sánchez de Arévalo, Alcaide de Sant'Angelo* (1973).

During his embassy to the court of Frederick III, Sánchez de Arévalo wrote his first book, *Dialogus de remediis schismatis* (Dialogue on Solutions for the Schism, 1440). Scholars have considered it an important work because of its strong defense of papal authority as well as its condemnation of the declared neutrality of Frederick's court on the findings of the Council of Basel. The work takes the form of a debate between Sánchez de Arévalo and a lawyer named Theodoric, and it probably represents an actual formal argument that took place during his stay at Frederick's court. In the work the two men argue the two central issues (the pontiff's absolute authority and the neutrality of the Germans). Sánchez de Arévalo gives himself the opportunity to demonstrate his considerable knowledge of the writings of the church fathers, as well as those of the philosophers.

By July 1441 Sánchez de Arévalo had returned to Burgos and to church business. There is evidence, however, that he might have spent less than a year there before traveling once again to Germany to attend meetings concerning the settlement of the schism. The evidence of his attendance at these conferences comes from a letter that Nicholas of Cusa, one of the most noted theologians of his time and an influential participant in the Council of Basel, wrote to his friend Sánchez de Arévalo. In the letter Cusa assumes that, given Sánchez de Arévalo's past fervor for unity within the church, he would be in attendance at the Diet of Frankfurt. There exists no other documentation to confirm his participation in these meetings.

Sánchez de Arévalo's clerical responsibilities in Burgos were typical of his office as archdeacon of Treviño (a post he first received in 1440): most of his work was administrative. He also edited the statutes of the cathedral chapter. By 1443 he had been promoted to vicar general of the diocese, second only to the bishop in importance as an overseer of diocesan administration. As vicar general he accompanied Bishop Alfonso de Cartagena on some of his official visits throughout Castile and participated in the adjudication of both civil and political disputes. Sánchez de Arévalo was particularly active during the renewed civil war between Navarre and Castile in the mid 1440s. Probably during this period either he or Alfonso de Cartagena wrote *De questionibus hortolanis* (On Garden Questions, circa 1443–1447), a text that recounts the discussions that took place at the bishop's palace in Burgos. Scholars have said that Sánchez de Arévalo's ideas on the subject of the debate–the primacy of the sense of sight over that of hearing–do not offer any new insight on the topic and that the work is best considered from a literary, rather than philosophical, perspective.

In 1447 Sánchez de Arévalo was elected dean of the cathedral of León. Unbeknownst to the cathedral chapter that had chosen him, the right to fill the position in reality belonged to the new pope, Nicholas V, because the former dean was attending the Curia at the time of his death. The Pope named a nephew of Cardinal Cervantes to the office, and a dispute ensued between the two candidates for the post. Sánchez de Arévalo found himself excommunicated because of his insistence on pursuing the matter, but in 1448 Juan II intervened on his behalf with Pope Nicholas. As a result of the king's involvement in the case, the pontiff annulled the naming of Cervantes' nephew to the deanship and granted it instead to Sánchez de Arévalo, who almost immediately left the kingdom for Rome. Juan II had not yet sent a delegation to the new pope, as was the custom. Sánchez de Arévalo probably headed the embassy that swore Castile's obedience to the new head of the church.

Sánchez de Arévalo did not return to Burgos to resume his responsibilities in the diocese until 1450. The purpose behind his prolonged residence in Italy is not easy to ascertain, but it seems that once again it was related to the schismatic issues that continued to plague the church. His biographer Teodoro Toni, however, believes that Juan II might have sent Sánchez de Arévalo to visit Nicholas V in order to inform him of Castilian plans to restart the war against the Moors of Granada, a campaign that had been temporarily postponed in the 1440s because of the internecine conflict between Navarre and Castile. Probably just before his arrival in Rome or shortly thereafter, Sánchez de Arévalo wrote his *Contra tres propositiones Concilii Basiliensis* (Against Three Propositions of the Council of Basel, circa 1447–1448), which contested the need for yet another convocation of the council in order to end the schism. Nicholas had been elected pope on the death of his predecessor, Eugene IV, in early 1477, but an antipope, Felix V, also had been chosen by the schismatics. A meeting to address the problem of two papacies was called several months later and ended in an agreement to seek the abdication of Felix.

In *Contra tres propositiones Concilii Basiliensis* Sánchez de Arévalo argues convincingly and logically against convoking yet another council; the text is a model defense of the primacy of papal authority. Toni offers a useful analysis in which he explains the four parts (not three, as the title suggests) that individually make the case for not calling a new assembly. He refers to the clear and logical exposition of the treatise and Sánchez de Arévalo's call for a renewed unity within the church, but there is no evidence that Sánchez de Arévalo's arguments influenced the parties debating these issues. It is clear, however, that Nicholas had confidence in the diplomatic abilities of the Spanish envoy, because he sent him to Burgundy in the late summer of 1448 to attempt to settle a dispute concerning the election of the abbot for a monastery. Despite the eloquent discourse that Sánchez de Arévalo delivered on behalf of the Pope before Duke Philip, he did not succeed in having Nicholas's choice for abbot appointed to the post.

Sánchez de Arévalo returned to Rome after the unsuccessful mission to Burgundy and remained there until the fall of 1450, when he returned to Burgos. Here he stayed for most of the next five years. During this period he wrote what has been considered his first truly humanistic work, *De arte, disciplina, et modo alendi et erudiendi filios, pueros, et iuvenes* (The Art, Discipline, and Manner of Encouraging and Instructing Infants, Children, and Young Men, 1453). It is also possibly the first trea-

*Castel Sant'Angelo, the papal fortress in Rome where Sánchez de Arévalo was appointed castellan in the mid 1460s*
*(from Samuel Ball Platner,* The Topography and Monuments of Ancient Rome, *1904;*
*Thomas Cooper Library, University of South Carolina)*

tise on education written in Spain. The inspiration for this short work apparently came through a visit from Alfonso de la Hoz, secretary to Enrique, Prince of Asturias. During the course of their conversation Alfonso admired Sánchez de Arévalo's considerable library, and the subject turned to education. When Alfonso expressed the desire to see his young son well educated, Sánchez de Arévalo promised to commit to paper his own ideas on the education of children. The book is divided into sections according to the various stages in the life of boys and the care and instruction that each of these stages demands. Sánchez de Arévalo touches on subjects such as nutrition, parental love, and discipline, as well as the more traditional question of the proper books for children at each stage of their lives.

On this topic Plutarch seems to be his most likely source of information. Sánchez de Arévalo also takes into account the individual capacities of each child and the importance of educating each one according to his needs, the talents with which nature endowed him, and his personal inclinations and preferences.

Antonio de Nebrija, the famous Spanish humanist and author of the first grammar of the Spanish language, wrote a similar educational treatise some fifty years after Sánchez de Arévalo composed *De arte, disciplina, et modo alendi et erudiendi filios, pueros, et iuvenes.* While Nebrija's version of the education of the young is considered more closely aligned with Renaissance ideals and humanism, José López de Toro has clearly shown that he borrowed liberally from Sánchez de

Arévalo's text in writing his own. The works are similar in form and content and in their interpretation of the concepts under discussion. López de Toro believes that through Nebrija, Sánchez de Arévalo's proposals for the education of children were disseminated throughout Spain in the sixteenth century.

At some time before his death in July 1454, Juan II of Castile asked Sánchez de Arévalo to travel to France on what was to be his last diplomatic mission for this monarch. The issue at hand was essentially a complaint against the new policy of the French court toward the English. Castile and France had been aligned against England since the mid fourteenth century, but of late the French had granted royal protection to the English for the purpose of conducting commerce. In Sánchez de Arévalo's oration before Charles VII of France he expressed his king's view that France should not grant safe-conducts to the English without the knowledge of her allied kingdom, Castile. Sánchez de Arévalo also addressed a border dispute with the French, about which Charles VII had already sent Juan II a letter. Both of these questions were resolved some time after Sánchez de Arévalo's embassy.

During this period Sánchez de Arévalo produced his first work in Spanish, *Suma de la política* (The Summa of Politics, circa 1454–1455). It was also the first of his works on the subject of politics. According to the prologue, *Suma de la política* resulted from conversations between Sánchez de Arévalo and Pedro de Acuña, honorary guard of the new king, Enrique IV, and brother of Alfonso Carrillo de Acuña, archbishop of Toledo. Pedro de Acuña had expressed interest in the topic of the establishment and security of cities and towns, as well as their effective government. Sánchez de Arévalo's treatment of the subject is divided into two sections. The first deals with where and how cities should be founded in order to ensure their efficient defense against an enemy. In this part he addresses the economic life of a city and reveals the rather antiquated opinion that agriculture is a more profitable endeavor than commerce. In fact, Sánchez de Arévalo speaks out against merchants and their interests at the same time that he praises the honorable work of the farmer. He goes on to suggest that a town cultivate only as much food as is needed by its residents, thus extolling the virtue of self-sufficiency. He also addresses the health and education of the citizens and explains his thoughts on the ideals of knighthood. The second section of *Suma de la política* is concerned with government and the importance of an administration based on justice. Here Sánchez de Arévalo explains his views on the role of those who govern, from the king down to the local officers of government, and the responsibility of the individual to ensure the success of the system. It has been said that this treatise is more theoretical than practical and that its principles are more medieval in orientation than other political tracts written during the same era.

The death of the Spanish Pope Nicholas resulted in a positive change for Spain, when Cardinal Alfonso Borja (in Italian, Borgia) was elected to succeed him in the spring of 1455. This was a particularly profitable moment for Sánchez de Arévalo, because the new pontiff, Callistus III, remembered him on the first day of his reign, as he did other Spaniards. Sánchez de Arévalo was given several revenue-producing ecclesiastical posts in Burgos, Segovia, and Seville, as well as two additional stipends tied to such positions. As was customary, the king of Castile sent a delegation to Rome to pay homage to the new pope. Sánchez de Arévalo once again found himself undertaking this duty, as he had for the previous king and pope. The visit, which took place the year after Callistus's election, was not solely ceremonial in purpose. Enrique IV had Sánchez de Arévalo deliver an oration before the Pope, expressing his desire to have two of the three powerful military orders–Alcántara and Santiago–assigned to the Crown of Castile instead of to an independent Master. The income of these orders was significant and would aid the ailing treasury of the kingdom. In addition, because of the unstable relationship between the king and his highest-ranking noblemen (who usually led the orders), Enrique wanted to keep for himself the post of Master. Callistus was sympathetic to this request. The mission to the court of Callistus was beneficial to Sánchez de Arévalo's career as well. The Pope gave him lifelong tenure as both archdeacon of Treviño and dean of León, and also granted him the new office of dean of Seville, which had a generous income associated with it. During this visit Sánchez de Arévalo was also referred to as a papal referendary, or official signer of the Pope's documents.

At this time in his life Sánchez de Arévalo was at work on his second treatise in Spanish, a text titled *Verjel de los príncipes* (Pleasance of Princes, circa 1456–1457), which he dedicated to Enrique IV. In this short tract Sánchez de Arévalo considers those "honest sports and virtuous exercises" in which kings should participate: arms, hunting, and music. This well-written text would surely have pleased Enrique, who, like his father before him, was more interested in these pursuits than in directly governing his kingdom.

Shortly after Sánchez de Arévalo's return to Burgos early in 1457, Callistus awarded him the title of bishop of Oviedo. This new station required him to resign his offices in Treviño, León, and Seville. The Oviedo diocese was rather poor and isolated from the centers of Castilian political power. Although he probably traveled there from time to time, Sánchez de Arévalo was essentially an absentee bishop, and the diocese was administered by a member of his staff. The title of bishop of Oviedo, therefore, is best considered a reward for services rendered to the papacy and not a duty posting, a type of arrangement not atypical in this period.

Despite his ecclesiastical duties in Spain, which changed and increased over the years, Sánchez de Arévalo spent most of his remaining life in Rome, working with the Holy See in various capacities. From there he oversaw the operations and problems of his home dioceses. Pius II succeeded Callistus in the summer of 1458, and Sánchez de Arévalo continued as Castilian ambassador to the Vatican, where his work in favor of Enrique IV's troubled reign was well considered. Despite Pius's apparent high regard for the bishop of Oviedo, he was not as willing to reward Sánchez de Arévalo with the personal favors that the latter desired. In particular, Sánchez de Arévalo wanted to be named bishop of León–certainly a more advantageous bishopric than Oviedo–but Pius adamantly turned him down. Sánchez de Arévalo fared much better in his career with Pius's successor, Paul II (Pietro Barbo), who became head of the church in 1464.

Paul gave Sánchez de Arévalo the most challenging assignments of his career, appointing him castellan of Castel Sant'Angelo, the Pope's strongest fortress and the repository of the papal treasury. As castellan his duties included the defense of the castle and the supervision of all aspects of life within the garrison–the conduct of the soldiers assigned to it, the supplies needed to keep it running, and responsibility for the prisoners kept within its walls. Although naming him to the post was a measure of Paul's faith in his abilities, Sánchez de Arévalo subsequently wrote that the office of castellan was terribly difficult to endure. Among the hardships was immobility: Sánchez de Arévalo had been a man in constant movement up to this point in his life. In a work that he composed during this time, *De castellanis et custodibus arcium* (On Castellans and Guards of Citadels, 1465?), he describes in great detail the work of the castellan and the many virtues that this office demanded of the man who held it.

His years as castellan marked a period of increasing literary production for Sánchez de Arévalo. He was commissioned by the Pope to write several treatises condemning certain heresies that were epidemic in Rome at the time. One of these treatises was *Libellus de paupertate Christi et apostolorum* (Book of the Poverty of Christ and the Apostles, 1466). He also wrote on the absolute authority of the papacy, in *Defensorium ecclesiae et status ecclesiastici* (Defense of the Church and the State of Ecclesiastics, 1466). Sánchez de Arévalo also kept a close watch on politics at home. In 1465 King Enrique had been dethroned in effigy by rebel nobles, who crowned his younger brother, Alfonso, in his place. Sánchez de Arévalo had always been a steadfast

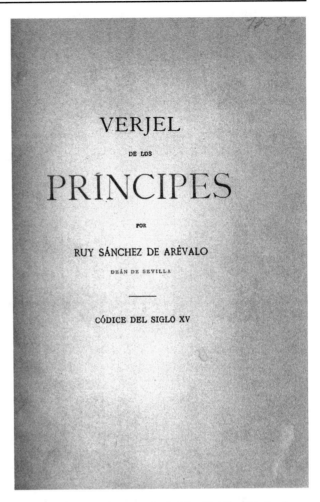

*Paperback cover for the standard edition (1900) of Sánchez de Arévalo's treatise on suitable avocations for royalty, written circa 1456–1457 (University of California at Los Angeles Library)*

defender of Enrique but was probably also worried about his own interests in Castile and what an abrupt change in government might do to his ecclesiastical offices and incomes. At this time he wrote *Liber de monarchia orbis et de differentia cuiusvis humani principatus tam imperalis quam regalis et de antiquitate et iustitia utriusque* (A Book about the Monarchy of the World and about Its Difference from a Sort of Human Preeminence as Imperial as Royal, and about the Antiquity and Justice of Either, 1467), in which he not only defended the cause of the unfortunate monarch but also identified the Pope as the only person with the authority to depose an anointed king. The problem was resolved in 1468 with the death of young Alfonso and the restored allegiance to Enrique of those who had opposed him.

Paul II twice transferred Sánchez de Arévalo to different bishoprics in Spain. In 1465, a year after he became castellan of Castel Sant'Angelo, the Pope shifted him from

Oviedo to Zamora, which was an older but even less financially endowed see. In any case, Sánchez de Arévalo remained an absentee bishop, and the income from his new diocese supplemented his stipend in Rome. Four years later Pope Paul decided to transfer him to Palencia, a wealthy diocese, but this time his designation was not well received by the administrators of the see. Paul prevailed, and Sánchez de Arévalo was consecrated bishop of Palencia, an office he held until his death in 1470.

Two works that Sánchez de Arévalo composed during the waning years of his life merit comment. The first is *Speculum vitae humanae* (Mirror of Human Life, 1468), a tract so popular that it went through sixteen print editions before 1500 and twenty-two thereafter. The book, intended to help those who are seeking guidance in choosing a career, is divided into two parts. In the first, Sánchez de Arévalo describes at length the secular occupations, from farming to royal service. The second part concerns ecclesiastical offices, where he draws greatly from his own experiences. In both parts he points out the virtues, vices, advantages, and pitfalls of the different professions. Scholars have commented on the evident medieval orientation of the work but also notice that the social order that Sánchez de Arévalo describes was an emerging Renaissance society, with new economic concerns.

The other text that Sánchez de Arévalo composed near the close of his life was the *Historia Hispanica* (1470), sometimes called the *Compendiosa historia Hispanica*. It is a patently medieval work in praise of all prominent Spaniards and was written from the perspective of a Castilian long absent from his homeland. The first three of the four parts are essentially reiterations of historical works that Sánchez de Arévalo consulted, such as Rodrigo Jiménez de Rada's *Historia de rebus Hispanie* (circa 1240), but the fourth, concerning the reign of Enrique IV, is the most noteworthy. Sánchez de Arévalo is reluctant to note the negative aspects of Enrique's monarchy (such as his failure to maintain absolute authority), but he tries to paint an impartial picture of the king and his realm. Because of Sánchez de Arévalo's absence from Castile during the times he describes, scholars generally put little stock in his version of events.

Rodrigo Sánchez de Arévalo died on 4 October 1470, after a brief illness that made it necessary for him to move from Castel Sant'Angelo. He was laid to rest first in the Spanish Church of Santiago in Rome, where an epitaph and sculpted figure of Sánchez de Arévalo were placed. The epitaph, written by two cardinals, describes him as a devoted servant to the Holy See and a doctor of both human and divine law. The epitaph and sculpture were later moved to the Church of Santa María de Monserrat in Rome, although it is not clear whether his remains accompanied them or not. A solemn funeral was held four years later in Palencia, where he held his last post as bishop.

**Biography:**

Teodoro Toni, *Don Rodrigo Sánchez de Arévalo, 1404–1470: Su personalidad y actividades* (Madrid, 1935).

**References:**

Nicolás Antonio, *Biblioteca hispana vetus* (1672), Biblioteca filológica hispana, no. 22 (Madrid: Visor, 1996);

Vicente Beltrán de Heredia, "La embajada de Castilla en el concilio de Basilea y su discusión con los ingleses acerca de la precedencia," *Hispania Sacra*, 10 (1957): 5–27;

Wolframe Benziger, ed., *Zur Theorie von Krieg und Frieden in der italianischen Renaissance* (Frankfurt & New York: P. Lang, 1996);

Geoffrey Butler, *Studies in Statecraft: Being Chapters, Biographical and Bibliographical, Mainly on the Sixteenth Century* (Cambridge: Cambridge University Press, 1920);

A. García, "Un opúsculo inédito de Rodrigo Sánchez de Arévalo: *De libera et irrefragabile auctoritate romani pontificis*," *Salmanticensis*, 4 (1957): 474–502;

H. Jedin, "Sánchez de Arévalo und die Konzilfrage unter Paul II," *Historisches Jahrbuch*, 73 (1953): 95–113;

Haywood Keniston, "A Fifteenth-Century Treatise on Education by Bishop Rodericus Zamorensis," *Bulletin Hispanique*, 32 (1930): 193–217;

Juan María Laboa, *Rodrigo Sánchez de Arévalo, Alcaide de Sant'Angelo* (Madrid: Fundación Universitaria Española, 1973);

José López de Toro, "El primer tratado de pedagogía en España (1453)," *Boletín de la Universidad de Granada*, 5 (1933): 259–275; 6 (1934): 153–171, 361–388; 7 (1935): 195–218;

Samuel Ball Platner, *The Topography and Monuments of Ancient Rome* (Boston: Allyn & Bacon, 1904), p. 495;

Julio Puyol, "Los cronistas de Enrique IV: Ruy Sánchez de Arévalo," *Boletín de la Real Academia de la Historia*, 78 (1921): 488–496;

Robert Brian Tate, "Rodrigo Sánchez de Arévalo and his *Compendiosa Historia Hispánica*," *Nottingham Medieval Studies*, 4 (1960): 58–80;

Teodoro Toni, "La realeza de Jesucristo en un tratado inédito del siglo XV," *Estudios eclesiásticos*, 13 (1934): 369–398;

Richard H. Trame, "Conciliar Agitation and Rodrigo Sánchez de Arévalo," in *Studies in Mediaevalia and Americana: Essays in Honor of William Lyle Davis, S.J.*, edited by Gerard G. Steckler and Leo Donald Davis (Spokane, Wash.: Gonzaga University Press, 1972), pp. 89–112;

Trame, *Rodrigo Sánchez de Arévalo, 1404–1470: Spanish Diplomat and Champion of the Papacy* (Washington, D.C.: Catholic University of America Press, 1958).

# Diego de San Pedro

*(fl. circa 1492)*

Sol Miguel-Prendes
*Wake Forest University*

WORKS: *La pasión trobada* (ca. 1480)

**Manuscript:** *Pasión trobada por Pedro [sic] de San Pedro a ruego duna dama,* in the *Cancionero de Oñate-Castañeda,* fols. 350r–372r.

**First publications:** *Coplas de la Pasión de Nuestro Redemptor,* in *Coplas de Vita Cristi: de la cena: con la Pasión; e de la Verónica: con la Resurrección de nuestro Redentor: e las siete Angustias: e siete Gozos de nuestra Señora, con otras obras mucho provechosas* (Saragossa: Paulo Hurus, 1492 [lost]; republished, 1495), fols. 35v–53v; *La pasión trobada,* broadside (Salamanca?: Leonardo Hutz & Lope Sanz?, 1496?).

**Editions:** *La pasión trobada de Diego de San Pedro: Edición paleográfica, según la versión manuscrita de Oñate-Castañeda,* edited by Dorothy Sherman Severin (Naples: Istituto Orientale, 1973); *Obras completas,* volume 3, edited by Keith Whinnom (Madrid: Castalia, 1973).

*Las siete angustias de Nuestra Señora* (ca. 1480)

**Manuscript:** *Las siete angustias de Nuestra Señora,* in *Cancionero de Pero Guillén de Segovia,* Madrid, Biblioteca Nacional MS. 4114, fols. 559r–573r.

**First publication:** In *Tractado de amores de Arnalte a [sic] Lucenda* (Burgos: Fadrique Alemán de Basilea, 1491); in *Coplas de Vita Cristi: de la cena: con la Pasión; e de la Verónica: con la Resurrección de nuestro Redentor: e las siete Angustias: e siete Gozos de nuestra Señora, con otras obras mucho provechosas* (Saragossa: Paulo Hurus, 1492 [lost]; republished, 1495).

**Edition:** In *Diego de San Pedro's* Tractado de amores de Arnalte y Lucenda: *A Critical Edition,* edited by Ivy A. Corfis (London: Tamesis, 1985), pp. 142–164.

**Electronic edition:** In *Tratado de amores de Arnalte y Lucenda* (ADMYTE 2. BOOST3 2297. TEXID 1753), a transcription of MS. 940 (Milan: Trivulziana, 1546. fols. 133v–222v) by Diane M. Wright and Stephen B. Raulston.

*Sermón* (ca. 1485)

**First publications:** *Sermón ordenado por Diego de Sant Pedro* (Alcalá de Henares: Arnaldo Guillén de Brocar, 1511); *Sermón ordenado por Diego de Sant Pedro porque dixeron unas señoras que le desseavan oyr predicar* (Burgos?: Juan de la Junta?, 1540?).

**Edition:** In *Obras completas,* volume 1, edited by Keith Whinnom (Madrid: Castalia, 1971), pp. 172–183.

*Tractado de amores de Arnalte y Lucenda* (1491)

**First publications:** *Tractado de amores de Arnalte a [sic] Lucenda* (Burgos: Fadrique Alemán de Basilea, 1491); *Arnalte e Lucenda. Tratado de Arnalte y Lucenda* (Burgos: Alonso de Melgar, 1522).

**Editions:** Transcribed by Raymond Foulché-Delbosch in *Révue Hispanique,* 25 (1911): 220–282; *Tratado de amores de Arnalte y Lucenda,* facsimile edition, prologue by A. G. de Amezúa (Madrid: Real Academia Española, 1952); *Diego de San Pedro's* Tractado de amores de Arnalte y Lucenda: *A Critical Edition,* edited by Ivy A. Corfis (London: Tamesis, 1985), pp. 33–173.

**Electronic edition:** *Tratado de amores de Arnalte y Lucenda* (ADMYTE 2. BOOST3 2297. TEXID 1753), a transcription of MS. 940 (Milan: Trivulziana, 1546. fols. 133v–222v) by Diane M. Wright and Stephen B. Raulston.

**Editions in English:** *A certayn treatye most wyttely deuised, orygynally written in the Spaynysshe, lately traducted in to Frenche entytled Lamant mal traicte de samye,* translated from French by John Clerke (London: Robert Wyre, 1543); *The pretie and wittie historie of Arnalt & Lucenda, with certen rules and dialogues set foorth for the learner of th' Italian tong,* translated from Italian by Claudius Hollyband (London: Thomas Purfoote, 1575); *A small treatise betwixt Arnalte and Lucenda entituled The evill-treated lover or, The melancholy knight,* verse translation from Italian by Leonard Lawrence (London: J. Okes, 1639).

*Cárcel de amor* (1492)

**First publications:** *Cárcel de amor* (Seville: Por Cuatro compañeros alemanes, 1492); *Cárcel de amor,* with a continuation by Nicolás Núñez (Burgos: Fadrique Alemán de Basilea, 1496).

**Editions:** *Diego de San Pedro's* Cárcel de amor: *A Critical Edition,* edited by Ivy A. Corfis (London: Tamesis, 1987); *Cárcel de amor,* facsimile edition, edited by Antonio Pérez y Gómez (Madrid: Soler, 1967).

**Standard edition:** *Cárcel de amor con la continuación de Nicolás Núñez,* edited by Carmen Parrilla (Barcelona: Crítica, 1995).

**Electronic edition:** *Cárcel de amor* (ADMYTE 2. BOOST3 2120. TEXID 1750), a transcription of the 1492 edition by Ivy A. Corfis.

**Editions in English:** *The castle of loue* (London: Printed by Robert Wyre for Richarde Kele, 1540); *The Castell of Loue,* translated by John Bourchier (London, ca. 1549); *The Castel of Love, 1549? A Translation by John Bourchier, Lord Berners, of* Cárcel de amor, *1492, by D. de San Pedro,* introduction by William G. Crane (Gainesville, Fla.: Scholars' Facsimiles & Reprints, 1950); *Prison of love, 1492: Together with the Continuation by Nicolás Núñez, 1496,* translated by Keith Whinnom (Edinburgh: Edinburgh University Press, 1979).

*Desprecio de la Fortuna* (ca. 1498)

**First publications:** In *Las CCC del famosíssimo poeta Juan de Mena con su glosa: y las cinqüenta con su glosa: y otras obras* (Saragossa: George Coci, 1509; Alcalá de Henares: Juan de Villanueva y Pedro de Robles, 1566), pp. 73–86; published, without prologue, in *Cancionero general recopilado por Hernando del Castillo* (Valencia: Cristóbal Kofman, 1511), pp. cvr–cxviir.

**Edition:** In *Obras completas,* volume 3, edited by Dorothy Sherman Severin and Keith Whinnom (Madrid: Castalia, 1985), pp. 270–297.

Minor Verse

**First publications:** Twenty-two of San Pedro's minor poems appear in *Cancionero general recopilado por Hernando del Castillo* (Valencia: Cristóbal Kofman, 1511; facsimile edition by Antonio Rodríguez-Moñino, Madrid: Real Academia Española, 1958), pp. cxiiir–cxvr, cxxiir, cxxiiir, cxxiiiv, cxxxiiir, ccxxviv; and six more in the second edition (Valencia, 1514); two ballads appear in Martin Nucio, *Cancionero de romances* (Amberes, 1550), pp. 245–246; facsimile edition by Ramón Menéndez Pidal, Madrid, 1914; reprinted, 1945).

**Editions:** *Obras,* edited, with an introduction, by Samuel Gili y Gaya (Madrid: Espasa-Calpe, 1950); *Obras completas,* volume 3, edited by Dorothy Sherman Severin and Keith Whinnom (Madrid: Castalia, 1985), pp. 241–269.

**Electronic edition:** *Cancionero de romances* (ADMYTE 2), a transcription of the 1550 edition

(New York: Hispanic Society) by Miles Becker and Antonio Cortijo Ocaña.

Diego de San Pedro achieved early recognition as the author of two sentimental fictions, *Tractado de amores de Arnalte y Lucenda* (The Story of the Loves of Arnalte and Lucenda, 1491; translated as *The pretie and wittie historie of Arnalt & Lucenda,* 1575) and *Cárcel de amor* (Prison of Love, 1492; translated as *The Castell of Love,* circa 1549). Their most distinctive feature is a complex analysis of sentimental love. Both works were quickly translated into French, Italian, and English. *Cárcel de amor,* also translated into Catalan, enjoyed unusual publishing success, with more than thirty prints and reprints in its original Castilian, more than twenty in seven other languages. The author was fully aware of the interest *Cárcel de amor* elicited. In his poem *Desprecio de la Fortuna* (Contempt of Fortune, circa 1498), he repented from his previous "obras livianas" (frivolous writings) and stated with remorse that the "salsa para pecar" (zest for sin) in *Cárcel de amor* "no tuvo en leerse calma" (had attracted excessively avid readers).

Besides his success as a popular fiction writer, San Pedro was also known in the sixteenth and seventeenth centuries as a skillful poet. Some court documents refer to him as "el trovador" (the troubadour), and Baltasar Gracián mentions San Pedro's poems in his *Agudeza y arte de ingenio* (1648; translated as *The Mind's Wit and Art,* 1964) as an example of the sharpest intellect and most subtle intricacy. San Pedro's *La pasión trobada* (The [Lord's] Passion in Verse, circa 1480) enjoyed tremendous popularity in Spain for more than four centuries and was still being printed in 1850 as a devotional pamphlet with broad popular appeal.

In contrast with the author's widespread literary reputation, little is known about his life. Keith Whinnom's exhaustive archival research was unable to ascertain San Pedro's identity, although it positively ruled out earlier identifications, such as Emilio Cotarelo y Mori's, that placed him at the court of Juan II of Castile. From what can be deduced from the works, particularly the prologues to the *Tractado de amores de Arnalte y Lucenda, Cárcel de amor,* and *Desprecio de la Fortuna,* San Pedro could not have begun writing before 1470. The *Tractado de amores de Arnalte y Lucenda* is dedicated to Isabel's ladies-in-waiting and includes a panegyric of the queen. In the second edition, the author identifies himself as a servant of Don Juan Téllez-Girón, Count of Urueña. Don Juan was one of the sons of Pedro Girón, a powerful grandee and favorite of King Enrique IV of Castile, Juan II's heir and half brother to Isabel (Isabella), whom she succeeded amid the revolts of opposing aristocratic factions. *Desprecio de la Fortuna* is dedicated to the count of Urueña, but here San Pedro addresses the count as "his lord," whom he served for twenty-nine years. *Cárcel de amor* is dedicated to another

Téllez-Girón connection, Diego Fernández de Córdoba, who was *alcaide de los donzeles,* or leader of a light-cavalry troop composed of young noblemen who enjoyed special privileges. The *alcaide* married Juana Pacheco, a niece of Téllez-Girón, sometime after 1475. Another person mentioned by name in the prologue to *Cárcel de amor* is Doña Marina Manuel. A member of the highest Castilian nobility, Doña Marina was also related by marriage to Téllez-Girón and served as one of Isabel's attendant ladies until 1490. Furthermore, the plot of *Cárcel de amor* unfolds in Peñafiel, a provincial estate in the Sierra Morena belonging to the Girón family. Taking the last possible approximate date for the composition of *Desprecio de la Fortuna* as 1498 and considering the twenty-nine years San Pedro served the count of Urueña, Carmen Parrilla notes that if the count and his servant were the same age, he would have been thirteen years old in 1469. Much more likely, Parrilla presumes, the poet was older than his young lord and a mature man by the end of the fifteenth century, when he composed *Desprecio de la fortuna,* in which he apologizes for the errors of his youth. Taking all this evidence into account, Parrilla places the author's career during the time when aristocratic unrest triggered by Enrique IV's succession had been stifled and powerful families such as the Téllez-Giróns bowed to Isabel—that is, around 1476. Therefore, San Pedro was writing in the 1480s and well into the 1490s for the entourage of the queen. His name disappears from documentary records after the composition of *Desprecio de la fortuna,* and his death passed unnoticed by a younger generation.

If San Pedro's association with noble circles is limited to the Téllez-Girón family and a few individuals related to it by marriage, his literary connections are not much broader. Whinnom adroitly notices that San Pedro's name does not appear in the tightly woven net of poetic *preguntas* (questions) and *respuestas* (answers) composed by the poets included in the *Cancionero general* of 1511 and concludes that he must have remained at the margin of the literary cliques of Isabel's court. The dedication to the ladies in *Tractado de amores de Arnalte y Lucenda* expresses openly the poet's "temor de vuestro burlar" (fear of their mockery), and one of his minor poems addresses a lady to whom he tendered a love letter in a glove, which she boldly showed to a group of gentlemen to scorn him. From this and other evidence, Whinnom sketches San Pedro's personality as that of an *hidalgo,* or member of the lower nobility, at the service of a grandee. He did as he was told, appears to have been exceedingly afraid of ridicule, and was willing to go to stylistic extremes to please his public. He obeyed any criticism made by the refined ladies-in-waiting of the queen and toiled over every word he wrote.

Another controversial point about San Pedro's biography is the *converso* (convert) status that might be implied

*Woodcut from the British Library copy of the 1496 Burgos edition of Diego de San Pedro's* Cárcel de amor, *first published in Seville in 1492. This edition is the first to include a continuation by the poet Nicolás Núñez that resolves the plot conflicts of the original poem. The title of the book appears on the scroll at the right (from* Diego de San Pedro's Cárcel de amor: A Critical Edition, *edited by Ivy A. Corfis, 1987; University of South Carolina Spartanburg Library).*

from his family name. It was a common practice for Jews who converted to Christianity to adopt a saint's name as a family name, but, as Whinnom points out, new and old Christians alike followed the same practice. San Pedro's presumed profession, as a sort of secretary to the count of Urueña, would also indicate that he was of Jewish stock, but no concrete evidence exists to support the claim. Still, several scholars subscribe to the *converso* theory: Marcel Bataillon bases his argument on the pathetic tone of his works; Francisco Márquez Villanueva, A. van Beysterveldt, Santiago Tejerina-Canal, and Regula Rohland de Langbehn have all suggested that the historical circumstances surrounding the composition of *Cárcel de amor* make it a literary response to the launching of the Inquisition; and Colbert I. Nepaulsingh notes in *Cárcel de amor* the apparent use of characters and attitudes borrowed from the Old Testament.

The dates ascribed to San Pedro's works are largely conjectural. The earliest appears to be *La pasión trobada*, probably composed in the late 1470s because it was included in an anthology assembled around the mid 1480s. It is dedicated to a nun for whom the poet declares his love, and it tells the story of the Passion of Christ in 248 stanzas of octosyllabic verses. It begins with the Agony in the Garden and ends before the Resurrection, an interesting fact if the poet was, in fact, Jewish. The manuscript version attributes the poem to Pedro de San Pedro and differs greatly from later printed editions in length and quality. If the name "Pedro" is not a copyist error, it can be assumed that Diego de San Pedro rewrote and polished a version of the Passion story composed by an inferior namesake. San Pedro added twelve introductory stanzas declaring his love for the nun and removed some sixty stanzas at the end that, according to Whinnom, are "pedestrian, based on noncanonical material, and metrically defective."

*La pasión trobada* follows closely the biblical narrative and phrasing of the Vulgate with only minor distortions to accommodate a rhyme or the required number of syllables. The canonical text, however, marked in the poem with the rubric "El texto evangelical" (The Gospel Text), is greatly expanded with apocryphal incidents. The most substantial additions include the legendary early life of Judas, and the episode in which Veronica compassionately wipes Jesus' face, later showing its imprint in the cloth to Mary. Parallel to Jesus' Passion, San Pedro also introduces the account of the passion of Mary, drawing from contemporary Marian devotion to assign Jesus' mother a much larger role than she is given in the Gospels. Finally, the author amplifies every detail of the Passion, focusing on its most horrifying aspects. As Whinnom notes, the gruesome details are not San Pedro's invention but taken from the *Meditationes vitae Christi* (Meditations on the Life of Christ, circa 1346–1364) by the Franciscan Juan de Caulibus. San Pedro follows the well-known technique of meditating on the humanity of Jesus, asking readers to reconstruct every detail of the scene to fill their hearts with devotion. A large portion of the material is presented as direct speech, either in soliloquy or dialogue, which is a characteristic of Franciscan preaching in the *Meditationes vitae Christi* as well.

The appeal of *La pasión trobada* as devotional literature was long lasting. The introductory stanzas in which the poet addresses the lovely nun were suppressed in the sixteenth century, and San Pedro's account of the Passion was actually performed as a play in 1566, which leads Dorothy S. Severin, in her 1964 essay "'La Passión trobada' de Diego de San Pedro y sus relaciones con el drama medieval de la Pasión" (Diego de San Pedro's Versified Passion and Its Relation to Medieval Passion Plays) to relate it to other medieval Passion plays in French, Ger-

man, and English. Scholars such as Marcelino Menéndez y Pelayo and Samuel Gili y Gaya, who had access only to the truncated versions that survived in loose leaves until the second half of the nineteenth century, dismiss *La pasión trobada* as archaic and lacking appeal to modern readers. More recently, Whinnom explains its popularity in both literary and nonliterary terms. *La pasión trobada* responds to an emotional need felt by an unsophisticated audience. It provides an accurate translation of the Gospel narrative and incorporates meditation techniques to allow the reader a visual reconstruction of the scene that would bring compassion and salvation. At the same time, it includes attractive materials, such as the accounts of the early life of Judas and Mary's passion. San Pedro's style is here deceptively simple. The most conspicuous features of *La pasión trobada* are its intensity and the effortless phrasing that builds the drama of the scenes.

*Las siete angustias de Nuestra Señora* (The Seven Sorrows of Our Lady) was likely composed around 1480, after *La pasión trobada*, from which the author takes eleven stanzas word for word and slightly varies a further six half-stanzas. San Pedro was one of the first Spanish poets to treat the subject of the Seven Sorrows, a series that matches Mary's Seven Joys. A feast commemorating the Seven Sorrows, also known as the Seven Swords or Knives, had been established by the Church in 1423. He seems to have selected several engaging stanzas from *La pasión trobada* and completed them with new material. The earliest extant printing of the poem is in the 1491 edition of *Tractado de amores de Arnalte y Lucenda*, which differs greatly from that in *Coplas de Vita Cristi: de la cena: con la Pasión; e de la Verónica: con la Resurrección de nuestro Redentor: e las siete Angustias: e siete Gozos de nuestra Señora, con otras obras mucho provechosas*, published in 1492 by Paulo Hurus. It is impossible to decide whether it was ever conceived as an independent poem or as a mere digression in *Tractado de amores de Arnalte y Lucenda*, in which Arnalte, rejected by Lucenda, composes the poem to forget his grief.

*Tractado de amores de Arnalte y Lucenda* and *Cárcel de amor* belong to the genre of *ficción sentimental* (sentimental romance), a term that is now more widely accepted than the confusing and outdated *novelas sentimentales* (sentimental novels) coined by Menéndez y Pelayo, who first categorized them in *Orígenes de la novela* (Origins of the Novel, 1905–1915). Sentimental romances are narrative works in prose, shorter than chivalric romances, that surfaced in Castile in the second half of the fifteenth century. Menéndez y Pelayo's explanation for the emergence of both genres, sentimental and chivalric romances, is the collapse of the medieval chivalric ideals that supported the feudal system and epic poetry and the subsequent rise of an aristocracy that preferred an idealized, escapist form of literature. Rohland de Langbehn notices that sentimental and chivalric romances emerge in Castile at a time when there is no evidence of any other genre of narrative fiction. They provided entertainment, along with chronicles, works in verse, old romances such as *El libro del caballero Çifar* (circa 1300; translated as *The Book of the Knight Zifar*, 1983) and *Amadís de Gaula* (Amadis of Gaul, circa 1300), and some well-known romances from the *matière de Bretagne*, or stories related to King Arthur's court. Chronologically, the first sentimental romances are Juan Rodríguez del Padrón's *Siervo libre de amor* (Free Slave of Love), the Constable of Portugal's *Sátira de felice e infelice vida* (Satire of a Happy and Unhappy Life), and the anonymous *Triste deleitación* (Sad Delight), all written around the mid 1400s. San Pedro's works are considered classics of this genre, which includes *Grimalte y Gradissa* (Grimalte and Gradissa, circa 1495), a sequel in part to Giovanni Boccaccio's *Elegia di Madonna Fiammetta* (1343–1344; translated as *The Elegy of Lady Fiammetta*, 1990), and *Grisel y Mirabella* (Grisel and Mirabella, circa 1495), both by Juan de Flores (flourished 1470–1500).

Scholars have yet to reach complete agreement on both the terminology and the generic ascription. Anna Krause places these romances in the formal category of the *tractatus* (treatise) and considers them primitive examples of experimentation in the novel. Bruno M. Damiani and Joseph Chorpenning concur, stressing their didactic quality. Pedro M. Cátedra regards them as a special type of the love treatise in the form of epistolary autobiography. Bruce Wardropper and Whinnom reject the *tractatus* labeling and its implied didactic intent. Whinnom explains that the term was used loosely in the fifteenth and sixteenth centuries and is more accurately translated as "story" or "romance." Finally, Alan Deyermond considers sentimental fictions a subgenre of romance; as chivalric romances, they narrate adventure stories, specifically sentimental adventures. In the same line and taking the argument one step further, Barbara F. Weissberger pronounces the sentimental romance genre, or subgenre, dead. Weissberger proposes to consolidate sentimental fictions and chivalric books into the single category of romance, ignoring the gendered and generic opposition of sentimental (feminine) and chivalric (masculine) created by Menéndez y Pelayo and regularly applied to romance by Hispano-medievalists.

The main problem sentimental romances pose is their lack of uniformity. Parrilla points out that their only consistent features are a similar treatment of love and a common effort to incorporate a multifaceted corpus on the theory and practice of human affection. Although they may vary greatly in form, however, sentimental romances share some of the following traits: they frequently take place in unfamiliar, remote places; and the duels, combats, and sieges that characterize chivalric fictions serve merely as a backdrop for an internal plot. This internal plot is carried through letters, poems, monologues, and dialogues that scrutinize the emotional extremes in a love relationship. Rohland de Langbehn identifies unity of action as a key structural element that sets sentimental fictions apart from chivalric romances; all episodes are subordinated to one narrative core, the experience of unrequited love. Stylistically, they share an autobiographical, sometimes even confessional, tone; narrative innovation; Latinizing syntax; and a rhetorically ornate style.

Since Menéndez y Pelayo's study, the earliest accepted precedents for the genre are Arthurian romances and Italian fiction, particularly Boccaccio's *Elegia di Madonna Fiammetta* and *Historia de duobus amantibus Eurialo et Lucrecia* (1444; translated as *The Tale of Two Lovers, Eurialus and Lucretia*, 1988), by Aeneas Sylvius Piccolomini, who later became Pope Pius II. More-recent studies have acknowledged the significance of *cancionero* poetry and Ovid's *Heroides*–Ovid's collection of epistolary writings translated into Castilian by Alfonse, el Sabio (the Learned, 1221–1289), and, later, by Rodríguez del Padrón–in the formation of the genre. Ovid's collection of fictional letters by classical heroines who fell victim to love was well known in Castile beginning in the thirteenth century. Rodríguez del Padrón, who wrote *Siervo libre de amor*, adapted them freely in the fifteenth century. Recently, Marina Brownlee has shown that the circulation of some romances belonging to the *matière de Troyes*, the Trojan stories inherited from classical antiquity and adapted to the medieval mind-set, facilitated the influence of the *Heroides* in Castile, since they include some of Ovid's letters. The impact of the *Heroides* can explain the central role of letters in sentimental fictions, while the tragic view of love, a defining characteristic in these works, is taken from the *Heroides, Elegia di Madonna Fiammetta*, and many *cancionero* poems, as is the autobiographical mode. Besides this detailed list of direct influences, Deyermond presumes a more complicated web of indirect stimuli, the most significant being Augustine's *Confessions*, the model for confessional autobiography throughout the Middle Ages; Peter Abelard's *Historia calamitatum* (circa 1130; translated as *The Story of My Misfortunes*, 1922), which adds an erotic component to the Augustinian model; and Boethius's *De Consolatione Philosophiae* (circa 524; translated as *The Consolation of Philosophy*, 1664), a medieval standard for self-consolation that alternates verse and prose.

Yet, the structure and concept of love presented in the *Heroides* and *Elegia di Madonna Fiammetta* do not seem to have exerted a direct influence on San Pedro's fiction, in particular on *Cárcel de amor*. Whinnom proposes, instead, French sources such as Guillaume de Machaut's *Le Livre de voir-dit* (circa 1363; translated as *The Book of the True Poem*, 1998), a love story narrated as autobiography that includes forty-six letters in prose and six poems connected by narrative couplets; and Christine de Pizan's *Le Livre du Duc des Vrais Amans* (circa 1403–1405; translated as *The*

*Book of the Duke of True Lovers,* 1908), which is formally similar to *Le Livre de voir-dit.* San Pedro's sentimental love resembles the courtly love of *cancionero* poetry, as Pamela Waley has shown; it is a moral principle that ennobles the individual, an unselfish gratuitous passion, an end in itself, love for the sake of love. The sentimental hero accepts and upholds the total supremacy of his beloved over him, men's loving loyalty is absolute, and love prevails always over reason.

*Tractado de amores de Arnalte y Lucenda* was published in Burgos on 25 November 1491 by Fadrique Alemán de Basilea. Whinnom dates its composition to the first years of the 1480s, when San Pedro must also have written the panegyric on the queen that is included in the book. Whinnom gives as terminus a quo 1479, the end of the civil wars, when the Téllez-Girón family had already capitulated to Isabel, and as terminus ad quem 1482, based on the author's references to peace in the realm and no mention of Isabel's crusade against Granada.

Addressed to the ladies of the queen, *Tractado de amores de Arnalte y Lucenda* is a story told in the first person by a narrator called "el autor" (the author) about his encounter with Arnalte, who relates his efforts to win the love of Lucenda. The narrator, far away from Castile, gets lost in a fearsome wilderness as the sun is setting. He sees smoke and finds a palace covered in black, where he observes a group of gentlemen also dressed in black. One of them invites him to come inside through a door with a sign proclaiming "Ésta es la triste morada / del que muere / porque muerte no le quiere" (This is the sad dwelling / of one who is dying / because death does not want him). The narrator is treated hospitably and given a bed but cannot sleep, agitated by the events he has witnessed and the constant, noisy lamentations of a knight. In the morning the narrator attends mass in the chapel, where a tomb has been prepared. After breakfast, the melancholy knight asks him if King Ferdinand has a queen worthy of him, which prompts the narrator to offer 210 stanzas of praise to Isabel. At the conclusion, the knight admits that he was already aware of the queen's fine reputation but wished to know if "el autor" would do her justice. Convinced of the narrator's discretion, the knight tells his own tale and asks "el autor" to make his heartbreaking story known. From this point on, the narrator is silent until he again addresses the ladies at the end.

Arnalte is a noble from Thebes, brought up at court. One day, while attending a funeral, he falls in love with Lucenda, the daughter of the deceased. He tries to reach her through all imaginable means, but she tears up his letters and rejects his advances, which become more and more forthright. Arnalte's sister, Belisa, is worried about him, but the hero refuses to confide in her. Instead, he reveals his love to his friend Elierso, who lives next door to Lucenda. Elierso is also in love with

Lucenda and eventually marries her. Arnalte finds out after he returns from a hunting holiday planned by his sister to restore his health. When Arnalte challenges Elierso to a duel, Elierso replies that he has married Lucenda to cure his friend of lovesickness. Arnalte chooses the weapons and requests that the king supervise the duel. Even in defeat, Elierso refuses to admit his fault, and Arnalte kills him. Arnalte writes to Lucenda, offering to take Elierso's place as her husband, but she makes no reply and takes her vows in a convent. Arnalte retires to the wilderness after seeing his sister married off. He concludes by repeating his request that the narrator share this story with compassionate women. The narrator then addresses the ladies of the court, reminding them that his purpose is to entertain them.

The physical events just described are a secondary part of the romance, and San Pedro devotes few pages to them. Instead, the most important part of the work is an internal plot consisting of the participants' arguments, feelings, and reactions. Monologues, speeches, and letters, rather than dialogue, describe in detail the psychological state of the speaker or writer.

The composition of *Cárcel de amor* can be dated sometime between 1482, the beginning of the campaign against Granada, and 1492, the date of its first printing, since there is no manuscript evidence. Since *Cárcel de amor* is dedicated to Fernández de Córdoba, *alcaide de los donzeles,* several scholars agree that the dedication could not have been written before 1483, the year when Don Diego, still quite young, took King Boabdil prisoner at the Battle of Lucena. The great success of *Cárcel de amor* increased when one of its most attentive readers, the poet Nicolás Núñez, composed a continuation that solved its conflict. Later editions in the sixteenth century consistently printed *Cárcel de amor* with Núñez's addition.

The story of *Cárcel de amor* echoes, to some extent, *Tractado de amores de Arnalte y Lucenda,* particularly at the beginning. The narrator, named "el autor" as in *Tractado de amores de Arnalte y Lucenda,* is returning home through the Sierra Morena after the summer's fighting. In the middle of the wilderness he encounters a fearsome knight, dressed in skins, who carries in his left hand a steel shield and in his right a stone carving that depicts a beautiful woman and radiates fire. The flames drag a prisoner, who begs the narrator to help him. The narrator confronts the ferocious warrior and learns that his name is Desire, chief officer of Love. He keeps away hope with his shield; the beauty of the stone image causes afflictions; and with them both he burns yet lives. He is taking a captive to die in the Prison of Love. The group disappears, and the narrator spends a sleepless night.

The following morning, he sees the prison on a mountain peak. He climbs to the tower and sees the prisoner ceaselessly burning in a chair of fire and being subjected to all kinds of torture. He is Leriano, son of the Duke Guersio and the Duchess Coleria of Macedonia, and is in love with Princess Laureola, daughter of King Gaulo. Leriano asks the narrator for help in winning over Laureola's heart. He agrees and makes his way to the court at Suria to tell the princess of Leriano's distressing state. Laureola is infuriated and threatens the narrator. He decides to pursue the case even at the risk of his life and mentions Leriano every subsequent time he sees her. He misinterprets her blushes and avoidance of company as love and persuades Leriano to write her a letter. She accepts the letter, and thus begins an epistolary exchange.

After being rescued from the Prison of Love by the narrator, Leriano returns to court and kisses Laureola's hand, but Persio, a friend of his who is also in love with Laureola, denounces them to the king, swearing that they are having intimate relations. The king sentences Laureola to death for causing dishonor. Leriano resolves to free Laureola, but the narrator advises him to safeguard Laureola's reputation. Leriano debates his loyalty to the king versus his love for Laureola. Love prevails, and Leriano and his men liberate the princess and kill Persio.

The king lays siege to Leriano's castle for three months, during which time Leriano and his men suffer terrible hardship. He captures one of the false witnesses who testified against Laureola. The false witness confesses the truth under the threat of torture. Leriano dispatches him to the king, who lifts the siege and receives Laureola back at court. Leriano, however, is asked to stay away from court until the situation has calmed down, and he deteriorates into his former state. He writes once more to Laureola, but she rejects his love. Her letter explains that she cannot continue their relationship since that would confirm Persio's accusation. She acknowledges her debt to Leriano and promises to repay him after her father dies.

Leriano resolves to die. His friend Tefeo tries to cure his lovesickness by citing examples of women's worthlessness. Infuriated by his friend's words, Leriano delivers an elaborate defense of women, presenting fifteen reasons for condemning men who speak ill of them, twenty reasons why men are indebted to them, and a catalogue of virtuous women. Fearing for the fate of Laureola's letters, he tears them into pieces and drinks them in a glass of water. The narrator declares that Leriano's death proves his faith and constancy and, after attending his funeral, returns to Peñafiel.

As in *Tractado de amores de Arnalte y Lucenda,* most of the incidents are covered in brief narrative, while letters and speeches make up the body of the work. *Cárcel de amor* is divided into forty-eight chapters of uneven length. Twenty are brief accounts of the events told by "el autor," who also reports all the speeches verbatim.

*Woodcut from the 1496 edition of* Cárcel de amor *depicting the narrator's first encounter with the fearsome knight Desire (from* Diego de San Pedro's Cárcel de amor: A Critical Edition, *edited by Ivy A. Corfis, 1987; University of South Carolina Spartanburg Library)*

Of twelve speeches, ten exchange opinions between two characters and two are monologues. There are seven love letters, one letter in which Laureola petitions her father for forgiveness, two challenge letters, a harangue to the troops, Duchess Coleria's *planctus* (lament) over her son's fate, and, finally, Leriano's speech disproving his friend Tefeo's accusations and defending women.

The early translations of *Tractado de amores de Arnalte y Lucenda* and *Cárcel de amor* into French, Italian, and English, and their many printings and reprints, attest to their remarkable success. In 1514 an Italian translation by Lelio Manfredi dedicated to Isabel D'Este was printed in Venice. This version was translated into French between 1525 and 1528 in Paris and Lyon as *Prison d'amour* (Prison of Love). The Musée de Cluny displays a tapestry that depicts the return of Laureola and her reception at court after Leriano frees her. It belongs to a series of nine representing scenes from *Cárcel de amor,* which Francis I gave to his sister-in-law Renée when she married Ercole D'Este, son of Isabel. Contemporary writers also took notice.

The influence of *Cárcel de amor* on Fernando de Rojas's *Comedia* (1499; revised in 1502 as the *Tragicomedia*) *de Calixto y Melibea,* later commonly known as *La Celestina* (1499–1502; translated as *The Spanish Bawd, represented in Celestina: or, The Tragicke-Comedy of Calisto and Melibea,* 1631) is well documented, and the letters composed for *Tractado de amores de Arnalte y Lucenda* would become rhetorical models, one of the English translations of the work being used as a manual of rhetoric. Moralists also bore witness to San Pedro's popularity. In his *De institutione foeminae christianae* (1523; translated as *The Instruction of a Christen Woman,* 1529), the Spanish humanist Juan Luis Vives listed *Cárcel de amor* as one of those "pestilent" books that sensible parents must keep away from honest daughters.

The modern reception of San Pedro's sentimental romances began with the studies of George Ticknor, Pascual de Gayangos, and José Amador de los Ríos, which grouped them with chivalric romances and unanimously criticized their rhetorical style and baffling structure. Menéndez y Pelayo was the first to acknowledge the merit of San Pedro's rhetorical style, as he revealed in *Orígenes de la novela.* In his opinion, rhetoric allowed the writer to craft a pathetic expression well suited to the new type of novelistic prose he was initiating. Less positive was Gili y Gaya in his introduction to the 1950 edition of San Pedro's works, in which he states that their pompous tone and learned pretentiousness deter modern readers.

Not until Wardropper's essay "El mundo sentimental de la *Cárcel de amor*" (1953) were San Pedro's romances placed in their proper context as a reflection of aristocratic longing for old-fashioned practices of heroic chivalry and courtly love. Whinnom has identified and elucidated the two main areas that alienate these works from modern sensibility: their concept of love and the role of rhetoric. The perplexing combination of letters and speeches in *Tractado de amores de Arnalte y Lucenda* and its lack of dialogue are a result of the fact that San Pedro follows the precepts of medieval rhetorical theory, which restrict dialogue exclusively to drama and some forms of fable and anecdote. San Pedro is also building on the tradition of *Heroides.* He became acquainted with this tradition most likely through the letters included in Leomarte's *Sumas de historia troyana* (Summary of Trojan History, 1300–1350), which was still circulating in manuscript form at the end of the fifteenth century. San Pedro set the stage for the first epistolary novel in Spanish, Juan de Segura's *Proceso de cartas de amores* (Exchange of Love Letters, 1548).

The overblown rhetorical style also provides an unintended comic element, at least for modern readers. San Pedro aimed to improve Castilian by following the medieval rhetoricians' precepts for writing in Latin. He wished to create a work that compared favorably with classical literature. For that purpose, monologues, letters, and speeches are set rhetorical pieces, and he adopts a heavily Latinized prose style. This ambition to rival Latin is a mark of the Renaissance writer, but, in San Pedro's case, it contradicts one of the principles of humanist good taste in that, as Elio Antonio de Nebrija points out, "no de manera que sea la salsa más que el manjar" (the sauce overpowered the meal). Particularly in *Tractado de amores de Arnalte y Lucenda,* San Pedro resorts to a highly Latinized syntax with the verb unnaturally placed at the end to achieve a rhyme. His prose is loaded with all the possible rhetorical ornaments, both *facile* (simple), such as *colores rhetorici* (rhetorical colors), with a preference for the "figures of sound" to produce an acoustic effect; and *difficile* (difficult), such as figures of thought and tropes, with a preference for *amplificatio* (amplification). The comic effect, however, is not a consequence of this accumulation of rhetorical devices but instead of a disjuncture of form and content.

Modern readers tend to find some of the episodes in *Tractado de amores de Arnalte y Lucenda* laughable. The hero disguises himself as a woman in order to stand next to Lucenda in church, and his page goes through Lucenda's garbage in search of his master's letter. Arnalte's hunting retreat to recover from his amorous passion, his offer to Lucenda to take her husband's place after he kills him, and his recitation of *Las siete angustias de Nuestra Señora* to forget his own pain all strike modern audiences as absurd. Still, Whinnom has traced many of these elements to literary models that are not comic at all. For instance, Arnalte masquerading as a woman derives from the story of Achilles and Deidamia in Ovid's *Ars amatoria* (The Art of Love). The motif of a man's supplanting the man he has killed has a long tradition, from the Oedipus myth to Chrétien de Troyes's *Yvain* and, in Spain, the late-thirteenth-century *Gesta de las mocedades de Rodrigo* (The Tales of the Cid's Youthful Exploits).

The source of hilarity lies in the absurd contrast between Arnalte's actions and the ostentatious idealism of his letters and speeches. Arnalte may not be the ideal lover but just a self-centered fool whose only concern is satisfying his desires. For that purpose, he follows faithfully the practical advice provided by Ovid's *Ars amatoria,* a book that is not really about love but about seduction techniques. His devotion to Lucenda is sincere but self-interested; he demands favors for his service, blames Lucenda for his suffering, and seeks remedy for his lovesickness by any means within his reach. Yet, for medieval readers, Arnalte's conduct is extravagantly generous and Lucenda's disdainful and diffident. Just for being in love, Arnalte is entitled to Lucenda's favors and she is indebted to him. Contemporary French and Italian translations provide praise for the melancholy knight's heroism and blame Lucenda's cruelty. Nonetheless, the bizarre disparity between the words' loftiness and the plot incidents this language is used to record, such as a page searching through the garbage, is so vast that it encourages laughter. Furthermore, San Pedro contradicts the principles of rhetoric, both medieval and humanist, that require a low style for low matters and a high style to portray high events. The individual letters and speeches, however, were used as rhetorical models until the seventeenth century in their Italian, French, and English versions, but only because translators eliminated a large amount of the stylistic ornament.

*Cárcel de amor* builds on the genre initiated with *Tractado de amores de Arnalte y Lucenda* but is a superior achievement. San Pedro had greatly improved his narrative technique, eliminating digressions, such as the panegyric on the queen or *Las siete angustias de Nuestra Señora,* and closely linking all the rhetorical elements (such as letters and speeches) to the subject matter of the work in a tighter, more credible plot. *Cárcel de amor* begins with an allegory of love, an old rhetorical device that performs several important functions. First of all, it provides a useful language for understanding and appreciating the discourse of love. San Pedro conveys his ideas on the psychology of love through a plastic representation that appealed to contemporary Castilian taste, as the success of Dante's writings and Íñigo López de Mendoza's love allegories indicates. It also sets the tone for the whole story. The allegorical introduction acts as an indication that the work is meant to be solemn and artistic. Finally, the lack of a clear-cut line between the world of ideas in the initial "perfect" allegory that the narrator sets in Spain and the world of events that take place in Macedonia, with which allegorical episodes interfere, envelops the whole *Cárcel de amor* in a dream atmosphere.

The style of *Cárcel de amor* abandons the Latinizing syntax of *Tractado de amores de Arnalte y Lucenda* and greatly reduces the use of acoustic conceits, but it is not less rhetorical. The acoustic conceits of *Tractado de amores de Arnalte y Lucenda* have matured into a rhythmic prose that is unsurpassed in its genre. As in the earlier work, the studied style of *Cárcel de amor* aspires to beauty, particularly in the letters and speeches, which are as polished as poems. Contrary to the bizarre incongruity between rhetorical style and mundane events in *Tractado de amores de Arnalte y Lucenda,* much of the ornamentation in *Cárcel de amor* derives from a balancing of thoughts so intricate that it is impossible to separate style from content.

Whinnom has also elucidated San Pedro's concept of love and traced all its sources. It stems from the rich European tradition of courtly love poetry, the psychological theory of love developed by Scholastic theologians, and the medical treatises on the sickness of love. The allegory that opens *Cárcel de amor* presents the theologians' theory as it had been accepted by the poets.

Love is a desire for beauty and a passion that prevents the lover from regaining his moral independence. The difference between true love and false love is constancy, defined as total obedience to the lady. *Tractado de amores de Arnalte y Lucenda* and *Cárcel de amor* present two lovers whose unhinged state is just a manifestation of their overwrought faithfulness. The allegory in *Cárcel de amor* describes Understanding, Reason, Memory, and Will agreeing to their enslavement, and Leriano has evolved from the selfish Arnalte into an ideal lover whose reason eventually will order him to die of love. Leriano's deathbed defense of women praises them as the source of all virtue and politeness, and his impassioned love leads him to contemplate the Passion of Christ. The contradictory nature of love brings forth a paradox that San Pedro expresses in tirades of antithetical couplets (such as love/death and fire/ice), as do most of his contemporary Castilian courtly poets. As for the lady, her most important virtue is compassion, and while Lucenda might be suspected of cruelty, Laureola's conduct is irreproachable. She is compassionate in spite of her fears and not ungrateful after her release from prison.

A great deal of controversy still surrounds several aspects of San Pedro's romances. The possible heretical implications of his concept of love have been studied by E. Michael Gerli. The main theme of love is closely linked to the subjects of honor and justice, a connection that led Wardropper to identify four codes of conduct: love, chivalry, honor, and virtue. Other unresolved questions concern the structure and the role of the narrator, "el autor." Studies by Harvey Sharrer and Deyermond point out San Pedro's debt to Arthurian tradition, the similarities of *Cárcel de amor* to the *Mort Artu* (Death of Arthur), and his adaptation of Arthurian materials with a different point of view. In spite of the disagreements, scholars concur that *Cárcel de amor* is the paradigm of the *ficción sentimental* genre in the fifteenth and sixteenth centuries.

*Sermón* was printed without an indication of year or press but can be dated around 1485, after the composition and circulation of *Tractado de amores de Arnalte y Lucenda,* when some ladies of the court requested a sermon from the author because they desired to hear him preach. San Pedro chose to write a burlesque parody on the passion of love following the rigid structure of a learned sermon. He begins with the *thema,* an obligatory quotation of the Holy Writ in Latin, that he, instead, fabricates out of genuine biblical phrases and attributes to "el Evangelista Afición" (the Evangelist Desire). A biblical-sounding Christian instruction, "In patientia vestra sustinete vestros dolores" (Bear your sorrows in patience), is manipulated for mundane purposes and will be repeated in Spanish—"En vuestra paciencia sostened vuestros dolores"—at the end of each section of the poem. The *thema* is followed by the *prothema,* in which the preacher explains the meaning of the

Latin quotation in the vernacular and entrusts his work to God. San Pedro entrusts his *Sermón* to Amor, the god of love.

The preacher tackles the subject by dividing the *Sermón* into three sections. The first section sets rules on how ladies should be served by their lovers, while the second offers advice that may help to console the afflicted lover. The fundamental rule is that lovers must observe absolute secrecy in order to protect the lady's honor. To soothe the aches of love, the lover must remember the superiority of the lady who is causing them and have hope for his own constancy. Furthermore, the lover must be willing to die of love to prove his faithfulness and must bear his sorrows in patience. In the third section San Pedro offers advice to the ladies on how to treat their suitors. A woman's role is loving and consoling, and ladies must act accordingly, relieving their lovers' suffering. If they do not, they commit four mortal sins: the sin of pride by abusing their power, the sin of avarice by taking a heart and giving nothing in return, the sin of anger when their lovers irritate them, and the sin of sloth when they refuse a kind word. The model of a compassionate woman is illustrated with the story of Pyramus and Thisbe. The *Sermón* concludes with the required Latin prayer, the brief "Ad quam gloriam nos perducat" (And may he lead us into glory), but, instead of God, the poet invokes Amor, and the word *gloria* has explicit sexual overtones in fifteenth-century Spanish love poetry.

The *Sermón* is a guide to lovers on how to behave, an *ars amatoria* in Ovid's style, a common form in the Middle Ages. Scholars, such as Ménendez y Pelayo, have considered the *Sermón* an inept parody that lacks any charm. Whinnom's interpretation underscores the fact that the structure of a sermon offers a meticulous configuration for the exposition of ideas and was used for nonreligious purposes on many occasions. Without rejecting the obvious burlesque component, Whinnom sees also some elements of seriousness in the context of San Pedro's sentimental romances. *Tractado de amores de Arnalte y Lucenda* stresses the Ovidian, comic ingredient, but *Cárcel de amor* develops the precepts to lovers with complete gravity. Besides revealing a transitional stage in San Pedro's ideas, the *Sermón* is well written, engaging, and funny.

San Pedro is also the author of approximately thirty short love poems that can be dated between 1480 and 1492, that is, during the time when he wrote to entertain the ladies and gentlemen at the court of the Catholic Monarchs. Their most conspicuous feature is their similarity—the subject is always love, and they all use octosyllabic verse and a restricted vocabulary. The variety of strophic forms, however, includes *canciones, esparsas, romances,* and *villancicos* (different types of ballads and popular lyrics) of varying lengths and styles. Their content is identical only superficially, and most of them are prompted by real or imaginary events. For instance, a crude poem rebukes a lady who replied with an obscenity when the poet requested a kiss; another acknowledges a gift of "un hilo" (a thread) (perhaps a linen handkerchief) from a lady; a third enlists the help of a gypsy woman to inform a lady of the poet's love. Three poems composed on the occasion of Palm Sunday, Easter Sunday, and Low Sunday celebrate his amorous passion. Two *romances* are contrafacta of traditional ballads, and the *villancicos* incorporate dialogues between idealized shepherdesses and gentlemen.

This type of courtly poetry is known as *cancionero* verse, because it was compiled in anthologies or *cancioneros*. San Pedro's minor poems were first printed in the *Cancionero general* (General Compilation), assembled by Hernando del Castillo in 1511. The large number of poems included in *cancioneros* is a testimony to the popularity this form enjoyed well into the seventeenth century. In 1648 Gracián commented on the merit of old poems by citing one of San Pedro's in his *Agudeza y arte de ingenio,* praising San Pedro's witty ideas and lively style that demands "si el percibir la agudeza acredita de áquila, el producirla empeñar en ángel" (the farsightedness of an eagle to decipher it and the mind of an angel to compose it).

Contemporary reception has not been so sympathetic. Menéndez y Pelayo finds most *cancionero* poems objectionable, and San Pedro's, in particular, are likened to "atendados poéticos contra el buen gusto y las buenas costumbres" (terrorist attacks on good taste and good manners). Whinnom's studies have raised an awareness of the significance of San Pedro's minor poems, releasing them from Romantic notions of what poetry ought to be. The irreverent use of religious subjects in erotic works is not exclusive to San Pedro. The later Middle Ages show evidence of an intimate relationship with God that motivates the use of religious motifs in mundane literature and that must be understood as an indication of affectionate informality with God and not intentional blasphemy.

As for its form, *cancionero* poetry employs a special language consisting of an extremely limited vocabulary of abstract terms, and the poems normally lack a temporal context. The craft of a *cancionero* poet lies in exploiting to the maximum the ambiguity inherent in abstract terms through parallelism and antithesis, a technique that makes it nearly impossible to translate all the simultaneous levels of meaning. San Pedro is one of the most skilled *cancionero* poets, as Gracián appreciated, but this same skill, along with the playful quality of his poems, has prevented his verse from being understood and appreciated by modern scholars. Furthermore, San Pedro uses the same poetic technique in the letters in *Cárcel de amor* to achieve rhetorical brevity. The letters persuade their addressees but also manipulate readers of the work to accept San Pedro's ideas on love and the amorous behavior that the letters scrutinize.

San Pedro's last work is *Desprecio de la Fortuna,* first published in 1506 in an edition of Juan de Mena's *Laberinto de Fortuna* (The Labyrinth of Fortune, also known as *Las trescientas,* The Three Hundred [Stanzas]). Its composition can be dated around 1498, when San Pedro's patron, Juan Téllez-Girón, retired from the court to his Andalusian estate after having lost his twin brother, Rodrigo, and most of his fortune in the campaign against Granada. The count devoted the rest of his life to charity and reading Boethius's *De Consolatione Philosophiae,* whose themes echoed his own misfortunes. San Pedro, who most likely followed his patron into exile, dedicated *Desprecio de la Fortuna* to him. The prologue reveals that the poet is acquainted with Boethius and some of Seneca's dialogues, such as *De vita beata* (On the Happy Life) and *De tranquillitate animi* (On Peace of Mind). The poem begins with a *palinode,* a formal retraction from his previous erotic works, that lists and describes each of them in detail. After invoking God's aid, he initiates his versified treatise on Fortune in 410 lines. In this short span, San Pedro tries to capture Boethius's genuine message, focusing on the theme of the miseries of this world. The poet discards strictly medieval motifs such as the catalogue of Fortune's victims, a list of possible disasters, and the allegory of the Wheel of Fortune. While a great distance mediates between the two works, in a remarkable way *Desprecio de la Fortuna* is able to come as close to Boethius as some translations. Most critics have ignored *Desprecio de la Fortuna* in spite of the fact that, as Whinnom notices, San Pedro's sober and effective stanzas render Boethius's thought without resorting to Petrarch or Boccaccio; he sensed in his public a new interest—the humanist thirst for close translations of the classics.

Diego de San Pedro's sensitivity to his public's preferences explains both his flaws and accomplishments. His aspiration to outshine everything and everyone led to the stylistic excesses of *Tractado de amores de Arnalte y Lucenda* or the tasteless short poems chastising snappish ladies. On the other hand, his *La pasión trobada* responds to a new spirituality, *Desprecio de la Fortuna* to the new humanist interest in the classics, and his fictions to a change in romantic codes. His knowledge of Latin and his desire to please the ladies at court inspired him to create a meticulously crafted prose style that became a rhetorical model for Europe.

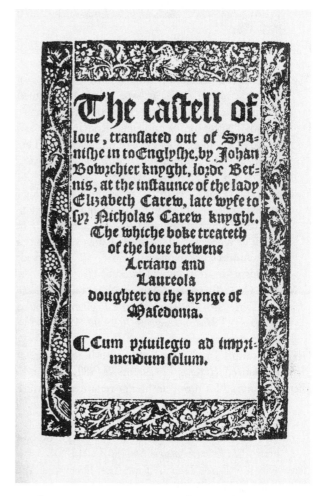

*Title page for an English translation (circa 1549) in the British Library of* Cárcel de amor *( from* The Castel of Love, *1549? A Translation by John Bourchier, Lord Berners, of* Cárcel de amor, *1492, by D. de San Pedro, 1950; Thomas Cooper Library, University of South Carolina)*

## References:

José Amador de los Ríos, *Historia crítica de la literatura española,* 7 volumes (Madrid: Rodriguez, 1861–1865), VI: 342–351;

Marcel Bataillon, "¿Melancolía renacentista o melancolía judía?" in *Estudios hispánicos: homenaje a Archer M. Huntington* (Wellesley, Mass.: Wellesley College, 1952), pp. 39–50;

Anthony van Beysterveldt, "La nueva teoría del amor en las novelas de Diego de San Pedro," *Cuadernos Hispanoamericanos,* 349 (1979): 70–83;

Marina Brownlee, *The Severed Word: Ovid's Heroides and the Novela Sentimental* (Princeton: Princeton University Press, 1990), pp. 145–175;

Pedro M. Cátedra, *Amor y pedagogía en la Edad Media: Estudios de doctrina amorosa y práctica literaria* (Salamanca: Universidad de Salamanca, 1989), pp. 120, 133, 137, 158, 162, 172, 175–176;

Joseph Chorpenning, "Rhetoric and Feminism in the *Cárcel de amor,*" *Bulletin of Hispanic Studies,* 54 (1977): 1–8;

Emilio Cotarelo y Mori, "Nuevos y curiosos datos biográficos del famoso trovador y novelista Diego de San

Pedro," *Boletín de la Real Academia Española,* 1 (1927): 305–326;

Bruno M. Damiani, "The Didactic Intention of the *Cárcel de amor,*" *Hispanófila,* 56 (1976): 29–43;

Alan Deyermond, "Estudio preliminar," in *Cárcel de amor con la continuación de Nicolás Nuñez,* edited by Carmen Parrilla (Barcelona: Crítica, 1995): pp. ix–xxxvii;

Deyermond, "Notes on Sentimental Romance, I: San Pedro, Cervantes, Shakespeare and Fletcher, Thebald: The Transformations of *Arnalte y Lucenda,*" *Anuario Medieval,* 3 (1991): 90–100;

Pascual de Gayangos, "Discurso preliminar y Catálogo razonado de los libros de caballería que hay en lengua castellana o portuguesa hasta el año 1800," in *Libros de caballerías,* edited by Gayangos, Biblioteca de Autores Españoles, no. 40 (Madrid: Rivadeneyra, 1857), pp. iii–lxxxvii;

E. Michael Gerli, "Leriano's Libation: Notes on the *Cancionero* Lyric, *Ars Moriendi,* and the Probable Debt to Boccaccio," *Modern Language Notes,* 96 (1981): 414–420;

Gerli, "Toward a Poetics of Spanish Sentimental Romance," *Hispania,* 72 (1989): 474–482;

Víctor Infantes, "La prosa de ficción renacentista: Entre los géneros literarios y el *género editorial,*" *Journal of Hispanic Philology,* 13 (1989): 115–124;

Anna Krause, "El tractado novelístico de Diego de San Pedro," *Bulletin Hispanique,* 54 (1952): 245–275;

Betty Kurth, "Three French Tapestries Illustrating the Spanish Love-Poem *Cárcel de amor,*" *Journal of the Warburg and Courtauld Institutes,* 5 (1942): 237–245;

Barbara E. Kurtz, "The Castle Motif and the Medieval Allegory of Love: Diego de San Pedro's *Cárcel de amor,*" *Fifteenth Century Studies,* 11 (1985): 37–49;

Francisco Márquez Villanueva, "Cárcel de amor, novela política," *Revista de Occidente,* 14 (1966): 185–200;

Marcelino Menéndez y Pelayo, *Antología de poetas líricos castellanos,* 13 volumes (Madrid: Hernando, 1891–1908), VI: cccliii;

Menéndez y Pelayo, *Historia de la poesia castellana en la edad media,* 3 volumes (Madrid: Suárez, 1911–1916), III: 169–190;

Menéndez y Pelayo, *Orígenes de la novela,* 4 volumes (Madrid: Bailly-Baillière, 1905–1915), II: 3–88;

Sol Miguel-Prendes, "Las cartas de la *Cárcel de amor,*" *Hispanófila,* 102 (1991): 1–22;

Antonio de Nebrija, *Gramática de la lengua castellana (Salamanca 1492),* edited by Ignacio González Llubera

(London & New York: H. Milford/Oxford University Press, 1926);

Colbert I. Nepaulsingh, *Towards a History of Literary Composition in Medieval Spain* (Toronto & Buffalo, N.Y.: University of Toronto Press, 1986), pp. 174–192;

Regula Rohland de Langbehn, "Desarrollo de géneros literarios: la novela sentimental española de los siglos XV y XVI," *Filología,* 21 (1986): 57–76;

Rohland de Langbehn, "El problema de los conversos y la novela sentimental," in *The Age of Catholic Monarchs, 1474–1516: Literary Studies in Memory of Keith Whinnom* [special issue of *Bulletin of Hispanic Studies*], edited by Alan Deyermond and Ian Macpherson (Liverpool: Liverpool University Press, 1989), pp. 134–154;

Carmelo Samonà, "Il romanzo sentimentale," in *La letteratura spagnola dal 'Cid' ai Re Cattolici,* edited by Alberto Vàrvaro and Samonà (Florence: Sansoni, 1972), pp. 185–195;

Dorothy S. Severin, "'La Passión trobada' de Diego de San Pedro y sus relaciones con el drama medieval de la Pasión," *Anuario de Estudios Medievales,* 1 (1964): 451–470;

Harvey Sharrer, "La fusión de las novelas artúrica y sentimental a fines de la Edad Media," *Anuarios de Filología Española,* 1 (1984): 147–157;

Santiago Tejerina-Canal, "Unidad en *Cárcel de amor:* El motivo de la tiranía," *Kentucky Romance Quarterly,* 31 (1984): 51–59;

George Ticknor, *History of Spanish Literature,* 3 volumes (New York: Harper, 1849), I: 424–427;

Pamela Waley, "Love and Honour in the *Novelas sentimentales* of Diego de San Pedro and Juan de Flores," *Bulletin of Hispanic Studies,* 43 (1966): 253–275;

Bruce Wardropper, "El mundo sentimental de la *Cárcel de amor,*" *Revista de Filología Española,* 37 (1953): 168–195;

Barbara F. Weissberger, "The Gendered Taxonomy of Spanish Romance," *La corónica,* 29, no. 1 (2000): 205–229;

Keith Whinnom, *Diego de San Pedro* (New York: Twayne, 1974);

Whinnom, "Hacia una interpretación y apreciación de las canciones del *Cancionero general* de 1511," *Filología,* 13 (1968–1969): 361–381;

Whinnom, "Nicolás Núñez's continuation of the *Cárcel de amor,*" in *Studies in Spanish Literature of the Golden Age Presented to Edward M. Wilson* (London: Tamesis, 1973), pp. 357–366.

# Íñigo López de Mendoza, Marqués de Santillana

### (1398 – 1458)

### Regula Rohland de Langbehn
*Universidad de Buenos Aires*

WORKS: *Defunsión de don Enrique de Villena* (1434)

**Manuscripts:** Locations and descriptions of Santillana's manuscripts are given in Brian Dutton, *El cancionero castellano del siglo XV, c. 1360–1520,* 7 volumes (Salamanca: Universidad de Salamanca, 1990–1991); Salamanca, Biblioteca Universitaria, MS. 2655; Madrid, Biblioteca Nacional, MS. 3677; and seven more manuscripts.

**Standard edition:** *Defunsión de don Enrique de Villena,* edited by Maximiliaan P. A. M. Kerkhof (The Hague: M. Nyhoff, 1977).

*Pregunta de nobles* (before 1436)

**Manuscripts:** Salamanca, Biblioteca Universitaria, MS. 2655; Madrid, Biblioteca Nacional, MS. 3677; and three more manuscripts.

**Standard edition:** "La pregunta de nobles del Marqués de Santillana: Edición crítica," edited by Kerkhof, *Crotalón: Anuario de filología española,* 2, no. 1 (1984): 331–357.

*Comedieta de Ponza* (ca. 1436)

**Manuscripts:** Salamanca, Biblioteca Universitaria, MS. 2655; Madrid, Biblioteca Nacional, MS. 3677; and twenty more fifteenth- and sixteenth-century manuscripts.

**Standard edition:** *La comedieta de Ponza,* edited by Kerkhof (Groningen: Rijksuniversiteit te Groningen, 1976); republished as *La Comedieta de Ponça* (Madrid: Espasa-Calpe, 1987).

*Proverbios o Centiloquio* (1437)

**Manuscripts:** The *Proverbios* (Proverbs) is the work by Santillana that exists in the most manuscripts: Salamanca, Biblioteca Universitaria, MS. 2655; Madrid, Biblioteca Nacional, MS. 3677; and nineteen fifteenth-century manuscripts.

**Early imprints:** There are about thirty early editions extant, including *Los proverbios* (Saragossa: P. Hurus, 1490); *Proverbios* (Seville: M. Ungut & S. Polono, 1494); *Proverbios* (Seville: J. Cromberger, 1516); and *Proverbios* (Seville: J. Cromberger, 1519).

**Edition in English:** *The Proverbes of the Noble and Woorthy Souldier Sir James Lopez de Mendoza Marques of Santillana,* translated by Barnabe Googe (London: R. Watkins, 1579).

*Questión fecha por el noble e magnífico señor don Íñigo López de Mendoza, Marqués de Santillana e Conde del Real, al muy sabio e noble perlado don Alfonso de Cartagena, obispo de Burgos* (1444)

**Manuscripts:** Seven fifteenth-century manuscripts.

**Standard edition:** "La Qüestión del Marqués de Santillana a don Alfonso de Cartagena," edited by Angel Gómez Moreno, *Crotalón: Anuario de filología española,* 2 (1985): 334–363.

*Bías contra Fortuna* (1448)

**Manuscripts:** Salamanca, Biblioteca Universitaria, MS 2655; and twelve more manuscripts.

**Standard edition:** *Bías contra Fortuna,* edited by Kerkhof (Madrid: Real Academia Española, 1982).

*Prohemio e carta qu'el Marqués de Santillana enbió al Condestable de Portugal* (1449)

**Manuscripts:** Extant in three of the personal *cancioneros* (Salamanca, Biblioteca Universitaria, MS. 2655; Madrid, Biblioteca Nacional, MS. 3677; and Madrid, Lázaro Galdiano, MS. 2341) and minor manuscripts.

**Standard editions:** *Il "Proemio" del Marchese di Santillana: Introduzione, testo, note critiche e indice storico-letterario,* edited by Luigi Sorrento (Como: C. Marzorati, 1946); *Prohemios y cartas literarias,* edited by Miguel Garci-Gómez (Madrid: Editora Nacional, 1984); *El Prohemio e carta del Marqués de Santillana y la teoría literaria del siglo XV,* edited by Gómez Moreno (Barcelona: PPU, 1990).

**Edition in English:** *Letter of the Marquis of Santillana to Don Peter, Constable of Portugal,* edited by Antonio R. Pastor and Edgar Prestage (Oxford: Clarendon Press, 1927).

*Favor de Hércules contra Fortuna* (ca. 1450)

**Manuscripts:** Salamanca, Biblioteca Universitaria, MS 2655; Madrid, Biblioteca Nacional, MS. 3677; and three more manuscripts.

**Standard edition:** "El 'Favor de Hércules contra Fortuna' del Marqués de Santillana," edited by Kerkhof, in *España, teatro y mujeres: Estudios dedicados a Henk Oostendorp,* edited by Martin Gosman and Hub Hermans (Amsterdam & Atlanta: Rodopi, 1989), pp. 191–201.

*Cancioneros* (ca. 1450–ca. 1650) courtly songs dating from 1423 onward, strophic courtly and allegorical poems (including *Triunfete de amor, Sueño,* and *Infierno de los enamorados*), and the *Serranillas* from the late 1420s onward, collected in five manuscript *cancioneros* of Santillana's works alone and more than twenty *cancioneros* of works by Santillana and others)

**Manuscripts:** The most complete manuscripts of Santillana's *cancioneros* are Salamanca, Biblioteca Universitaria MS. 2655 (ca. 1456)–facsimile edition, *Cancionero del Marqués de Santillana: B.U.S., Ms. 2655,* edited by Pedro M. Cátedra and Javier Coca Senande (Salamanca: Universidad de Salamanca, 1990); and Madrid, Biblioteca Nacional MS. 3677 (early sixteenth century).

*Coplas contra Don Alvaro de Luna* (before 1453)

**Manuscripts:** *Cancionero de Oñate-Castañeda* (ca. 1485), Cambridge, Mass., Harvard University, Houghton Library, MS. Sp 97.

**Standard edition:** "De tu resplandor, o Luna," edited by Francisco R. de Uhagón, *Revista de Archivos, Bibliotecas y Museos,* 4 (1900): 333–338.

*Refranes que dicen las viejas tras el fuego* (undated; attribution uncertain)

**Early imprints:** There are five sixteenth-century editions, including *Inigo Lopez de Mendoça a ruego del Rey don Iuan ordeno estos refranes que dizen las viejas tras el fuego & van ordenados por el a.b.c.* (ca. 1510).

**Standard editions:** *Refranes que dizen las viejas tras el fuego,* edited by Raymond Foulché-Delbosc (as Urban Cronan), *Revue Hispanique,* 25 (1911): 134–219; *Refranes que dizen las viejas tras el fuego,* edited by Hugo O. Bizzarri (Kassel: Reichenberger, 1995).

**Editions and Collections:** *Rimas inéditas de don Íñigo López de Mendoza, Marqués de Santillana, de Fernán Pérez de Guzmán, señor de Batres y de otros poetas del siglo XV,* edited by Eugenio de Ochoa (Paris: Fain & Thunot, 1844); *Obras de Don Íñigo Lopez de Mendoza, marqués de Santillana, ahora por vez primera comp. de los códices originales, é ilustradas con la vida del autor,* edited by José Amador de los Ríos (Madrid: Rodríguez, 1852); *Canciones y decires,* edited by Vicente García de Diego (Madrid: Ediciones de La Lectura, 1913; reprinted, Madrid: Espasa-Calpe, 1964); *Prose and Verse [by the] Marqués de Santillana,* edited by J. B. Trend (London: Dol-

phin Bookshop Editions, 1940); Jules Piccus, ed., "Rimas inéditas del Marqués de Santillana, sacadas del *Cancionero de Gallardo* (o de *San Román*), Academia de la Historia, Si. 2-7-2, ms. 2," *Hispanófila,* 1 (1957): 19–29; *Poesías completas,* edited by Manuel Durán, 2 volumes (Madrid: Castalia, 1975, 1980); Miguel Angel Pérez Priego, ed., "Composiciones inéditas del Marqués de Santillana," *Anuario de Estudios Filológicos,* 3 (1980): 151–158; *Poesía lírica,* edited by Pérez Priego (Madrid: Cátedra, 1983; revised, 1999); *Poesías completas,* edited by Pérez Priego, 2 volumes (Madrid: Alhambra, 1983, 1991); R. Lapesa, ed., "'Las Serranillas' del Marqués de Santillana," in *El comentario de textos, 4: La poesía medieval,* edited by Manuel Alvar and others (Madrid: Castalia, 1983), pp. 243–276; *Los sonetos "al itálico modo" de Íñigo López de Mendoza, marqués de Santillana,* edited by Kerkhof and Dirk Tuin (Madison, Wis.: Hispanic Seminary of Medieval Studies, 1985); *Obras completas,* edited by Gómez Moreno and Kerkhof (Barcelona: Planeta, 1988); *El cancionero de Toledo del Marqués de Santillana,* edited by José Luis Pérez López (Toledo: Caja de Toledo, 1989); and *Comedieta de Ponza, sonetos, serranillas y otras obras,* edited by Regula Rohland de Langbehn, with a preliminary study by Vicente Beltrán (Barcelona: Critica, 1997).

Íñigo López de Mendoza, Lord of Hita and Buitrago, was granted the titles of conde del Real and marqués de Santillana by King Juan II of Castile after the Battle of Olmedo (1445). He is best known by the second title, marqués de Santillana. He belonged to one of the great families that were promoted to the circles of power after the murder of Pedro I by his illegitimate half brother, Enrique de Trastámara (Enrique II), during the second half of the fourteenth century.

When he was five years old López de Mendoza lost his father, Diego Hurtado de Mendoza, admiral of Castile under Enrique III. He was raised by his mother, Leonor de la Vega, and his grandmother Mencía de Cisneros. Among the boy's tutors was one of the most powerful men of Castile, Chancellor Pedro López de Ayala, who was also one of the main intellectuals and writers of the period.

While still a young boy López de Mendoza attended the crowning of Fernando de Antequera as King Fernando I of Aragon in 1412. He formed part of the household of Prince Alfonso de Trastámara (the future Alfonso V of Aragon) as *cuchillo* (knife) or *trinchero* (carver), and, later, *copero mayor* (principal cupbearer), all offices in the royal house. During his stay in Aragon, López de Mendoza must have met some of the court poets, such as Jordi de Sant Jordi (who also held a court office), and established relations with one of the most outstanding intellectuals of his time, Enrique de Villena, who dedicated his translations of Dante's *Commedia* and Virgil's *Aeneid* to Santillana.

Even though there is no personal chronicle of Santillana's life, such as those surviving for Alvaro de Luna and Pero Niño, the essential events of his life and character are reflected in legal documents published in the twentieth century and in literary works that mention or are dedicated to him. His political life can also be traced through the chronicles of the period. The most complete contemporary literary portrait of Santillana is that of Hernando del Pulgar, in his *Claros varones de Castilla* (Illustrious Noblemen of Castile, 1486). After mentioning Santillana's sexual habits and occasional irascibility arising from his sanguine nature, Pulgar praises Santillana's self-control, his excellence as an administrator of his possessions and judge of his subjects, his erudition, and his literary gifts.

As a young man López de Mendoza was one of the supporters of the ambitious Prince Enrique of Aragon. He was in Enrique's company when the latter kidnapped the young Juan II of Castile in Tordesillas. López de Mendoza's partiality to Enrique and the other infantes (princes) of Aragon came to an end in 1428, when Juan II pacified Castile. Once allied with his natural lord, the king of Castile (López de Mendoza's properties, Hita, Buitrago, and Real de Manzanares, were part of Castile), he distinguished himself in the wars between Castile and Aragon that took place in the years 1429–1430 as well as in the war of 1438 against Granada. In 1445 López de Mendoza took part in the Battle of Olmedo, which ended in the defeat of Prince Enrique of Aragon.

Santillana's personality has provoked varying opinions. In *La obra literaria del Marqués de Santillana* (The Literary Work of the Marquess of Santillana, 1957) Rafael Lapesa attributes to him a greater sympathy with the goals pursued by the infantes of Aragon than is found in contemporary sources. This sympathy is corroborated by Santillana's "Decir contra los Aragoneses" (Poem against the Aragonese, 1429), by a burlesque poem written by Juan de Dueñas, and by a reference in the correspondence of Alfonso V of Aragon.

María Rosa Lida de Malkiel doubts the sincerity of the stoicism that increasingly pervades Santillana's work because of his thirst for possessions and power for himself and his family. She does not recall that the rank to which Santillana had been born not only provided him with a life of material ease but also with several obligations that he had to fulfill. During the Middle Ages the administration of justice in noble lands was in the hands of the high nobility. Santillana's rank meant that he administered justice in his vast patrimony. In addition, with his wife, Catalina Suárez de Figueroa, he had ten children, and he tried to provide all of them, male and female, with positions and rents. The couple's youngest son was Pedro González de Mendoza, later cardinal (he was known as the "Great Cardinal") and archbishop of Toledo under the Catholic Monarchs, Isabel I (Isabella) and Fernando II (Ferdinand). Santillana's duties demanded much of him, and his compliance with them provided the basis for the assessments of his contemporaries. Far from being exercises in flattery, as Lida de Malkiel supposes, these assessments demonstrate that there is not a single great lord of the period of whom fewer vices are known and who was the object of such general praise.

Helen Nader describes the increase in power of the Mendoza house in the fifteenth century and considers part of this increase to be owing to Santillana, who was an able litigant in support of his family. The increase in the fortune of the Mendozas was not the result of his deference to Juan II, nor of royal munificence or friendship. Santillana kept himself as far away from the court as he could for almost thirty years because of his aversion to Álvaro de Luna, the royal favorite. Santillana never held a post at the king's court, even though Alfonso de Cartagena in his *Respuesta a la Qüestión fecha por el Marqués de Santillana* (Response to the Question Formulated by the Marquess of Santillana, 1444) calls Santillana "uno de los prinçipales mienbros que a nuestro muy soberano prínçipe, que nuestra cabeça serviendo ha de sostener e ayudar a la direcçión de la real poliçía" (one of the principal knights who by his service should sustain our head and help direct the royal policy of our master).

Many important intellectuals and authors stemmed from the high nobility of Castile during the Middle Ages, including Alfonso X, Juan Manuel, López de Ayala, Villena (the only one to devote his entire life to study), and Santillana. These men usually had to combine civic duties with their passion for study and poetry. These two facets of Santillana's personality were the object of several testimonies by his contemporaries. They allow him to be viewed as the ideal incarnation of a man devoted to the pursuit of arms and letters (a frequent topos of the day). He was not, however, as erudite as Villena. Santillana's pursuit of letters first manifested itself in the then-fashionable area of courtly poetry, but, in the second half of the 1430s, when he composed works in *arte mayor* (poems composed in lines of more than eight syllables) and the *Proverbios o Centiloquio* (Proverbs or a Hundred Sayings, 1437), he branched out into weightier verse. Moral, political, and religious themes gradually captured more of his attention.

Santillana's alleged lack of learning has been the subject of much critical debate. He himself confessed that he did not know Latin when he asked one of his sons to translate Homer's *Iliad* (which he owned in the Latin version of Leonardo Bruni and Pier Candido Decembri) into Castilian. A similar statement about Santillana's lack of instruction in Latin appears in several prologues to translations into Spanish for his library. This deficiency is difficult to understand, because Santillana compiled one of the most important libraries of his time; it included many works in Latin as well as Romance languages, among them the *Roman de la rose* and Dante's *Commedia,* as Mario Schiff has shown. Still, however obtained, knowledge of poetic, moral, religious, and juridical texts in Latin informs the background of many of Santillana's own works. An insatiable thirst for knowledge led him to enlarge his library through costly purchases of manuscripts abroad. Nuño de Guzmán, the subject of a study by Jeremy N. H. Lawrance, was Santillana's Florentine agent in charge of buying books, and in his palace in Guadalajara, Santillana maintained a scriptorium to which important clergymen were attached. His well-known collection was kept in Guadalajara until it became the core collection of the Biblioteca Nacional in Madrid.

Santillana's attraction to learning was coupled with a sure command of the Spanish language that allowed him to create both highly rhetorical and visionary poetry, as well as verses of great intimacy and simplicity. He was one of the most original writers of the courtly school of poetry that flourished anew in his time under the inspiration of the Provençal school. The Santillana's work ranges widely in form and content, and his letters and prologues to collections of his writings demonstrate an unusual awareness about his craft.

No originals of Santillana's works have survived; they were copied in later *cancioneros* (songbooks or collections), some of which were produced in his lifetime but probably not under his supervision. Some of these collections include works by various authors (collective *cancioneros*), while others consist of works by Santillana alone (personal *cancioneros*). His works did not have equal diffusion. Two groups of works, the *serranillas* (pastoral songs, circa 1423–1440) and the *sonetos fechos al ytalico modo* (sonnets made in the italian manner, circa 1438–1455), though remarkable collections of poetry, were seldom copied in his time; others had a more ample reading public and have survived in twenty or more manuscript copies. Some of his briefer works circulated in the sixteenth century as *pliegos sueltos* (chapbooks) and are among the folkloric materials that were used or alluded to by poets of the Golden Age in Span-

ish literature, as is the case with the "Vaquera de Moraña" (Cowgirl from Morana), which is hinted at by the title *El vaquero de Morana* (The Cowboy from Morana, 1617), by Lope de Vega. There is still no complete, fully reliable edition of Santillana's collected works.

A lover of all kinds of linguistic fireworks, Santillana experimented with some of the forms he inherited from Provence through Gallego-Portuguese poetry. Thus, he occasionally employed *maestria mayor* (the repetition of the same rhyme in all of the stanzas of a poem), *maestria menor* (the repetition of the same rhyme in some of the lines of each stanza), *lexapren* (beginning a stanza with the last word of the previous stanza), *encadenados* (beginning of a stanza by repeating the entire last line of the previous stanza), and *manzobre* (the repetition of words derived from the same root), instead of rhyme. Santillana used these figures in his *canciones* (songs) and brief *decires* (strophic poems) and mentions them in the famous proem he wrote to don Pedro, constable of Portugal.

The *serranillas,* the courtly *canciones* and *decires,* and, later, the more solemn allegorical and courtly poems in *arte mayor*–mainly the *Defunsión de don Enrique de Villena* (Death of don Enrique de Villena, 1434) and the *Comedieta de Ponza* (circa 1436)–are characteristic of the beginning of Santillana's literary career, while the moral and religious poems, as well as the sonnets, belong to the end. The genre in which he wrote most extensively is that of the *decir,* a form of variable verse and stanza length (from a few to more than one hundred stanzas). Santillana's *decires* are no exception, ranging widely in length, verse, and theme. His longer *decires*–the *Proverbios o Centiloquio,* the *Comedieta de Ponza,* and the *Bías contra Fortuna* (Bias against Fortune, 1448)–are complex in their message and formal organization. Those of middling length–such as the *Sueño* (Dream, late 1420s), *Infierno de los enamorados* (Hell of Lovers, after 1428), and *Doctrinal de privados* (Rule Book for Favorites, 1454), which are all more than fifty stanzas long–merit attention for their expert development of thought, as well as for the information and the learned vocabulary they include.

Santillana has been accused of using poetry to defend the power of his family and political party, particularly in his poems on the downfall of Luna. These poems seem to have been written near the time of the events recounted in them. They illustrate the rancor that existed between the powerful favorite and other great nobles, but commentators have noted that the ethical and moral elements that Santillana expresses in them gradually move beyond the example of Luna's life.

Santillana's first poems belong to the Gallego-Portuguese and Provençal traditions of the *cantiga* (canticle or song). The *villancicos* (folk carols) and the courtly *canciones,* new fifteenth-century genres, derived from the *cantigas* of the previous century, which combined music and song. By the fifteenth century, however, lyric poets were no longer necessarily musicians as well as poets. Although as a young courtier Santillana received a harp as a gift from Alfonso de Trastámara, scant evidence of his musical ability survives. Excepting the appearance of two *canciones* in songbooks and the survival of two *serranillas* in the oral tradition, which suggest that they were actually sung, his poems survive only as written lyrics.

Santillana's fame today is based mainly on his *serranillas*. Some of them will be found in every anthology and history of Spanish literature. Best known is the *serranilla* that begins "Moza tan fermosa / non vi en la frontera / como esa vaquera / de la Finojosa" (Never did I see as beautiful a maid as that cowgirl from the Finojosa).

The *serranillas,* as well as "Cantar a sus fijas loando su fermosura" (Song for His Daughters, Praising Their Beauty) and "Villancico a tres fijas suyas" (Carol That He Made for Three of His Daughters, 1444–1445), are preserved only in the two most important manuscripts of Santillana's works (the personal *cancioneros* conserved in Salamanca and Madrid). Nevertheless, as Miguel Ángel Pérez Priego noted in 1987, they must have been transmitted orally, with occasional traces of their passing in *pliegos sueltos* from the beginning of the sixteenth century. They entered the awareness of the reading public when José Amador de los Ríos published them in *Obras de Don Íñigo Lopez de Mendoza, marqués de Santillana* (1852), the first philological edition of Santillana's works.

The *serranillas* consist of eight poems plus two loose stanzas that are part of collective poems; that is, poems to which several authors contributed stanzas. They are written in hexasyllabic or octosyllabic lines, like the *cantiga* or *villancico,* and are preceded by an *entrada* (beginning) or *tema* (theme), followed by several stanzas in which the initial *entrada* reappears or is alluded to by the rhyme. They have the structure of a sung poem, which accounts for their survival in the oral tradition. In addition, the first *serranilla,* also known as "La Serrana de Voxmediano" (The Cowgirl of Voxmediano) or the "Serranillas de Moncayo" (You Cowgirls of Moncayo) includes a *finida* (concluding stanza half the length of the preceding stanzas).

The *serranilla* genre is connected to the Provençal *pastorela,* to the French *pastourelle,* and to the *serranas* (cowgirl songs) of Juan Ruiz's *Libro de buen amor* (Book of Good Love, circa 1330), although Santillana's *Serra-nillas* are distinctly his own. Each poem tells of an encounter between a knight and a lower-class maid. The two proceed to exchange pleasantries, with the girl sometimes willing and sometimes refusing to enter into a romantic relationship. In no case do Santillana's *serranas* force themselves on the marquess (as is the case with the *serranas* in the *Libro de buen amor*), although Menga de Manzanares comes close. The narrator in some of Santillana's poems finds his erotic needs satisfied, while in others he is rejected, according to the personality of the *serrana,* as Lapesa notes in a 1983 article. The narrator addresses the *serranas* rather freely and explicitly, though often in a courtly manner. The women's responses range from the emphatic "No" of those who already have a boyfriend (as in "La vaquera de Morana") or do not desire a tryst ("La vaquera de la Finojosa"), to those who readily accept the marqués's advances ("La serrana de Voxmediano"), or else their answer is so elegant as to make the narrator mention the possibility that the maids might be of noble extraction ("Yllana, la serrana de Lozoyuela").

Although the *serranilla* genre admits courtly elements in the description of the place or the girl, the brevity of the poems does not allow for extensive descriptions. More than any other poems of the era, however, Santillana's *serranillas* evoke the countryside; each of them mentions concrete places where the encounters take place. The narrator travels "encima de Voxmediano" (above Voxmediano); in the Moncayo mountains; in the pine forest near Bovalo; near Salloçar, "entre Torres y Canena" (between Torres and Canena); or wanders lost "por tierra fragosa" (in difficult land) on the way to the lands of Calatrava and the church of Santa Maria. The girls also appear in their regional attire, as in "La vaquera de Morana": "saya apretada / muy bien fecha en la cintura / a guisa de Extremadura, / cinta e collera labrada" (a tight skirt, very well-made in the waist, in the manner of Extremadura, with an embroidered ribbon and neckpiece).

Some of the *serranillas* date from Santillana's military campaigns against the Aragonese in 1429 ("Serranillas de Moncayo" and "La vaquera de Morana") and against the Moors, a campaign that culminated in the taking of Huelma in 1438 ("La moza de Bedmar" [The Girl of Bedmar] and, probably, "La vaquera de la Finojosa"). The other *serranillas* can be attributed to the nobleman's visits to his properties. In their totality, they provide an erotic (and probably fictitious) biography of Santillana. The last *serranilla,* the "Moza lepuzcana" (Girl of Guipuzcon) which dates from about 1440, recapitulates this biography by naming the *serranas* of the seven earlier poems.

The closeness of Santillana to musical compositions can be observed in poems in which he incorporates fragments of existing songs. Related to the *serranillas* but more markedly courtly is the "Villancico que fizo a tres hijas suyas." Of doubtful attribution, since important philologists attribute it to Suero de Ribera, the "Villancico que fizo a tres hijas suyas" consists of four stanzas with quotations taken from traditional songs. The poet pretends to overhear from behind some bushes three *serranas* singing the quoted songs and remembering their loves. When he abandons his hiding place, the women ask him to join them in song, even though he is not the person they were looking for. He then sings a fourth song, similarly quoting an older work; this last song gives the "Villancico que fizo a tres hijas suyas" a witty turn. Although the title appears in early manuscripts, the poem is not formally a *villancico*. The main device used in the work, the quotation of earlier texts, was common from the beginning of Provençal poetry and was also used by Petrarch and by Sant Jordi. Santillana employed this device with equal success in two other works: "Querella de amor" (Quarrel of Love) and the *decir* "En mirando una ribera" (On Seeing a Shore), both written between 1430 and 1447.

Nineteen *canciones corteses* (courtly songs) by Santillana appear in *Obras completas* (1988), edited by Angel Gómez Moreno and Maximiliaan P. A. M. Kerkhof, but only fifteen of these are actually *canciones*. In Santillana's generation the courtly songs were still composed of several stanzas, like their immediate ancestors, the *cantigas*. Santillana, however, was already moving in the direction in which the form was evolving: several of his songs have only one stanza, concluding with the *estribillo* (refrain). This form became standard in the second half of the fifteenth century.

Most of Santillana's *canciones* are confessions of love, written with the same apparent facility and elegance as the *serranillas*. As is the case with courtly songs, however, they are more contrived, lacking the concreteness of the *Serranillas*. Several *canciones* share themes with some of Santillana's *decires*. "Quién será que se detenga?" (Who might stop here?) is a brief allegory that in two stanzas recapitulates the battle of Love, using some of the same terms as Santillana's long allegories, for example, the *Sueño*. The two songs dedicated to historical personages (Princess Blanca de Navarra and Queen Isabel de Portugal) are poems of praise that have counterparts among the *decires*. Though not love poems, both are based on a central concept, a characteristic feature of the *canción* genre. Thus, the poem for Isabel applies to her the concept of *calocagatía* (ideal coincidence of beauty and virtue), which supposes that beauty and virtue have to reside in the same person, so the greater the beauty, the greater the virtue: "Siempre la virtud huyó / a la extrema fealdad, / e creemos se

halló / en conpaña de beldad . . ." (Virtue always fled extreme ugliness and found company, we believe, in Beauty).

The *decires* are poems of variable stanzaic length. They have no *estribillo* but do have a *finida*. The stanzas in a *decir* can range from eight to twelve octosyllabic lines in length, with varying rhyme schemes. Their structure is not based on any musical form, but rather, as the name *decir* (to say) indicates, the poems have their root in spoken poetry, like the French *dits* (spoken narrative poems), and they are related to gnomic sayings, as well as to the French *sirventés* (satirical lyrics treating moral, political, personal, or didactic subjects). During the fifteenth century, *decires* were used as vehicles for amorous, moral, or political verse. Santillana's *decires* are a rich source of Latin, French, or Italian neologisms. In this he is comparable to his friend Juan de Mena, but, whereas the latter's vocabulary has been carefully studied by Lida de Malkiel in her book *Juan de Mena, poeta del prerrenacimiento español* (Juan de Mena, Poet of Pre-Renaissance Spain, 1950), that of Santillana, though described in several articles by María Isabel López Bascuñana, has taken second place to the study of the graceful and elegant style of his verses, with the result that there has been no comprehensive assessment of his neologisms.

The *decires líricos* (lyrical *decires*) are love or praise poems. If their style is more rhetorical than that of the *canciones*, it is not because of their complex syntax or vocabulary but because of the more erudite comparisons made in them. The images employed in the *decires líricos* disguise courtly concepts with mythological comparisons that make a puzzle of some of the stanzas. For example, in the fourth of the *decires líricos* Santillana personifies his sighs by wishing that they had the capacity to speak: "¡O, si fuesen oradores / mis sospiros e fablasen, / porque vos notificasen / los infinitos dolores / que mi triste coraçón / padesçe por vos amar" (Oh, if only my sighs were prayers and could talk so that they could tell you of the infinite pain that afflicts my sad heart on account of loving you!).

The ten compositions that are called *decires líricos* by modern editors have between three and twelve stanzas, with an occasional *finida*. Most are octosyllabic, but two employ *quebrados* (half lines) in the second half of each stanza. One is a poem in praise of Juana de Urgel, condesa de Fox. Another is a *decir amatorio* (poem about love) written on behalf of Santillana's cousin, Fernando de Guevara, and replete with oxymora: "Las fieras tigres farán / antes paz con todo armento ['cattle,' a flagrant Latinism used by someone who supposedly knew no Latin], / habrán las arenas cuento, / los mares s'agotarán, / que me haga la fortuna / si non tuyo / ni me pueda llamar suyo / otra alguna" (The ferocious tigers will make peace with all cattle, the sands will be counted, the seas will run dry, if Fortune were able to make me follow another lady or another lady call me hers).

Modern editors distinguish ten *decires narrativos* (narrative *decires*) from the *decires líricos* by their length, but it is not easy to trace an exact boundary between Santillana's lyrical and narrative *decires*. The *decir* "Por un valle deleytoso" (Through a Delightful Valley, before 1437), a brief poem of six stanzas, introduces the figure of the *cuco* (cuckoo), a word that Santillana borrowed from the French. The narrator has been wronged by his lady and asks the cuckoo to take him into his service. The cuckoo agrees, saying "que tú seas en mi sala / el mayor que puede ser" (that you be in my household the most important servant [cuckold]). The word *cuco* is elided in Spanish, which allows Santillana to maintain a certain lack of clarity about what he is saying. In the *finida* the cuckoo returns to its perch to tend to the "añagacias" (lures) with which he hopes to trap other unwary lovers. This *decir* is a burlesque poem that could as well be ranged among Santillana's jocose works.

In the highly lyrical "Querella de amor" the narrator relates the vision of a lover who dies the death of love. At the end of each of seven stanzas, seven poems by other authors are cited. Several of these are by Macías, the exemplary medieval Spanish martyr for love. The *fin* (final stanza) of this *decir* repeats a gnomic statement: "quien me creyere / castigue en cabeza ajena, / e non entre en tal cadena / do non salga, si quisiere" (Whosoever believes me should learn by the example of others and not enter in such a service, for maybe there is no exit if he were to wish to leave). Santillana's recourse to learned or popular sayings like the one he employs here–"castigue en cabeza ajena"–conveys his interest in language.

The majority of the *decires narrativos* are long and, by theme, can be classified either as love visions or poems of praise. To the latter belong the *Planto a la reina Margarida de Prades* (Lament for Queen Margarita de Prades, 1431), the courtly widow of Martin the Humane (King Martin I of Aragon), and the *Coronación de Mossén Jordi de Sant Jordi* (The Coronation of Jordi de Sant Jordi, 1430), in which the Catalan writer is crowned by other great poets as their equal. It is the first example of the use of this motif in Spanish letters.

The most famous of Santillana's *decires* are the *Triunfete de amor* (Little Triumph of Love, before 1428), the *Infierno de los enamorados,* and the *Sueño.* All three examine love from different perspectives and exist in two versions, an earlier one that is more extensive, and a later one that has survived in only two of the *cancioneros* dedicated to Santillana, those conserved in Salamanca and Madrid.

The *Triunfete de amor* is a free rendering of Petrarch's *Triunphus Cupidinis* (Triumph of Love), from the *Trionfi* (Triumphs, begun in 1350). The narrator witnesses a procession of Venus and her court that is interrupted and ends with the goddess shooting a *flecha inficionada* (poisoned arrow) at the narrator; this makes him sad because in the place of the goddess he sees "la señora mía / contra mí desmesurada" (my lady mad at me). This ending transforms the allegory into the thing to which it alludes, as is the case in some other fifteenth-century allegories. Santillana's *Triunfete de amor* lacks the philosophic depth of Petrarch's *Trionfi.* Santillana focuses on the spectacular allure of the allegorical figures portrayed, whereas Petrarch mainly presents a world of pain and apprehension. Although the general scheme of the *Triunfete de amor* is based on *Triunphus Cupidinis,* it can be clearly shown that in Petrarch's text the allegorical cortege is derived from other sources, particularly Ovid's *Metamorphoses* and Valerius Maximus's *Dictorum Factorumque Memorabilia* (circa A.D. 30). The catalogue of famous lovers appears only in Santillana's later version, where they are much more in keeping with the subject than the examples they replace; the substituted examples derive directly from the *Triunphus Cupidinis* of Petrarch and canto 5 of Dante's *Inferno.*

The most popular of Santillana's courtly allegories in the fifteenth century was the *Infierno de los enamorados.* It survives in sixteen manuscript *cancioneros,* most of them collective, and was imitated again and again in the fifteenth and at the beginning of the sixteenth centuries. The title identifies it with the first canto of Dante's *Commedia.* Santillana's poem, however, emulates neither the complexity nor the bitter criticism of society in Dante's work. The *Infierno de los enamorados* is a courtly poem. Santillana plays with allusion in a way that is almost parodic. In contrast to Dante's subterranean world, he presents a wild place at night, populated by wild beasts, where the first-person narrator is lost. When day breaks, the narrator finds that he is in a jungle, where he eventually finds a hunter in pursuit of a wild boar. The hunter is a handsome and elegant young knight who, after killing his prey, is addressed by the narrator. The knight, Hippolytus, has died "según murieron / otros, non por su pecado, / que por donas padescieron" (like others died, not for their sins, but because of their ladies) and is condemned to spend his afterlife as a hunter in an inverted *locus amoenus* (pleasant place), a dismal and rough locality, in which he shines by contrast as an exemplar of courtliness. The passionless hunter is at the same time rewarded and purged because he resisted the power of love. Hippolytus offers to be the narrator's guide so that he can see "en qué trabajades, / e la gloria qu'esperades" (what your suffering is and the fate that awaits you).

*Íñigo López de Mendoza, Marqués de Santillana; detail from an altarpiece painted by Jorge Inglés in 1455 (from Alan D. Deyermond, ed.,* Santillana: A Symposium, *2000; University of New Hampshire Library)*

For a long time the two follow a trail, eventually coming to a "castillo espantoso" (horrible castle) surrounded by fire and dimmed by smoke. Hippolytus reassures the narrator that the flames will not burn him, and they enter and reach the door of the castle. Above it they see an inscription that alludes to the one above the door in Dante's *Inferno;* they read, "El que por Venus se guía / venga penar su pecado" (He who takes Venus as a guide should come here to expiate his sin). In stanza 49 Hippolytus reassures his ward once more with another allusion to Dante: "el título que mirades / al ánima se dirige; / tanto qu'el cuerpo la rige / de sus penas non temades" (the sign that you see here is directed to the soul; do not fear its threats while the body is in control). In stanza 50 (out of a total of 68 stanzas) they enter Hell. After pausing to invoke Apollo for help in telling what he has seen, the narrator presents a series of examples of the ancient and modern lovers he has met there: Phyllis and Demophon, Paris and Helena, Achilles and Polixene, and Francesca de Rimini (who appears in canto 5 of the *Inferno* and in stanza 55 of Santillana's poem) and Paolo Malatesta.

The narrator then hears steps approaching (another incident reminiscent of Dante). It is Macías,

who speaks to him in Castilian to explain that "La mayor cuita que haber / puede ningún amador / es menbrarse del plaçer / en el tiempo del dolor" (The greatest pain that afflicts any lover is to remember pleasure at a time of sorrow). The narrator confesses to Macías that "tus esquivas tormentas / me hacen llaga incurable" (Your bitter torments cause me an incurable pain), but since only God can remedy damnation for love's sake, he asks Macías to forgive him. The narrator must then return to his road because "ya non me da lugar / el tiempo que me detarde" (I do not have time to tarry). When he tries to find the way and looks out for his guide, however, he is ravished like Ganymede, and, back on earth, suddenly finds himself free from his love service. The poem ends with the assertion that "lo procesado / de todo amor me desparte, / ni sé tal que no se aparte / si no es loco probado" (the events witnessed have cured me of love; I do not know of anyone who would not put aside love other than a proven madman). Instead of engaging in the more common complaint about unrequited service to love, the ending of the poem counsels men not to love. The former approach is that taken by imitators of Santillana in their own *infiernos* (poems about hell).

The Italianate *Infierno de los enamorados* is in some ways opposed to the *Sueño,* which takes its inspiration from the French courtly tradition and has roots in the allegorical battles of the *Roman de la rose* and, ultimately, in the fourth-century *Psychomachia* of Prudentius. In the *Sueño* the narrator dreams that his harp has become a "sepes," a venomous serpent that bites him. He realizes, however, the deceitful nature of the bite: "engañosa / la dolor que me penaba, / e sentí que me soñaba / en tal pena congoxosa" (the pain afflicting me was deceiving, and I felt that I dreamed myself in that state of suffering). At daybreak the narrator listens to news of how Love and his host are approaching, and his reason and heart enter into a dispute that ends in the victory of the heart. He then leaves and travels through "selvas inusitadas / e tierras que non sabía" (unusual jungles and lands that I did not know), until he comes upon an honestly dressed old man, whom he tells how he has left his dwelling, Tranquilidad (Tranquility, an allegorical place), because of an unsettling dream. The old man reveals himself to be the Theban Tiresias—a seer who appears in a variety of medieval texts as arbiter in disputes on love and sex because in classical myth he was changed into a woman. Tiresias reminds the narrator that in order to counter the effects of Fortune, "quédanos tan solo . . . el libre albedrío" (the only thing we have at our disposal is free will), and he counsels him to look out for Diana, the goddess of chastity, because only she is capable of extinguishing the arrows of Love. The lover parts company with Tiresias and eventually encounters a group of beautifully dressed "vírgenes que cazaban / e los alpes atronaban / con la su grand vocería" (virgins hunting, whose tumultuous voices reached the heights of the Alps), while others hunt from boats. The reader is presented with a courtly hunt taking place in an artificially cultivated garden, with "calles fermosas, / las cuales murtas e rosas / cubren odoriferando" (beautiful paths covered with sweet-smelling myrtles and roses). The wayfarer is reassured by this sight, and his fears vanish. The goddess Diana promises him her military support against the host of Love, which is compared to the heroes in the siege of Troy. The ensuing battle is couched in allegory, with personifications fighting against one another in a manner that recalls the *Roman de la rose.* Perfect Beauty and Reason vanquish Shame and Measure; Ability and Nobility fight Sloth and slow Understanding. Pleasing Semblance and Youth attack from another side, but Diana's fury increases—she is compared to a furious lioness defending her cubs, to a curious stone frozen by the winds, and to the Theban tigress, She incites her troops to resist until they vanquish Cupid. The latter, however, receives reinforcements from Venus and Jupiter, so that the narrator is "de mortal golpe llagado / en el pecho, e mal herido" (hit and wounded with a mortal wound to the chest) and declares that he now lives "aprisionado / en gravísimas cadenas" (imprisoned by heavy chains).

In spite of their different lengths, *Triunfete de amor* (twenty stanzas), *Infierno de los enamorados* (fifty-eight stanzas) and *Sueño* (fifty-seven stanzas in the second, six more in the first version) have been interpreted as a trilogy. It has also been proposed that the two longer poems form a series and that *Sueño* replaced *Triunfete de amor* in a dyptich. The internal logic of these poems and their textual transmission argue for their individuality, however, since they were not transcribed together in a fixed order and they are not conserved in the same codices (*Triunfete de amor* being conserved in eleven, the *Sueño* in seven, and *Infierno de los enamorados* in sixteen manuscripts). Thus, these groupings seem to have arisen from modern interpretations.

To the group of narrative *decires* the 1988 Gómez Moreno and Kerkhof edition adds two *decires historicos* (historical *decires*) in *arte mayor:* the *Defunsión del don Enrique de Villena* and the *Comedieta de Ponza.* Both these poems are further distinguished from the other ten narrative *decires* by their historical content, length, and solemn tone. The reader's attention is captured not by the sentimental experiences of a lyric first-person narrator but by events the narrator purports to have witnessed.

The *arte mayor* stanza employed is highly contrived. It was created at the beginning of the fifteenth century as a vehicle for more-elevated subjects and required an elevated vocabulary as well. The stanza is composed of eight twelve-syllable lines that employ three rhymes in the pattern *abbaacca*. A regular caesura subdivides the lines into two half lines of six syllables each, which means it has accents on the fifth and eleventh syllables. This fixed accentuation constrains the pattern of accents that would otherwise be available in a line of this length. The *arte mayor* stanza sets the rigidity of the verse form against a complicated syntax that uses hyperbaton (transposition or inversion of usual word order). In spite of the complexity of the form, poets tend to respect the structure of the stanza, forcing their syntax into the rhythmic structure of the verse and avoiding the use of run-on lines, which tend to the colloquial. Santillana uses this feature with utmost regularity. His *arte mayor* verse flows with a slow majesty, but its grace also stems in part from the unusual and evocative images and the learned metaphors, concepts, and vocabulary he tends to employ.

The two longer poems—according to medieval standards, long poems are those composed of twenty or more stanzas—in which Santillana employs this verse form, the *Defunsión de don Enrique de Villena* and the *Comedieta de Ponza,* can be dated by the events they relate.

The marqués de Villena was a distant relative of Santillana and a relative also of the Trastámara kings of Castile and Aragon. Villena's death occurred in 1434. If there are many Latinisms in the praise poem *Coronación de Mossén Jordi de Sant Jordi,* in which Santillana praises a young fellow poet he came to know at the Aragonese court, with more reason one finds rhetorical *ornatus* (aesthetic decoration of language) and a carefully chosen vocabulary in the *Defunsión de don Enrique de Villena,* a *planto* (remembrance poem) for one of the most learned men of his time.

The *Defunsión de don Enrique de Villena* is Santillana's most difficult poem, not because of the vocabulary, which includes a moderate amount of neologisms and Latinisms, but because of the mythological allusions and images, some of which are nearly incomprehensible:

> Quebraban los arcos de hueso, corvados
> con la humana cuerda de aquella manera
> que hacen la seña o noble bandera
> del magno difunto los nobles criados;
> rompían las trozas y goldres manchados
> del peloso cuero con tanta fereza
> ca dubdo si Hécuba sintió más graveza
> en sus infortunios que Homero ha contados.

(The bony and curved arches were broken by a human rope such as the noble kin are wont to make for the ensign or noble flag of the prominent deceased. They broke loose their hair with such force that I doubt that Hecuba, wife of Priam—as Homer has told us—felt the depth of her misfortune more.)

The *arcos de hueso,* one presumes, are the curved spinal columns of crying people. Their hair is the *humana cuerda* that hangs loosened as they tear at it, and it is compared to the flag or ensign that accompanies the noble dead to their resting place. This company's mourning is likened to Hecuba's reaction at the news of the death of her sons in the Trojan War, which was known to the fifteenth century through the *Historia troyana* (History of Troy), the Spanish version of Benoît de Sainte-More's twelfth-century *Roman de Troie,* and the *Metamorphoses* of Ovid. The *Defunsión de don Enrique de Villena* also includes comparisons between the grief inspired by Villena's death and various situations taken from real life: a feeling of desolation is compared to the feeling experienced by an infant taken from his crib (stanza 4), the multitudes who climb Parnassus are compared to the pilgrims who come together on their final approach to Santiago de Compostela (stanza 16), and a night lit by torches recalls the Feast of the Virgin of Candelaria (stanza 17). At the outset the narrator is transported to a barren and desolate place, where he finds, one after another, "fieras diformes y animalias brutas" (deformed beasts and brute animals), the servants of the dead man, and other men mourning in a field. He climbs a narrow trail that leads him through these people until he reaches a prominence, where he comes upon a richly decorated coffin. There he sees the Muses lamenting the death of several poets who have left the world and finally reaching the name of Villena. The news of Don Enrique's death prompts the narrator to curse the Parcae (the Roman goddesses of fate) and add his lament to that of the people around him. The *finida,* laconic as in many of the endings in Santillana's poems, relates how Aurora (dawn) took the vision away, and the narrator suddenly awoke in bed.

Santillana's other historical or political poem, the *Comedieta de Ponza,* consists of 120 stanzas of *arte mayor,* that is, of 960 lines. This length gives considerable weight to the poem. It was composed several years earlier than the most famous Castilian poem of the fifteenth century, Mena's *Laberinto de Fortuna* (Labyrinth of Fortune, 1444), which shares many characteristics with the *Comedieta de Ponza.* The immediate subject of Santillana's poem was the defeat of the Aragonese fleet by the Genoese on 5 August 1435 near the island of Ponza. The Aragonese fleet was conveying Alfonso V and his three brothers (Juan, Enrique, and Pedro), the infantes of Aragon, to Naples. The royal party had overloaded their ships in such a way that they were not able to maneuver freely. Only Pedro managed to escape the Genoese. Alfonso and Enrique were kept in Milan, while Juan first went to Genoa in the company of many of his nobles. The three brothers were soon released by the duke of Milan, Filippo Maria Visconti, who treated Alfonso with great honors. The poem relates how word of the infantes' defeat and capture reached doña Leonor de Alburquerque, the mother of the princes, and how she died as a consequence of the news. In fact, almost half a year elapsed between the two events, but Santillana makes them immediately sequential, thus achieving a poetic truth, which—according to Aristotle—is more truthful than history.

Stylistically, the *Comedieta de Ponza* is related to the *Defunsión de don Enrique de Villena,* but its structure is more complex. The poem employs several devices that function independently of each other. As the dream vision begins, the narrator comes upon four ladies: the queen mother (Leonor) and her three daughters-in-law, Blanca of Navarre (wife of Juan), Maria of Castile (wife of Alfonso V), and Catalina of Castile (wife of Enrique). They complain to Giovanni Boccaccio, the Florentine poet, asking that he write of their plight. Boccaccio asks them to relate the events that have transpired. At this point the poem employs another device current in fifteenth-century literature, the literary portrait, as the queen mother describes her four sons and two daughters and talks of her fears for the future of the dynasty, because she has been frightened by some presentiments and signs she has seen. Even though Leonor's ladies-in-waiting attempt to distract her with "novelas e plazientes cuentos" (novels and pleasing tales)—this is the first documented occurrence of the term *novela* (narrative fiction) in Spanish—she is disturbed because she has dreamed about a ship that has foundered in a terrible storm. When she awakens, her servants approach her with a letter from her daughters, Queen Mary of Castile and Queen Leonor of Portugal. The queen mother then proceeds to read the letter, which constitutes a third level in the narrative. After an exordium, the letter tells of the Battle of Ponza and of the king and princes' imprisonment.

The narrator relates how Leonor died after she finished reading the letter and how her three daughters-in-law began their lament: "el más dolorido / duelo . . . que jamás se falla / ser fecho en el mundo" (the deepest lament . . . that has ever been witnessed by the world). Then Fortune, in the shape of a woman, comes to console them, followed by a great cortege composed of worthies taken from classical and biblical literature. While the names of the men are taken from diverse sources, it has been shown that all the sixty women mentioned in this catalogue come from Boccaccio's *De claris mulieribus* (On Prominent Women, circa 1362). Fortune prophesies that

> no solamente serán delibrados
> e restituïdos en sus señorías,
> mas grandes imperios les son dedicados,
> regiones, provincias, ca todas son mías.
> Y d'este linaje, infinitos días
> vendrá quien posea grand parte del mundo.
> . . . . . . . . . . . . . . . . . . . . . . . . . . . . . . . .
> Los cuales, demás de toda la España
> habrán por heredo diversas partidas
> del orbe terreno. . . .
> Al su yugo e mando vendrán, sometidas
> las gentes.

(not only will they be returned to their kingdoms, but they will have command of greater empires, regions, and provinces, for they are all subject to me. And from this lineage will eventually come the possessor of a great part of the earthly orb. . . . They will inherit not only all of Spain but also different parts of the whole earth. . . . The peoples of the world will be subjected to his yoke and command.)

Once this prophecy is delivered, the four men who are the subject of the poem appear in person, and morning frightens away Fortune and her company.

The *Comedieta de Ponza* includes some other significant topics and motifs, such as the veracity of dreams, arms and letters, fortune as providence, the Horatian *beatus ille* (happy is he), and others. But above all, it is a political poem that portrays the Aragonese branch of the Trastámara family. It is severely critical of the sons of Fernando de Antequera (the infantes of Aragon), who are described as profligate or unduly ambitious. The final prophecy may be interpreted as a justification for the actions of the infantes, but it is more likely that it should be read as a justification of the Trastámaras of Castile, where Santillana's domains as lord of Hita and Buitrago were located and whose policies he had backed since 1428.

Santillana's fourth group of poems, the moral and didactic *decires,* includes two of his longest works: the *Proverbios o Centiloquio* and *Bías contra Fortuna.* Present-day readers tend to react strongly against ethical poetry, but critics generally consider it an important part of the medieval literary output. The *Proverbios o Centiloquio* and *Bías contra Fortuna* have been criticized as pretentious, dishonest, and lacking in originality. Such prominent critics as Lida de Malkiel and Nader consider that some of the lessons in these works promote a hidden agenda that advocates the weakening of the royal house of Castile. It might be the case, however, that in these poems Santillana actually argues for a strengthening of royal power.

The *Pregunta de nobles* (Question of the Nobles, before 1436), probably the earliest of the *decires morales,* is composed of ten *arte mayor* stanzas and a *finida.* The poem asks about "aquellos que fueron / subjugadores del siglo mundano" (those who were subjugators of the world) and, in an extensive catalogue, enumerates heroes taken from the Bible, the Trojan tradition, and Greek and Roman mythology. The catalogue does not reach Santillana's own time, as it did two generations later in *Coplas a la muerte de su padre* (Stanzas on the Death of His Father, circa 1476–1479), by his great-nephew Jorge Manrique. Another of Santillana's *decires morales,* the *Favor de Hércules contra Fortuna* (Plea of Hercules against Fortune, circa 1450), employs six stanzas and a *fin* to consecrate Hercules as a just man, in opposition to the disorder created by Luna.

The *Proverbios o Centiloquio* (the latter part of the title refers to the fact that it has one hundred stanzas) was commissioned by the crown in 1437 for the moral instruction of the crown prince of Castile, the future Enrique IV. In the proem Santillana compares his enterprise to Proverbs, a biblical book with the same objective: to provide lessons for a son who is learning to control himself: "¿cómo puede regir a otro el que a sí mismo no rige? ¿ni cómo se regirá ni gobernará aquel que no sabe ni ha visto las gobernaciones y regimientos de los bien regidos y gobernados?" (How can someone rule another man if he cannot rule himself? How will a person rule or govern if he does not know, nor has he seen, the rule and government of those who are well-ruled and well-governed?). In the proem Santillana also quotes from one of his own writings, now lost—"la ciencia no embota el fierro de la lanza, ni hace floja la espada en la mano del caballero" (learning does not dull the iron of a lance, nor does it weaken the sword in the hand of the knight)—a saying that could well serve as a motto for the writer himself. The stanzas of the *Proverbios o Centiloquio* are composed of octosyllabic lines with *quebrados*. The majority begin with an iambic rhythm that gives the verse a feeling of agility coupled with weight, the cadencing corresponding to that of a twelve-syllable line with a marked caesura after the eighth syllable.

Right at the beginning the prevailing character of the poem is made known:

Fijo mío mucho amado,
para mientes
e non contrastes las gentes
mal su grado;
ama e serás amado,
y podrás
hacer lo que no harás
desamado.

(Beloved son, stop and consider, do not treat people differently, despite their rank; love and you will be loved, [love] and you will accomplish that which would be impossible if you were not loved.)

The poem is seemingly dedicated to the moral qualities that anyone should have and not only princes such as Enrique: one should avoid all vices; make oneself loved, not feared; be courteous in answering; avoid listening to evil tongues or "noveleros decidores" (newsmongers); judge only after listening to both sides of a plea; listen to counsel; fear God; and be just in the exercise of the law. One should be studious and yet not covet learning for itself, but as an instrument to admonish sin, because

El comienzo de salud
es el saber
distinguir y conocer
cuál es virtud;
quien comienza en juventud
a bien obrar,
señal es de non errar
en senectud.

(The beginning of health is knowledge of how to distinguish and know virtue; if you begin with good deeds in youth this shows you will not err in old age.)

Some of the advice, however, seems of particular relevance to the young crown prince: "non blasfemes del rey / en escondido; / huya tu lengua y sentido / tales redes" (do not blaspheme against the king in private, let your tongue and sense avoid such traps). In counsel and in judgment one should be free of wrath, console the afflicted, and forgive sin because "las armas del culpable / son piedad" (the arms of the culprit are pity). Santillana insists on clemency:

Siempre me plugo loar
al que perdona,
como sea gran corona
sin dudar;
e no menos reprobar
pena de fierro,
ca si pasa, non es yerro
de emendar.

(I always praised the person who forgave, this doubtlessly is a great merit, and not less to reprove capital punishment, because, if it comes about by error, you can not make amends.)

Santillana hurries to declare, however, that there are precise limits to pardoning:

No se entienda perdonar
los torpes hechos,
ni las leyes y derechos
usurpar,
ca no es de tolerar
al que mató,
si de lejos contrayó
damnificar.
. . . . . . . . .
Ca sería crueldad
el tal perdón
e contrario a la razón
de humanidad.
Non se nombra piedad
mal permitir
mas dañar y destruir
autoridad.

(Do not think that we want evil deeds to be pardoned, nor usurp laws and rights, because our intent is not to tolerate the murderer, if he premeditated his crime. . . . Because to pardon such would be cruel and contrary to human reason. Pity is not leniency to the bad person, for this would injure and destroy authority.)

After this section on justice Santillana proceeds to name the sins of gluttony, sloth, and lust (he follows Ovid in linking two vices—one should flee sloth in order not to be tempted by the flesh). The following section combines an injunction to be chaste with a praise of women and introduces a catalogue of saintly and chaste pagan and Christian women. Next, Santillana reviews constancy, personal courage, avoidance of praise, liberality, prodigality, charity, truthfulness, cupidity and ambition, envy, good counsel, filial obedience, and reverence for the old. The section ends with an admonition: "grand locura / es que piense la criatura / ser nacida / para siempre en esta vida / de amargura" (it is madness for a creature to think that it was born to live forever in this vale of tears).

A last brief section contrasts the theme of death and eternal life, the *vida inmensa* (unmeasured life) where "vivirás y sin ofensa / nin castigo" (you will live without harm or punishment). Of particular note is the theme of possible irreverence on the part of the prince toward his father and toward the king; these stanzas might allude to hidden purposes attributed by Santillana to the young prince.

*Proverbios o Centiloquio* is the only poem in which Santillana explains in glosses or explanatory notes his many classical and biblical examples, making explicit their connection to historical, biblical, and mythological people and events. Alfonso V, in turn, asked another commentator, Pero Díaz de Toledo, to add his learned commentary to the *Proverbios o Centiloquio*. Thus, there exists a supplementary source that explains the examples Santillana employed and elucidates contemporary values. Díaz de Toledo's commentary is transcribed in volume two of Pérez Priego's edition of Santillana's *Poesías completas* (1991). The work is also accompanied by a proem in which Santillana defends himself against the charge of having plagiarized ancient poets and philosophers. He argues that knowledge belongs to a tradition and not to individuals: "estos que dicho he, de otros lo tomaron, e los otros de otros, e los otros de aquellos que por luenga vida y sutil inquisición alcanzaron las experiencias y causas de las cosas" (the men I mentioned took it from others, and the others from others, and these from those who, because of their long life and subtle intellect, reached into the experience and cause of things). In reality, both the *Proverbios o Centiloquio* and *Bías contra Fortuna* are in great measure based on Walter Burley's *De vita et moribus philosophorum* (On the Life and Morals of the Philosophers, 1325–1337) and on examples taken from Valerius Maximus.

*Bías contra Fortuna,* a long poem in dialogue form, is dedicated to Santillana's cousin Fernan Alvarez de Toledo, conde de Alva, whom Luna had taken prisoner in 1448, confiscating his goods. Alvarez de Toledo remained in prison until after the death of Juan II in 1454, when the new king, Enrique IV, restored his freedom and patrimony. While in prison, Alvarez de Toledo had asked Santillana to send to him some of his poems. The marqués responded with *Bías contra Fortuna*, one of his chief works.

*Bías contra Fortuna* begins with a prologue in which Santillana discusses his lifelong friendship with Alvarez de Toledo and recalls the latter's victories against the Aragonese and the Moors. Santillana then describes the life and deeds of the philosopher Bias of Priene (fl. circa 570 B.C.) and his Stoic principles, so that readers can understand why this character argues with Fortune in the poem. Sayings attributed to Bias circulated in the vernacular collections of apothegms attributed to the "siete sabios de Grecia" (seven wise men of Greece), to whom he belonged, but it can be shown that Santillana followed Burley's *De vita et moribus philosophorum*. Burley's work (which Santillana does not mention) was the real source of the citations of Valerius Maximus and Diogenes Laertius in the prologue.

The short-verse form used by Santillana, octosyllables with one *quebrado* per stanza, produces a lively dialogue. Fortune repeatedly threatens Bias, who shows himself unafraid of losing possessions, loved ones, wars, or even life to her. In order to counteract the threats of Fortune, Bias gives her lengthy examples, arguing that his friends, the philosophers (if only the memory of their writings), will keep him company in prison. He recalls the story of the Creation before reaching a famous stanza:

> E la bibliotheca mía
> allí se desplegará;
> allí me consolará
> la moral maestra mía.
> E muchos de mis amigos
> mal tu grado
> serán juntos a mi lado,
> que fueron tus enemigos.

(And my library will be fully used, and my mistress, Moral, will console me. And many of my friends, who were your former enemies, will keep me company.)

After Bias speaks, Fortune asks, "Di, ¿non temes los bramidos / de la entrada tenebrosa, / nin de la selva espantosa / los sus canes y ladridos?" (Tell me, don't you fear the roar of the tenebrous entrance, nor the horrible jungle with its dogs and barks?). Bias laconically answers, "Temer se deven las cosas / que han poder / de nuzir o mal hacer, / otras no son pavorosas" (We should fear the things that can harm or endanger us, others are not to be feared). Replacing his Stoic philosophy with an anachronistic Christian view, Bias imagines a beautiful place to which he will come after death, where "cantando / viviré, siempre gozando, / do cesan todas mudanzas" (singing I will live, always in enjoyment, where all change ceases), and where "las ánimas benditas / tienen sus sillas conscriptas, / . . . do triunphan los virtuosos / e buenos en todos genos" (the blessed souls have their assigned chairs . . . where the good and the virtuous triumph in every way).

The two *decires* concerning Luna have been interpreted as rancorous or vengeful poems. From internal evidence it can be deduced that one must have been written in 1453, after Luna's fall, and the other after his death in 1454. The *decir* beginning "De tu resplandor, o Luna, / te ha quitado la Fortuna" (Fortune has deprived you of your splendor, oh Moon!), also known as *Coplas contra Don Álvaro de Luna* (Stanzas against don Álvaro de Luna), must have been written immediately after Luna's imprisonment. The delight taken in the plight of the powerful favorite, viewed in light of the sentiments expressed in the *decires doctrinales* (moral *decires*), can be understood only if Luna is seen as the embodiment of everything that Santillana opposed. Santillana settles old scores with Luna and attributes to him sins commonly assigned to Luna by his opponents, for they are echoed in the *Generaciones y semblanzas* (Lineages and Likenesses, circa 1450–1455) of Fernán Pérez de Guzmán. Twenty-four of the forty-nine stanzas in Santillana's *decir* relate the deeds of Luna and chide him for not paying due deference to Juan II. Luna is reprehended for his prominence, for depriving the king of his liberty, for making the king a perjurer and diminishing his fame, for dismantling the royal patrimony, for making the king hate his wife and children, and for taking away the king's free will. Luna is also accused of banishing the king's relatives and natural vassals in order to take their possessions "con garganta insaciable" (with an insatiable gullet), reducing everything to his ambition and driving loyalty out of Spain. Santillana compares Luna's pride to that of Lucifer, but Luna's is now broken on Fortune's wheel:

Por medida que medías
ciertamente eres medido,
aquellos que abatías
ya te traen abatido.
Abaxabas, ya te abaxan;
aquexabas, ya te aquexan;
tú tajabas, ya te tajan
y jamás nunca te dexan.

(You are measured by the same measure you used, those that you diminished now diminish you; you brought them down, now they bring you down; you afflicted them, now they afflict you; you cut them, now they cut you, and they never let up.)

The concluding stanza of this section recalls the initial invocation: "¡O luna eclipsada / y llena d'oscuridad, / tenebrosa y fuscada, cumplida de ceguedad! . . . gualardón equivalente / recibes según mereces" (Oh, eclipsed and shadowed Moon, faint and gloomy, full of blindness! . . . you merited what you got in full). The rest of the poem calls on God and Juan II, Queen Isabel of Portugal (she was a great adversary of Luna and is compared in the poem to Judith, Esther, and the Virgin Mary), and the crown prince; a total of twenty-nine stanzas and a *fin* are devoted to remedying the wrongs the Castilian people have suffered.

*Coplas contra Don Álvaro de Luna* has survived in a unique version in the *Cancionero de Oñate-Castañeda* (circa 1485) and was not known to Amador de los Ríos. It was first published in 1900 by Francisco R. de Uhagón. The attribution of this poem to Santillana has been questioned, but, as Michèle de Cruz-Sáenz has demonstrated, its structure is similar to that of his *Doctrinal de privados*. The brief catalogue of feminine names that appears in stanzas 27–29 of "De tu resplandor, o Luna" is similar to the one found in stanza 51 of the *Proverbios o Centiloquio,* and the poem employs word games that accord with Santillana's practice. The work is mainly political in nature, dedicated to the restitution of the law. Santillana defends traditional order, which he considers to have been subverted by the immense personal power of Luna, the ostensible dedicatee, when Juan II was left only with a pen to sign what he, Luna, wished ("solo pluma le quedó / a firmar lo a ti plaziente"; *a ti* refers to Luna). According to Santillana, the moment had come to redress these wrongs by "los perversos expeliendo, / los presos desagraviando / y a opresos oprimiendo" (expelling the perverse, making reparations to prisoners, and oppressing the oppressors). He addresses the future Enrique IV, admonishing him: "los contritos desterrados / quered reconciliïar / y cruelmente dañad / los perversos obstinados" (reconcile yourself with the banished who are contrite and ruthlessly combat the obstinate perverse men).

The other poem on Luna, *Doctrinal de privados,* is one of the most widely disseminated works by Santillana. The mention in the penultimate stanza of "Maestre Espina"–Francisco de Espina, the author of the anti-Jewish tract *Fortalitium Fidei* (In Defense of the Faithful, 1451) and Luna's final confessor–means that the entire poem should be read as a confession. Luna is shown in his last moments before climbing onto the execution platform. He renounces his covetousness, ambition, and pride, which led him to consider himself superior to his lord and everyone else.

He counsels others with the wisdom he acquired in his fall:

> Todo omne sea contento
> de ser como fue su padre;
> la muger, cuanto su madre . . .
> . . . . . . . . . . . . . . . . . . . . . .
> E quiera la medianía
> de las gentes y segure,
> no le plega ni procure
> extrema soberanía.

> (Every man should be content to be like his father; the woman to be like her mother. . . . He should be content of the security of the middle rank, and never seek or desire extreme sovereignty).

Lida de Malkiel sees Santillana's pride in his birth and privileges reflected in this passage. This pride cannot be denied; Santillana was an aristocrat, the product of his birth and upbringing, but one should also note the rhetorical thrust of the passage, for the intention is to decry the prerogatives of an aristocracy whose power was based on neither merit nor tradition but on favors and factional manipulation. Santillana's Luna recognizes the justice of his impending execution; he praises moderation and takes a liberal stance on the nature of power:

> Son diversas calidades:
> non menos en los mayores
> que medianos e menores,
> . . . . . . . . . . . . . . . . . .
> Unos quieren reposar,
> a otros plazen las guerras
> a otros campos e sierras,
> los venados e caçar.
> Justas otros tornear,
> juegos deleitosos, danças;
> otros, tiempos de bonanças,
> sacrifiços contemplar.

> (Differences exist equally in the great, middle, and lower ranks of society. . . . Some want to take their ease, others like war, still others like fields and mountains where they can hunt deer. Others like to fight in tournaments, to play delightful games, to dance, and still others use their leisure time for religious contemplation).

Luna's most important advice is that positions in the royal council and judiciary not be granted as a reward for service or by petition, and that those who do obtain these positions should not let preferences, fears, or money affect their decisions. In the last twelve stanzas of *Doctrinal de privados,* which bear the subtitle *Confesión* (Confession), Luna attributes to himself all the sins mentioned; he shows contrition, invokes divine mercy, and begs that all people pray for him. He is contrite and will be redeemed; Santillana's enemy will not suffer condemnation, as do Dante's enemies in *Commedia.* The *Doctrinal de privados* may be read as a poem of blame, but Santillana leaves the door open for Luna's redemption. By subject matter this poem, more than the *Coplas contra Don Alvaro de Luna,* belongs to the group of *decires doctrinales.* The author himself probably would have grouped both works among his "satires."

Santillana's religious poetry, including his religious sonnets, bear witness to his particular devotion to the Virgin Mary. His motto, *Dios y vos* (God and you), refers to her. It is not surprising, then, that some of his lyrics also sing her praises. In the "Gozos de Nuestra Señora" (Joys of Our Lady, before 1455) he treats a poetic subject that had been used in Latin songs from the twelfth century onward, the seven joys of Mary: Annunciation, Conception, Virgin Birth, Adoration of the Magi, Resurrection, Ascension, and Descent of the Holy Spirit. At the beginning of the fifteenth century, however, these joys were extended to twelve. To the traditional seven were added the presentation of Jesus at the temple, his dispute with the priests there, the wedding at Canaan, and other motives that can vary in the different cases, taken from the prayer books. Santillana's poem follows this amplified division into twelve. He cites some Latin phrases connected with the Marian cult—for example, "por el oído / *concepisti, pulcra e decora, inviolata permansiste,* and *gracia plena*" (you conceived through the ear, chaste and decorous, remained a virgin, full of grace)—which, of course, provide no evidence of his knowledge of Latin since they are part of the daily service.

According to Pérez Priego, during the fifteenth century, prayers and songs in praise of the Virgin came to replace Marian examples and miracles. The prayer "A Nuestra Señora de Guadalupe" (To Our Lady of Guadalupe, 1455) corresponds to a pilgrimage Santillana made to Guadalupe in 1445, after his return from the frontier with Granada. The prayer is noted for the use of traditional language to express the inexpressible:

> Inefable, más hermosa
> que todas las muy hermosas,
> tesoro de santas cosas,
> flor de blanco lirio closa,
> abundante fructuosa
> de perfecta caridad,
> palma de gran humildad,
> esfuerzo de humanidad,
> armas de la cristiandad
> en cualquier hora espantosa.

(Inneffable, the most beautiful of all beauties, treasure of holy things, enclosed white lily, fruitful and abundant, of perfect charity, palm of great humility, humanity's effort, weapons of Christendom, terrifying always.)

Santillana employs a dream vision in "Canonización de San Vicente Ferrer y Fray Pedro de Villacreçes" (Canonization of San Vicente Ferrer and Fray Pedro de Villacreces, 1455) to suggest that the Valencian and Franciscan preachers be canonized. The narrator travels to Paradise, where he sees the nine celestial choirs that Dante visited when guided by Bernard of Clairvaux (as recounted in canto 21 of Dante's *Paradiso*). Santillana defines these choirs using names taken from Dionysus the Areopagite. There is an immense catalogue of the saints he sees on his way to the top, where

> como los cantores
> çessan quando el preste canta,
> cessó la familia sancta
> los triples, contras, tenores . . . todos inclinados
> al Señor de los señores.

(Like singers stop when a priest sings the Mass, the holy family stopped, sopranos, contras, tenors . . . all inclined before the Lord of Lords.)

St. Dominic intercedes, promoting the canonization of the two Spanish candidates, Ferrer and Villacreces, and the voice of the archangel Gabriel announces the divine decision.

This *decir* exists in two versions. The first argues only for the canonization of Ferrer, which took place in June 1445. The second version must have been written after that year, for Gabriel announces two canonizations: "que a Ferrer y Villacreçes / honoren sollepnizando" (let Ferrer and Villacreces be honored with solemnity). The same theme appears in sonnet 41 of the *sonetos fechos al ytalico modo*, which "el Marqués fizo a Sant Viçente, de la orden de los predicadores" (the Marquess made to Saint Vicente, of the Order of Preachers). Pope Callistus III, of the Valencian house of the Borgia family, had canonized Ferrer, his fellow Dominican priest and native of Valencia. In sonnet 41 Santillana tells Callistus to do the same with Juan II's Franciscan confessor, Villacreces, who had already been canonized in the eyes of the people.

Unlike Santillana's serious works, his *poemas de burlas* (festive and burlesque poems) have not found a secure place in the eyes of critics. They appear in the personal Salamanca *cancionero,* as is the case with the two collective *serranillas* and several *preguntas* (questions) and *respuestas* (answers) Santillana exchanged with Mena. They also appear in other *cancioneros,* such as the *Cancionero de san Román,* which includes the *pregunta* "El

que a la nieta de Egeo." The *preguntas y respuestas* were a rather popular genre of poetry in the early fifteenth century. They can be serious, such as the composition that begins "Grant retórico eloqüente" (Great and eloquent rhetorician), in which Santillana asks about the limitations of time in the universe; and the question about the harpy, symbol of covetousness, that is directed to Mena: "Dezid, Juan de Mena, e mostradme quál" (Tell me, Juan de Mena, and show me which one). Most of the response poems seem intended to provoke quick, ingenious answers. Others show a festive quality, such as "Cuartana del rey Juan II" (The Fever of King Juan II) and the little poem "Subí acá, Juan de Mena" (Get up here, Juan de Mena). Some poems that Santillana's editors place in other genres should certainly be included in the *poemas de burlas,* such as "Por un valle deleytoso" (a *decir narrativo* according to Gómez Moreno and Kerkhof) and the *copla esparsa* (single strophe) beginning "Por vuestra descortesía" (By your lack of courtesy). Still, though one cannot deny the ingeniousness of some of the examples, Santillana seems not to have preferred this type of poetry.

The last group of poems are Santillana's *sonetos fechos al ytalico modo* (as they are called in the Madrid and Salamanca personal *cancioneros*), of which there are forty-two. They mark the first appearance of the Italian form in Spanish poetry, some eighty years before Garcilaso de la Vega's verse. Santillana wrote sonnets from the late 1430s (the second sonnet is dedicated to the death of Prince Pedro de Trastámara, who died in 1438), until a few years before his own death in 1458.

With one exception the sonnets were transmitted only in manuscript form (there are differing manuscript traditions for groups of them) until Eugenio de Ochoa published them in his *Rimas inéditas de don Íñigo López de Mendoza, Marqués de Santillana, de Fernán Pérez de Guzmán, señor de Batres y de otros poetas del siglo XV* (1844). In 1852 Amador de los Ríos included all of the sonnets in his edition of the complete works of Santillana. The one exception is sonnet 19, "Lexos de vos e çerca de cuidado" (Far from you and next to care), which was included in the first note to Fernando de Herrera's annotated 1580 edition of the works of Garcilaso de la Vega. The sonnets are now available in more critical editions than any other of Santillana's works, but, though the manuscript transmission is less complicated than that for many of his other poems, Jane Whetnall points out in a contribution to *Santillana: A Symposium* (2000), edited by Alan D. Deyermond, that no edition exists that that solves all the textual problems posed by the sonnets.

The sonnets were edited many times in the twentieth century, and they have been grouped in various ways. The Salamanca and Madrid personal *cancioneros* group the sonnets in a sequence that seems to correspond to their dates of composition. Later critical editions of Santillana maintain the order of the ancient manuscripts, but *Poesías completas* (1975, 1980), edited by Manuel Durán, uses a different ordering.

The subject matter of the sonnets is the same found in the rest of Santillana's poetry: love, politics, morals, and religion. The love, political, and moral sonnets were written early in his career. The last nine (seven of them conserved in the Madrid personal *cancionero* only) are religious poems, although even here one can detect an occasional allusion to love. In sonnet 37 Santillana writes that the hearts of the Apostles "non se turbaron punto más que yo, / por mí sabidas vuestras estaciones, / vuestro camino, . . . aunque, si vuestro era, vuestro só" (were not perturbed a whit more than mine, for I knew your stations, your way, . . . though if I was yours then I am yours now). In sonnet 40 he thanks St. Andrew for taking him before his beloved,

> aquella que en niñez me conquistó,
> a quien adoro, sirvo e me guerrea,
> e las mis fuerças del todo sobró:
> a quien deseo e non me desea,
> a quien me mata, aunque suyo só.

> (she who conquered me as a child, she whom I adore, serve, and does constant battle against me, and who compelled my strength; she whom I desire, and who desires me not, she who kills me, even though I am hers.)

This constant use of courtly language could only with difficulty be attributed to Marian devotion. Such usage confers upon the religious poems a trace of frivolity that will be understood only when the sonnets are more accurately dated.

The Petrarchan elements in the sonnets—mythological, biblical, and historical names; the deification of the beloved and her physical description; the identification of love with a lesion; words taken from Italian, such as *punto* (point in time) and *gentil* (gentle)—have received increased attention in such Santillana editions as Pérez Priego's *Poesías completas* and Regula Rohland de Langbehn's *Comedieta de Ponza, sonetos, serranillas y otras obras* (1997). The influence of the French courtly lyric, which includes some borrowings from Guillaume de Machaut, is less significant. With the exception of Lapesa's *La obra literaria del Marqués de Santillana*, studies have paid little attention to the sonnets for their intrinsic merit. The internal structure of the poems is generally centered on an image, an exemplum, or a moral saying focusing the theme. The focus on a single theme gives the sonnets a different tone from that of the courtly lyrics.

Much critical ink has been spilled, from Amador de los Ríos's 1852 edition onward, over Santillana's versification in the sonnets. Simply stated, the problem is whether his endecasyllables (eleven-syllable lines) should be considered defective because they do not follow the patterns that were introduced in Spain by Garcilaso de la Vega and Juan Boscán many years later. The stress pattern of Santillana's sonnets falls regularly on the fourth, seventh, and tenth syllables, coinciding with the stress pattern of *arte mayor* verses and also with Dante's usage but not with that of Petrarch or the Spanish sonneteers of the sixteenth century, who typically stressed the sixth or eighth and the tenth, as Lapesa has noted. There are, however, two devices in Santillana's sonnets by which rhythmic structure is amplified, both characteristic of two-thirds of Dante's as well as Petrarch's endecasyllables: the acute accent before the caesura and the use of synaloepha (the omission of one of two vowels that occur together at the end of one word and the beginning of another). These features appear in only 25 percent of Santillana's verses. After long debate, critics such as Mario Penna, Derek C. Carr, Martin J. Duffell, and Javier Gutiérrez Carou have assessed Santillana's versification according to its place in the evolution of literary history by comparing the stress pattern he employed to that of Dante and not to that of later Spanish sonneteers, who regularized stress patterns more than their Italian models did.

Seventeen of the first sonnets have rubrics (titles explaining their content). These rubrics have been attributed to Santillana, but since some of them do not match the sense of the sonnets they introduce, they are now considered to be contemporary commentaries and not necessarily the work of Santillana.

In the sonnets, as in his other works, Santillana alludes to many mythological, historical, and literary figures and employs interesting linguistic devices. His endecasyllable is more malleable than the other traditional Castilian lines of verse (the octosyllable and the dodecasyllable with caesura, for example), which exhibit a lesser variety of stresses. Santillana attempted to develop a more natural poetic rhythm, as can be seen in sonnet 20: "Doradas ondas del famoso río / que baña entorno la noble çibdad / do es aquella cuyo, más que mío, / soy e posee la mi voluntad" (Golden waves of the famous river that beats around the noble city where she is, to whom I belong more than to myself and who possesses my will). These lines feature hyperbaton ("cuyo, más que mío, / soy") and elision ("y [quien] posee"), yet they flow smoothly and are perfectly understood because of their stresses. There are occasional perfectly stressed lines, but they alternate with others in which the caesura and hyperbaton become much more obvious and interrupt the flow of words.

Perhaps the most intriguing aspect of the sonnets are the political, moral, and religious doctrines found in many of them. This aspect has yet to be fully explored by critics. The sonnets have not been examined as didactic literature, though it is an important aspect of this group of poems. This important facet of the sonnets is corroborated by the fact that the personal *cancionero* of Madrid separates both types of text, grouping the doctrinal sonnets with Santillana's serious poetry and the amatory ones with the love poetry. In contrast, the political and amatory sonnets alternate with each other in the Parisian and Salmantine manuscripts.

There are thirteen political sonnets, all dealing with government administration and many showing a special concern for the Trastámaras. Sonnet 2 is a lament for the death of Prince Pedro; sonnet 5 is a lament for Doña Catalina, wife of Enrique de Trastámara; and sonnet 13 centers on the fact that the deeds of Alfonso V of Aragon have not received due attention from poets. In other sonnets Santillana admonishes Juan II of Castile to persevere in his endeavors (sonnet 30) and Enrique IV to display more clemency (sonnet 33). Santillana laments the factionalism that characterizes Castilian politics and the harm it brings to Spain (sonnet 18)—a theme that he also treats in the short prose work *Lamentación de España* (Lament for Spain) and in the gallant *Visión*—and he devotes three sonnets (10, 15, and 17) to his own military faction, chiding the men for tardiness in action. In the remaining political sonnets he urges men to live according to principle (sonnet 22), asks European rulers to come to the defense of Constantinople (sonnet 31), and petitions Callistus III to sanctify Villacreces (sonnet 41). Sonnet 32 is dedicated to the praise of Seville.

Petrarch's influence is felt everywhere in the love sonnets. Santillana echoes Petrarch with expressions such as "Si el pelo por ventura voy trocando" (If by chance I am changing my hair) and "Si la vida biviesse de Noé" (If I were to live Noah's life), both from sonnet 24. On occasion he contracts or expands a Petrarchan image, such as "el punto e hora" (the moment in time and the hour), from sonnet 1, which can become "el año, / el mes, nin la semana, nin el día, / la hora, el punto" (neither the year, week, day, hour, or moment in time), from sonnet 22. But Petrarch's influence is always combined with mythological and biblical images from diverse sources.

Santillana's work also includes some prose. His commentaries on the *Proverbios o Centiloquio* and some letters, among them the *Questión fecha por el noble e magnífico señor don Íñigo López de Mendoza, Marqués de Santillana e Conde del Real, al muy sabio e noble perlado don Alfonso de Cartagena, obispo de Burgos* (Question Formulated by the Noble and Magnificent Gentleman Don Iñigo Lopez

De Mendoza, Marquess of Santillana and Count of El Real, to the Very Wise and Noble Don Alfonso of Cartagena, Bishop of Burgos, 1444) directed to Cartagena, are extant. Only one independent essay still exists: the *Lamentación de España*.

The *Lamantación de España* comments on political trends features a prophecy about the evil that is to come because of the deterioration of morals and the practice of vices in Spain. The forgiveness of Heaven hinges on a return to the old ways, ancient customs, faith, truth, and loyalty. The moment of composition was a time of civil war: "no ves tus gentes, e tus pueblos contra tus pueblos, e los padres contra los fijos . . . ?" (don't you see people and towns opposing each other, and parents against children . . . ?). The reference could be to the disturbances caused by the four infantes of Aragon, to whom the image of the *quatro leones* (four lions) in the *Lamentación de España* could refer. More than once in this essay the corruption of morals is called *ytálica* (Italian). Italy mostly figures as the birthplace of culture and the arts, but in this text it is taken to be the source of all evils because Santillana considered it to be the political precursor of Spain. Italy succeeded Greece, and Spain was the next inheritor of ancient power, according to the theory of *translatio imperii* (transfer of empire); but in Santillana's essay Italy acquires a negative connotation: "non vees los titulos ytálicos que engendraste en ti, los quales nunqua fueron en memoria de las tus gentes, con crueles fuegos divinales estar sobre ti para te quemar?" (don't you see that the Italian honors that you bore, such as your people cannot ever remember, have come upon you with divine fury to burn you?).

In the *questión* dedicated to Cartagena, Santillana, who, as his library proves, was interested in all matters related to chivalry and law, asks the bishop of Burgos to instruct him in the rules of chivalry. He wants guidance because the political upheavals and deep divisions of Spain cause him great preoccupation. Cartagena's answer, *Respuesta a la Qüestión fecha por el Marqués de Santillana,* includes a wonderful portrait of Santillana as a man of politics who in spite of his duties, finds the time to devote himself to letters, delighting in intellectual pursuits and seeking to achieve fame through his writings. Cartagena's answer is also a treatise on chivalry, the ceremonies related to the dubbing of knights, the oath of fealty, and the rights of knights.

The great artistic merit of Santillana's work, its formal and thematic variety, as well as its volume, reveals him to be a person of true poetic vocation. This vocation can also be traced in the prologues and scattered comments that accompany some of his works. Prologues introduce the *Proverbios o Centiloquio, Bías contra Fortuna,* and some of the *cancioneros* that he dedicated to his friends. The recipients of these works belong to the highest nobility, among them Violante de Prades, condesa de Prades and Cabrera, and the Constable don Pedro of Portugal, a pretender to the Aragonese crown. These addressees exemplify the profound interest of the Spanish aristocracy in letters. Characteristic of the times is the dedication of literary works to women, since they formed a considerable segment of the literary public, as is nicely illustrated in stanzas 44–48 of the *Comedieta de Ponza.*

Though unsystematic, the surviving prologues allow a glimpse into Santillana's literary craft to a degree found in no other fifteenth-century writer's works. He thus occupies a singular place in the evolution of literary history. There is only one other text comparable to the prologues of Santillana, the "Prologus Baenensis" (Baena's Prologue), written by Juan Alfonso de Baena to introduce his important compilation, the *Cancionero de Baena* (1440). Santillana's prologues are in line with the humanist principles found in Villena and Mena, both preserved in their commentaries to learned poems: Villena's translation of the *Aeneid* and Mena's *La Coronación* (The Coronation, 1438), dedicated to Santillana himself. The poetic principles of this group of poets, their handling of concepts such as *integumentum* (covering), and their dedication to literature written in a Romance language have been studied by Julian Weiss.

The prologue to the *Proverbios o Centiloquio* is the oldest of Santillana's prologues. It gives greater weight to the moral content of the poem by treating two concepts: the need to know and govern oneself before attempting to govern others and the possibility of uniting the practices of arms and letters. A long passage dedicated to great warriors of antiquity ends with a singular praise of Scipio Africanus and Julius Caesar for their practice of both arms and letters. Santillana also refers to questions of originality, plagiarism, and other matters related to writing, but, above all, to the need of not repeating rhymes within a group of twenty stanzas. This last is a principle that dates back to the Provençal school of poetry, whose rules Santillana was familiar with. In this prologue he answers the charge of not knowing versification well because, being more than twenty stanzas long, the *Proverbios o Centiloquio* "pueda ser más dicho libro o tractado que dezir nin cançion, balada, rondel, nin virolay" (might be called a book or treatise more than a *dezir,* or *canción,* ballad, rondeau, or virelay)—terms of versification that appear again in the *Prohemio e carta al Condestable de Portugal* (Proem and Letter to the Constable of Portugal, 1449). Santillana shows the care taken with his stanzas in keeping "el cuento de las sílabas e las últimas e penúltimas e en algunos logares las antepenúltimas, los yerros de los diptongos e las vocales en aquellos logares donde se pertenesçen" (the count of syllables and whether the accent falls in the last, the penultimate, or the antepenultimate syllable, the errors committed in counting the diphthongs and vowels according to their placement).

There is more evidence concerning Santillana's poetic practice in the *Carta a doña Violante de Prades* (Letter to doña Violante de Prades, 1443), sent to accompany copies of the *Comedieta de Ponza,* the *Proverbios o Centiloquio,* and some sonnets written *al itálico modo* (in the Italian manner). In the letter he defines the nature of tragedy ("contiene en sí caídas de grandes reys e príncipes" [it treats of the fall of great kings and princes]), satire ("es aquella manera de fablar que tovo un poeta que se llamó Sátiro, el qual reprehendió muy mucho los viçios e loó las vyrtudes" [it is that kind of speech that was used by a poet named Satyr, who scolded very much the vices and praised the virtues]), and comedy ("cuyos comienços son trabajosos e tristes, e después el medio e fin de sus días alegre, gozoso e bienaventurado" [whose beginnings are fraught with hardships and great woes, and then its middle and end are happy, joyful, and blissful]). According to this definition, one should call Santillana's moral works satires.

The European context of Santillana's literary theory, which has been studied by Weiss and by Gómez Moreno in *El Prohemio e carta del Marqués de Santillana y la teoría literaria del siglo XV* (1990), is best seen in the *Prohemio e carta al Condestable de Portugal,* the writer's most extensive essay on the nature of literature and one of his chief works. Santillana first undertakes a brief description of the evolution of poetry, from the Bible to classical antiquity. He then presents an historical panorama, the first ever written, of Spanish poetry, and places it in a European context. This survey secures Santillana a prominent place in the historiography of medieval literature after Dante's *De vulgari eloquentia* (On the Vulgar Tongue), although both of these accounts were forgotten until they were published in modern times by historical philologists. Santillana's views refer above all to the nature of poetry, or, as he calls it, the *gaya sciencia* (gay science), a name that reveals the Provençal roots of Castilian courtly poetry. He defines poetry as "un zelo çeleste, una afecçion divina, un insaçiable çibo del ánimo" (an unearthly zeal, a divine affection, an insatiable thirst of the soul) that "buscaron nin se fallaron sinon en los ánimos gentiles, claros ingenios, e elevados spíritus" (is only to be found in gentle souls, clear intellects, and elevated spirits) and is "un fingimiento de cosas útiles, cubiertas o veladas con muy fermosa cobertura, conpuestas, distinguidas e scandidas por çierto cuento, peso e medida" (a feigning of useful things, covered or veiled with a very pleasant envelope, composed, distinguished, and scanned by their number, weight, and measurement). The terms employed by Santillana reveal his knowledge of European poetry, not only to Provençal antecedents but also to Italian poetry ("ánimos gentiles"), Latin verse ("peso," the "pondus" [weight] in Horace's *Ars poetica,* line 320), the Bible ("çierto cuento, peso, y medida," from the apocryphal Wisdom of Solomon 11:20, "omnia in mensura, numero et pondere disposuisti" [thou hast ordered all things in measure, number and weight]), and that favorite medieval device, allegory (*fingimiento*).

At the beginning of the *Prohemio e carta al Condestable de Portugal* Santillana encourages the young constable to continue in the practice of poetry because it belongs to the "sçiençias de arriba infusas" (sciences inspired from above) and to "onbres bien nasçidos e doctos" (well-born and learned men). As an introduction to the history of poetry, the central theme of the *Prohemio e carta al Condestable de Portugal,* Santillana documents the origin of poetry with biblical examples. As he develops his theme, he reviews the poetic forms used by his predecessors, particularly those poets nearest to his own time. Besides important definitions of verse forms, the work includes a valuable listing of the medieval poets that were known to Santillana.

An undated work titled *Refranes que dicen las viejas tras el fuego* (Refrains Told by Old Women by the Fire) is sometimes attributed to Santillana, but his authorship is uncertain. Hugo O. Bizzarri, editor of a 1995 edition of the work, mentions the possibility that Santillana wrote it but does not definitively attribute it to him, although Santillana's name appears on the cover of the edition. Behind the attribution lies a printing tradition that began with some incunabula and extended to the middle of the sixteenth century; in these printed collections the work is invariably assigned to Santillana. The attribution is credible in view of his interest in popular sayings and proverbs, manifest in the *Proverbios o Centiloquio* and traceable throughout his other works. Santillana may thus be seen as continuing an old tradition in which sayings from folk literature were incorporated into written works. There survives one other contemporary collection, *Seniloquium* (Sayings of the Old), in which the sayings are accompanied by extensive Latin commentaries. Collections of this type demonstrate the interest of fifteenth-century intellectuals in bringing the oral tradition to the same level of estimation as other collections of Latin or Greek sayings. The task of gathering popular proverbs marks the introduction of humanism into Spanish letters. It affected the evolution of the Spanish language, which was already being expanded by many neologisms based on Latin and on the Romance languages of neighboring regions. Since many traces of this interest are found in Santillana's

other works, the attribution of *Refranes que dizen las viejas tras el fuego* may well be correct.

Santillana's works enjoyed great prestige during his lifetime and for a century thereafter. Several *cancioneros* are devoted to it, particularly a precious manuscript that was produced in his own scriptorium and is kept in Salamanca. A facsimile, *Cancionero del Marqués de Santillana: B. U. S., Ms. 2655,* edited by Pedro M. Cátedra and Javier Coca Senande, was published in 1990. Certainly, Santillana's condition and means allowed him to have his works copied and give them away freely. But they also found their way into most of the collective *cancioneros.* Although Santillana is not represented in the *Cancionero de Baena* (compiled in 1440 but featuring only poetry written up to 1425), later songbooks, from the *Cancionero de Stúñiga* (circa 1465) to the *Cancionero General* of 1511 and subsequent editions, include many examples of his *canciones* and *decires.* In his own time Santillana's moral poetry enjoyed at least the same prestige as his allegorical and visionary poems. Most of the sonnets and the *serranillas* were transmitted more rarely.

Santillana is mentioned in the works of such eighteenth-century antiquarians as Nicolás Antonio and Rafael Floranes, but his work began to come into its own with the mid-nineteenth-century editions prepared by Ochoa and Amador de los Ríos. Santillana's initial fame was eclipsed by that of Mena, whose *Laberinto de Fortuna* was the object of erudite editions and commentaries from the end of the fifteenth century onward. Santillana's comparable poems, above all the *Comedieta de Ponza,* did not attract the attention of Renaissance philologists. Santillana is now most often edited and cited for his *serranillas* and the *Prohemio e carta al Condestable de Portugal;* the sonnets and long poems are also the subject of current studies.

**Biographies:**

José Amador de los Ríos, *Vida del Marqués de Santillana* [1852] (Buenos Aires: Espasa-Calpe, 1947);

Rogelio Pérez Bustamante and José Manuel Calderón Ortega, *El marqués de Santillana: Biografía y documentación* (Santillana del Mar: Taurus, 1983).

**References:**

Diego de Burgos, "Triunfo del Marqués," in *Cancionero Castellano del siglo XV,* edited by Raymond Foulché-Delbosc, 2 volumes (Madrid: Bailly-Baillière, 1912, 1915), II: 353–559;

Giovanni Caravaggi, "Petrarch in Castile in the Fifteenth Century: The *Triunphete de Amor* by the Marquis of Santillana," in *Petrarch's Triumphs: Allegory and Spectacle,* edited by Amilcare A. Iannucci and Konrad Eisenbichler (Ottawa: Dovehouse, 1988), pp. 291–306;

Derek C. Carr, "Another Look on the Metrics of Santillana's Sonnets," *Hispanic Review,* 46 (1978): 41–53;

Michèle de Cruz-Sáenz, "The Marqués de Santillana's *Coplas* on Don Alvaro de Luna and the *Doctrinal de Privados,*" *Hispanic Review,* 49 (1981): 219–224;

Alan D. Deyermond, "The Double Petrarchism in Spain," *Journal of the Institute of Romance Studies,* 1 (1993): 69–85;

Deyermond, "Santillana's Love-Allegories: Structure, Relation, and Message," in *Studies in Honor of Bruce W. Wardropper,* edited by Dian Fox, Harry Sieber, and Robert Ter Horst (Newark, Del.: Juan de la Cuesta, 1989), pp. 75–90;

Deyermond, ed., *Santillana: A Symposium* (London: Department of Hispanic Studies, Queen Mary and Westfield College, 2000);

Pero Díaz de Toledo, "Diálogo e razonamiento en la muerte del Marqués de Santillana," in *Opúsculos literarios de los siglos XIV a XVI,* edited by Antonio Paz y Mélia (Madrid: Sociedad de Bibliófilos Españoles, 1892), pp. 247–360;

Martin J. Duffell, "The Metre of Santillana's Sonnets," *Medium Aevum,* 56 (1987): 276–303;

Duffell, "The Origins of Arte Mayor," *Cultura Neolatina,* 45 (1985): 105–123;

Foulché-Delbosc, "Testament du Marquis de Santillane," *Revue Hispanique,* 25 (1911): 114–133;

Luis García de Valdeavellanos, "Una carta particular inédita del Marqués de Santillana," in *Homenaje a Xavier Zubiri* (Madrid: Moneda y crédito, 1970), pp. 627–646;

Javier Gutiérrez Carou, "Métrica y rima en los sonetos del Marqués de Santillana," *Revista de Literatura Medieval,* 4 (1992): 123–144;

Werner Krauss, "Wege der spanischen Renaissancelyrik," *Romanische Forschungen,* 49 (1935): 183–184;

Rafael Lapesa, *La obra literaria del Marqués de Santillana* (Madrid: Insula, 1957);

Lapesa, "Los *Proverbios* de Santillana: Contribución al estudio de sus fuentes," *Hispanófila,* 1 (1957): 1–15;

Lapesa, "'Las Serranillas' del Marqués de Santillana," in *El comentario de textos, 4: La poesía medieval,* edited by Manuel Alvar and others (Madrid: Castalia, 1983), pp. 243–276;

Jeremy N. H. Lawrance, "Nuño de Guzmán and Early Spanish Humanism: Some Reconsiderations," *Medium Aevum,* 51 (1982): 55–84;

María Rosa Lida de Malkiel, *La idea de la fama en la Edad Media Castellana* (Mexico: Fondo de Cultura Económica, 1952);

María Isabel López Bascuñana, "Cultismos, arcaísmos, elementos populares y lenguaje paremiológico en la obra del Marqués de Santillana," *Anuario de Filología,* 3 (1977): 279–314;

Juan de Lucena, "Libro de vita beata," in *Opúsculos literarios de los siglos XIV a XVI,* edited by Antonio Paz y Mélia (Madrid: Sociedad de Bibliófilos Españoles, 1892), pp. 105–205;

Alejandro Medina Bermúdez, "El diálogo *De vita beata* de Juan de Lucena: Un rompecabezas histórico," *Dicenda,* 15 (1997): 251–270; 16 (1998): 135–170;

Juan de Mena, "La Coronación," in *Cancionero Castellano del siglo XV,* I;

Helen Nader, *The Mendoza Family in the Spanish Renaissance, 1350 to 1550* (New Brunswick, N.J.: Rutgers University Press, 1979);

Marçal Olivar, "Documents per la biografia del Marquès de Santillana," *Estudis Universitaris Catalans,* 11 (1926): 110–120;

Mario Penna, "Notas sobre el endecasílabo en los sonetos del Marqués de Santillana," in *Estudios dedicados a Menéndez Pidal,* volume 5 (Madrid: Consejo Superior de Investigaciones Científicas, 1954), pp. 253–282;

Rogelio Pérez Bustamante, *Íñigo López de Mendoza, Marqués de Santillana (1398–1458)* (Santillana del Mar: Fundación Santillana, 1981);

Miguel Ángel Pérez Priego, "De Dante a Juan de Mena: Sobre el género literario de *comedia* en 1616," *1616: Anuario de la Sociedad Española de Literatura General y Comparada,* 1 (1978): 151–158;

Pérez Priego, "La escritura proverbial de Santillana," in *Actas, II Congreso Internacional de la Asociación Hispánica de Literatura Medieval,* edited by José Manuel Lucía Megías, Paloma Gracia Alonso, and Carmen Martín Daza (Alcalá de Henares: Universidad de Alcalá de Henares, 1992), pp. 644–651;

Pérez Priego, "Formas del discurso en los poemas mayores de Santillana," in *Homenaje al profesor José Fradejas Lebrero,* 2 volumes, edited by José Romera, Ana Freire López, and Antonio Lorente Medina (Madrid: UNED, 1993), I: 173–180;

Pérez Priego, "Sobre la transmisión y recepción de la poesía de Santillana: El caso de las serranillas y los sonetos," *Dicenda,* 6 (1987): 189–197;

Hernando del Pulgar, "Título IV: El Marqués de Santillana," in his *Claros varones de Castilla,* edited by Jesús Domínguez Bordona, Clásicos Castellanos, no. 49 (Madrid: Ediciones de La Lectura, 1923), pp. 36–47;

Arnold G. Reichenberger, "The Marqués de Santillana and the Classical Tradition," *Iberorromania,* 1 (1969): 5–34;

Regula Rohland de Langbehn, "Problemas de texto y problemas constructivos en algunos poemas de Santillana: La *Visión*, el *Infierno de los enamorados*, el *Sueño*," *Filología*, 17–18 (1976–1977): 414–431;

Rohland de Langbehn, "Santillana y sus fuentes: Anotaciones sobre sus procedimientos poéticos," in *Studia Hispanica Medievalia III: Actas de las IV Jornadas Internacionales de Literatura Española Medieval, Agosto 19–20, 1993, Buenos Aires, Argentina,* edited by Rosa E. Penna and María A. Rosarossa (Buenos Aires: Universidad Católica Argentina, 1995), pp. 158–168;

Nicholas G. Round, "The Antiquary Reassessed: Floranes and the Liberal Tradition," *Bulletin of Hispanic Studies,* 68 (1991): 107–123;

Round, "Exemplary Ethics: Towards a Reassessment of Santillana's *Proverbios*," in *Belfast Spanish and Portuguese Papers,* edited by P. S. N. Russell-Gebbett, Round, and A. H. Terry (Belfast: Queen's University of Belfast, 1979), pp. 217–236;

Round, *The Greatest Man Uncrowned: A Study of the Fall of Don Alvaro de Luna* (London: Tamesis, 1986);

Round, "Renaissance Culture and Its Opponents in Fifteenth-Century Castile," *Modern Language Review,* 57 (1962): 204–215;

Luis Rubio García, *Documentos sobre el Marqués de Santillana* (Murcia: Universidad de Murcia, 1983);

Mario Schiff, *La Bibliothèque du Marquis de Santillane* (Paris: Bouillon, 1905);

Joseph Seronde, "Dante and the French Influence on the Marqués de Santillana," *Romanic Review,* 7 (1916): 194–221;

Seronde, "A Study of the Relations of Some Leading French Poets of the XIV and XV Centuries to the Marqués de Santillana," *Romanic Review,* 6 (1915): 60–86;

Colin Smith, "Los cultismos literarios del Renacimiento, breve adición al *Diccionario crítico etimológico* de Corominas," *Bulletin Hispanique,* 61 (1959): 236–272;

Jesús Angel Solórzano Telechea and Lorena Fernández González, *Conflictos jurisdiccionales entre la villa de Santander y el marquesado de Santillana en el siglo XV* (Santander: Fundación Marcelino Botín, 1996);

Julian Weiss, *The Poet's Art: Literary Theory in Castile, c. 1400–60* (Oxford: Society for the Study of Mediaeval Languages and Literature, 1990);

Jane Whetnall, "Editing Santillana's Early Sonnets: Some Doubts about the Authority of SA8," in *Santillana: A Symposium,* edited by Alan D. Deyermond (London: Department of Hispanic Studies, Queen Mary and Westfield College, 2000), pp. 54–80.

# Diego de Valera

*(1412 – 1488)*

### Noel Fallows
*University of Georgia*

WORKS: Epistles (1441–1487)

**Manuscripts:** Madrid, Biblioteca Nacional 1341, 9263, 10445.

**Standard editions:** *Epístolas,* in *Epístolas de Mosén Diego de Valera enbiadas en diversos tiempos é á diversas personas: Publícalas juntamente con otros cinco tratados del mismo autor sobre diversas materias la Sociedad de Bibliófilos Españoles,* edited by José Antonio de Balenchana (Madrid: Sociedad de Bibliófilos Españoles, 1878), pp. 1–121; and *Epístolas,* in *Prosistas castellanos del siglo XV,* volume 1, edited by Mario Penna (Madrid: Rivadeneira, 1959), pp. 3–51. Epistles numbers 24 and 25, omitted from Balenchana's and Penna's editions, have been edited by Juan de Mata Carriazo Arrioquia in his editions of two fifteenth-century chronicles. For epistle 24, see Pedro Carrillo de Huete, *Crónica del halconero de Juan II,* edited by Carriazo Arrioquia (Madrid: Espasa-Calpe, 1946), pp. 317–319. For epistle 25, see Valera, "Crónica abreviada de España," in *Memorial de diversas hazañas, crónica de Enrique IV, ordenada por mosén Diego de Valera,* edited by Carriazo Arrioquia (Madrid: Espasa-Calpe, 1941), pp. 324–325.

*Espejo de verdadera nobleza* (ca. 1441)

**Manuscripts:** There are six extant manuscripts, four in Madrid, Biblioteca Nacional (1341, 12672, 12690, and 12701); one in El Escorial, Biblioteca de San Lorenzo de El Escorial (N-I-13); and one in New York, Hispanic Society of America (HC397/762).

**Standard editions:** *Espejo de verdadera nobleza,* in *Epístolas de Mosén Diego de Valera enbiadas en diversos tiempos é á diversas personas: Publícalas juntamente con otros cinco tratados del mismo autor sobre diversas materias la Sociedad de Bibliófilos Españoles,* edited by José Antonio de Balenchana (Madrid: Sociedad de Bibliófilos Españoles, 1878), pp. 167–231; and *Espejo de verdadera nobleza,* in *Prosistas castellanos del siglo XV,* volume 1, edited by Mario Penna (Madrid: Rivadeneira, 1959), pp. 89–116.

*Tratado en defenssa de virtuossas mugeres* (ca. 1445)

**Manuscripts:** The text is extant in Madrid, Biblioteca Nacional 1341, 9985, and 12672; and Biblioteca de San Lorenzo de El Escorial N-I-13.

**Standard editions:** *Tratado en defensa de virtuossas mugeres,* in *Epístolas de Mosén Diego de Valera enbiadas en diversos tiempos é á diversas personas: Publícalas juntamente con otros cinco tratados del mismo autor sobre diversas materias la Sociedad de Bibliófilos Españoles,* edited by José Antonio de Balenchana (Madrid: Sociedad de Bibliófilos Españoles, 1878), pp. 123–166; *Tratado en defenssa de virtuossas mugeres,* in *Prosistas castellanos del siglo XV,* volume 1, edited by Mario Penna (Madrid: Rivadeneira, 1959), pp. 55–76; *Texto y Concordancias de la "Defenssa de virtuossas mugeres" de Mosén Diego de Valera. MS. 1341 de la Biblioteca Nacional,* 3 microfiches, edited by María Isabel Montoya Ramírez (Madison, Wis.: Hispanic Seminary of Medieval Studies, 1992); and Diego de Valera, *Tratado en defensa de las virtuosas mujeres,* edited by María Angeles Suz Ruiz (Madrid: El Archipiélago, 1983).

*Tratado de Providencia contra Fortuna* (ca. 1445–1448)

**Manuscripts:** There are four extant manuscripts in Madrid, Biblioteca Nacional (1341, 10445, 12672, and 12701) and one in London, British Library (G11272).

**Standard edition:** *Tratado de Providencia contra Fortuna,* in *Prosistas castellanos del siglo XV,* volume 1, edited by Mario Penna (Madrid: Rivadeneira, 1959), pp. 141–146.

*Breviloquio de virtudes* (ca. 1447–1448)

**Manuscripts:** There are three manuscripts in Madrid, Biblioteca Nacional 1341, 12672, and 12701.

**Standard edition:** *Breviloquio de virtudes,* in *Prosistas castellanos del siglo XV,* volume 1, edited by Mario Penna (Madrid: Rivadeneira, 1959), pp. 147–154.

Poetry (1447–ca. 1460)

**Manuscripts:** Valera's poetry is extant in thirteen manuscript collections of *cancionero* poetry.

**Standard edition:** *El Cancionero del siglo XV, c. 1360–1520,* 7 volumes, edited by Brian Dutton (Salamanca: Universidad de Salamanca, 1990–1991).

*Exortación de la pas* (ca. 1448)

**Manuscripts:** There are two extant manuscripts in Madrid, Biblioteca Nacional 1341 and 9263.

**Standard edition:** *Exortación de la pas,* in *Prosistas castellanos del siglo XV,* volume 1, edited by Mario Penna (Madrid: Rivadeneira, 1959), pp. 77–87.

*Origen de Troya y Roma* (ca. 1455–1460)

**Manuscript:** There is one extant manuscript, in Madrid, Biblioteca Nacional 12672.

**Standard edition:** *Origen de Troya y Roma,* in *Prosistas castellanos del siglo XV,* volume 1, edited by Mario Penna (Madrid: Rivadeneira, 1959), pp. 155–159.

*Genealogía de los Reyes de Francia* (ca. 1455–1460)

**Manuscripts:** There are two extant manuscripts: Madrid, Biblioteca Nacional 1341; and Vienna, Österreichische Nationalbibliothek 5612.

*Ceremonial de príncipes y caballeros* (ca. 1458–1460)

**Manuscripts:** The text is extant in Madrid, Biblioteca Nacional 1159, 1341, 9782, 9942, 10445, 12672, 12701, and Res. 125; Madrid, Biblioteca de Palacio II/1341; Biblioteca Pública de Toledo 208; and Barcelona, Biblioteca de Cataluña 529 and 3841.

**Standard editions:** *Cirimonial de príncipes,* in *Epístolas de Mosén Diego de Valera enbiadas en diversos tiempos é á diversas personas: Publícalas juntamente con otros cinco tratados del mismo autor sobre diversas materias la Sociedad de Bibliófilos Españoles,* edited by José Antonio de Balenchana (Madrid: Sociedad de Bibliófilos Españoles, 1878), pp. 305–322; and *Cirimonial de príncipes y caballeros,* in *Prosistas castellanos del siglo XV,* volume 1, edited by Mario Penna (Madrid: Rivadeneira, 1959), pp. 161–167.

*Tratado de las armas* (ca. 1462–1465)

**Manuscripts:** There are at least fourteen extant manuscripts of this text, including Madrid, Biblioteca Nacional 1341.

**Standard editions:** *Tratado de las armas,* in *Epístolas de Mosén Diego de Valera enbiadas en diversos tiempos é á diversas personas: Publícalas juntamente con otros cinco tratados del mismo autor sobre diversas materias la Sociedad de Bibliófilos Españoles,* edited by José Antonio de Balenchana (Madrid: Sociedad de Bibliófilos Españoles, 1878), pp. 243–303; *Tratado de las armas,* in *Prosistas castellanos del siglo XV,* volume 1, edited by Mario Penna (Madrid: Rivadeneira, 1959), pp. 117–139; *Textos y Concordancias del "Tratado de las armas" de Diego de Valera. Rome, Casanatense MS. 1098, BNM MS. 1341,* 4 microfiches, edited by Francisco Gago Jover (Madison, Wis.: Hispanic Seminary of Medieval Studies, 1994).

*Doctrinal de príncipes* (ca. 1474–1476)

**Manuscripts:** Madrid, Biblioteca Bartolomé March 1916/3; Madrid, Biblioteca Nacional 1341, 7099, 10445, 12672, and 17804; New York, Hispanic Society of America B2572; Parma, Biblioteca Nazionale Palatino 86.

**Standard editions:** *Doctrinal de príncipes,* in *Prosistas castellanos del siglo XV,* volume 1, edited by Mario Penna (Madrid: Rivadeneira, 1959), pp. 173–202; and *Doctrinal de príncipes,* edited by Silvia Monti (Verona: Università degli studi di Verona, Facoltà di economia e commercio, Istituto di lingue e letterature straniere, 1982).

*Preheminencias y cargos de los oficiales de armas* (ca. 1480)

**Manuscripts:** Extant manuscripts include Madrid, Biblioteca Nacional 1341 and 7099.

**Standard editions:** *Preheminencias y cargos de los oficiales darmas,* in *Epístolas de Mosén Diego de Valera enbiadas en diversos tiempos é á diversas personas: Publícalas juntamente con otros cinco tratados del mismo autor sobre diversas materias la Sociedad de Bibliófilos Españoles,* edited by José Antonio de Balenchana (Madrid: Sociedad de Bibliófilos Españoles, 1878), pp. 233–241; and *Preheminencias y cargos de los oficiales de armas,* in *Prosistas castellanos del siglo XV,* volume 1, edited by Mario Penna (Madrid: Rivadeneira, 1959), pp. 169–171.

*Crónica abreviada de España [Valeriana]* (1481)

**Manuscripts:** There are at least eighteen early printed editions and one extant manuscript (British Library Egerton 286), which is copied from the first printed edition (Seville: Alonso del Puerto, 1482).

**Standard edition:** *Crónica abreviada de España,* in *Memorial de diversas hazañas,* edited by Juan de Mata Carriazo Arrioquia (Madrid: Espasa-Calpe, 1941), pp. 299–337.

*Memorial de diversas hazañas* (ca. 1482–1488)

**Manuscripts:** There are seven extant manuscripts, six of which are in European libraries—including Seville, Biblioteca Colombina (84-5-11); Madrid, Biblioteca Nacional (1210 and 18219); the Biblioteca de San Lorenzo de El Escorial (M-I-23); London, British Library (Egerton 302); and Madrid, Real Academia de la Historia (D-118)—and one of which is in Bristol, private collection of Professor David Hook (C-1).

**Standard editions:** *Memorial de diversas hazañas,* edited by Juan de Mata Carriazo Arrioquia (Madrid: Espasa-Calpe, 1941); *Memorial de diversas hazañas,* in *Crónica de los reyes de Castilla, III,* edited by Cayetano Rosell, Biblioteca de Autores Españoles, no. 70 (Madrid: Rivadeneira, 1953), pp. 1–95.

*Crónica de los Reyes Católicos* (ca. 1487–1488)

    **Manuscripts:** Bristol, private collection of Professor David Hook, C-1; El Escorial, Biblioteca de San Lorenzo de El Escorial L.I.6; London, British Library Egerton 303. The standard edition is based on a collation of Escorial L.I.6 and Egerton 303.

    **Standard edition:** *Crónica de los Reyes Católicos, Revista de Filología Española,* Anejo 8, edited by Juan de Mata Carriazo Arrioquia (Madrid: José Molina, 1927).

TRANSLATION: Honoré Bouvet, *Arbol de batallas* (ca. 1445; attribution uncertain)

    **Manuscripts:** Manuscripts include Madrid, Biblioteca Nacional 764, 1341, and 1502.

Early-twentieth-century biographers of Diego de Valera such as Lucas de Torre y Franco-Romero and José Antonio de Balenchana tend to dismiss Valera as little more than a pedant and a brigand. This portrait has been extensively revised by scholars such as César Real de la Riva, Nicasio Salvador Miguel, and Jesús D. Rodríguez Velasco in his well-documented treatment of Valera's life and works in *El debate sobre la caballería en el siglo XV: La tratadística caballeresca castellana en su marco europeo* (The Debate on Chivalry in the Fifteenth Century: Castialian Treatises on Chivalry in Their European Context, 1996). Valera's exact birth date is unknown, but it is clear that he was born in the year 1412 in Cuenca. He was the youngest son of Alfonso Chirino, personal physician to King Juan II of Castile, by Chirino's first wife, María de Valera. Both Rodríguez Velasco and Marcelino Amasuno Sárraga, in his study of Alfonso Chirino, provide much documentary evidence to support the contention that Diego de Valera was of *converso* stock. Becaue of his father's obligations at court, Valera was essentially raised by his mother, and he chose to adopt her surname. Rodríguez Velasco conjectures that Valera adopted this surname not only because his relationship with his father was somewhat strained but also because Valera wished to distance himself as much as possible from his Jewish ancestry.

From 1427 to 1435 Valera was a *doncel,* that is, a royal page, in the court of Juan II of Castile, a post he attained most probably through his father's connections. Still in his teens, he found himself at the political and cultural epicenter of Castile. It is now known that as a *doncel* Valera was not simply a servant but a member of the "Orden de los Donceles" (Order of Royal Pages), a military order noted for prowess in battle. Indeed, Valera

acquitted himself with distinction in Juan II's campaigns in Granada, and he was present at the Battle of La Higueruela in 1431. By 1435, on the eve of the siege of Huelma, he was dubbed a knight. Rodríguez Velasco contends that this moment was decisive in Valera's life, for although he was invested, he was not invested by the king himself. Rather, Valera's knighthood was conferred on him by Fernán Alvarez de Toledo, a fellow knight. It is quite possible that this incident, when conjoined with the issue of his Jewish ancestry, sowed the seeds for many of Valera's future writings, in which he ponders whether the king also confers nobility upon those he dubs knights. It should be stressed, however, that while Valera does grapple in many of his treatises with concepts of nobility, he does not express moral disaffection or rancor against those who persecute *conversos*. As in the case of Alfonso de Cartagena and other *conversos* of the epoch, although Valera's heritage undoubtedly influenced his way of thinking, readers of his works must be cautioned, especially in light of recent scholarship, against seeking a unifying "*converso* voice" or attitude throughout his works.

By 1437 Valera was pursuing the ideal life of the knight-errant, traveling extensively throughout Europe. Specifically, on the pretext of minor diplomatic missions, he visited France and Bohemia. He did not return to Castile until the early 1440s, by which time he had participated in the siege of Montreux with the army of King Charles VII of France and the wars against the Hussites with the army of King Albert of Bohemia. Valera's modern biographers have debunked the myth of him as a brigand, noting that he categorically refused payment for his services to both monarchs. In his travels Valera had also proven himself to be a skilled orator and rhetorician, at least according to a passage in the *Crónica de Juan II* (Chronicle of Juan II, late fifteenth century). The passage in question, which some critics believe was penned by Valera himself, describes how during his visit to Bohemia, Valera gained notoriety for an incident in which he responded to Count Ulrich of Cilli at a banquet in Prague. When the count made a pointed comment about the ignominious loss of the king of Castile's colors at the Battle of Aljubarrota in 1385, Valera responded, citing Bartolus of Sassoferrato as a point of departure, that although the colors were indeed lost, the king's noble lineage was not tarnished, proof of which lay in the fact that since Aljubarrota the Castilians had won many battles against the Muslims in the Iberian Peninsula. Those at table, including the host, King Albert, were suitably convinced, with the result that the count was forced to retract his insult.

The year 1441, upon Valera's return to Castile, was eventful in that the honorific title *Mosén* was conferred on the knight-errant by Juan II. According to the

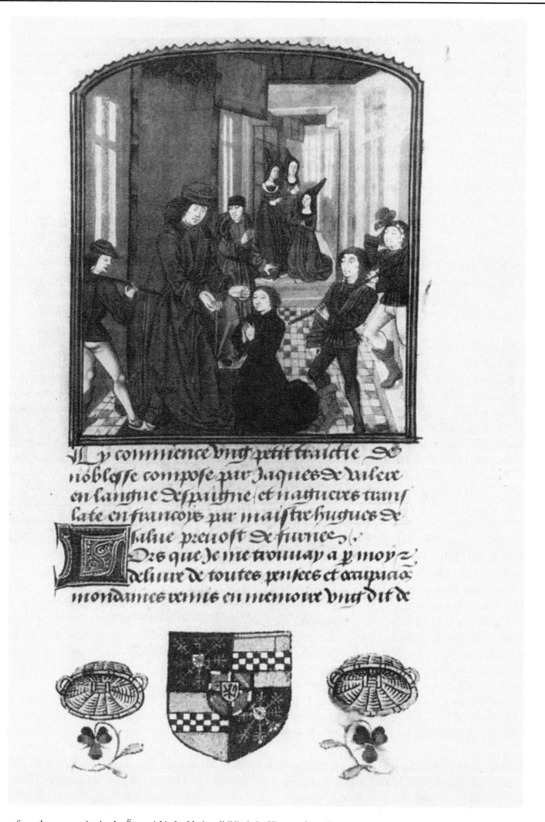

*Page from the manuscript in the Österreichische Nationalbibliothek, Vienna, for a French translation, circa 1481, of Diego de Valera's*
Espejo de verdadera nobleza, *composed circa 1441 (from Arie Johan Vanderjagt,* "Qui sa vertu anoblist":
The Concepts of "Noblesse" and "Chose Publicque" in Burgundian Political Thought, *1981;*
*Thomas Cooper Library, University of South Carolina)*

*Crónica de Juan II,* the title was just one of many honors heaped on Valera for his eloquent defense of the Castilian monarchy in Bohemia. *Mosén,* used more frequently in Catalonia than in Castile, is possibly a calque on the French *monseigneur.* As well as being a sign of respect reserved for knights and members of the clergy, the honorific title underscores Valera's affiliation with courts in Burgundy and France, and, perhaps more importantly, the conferral of the title by the ruling monarch represents royal recognition of Valera's knighthood. The year 1441 was also eventful from a literary point of view, for Valera wrote his first epistle in defense of the concept of monarchy and the importance of the king's suzerainty, in opposition to the power the king was relinquishing and conceding to his favorite, Alvaro de Luna. The letter is the first in a relatively large body of correspondence that Valera sent to Castilian monarchs, lending support to or expressing disapproval of a variety of political initiatives. As well as epistles, Valera composed a short treatise on knighthood around 1441, *Espejo de verdadera nobleza* (Mirror of True Nobility), which concerns a discussion of the origin and purpose of the institution of chivalry. The book is also a product of its time in the sense that Valera sues for peace, and he reminds the nobles of Castile, most of whom were involved in petty feuds of one sort or another, that the mission of knights is above all to defend the state.

More diplomatic missions followed, first to Denmark, then to England and Burgundy. Under the patronage of Philip the Good, Duke of Burgundy, and Philip's natural son Anthony of Burgundy, Valera fought with distinction in a spectacular tournament called the Pas de l'Arbre de Charlemagne (Passage of Arms at the Tree of Charlemagne), held near Dijon in 1443. From this moment forth Valera was a devout Francophile, even to the extent that he christened his son not Carlos but the French-Burgundian equivalent, Charles. If the Burgundians made a lasting impression on Valera, so too did he have a profound impact on the Burgundian court. Charity Cannon Willard has discussed the enduring influence on Burgundian court politics of the lavishly illuminated manuscript translations of Valera's *Espejo de verdadera nobleza* and *Tratado de las armas* (Treatise on Arms), commissioned by Philip the Good in the early 1460s. The translations–titled, respectively, *Ung petit traictyé de noblesse* and *Traitté intitulé des drois d'armes*–are also discussed by Arie Johan Vanderjagt in his *"Qui sa vertu anoblist": The Concepts of "Noblesse" and "Chose Publicque" in Burgundian Political Thought* (1981). After taking his leave of the Burgundian court, en route for Castile, Valera visited France for the second time, where he deployed his diplomatic skills and successfully negotiated the release of the count of

Armagnac, who was in the service of Juan II when he had been imprisoned by Charles VII.

By 1445 Valera was back in Castile. In this year he took a detour from his usual line of inquiry and composed *Tratado en defenssa de virtuossas mugeres* (Treatise in Defense of Virtuous Women). Works that praise or censure the female sex constitute a commonplace in the literature of western Europe during the Middle Ages. The feminist-misogynist polemic piqued the interest of a variety of medieval Castilian writers, from Valera to the king's favorite, Luna, who wrote his own *Libro de las claras e virtuosas mujeres* (Book on Illustrious and Virtuous Women) in 1446, to Fray Martin de Córdoba, author of *Jardín de nobles donzellas* (Garden of Noble Ladies), composed in 1468. *Tratado en defenssa de virtuossas mugeres* engages in the feminist-misogynist polemic of the day, and the book is a testimony to Valera's multifaceted talents as a writer. It is dedicated to Queen María of Castile and is addressed to a courtly public, one that would be familiar with the polemic. In the treatise Valera refutes the arguments postulated by the misogynists. Specifically, he takes issue with Giovanni Boccaccio because of the rhetorical contradiction inherent in two of Boccaccio's works. On the one hand, Boccaccio composed *De mulieribus claris* (On Illustrious Women, 1362), a profeminist text on womanly virtues, but on the other hand, he wrote *Il Corbaccio* (The Old Crow, 1365), a misogynist work in which he launches a vitriolic attack against the evils of the female sex. Nicholas G. Round, in his 1989 essay "The Presence of Mosén Diego de Valera in *Cárcel de Amor,*" has further pointed to the links between profeminist treatises and the sentimental fiction that was popular reading matter at the time. In the case of *Tratado en defenssa de virtuossas mugeres* Round shows that there are clearly rhetorical affinities between this treatise and Diego de San Pedro's *Cárcel de Amor* (Prison of Love), which was first published in 1492, some forty-seven years after Valera's treatise, and which, like the Burgundian translations undertaken in the 1460s, underscores the enduring influence of Valera's literary production.

Around the same time he composed *Tratado en defenssa de virtuossas mugeres,* Valera also probably translated Honoré Bonet's *L'Arbre des batailles* (Tree of Battles). Originally composed circa 1387, *L'Arbre des batailles* was translated into Castilian twice in the fifteenth century. One translator is known to be Antón de Zorita. Carlos Alvar in particular, in his 1989 essay "Traducciones francesas en el siglo XV: El caso del *Arbol de batallas* de Honoré Bouvet," argues that the other translator is Valera, although Rodríguez Velasco casts doubt on this assertion on the grounds that since the book is dedicated to Álvaro de Luna, and Luna and Valera

*Tomb of Don Juan Pacheco, the socially ambitious marquis for whom Valera wrote his* Ceremonial de príncipes y caballeros *circa 1458–1460 ( from Juan de Mata Carriazo Arrioquia, ed.,* Memorial de diversas hazañas, *1941; Thomas Cooper Library, University of South Carolina)*

were known enemies, it is unlikely that Valera would have dedicated a book to the king's favorite. It should also be taken into consideration, however, that the 1440s in Castile was a decade characterized by constantly shifting loyalties, so it is not impossible that Valera should dedicate a work to a man he ultimately came to despise. The Castilian translation, *Arbol de batallas,* was subsequently diffused throughout the Iberian Peninsula. The book is essentially a collection of hypothetical situations, mostly problematic, that pertain to knighthood, to which Bouvet proposes a solution or challenges the accepted solution with his own views, based primarily on a reading of civil and canon law.

*Tratado de Providencia contra Fortuna* (Treatise on Providence against Fortune), composed circa 1445–1448, is an occasional treatise, inspired by the catastrophic defeat at the Battle of Olmedo (19 May 1445) of the Castilian noble faction that opposed and defied the king. Based on a reading of Seneca, Cato, and the Psalms, the work, perhaps not surprisingly, is a treatise on the fickle nature of fortune in which Valera advocates for absolute loyalty to the reigning monarch as well as the benefits of this loyalty to the state as a whole. The treatise *Breviloquio de virtudes* (Opuscule on Virtue) followed, circa 1447–1448. Not unlike the *Tra-*

*tado de Providencia contra Fortuna,* the *Breviloquio de virtudes* is a treatise on virtue, following the teachings of Aristotle, Cicero, Seneca, and St. Augustine, the purpose of which is to denounce tyranny and advocate for clemency, doubtless with the fate of those who were vanquished at Olmedo firmly in mind.

As well as composing political treatises and participating in literary debates such as the feminist-misogynist polemic, Valera tried his hand at poetry in the mid 1440s, true to the stereotypical image of the medieval courtly knight. Valera is known to have written twenty-one poems, and Brian Dutton attributes another two to him in his edition of fifteenth-century *cancionero* poetry, *El Cancionero del siglo XV, c. 1360–1520* (1990–1991). Most recently Alvar has divided Valera's poetry into three groups, representing three distinct periods of poetic activity: from 1447 to 1453; from 1450 to 1459; and circa 1460. The first group of poems is moral and political in nature; the second group consists primarily of love poems; and the third group, according to Alvar, represents a period of crisis in Valera's personal life. Certainly the tone of many of the poems in the third group, in contradistinction to *Tratado en defenssa de virtuossas mugeres* and Valera's earlier criticism of Boccaccio, is decidedly misogynist.

By the late 1440s Valera returned to his preferred medium of political commentary. In *Exortación de la pas* (Exhortation for Peace, circa 1448), Valera offers solutions to the contentious and unstable political situation in Castile precipitated, in his opinion, by the rivalries between noble factions and the king. The issue in the disputes between the king and his nobles revolved almost exclusively around Luna and his role, as royal favorite and constable of Castile, in the government of the kingdom of Castile. Valera refers to the Muslims of Granada, who had already taken advantage of the situation by making several incursions into Christian-occupied territory. While these incursions were largely abortive, as Valera points out, Castile's political instability leaves its borders open to attack with the potential for disastrous consequences. John Edwards analyzes this text in conjunction with the epistles Valera wrote to Juan II in the 1440s as another appeal for clemency toward the king's opponents, who were on the losing side at the Battle of Olmedo. *Exortación de la pas* is the last work (except the ubiquitous epistles) that Valera wrote during the reign of Juan II, which ended with the king's death in 1454.

The power of Valera's intellect, when conjoined with his obvious physical prowess as a knight, has meant that his position in the context of the fifteenth-century debate between arms and letters is viewed by critics from a variety of different perspectives. Round, in his "Renaissance Culture and Its Opponents in

*First page of a manuscript in the Biblioteca Nacional, Madrid, for Valera's* Doctrinal de príncipes *(circa 1474–1476), dedicated to Prince Fernando, in which he advocates that princes use violence judiciously (from Juan de Mata Carriazo Arrioquia, ed.,* Memorial de diversas hazañas, *1941; Thomas Cooper Library, University of South Carolina)*

Fifteenth-Century Castile" (1962), takes issue with the assumption that arms and letters went hand in hand at the court of Juan II. He contends that the study of literature was considered an unworthy pursuit for members of the nobility during the reign of Juan II because it detracted from time better spent in battle or in sport. As far as Round is concerned, Valera constitutes an exception to the general rule that knights were an uneducated lot, dedicated to vainglorious quests for recognition and legitimization. Valera forms part of what Round calls a "cultured minority." Peter E. Russell follows the same line of argument, noting that with few exceptions members of the nobility during the reign of Juan II lacked interest in the pursuit of literature. On the other hand, in *El humanismo castellano del siglo XV* (1976) Ottavio Di Camillo maintains that figures such as Alfonso de Cartagena—author of the *Doctrinal de los caballeros* (Catechism of Knighthood, circa 1440)—and Valera are representative of the fact that arms and letters were in fact compatible. Di Camillo argues that Valera belonged to an "association" of intellectuals who were defined not so much by their social caste as by their ability to communicate effectively. Jeremy N. H. Lawrance also challenges the contention that there really was a prejudice against letters in mid-fifteenth-century Castile and maintains that many princes and noblemen, including Valera, were in fact avid, well-educated readers. As more and more noblemen became involved with governance and polity, argues Lawrance, so they became more aware that a well-rounded literary education was an essential part of their training. E. Michael Gerli has offered a new twist to these contrasting theories. Gerli argues persuasively that Valera is an example of "performing nobility," that is, he was just as violent and contentious as other noblemen of his day, but he is an exception to a general rule to the extent that he sought validation and legitimization through his literary interpretation of his own deeds. He thus went a step further than most ordinary knights, who depended on others to write about their deeds. In his literary quest for legitimization and his self-portrayal as an authority on questions of nobility and honor, argues Gerli, Valera presses home the idea that those who convert from Judaism to Christianity are not automatically excluded from the ranks of the nobility.

Between 1455 and 1465, during the first ten years of the reign of Juan II's successor, Enrique IV, Valera wrote four works that illustrate above all the extent of his knowledge of European history, culture, and customs: *Origen de Troya y Roma* (The Origin of Troy and Rome, circa 1455–1460); *Genealogía de los Reyes de Francia* (Genealogy of the Kings of France, circa 1455–1460); *Ceremonial de príncipes y caballeros* (Ceremonial on

Princes and Knights, circa 1458–1460); and *Tratado de las armas* (circa 1462–1465).

*Origen de Troya y Roma* is a brief excursus on the mythological foundation of Troy and Rome, written at the request of Juan Hurtado de Mendoza. Rebeca Sanmartín Bastida has shown that the treatise is based primarily on Valera's reading of Leomarte's fourteenth-century *Sumas de historia troyana* (Summary of Trojan History). Never one to stray too far from his own political agenda, Valera uses the two cities as a pretext for a disquisition on the fall of great empires through civil wars and dynastic disputes. Geographically closer to home, the *Genealogía de los Reyes de Francia* is a straightforward genealogical history of the kings of France, paraphrased from a Latin chronicle that stops in 1320, in which the French royal lineage is traced from Japhet to Philippe V.

*Ceremonial de príncipes y caballeros* is a rather self-serving disquisition written at the behest of Juan Pacheco. It is written on the pretext of describing the differences between noble titles in Europe, such as *marquis, count, duke, viscount,* and *baron.* In almost every western European country except Castile, argues Valera, a marquis takes precedence over a duke. It is no coincidence that the dedicatee of the work, the aggressive social upstart Pacheco, also was marquis of Villena, and Valera essentially insinuates that Enrique IV is mistaken to confer more power on his counts than on the marquis of Villena. Finally, *Tratado de las armas,* which is sometimes referred to as *Tratado de los rieptos y desafíos* (Treatise on Jousts and Challenges), is a treatise on armor, arms, heraldic devices, and the etiquette that should be observed by those who participate in jousts and tournaments. The manuscripts and the content of this treatise are discussed at length in a series of articles by María Lourdes Simó, who underscores Valera's impressive knowledge not just of Castilian but also of western European heraldic customs and courtly etiquette. It should not be forgotten that Valera also continued writing epistles in which he often submitted unsolicited advice to the reigning monarch. He survived the turbulent reign of Enrique IV intact, and despite the fact that in his epistles he repeatedly voiced concern and criticism about Enrique's abilities as a monarch and a politician, in 1467 he was appointed *maestresala,* that is, steward of the royal hall, a testimony to Enrique's tolerance even of his most critical subjects.

After Enrique IV's death in 1474 Valera lent his support to Fernando (Ferdinand) and Isabel (Isabella), the Catholic Monarchs. He continued to serve as *maestresala* to Fernando and Isabel, even though he had now practically withdrawn from court life and spent most of his time as governor of Puerto de Santa María,

*Page from the first edition (1482), in the Biblioteca Nacional, Madrid, of Valera's* Crónica abreviada de España,
*which chronicles Spanish history from the Dark Ages to the reign of King Juan II, the father of then-ruler
Queen Isabel (from Juan de Mata Carriazo Arrioquia, ed.,* Memorial de diversas hazañas, *1941;
Thomas Cooper Library, University of South Carolina)*

near Cádiz. A united Christian Spain with two young monarchs at the helm constituted an ideal pretext for offering advice on how to govern, and perhaps because of his withdrawal from court life in the north, the early years of the reign of the Catholic Monarchs coincide with Valera's most prolific period of letter writing. Although Valera's letters were unsolicited, with the result that his suggestions were largely ignored, John Edwards has shown that his strategic advice to Fernando and Isabel, as well as to their predecessors Juan II and Enrique IV, was sound, and that the Reconquest would probably have ended sooner had his advice in fact been heeded.

Gino V. M. de Solenni showed that sometime between 1474 and 1476 Valera composed the *Doctrinal de príncipes* (Catechism of Princes), which he dedicated to the young prince Fernando. In this treatise Valera, who had been admonished in his correspondence with Juan II for his supposedly pacifist views, develops ideas he had touched upon in *Breviloquio de virtudes*. He addresses the question of whether human beings are intuitively violent or in fact able to control violent impulses. The answer is based primarily on a reading of Aristotle's *Nicomachean Ethics* and Giles of Rome's *De Regimine principum* (On the Government of Rulers), peppered with much of Valera's own material concerning such chivalric pursuits as jousting and warfare. Violence, argues Valera, can and must be controlled, especially if the prince understands the notion of legally binding friendship *(amicitia),* as well as Greek and Roman ideas on the political society. Blessed with a well-rounded education and skill in the martial arts, in particular the ability to wield sword and lance, Valera's ideal prince is never tyrannical, always a model of clemency and magnanimity.

Valera was as active in the twilight years of his life as he was in his prime. In 1480 he wrote his last short treatise, *Preheminencias y cargos de los oficiales de armas* (Prerogatives and Duties of Officials of Arms), a work that dwells primarily on the intricate duties of kings of arms and heralds. A year later, in 1481, he addressed *Crónica abreviada de España* (Brief Chronicle of Spain), also known as *Crónica Valeriana,* to Isabel of Castile. This chronicle was probably composed with the newly invented printing press firmly in mind, the virtues of which Valera the self-publicist not surprisingly extols in the prologue. The chronicle covers Spain's Visigothic heritage up to the end of the reign of Isabella's father, Juan II. The many early printed editions of this chronicle, discussed in articles by David Mackenzie and Julián Martín Abad, attest to the popularity and wide diffusion of this work.

Two more chronicles followed. The first was *Memorial de diversas hazañas* (Memorial on Miscellaneous Deeds), written circa 1482–1488 and dedicated to the reign of Enrique IV. A manuscript copy of the *Memorial de diversas hazañas* in the private collection of Professor David Hook of the University of Bristol includes sundry marginal annotations that attest to its popularity in subsequent centuries. The second chronicle, *Crónica de los Reyes Católicos* (Chronicle of the Catholic Monarchs), was composed circa 1487–1488. It is dedicated to the reign of Ferdinand and Isabella, specifically the years from 1474 to 1488. Naturally the chronicles depict history according to Valera, and the *Crónica de los Reyes Católicos* especially is a propagandistic work in favor of the Catholic Monarchs' expansionist and imperialistic political agenda.

Diego de Valera died at the age of seventy-six in his beloved Puerto de Santa María. He had the singular distinction of living, writing, and fighting his way through the reigns of Juan II, Enrique IV, and most of the reign of the Catholic Monarchs. As such his treatises and his epistles reveal a man—one of the few—who truly understood the complex politics of fifteenth-century Castile. While it is true that his opinions were often unsolicited, it is also true that Valera was never a sycophant and certainly always a Castilian patriot. Real de la Riva sums his career up best when he describes Valera not as a pedant but as a true "mentor." Throughout his literary career Valera stubbornly refused to be fettered intellectually, while he continued to ponder, define, and legitimize his own social position with respect to the monarchs he loyally served.

**References:**

Julián Martín Abad, "Las ediciones salmantinas de la *Crónica abreviada de España* de Diego de Valera en 1499 y 1500," *Revista de Literatura Medieval,* 6 (1994): 125–131;

Carlos Alvar, "La poesía de mosén Diego de Valera," in *Filologia romanza e cultura medievale: Studi in onore di Elio Melli,* 2 volumes, edited by Andrea Fassò, Luciano Formisano, and Mario Mansini (Alessandria: Edizioni dell'Orso, 1998), I: 1–13;

Alvar, "Traducciones francesas en el siglo XV: El caso del *Arbol de batallas* de Honoré Bouvet," in *Miscellanea di Studi in onore di Aurelio Roncaglia a cinquant'anni dalla sua laurea* (Modena: Mucchi, 1989), pp. 25–34;

Marcelino Amasuno Sárraga, *Alfonso Chirino, un médico de monarcas castellanos* (Salamanca: Junta de Castilla y León, 1993);

Ottavio Di Camillo, *El humanismo castellano del siglo XV* (Valencia: J. Doménech, 1976), pp. 137–193;

Di Camillo, "Las teorías de la nobleza en el pensamiento ético de Mosén Diego de Valera," in *Nunca fue pena mayor: Estudios de literatura española en homenaje a Brian Dutton,* edited by Ana Menéndez Collera and Victoriano Roncero López (Cuenca: Ediciones de la Universidad de Castilla-La Mancha, 1996), pp. 223–237;

John Edwards, "War and Peace in Fifteenth-Century Castile: Diego de Valera and the Granada War," in *Studies in Medieval History Presented to R. H. C. Davis,* edited by Henry Mayr-Harting and R. I. Moore (London: Hambledon Press, 1985), pp. 283–295;

E. Michael Gerli, "Performing Nobility: Mosén Diego de Valera and the Poetics of *Converso* Identity," *La corónica,* 25, no. 1 (1996): 19–36;

David Hook, "Method in the Margins: An Archaeology of Annotations," in *Proceedings of the Eighth Colloquium: Papers of the Medieval Hispanic Research Seminar,* volume 5, edited by Andrew M. Beresford and Alan Deyermond (London: Department of Hispanic Studies, Queen Mary and Westfield College, 1997), pp. 135–144;

Jeremy N. H. Lawrance, "On Fifteenth-Century Spanish Vernacular Humanism," in *Medieval and Renaissance Studies in Honour of Robert Brian Tate* (Oxford: Dolphin, 1986), pp. 63–79;

David Mackenzie, "Spaniards, 'Germans,' and the Invention of Printing: Diego de Valera's Eulogy in the *Crónica abreviada,*" in *New Frontiers in Hispanic and Luso-Brazilian Scholarship. "Como se fue el maestro": for Derek W. Lomax in Memoriam,* edited by Trevor J. Dadson, R. J. Oakley, and P. A. Odber de Baubeta (Lewiston, Pa.: Edwin Mellen Press, 1994), pp. 87–103;

César Real de la Riva, "Un mentor del siglo XV. Diego de Valera y sus epístolas," *Revista de Literatura,* 20, nos. 39–40 (1961): 279–305;

Jesús D. Rodríguez Velasco, *El debate sobre la caballería en el siglo XV: La tratadística caballeresca castellana en su marco europeo* (Salamanca: Junta de Castilla y León, 1996), pp. 195–274;

Nicholas G. Round, "The Presence of Mosén Diego de Valera in *Cárcel de Amor,*" in *The Age of the Catholic Monarchs, 1474–1516: Literary Studies in Memory of Keith Whinnom,* edited by Deyermond and Ian Macpherson (Liverpool: Liverpool University Press, 1989), pp. 144–154;

Round, "Renaissance Culture and Its Opponents in Fifteenth-Century Castile," *Modern Language Review,* 57 (1962): 204–215;

Peter E. Russell, "Las armas contra las letras: para una definición del humanismo español del siglo XV," in *Temas de "La Celestina" y otros estudios: Del "Cid" al "Quijote"* (Barcelona: Ariel, 1978), pp. 207–239;

Nicasio Salvador Miguel, *La poesía cancioneril: El "Cancionero de Estúñiga"* (Madrid: Alhambra, 1977);

Rebeca Sanmartín Bastida, "El tema troyano en *Origen de Troya y Roma* de Diego de Valera," *Cuadernos de Filología Clásica: Estudios Latinos,* 14 (1998): 167–185;

María Lourdes Simó, "Acerca de los manuscritos del *Tratado de las armas* de Mosén Diego de Valera," *Incipit,* 18 (1998): 65–80;

Simó, "Los conocimientos heráldicos de Mosén Diego de Valera," *La corónica,* 22, no. 1 (1993): 41–56;

Simó, "El Ms. 529 de la Biblioteca Nacional de Cataluña y el *Tratado de las armas* de Mosén Diego de Valera," *Incipit,* 13 (1993): 153–169;

Gino V. M. de Solenni, "On the Date of Composition of Mosén Diego de Valera's *El doctrinal de príncipes,*" *Romanic Review,* 16 (1925): 87–88;

Lucas de Torre y Franco-Romero, "Mosén Diego de Valera: Su vida y obras," *Boletín de la Real Academia de la Historia,* 64 (1914): 50–83, 133–168, 249–276, 365–412;

Arie Johan Vanderjagt, *"Qui sa vertu anoblist": The Concepts of "Noblesse" and "Chose Publicque" in Burgundian Political Thought* (Groningen: Jean Miélot, 1981), pp. 225–283;

Charity Cannon Willard, "The Concept of True Nobility at the Burgundian Court," *Studies in the Renaissance,* 14 (1967): 33–48.

# Enrique de Villena

(circa 1382–1384 – 15 December 1434)

Sol Miguel-Prendes
*Wake Forest University*

WORKS: *Los dotze treballs de Hèrcules* (1417)

**First publication:** *Los dotze treballs d'Hèrcules* (Valencia: Printed by C. Cofman, 1514).

*Los doce trabajos de Hércules* (1417)

**Manuscripts:** The text is extant in several fifteenth-century manuscripts: Madrid, Biblioteca Nacional MS. 6526, fols. 5ra–60vb, tablas 2ra–4va; MS. 17814, fols. 65r–97r; MS. 27, fols. 158ra–194ra; and MS. 6599, fols. 49r–110r; Geneva, Bibliotheca Bodmeriana cod. 167, fols. 1–31; El Escorial, Biblioteca de San Lorenzo de El Escorial MS. Q.I.20; Madrid, Real Academia Española V-6-64, fols. 63r–101v. Eighteenth-century copies are extant in Madrid, Biblioteca Nacional MS. 8546; Madrid, Real Academia Española MS. 158, fols. 1–267; Madrid, Real Academia de la Historia 9-27-4/5218, fols. 3r–54v.

**Early imprints:** *Los doze trabajos de Hércules* (Zamora: Antonio de Centenera, 1483)–facsimile edition, *Los doce trabajos de Hércules* (Valencia: Vicent García Editores / Madrid: Biblioteca Nacional, 1995); *Los doze trabajos de Ercules copilados por don enrrique de villena . . . y un tractado muy provechoso dela vida bienaventurada* (Burgos: Juan de Burgos, 1499).

**Modern editions:** *Los doze trabajos de Hércules,* edited by Margherita Morreale (Madrid: Real Academia Española, 1958); *Texto y concordancias de Los doze trabajos de Hércules,* edition of Biblioteca Nacional MS. 27, edited by Francisco Gago Jover (Madison, Wis.: Hispanic Seminary of Medieval Studies, 1991).

*Tratado de la lepra* (ca. 1421–1422)

**Manuscripts:** There are three fifteenth-century manuscripts: Madrid, Biblioteca Nacional MS. 6599, fols. 127v–140r; Madrid, Academia Española V-6-64, fols. 114v–123r; Geneva, Bibliotheca Bodmeriana.

*Tratado de aojamiento* or *Tratado de la fascinación* (ca. 1422–1425)

**Manuscripts:** Madrid, Biblioteca Nacional MS. 6599, fols. 140r–150v; Madrid, Real Academia Española V-6-64, fols. 124r–131r; eighteenth- century copies, Madrid, Real Academia de la Historia 9-27-4/5218; Geneva, Bibliotheca Bodmeriana.

**Modern edition:** *Tratado de aojamiento,* edited by Anna Maria Gallina (Bari: Adriatica, 1978).

*Arte cisoria* (1423)

**Manuscripts:** A copy made in Iniesta by Gabriel Gutiérrez de Bernido (28 October 1424) is in Santander, Biblioteca de Menéndez Pelayo M-103, fols. 1r–44v; a fifteenth-century copy is in El Escorial, Biblioteca de San Lorenzo de El Escorial f.IV.1, fols. 1r–84v; there are two eighteenth-century copies: Madrid, Biblioteca Nacional MS. 7843; El Escorial, Biblioteca de San Lorenzo de El Escorial J.II.28.

**First publication:** *Arte cisoria, o, Tratado del arte del cortar del cuchillo* (Madrid: Oficina de Antonio Marin, 1766)–facsimile edition, *Arte cisoria, o, Tratado del arte del cortar del cuchillo* (Madrid: G. Blázquez, 1981).

**Modern editions:** *Arte cisoria, de d. Enrique de Villena, con varios estudios sobre su vida y obras y muchas notas y apendices,* edited by Felipe Benicio Navarro (Madrid: Murillo, 1879); *Arte cisoria,* edited by Russell V. Brown (Barcelona: Humanitas, 1984); *The Text and Concordance of Escorial Manuscript f.iv.1, Arte Cisoria,* edited by John O'Neill (Madison, Wis.: Hispanic Seminary of Medieval Studies, 1987); *Arte cisoria, o, Arte de cortar los alimentos y servir la mesa,* edited by José Luis Martín (Salamanca, 1997).

*Exposición del salmo Quoniam videbo* (1424)

**Manuscripts:** Six from the fifteenth century, including Chicago, University of Chicago Library MS. 1154, fols. 18r–25r; Madrid, Biblioteca Nacional MS. 17814, fols. 125r–145r; Biblioteca Nacional MS. 6599, fols. 110v–127r; and four eighteenth-century copies.

**Modern edition:** *Exégesis, ciencia, literatura: La Exposición del Salmo "Quoniam videbo" de Enrique de Villena,* edited by Pedro M. Cátedra (Madrid: El Crotalón, 1985), pp. 85–123.

*Tratado de consolación* or *Consolatoria a Juan Fernández de Valera* (1424)

**Manuscripts:** There are several fifteenth-century copies, including Chicago, University of Chicago Library MS. 1154, fols. 1–18r; Madrid, Biblioteca Nacional Res. 385; Madrid, Biblioteca de Fundación Lázaro Galdiano 208, fols. 62r–107r; Madrid, Biblioteca Nacional MS. 6599, fols. 1r–48v; Madrid, Real Academia Española V-6-64, fols. 130r–163v; Santander, Biblioteca Menéndez Pelayo M-279, fols. 100r–173v.

**Modern edition:** *Tratado de la consolacion,* edited by Derek C. Carr (Madrid: Espasa-Calpe, 1976).

*Arte de trovar* (ca. 1417–1428)

**Manuscripts:** Fragments copied by Alvar Gómez de Castro (ca. 1500–1550), El Escorial, Biblioteca de San Lorenzo de El Escorial K.III.31, fols. 69r–89r; another sixteenth-century copy, Madrid, Biblioteca Nacional MS. 1966, fols. 1r–11r; a seventeenth-century copy by Juan Francisco de Uztarroz, Salamanca, Biblioteca Universitaria de Salamanca 2147, fols. 4r–15v.

**First publication:** "El *Arte de trobar* de Enrique de Villena, apuntado por incierto autor coetáneo," in *Orígenes de la lengua española compuesto por varios autores,* edited by Gregorio Mayans y Siscar (Madrid: Juan de Zúñiga, 1737; reprinted, Madrid: V. Suárez, 1873; reprinted, Valencia: Librerías París-Valencia, 1980).

**Modern editions:** *Arte de trovar,* edited by F. J. Sánchez Cantón (Madrid: V. Suárez, 1923; reprinted, Madrid: Visor, 1993); *Arte de trovar,* in *Villena, Lebrija, Encina: Selections,* edited by Theodore W. I. Bullock (Cambridge: Cambridge University Press, 1926).

*Epístola a Suero de Quiñones* (1427–1434)

**Manuscript:** Santander, Biblioteca Menéndez Pelayo M-279, fols. 174r–181r.

**Modern editions:** "La 'Epístola que enbio Don Enrrique de Villena a Suero de Quiñones' y la fecha de la *Crónica sarracina* de Pedro de Corral," edited by Carr, in *University of British Columbia Hispanic Studies,* edited by Harold Livermore (London: Tamesis, 1974), pp. 1–18; *Epistolario de Enrique de Villena Epistolario de Enrique de Villena,* edited by Cátedra and Carr (London: Department of Hispanic Studies, Queen Mary, University of London, 2001), pp. 58–68.

**Collection:** *Obras Completas,* edited by Pedro M. Cátedra, 3 volumes (Madrid: Fundación José Antonio de Castro/Turner, 1994–2000).

TRANSLATIONS: *Traducción de la Divina comedia* (1427–1428)

**Manuscript:** Madrid, Biblioteca Nacional MS. 10186, fols. 1r–194v; Dante's Italian text with Spanish translation in the margin; glosses are probably by Iñigo López de Mendoza, Marqués de Santillana.

**Modern edition:** *La traducción de la 'Divina comedia' atribuida a D. Enrique de Aragón: Estudio y edición del Infierno,* edited by José A. Pascual (Salamanca: Universidad de Salamanca, 1974).

*Traducción y exposicion del soneto de Petrarca* (1427–1428)

**Manuscript:** Translation and commentary of the Petrarch sonnet "Non Po, Tesin, Varo, Arno, Adige, e Tebro," Madrid, Biblioteca Nacional MS 10186, fols. 196r–199r.

*Traducción y glosas a la Eneida* (1427–1428)

**Manuscripts:** Translation of books 1–6 of Virgil's *Aeneid* without glosses, Seville, Biblioteca Colombina 82-1-1; letter to Juan II of Navarre, proem, and translation of books 1–3 with glosses, Madrid, Biblioteca Nacional 17975; glosses only, Madrid, Biblioteca Nacional 10111; translation of books 4–12 without glosses, Paris, Bibliothèque Nationale Esp. 207; proem and translation of books 1–3 without glosses, Santander, Biblioteca Menéndez Pelayo M-102, fols. 1r–108va; eighteenth-century copy of Biblioteca Colombina 82-1-1, Madrid, Biblioteca Nacional MS. 1874.

**Modern editions:** *La primera versión castellana de La Eneida de Virgilio: Los libros I–III traducidos y comentados por Enrique de Villena (1384–1434),* translation without glosses, edited by Ramón Santiago Lacuesta, Anejos del Boletín de la Real Academia Española, no. 38 (Madrid: Real Academia Española, 1979); *Traducción y glosas a la Eneida,* books 1–3 of the translation with glosses, edited by Pedro M. Cátedra, 2 volumes (Salamanca: Diputación de Salamanca, 1989).

Enrique de Villena is recognized today as one of the leading intellectual figures of early-fifteenth-century Castile, in spite of a pervasive reputation as a necromancer in his own time that transformed him into a grotesque character in some comedies written during the Golden Age of Spanish literature. He was an intellectual pioneer in a period when Castilian intellectual life was moving away from French toward Italian models. Vernacular humanism, the translation and adaptation of classical works for the entertainment and instruction of nobles, played a significant role in this transformation by changing secular elite attitudes toward reading and the classics. Villena did not belong to the world of official academic culture but mediated between official learning and vernacular lay culture and promoted Italian humanist thought in Castile.

Villena's real name was Enrique de Aragón. Born between 1382 and 1384, he was the second son of Juana of Castile, illegitimate daughter of King Enrique II, and Pedro de Villena. Pedro's own father was Alfonso, Condestable (Constable) of Castile, Marqués of Villena, Duke of Gandía, Count of Denia and Ribagorza, who was a direct descendant of King Pedro *el Ceremonioso* (the Ceremonious) of Aragon and had an unbroken lineage tracing back to such ninth-century counts of Barcelona as Wifredo *el Velloso* (the Hairy). Enrique was thus connected to the most powerful members of the aristocracy in Castile and Aragon. His paternal grandfather, Alfonso, one of the most prominent figures of the period, was deeply indebted to the first king of the new Trastámaran dynasty in Castile, Enrique II, who had rewarded Alfonso with the *señorío* (seigniory) of Villena for his firm support against King Pedro I *el Cruel* (the Merciless) in the Castilian civil war. When his son Pedro died at the battle of Aljubarrota in 1385, Alfonso took charge of Enrique, heir to the marquessate of Villena. Alfonso's family, however, was rapidly losing influence at the Castilian court by the end of the fourteenth century. Alfonso lost the marquessate of Villena in 1398. In spite of continued efforts, his grandson Enrique, as a consequence of the Castilian Crown's political reshuffling, was unable to regain the title. Two key events instigated the political defeat of the dissident Trastámaran aristocrats and the Aragonese party to which Don Alfonso and Enrique belonged. The first was the regency of Catherine of Lancaster, descendant of Pedro I, who encouraged anti-Trastámaran sentiment, especially on the death of her husband, Enrique III. The second event was the transfer in 1412 of the crown of Aragon to the Infante Fernando de Antequera, Enrique III's brother. (Fernando had also served as coregent with Catherine following his brother's death.) Villena was to spend half of his life trying to win back his pretended rights to the marquessate, for although he is commonly known as Enrique de Villena, or the marquess of Villena, and signed documents under that name, the title did not legally belong to him.

Villena spent his early years at his paternal grandfather's seigneurial court in Valencia. There he met the leading literary and intellectual figures of the time, who were to leave a strong imprint on his later work. Members of the March family—the brothers Pere and Jacme and the famous poet Ausiàs March (circa 1397–1459), Pere's son—were in his grandfather's service. The Franciscan friar Francesc Eiximenis dedicated the *Dotzè del crestià* (Twelfth Book of the Christian, 1484), about the education of the ruling class, to Alfonso. The Dominican Antoni Canals, translator of the classics and one of the reformers of Cata-

lan prose at the end of the fourteenth century, likewise dedicated his *Scipió e Aníbal* (Scipio and Hannibal, circa 1399), a Catalan prose version of book 7 of Petrarch's *Africa,* to Alfonso. In 1387 Queen Violant de Bar invited don Enrique, still a young child, to spend some time at the royal court of Barcelona, where he came into contact with the Catalan literary world. Two extant letters dated 6 April 1396 from Gandía and addressed to the king of Castile and the royal council, respectively, relate don Enrique and his brother Alfonso's unsuccessful efforts to regain the rights to the marquessate of Villena. The letters were written by the chancellery clerks who worked for Enrique's grandfather; Enrique and his brother signed them.

In the first years of the fifteenth century, Villena probably traveled to Castile and married María de Albornoz, a wealthy heiress from Cuenca. He received the title of count of Cangas and Tineo from his cousin Enrique III but did not benefit from the rents for long. In 1404 Villena decided to abandon the court and travel the world, but that same year, the position of master of the Order of Calatrava, a powerful religious and military order, became vacant, and he applied for it. In this obscure episode he divorced his wife, claiming impotence, and renounced his title of count in order to become a friar of Calatrava. Finally, Enrique III forced the *comendadores* (commanders) of the order to elect Villena as their master. Contemporary chroniclers suggest that Enrique III favored his cousin's candidacy because he was having an amorous relation with Villena's wife, but, as Pedro M. Cátedra indicates in his introduction to volume one of the *Obras completas* (1994), the royal support was more likely a result of the monarch's interest in controlling the influential orders by positioning individuals connected to him by family ties in key offices. The election, however, divided the order, which voted a new master in Castile two years later, right after the king's death. In any case, Villena was an incompetent officer. His contemporary Fernán Pérez de Guzmán portrays him as a learned man, but without the political savvy his aristocratic position demanded. The fall from grace at the Castilian court of the Trastámaran faction with Aragonese ties did not help his claim, either.

When Infante Fernando was made king of Aragon in 1412, Villena followed his cousin and enjoyed some years of peace at the Aragonese court. At the coronation in Saragossa he marched by the king's side with other noblemen, carrying the reins of the monarch's horse; performed minor ambassadorial functions at court, and played an active role as carver-at-table and butler; and was rewarded with a small rent to cover his economic needs. In 1413 Fernando put Villena in charge of reinstating in Barcelona the Consistori de la Gaya Ciència (Consistory of Poetry), a solemn assembly of poets, and organizing its elaborate prize-giving ceremonies, in which the whole court and some religious orders participated.

In 1416 Villena found his nomination as master of Calatrava invalidated. After the death of King Fernando that same year, not being on good terms with Fernando's successor, Alfonso V, Villena returned to Castile and withdrew to his wife's estates in Cuenca to take care of family affairs. Carr and Cátedra's archival research in *Epistolario de Enrique de Villena* (2001) has brought to light several documents showing that the town of Cuenca greatly appreciated Villena's legal expertise and diplomatic skills. His divorce had been annulled by the Pope, and, as for his impotence, it was either feigned or was really a reflection of his wife's inability to bear children, since Villena later had two daughters out of wedlock, the second of whom, Leonor, born in 1430, took the veil under the name of Sor Isabel de Villena and wrote a *Vita Christi* (Life of Christ), published posthumously in 1497.

In 1417, when Villena was about to depart from the Aragonese court, he wrote in Catalan the *Los dotze treballs de Hèrcules* (Twelve Labors of Hercules) at the request of Mosén Pero Pardo. Months later, at the request of Juan Fernández de Valera, a clerk at the Castilian court who was in his service in Cuenca, Villena translated the work into Castilian, with minor additions, as *Los doce trabajos de Hércules*. The Castilian version differs slightly from the Catalan original in its use of overtly Latinizing terminology. It also includes more information on the acquisition of knowledge, because Villena was adapting his work to a readership interested in philosophy and theology. In tune with his public's curiosity, Villena also makes reference to a work he was planning to write, to be titled "El libro de los fuegos inextinguíbiles" (The Book of Inextinguishable Fires), about Greek fire and its military applications. The *Los doce trabajos de Hércules* represents a first step in the massive *translatio studii,* or assimilation of Latin culture and its intellectual habits and tools into the vernacular lay world, that Villena was to attempt in his translation of and commentary on Virgil's *Aeneid.*

In *Los doce trabajos de Hércules* Villena interprets the adventures of the mythological Greek hero using the methods of medieval biblical exegesis; that is, he interprets them literally, allegorically, and morally. Hercules is the allegorical representation of the wise man, and his actions are related to the acquisition of knowledge. The moral interpretation offers a practical guide for life, and although Villena does not expressly mention the fourth biblical sense—anagogy, or spiritual sense—the work as a whole creates the impression that he considered reading a process through which man sharpens his intellect and lifts it to a higher purpose. The act of reading, along with the scientific study it demands, is presented

as a key component in the nobleman's education. In Villena's ideology noblemen are the arms of the mystic social body, in charge of carrying out divine laws. The book is conceived as a mirror, or speculum. The reading of Hercules' labors is meant to instruct prospective rulers of the state by example. It presents them with a gallery of behavioral patterns: the weak woman, the humble hermit, the magnanimous patrician, and so forth. Like the work of Villena's Italian predecessors—particularly Coluccio Salutati (1331–1406), whose *De seculo et religione* (On Secular and Religious Life) he had read—*Los doce trabajos de Hércules* displays the social and political interests of early humanism.

Around this same time, Villena might have written his *Arte de trovar* (Art of Composing Poetry), also known as *Libro de la sciençia gaya* (Book on the Science of Poetry), although it is impossible to date the work with any accuracy because it has survived only in a few fragments reconstructed from humanist Alvar Gómez de Castro's notes. Emilio Cotarelo y Mori advocates an early date, between 1412 and 1417, but Sánchez Cantón and Cátedra (in his introduction to volume one of the *Obras completas*) date it from the years that Villena was translating the *Aeneid,* 1427 to 1428. *Arte de trovar* is dedicated to the Castilian grandee Íñigo López de Mendoza, Marqués de Santillana, a prime example of the emerging type of learned noblemen who successfully combined the exercise of "arms and letters." Santillana was a famous warrior, talented poet, and patron of the arts who possessed a magnificent library of Florentine manuscripts. The term *gaya sciençia* in the title refers to the art of composing verse and emphasizes that poetry is a branch of knowledge in its own right because it possesses a set of rules. Accordingly, *Arte de trovar* begins with the assertion that lucid and obtuse minds no longer differ when composing poetry, because even fine poets ignore the *sciençia,* the set of rules. Villena dedicated his treatise to Santillana, already a famous troubadour, whose imperfect knowledge of the rules of poetic science prevented him from communicating his God-given talents. As Julian Weiss has noted, Villena believed in an intellectual hierarchy imposed by God that is revealed in one's ability to cope with the rules of poetry. A wise man's most important test is his ability to communicate properly; hence, the importance Villena assigns to accurate knowledge of the rules.

In another fragment of *Arte de trovar* Villena presents a short history of the Provençal-Catalan consistories of Toulouse and Barcelona up to Villena's time and describes in great detail the solemn ceremonies he helped to organize. This section is historically inaccurate, presenting instead, in Weiss's words, "an idealized picture of the nature and development of vernacular poetics," because Villena is not interested in historical

ya concordia paresçe la significaçion
enla manera que se sygue.
¶ Hystoria nueua. ¶ Es en greçia
vna grande selua τ espesura de arbo
les antigua τ espantable τ esquiua
τ no abitada τ aspera de peñas τ a
sopada de cueuas sombrosas τ escu
ras dicha montña. acompañada de fie
ras τ saluajes bestias. entre las quales
auia vn leon muy grande τ brauo gas
t idor delos pobladores τ delos de alli
vezinos por miedo del qual los vian
dantes desmáparauá los caminos q
pasauan açerca de aquel lugar τ los
labradores cõ los bueyes no osauá re
boluer la tierra dura ni écomédar las
simientes al labrado campo. Los pa
stores dexauan los ganados sin osar
los boluer quándo se llegauan a aqlu
gar. τ los moradores enlas caserias

τ aldeas dexauan su labrança ençer
rátose enel fuerte muro delos mayo
res lugares recogiendose enlas forta
lezas τ casas altas tanto era el temor
q del dicho leon auiá τ no menos da
ño auido τ conçebido auian. Oyendo
esto el virtuoso hercules τ cauallero
valiente corrio τ ayudo al hermami
ento τ daño que resçebiã los de aqlla
tierra. no auiendo miedo maguera o
pera dezir de otros muchos caualle
ros que antes del auian dubdado ma
tar el dicho leon τ avn algunos quelo
prouaró fenesçieron ay sus dias entre
los dientes del leon. τ la suya syn de.
fesion perdieron arrebatada méte vi
da. Hercules con vtud sobrada ándo
do ala selua ya dicha buscãdo el espá
table leon conbidádolo que veniese a
el por bozes τ amenazas fasta q llego

*Pages from the 1483 edition of Enrique de Villena's* Los doze trabajos de Hércules
*in the Biblioteca Nacional, Madrid (from* Los doze trabajos de Hércules,
*edited by Margherita Morreale, 1958; Thomas Cooper Library,*
*University of South Carolina)*

Ca ēbarga el sossiego dla cīuil vida. no tema por tales escādalos amar z vel echar dela su comunidad contradizīendo alos mas fuertes parando mīetes a hercules quādo no dubdo al rey orto contradezir·sacando de su poder a proserpina. ni temio al can çeruero. z saluaje. Ca no menos vesto el buen çibdadano deue procurar z quitarse afuera echando toda espeçie de gula crapula z golosina dela su çibdad. Ca esto es abismo de muchos viçios graue mente nozibles ala çibdad o allega miento. E puede bien este mismo cō uenir exēplo al de mercader estado ḡ deue desordenada cobdiçia z soberja nia z rapina z avn goloso benir arre drar desi biuiendo leal mente z llana enla mercadozia·si quier que del su estado sien. z asi dlos otros en su ma

xij

nera. segūo no dubdo la sabieza vfa aplicar deduzir z multiplicar sabza por lo que menos bien es en aqueste sumado capitulo.

❡Capitulo. vj. como fue la crueldad de diomedes castigada z penada eñl mesmo.
     ❡Estado de mercader.
       L sexto trabajo de her cules fue quando por la crueldad de diomedes rey de traçia refreno a quella · si quier le puso fin. dādo carne humana alos sus ca uallos por viāda  ❡Hystoria nuda ❡La fictiō por los poetas desto fue asy ordenada. Diomedes tornādo dl cerco de tropa·como en su reyno no fuese resçebido fue a traçia. z seyēdo

precision but in outlining the image of a royal patron who can help in transferring knowledge. Villena insists on the educational role of poetry in creating an intellectual elite. As he also suggests in the *Los doce trajos de Hércules,* the models for this elite are Julius Caesar and Augustus, whose generous minds were able to bestow invaluable services on the Roman Republic. The social function that Villena assigns to poetry may betray the influence of Italian civic humanism, a hypothesis advanced by Ottavio Di Camillo, but Weiss shows that this aspect of Italian humanism conforms closely to the precepts of Provençal-Catalan poetry. Finally, there is a highly incomplete set of considerations dealing with orthography, punctuation, grammar, and etymology.

*Los doce trabajos de Hércules* and *Arte de trovar,* like most of Villena's works, reveal the author's aspiration to exert some influence at the Castilian court of Juan II. Villena's life in Castile between 1420 and 1425 is not documented but can be inferred from his writings. During these years he wrote *Arte cisoria* (Art of Carving at Table, 1423) and a series of treatises in the epistolary genre. They are addressed to the members of the court and their assistants, revealing a new taste and interest on the part of his Castilian readership. Three of them, the *Tratado de la lepra* (Treatise on Leprosy, circa 1421–1422), the *Exposición del salmo Quoniam videbo* (Commentary on the Psalm "Quoniam videbo," 1424), and the *Tratado de fascinación o de aojamiento* (Treatise on the Evil Eye, circa 1422–1425), expound biblical fragments.

Villena wrote *Arte cisoria* in September 1423 at the request of Sancho de Jarava, who was the official *cortador,* or carver-at-table for the king. It is both a book on the etiquette of princes at table and the oldest gastronomic inventory in Spain. For instance, Villena suggests the use of silver or gold instead of iron or steel utensils to cut fish and describes a meticulous system for the preparation of cooked partridges. He also provides illustrations for the various instruments used in this art. The treatise affords an indirect look at Castilian manners; for example, Villena advises readers to refrain from gnawing at the bones of birds served in the royal chamber and observes that if a piece of meat is so large that it requires vigorous biting, it is preferable to cut it with a knife. Villena considers carving a science that complements medicine, and his treatise spells out its rules.

The *Tratado de la lepra* is addressed to Alfonso Chirino, Juan II's doctor, who converted from Judaism to Christianity. It answers a question Villena himself posed regarding the reliability of the text of Leviticus on leprosy outside the human body. Chirino deemed impossible a literal reading and propounded a spiritual interpretation. Villena, in contrast, tries to justify "the letter of the law" with rationalistic methods, supporting his analysis with medical and Talmudic authorities.

*Exposición del salmo Quoniam videbo,* an analysis of the fourth line of Psalm 8, was written for Juan Fernández de Valera, who requested an explanation for why the psalm mentions the moon and the stars but not the sun. In his introduction to *Algunas obras perdidas de Enrique de Villena con consideraciones sobre su obra y su biblioteca* (1985), Cátedra dates the treatise to 1423–1424, when Juan II's favorite, Alvaro de Luna, eclipsed royal power at the Castilian court, supporting an allegorical interpretation for Fernández de Valera's question. Villena begins his exposition with a conventional prologue of the kind used in schools to introduce the study of auctorial works. He mentions the author, the efficient cause, and the final cause; that is, he follows the structure of a fourteenth-century biblical *accessus ad auctores* (prologue or introduction to a work). Then, he analyzes the literal meaning of the psalm word by word, following the scholarly procedure for answering a *quaestio* (question raised during the scholarly reading of a text). In the exposition he endeavors to unveil the secrets hidden in the words of the prophet, which, for Villena, are always of a scientific nature; to understand them, he resorts to all the branches of knowledge available to him, even the Cabala. His knowledge of the Cabala is not, as it might seem, a confirmation of his reputation as a necromancer; on the contrary, Villena was adopting a method widely used by theologians. For instance, a biblical scholar as respected as Nicholas de Lyra (circa 1270–1349) proposes in the prologue to his *Postillae perpetuae in vetus et novus Testamentum* (Glosses on the Old and New Testament) to make use of Hebrew scholarship to clarify the literal meaning of the Scriptures in hopes of converting Jews to the Catholic faith. Villena, on the other hand, was motivated by a deep interest in science, which he shared with those contemporaries for whom he wrote his learned works.

*Tratado de fascinación o de aojamiento* is also addressed to Fernández de Valera. The reading of a remark regarding "either corporal or intellectual vision" in the *Exposición del salmo Quoniam videbo* had suggested to Fernández de Valera an analogous question on the evil eye. Villena's reply, written from his retreat at Torralva, begins with a description of the evil-eye phenomenon and an explanation of the origin and meaning of the expression. He names the three steps in the therapy for it—prevention, identification, and cure—and, for each step, lists three methods used in the past and in the present. For each of them Villena marshals Arabic, Persian, and Jewish authorities, along with the more orthodox names of Aristotle and Albertus Magnus. *Tratado de fascinación o de aojamiento* was extraordinarily popular in the fifteenth century, to the extent that Cátedra has advanced the hypothesis in his introduction to volume one of the *Obras completas* that Alfonso Fernández de

Madrigal's long excursus on the evil eye in *Las çinco figuratas paradoxas* (The Five Figured Paradoxes, 1437) is likely a rebuttal of Villena's position.

In these three treatises Villena combines non-canonical, scientific sources and literal exposition traditionally linked to scientific research. In his introduction to volume one of the *Obras completas* Cátedra stresses the heterodox, unstructured nature of Villena's knowledge, which represents a link with the intellectual enterprise of Alfonso X the Learned and the *translatio studii* of the thirteenth century.

During these same years Villena wrote the *Tratado de consolación* (Treatise on Consolation, 1424) for Fernández de Valera, who, in a letter to Villena dated December 1422, communicated the loss of his entire family to the Black Death that was ravaging Cuenca. Ailing in solitude, Fernández de Valera requests "true consolation" from his friend's "elaborated words laden with profound scientific treasures." Hesitating at first between a short formal letter and a longer exposition, Villena decided to compose a wide-ranging treatise in which he turned to the consolatory classics from antiquity and the Middle Ages. In *Letters and Society in Fifteenth-Century Spain* (1993), Cátedra considers the *Tratado de la consolación* one of the first Stoic expressions in a Romance tongue, in which Villena initiates a novel reading of Seneca the Younger and Petrarch.

Between 1425 and 1429 Alfonso V *el Magnánimo* of Aragon, in a move that contradicts his epithet, disqualified Villena as heir to the duchy of Gandía in favor of his own brother, Juan II of Navarre, on the pretext that he had supported Juan II of Castile in some recent border hostilities. Faced with a possible separation from his wealthy wife, Villena was forced to turn to his nephew Juan II of Castile for economic support. The king bestowed on him the seigneury of Iniesta, where Villena resided until his death in 1434.

From 1427 on, Villena devoted his efforts to translating the classics: the pseudo-Ciceronian *Rhetorica ad Herennium*, Titus Livius's fragments, the *Aeneid*, Dante's *Commedia*, and Petrarch. Only a few of these translations have survived: the twelve books of the *Aeneid*, Dante's *Commedia*, and a Petrarchan sonnet. The translations of the *Commedia* and Petrarch's sonnet appear in the same manuscript and were credited to Villena after studies by Ramón Santiago Lacuesta, Derek C. Carr, and Weiss.

The translation of the *Aeneid* represents the culmination of Villena's endeavors. Juan II of Navarre, commissioned it; he was one of the infantes of Aragon and often referred to as Villena's nephew, although both Juan II of Navarre and Juan II of Castile are children of Villena's cousins (Enrique III and Faernando de Antequera), not of Villena's siblings. It is the first complete translation of Virgil's epic into a Romance tongue, as Villena proudly declares in the introduction, and it took him from 28 September 1427 to 10 November 1428 to complete the first version. Later, perhaps at the request of Santillana, for whom he translated the *Commedia*, Villena corrected the first version and added an enormous commentary that stops at the end of the third book.

The *Commedia* and the *Aeneid* are closely associated. The interest of Juan II of Navarre in Virgil's poem surfaced while he was reading Dante's work. The character of Virgil in the *Commedia* is a synthesis of medieval ideas about the Roman poet: he is a divinely inspired author who possesses unlimited knowledge. Moreover, he was Christ's contemporary and involuntary prophet. The *Aeneid* was viewed as a book full of wisdom, resembling the Psalms in both beauty and depth, that told about man's search for perfection in terms similar to those of the *Commedia* and could thus be subject to allegorical interpretation. A commentary was necessary since the vernacular reader needed help in understanding what Villena calls the "ocean of knowledge" veiled under Virgil's poetry. For this purpose Villena resorted to the methods and tools of the schools. He begins his translation and commentary with a letter to Juan II of Navarre, followed by a proem, and what he calls "advice for the beginning reader." He divides the *Aeneid* into chapters (366 in total, to help the "lazy reader") and adds titles, glosses, and summaries at the beginning of each book and each chapter.

In the letter Villena obliquely mentions his economic and administrative difficulties with his Aragonese royal relatives. He offers the translation to Juan II of Navarre in exchange for his efforts to defend Villena's interests. In 1429, however, losing all hope of regaining the duchy of Gandía, Villena decided not to send the translation to the king of Navarre and chose instead "to present it to some gentlemen who wanted to see it," adding the commentary at this time.

In the proem Villena justifies the need for such a long introduction with the *auctoritas*, or intrinsic worth of the poem, and the obscurity of its meaning. Since vernacular readers did not understand Latin, they were also not acquainted with the tools to which any Latinate scholar could resort while reading Virgil. These tools are found in the commentaries, glosses, or expositions that generally accompany Virgil's text. Villena summarizes the necessary information for his lay readers. The proem follows the well-known pattern of an *accessus ad auctores* of the type that medieval scholars generally associated with Servius, the fourth-century Latin grammarian. It includes all the information related to the standard headings: the title of the work; the author's name; a life of the author, taken from Aelius Donatus's biography of Virgil (and Servius's commentary upon that work), in which Villena lists some of Virgil's apocryphal poems, which he claims to have introduced for the first time in Castile, such as "De culiçe" (On the Gnat) and "De rosa" (On the Rose); the author's intention and didactic method, or *modus agendi;* the area of philosophy to which the work belongs; and the *utilitas,* or utility, of the work–that is, considerations of its ultimate usefulness.

This *accessus* presents the Roman emperor Augustus as the ideal prince and Virgil as the quintessential poet. Virgil's style in the *Aeneid,* comments Villena, is the poetic mode that speaks *per integumentum;* that is, it speaks obscurely, under a veil, to hide the many secrets of the poem from the ignorant and to entice the wise to penetrate its depths. The usefulness of the work lies in its moral aims: it reprehends vice and recommends virtue; therefore, it belongs to the branch of philosophy known as ethics, to which all nonbiblical works were conventionally assigned during the Middle Ages. The *Aeneid* is presented, then, as a mirror, the moral value of which can "illuminate chivalrous knowledge and maintain political life."

The depth of Virgil's epic, however, is such that its hidden knowledge is not constrained to the field of ethics. Villena says in a gloss that the *Aeneid* offers "benefits and usefulness both general and specific." The list of the possible benefits that may be drawn from reading the *Aeneid* outlines the exegetical method that Villena follows in his commentary. The specific benefits correspond to the analysis of the letter, or literal sense, which is clearly of a practical nature. Aeneas's stories and speeches are models of noble behavior and the rhetorical ideal. Villena comments on the literal meaning of these stories to teach the courtier how to perform in almost every situation in order to improve Castilian society. The general benefits, on the other hand, are of an esoteric nature, both scientific and moral. The inner core of the allegory conceals scientific learning and moral teaching, designated respectively as "the secret" and "the morality." The secret physical knowledge in the *Aeneid* includes information about astronomy and astrology. The moral meaning explains events, reworking Servius's interpretation of the ages of man into man's fall from grace and his recovery after a *psychomachia* (battle between vices and virtues), in order to teach laymen how to master their passions and save themselves. Villena regards scientific and moral knowledge as inseparably bound; they correspond to the macrocosm and the microcosm, and by knowing the way they operate, wise men may control their destiny.

Reading is a meditation on the word that leads to a state of inner reflection. The literal sense is the base on which the walls of the spiritual sense are built. Accordingly, Villena's commentary is copious at the beginning in glosses that instruct his readers on how to interpret some terms and recognize figures of speech.

He even provides a system of punctuation to teach the reader to breathe, and by dividing his text into chapters, he gives his reader time to meditate on the meaning of the text. The punctuation system, unfortunately, was never used in any of the manuscripts, although Villena describes it at length in the "advice for the beginning reader." He considers reading a major element in the education of the aristocratic elite: only the learned are in full control of their passions and, therefore, conveniently prepared to govern the republic. The *Aeneid* becomes a point of departure for intellectual speculation, and the act of reading has serious intellectual and ethical implications supporting Villena's ideal of knighthood based on arms and letters. The ideal nobleman stands above the ignorant masses about whom Villena complains in his *Arte de trovar.*

The translation and commentary on the *Aeneid* appear as a typical product of vernacular humanism. Villena approaches the poem with the help of medieval interpretive tools and translates it into the vernacular culture of his aristocratic patrons and friends, reworking the content and appropriating it for his political purposes. In *El espejo y el piélago: La Eneida castellana de Enrique de Villena* (The Mirror and the Sea: The Castilian *Aeneid* of Enrique de Villena, 1998) as well as *Translation, Authority and Authorship in the Works of Enrique de Villena and Juan de Mena* (1996), Sol Miguel-Prendes argues that Villena's translation and commentary do not simply translate a textual authority by copying its Latin style: they reconfigure the *Aeneid* through paraphrase and allegorical interpretation, achieving a difference from it and from previous commentaries. Villena creates a vernacular *Aeneid* that claims for itself and its author a canonical status; author and work become a vernacular *auctoritas*– a new Virgil–in a process carried later to its full extent by one of the most prominent figures of fifteenth-century Castile, the courtly poet and royal secretary of Latin letters Juan de Mena.

Villena's last work is the *Epístola a Suero de Quiñones* (Epistle to Suero de Quiñones), recovered in 1895 by Cotarelo y Mori, who dates it to 15 March 1434, although Cátedra and Carr propose in *Epistolario de Enrique de Villena* (2001) an indeterminate date between 1427 and 1434. Suero de Quiñones was the celebrated knight-errant who in 1433 defended the bridge over the Orbigo River on the Camino de Santiago for thirty days against any knight who would not acknowledge the preeminent beauty of his lady. Sancho de Jarava informs don Enrique. The knight, always afflicted by amorous passion, requests advice for his lovesickness from Villena. Anticipating Quiñones's letter, Villena writes a reply. In his letter Villena cites examples of other unfortunate lovers and gives a detailed analysis of astrological influences on the illness.

He rejects traditional herbal remedies or more-unusual therapies involving, for instance, the heart of a vulture and proposes instead, citing Seneca, learning to endure what is unavoidable with the help of scientific study.

Villena suffered from gout; as Pérez de Guzmán recounts, this illness, complicated by a severe fever, finally killed him in Madrid on 15 December 1434. Villena's nephew Juan II of Castile arranged for his burial with great ceremony at the convent of San Francisco, but soon after, the king appropriated Villena's library and assigned the evaluation of the volumes to Friar Lope de Barrientos. Some of them were deemed dangerous and were burned; others ended up in Santillana's hands, and most went to the king's library. Elena Gascón Vera has studied the burning of Villena's books and attributes it to an anti-Semitic political ploy. Perhaps one of the volumes was the *Tratado de astrología* (Treatise on Astrology), wrongly attributed to Villena, which Cátedra includes in his edition of Villena's complete works, *Obras Completas* (1994–2000), as an example of the type of books that Villena's library might have contained.

Contemporary poets deplored Villena's death. Santillana considered him "the only pillar in the temple of the Muses," and Mena referred to him as "illustrious sage" and an "honor for Spain and for his century." Villena's fame in the following centuries was based on a few tales that elaborated on his reputation as a necromancer, some of them by Francisco de Quevedo (1580–1645), the last scholar to read a complete version of the *Arte de trovar*. The humanist Antonio de Nebrija criticized Villena's highly Latinized syntax, with its unnatural placement of words. Father Juan de Mariana (1536–1624) was also dismayed at Villena's style, which he described as a pretentious and horrific mixture of Latin and Spanish. The tales about his magic powers, which persisted in some twentieth-century studies, were already regarded as "the same old-women stories repeated by slackers" in *Bibliotheca hispana vetus* (Old Spanish Library, 1788), by Nicolás Antonio, the first scholar to give an objective account of Villena's significance.

Villena's modern reception began with Cotarelo y Mori, who sketched his biography in an attempt to reconstruct his library. Carr and Cátedra have solved most of the questions related to Villena's biography, published his complete works, and illuminated the sources of his stylistic choices. The novel use of classical and humanist authors and the artificiality of his expression are characteristic of the Catalan *dictatores,* chancellery clerks who wrote according to the rules of the *artes dictandi,* medieval manuals on how to write letters. Weiss has elucidated Villena's poetics and his notions of eloquence as a civic virtue. Controversy surrounds his connection with Italian humanism, particu-larly his translations. Peter E. Russell considers his work entirely medieval. In "Enrique de Villena y algunos humanistas" (1983) Cátedra concurs but identi-fies in it some humanistic traits. Finally, Jeremy N. H. Lawrance and Weiss embrace a wider definition of humanism and consider Villena a "vernacular human-ist." Others debate the discrepancy between Villena's fame as a poet and his lack of poetic production. John K. Walsh and Alan Deyermond believe Villena's poetic reputation is a myth, while Miguel-Prendes suggests in *El espejo y el piélago* that the term *poet* should be under-stood to have meant an interpreter of the classics, skilled in rhetoric, in Villena's literary circles.

Enrique de Villena's literary production is medi-eval in its aims and purposes; yet, his efforts prepared the way for philological humanism by enabling private readers to understand and enjoy the classics. His writ-ings had a practical purpose: to prepare noblemen to perform their role in society, a social and political inter-est that Villena shared with early Italian humanism and the Provençal-Catalan schools of poetry. Villena and his work are poised on the threshold between the Mid-dle Ages and the Renaissance, mediating between the clerical and the secular world toward which Castilian culture inevitably began to drift.

## References:

Nicolás Antonio, *Bibliotheca hispana vetus* (1696), 2 vol-umes (Madrid: Printed by the widow and heirs of D. Joaquín Ibarra, 1788; reprinted, Madrid: Visor, 1996);

Russell V. Brown, "Ceremony and Stylistic Awareness in Enrique de Villena's 'Arte Cisoria'," *Revista de Estudios Hispánicos,* 15.1 (1981): 75–83;

Derek C. Carr, "La 'Epístola que enbio Don Enrique de Villena a Suero de Quiñones' y la fecha de la *Crónica sarracina* de Pedro de Corral," *University of British Columbia Hispanic Studies,* edited by Harold Livermore (London: Tamesis, 1974), pp. 1–18;

Carr, "A Fifteenth-Century Castilian Translation and Commentary of a Petrarchan Sonnet: Biblioteca Nacional Ms. 10186 ff 196r–199r," *Revista Cana-diense de Estudios Hispánicos,* 5 (1981): 123–143;

Carr, "Pérez de Guzmán and Villena: A Polemic on Historiography?" in *Hispanic Studies in Honor of Alan D. Deyermond: A North American Tribute,* edited by John S. Miletich (Madison, Wis.: Hispanic Seminary of Medieval Studies, 1986), pp. 57–70;

Carr and Pedro M. Cátedra, "Datos para la biografía de Enrique de Villena," *La corónica,* 11 (1983): 293–299;

Pedro M. Cátedra, "Algunas obras perdidas de Enrique de Villena con consideraciones sobre su obra y su biblioteca," *Crotalón: Anuario de Filología Española,* 2 (1985): 53–75;

Cátedra, "Un aspecto de la difusión del escrito en la Edad Media: La autotraducción al romance," *Atalaya,* 2 (1992): 67–84;

Cátedra, "Los *Doce trabajos de Hércules* en el *Tirant* (Lecturas de la obra de Villena en Castilla y Aragón)," in *Actes del Symposion Tirant lo Blanc* (Barcelona: Quaderns Cremà, 1993), pp. 171–205;

Cátedra, "Enrique de Villena y algunos humanistas," in *Nebrija y la introducción del Renacimiento en España,* edited by Víctor García de la Concha (Salamanca: Universidad de Salamanca, 1983), pp. 187–203;

Cátedra, "Escolios teatrales de Enrique de Villena," in *Serta Philologica F. Lázaro Carreter: Natalem diem sexagesimum celebranti dicata,* edited by Emilio Alarcos and others (Madrid: Cátedra, 1983), pp. 127–136;

Cátedra, "Prospección sobre el género consolatorio en el siglo XV," in *Letters and Society in Fifteenth-Century Spain: Studies Presented to P. E. Russell on his Eightieth Birthday,* edited by Alan Deyermond and Jeremy N. H. Lawrance (London: Dolphin, 1993), pp. 1–16;

Cátedra, "Sobre la biblioteca del Marqués de Santillana: La *Iliada* y Pier Candido Decembrio," *Hispanic Review,* 51 (1983): 23–28;

Cátedra, "Sobre la obra catalana de Enrique de Villena," in *Homenaje a Eugenio Asensio,* edited by Luisa López Grigera and Augustin Redondo (Madrid: Gredos, 1988), pp. 127–140;

Cátedra and Derek C. Carr, *Epistolario de Enrique de Villena* (London: Department of Hispanic Studies, Queen Mary, University of London, 2001);

Marcella Ciceri, "Enrique de Villena traduttore dell'*Eneide* e della *Commedia,*" *Rassegna Iberistica,* 15 (1982): 3–24;

Ciceri, "Per Villena," *Quaderni di Lingue e Letterature,* 3–4 (1978–1979): 295–335;

Emilio Cotarelo y Mori, *Don Enrique de Villena: Su vida y obras* (Madrid: Sucesores de Rivadeneyra, 1896);

Carla De Nigris, "La classificazione delle arti magiche di Enrique de Villena," *Quaderni ispano-americani,* (1981): 289–298;

De Nigris, "Puntuación y pausas en Enrique de Villena," *Medioevo Romanzo,* 9 (1984): 421–442;

Ottavio Di Camillo, *El humanismo castellano del siglo XV* (Valencia: F. Torres, 1976);

Elena Gascón Vera, "La ceremonia como ciencia: 'El arte cisoria' de Enrique de Villena," *Actas del VIII Congreso de la Asociación Internacional de Hispanistas* (Madrid: Istmo, 1986), pp. 587–595;

Gascón Vera, "La quema de libros de don Enrique de Villena: Una maniobra política y antisemítica," *Bulletin of Hispanic Studies,* 56 (1979): 317–324;

Angel Gómez Moreno, *España y la Italia de los humanistas: Primeros ecos* (Madrid: Gredos, 1994);

R. G. Keightley, "Boethius, Villena and Juan de Mena," *Bulletin of Hispanic Studies,* 55 (1978): 189–202;

Keightley, "Enrique de Villena's *Los doce trabajos de Hércules:* A Reappraisal," *Journal of Hispanic Philology,* 3 (1978–1979): 49–68;

Jeremy N. H. Lawrance, "Humanism in the Iberian Peninsula," in *The Impact of Humanism in Western Europe,* edited by Anthony Goodman and Angus MacKay (London & New York: Longman, 1990), pp. 220–258;

Lawrance, "On Fifteenth-Century Spanish Vernacular Humanism," in *Medieval and Renaissance Studies in Honour of Robert Brian Tate,* edited by Ian Michael and Richard A. Cardwell (Oxford: Dolphin, 1986): 63–79;

Lawrance, "The Spread of Lay Literacy in Late Medieval Castile," *Bulletin of Hispanic Studies,* 62 (1985): 79–94;

Sol Miguel-Prendes, *El espejo y el piélago: La Eneida castellana de Enrique de Villena* (Kassel: Reichenberger, 1998);

Miguel-Prendes, "Translation, Authority, and Authorship in the Works of Enrique de Villena and Juan de Mena: The Vernacular Author in Fifteenth-Century Castile," *Allegorica,* 17 (1996): 17–31;

Margherita Morreale, "Coluccio Salutati's *De laboribus Herculis* (1406) and Enrique de Villena's *Los doze trabajos de Hércules* (1417)," *Studies in Philology,* 51 (1954): 95–106;

Fernán Pérez de Guzmán, *Generaciones y semblanzas,* edited by R. B. Tate (London: Tamesis, 1965);

Nicholas G. Round, "Five Magicians, or the Uses of Literacy," *Modern Language Review,* 64 (1969): 793–805;

Peter E. Russell, *Traducciones y traductores en la Península Ibérica, 1400–1550* (Bellaterra: Universidad Autónoma de Barcelona, 1985);

Antonio Torres-Alcalá, *Don Enrique de Villena: Un mago en el dintel del Renacimiento* (Madrid: J. Porrúa Turanzas, 1983);

John K. Walsh and Deyermond, "Enrique de Villena como poeta y dramaturgo: Bosquejo de una polémica frustrada," *Nueva Revista de Filología Hispánica,* 28 (1979): 57–85;

Julian Weiss, *The Poet's Art: Literary Theory in Castile c. 1400–60* (Oxford: Society for the Study of Medieval Languages and Literature, 1990).

# Appendix:
# Literary Genres in
# Fifteenth-Century Spain

# Aljamiado Literature

Vincent Barletta
*University of Colorado, Boulder*

WORKS: *Poema de Yuçuf* (ca. fourteenth–fifteenth centuries)
**Manuscripts:** Madrid, Biblioteca Nacional, MS. Res. 247; Madrid, Real Academia de la Historia, MS. 11/9409.
**Editions:** *El Poema de José, nach der Handschrift der Madrider Nationalbibliothek,* edited by Heinrich Morf (Leipzig: Drugulin, 1883); *Poema de Yuçuf: Materiales para su estudio,* edited by Ramón Menéndez Pidal (Madrid: Revista de Archivos, Bibliotecas y Museos, 1902; republished, Granada: Universidad de Granada, 1952); *The Poema de José: A Transcription and Comparison of the Extant Manuscripts,* edited by William Weisiger Johnson (University, Miss.: Romance Monographs, 1974).

Yçe de Gebir (Yça of Segovia, Yça Gidelli) (fl. 1450), *Breviario sunni*
**Manuscripts:** Madrid, Biblioteca Nacional, MS. 2076; Biblioteca Nacional, MS. 6016; Biblioteca Nacional, MS. 5301; Madrid, Real Academia de la Historia, MS. 11/9396; Madrid, Escuela de Estudios Árabes (Consejo Superior de Investigaciones Científicas), MS. 1; Escuela de Estudios Árabes, MS. 60.
**Editions:** *Tratados de legislación musulmana: 1. Leyes de moros, del siglo XIV; 2. Suma de los principales mandamientos y devedamientos de la ley y çunna, por don Içe de Gebir, alfaqui mayor y mufti de la aljama de Segovia, año de 1462,* edited by Pascual de Gayangos (Madrid: Real Academia de la Historia, 1853); *Islamic Literature in Spanish and Aljamiado: Yça of Segovia (fl. 1450), His Antecedents and Successors,* by Gerard Wiegers (Leiden & New York: Brill, 1994).

*Historia de los amores de París y Viana* (ca. fifteenth century)
**Manuscript:** Madrid, Real Academia de la Historia, MS. 11/9416.
**Edition:** *Historia de los amores de París y Viana: Edición, estudio y materiales,* edited by Alvaro Galmés de Fuentes (Madrid: Gredos, 1970).

Mancebo de Arévalo (circa 1498–1550), *Breve compendio de la santa ley i sunna*
**Manuscript:** Cambridge, University Library, Dd 9.49.
**Edition:** "Un manuscrito aljamiado en la Biblioteca de la Universidad de Cambridge," by L. P. Harvey, *Al-Andalus,* 22 (1958): 49–74.

Mancebo de Arévalo, *Tafçira*
**Manuscript:** Madrid, Escuela de Estudios Árabes (Consejo Superior de Investigaciones Científicas), MS. 62.
**Edition:** "La *Tafsira* del Mancebo de Arévalo: transcripción y estudio," edited by María T. Narváez, Ph.D. thesis, Universidad de Puerto Rico, Río Piedras, 1988.

Mancebo de Arévalo, *Sumario de la relación y ejercicio espiritual*
**Manuscript:** Madrid, Biblioteca Nacional, MS. Res. 245.
**Edition:** "Sumario de la relación y ejercicio espiritual sacado y declarado por el mancebo de Arévalo en nuestra lengua castellana," edited by Gregorio Fonseca Antuña, Ph.D. thesis, Universidad de Oviedo, 1988.

*Libro de dichos maravillosos* (ca. sixteenth century)
**Manuscript:** Madrid, Escuela de Estudios Árabes (Consejo Superior de Investigaciones Científicas), MS. 22.
**Edition:** *Libro de dichos maravillosos: Misceláneo morisco de magia y adivinación,* edited by Ana Labarta (Madrid: Consejo Superior de Investigaciones Científicas, 1993).

*Libro de las batallas* (ca. sixteenth century)
**Manuscript:** Madrid, Biblioteca Nacional, MS. 5337.
**Edition:** *El Libro de las batallas: Narraciones épico-caballerescas,* edited by Alvaro Galmés de Fuentes (Madrid: Gredos, 1975).

*Libro de las luces* (ca. sixteenth century)
**Manuscripts:** Madrid, Biblioteca Nacional, MS. 4955; Madrid, Real Academia de la Historia, MS. 11/9413; Real Academia de la Historia, MS. 11/9414; Madrid, Biblioteca del Palacio Real, MS. 3225.

**Editions:** "Noticias y extractos de algunos manuscritos árabes y aljamiados de Toledo y Madrid," edited by Angel González Palencia, in *Miscelánea de estudios y textos árabes* (Madrid: Maestre, 1915), pp. 117–145; "Libro de las luces," in *Aljamiado Texte,* volume 2, edited by Reinhold Kontzi (Wiesbaden: Steiner, 1974), pp. 799–837.

*Libro del baño de Zaryab* (ca. sixteenth century)
**Manuscripts:** Madrid, Real Academia de la Historia, MS. 11/9409; Madrid, Escuela de Estudios Árabes (Consejo Superior de Investigaciones Científicas), MS. 4.
**Editions:** "Libro del baño de Zaryab," in *Colección de textos aljamiados,* edited by Pablo Gil, Julián Ribera, and Mariano Sánchez (Zaragoza: Comas, Guerra y Bacque, 1888), pp. 97–114; "Estudio y edición del códice misceláneo aljamiado-morisco num. IV de la Junta para la Ampliación de Estudios, Madrid," edited by Mohamed Ali ben Mrad, dissertation, Universidad Complutense de Madrid, 1991.

*El rekontamiento del rey Alisandere* (ca. sixteenth century)
**Manuscript:** Madrid, Biblioteca Nacional, MS. 5254.
**Edition:** "El rekontamiento del rey Alisandre," edited by A. R. Nykl, *Revue Hispanique,* 77 (1929): 409–611.

The term *aljamiado* (from the Arabic *a'jamiyya:* "barbarian, non-Arabic, foreign") refers to the Hispano-Romance dialect spoken and written by communities of Muslims, Christians under Muslim rule, and Muslim converts to Christianity during the medieval and early-modern periods in Spain. The earliest known traces of the use of this dialect by non-Christians date to the first half of the ninth century, though it is probable that *aljamiado* speech came to form a part of the linguistic repertoire of Andalusi Muslims nearly a century earlier.

From the point of view of modern literary scholars, *aljamiado* is primarily used to describe a large corpus of handwritten Castilian and Aragonese texts composed using an idiosyncratic form of Arabic and, to a much lesser extent, Hebrew script. The overwhelming majority of extant *aljamiado* documents date from the sixteenth to early seventeenth centuries, a period during which Muslim communities—nominally Christian after their compulsory conversion—suffered widespread discrimination, forced relocations, and eventual expulsion from Spain. These *aljamiado* texts, which range from practical religious guides to complex narrative works rooted in the Qur'an as well as in Western literary traditions, represent the literary production of the last remnants of a Hispano-Muslim culture that had taken root in the Iberian Peninsula at the start of the eighth century.

An important early example of *aljamiado* literature is the small collection of Hispano-Romance couplets called *kharjas* that were placed at the end of Andalusi strophic poems known as *muwashshahat*. These couplets have been widely studied by scholars of Arabic, Hebrew, and Romance literatures and linguistics, though a consensus about their nature and function within the *muwashshahat*–or within the broader cultural context of Muslim Spain–has not yet been reached. What is largely agreed upon is that the *kharjas* function as representations of the popular speech of the Christian *(Mozarab)* minority in al-Andalus composed by highly learned poets writing in classical Arabic and, in some cases, Hebrew. Their apparently lower register places the *kharjas* on a different social footing from the much larger corpus of *aljamiado* texts written in Spain toward the end of the medieval period and into the seventeenth century. Rather than recontextualizing the speech of minority Christians living under Muslim rule within the courtly lyric, these later *aljamiado* texts make wide use of the written and spoken language of a Muslim minority operating within a predominantly Christian social milieu.

The factors that led to the steady ebb of literacy in classical Arabic within the Iberian Peninsula throughout the last three centuries of the medieval period have their roots in the series of Christian military conquests that began in the first quarter of the thirteenth century. In 1212 a joint Castilian, Navarrese, and Aragonese force succeeded in taking the important mountain pass at Las Navas de Tolosa, opening up the southern portion of the peninsula to Christian military advance. By 1250, important Muslim cities such as Seville, Córdoba, Jaén, Murcia, and Cádiz–in all, roughly fifty-six thousand square miles of formerly Muslim land–had fallen under the rule of Christian kings. With the defeat of the Merinids at the battle of Salado in 1340, Christian forces effectively took control of Gibraltar and closed off the possibility of renewed invasions by North African forces seeking to shore up the waning Muslim kingdoms of the Iberian Peninsula. While a certain percentage of the Muslim inhabitants of cities taken by Christian forces retreated to unconquered territories such as the kingdom of Granada or left the Iberian Peninsula altogether, many remained to live out their lives within a political and social system characterized by multiple jurisdictions, labyrinthine legal codes, and overlapping, semi-autonomous, multilingual communities.

The Muslims who remained within the newly conquered Christian territories were known as Mudejars. They were allowed by law to practice their religion

*Two pages of sura 79 from a sixteenth-century aljamiado copy of the Qur'an in the Biblioteca Nacional, Madrid (from Consuelo Lopez-Morillas,*
*The Qur'an in Sixteenth-Century Spain, 1982; Thomas Cooper Library, University of South Carolina)*

(which implied the use of classical Arabic for devotional and exegetical purposes) and in general enjoyed a significant degree of political, spiritual, and economic autonomy. The existence of such autonomy, however, should by no means be taken to suggest that the Mudejars were isolated from the ways of life of their Christian neighbors. Intermarriage between Muslims and Christians was far from an isolated occurrence, and there is a wealth of historical evidence supporting the notion that a high level of social interaction between the Mudejar communities and their Christian neighbors took place. In addition, literary works such as Juan Ruiz's *Libro de buen amor* (Book of Good Love) and Don Juan Manuel's *El conde Lucanor* (Count Lucanor), both redacted in or near Toledo during the fourteenth century, provide ample narrative accounts of such cross-cultural interaction.

During this period—most likely sometime during the fourteenth century—copies of the *Poema de Yuçuf* (Poem of Joseph), an *aljamiado* version of the Qur'anic story of Joseph, the son of Jacob, were first produced. Composed in unrhymed *cuaderna vía*, a strophic form based on the French alexandrine that was developed by clerical poets in Castile early in the thirteenth century, the *Poema de Yuçuf* is extant in two manuscripts. The first, referred to as *A* in Ramón Menéndez Pidal's influential 1902 study and transcription of the *Poema de Yuçuf,* is currently in the archive of the Real Academia de la Historia in Madrid. It consists of seventy-seven folios of badly deteriorated paper, twenty by fourteen centimeters, and includes eighteen different texts.

A portion of the *Poema de Yuçuf,* copied out as prose toward the end of the fourteenth century or the beginning of the fifteenth, takes up the first nine folios (the eighth folio is missing) of this manuscript. It is directly followed by a short narrative dealing with another Qur'anic theme, Abraham's near sacrifice of his son Ishmael. Other texts included in the manuscript are the *Historia del nacimiento de Mahoma* (Story of Mohammed's Birth), *Historia de un solitario israelita* (Story of a Lone Israelite), *El castigo de 'Umar a su hijo* (The Moral Teaching of 'Umar to his Son), *Alhadiç del legarto* (The Story of the Lizard), *Alhadiç de Bilal* (The Story of Bilal), *La disputa con los cristianos* (The Dispute with the Christians), *Alhadiç del baño de Zarieb* (The Story of the Bath of Zarieb), *Alhadiç de Tamim* (The Story of Tamim), *Explicación de unas palabras de una obra de al-Ghazali* (Explanation of a Few Words from a Work of al-Ghazali, in Arabic), *Dos jutbas* (Two Sermons), and *Texto y traducción del capítulo 36 del alcorán* (Text and Translation of Chapter 36 of the Qur'an).

The second manuscript (*B,* in Menéndez Pidal's study) is an acephalous but more extensive version of the *Poema de Yuçuf,* now in the custody of the Biblioteca Nacional in Madrid. This text consists of fifty folios (14.2 by 21.2 centimeters) and is preserved in much better condition than manuscript *A,* which it postdates by at least a century. Menéndez Pidal also makes mention of the existence of a single folio of the *Poema de Yuçuf* that includes, in the same scribal hand, several of the verses of manuscript *B.*

The *Poema de Yuçuf* is closely based on the Joseph story found in sura 12 of the Qur'an. It begins with Joseph as a small boy relating a dream to his father, Jacob, in which eleven planets, the sun, and the moon all bow before the young boy to pay homage. At the same time Joseph's half brothers, consumed by the fear that their father prefers Joseph and his younger brother, Benjamin, to them, plot to rid themselves of Joseph. They take him far away with them one day and throw him into a pit, leaving him there to die. They return to Jacob in tears, claiming that Joseph has been eaten by a wolf. In the meantime, Joseph is saved from the pit and taken to Egypt, where he is bought by an Egyptian who has every intention of raising Joseph as his own son. Upon reaching maturity, however, Joseph is approached by the Egyptian's wife, who attempts to seduce him. Joseph resists, but, because of the woman's treachery, he is placed in prison, where he spends many years. Owing to Joseph's powers of dream interpretation, he is eventually cleared of all charges and released into the service of the pharaoh, with control over the treasures and stores of Egypt. In a time of lean harvest, Jacob sends his remaining sons to Egypt to buy grain. Upon seeing Joseph they do not recognize him, though he knows who they are. Rather than punish them for their cruelty, Joseph shows mercy to them. They come to admit their treachery and repent, while the elderly Jacob—having recovered the sight taken from him—comes to Egypt to be reunited with Joseph.

The Qur'anic text is greatly expanded in the *Poema de Yuçuf.* The setting is presented in much greater detail, and the dramatic dialogue is given a heightened development in the *aljamiado* text, reflecting a narrative tradition quite independent from the practice of Qur'anic exegesis and commentary that continued among learned Muslims in Spain until the time of expulsion. The *Poema de Yuçuf,* like the majority of *aljamiado* narrative texts, operated within the tradition of popular Islam rather than that characterized by learned Qur'anic commentary and the Hadith system of Islamic jurisprudence.

Another important *aljamiado* text, produced during the middle third of the fifteenth century, is the *Breviario sunni,* or *Memorial y sumario de los principales mandamientos y devedamientos de nuestra santa ley y sunna* (Survey and Summary of the Principle Commandments and Obligations of Our Holy Law and Practice), of Yçe de Gebir. This work, a compendium of religious customs and practices meant to guide communities of Muslims living in Spain under Christian rule, continued to be an influential text within these communities even as they went into exile at the beginning of the seventeenth century. Because of its usefulness and direct, clear style, the *Breviario sunni* is extensively cited in the *aljamiado* documents used by crypto-Muslim communities throughout the sixteenth century. As the title suggests, the *Breviario sunni* is an abridged manual of Islamic faith and practice, consisting mostly of practical material concerning daily life. A sampling of this material, briefly studied by L. P. Harvey in his 1993 survey of Morisco culture and history, demonstrates the general tone of the text (Harvey's translation):

> It is your Creator alone whom you must adore, attributing to him no likeness or semblance, and honoring his well-chosen and fortunate Muhammad.
>
> Keep clean at all times by ritual ablutions and by purity; observe the five hours of prayer.
>
> Obey your father and mother, even though they be unbelievers.
>
> Pay alms *(zakat);* fast thc honored month of Ramadan; carry out the pilgrimage.
>
> Honor scholars.
>
> Defend the religion with your person and property.
>
> Honor your neighbor, though he be an outsider *(estraño),* a relative, or an unbeliever.
>
> Do not eat ham, or carrion flesh, or blood, or any dubious or improperly slaughtered thing, or anything offered up on an altar to God's creature.
>
> Be truthful to your lord, even though he be a non-Muslim, for, should you not have an heir, he will inherit from you: pay him his due.
>
> Honor the rich, do not despise the poor, avoid envy and anger, and be patient.
>
> Do not live in the land of the unbelievers, nor in any land devoid of justice, nor among evil neighbors, and do not keep company with bad Muslims.
>
> Forgive him who leads you astray, and ask forgiveness of anybody whom you lead astray.
>
> Learn the Law, and teach it to everybody, for you may be called to account for this on Judgment Day, and cast into the fire.
>
> Do not follow the practices, uses, or customs of the Christians, nor use their clothing, nor their likenesses, nor those of sinners, and you will be free from the sins of hell.

As Harvey points out, there is a striking paradox in the admonition against living "in the land of the unbelievers" when the purpose of the book is to instruct those Muslims living within such a cultural context. Such a paradox aside, this work serves as an important textual axis around which a great number of later *aljamiado* texts revolve.

*Prayer hall of the Great Mosque of Cordoba, begun in 784, expanded in the ninth and tenth centuries, and used as a Christian cathedral beginning in 1236 (courtesy of Frank A. Domínguez)*

Shortly after the fall of the independent Nasrid kingdom of Granada to the Catholic Monarchs in 1492, the social context in which *aljamiado* literature was produced and made use of by its Muslim readers changed radically. As with other Muslim cities that had fallen to Christian armies over the preceding several hundred years, the inhabitants of Granada were at first afforded a certain amount of latitude and autonomy with respect to their customs, language, and religious practices—an arrangement that starkly contrasts with the dire situation in which Jewish communities found themselves in 1492. By the beginning of the sixteenth century, however, these liberal terms of surrender had all been summarily revoked. The annulment of the Capitulations of 1492—in effect, the revocation of the legal document that served as the main social contract between the people of Granada and their Christian conquerors—was the first step in a process that was eventually to leave Muslim communities residing in Spain with the same choice that had faced Jewish communities a decade earlier: convert to Christianity or leave Spain.

While many Muslims did convert to Christianity, the majority continued to practice Islam in secret. Modern scholarship commonly refers to these converts as Moriscos, though this term seems not to have been applied to them in Spain (or elsewhere) until well into the sixteenth century. Even as late as the seventeenth century, playwrights such as Lope de Vega used the terms *morisco* and *moro* (a term generally understood to apply to Muslims, not Christian converts from Islam) interchangeably.

From the perspective of state and church authorities, these Morisco communities had ceased being Muslim in any legal sense upon their religious conversion, a conversion in most cases forced upon them. As Christian converts, crypto-Muslims as well as willing *cristianos nuevos* (new Christians) were subject to several laws that sought to control the manner in which they dressed, ate, spoke, and gathered. Moriscos were not allowed even to shut the doors to their homes on *jum'aa* (Fridays), the traditional Muslim holy day, for fear that they would secretly gather together to pray. These communities also fell within the jurisdiction of the Spanish Inquisition, which prosecuted an aggressive campaign against crypto-Muslims and their Jewish counterparts throughout the sixteenth century and until their eventual expulsion in 1609–1611. It is within this context of persecution, secrecy, and cultural decline that *aljamiado* literature during the sixteenth and seventeenth centuries must be understood.

Many *aljamiado* texts from the sixteenth and seventeenth centuries are translations of material originally written in Arabic or in Romance languages, as in the case of the *Historia de los amores de París y Viana* (History of the Loves of Paris and Viana), a popular chivalric romance originally composed in French. Such is the case with the *Libro de las luces* (Book of the Lights), a translation of the Arabic *Kitab al-anwar,* by Egyptian scholar Ahmad ibn Muhammad abu-l-Hasan al-Bakri (1493–1545). This book, about the foretelling of the birth of Muhammad through a light that appeared on Adam's head at the time of his creation, fits within a large tradition of *aljamiado-morisco* texts that deal with the birth, life, and death of the Prophet. Other texts in this tradition include Aragonese poet Mohammed Rabadán's *Discurso de la luz* (Discourse on Light, modeled on al-Bakri's text), as well as works by others, such as *Alhadiç del annabi* (The Story of the Prophet), *Predicación en el nacimiento del annabi* (Preaching on the Birth of the Prophet), *Historia de naçimiento de Muhammad* (Story of Muhammad's Birth), *Historia de la conquista de*

*la casa de Meca* (History of the Conquest of the House of Mecca), *Libro de las batallas* (Book of the Battles), *Historia del puyomiento del annabi* (History of the Prophet's Advance), and *Historia de la muerte del annabi* (History of the Prophet's Death).

While the vast majority of *aljamiado* texts were composed and recopied anonymously, three important works were composed by a figure known as the Mancebo de Arévalo. These texts are learned in style and reflect a subtle grasp of the precepts and customs of Islam, as well as a good understanding of Qur'anic commentary. The first of these works is the *Breve compendio de la santa ley i sunna* (Brief Compendium of the Holy Law and Practice), composed in collaboration with Baray de Remendio, a *faqih* (scholar of Islamic jurisprudence) from Cadrete. The *Breve compendio de la santa ley i sunna* presents and comments upon a great deal of the same material as Yçe de Gebir's *Breviario sunni,* a text upon which it draws liberally. The Mancebo de Arévalo's *Tafçira* (from the Arabic *tafsir,* "Qur'anic commentary") coincides with much of the material in his *Breve compendio de la santa ley i sunna* and was composed, according to the introduction, at the urging of a group of pious men who felt the need to have access to a reliable and practical guide for Qur'anic study. The last of the Mancebo de Arévalo's works is the complex *Sumario de la relaçion y ejercicio espiritual* (Summary of the Relation and Spiritual Exercise). This work, which includes only a small amount of material from the *Breviario sunni* (in contrast to the *Breve compendio de la santa ley i sunna*), features long passages of first-person narrative regarding the author's experiences among other crypto-Muslims in sixteenth-century Spain as well as many penetrating comments regarding the state of Hispano-Muslim culture during this period. In a frequently cited passage, the Mancebo de Arévalo reports the comments of Yuçe Banegas, a learned Muslim from Granada who, lamenting the lack of faith shown by Christian authorities after the conquest of Granada, asks, "If the king of the conquest doesn't keep his word, what can we expect of his successors?"

Beyond the difficulties that come with any attempt to account for the complex and ever shifting social contexts in which *aljamiado* literature was redacted and made use of during the late-medieval and early-modern periods, these texts also present enormous challenges at the level of generic analysis. Extremely wide in generic and stylistic scope, *aljamiado* literature—at its core a secret literature composed and recopied by and for small, intricately connected communities of readers—presents few interpretive clues for the modern researcher. Most of the extant manuscripts, in fact, lack any sort of marginal commentary or annotation that might provide concrete information regard-

*Leyes de Moros.*

Entre los mss. que se guardan en la
biblioteca del colegio mayor de S. Ylde-
fonso de Alcala de Henares, se halla
uno en fol. del qual daremos razon.
Es un quaderno de leyes en castellano antiguo, mesclado de palabras
arabigas para el uso y govierno de
los moros. No consta su autor, ni el
tiempo en que se escribieron, pero
parece fue cerca de fines del siglo
XIII. y el caracter de la letra del
ms. se vée en este especimen.

O pasa el casamjento q̃ feziere el padre sobre la fija
pequeña sea virgen o non ⁌ Et pasa el casamjento
que feziere el padre sobre la virgen de hedat
sy en su consejo ⁌ Pero derecho q̃ la pregunten antt
que atorgue su casamjento ⁌ Et otrosy la muger virgen y en
uerdat y es muger de entendimjento ay en esto dos departimjen
tos.

*Page from a manuscript of the Moorish legal code (photograph by Ricardo Leoz; from Alvaro Galmes de Fuentes,*
Los manuscritos aljamiado-moriscos de la Biblioteca de la Real Academia de la Historia, *1998;*
*Thomas Cooper Library, University of South Carolina )*

ing the manner in which these texts were interpreted and applied by individuals in such communities. Alvaro Galmés de Fuentes, having spent decades studying both *aljamiado* and Arabic literature, offered a detailed portrait of the principal genres of *aljamiado* literature in 1978. These include:

Prose narratives (divisible into romances, short stories, and legends): *Rekontamiento del rey Alisandere* (Story of King Alexander), *Historia de los amores de París y Viana, Libro de las batallas, Leyenda de 'Ali ibnu abi Talib y las cuarenta doncellas* (Legend of 'Ali ibnu abi Talib and the Forty Damsels), *El baño de Zarieb,* and *Leyenda de Yuçuf* (Legend of Joseph).

Eschatological texts: *Estoria del dia del juicio* (Story of the Day of Judgment) and *Ascención de Mahoma a los cielos* (Ascension of Muhammad to the Heavens).

Biblical legends: *La leyenda de Ibrahim* (The Legend of Abraham), *Historia del sacrificio de Ismael* (Story of the Sacrifice of Ishmael), *Las demandas de Muça* (The Questions of Moses), *Leyenda de Muça con la paloma y el halcón* (Legend of Moses with the Dove and the Falcon), *Muerte de Muça* (Death of Moses), *Historia de Ayub* (Story of Job), *Recontamiento de Çulayman* (Story of Solomon), *Nacimiento de Iça* (Birth of Jesus), *Jesús resucita a Sem hijo de Noe* (Jesus Resuscitates Shem, Son of Noah), and *Historia del rey Jesús* (Story of King Jesus).

Travel literature: *Itinerario de España y Turquía* (Itinerary of Spain and Turkey) and *Avisos para el caminante* (Warnings for the Walker).

Didactic prose: *Los castigos de 'Ali* (The Moral Teachings of 'Ali), *Los castigos de Alhaquim a su hijo* (The Moral Teachings of al-Hakim for His Son), *Los castigos del hijo de Edam* (The Moral Teachings of the Son of Edam), *Libro y translado de buenas doctrinas y castigos y buenas costumbres* (Book of Good Doctrine, Moral Teachings, and Good Habits), and *Libro de predicas y examplos y doctrinas para medecinar el alma y amar la otra vida y aborrecer este mundo* (Book of Preachings, Exempla, and Doctrine to Heal the Soul, Love the Life to Come, and Abhor This World).

Treatises on popular beliefs and superstitions: *Libro de dichos maravillosos* (Book of Marvelous Sayings), *Libro de las suertes* (The Book of Fortunes), and *Libro de los sueños* (Book of Dreams).

Anti-Christian and anti-Jewish polemics: *Disputa contra los judíos y disputa contra los cristianos* (Dispute against the Jews and Dispute against the Christians) and *Preguntas de unos judíos a Muhammad* (Questions of Some Jews to Muhammad).

Ascetic and mystical literature: *Tafçira* and *Sumario de la relación y ejercicio espiritual.*

Legal texts: *Leyes de moros* (Laws of Moors) and *El Atafría* (Kitab Al-Tafri, an Islamic legal text written by Iraqi *faqih* Ubayd Allah ibn al-Husayn Ibn al-Jallab during the tenth century).

Poetic works: *Poema de Yuçuf, Almadha de alabança al annabi Muhammad* (Poem of Praise for the Prophet Muhammad), *Historia genealógica de Mahoma* (Genealogical History of Muhammad), and *Coplas en alabança del-adín del-aliçlam* (Verses in Praise of the Religion of Islam).

While the generic categorizations that Galmés de Fuentes offers are at best provisional (Anwar Chejne offers a different framework in his 1983 study of Morisco literature and culture), they do offer a rough sketch of the wide body of texts that make up the bulk of *aljamiado* literature produced between 1492 and 1611. It is from such a sketch, as Galmés de Fuentes readily admits, that further refining should take place.

To develop a global view of *aljamiado* literature from its earliest examples to the literary production of crypto-Muslim communities in Spain (and beyond, as texts exist that were produced after 1611 by Moriscos exiled in North Africa, as well as many by Jews working in Amsterdam and throughout the Mediterranean region) is a particularly difficult task. The dynamic social changes that took place for Muslim and Jewish communities throughout the medieval period in Spain make *aljamiado* literature a protean body of texts designed to serve within ever changing social contexts. That much of this literature is concerned with traditional legends and the practical issues of religious life has certainly come as no surprise to scholars working with this literature. What remains, however, as the careful philological work continues, is to understand how this Romance literature fit into the ways of life practiced in these communities at the end of the medieval period and beyond.

**Bibliography:**

Luis F. Bernabé Pons, *Bibliografía de la literatura aljamiado-morisca* (Alicante: Universidad de Alicante, 1992).

**References:**

J. Oliver Asín, "Un morisco de Túnez, admirador de Lope de Vega," *Al-Andalus,* 1 (1933): 409–450;

Anwar Chejne, *Islam and the West: The Moriscos, a Cultural and Social History* (Albany: State University of New York Press, 1983);

Antonio Domínguez Ortiz and Bernard Vincent, *Historia de los moriscos: Vida y tragedia de una minoría* (Madrid: Revista de Occidente, 1978);

Alvaro Galmés de Fuentes, *Glosario de voces aljamiado-moriscas* (Oviedo: Universidad de Oviedo, 1994);

Galmés de Fuentes, "Lengua y estilo en la literatura aljamiado-morisca," *Nueva Revista de Filología Hispánica,* 30 (1981): 420–444;

Galmés de Fuentes, *El Libro de las batallas (narraciones caballerescas aljamiado-moriscas): Discurso inaugural del año académico 1967–68* (Oviedo: Universidad de Oviedo, 1967);

Galmés de Fuentes, *Los manuscritos aljamiado-moriscos de la Biblioteca de la Real Academia de la Historia* (Madrid: Real Academia de la Historia, 1998);

Galmés de Fuentes, ed., *Actas del coloquio internacional sobre literatura aljamiada y morisca: Departamento de Filología Románica de la Facultad de Filosofía y Letras de la Universidad de Oviedo, 10 al 16 de julio de 1972* (Madrid: Gredos, 1978);

Ignasi González Llubera, ed., *Coplas de Yoçef: A Medieval Spanish Poem in Hebrew Characters* (Cambridge: Cambridge University Press, 1935);

L. P. Harvey, "The Literary Culture of the Moriscos, 1492–1609: A Study Based on the Extant Manuscripts in Arabic and Aljamía," dissertation, Oxford University, 1958;

Harvey, "El mancebo de Arévalo y la tradición cultural de los moriscos," in *Actas del coloquio internacional sobre literatura aljamiada y morisca,* pp. 20–41;

Harvey, "The Political, Social, and Cultural History of the Moriscos," in *The Legacy of Muslim Spain,* 2 volumes, edited by Salma Khadra Jayyusi, second edition (Leiden & Boston: Brill, 1994), I: 201–234;

Ursula Klenk, ed., *La Leyenda de Yusuf: Ein Aljamiado-text* (Tübingen: Niemeyer, 1972);

Moshe Lazar, ed., *Joseph and His Brethren: Three Ladino Versions: Poema de Yosef, Coplas de Yosef ha-Saddiq, Sefer ha-Yasar* (Culver City, Cal.: Labyrinthos, 1990);

Luce López Baralt, "Crónica de la destrucción de un mundo: La literatura aljamiado-morisca," *Bulletin Hispanique,* 82 (1980): 16–58;

López Baralt, "El oráculo de Mahoma sobre la Andalucia musulmana de los últimos tiempos en un manuscrito aljamiado-morisco de la Biblioteca Nacional de Paris," *Hispanic Review,* 52, no. 1 (1984): 41–57;

Consuelo López-Morillas, "Lexical and etymological studies in the Aljamiado Koran based on manuscript 4938 of the Biblioteca Nacional, Madrid," dissertation, University of California, Berkeley, 1974;

López-Morillas, *The Qur'an in Sixteenth-Century Spain: Six Morisco Versions of Sura 79* (London: Tamesis, 1982);

Francisco Márquez Villanueva, *El problema morisco: Desde otras laderas* (Madrid: Libertarias, 1991);

Alberto Montaner Frutos, *"El baño de Ziryab:* De apólogo oriental a relato aljamiado morisco," in *Actas del Primer Congreso Anglo-Hispano,* 2 volumes, edited by Ralph Penny and Alan Deyermond (Madrid: Castalia, 1993), I: 121–135;

Montaner Frutos, *El recontamiento de al-Miqdâd y al-Mayâsa: Edición y estudio de un relato aljamiado-morisco aragonés* (Zaragoza: Institución Fernando el Católico, 1988);

A. R. Nykl, ed., *A Compendium of Aljamiado Literature* (New York & Paris: Protat, 1929);

José María Perceval, *Todos son uno: Arquetipos, xenofobia y racismo—La imagen del morisco en la monarquía española durante los siglos XVI y XVII* (Almería: Instituto de Estudios Almerienses, 1997);

Eduardo Saavedra, *Discursos leídos ante la Real Academia Española en la recepcion pública* (Madrid: Impresores y Libreros, 1878);

Mercedes Sánchez Alvarez, "La lengua de los manuscritos aljamiado-moriscos como testimonio de la doble marginación de una minoría islámica," *Nueva Revista de Filología Hispánica,* 30, no. 2 (1981): 441–452;

Michael Schmitz, "Über das altspanische *Poema de José,*" *Romanische Forschungen,* 9 (1901): 357–410;

Abdeljelil Temimi, ed., *Les actes de la première table ronde du C.I.E.M. sur la littérature aljamiado-morisque: hybridisme linguistique et univers discursif* (Tunis: Centre de Recherches en Bibliothéconomie et Sciences de l'Information, 1986);

Antonio Vespertino Rodríguez, ed., *Leyendas aljamiadas y moriscas sobre personajes bíblicos* (Madrid: Gredos, 1983).

# Cancioneros

Jane Whetnall
*Queen Mary, University of London*

WORKS: *Cancionero de Baena* (circa 1430)

**Manuscript:** Paris, Bibliothèque Nationale, Esp. 37.

**Editions**: *El cancionero de Juan Alfonso de Baena (siglo XV). Ahora por primera vez dado a luz con notas y comentarios,* edited by Pedro José Pidal, Eugenio de Ochoa, Pascual de Gayangos, and Agustín Durán (Madrid: Rivadaneyra, 1851; Buenos Aires: Anaconda, 1949); *Cancionero de Baena,* 2 volumes, edited by Francisque Michel (Leipzig: Brockhaus, 1860); *Cancionero de Baena: Reproduced in Facsimile from the Unique Manuscript in the Bibliothèque Nationale,* foreword by Henry R. Lang (New York: Hispanic Society of America, 1926); *Cancionero de Juan Alfonso de Baena,* 3 volumes, edited by José María Azáceta, Clásicos Hispánicos, series 2, volumes 10-12 (Madrid: Consejo Superior de Investigaciones Científicas, 1966); *El cancionero del siglo XV, c. 1360-1520,* 7 volumes, edited by Brian Dutton and Jineen Krogstad, Biblioteca Española del Siglo XV, Serie Maior, nos. 1-7 (Salamanca: Biblioteca española del siglo XV & Universidad de Salamanca, 1990-1991), III: 72-327; *Cancionero de Juan Alfonso de Baena,* edited by Dutton and Joaquín González Cuenca, Biblioteca Filológica Hispana, no. 14 (Madrid: Visor, 1993).

*Cancionero de Palacio* (circa 1437-1442)

**Manuscript:** Salamanca, Biblioteca Universitaria, 2653 (formerly Madrid, Biblioteca de Palacio, 594).

**Editions:** *El cancionero de Palacio (manuscrito no. 594),* edited by Francisca Vendrell de Millás (Barcelona: Consejo Superior de Investigaciones Científicas, 1945); *Cancionero de Palacio: Ms. 2653 Biblioteca Universitaria de Salamanca,* edited by Ana María Álvarez Pellitero (Salamanca: Junta de Castilla y León, Consejería de Cultura y Turismo, 1993).

**Excerpts:** *Colección de poesías de un cancionero inédito del siglo XV existente en la biblioteca de S. M. el Rey D. Alonso XII,* edited by Alfonso Pérez Gómez Nieva (Madrid: Tipografía de Alfredo Alonso, 1884); *El*

*cancionero del siglo XV, c. 1360-1520,* edited by Dutton and Krogstad, IV: 84-179–includes all the texts except Íñigo López de Mendoza, Marqués de Santillana's *Infierno de los amadores.*

*Cancionero de París 313,* also known as "Paris H" and "Ph" (1444-1448)

**Manuscript:** Paris, Bibliothèque Nationale, Esp. 313.

**Edition:** *Texto y concordancias del* Cancionero castellano de París (Bibliothèque Nationale, Paris, ms. Esp. 313), microfiche, edited by Javier Coca, Spanish Series, no. 45 (Madison, Wis.: Hispanic Seminary of Medieval Studies, 1989).

**Excerpts:** Caroline B. Bourland, ed., "The Unprinted Poems of the Spanish *Cancioneros* in the Bibliothèque Nationale, Paris," *Revue Hispanique,* 21 (1909): 460-566; *El cancionero del siglo XV, c. 1360-1520,* edited by Dutton and Krogstad, III: 438-470.

*Cancionero de Gallardo-San Román* (circa 1454)

**Manuscript:** Madrid, Real Academia de la Historia, MS. 2 (formerly MS. 2-7-2).

**Excerpts:** "El cancionero de Gallardo de la Real Academia de la Historia," edited by Azáceta, *Revista de Literatura,* 6 (1954): 239-270; 7 (1955): 134-180; 8 (1955): 271-294; "Las poesías inéditas de Juan de Dueñas," edited by Vendrell, *Revista de Archivos, Bibliotecas y Museos,* 64 (1958): 149-240; *El cancionero del siglo XV, c. 1360-1520,* edited by Dutton and Krogstad, I: 430-542.

*Libro de las veynte cartas e qüistiones* (1456-1465)

**Manuscript:** Madrid, Biblioteca Nacional, 18041.

**Editions:** Fernando de la Torre, *Cancionero y obras en prosa,* edited by Antonio Paz y Melia, Veröfftenlichungen der Gesellschaft, no. 16 (Dresden: Gesellschaft für romanische Literatur, 1907); *La obra literaria de Fernando de la Torre,* edited by María Jesús Díez Garretas (Valladolid: Universidad de Valladolid, 1983).

**Excerpts:** *El cancionero del siglo XV, c. 1360-1520,* edited by Dutton and Krogstad, II: 260-288.

*Cancionero de Herberay* (circa 1463)

**Manuscript:** London, British Library, Add. 33.382.

**Edition:** *Le Chansonnier espagnol d'Herberay des Essarts (XV^e siècle),* edited by Charles V. Aubrun, Bibliothèque de l'Ecole des Hautes Etudes Hispaniques, no. 25 (Bordeaux: Féret, 1951).

**Excerpts:** *El cancionero del siglo XV, c. 1360–1520,* edited by Dutton and Krogstad, I: 276–358.

*Cancionero de Stúñiga* or *Estúñiga* (circa 1465)

**Manuscript:** Madrid, Biblioteca Nacional, Vitrina 17.7.

**Editions:** *Cancionero de Lope de Stúñiga, códice del siglo XV,* edited by the Marqués de la Fuensanta del Valle and José Sancho Rayón, Colección de Libros Españoles Raros o Curiosos, no. 4 (Madrid: Rivadaneyra, 1872); *Cancionero de Estúñiga: Edición paleográfica,* edited by Manuel Alvar and Elena Alvar, Publicaciones de la Institución Fernando el Católico, no. 821 (Saragossa: Consejo Superior de Investigaciones Científicas, 1981); *Cancionero de Estúñiga,* edited by Nicasio Salvador Miguel (Madrid: Alhambra, 1987).

**Excerpts:** *El cancionero del siglo XV, c. 1360–1520,* edited by Dutton and Krogstad, II: 298–365.

*Cancionero de Modena* (circa 1466)

**Manuscript:** Modena, Biblioteca Estense, α.R.8.9.

**Edition:** *El cancionero castellano del s. XV de la Biblioteca Estense de Módena,* edited by Marcella Ciceri, Textos Recuperados, no. 12 (Salamanca: Universidad de Salamanca, 1995).

**Excerpts:** Karl Vollmöller, "Der *Cancionero von Modena,*" *Romanische Forschungen,* 10 (1899): 449–470; G. Bertoni, "Catalogo dei codici spagnuoli della Biblioteca Estense in Modena," *Romanische Forschungen,* 20 (1907): 321–392; *Il canzoniere spagnuolo di Modena,* edited by Ferruccio Blasi (Messina: Ferrara, 1956); *El cancionero del siglo XV, c. 1360–1520,* edited by Dutton and Krogstad, I: 379–429.

*Cancionero de Roma* (circa 1470)

**Manuscript:** Rome, Biblioteca Casanatense, 1098.

**Edition:** *El cancionero de Roma,* 2 volumes, edited by M. Canal Gómez, Biblioteca Hispano-Italiana, nos. 2, 3 (Florence: Sansoni, 1935).

**Excerpts:** *El cancionero del siglo XV, c. 1360–1520,* edited by Dutton and Krogstad, IV: 1–74.

*Cancionero de la Marciana* or *de Venecia* (circa 1470)

**Manuscript:** Venice, Biblioteca Marciana, Str. App. XXV.

**Edition:** *El cancionero del siglo XV, c. 1360–1520,* edited by Dutton and Krogstad, IV: 327–370.

**Excerpts:** *Il* Cancionero *marciano (Str. App. XXV),* edited by Alfredo Cavaliere (Venice: Zanetti, 1943).

*Cancionero de Pero Guillén de Segovia* (circa 1480)

**Manuscript:** Madrid, Biblioteca Nacional, 4114 (eighteenth-century copy of lost original of circa 1480).

**Excerpts:** Henry R. Lang, "The So-Called *Cancionero de Pero Guillén de Segovia,*" *Revue Hispanique,* 19 (1908): 51–81; *El cancionero del siglo XV, c. 1360–1520,* edited by Dutton and Krogstad, II: 103–193.

*Cancionero de Oñate-Castañeda* (circa 1485)

**Manuscript:** Harvard University, Houghton Library, Sp. 97.

**Edition:** *El Cancionero de Oñate-Castañeda,* edited by Dorothy Sherman Severin and Fiona Maguire, introduction by Michel Garcia, Spanish Series, no. 36 (Madison, Wis.: Hispanic Seminary of Medieval Studies, 1990).

**Excerpts:** Francisco R. de Uhagon (Marqués de Laurencín), "Un cancionero del siglo XV, con varias poesías inéditas," *Revista de Archivos, Bibliotecas y Museos,* 4 (1900): 321–338, 390–403, 516–535; Michel Garcia, "Le *Chansonnier d'Oñate y Castañeda,*" *Mélanges de la Casa de Velázquez,* 14 (1978): 107–142; 15 (1979): 207–239; 16 (1980): 141–149; *El cancionero del siglo XV, c. 1360–1520,* edited by Dutton and Krogstad, I: 94–129.

*Cancionero de Ramón Llavia* (circa 1486)

**Early edition:** *Cancionero de Ramón de Llavia* (Saragossa: Juan Hurus, n.d.).

**Editions:** *Cancionero de Ramón de Llavia,* edited by Rafael Benitos Claros, Sociedad de Bibliófilos Españoles, segunda época, no. 16 (Madrid: Sociedad de Bibliófilos Españoles, 1945).

**Excerpts:** *El cancionero del siglo XV, c. 1360–1520,* edited by Dutton and Krogstad, V: 5–8.

*Cancionero musical de la Colombina* (circa 1495)

**Manuscript:** Seville, Biblioteca Colombina, 7-1-28.

**Editions:** *Cancionero musical de la Colombina (siglo XV),* edited by Miguel Querol Gavaldá, Monumentos de la Música Española, no. 33 (Barcelona: Consejo Superior de Investigaciones Científicas, Instituto Español de Musicología, 1971); *El cancionero del siglo XV, c. 1360–1520,* edited by Dutton and Krogstad, IV: 288–301.

*Cancionero musical de Palacio* (1495–1520)

**Manuscript:** Madrid, Biblioteca de Palacio, 1335.

**Editions:** *Cancionero musical de los siglos XV y XVI,* edited by Francisco Asenjo Barbieri (Madrid: Real Academia de las Bellas Artes de San Fernando, 1890); (texts and music) *La música en la*

*Folios 3v and 4r from the manuscript for the* Cancionero de Baena, *compiled between 1426 and 1430.
This manuscript was copied from an earlier one, now lost, between 1460 and 1500
(Bibliothèque Nationale, Paris; courtesy of Jane Whetnall).*

# Cantigas Alfon: Aluares.

*corte de los Reyes Católicos,* parts 2 and 3: *Polifonía profana: Cancionero Musical de Palacio (siglos XV–XVI),* 2 volumes, edited by Higinio Anglés, Monumentos de la Música Española, nos. 5, 10 (Barcelona: Consejo Superior de Investigaciones Científicas & Instituto Español de Musicología, 1947, 1951); *La música en la corte de los Reyes Católicos,* part 4: *Cancionero Musical de Palacio (siglos XV–XVI),* volume 3, 2 volumes, edited by José Romeu Figueras, Monumentos de la Música Española, no. 14 (Barcelona: Consejo Superior de Investigaciones Científicas, Instituto Español de Musicología, 1965); *El cancionero del siglo XV, c. 1360–1520,* cditcd by Dutton and Krogstad, II: 503–600.

*Cancionero de las obras de Juan del Enzina* (Salamanca: [printer unknown], 1496)

    **Editions:** *Cancionero de Juan del Encina. Primera edición. 1496. Publicado en facsímile por la Real Academia Española,* prologue by E. Cotarelo (Madrid: Tipografía de la *Revista de Archivos, Bibliotecas y Museos,* 1928); Juan del Encina, *Obras completas,* edited by Ana María Rambaldo, 4 volumes (Madrid: Espasa-Calpe, 1978–1983).

    **Excerpts:** *El Cancionero del siglo XV, c. 1360–1520,* edited by Dutton and Krogstad, V: 24–86.

*Cancionero de Juan Álvarez Gato* (circa 1507)

    **Manuscript:** Madrid, Real Academia de la Historia, C.114.9 / 5535.

    **Edition:** Juan Álvarez Gato, *Obras completas,* edited by Jenaro Artiles Rodríguez, Los Clásicos Olvidados, no. 4 (Madrid: Editorial Ibero-Americana, 1928).

    **Excerpts:** *Cancionero inédito de Juan Álvarez Gato, poeta madrileño del siglo XV,* edited by Emilio Cotarelo (Madrid: Revista Española, 1901); *El cancionero del siglo XV, c. 1360–1520,* edited by Dutton and Krogstad, I: 543–379.

*Cancionero general recopilado por Hernando del Castillo* (Valencia: Cristóbal Kofman, 1511).

    **Editions:** *Cancionero general de Hernando del Castillo* (Madrid: Sociedad de Bibliófilos Españoles, 1882); *Cancionero general recopilado por Hernando del Castillo (Valencia, 1511),* facsimile edition, edited by Antonio Rodríguez-Moñino (Madrid: Real Academia Española, 1958).

    **Excerpts:** *El cancionero del siglo XV, c. 1360–1520,* edited by Dutton and Krogstad, V: 117–538.

    Ian Macpherson, "Secret Language in the *Cancioneros:* Some Courtly Codes," *Bulletin of Hispanic Studies,* 62 (1985): 51–63;

*Cancionero de la British Library,* also known as *Cancionero de Londres* and *Cancionero de Rennert* (circa 1515)

    **Manuscript:** London, British Library, Add. 10431.

    **Edition:** *El cancionero del siglo XV, c. 1360–1520,* edited by Dutton and Krogstad, I: 131–275.

    **Excerpts:** Hugo Albert Rennert, "Der spanische *Cancionero* des British Museums (MS. Add. 10431)," *Romanische Forschungen,* 10 (1895 [i.e., 1899]): 1–176.

    John Gornall, *The* Invenciones *of the British Library* Cancionero, Papers of the Medieval Hispanic Research Seminar, no. 41 (London: Department of Hispanic Studies, Queen Mary, University of London, 2003);

*Cancionero de obras de burlas provocantes a risa* (Valencia: Juan Viñao, 1519)

    **Editions:** *Cancionero de obras de burlas provocantes a risa,* ed. Luis de Usoz y Río (London: Pickering, 1841–1843); facsimile edition by Antonio Pérez Gómez (Valencia, 1951); Pedro Jauralde Pou and Juan Alfredo Bellón Cazabán Pou, eds., *Cancionero de obras de burlas provocantes a risa* (Madrid: Akal, 1974).

    **Excerpts:** *El Cancionero del siglo XV, c. 1360–1520,* edited by Dutton and Krogstad, VII: 631–637.

OTHER COLLECTIONS: Henry R. Lang, ed., *Cancionero Gallego-Castelhano: The Extant Galician Poems of the Gallego-Castilian Lyric School (1350–1450),* volume 1 (New York: Scribners / London: Arnold, 1902);

Raymond Foulché-Delbosc, ed., *Cancionero castellano del siglo XV,* 2 volumes, Nueva Biblioteca de Autores Españoles, nos. 19, 22 (Madrid: Bailly-Baillière, 1912, 1915);

Marcelino Menéndez y Pelayo, *Antología de poetas líricos castellanos,* 10 volumes, Edición Nacional de las Obras Completas de Menéndez Pelayo, edited by Enrique Sánchez Reyes, volumes 17–26 (Santander: Consejo Superior de Investigaciones Científicas, 1944–1945); first edition, 13 volumes (Madrid: Viuda de Hernando, 1890–1908);

Dámaso Alonso and José Manuel Blecua, eds., *Antología de la poesía española: Poesía de tipo tradicional* (Madrid: Gredos, 1956; corrected, 1964);

José María Azáceta, "El *Pequeño cancionero,*" in *Estudios dedicados a Menéndez Pidal,* volume 7 (Madrid: Consejo Superior de Investigaciones Científicas, 1957), pp. 83–112;

Antonio Rodríguez-Moñino, ed., *Suplemento al* Cancionero general *de Hernando del Castillo (Valencia, 1511) que contiene todas las poesías que no figuran en la primera edición y fueron añadidas desde 1514 hasta 1557* (Valencia: Castalia, 1959);

Álvaro Alonso, ed., *Poesía de cancionero,* Letras Hispánicas, no. 247 (Madrid: Cátedra, 1986);

Víctor de Lama de la Cruz, ed., *Cancionero musical de la Catedral de Segovia* (Salamanca: Junta de Castilla y León, 1994);

E. Michael Gerli, ed., *Poesía cancioneril castellana,* Nuestros Clásicos, no. 7 (Madrid: Akal, 1994);

Ricardo Polín, *Cancioneiro Galego-Castelán (1350–1450): 'Corpus' lírico da decadencia,* Publicacións do Seminario de Estudos Galegos, 3 (Sada, Corunna: O Castro, 1997);

Dorothy Sherman Severin, ed., *Two Spanish Songbooks. The* Cancionero Capitular de la Colombina *(SV2) and the* Cancionero de Egerton *(LB3).* Editorial Assistant Fiona Maguire. Hispanic Studies TRAC (Textual Research and Criticism) Volume 11 (Liverpool: Liverpool University Press / Seville: Institución Colombina, 2000);

Paola Elia, ed., *El "Pequeño Cancionero" (MS. 3788 BNM),* Biblioteca Filológica, no. 11 (Noia: Toxosoutos, 2002).

*Cancionero* (songbook or collection of lyrics) is a calque from the French *chansonnier* or Italian *canzoniere* and was used by fifteenth-century writers to refer to collections of poetry in book form. By extension, it has come to refer to the kind of poetry–*poesía de cancionero* or *cancioneril*–that is collected in these books and, therefore, to all the Spanish court poetry of the late Middle Ages. The earliest known extant *cancionero,* which dates from the 1430s, includes verse from as early as 1360 and must have been largely dependent on written sources. Around sixty contemporary manuscript *cancioneros* survive, along with a dozen sixteenth-century or later copies of lost collections. Fourteenth- and fifteenth-century court lyric is also found in a wide variety of other sources–foreign songbooks, prose miscellanies, sentimental fiction–and in *pliegos sueltos* (chapbooks) and printed anthologies from the 1470s onward. Altogether, these sources–which are probably a fraction of what was in circulation at the time–include many thousands of poems by more than five hundred poets. Among these poets are nearly all of the well-known men of letters of the fifteenth century–Fernán Pérez de Guzmán (1376–circa 1460); Íñigo López de Mendoza, Marqués de Santillana (1398–1458); Juan de Mena (1411–1456); Gómez Manrique (1412–1490); Jorge Manrique (circa 1440 – 24 April 1479); and Fray (Friar) Íñigo de Mendoza (fl. 1475–1500), as well as writers who are better known for their prose works, such as Juan Rodríguez del Padrón (fl. 1430–1450), Diego de Valera (fl. 1412–1488), and Diego de San Pedro (1477–circa 1492) and a host of secondary figures. Only a handful of poems are by women. Nothing is known of the great majority of the poets but their names.

The typical *cancionero* is a collection of poems by various poets, but "personal" *cancioneros* devoted to the works of one individual also exist. Almost all of the surviving manuscripts are copies, as opposed to compilations in the hand of the original compiler or his or her amanuensis. Physically they range from costly presentation volumes in pristine condition to fragments of humbler manufacture that have been literally read to pieces. Awareness of the composition and structure of the extant artifact is essential to a proper understanding of the transmission and reception of its contents.

Implicitly, all the verse was written for the members of a court by poets in some way associated with that court. References to personalities, places, and events in occasional poems conjure up, for example, the Aragonese royal court at Naples in the late 1440s and 1450s and the royal court of Navarre in the 1460s. Smaller centers, such as the court of a duke or prelate, could also foster poetic activity.

Despite a tendency among critics to treat all the poetry of a 150-year period as an undifferentiated mass, great differences are apparent over time, from place to place, across genres, and even within the output of a given individual. Court poetry encompasses a variety of types, modes, and genres: religious, politico-historical, didactic, elegiac, panegyric, and satirical. The term *poesía de cancionero,* however, is most generally applied to the love poetry.

For all of the texts it includes, the *cancionero* represents the final phase of a drawn-out publication process. At least two initial reception contexts can be envisaged: one oral and public, the other written and private. These contexts are not mutually exclusive: some poems would have been read aloud or declaimed in front of an audience in competitive debates or semistaged recitals; others would have been set to music and sung. The performance of songs was a central part of court life, but musical notation is not found in the poetry collections. One must take it on faith that poems labeled *canción* (song), *romance* (ballad), or *villancico* (carol) or lyrics with certain fixed patterns were written to be sung, either to preexisting tunes or to specially composed settings. Whoever committed these shorter pieces to writing may well have done so from memory. The length and complexity of some polemical texts, on the other hand, suggest that they circulated from the beginning as written documents and that the responses they solicited were likewise passed from hand to hand before being given a public airing. And it is possible that most of the love poems had, like love letters, a primary communicative function in wooing rituals. How and by whom these disparate tokens of private and public intercourse were subsequently gathered up and recorded remains a subject for investigation.

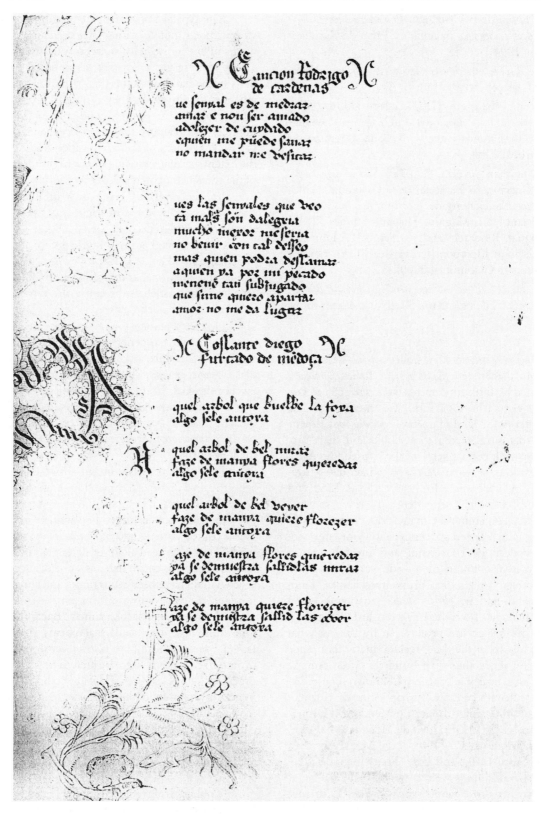

*Folio 6v from the* Cancionero de Palacio, *compiled between 1437 and 1442 and comprising nearly 370 poems (Biblioteca Universitaria, Salamanca; courtesy of Jane Whetnall)*

Hardly a *cancionero* exists that does not have its peculiar contribution to make to the panorama of late-medieval Castilian lyric. Moreover, *cancionero* studies are a major growth area, and the ground is shifting. Given the present state of knowledge, any selective account must be arbitrary. Collections that seem important today may not seem so in ten years; others that are only ciphers may prove to be fundamental; still others may await discovery or rediscovery.

The *Cancionero de Baena* is the oldest known extant fifteenth-century compilation and also the largest. Juan Alfonso de Baena (circa 1375–1435) was a scribe in the service of King Juan II (1405–1454). He assembled this vast compendium of nearly six hundred poems, many of which are quite long, over a period of about five years beginning in 1426. The Paris manuscript is a copy of a defective exemplar, which was itself probably a copy of the original *cancionero* presented to Juan II. According to Brian Dutton and Joaquín González Cuenca, the Paris manuscript is the work of five different hands; the bulk was copied from 1460 to 1465, with additions and foliation by a scribe working around 1500.

The volume opens with Baena's dedicatory preface addressed to Juan II; a prologue, which is truncated; and a table of contents naming seventeen poets. Baena places himself at the end of the list: with eighty compositions under four headings, he is the second-best-represented author in the *cancionero*. In the text itself another thirty poets are included, mainly as authors of replies to works of one or another of the poets in the table of contents. Except for two cycles of poems commemorating the death of King Enrique III and the birth of Juan II, the texts are organized by author. Lengthy rubrics provide background information on the personal life or status of the poet, the circumstances of composition, and, in some cases, a critical evaluation of the verse.

The prologue is a conventional defense of reading and poetry as courtly pursuits. The mismatch between the actual contents of the collection and Baena's insistence on the aristocratic and divine nature of the poetic gift and the importance of love has been pointed out by Julian Weiss: many of the poets are clerics or bureaucrats, and only a small proportion of the works are love lyrics. The collection reflects what Dutton, in "Spanish Fifteenth-Century *Cancioneros:* A General Survey to 1465" (1979), calls "the rather pompous taste of bourgeois clerks, scribes and officials."

Largely retrospective, the *Cancionero de Baena* comprises poetry written during the reigns of the five kings from Pedro I to Juan II. The compositions can be divided into two main categories, *cantiga* (song) and *dezir* (poem), but the boundaries are not clear-cut; each category embraces a wide variety of forms, meters, and subject matters. There are Marian hymns, political allegories, theological debates on topics such as predestination, riddles, testaments and mock testaments, and a few scurrilous exchanges in the style of the *cantigas de escarnho e de maldizer* (songs of mockery and slander of Galician-Portuguese tradition). There is one rustic wooing song, "Menga dame el tu acorro" (Menga, give me your protection), by Santillana's grandfather, Pero González de Mendoza (circa 1340–1385).

Despite its wide chronological scope, the volume is by no means comprehensive. Other sources, such as Santillana's *Prohemio e carta al Condestable de Portugal* (Preface and Letter to the Constable of Portugal, 1449), and even references within the *Cancionero de Baena* itself provide evidence of the existence of late-fourteenth-century poets and poetic circles who are not represented. The younger generation has been deliberately ignored: apart from Baena himself and Pérez de Guzmán, most of the authors listed in the table of contents were dead by 1430.

The emphasis on history in Baena's prologue favors the assumption that he was recording for posterity the output of the milieu in which he received his training as a professional rhymester. The volume can be regarded as a tribute to Alfonso Álvarez de Villasandino (circa 1345–1425) and a monument to a vanished world. One feature of this world was the importance of Seville as a center for poetry: ten authors are from Seville or other parts of the south. Another feature is the presence of a small number of compositions in the hybrid literary dialect that has been dubbed "Galician-Castilian." Forty-eight such poems in the *Cancionero de Baena* by seven poets–Villasandino, González de Mendoza, Macías (fl. 1350–1370), the archdeacon of Toro Gonzalo Rodríguez (fl. 1360–1390), Pero Vélez de Guevara (fl. 1400–1420), Garci Ferrández de Jerena (fl. 1385–1410), and an unnamed "Bachiller en Artes" (Bachelor of Arts)–have given rise to the hypothesis of a school of poetry that bridged the transition from Galician-Portuguese to Castilian as the language of lyric in Spain. After the *Cancionero de Baena,* poems in Galician or with Galician traits are few and far between.

The earliest poet in the *Cancionero de Baena* is a Galician troubadour, whose dates are completely speculative. The misty, luminous figure of Macías was synonymous with the tragic lover until well into the Golden Age (circa 1530–1680); by then the story of his martyrdom for love had long since eclipsed the fame of his songs. Only five can be attributed to him with any certainty, and they are all in the *Cancionero de Baena*. His most commonly cited and anthologized lyrics are "Cativo de miña tristura" (Captive of my sorrow) and "Amor cruel e brioso" (Cruel and capricious Love), but

*Medal cast in 1449 by the Italian artist Pisanello (Antonio Pisano)*
*of King Alfonso V of Aragon. Pedro de Santa Fe, forty-seven*
*of whose works are included in the* Cancionero
*de Palacio, was attached to his court (Museo*
*Arqueológico Nacional, Madrid; courtesy*
*of Jane Whetnall).*

the legend of his murder by an outraged husband probably derives from a literal interpretation of the metaphor in "Ay señora en que fiança" (O Lady in whom I trust): "Aquesta lança sin falla / ¡ay coitado! / non me la dieron del muro / nin la prise yo en batalla . . ." (This unerring lance thrust, / woe is me!, / did not come at me from the rampart / nor in the thick of battle . . .).

The lyrical heir to Macías is Villasandino, by far the best-represented poet in the *Cancionero de Baena* and also the most prolific poet of the *cancionero* period. More than two hundred poems are attributed to him, including twenty-four in Galician. Villasandino was a master of many styles and prided himself on his virtuosity and craftsmanship. He produced poems for state and civic occasions, love poems on commission to the mistresses of Enrique II, wooing poems on behalf of Conde (Count) Pero Niño and Adelantado (frontier governor) Pero Manrique to their future wives, and seventy-two begging poems on his own behalf to nineteen patrons. He was not averse to making his own marital problems the subject of his verse. The Villasandino text that appears most often in later collections, a protest on the *contemptu mundi* (contempt for the world) theme, is not included in the *Cancionero de Baena*. Four or five of his love lyrics had longer lives as quotations. One that is popular with anthologists occurs without a rubric in the manuscript, but Villasandino's authorship has never been in doubt: "Quien de lynda se enamora / atender

deve perdón / en caso que sea mora" (He who falls in love with a pretty woman / must sue for pardon / should she be a Muslim).

Micer Francisco Imperial (fl. 1394–1407), probably the most distinguished author represented, is singled out by Santillana in his *Prohemio e carta al Condestable de Portugal* for the accolade of *poeta:* "al qual yo no llamaría dezidor o trobador mas poeta" (whom I would call not a writer of verse or a troubadour but a poet). Imperial came from a well-to-do family of Genoese merchants, recent immigrants to Seville, and held office under Enrique III. His year of birth is unknown, but there is documentary evidence that he was dead by April 1409. Imperial is the author of nineteen extant compositions, all but one of which are included in the *Cancionero de Baena;* some are in octosyllabic meter and others in *arte mayor,* but he is best known for introducing the Italian hendecasyllable, along with echoes of Dante's *Divina commedia,* into his long, allegorical *Dezir a las siete virtudes* (Poem of the Seven Virtues). In several poems he refers to his lady by the *senhal* (pseudonym) Estrella Diana (Day or Morning Star), borrowed from the Italian *stilnovisti* poet Guido Guinizelli (the *stilnovisti* [new stylists], a movement of which Dante was a member, developed a "sweet new style" that replaced the wordplay and often harsh rhetoric of earlier poetry with simplicity and elegance). In a series of exchanges in the *Cancionero de Baena* Imperial's extravagant praise of Estrella Diana is challenged in successive poems by Pérez de Guzmán and Diego Martínez de Medina. He retaliates with "Ante la muy alta corte" (Before the high court), in which he asks her permission to arm himself with her beauty: "Vuestra nariz afilada / sea flecha muy polida, / con las pestañas, mi vida, / ricamente enplumada" (Let your dainty nose / be a delicate arrow, / richly feathered / with your eyelashes, darling). Notwithstanding his sparse appearances in collections after the *Cancionero de Baena,* Imperial exercised considerable influence over younger poets such as Santillana and Mena.

Because it was the first manuscript collection to be published in a modern edition (1851) and remains the one that has been most extensively studied, the *Cancionero de Baena* has been allowed to stand as a paradigm for the fifteenth-century *cancionero*. But it is atypical in several respects: it is the only manuscript collection with a known compiler, and the level of organization, intervention, and control he exercised was not repeated until Hernando del Castillo's *Cancionero general* of 1511. Critics often use the *Cancionero de Baena* as a point of reference for later developments, but it is unclear how widely the collection or the individual poems in it circulated in the fifteenth century.

Internal evidence points to a date between 1437 and 1442 for the *Cancionero de Palacio* (of Salamanca). A large-format volume of 178 leaves, copied by four or five hands, it has several styles of decoration, including some sexually explicit marginal drawings that have been described by some as erotic and by others as obscene. For a collection assembled only a few years later, it could not be more unlike the *Cancionero de Baena*. There is no preface, no prologue, no table of contents, and no sign of internal organization; rubrication is relatively spare. The manuscript is in an irremediable state of disorder: whole quires and single leaves were already out of sequence when it was foliated in Roman numerals during the fifteenth century.

The *Cancionero de Palacio* includes nearly 370 texts, but the overlap with the *Cancionero de Baena* amounts to little more than a few poems by Macías and Villasandino. Older poets include Imperial, with a dream-vision poem, "Solo en l'alva pensoso estando" (Alone and rapt in thought at dawn), and Santillana's father, Diego Hurtado de Mendoza (1364–1404), with the parallelistic *cossaute* (dance song) "Aquel árbol que buelbe la foxa" (That tree whose leaves are stirring). The admiral of Castile Alfonso Enríquez (1354–1429) is represented by seven poems, including the famous *Vergel del pensamiento* (Grove of Thought) "Por la muy aspera vía" (Along the rugged way), an interior monologue with an allegorical frame, and a mock *testamento*. Other poems destined to become *cancionero* standards are Villasandino's "¿Qué se fizo lo pasado?" (What became of days gone by?) and a lively *Dezir de la muerte* (Ode to Death), "Muerte que a todos conbidas / dime que son tus manjares" (Death, who keep open house, / tell me your bill of fare).

The *Cancionero de Palacio* gives precedence, however, to poets born in the 1390s or the early 1400s who were writing in the 1410s and 1420s. Santillana makes his debut here with sixteen poems, among them the earliest versions of his *Querella de amor* (Complaint to Love), *Triunphete de amor* (Little Triumph of Love), and *Infierno de los enamorados* (Lovers' Hell). This collection also marks the first appearance of Rodríguez del Padrón's classic *Siete gozos de amor* (Seven Joys of Love), alongside poems by men who are better represented in later *cancioneros*: Juan Agraz (fl. 1430–1450), Juan de Dueñas (circa 1400–circa 1460), Juan de Tapia (fl. 1430–1460), Hugo de Urriés (circa 1405–circa 1490), and Juan de Villalpando (fl. 1440–1460).

Although this collection has a much more modern feel than the *Cancionero de Baena*, it too reflects a vanished world. More than half of the eighty poets named in the rubrics are credited with only one or two poems; about some of the more promising names–García de Pedraza and Gonçalvo de Torquemada–nothing is known, and they are never heard from again. Apart

from the minstrel Martín el Tañedor and his brother Diego, most of them are from the ranks of the aristocracy: a king, a prince, a duke, a count, a *comendador* (military commander), and knights such as Suero de Quiñones, Juan de Merlo, and Alonso de Deza, who are better known for their roles in the Paso Honroso jousting tournament at the Bridge of Órbigo in 1434. Unlike the *Cancionero de Baena,* the *Cancionero de Palacio* boasts not a single cleric among its authors.

A more significant, and perhaps related, difference is that two-thirds of the contents of the *Cancionero de Palacio* are love lyrics. Juan II is ascribed four *canciones,* including one that became famous: "Amor, yo nunca pensé, / aunque poderoso eras, / que podías tener maneras / para trastornar la fe, / fasta agora que lo sé" (O, Love, I never knew, / all-powerful though you might be, / that you had ways / of overturning faith; / but now I do). Álvaro de Luna (1388–1453), author of fifteen lyrics in the *Cancionero de Palacio,* is responsible for one of the most blatant examples of the phenomenon for which María Rosa Lida de Malkiel in 1946 coined the term *hipérbole sagrada* (sacred hyperbole): "Si Dios nuestro salvador / oviera de tomar amiga / fuera mi conpetidor" (If God our savior / were to take a mistress / he would be my rival). In a similar vein, Francisco de Villalpando (fl. 1420–1440) casts Psalm 51 ("Have mercy on me") in an entirely amatory light: each phrase of the Vulgate text is glossed by a stanza applying the Psalmist's words to the poet's lovelorn condition.

Liturgical refrains are a feature of the lyrics of Pedro de Santa Fe (fl. 1418–1434), who with forty-seven texts is the best-represented poet in the *Cancionero de Palacio.* Cleofé Tato has constructed a new identity for him, correcting some of the assumptions of Francisca Vendrell. A university-educated native of Aragón, Santa Fe was employed to buy books for Alfonso V on at least one occasion. He was attached to the Aragonese royal household from 1419 until 1430, when Alfonso awarded him an annuity. His poems can be divided roughly into three groups: love lyrics to a lady to whom he refers by the *senhal* Aymía (Beloved), occasional poems to named female patrons such as Doña Timbor de Cabrera, and a sequence celebrating Alfonso's majesty and major incidents in the first Neapolitan expedition of 1420 to 1423. His imaginative recreation of the leave-taking between Alfonso and Queen María is one of the highlights of the *Cancionero de Palacio.* Given his prominence in this collection, Tato argues, he must have been a much more significant figure than the sparse available evidence indicates.

More typical of the collection as a whole is Juan de Torres (fl. 1420–1450); he comes second to Santa Fe numerically with thirty-four poems, most of them *can-*

Quie mas vos ama no yerra
de qntos vos soes amada
donzella destraña tierra
enesta bre empleada
no vse de voluntad
elq mas vro se llama
no yerra qen mas vos ama

Lope destuniga

Si mis tstes pesamientos
dolor etristes cuydados
enojos
no fuesen grades tormetos
emales desesperados
trabajos
oq pesar cola muerte
qndo me fuese vemda
tomaria
mas es la llaga ta fuerte
q fin de ta mala vida
bien seria

*Folio 11r from the* Cancionero de París 313. *It is unusual among* cancioneros *in that it includes two works of
prose fiction along with the poems (Bibliothèque Nationale, Paris; courtesy of Jane Whetnall).*

*ciones.* He was principally the author of love lyrics, presumably songs, and his work was widely quoted—by the Catalan Pere Torroella (fl. 1430–1465), known as Pedro Torrellas in the Spanish *cancioneros;* by the Conde de Mayorga Juan Pimentel (1409–1437); and in one anonymous *dezir de estribillos* (quoting poem)—although it rarely appears in subsequent *cancioneros.* The verse itself offers few clues to his identity beyond an association with Luna and Juan de Padilla. The proliferation of similar names in chronicles and other documents makes it impossible to establish a biography for him.

Little is known about the life of Suero de Ribera (fl. 1420–1460) except that he participated in both of Alfonso's Neapolitan campaigns. Twenty poems are ascribed to him in sixteen manuscripts, as well as in the *Cancionero general.* His most controversial work is a *misa de amor* (Lovers' Mass) which was mutilated by censors in most of the manuscripts in which it appeared—including the *Cancionero de Palacio.* But he may have been better known to his contemporaries for his *canciones* and for two long *dezires*—a spirited response to Torrellas's misogynistic "Quien bien amando persigue" (Pursuing a lady for love) and an ironic *doctrinal de gentileza* (Guide to Good Conduct), both of which are preserved in multiple copies. He has yet to receive due recognition for having written one of the best-known lyrics of the fifteenth century, *Villancico para unas tres fijas suyas* (Carol that He Made for Three of His Daughters), which was long regarded as Santillana's:

> En una linda floresta
> de muchas flores e rosas
> vi tres donzellas fermosas
> que d'amores han reqüesta;
> et yo con voluntad presta
> lleguéme por conocellas,
> dixo la mayor de ellas
> esta canción muy honesta:
> "Aguardan a mí,
> nunca tales guardas vi."

> (In a pretty grove
> full of roses in bloom
> I saw three fair maidens
> complaining about love;
> and I with ready heart
> made to approach them,
> when the eldest of them
> sang this chaste ditty:
> "They're guarding me,
> guardians like I've never seen.")

The poem is attributed to Santillana in three late printings. Ribera's prior claim only came to light with Vendrell's edition of the *Cancionero de Palacio* in 1945; but, though it was soon supported by the publication of a second early source, Santillana editors have been slow to yield precedence to Suero. His complete poems were edited by Blanca Periñán in 1968.

There is evidence for the existence, about a decade after the monumental endeavor of Baena and the haphazard accumulation of the *Cancionero de Palacio,* of multiple copies of much smaller compilations that can be classified as anthologies. This evidence takes the form of a batch of *cancioneros* from the Aragonese royal library at Naples that today are in the Bibliothèque Nationale in Paris. Together with six manuscripts scattered in other European libraries, they make up three families that were described and analyzed by Alberto Vàrvaro in 1964. One of these families, which he calls *a,* derives from an archetype of Peninsular origin that was copied and cannibalized in Naples during the 1460s and 1470s. The best surviving example is *Cancionero de París 313* in the Bibliothèque Nationale; it is little studied because the quality of the texts is poor, and none is unique to it. Nonetheless, it represents a milestone in the history of the *cancionero.* It is a small quarto volume of 193 paper leaves comprising nineteen of what were originally twenty quires, neatly copied in the same hand throughout from an exemplar that was evidently in the same format. Aside from the first quire, only 1 leaf is missing. The four prose pieces and seventy poems that make up the work can be dated from the mid to late 1440s: a terminus a quo of 1444 is provided by Santillana's letter of dedication that accompanies his *Comedieta de Ponza* (Little *comedia* of Ponza).

The first half of the anthology consists of a mixture of standard long and short love poems, a more sober section headed by Pérez de Guzmán's *Proverbios* (Proverbs), and an exchange of letters in the style of Ovid's *Heroides* between Troilo and Bresaida (Troilus and Cressida) by Rodríguez del Padrón. A block of Santillana texts—the *Proverbios,* the *Comedieta de Ponza,* and the Sonnets—recognizable as the collection he sent to Violante de Prades, take up most of the second half of the manuscript, which ends with a further miscellany of love poems. Since there is no obvious sign of compiler intervention—organization by author or genre, for example—it remains a matter of surmise whether the ensemble represents a deliberate selection or an accidental coming together of disparate elements that had previously circulated independently. The inclusion of prose fiction is unusual; along with the small size of the collection, it points to a product designed for a private, probably female, readership.

The contents of this *cancionero* show continuity with the *Cancionero de Palacio* in, for example, Enríquez's *Testamento,* Santillana's *Infierno de los enamorados* and *Querella de amor,* Suero de Ribera's *Misa de amor,* and Rodríguez del Padrón's *Siete gozos de amor.* They are

*Folio 350r from the manuscript for the* Cancionero de Gallardo-San Román, *copied around 1454.*
*At least 80 of the more than 474 leaves are missing (Real Academia de la Historia,*
*Madrid; courtesy of Jane Whetnall).*

joined by new poems, many of which became classics. Mena, Lope de Stúñiga (or Estúñiga, circa 1407–1477), and the Bachiller Alfonso de la Torre (fl. 1440–1460) emerge as the leading lights of the 1440s.

Although they have not received the critical acclaim accorded to his moral and political works, several of Mena's love poems were extremely popular with his contemporaries and survive in ten or more manuscripts. "Ya no sufre mi cuidado" (No more will my mind be prey) is one of a pair of *dezires* that stand out from the rest of his lyrics because they carry the poet's signature in the *fin* or *cabo* (envoi); the other, "Guay d'aquel hombre que mira" (Woe betide the man who gazes), would have been in the missing first quire of the *Cancionero de París 313*. (It is known that this poem–and four others–are missing because in two related manuscripts that have survived intact the opening sets of poems are in identical sequence with each other and with the corresponding part of the *Cancionero de París 313*.) "Ya no sufre mi cuidado," the longer and better known of the two, consists of an urgent but strangely detached catalogue of pleas for kinder treatment from the beloved, involving arcane imagery and some discreet echoes of Virgil and Dante.

The author of twenty-five extant poems, Lope de Stúñiga was the most successful love poet of the manuscript era (1430 to 1480). A grandson of Charles III of Navarre, he was one of the codefenders with Suero de Quiñones of the Paso Honroso joust in 1434 and has a well-documented and turbulent life story to match his literary persona. Apart from a fleeting appearance at the end of the *Cancionero de Palacio* that is thought to be a late addition to the manuscript, he formally enters the records in this Paris *cancionero* with eight poems, including his four best-known *dezires*.

Stúñiga's contemporary reputation evidently rested on his consummate rendering of the lyric complaint, which he refined in a display of verbal pyrotechnics–occasionally at the expense of meaning, as in "Llorad, mis llantos, llorad" (Weep, my sobbing, weep). His best-known poem, "Si mis tristes pensamientos" (If my sad thoughts), is important today as the first widely disseminated example of the *sextilla doble con pie quebrado* (twelve-line stanza with half-lines, rhyming *abcabcdefdef*), which Jorge Manrique adopted for his *Coplas a la muerte de su padre* (Elegy on the Death of His Father, circa 1476–1479). It provoked an indignant *respuesta por consonantes* (rhyme-for-rhyme reply) by his contemporary Pero Guillén de Segovia "porque [Stúñiga] se loó de mucho amador" (because Stúñiga boasted that he was a great lover); stanza 4 was quoted by Torrellas; Lucrezia Borgia copied stanza 5 in a letter to Pietro Bembo; and Gómez Manrique deplored the fickle posture of stanza 3:

Yo quise mudar amor
en otra filosomía
no tan buena;
mas no se mudó dolor,
ni jamás se mudaría
de mi pena;
lo qual muestra la gloria
de que só meresçedor,
es a saber:
que siempre quede memoria
yo ser el más amador
que puede ser.

(I tried to switch my love
to another face,
less fair;
but the pain did not shift,
and would never shift
from my grief;
all of which goes to show
the glory I have earned,
and it is this:
to be remembered always
as the greatest lover
who has ever lived.)

"El triste quc más morir" (The wretch who would sooner die) is the longest-lived love *dezir* of the Spanish Middle Ages: it is preserved in eleven fifteenth-century and four sixteenth-century manuscript collections, as well as in successive editions of the *Cancionero general*. In this collection it is mistakenly attributed to Stúñiga. The real author, el Bachiller Alfonso de la Torre, is a more shadowy figure, despite having written one of the first best-sellers of Spanish literature, the *Visión deleitable* (Vision of Delight, circa 1450), and serving as tutor to Carlos, prince of Viana (d. 1461). He is credited with a further nine poems in other sources, but his poetic reputation rests on this one long *dezir* of twenty-five *décimas* (stanzas of ten octosyllabic lines) and a five-line *fin*. "El triste que más morir" is framed as a letter of farewell to his mistress. It is unusual in expressing gratitude for favors received, which challenges modern assumptions about the courtly love ethic in *cancionero* poetry:

Ay, señora, por te amar
yo me vi tanto penado
que pensé desesperar
no entendiendo de alcançar
que fuesse de ti amado;
y después, tu señoría
sabe el grand bien que me diste,
queriendo la dicha mía
que alegre fuesse un día
y toda mi vida triste.

(O lady, for love of you
I was in such pain
I almost despaired,

never thinking I could attain
your love and affection;
and then, you know,
a great favor you granted:
it was just my luck
to be happy for one day
and wretched for the rest of my life.)

Torre is one of the few *cancionero* poets to be cited with approval by Juan de Valdés; he is praised by Juan Boscán (circa 1495–1542) for the "fuerça de su estilo" (power of his style).

Assembled around 1454, about ten years after the *Cancionero de París 313,* the *Cancionero de Gallardo-San Román* presents yet another paradigm. It resembles nothing so much as a work-in-progress compilation that could have been part of the stock of a commercial copy shop. A first scribe started a fresh quire for each author, leaving the rest of the quire blank. Other hands intervened to complete poems, to add new poems and new poets, and also to tear out leaves before the collection was bound and foliated; once bound, it suffered further depredations and additions. The initial project was evidently abandoned: the manuscript has lost more than 80 of its original complement of more than 474 leaves. Until a proper analysis has been completed, one can only speculate about its parameters, the original sequence of texts, or the nature of its sources. With nearly 300 poems, including some quite long ones, the *Cancionero de Gallardo-San Román* must have have been, in intention at least, a compilation to rival the *Cancionero de Baena.* As though to mark that intention, the volume opens with a *dezir* of 218 stanzas by Baena, "Para rey tan excelente" (For so Excellent a King), which exists in no other source. (Dutton and González Cuenca include it in the appendix to their 1993 edition of the *Cancionero de Baena.*)

Famous poems by established names of the first half of the century–Pérez de Guzmán, Santillana, Mena, and Stúñiga–are present in considerable numbers; trailing them are some minor figures whose works had been collected only sporadically in previous compilations. This *cancionero* is an important source for the works of Valera and of Agraz, an accomplished occasional poet who specialized in elegies. Although it is organized in principle by author, the scheme is punctuated at various points by themed series. Toward the end of the manuscript a series on the birth of Juan II ushers in a concentration of approximately thirty texts by *Cancionero de Baena* veterans Imperial, Villasandino, Fray Diego de Valencia, Gonzalo Martínez de Medina, and Ruy Páez de Ribera, sometimes with new attributions. Earlier in the manuscript two clusters of poems on the death of Luna and the birth of the Infante

Alfonso in 1453 provide an approximate terminus a quo for the collection.

The lyrical center of the *Cancionero de Gallardo-San Román* is a miscellany of the works of individuals such as Manuel de Guzmán and Toledo, for whom it is the only source, and Urriés and Pedro de Escavias, who are represented more fully in other collections. The manuscript includes important *dezires de estribillos* by the Conde de Mayorga and Francisco Bocanegra (fl. 1430–1450) and a gloss by Pedro de Quiñones (fl. 1430–1450) one of the oldest *cancionero* lyrics, a fourteenth-century Galician song, "Ay donas porque tristura." (O ladies for whom in sorrow). It also includes probably the earliest extant texts of two *cancionero* standards. Suero de Ribera's "Non teniendo que perder" (With nothing to lose) is a satire advising readers how to emulate the ideal gallant or man-about-court's melancholic posture, dress code, and tastes in literature, food, and music. It is preserved in seven other sources, including the first two editions of the *Cancionero general.* In terms of popularity, however, it is no match for the other standard, Torrellas's misogynistic diatribe, "Quien bien amando persigue," which exists today in more than sixteen manuscripts.

Torrellas was one of the first fifteenth-century Catalan poets who also composed in Castilian. (Twenty-four bilingual Catalan-Castilian poets are listed by Montserrat Ganges Garriga.) He was a distinguished man of letters, an author of literary epistles and prose treatises, and a pivotal figure bridging the Catalan-Castilian divide. "Quien bien amando persigue" is by far his best-known work. It provoked four contemporary *respuestas por consonantes* and made him go down in history as a woman hater, a posthumous reputation for which his fictional persona pays dearly in Juan de Flores's "Grisel y Mirabella" (Grisel and Mirabella, 1474–1475?). To judge from their relatively low survival rate–only about eighteen are extant–his Spanish love *dezires* circulated rather less widely, but the full extent of Torrellas's influence in Castile has still to be assessed. Of great interest from the literary-historical point of view is one of his Catalan poems, "Tant mon voler s'és dat amors" (So much in thrall to love), which quotes eight *cancionero* poets as authorities on love.

The *Cancionero de Gallardo-San Román* reveals Juan de Dueñas as one of the most versatile and prolific poets of his generation, equally at ease with allegorical narrative, semitheatrical dialogues, and simple love lyrics. From historical documents and from his occasional poems Vendrell was able in 1933 to trace the profile of an energetic courtier in service successively with the kings of Castile, Navarre, and Aragón. Most of his seventy extant compositions are found in this *cancionero;* nine are in the *Cancionero de Palacio,* but, with the excep-

*Page from a fifteenth-century manuscript for* Le Livre des echecs amoureux, *with an illustration of the author meeting the goddess Diana. Situations in which narrators encounter pagan divinities occur in many Spanish dream-vision poems, including Íñigo López de Mendoza, Marqués de Santillana's "El Sueño" in the* Cancionero de Gallardo-San Román *(Bibliothèque Nationale, Paris; courtesy of Jane Whetnall).*

tion of *La nao de amor* (The Ship of Love) which is copied in thirteen manuscripts, they occur only sporadically elsewhere. "En altas ondas de amar" (On the high seas of loving) is an amatory allegory with, according to Marco Presotto, a political subtext relating to the poet's capture and imprisonment by the Genoese in 1439. His *Misa de amores* is longer and more elaborate than Suero de Ribera's *Misa de amor;* no signs of influence either way have been detected. The literary allusions in this and other poems by Dueñas are a useful guide to the currency of chivalric romances in the mid fifteenth century.

The *Cancionero de Herberay* (named after a sixteenth-century owner, Nicolas de Herberay des Essarts) is a collection that is clearly rooted in a particular location–the Navarrese court–at a particular time: circa 1463 is the date given to it by Charles V. Aubrun, who edited it in 1951. It is a fine manuscript of 212 leaves, copied in a single hand, comprising 7 short prose pieces and 202 poems. It has an extant cousin in the *Cancionero de Modena* (circa 1466), and this relationship has allowed some reconstruction of its compositional history.

At the heart of the collection is a nucleus of about ninety poems that make up almost the whole of the *Cancionero de Modena*. This core, which is more complete in the *Cancionero de Modena,* comprises a selection of love poems of the period 1420 to 1440 by authors such as Mena, Stúñiga, Torrellas, and Santa Fe. It includes a run of *canciones* and four sonnets by Juan de Villalpando (fl. 1450–1470), the only fifteenth-century Spanish poet besides Santillana to have attempted that form. Whereas the *Cancionero de Modena* gives gravitas to this predominantly lightweight selection by sandwiching it between Santillana's *Proverbios* and Mena's *Canta tú christiana musa* (Sing Christian Muse), in the *Cancionero de Herberay* the core is embedded in more varied material of local provenance. The prose miscellany that opens the volume features work by Santillana and Torrellas and an unattributed piece of quasi-Ovidian fiction by Rodríguez del Padrón, *Epístola de Madreselva a Mauseol* (Epistle from Madreselva to Mauseolus). The anonymous treatise *Leyes de amor* (Laws of Love) is probably also by Torrellas. A second element in the *Cancionero de Herberay* that is alien to the *Cancionero de Modena* is the handful of occasional poems by Diego de Sevilla (fl. 1450–1470), a mystery woman called Vayona, and Juan de Valladolid (circa 1403–circa 1475), all of them unique. These poems, some of which occur after the prose pieces, others at the end of the volume, link the collection to the circle of Leonor, Condesa de Foix, who had become heiress to the crown of Navarre when her sister, Blanca, died in 1464. (Leonor became queen on 19 January 1479 but died fifteen days later.) Part of the same group is the anonymous *juego trobado* (parlor game in verse) "En

Ávila por la A" (In Avila for A), a burlesque narrative describing the mock journey of a king from town to town. It is an alphabet poem: each town the king visits is named for a letter of the alphabet, A through Z, and in successive pairs of stanzas a different letter provides the initial for the names of his host and hostess, the food they prepare for him, the wood of the tree they burn, a proverb, and a song that is sung for his entertainment. Aubrun has identified some of the characters mentioned as mostly minor figures who belonged to the Navarrese court between 1450 and 1462.

Interleaved with the Navarrese poems is a block of some forty anonymous *dezires* and *canciones* that Aubrun ascribes to Urriés, who is named in the *cabo* to one of them and can safely be identified with the "Mossén Ugo" to whom *Leyes de amor* is dedicated. Among the love lyrics and longer poems of social comment is an evidently autobiographical account of a real-life courtship: the narrator of the *Dezir del casado,* (Poem of the Married Man), tells how he wooed and won the girl who became his wife. As Aubrun surmises, many of the surrounding poems can be read as part of this autobiography. In "Unmasking the Devout Lover: Hugo de Urriés in the *Cancionero de Herberay*" (1997) Jane Whetnall shows that poems ascribed to Urriés in the *Cancionero de Gallardo-San Román,* for example, that display the same rather puritanical devoutness and interest in the phenomenology of love conform stylistically to the anonymous *dezires* in the *Cancionero de Herberay*.

Another component that the *Cancionero de Herberay* adds to the nucleus it has in common with the *Cancionero de Modena* is a cluster of traditional-style lyrics and the contrafactum (a song produced by setting new words to an existing melody) of a ballad from the Roncesvalles cycle. Whether authentic cullings from the folk repertoire or learned imitations, seven poems from the *Cancionero de Herberay* were included in Dámaso Alonso and José Manuel Blecua's 1956 anthology of *poesía de tipo tradicional* (traditional poetry). Whetnall argues that the various components of the *Cancionero de Herberay,* in the form of loose sheets, booklets, and a *Modena*-style *cancionero,* had been the property of Urriés's wife and that at some point, perhaps after her death, they were copied into a seamless whole. The extant manuscript is a copy of a copy of this library-in-miniature.

Fernando de la Torre (circa 1416–circa 1475) was a native of Burgos who traveled widely in his youth and lost his right arm fighting in the service of Juan II. His *Libro de las veynte cartas e qüistiones* (Book of Twenty Letters and Debates, circa 1456–1465), a *cancionero* in all but name, provides an extremely important window on fifteenth-century cultural practices. Incorporating more prose than verse, it is primarily a record of the literary

*Folio 196r from the* Cancionero de Herberay, *compiled in the Navarrese court around 1463. It includes poems
by Diego de Sevilla, a woman known only as Vayona, and Juan de Valladolid that are
found in no other collection (British Library; courtesy of Jane Whetnall).*

letters exchanged between the poet and about fifteen correspondents of both sexes, including the young Enrique IV. The second half of the manuscript is taken up by more than 120 short fixed-form lyrics, about a quarter of which are only four- or five-line *esparsas,* but notable also are the rubrics denoting lyric forms—*cossaute, repullón* (witty gibe), *rondel* (Fr. *rondeau*)—found rarely, if at all, elsewhere. The sociocultural value of this collection is paramount, from the dedicatory preface to Leonor, Condesa de Foix, which tells of Fernando de la Torre's role as purveyor of reading matter to the ladies in his circle, to the occasional verse exchanged with his fellow poets Stúñiga, Francisco Bocanegra, and Alfonso de la Torre. His poetry is little known outside this manuscript, except for the *Juego de naipes* (Game of Cards) "Magnificencia y virtud" (Magnificence and virtue), which he dedicated to Mencía Enríquez, Condesa de Castañeda. It belongs to the genre of parlor-game compositions and is accompanied by prose instructions specifying how the deck of cards is to be illustrated.

Varvaro suggests 1465 as the date for a lost Neapolitan compilation that he labels *an,* which was the parent of three magnificent *cancioneros* copied in mainland Italy in the 1460s or 1470s. All three are deluxe folio volumes, with illuminated frontispieces and decorated initials, copied on vellum in a fine humanistic script. They are superior in execution to any extant *cancionero* produced in Spain. Of the three, the *Cancionero de Roma* (circa 1470) has the most reliable texts, but it has dropped more than thirty poems from the common archetype. The *Cancionero de la Marciana* or *de Venecia* (circa 1470) is even more reduced, partly because of mutilations caused by the removal of Suero de Ribera's *Misa de amor.* It provides, however, parallel-text translations into Italian verse of about the first dozen poems.

The most complete reflection of the parent compilation is the *Cancionero de Stúñiga* or *Estúñiga* (circa 1465), so named because the first piece is by Stúñiga. It comprises 162 items and is a composite of two main sources, a selection of forty-five poems from the *a* tradition, of which the *Cancionero de París 313* is the best extant example, and a larger number of texts, the *n* tradition, of Neapolitan provenance. The Peninsular component is made up of predictable standards from the *a* family: love poems by Mena, Lope de Stúñiga, Santillana, and Rodríguez del Padrón, and a few strays from other sources, such as Fernando de la Torre's *Juego de naipes.* These pieces are grafted onto a block of more-recent poems composed in Naples by a small group of expatriate Spaniards who formed part of Alfonso's court in the late 1440s and 1450s and stayed on into the reign of his successor, Ferrante (Fernando I, king of Naples, 1458–1494).

Not all of the poets in this group have been securely identified. Juan de Andújar (fl. 1445–1460), for example, is unknown except as the author of four poems, one of them a Lovers' Hell, "Como procede Fortuna" (When Fortune goes into action), based on Santillana's *Infierno de los enamorados.* Juan de Tapia, on the other hand, has a well-documented life. He participated in Alfonso's second expeditionary force to Naples in 1432 and was taken captive after the naval defeat at Ponza in 1435. He is represented by six poems in the *Cancionero de Palacio,* most notably a *dezir* written in prison in Genoa. After his release he stayed on in Naples. The sixteen poems in the *Cancionero de Stúñiga* are a mix of *canciones* and occasional poems addressed to individual ladies of the court and to Ferrante after the death of Alfonso. Tapia is one of many Neapolitan literati to compose in honor of Alfonso's mistress, Lucrezia d'Alagno.

Carvajales (fl. 1445–1460) is the most prominent poet of the group and leaves a legacy of more than fifty poems. Nothing is known about his life, and even the form of his name is uncertain: he calls himself simply Carvajal in the text of one autobiographical poem, but the rubrics in all three *cancioneros* refer to him consistently as Carvajales. His technical and emotional range is considerable. He wrote wooing poems to Lucrezia d'Alagno on behalf of Alfonso, as well as a long prose epistle to Alfonso purporting to be from Alfonso's grass widow, María de Castilla, and a lament for the death of one of Ferrante's captains, Jaumot Torres, in 1460. The bulk of his corpus is made up of *canciones,* two of them in Italian. He is also the author of two ballads and several pastourelles in a range of styles that at times recall the *cantigas de serrana* of the *Libro de buen amor* (Book of Good Love, ascribed to Juan Ruiz, the archpriest of Hita, circa 1283–circa 1350) and at others the more enigmatic and decorous encounters of Francisco Imperial's dream-vision poems. In one of them a squire despairing of his lady's love is offered some cynical advice: "Amad, amadores, muger que non sabe, / a quien toda cosa paresca ser nueva; / que quanto más sabe muger, menos vale, / segund por exemplo lo hemos de Eva" (Take care to love an ignorant woman, / to whom all things seem fresh and new; / for as the example of Eve shows, / the more a woman knows, the worse it is for you). Carvajales's evident indebtedness to native models such as Santillana and Juan Ruiz and motifs such as the *niña precoz* (child woman) and the *fonte frida* (cold spring) has to be weighed alongside an equally clear debt to Petrarch. Although he was susceptible to influences of all kinds, Carvajales's poetry is unlikely to have left any trace on the poetry of mainland Spain. Only two of his lyrics, both *canciones,* are found in Peninsular sources.

*Folio 1r from the manuscript for the* Cancionero de Stúñiga, *so called because the first poem in the collection is by Lope de Stúñiga.*
*The collection was compiled circa 1465 (Biblioteca Nacional, Madrid; courtesy of Jane Whetnall).*

The majority of extant *cancioneros* record the poetic production of the period 1430 to 1465. After about 1470 a marked falling off in the register of poetic manuscripts can be observed; *cancioneros* went on being made, especially *cancioneros* of individual poets, but no contemporary collection of love lyric has survived from the reigns of Enrique IV or Fernando and Isabel (the Catholic Monarchs).

One of the best witnesses to the poetry of this time, the *Cancionero de Pero Guillén de Segovia,* is extant only in an eighteenth-century copy, full of gaps and misreadings, from a lost manuscript that must have been compiled around 1480. Although the scribe was scrupulous in assigning nearly every piece to a single source, one cannot be sure that his exemplar was not itself a composite of several parts. A large compendium of more than two hundred poems, it is relatively compact in its chronological range, being made up almost entirely of verse from the 1460s and 1470s by Gómez Manrique and his circle. As John G. Cummins points out in "Pero Guillén de Segovia y el ms. 4.114" (1973), this collection reflects a milieu akin to that of the *Cancionero de Baena.* Much of the poetry is occasional, interactive, featuring bureaucrats and clerics in battles of wit with the landed aristocracy. As well as a series of long single masterworks such as Guevara's *Sepultura de amor* (Burial of Love), Diego de San Pedro's *Siete angustias* (Seven Sorrows), Fray Íñigo de Mendoza's *Vita Christi* (Life of Christ), and an incomplete text of Jorge Manrique's *Coplas,* it includes verse by three poets who in different ways characterized the literary establishment of the time: Pero Guillén de Segovia (circa 1413–circa 1475), Antón de Montoro (1404–1477), and Juan Álvarez Gato (circa 1440–circa 1510). All three were long-lived, productive, professional writers of *converso* (Jewish convert to Christianity) origin.

Prose and verse by Pero Guillén de Segovia occupy the first third of the collection that bears his name. His biography has been largely pieced together from the prologues and rubrics in this and another eighteenth-century copy of a lost *cancionero.* Born in Seville, he spent the early part of his career at the court of Juan II but fell on hard times after the disgrace of Luna, who was probably his patron; he emerged from penury a decade later, in 1463, when he was taken into the household of Alonso Carrillo, the archbishop of Toledo, who gave him employment as an accountant. He is the author of love poems, a rare composition in defense of Luna (1453), and one on Enrique IV's accession (1454). Like Manrique, Guillén wrote a continuation to "Canta tú christiana musa," which Mena had left unfinished at his death; also like Manrique, Guillén took exception to the extravagant boast of Stúñiga's "Si mis tristes pensamientos." Serious, learned, and devout, he

is probably best known today for his verse translations of the Seven Penitential Psalms. Most of his major works are too long for modern anthologists; his longest composition–230 stanzas of *arte mayor*–is "Oyd maravillas del siglo presente" (Hear marvels of the present time) is a poem of epic proportions based on Alfonso de la Torre's *Visión deleitable.* Toward the end of his career Guillén compiled a *Gaya ciencia* (Art of Poetry), a dictionary of rhymes that survives in one fifteenth-century manuscript.

Montoro evidently depended on writing to supplement his income as a *ropero* (tailor or secondhand-clothes dealer) in Córdoba. With more than 160 poems to his credit, he is one of the most prolific *cancionero* authors after Villasandino, and his work was widely disseminated: it is extant in more than twenty manuscripts and printed volumes. Disreputable and disputatious, he is best known for many ad hominem exchanges with other poets, some of them undoubtedly stage-managed, in which he fields insults about his Jewish ancestry. He also wrote begging poems, devotional poems, and pointed love lyrics. He created an outcry with his blasphemous tribute to Isabel: "Alta reyna soberana, / si fuérades antes vós / que la hija de Santana, / de vós el hijo de Dios / recibiera carne humana" (High sovereign queen, / if you had been born / before the daughter of St. Anne, / from you the Son of God would have / received his human form). Four modern editions of his poetry have been published.

Guillén's and Montoro's younger contemporary, Álvarez Gato of Madrid, is not as well represented in the *Cancionero de Pero Guillén de Segovia* as they are, but a personal *cancionero* exists for him. From the information provided in his prose works and epigraphs his writing career can be divided into two phases: the love poems and sociopolitical verse he composed for his friend Hernán Mexía of Jaén and members of the Manrique clan, and the religious verse to which he devoted himself after undergoing a spiritual conversion: "D'aquí adelante no hay cosa trobada ni escrita syno de devoción y buena dotrina" (From this point onward there is no piece of writing, prose or verse, that is not religious or of sound doctrine). His down-to-earth poetic diction is larded with proverbs, and he is also one of the earliest court poets to have found inspiration in folk song. His *a lo divino* glosses (reworkings of known texts in a spiritual register) and *contrafacta* provide the first documentation of several traditional lyrics, such as "Nuevas te traigo carillo" (News I bring, sweetheart) and "Amor no me dejes / que me moriré" (Love, do not leave me, I shall die). In contemplative or moralistic veins he is persuasive and lyrical, but he is at his best in epigram mode. The poem that has received most attention from critics and anthologists is his *esparsa* on being proposed to by his mistress: "Dezís: 'Casémonos los dos / por que d'este mal no muera." / Señora, no plega a Dios, / syendo mi señora vós, / c'os haga mi compañera" (You say "Let's get married, / lest this illness kill me": / Lady, God forbid / that, having you as my lady, / I should make you my mate).

Poems by Guillén, Montoro, and Álvarez Gato also found their way into the *Cancionero de Oñate-Castañeda* (named for two successive owners of the manuscript, the Condes de Oñate and the Condesa de Castañeda). Compiled and copied in the mid 1480s, it is another large volume, comprising more than ninety works by sixteen poets. In his introduction to the 1990 edition of the *Cancionero de Oñate-Castañeda,* edited by Dorothy Sherman Severin and Fiona Maguire, Michel Garcia says that the work consists of a carefully chosen sample of the most weighty poems of the previous half-century, starting with what amounts to a personal *cancionero* of Pérez de Guzmán and including works by Santillana, Mena, Gómez Manrique, one of the few manuscript copies of Jorge Manrique's *Coplas a la muerte de su padre,* Guillén's Penitential Psalms, and what appear to be early drafts of Fray Íñigo de Mendoza's *Vita Christi* and San Pedro's *Pasión trobada* (Passion in Verse).

Given the overwhelmingly elegiac character of the collection, the presence of two lyric interludes is refreshing. The poet known as Costana (fl. 1470–1504) is the principal casualty of the mutilation suffered by the manuscript, as the four last stanzas of his long dream-vision poem "Al tiempo que se levanta" (At the hour of reveille) occur after a lacuna of twelve leaves. More complete is *Conjuros que fizo Costana a su amiga* (Oaths which Costana Swore to His Mistress), as the poem is titled in a later source. "La grandeza de mis males" (The magnitude of my sufferings), (the stanza form of Manriqué's *Coplas*) in twenty-four *coplas manriqueñas,* is the palinode to end all palinodes: invoking a litany of lovelorn bestiary creatures and mythical heroines, the poetic voice wishes all manner of horrible fates on his ungrateful mistress—only to retract all of it contritely at the end. Costana's contribution to the poetry of the period is small but significant, and he is one of the growing number of late-fifteenth-century poets in whom Petrarchan influence has been detected. The historical man was an elusive figure known, like so many other *cancionero* poets, by surname only until an almost certain identity was found for him in 2000 by Vicenç Beltran. According to Beltran, he was Comendador Francisco de Costana, a member of the royal chapel who was on Isabel's payroll from 1484 until his death in 1504.

The second incongruous lyric interlude in the *Cancionero de Oñate-Castañeda* occurs at the end of the manuscript, the place conventionally reserved for the compiler's own works. Pedro de Escavias (circa 1417–circa 1485), mayor of the frontier town of Andújar and author of the prose works *Repertorio de príncipes de España* (Register of the Princes of Spain, circa 1475) and probably of the anonymous *Hechos del Condestable don Miguel Lucas de Iranzo* (Deeds of the Constable Don Miguel Lucas de Iranzo, 1473–1474), also wrote at least nineteen poems. Five are preserved in the *Cancionero de Gallardo-San Román;* the *Cancionero de Oñate-Castañeda* collects four of these and fourteen more under the heading "coplas y canciones de pedro descauias syendo paje de el Rey y harto mochacho" (poems and songs by Pedro de Escavias when he was page to the king and quite young). They are mostly love lyrics but include what appears to be an authentic *romance noticiero* (broadsheet ballad), "Yo me só el ynfante Enrique" (I am Prince Henry), which must have been composed soon after the death of the Infante of Aragón from a wound sustained in the Battle of Olmedo in 1445. The manuscript breaks off in the middle of "Virtuoso condestable" (Virtuous constable), a rousing poem in praise of Miguel Lucas de Iranzo's frontier exploits with extensive prose commentaries by an eyewitness to the events—presumably Escavias himself. Four of the lyrics in the *Cancionero de Oñate-Castañeda* show clear signs of authorial reworking. The witty *pastourelle* "Llegando cansado yo" (Arriving Weary) acquires six stanzas not present in the *Cancionero de Gallardo-San Román* version, and a surprise ending. Whether Escavias was the compiler of the collection has yet to be proved.

The sobriety of the *Cancionero de Oñate-Castañeda* brings it close in mood to the kind of poetry that was being produced by the early Spanish presses. Among the earliest material printed—as far as records show—are *pliegos sueltos* (chapbooks, or small booklets of verse); more than eighty verse items published between 1474 and 1511 are extant, the majority devotional or moralizing works. It would be a mistake to infer too much from these figures about changes in readership brought about by printing. The preponderance of religious verse could simply mean that religious ephemera—the more respectable end of the market—has a better chance of survival than other ephemera. In any case, printers took advantage of the availability of free copy by recycling national treasures such as Mena's *Laberinto de Fortuna* (Labyrinth of Fortune) and the *Proverbios* of Santillana, which were soon joined by Manrique's *Coplas.* Successive editions of the selected works of Fray Íñigo de Mendoza grew in size, perhaps in response to a favorable reception, and were bulked out with texts by other poets.

The first substantial printed anthology, the *Cancionero de Ramón de Llavia,* was published in Saragossa between 1484 and 1488. The compiler, Llavia, boasts

*Folios 152v and 153r of the manuscript for a dictionary of rhymes compiled by Pero Guillén de Segovia, for whom a cancionero is named (Biblioteca Nacional, Madrid; courtesy of Jane Whetnall)*

in his dedication to Francisquina de Bardaxí of his "diligencia en hauer escogido de muchas obras catholicas puestas por coplas las más esmeradas y perfectas" (zeal in having picked out the most polished and excellent of the many Catholic poetic works in circulation). This claim to eclecticism is borne out by the contents: twenty-four poems by twelve authors and a chronological range that spans the entire century. The poems are nearly all long, devotional or moralistic in character, and include some established favorites of the early printing market. The selection also displays a markedly feminine bias: hymns on the Joys, Sorrows, and Coronation of the Virgin Mary; Pérez de Guzmán's *Doctrina que dieron a Sarra* (Instruction Given to Sara); and Fray Íñigo de Mendoza's contribution to the *querelle des femmes,* "the woman question," the centuries-long debate on the merits or demerits of the female sex, "En este mundo disforme" (In this misshapen world). The lively *arte mayor* debate with a *donzella* (maiden) by Fernán Sánchez Calavera (fl. 1400–1410), "Señora muy linda, sabed que vos amo" (Most fair lady, know that I love you) otherwise only preserved in the *Cancionero de Baena,* is a protofeminist text in which the lady has the last word.

The last two decades of the fifteenth century also encompass the first examples of another kind of *cancionero: cancioneros musicales* (songbooks with musical notation) that record the polyphonic repertoire of the singers and instrumentalists that made up a court or cathedral chapel. Sacred pieces in Latin and vernacular hymns and carols are found alongside secular songs of all kinds, both courtly and traditional. Many French and Italian songbooks survive from the second half of the fifteenth century, and more than twenty include one or two Spanish songs. The earliest extant songbook of Hispanic provenance comes from the court of Naples and includes a typical mixture of three- and four-voice part-songs in Latin, French, and Italian, as well as Spanish. In songbooks the lyrics are usually incomplete, often garbled, and always unattributed; only the composer or arranger of the music is named. Although the textual concordance with poetry collections is small, the *cancionero musicales* confirm that several short lyrics collected as poems were also performed as songs.

The earlier of the two principal fifteenth-century Spanish songbooks, the *Cancionero musical de la Colombina,* so named because the manuscript is in the Biblioteca Colombina in Seville, was compiled in the 1490s. In its present state it includes settings for nearly one hundred items: love songs, Christmas carols, and Latin motets. Among the unattributed courtly pieces that make up the first half of the collection are many of the well-known lyrics of the day, such as "Nunca fue pena mayor" (No greater sorrow), a favorite subject for gloss and quotation, and one *canción* each by Rodríguez del Padrón, Santillana, and Mena. The traditional repertoire is represented by the first appearance of "Niña y viña / peral y habar / malo es de guardar" (Young girl and vineyard / peartree and bean patch / need a watchful eye) and a setting for the Easter Sunday trope glossed by Álverez Gato, "Dic nobis, Maria / quid vidisti in via" (Tell us, Mary, what did you see on the way?).

More important, because of its size, is the *Cancionero musical de Palacio,* which is the musical record of King Fernando's royal chapel. It was copied in phases from the 1490s to 1520, mostly by a single hand, and incorporates additions to the chapel repertoire following the death of Isabel in 1504. It includes the settings for more than 450 texts; the table of contents lists nearly 100 more, lost with their missing leaves, some of which have been identified or even recovered from other sources. The concordance with poetry collections is much higher than for the *Cancionero musical de la Colombina;* the author best represented is Juan del Encina (1468–1529 / 1530), who is also named as composer of more than seventy arrangements. The contents are incontrovertible evidence of the importance of folk song in court circles: the *Cancionero musical de Palacio* preserves settings for thirty-eight traditional ballads and countless *villancicos* (popular lyric with opening refrain), including "En Ávila, mis ojos" (In Ávila, in light of my eyes), "Tres morillas m'enamoran" (Three Moorish girls have captured my heart), and "Al alba venid, buen amigo" (Come at dawn, sweet friend).

The *Cancionero de Ramón de Llavia* included a few living poets in its selection: Álvarez Gato, Fray Íñigo de Mendoza, and Gómez Manrique. By the 1490s other new writers, such as San Pedro, Rodrigo de Reinosa, and the Comendador Román, were alert to the impact of printing and the opportunity it afforded for quality control and protection from plagiarism. One major author who was quick to take advantage of the new technology was Encina, who became the first European poet to supervise the printing of his own works. The first edition of his individual *cancionero* appeared in 1496, before he was thirty.

Throughout this period the presses had been constant in their tendency to promote moral and doctrinal works. When the *Cancionero general* was published in 1511, it filled a yawning gap in both the early printed and the manuscript provisions for love poetry. Hernando del Castillo amassed material for twenty years before he handed his manuscript to the typesetters in December 1509: it included more than 1,000 compositions by more than 180 poets. Castillo explains the rationale of this extraordinarily ambitious undertaking in a prologue dedicated to his patron, the second Conde de Oliva, Serafín de Centellas y Cardona. His aim, he says, was to assemble all the verse he could find by authors from Mena onward "que en este género de escrevir auctoridad tienen en nuestro tiempo" (who in this field of writing have some authority in our era). To date none of Castillo's sources has been identified. Since more than half the contents of the *Cancionero general* are known only through this collection or one of its derivatives, the constraints on Castillo's selection and the criteria for inclusion are little understood. He avoids much that was already in print: for example, Jorge Manrique's *Coplas,* Santillana's *Proverbios,* Mena's *Laberinto de fortuna,* anything by Fray Íñigo de Mendoza or Fray Ambrosio Montesino, and all but a few poems by Encina. He also shows a clear preference for love lyric and recreational, rather than moral-didactic or political, poetry.

The texts are arranged in part by author, in part by genre. A modest opening section of devotional poems leads into the first group of individual sections, headed by Santillana and including Stúñiga, Mena, and Gómez Manrique among the old names and Luis de Vivero, Diego López de Haro, and Lope de Sosa among the new ones. Just before the halfway point the compilation diversifies into seven generic sections: *canciones, romances, letras de justador* or *invenciones* (two- or three-line rhyming aphorisms couched as riddles to mystify or to explain the pictorial device worn on a jouster's helmet), *glosas de motes,* (short lyric on the theme of a *mote* or motto), *villancicos,* and *preguntas* (question poems, usually one or two stanzas of *arte mayor,* requiring a reply) with their corresponding *respuestas.* Castillo might have borrowed the idea for some of these divisions from the *cancionero* of Encina, or he might have taken them wholesale from one of his sources. The *invenciones* section shows a high coincidence with material in another anthology, the *Cancionero de la British Library* (British Library Cancionero, circa 1515); clearly, such texts circulated as independent collections. Similarly, the *glosas de motes* have all the features of an improvised parlor game and are likely to have been gathered up afterward by one of the participants.

After the *preguntas,* Castillo resumes his survey of individual poets with further contemporary figures, gradually shifting from Castile to the Valencian court and authors in the circle of the Conde de Oliva, who was himself an occasional poet. The compilation is rounded out by a final generic section of *obras de burlas,* (works in jest) a mixture of mild abuse and frank obscenity that was awarded more space and recognition in a separate volume of *Cancionero de obras de burlas provocantes a risa* (*Cancionero* of Works in Jest and Conducive to Laughter) published in Valencia in 1519.

The *Cancionero general,* therefore, offered something to satisfy all tastes. It was arranged with decorum—piety at the beginning and humor at the end—and designed with every consideration for the reader's comfort. Castillo's prologue is followed by a nine-page table of contents and an index of authors, listed in order of rank from the Maestre de Calatrava to Maestre Juan el Trepador (Master John the Acrobat). And it remains an extraordinarily rich collection of verse, testifying to a wide spectrum of inspiration and practice. For his all-purpose *juego trobado,* "Tome vuestra magestad" (Accept, your majesty), for example, Jerónimo Pinar composed a stanza for each of forty-six participants at a royal gathering, telling their fortunes in love with an apposite proverb and song title. A more pessimistic view of love informs Rodrigo Cota's *Diálogo entre el Amor y un viejo* (Dialogue between Love and an Old Man), one of a small band of *Cancionero general* texts that point to an active secular theater. Meanwhile, the exploitation of sacred subjects for profane purposes continues to add an irreverent edge to amorous themes. Nicolás Núñez's version of the canonical hours incorporates a *misa de amor,* and the deification of the beloved is a trademark motif of a poet known only as Tapia (not to be confused with the Juan de Tapia mentioned above). Nearly all the extant love poems of San Pedro and Jorge Manrique are preserved uniquely in the *Cancionero general.* Holding their own in this exalted company are two lyric masterpieces: the *canción* "Ven, muerte, tan escondida" (Come, death, so secretly) by the Comendador Escrivá (tentatively identified as Joan Escrivà), and the *coplas* "Esperança mía, por quien" (My Hope, for sake of whom) by the Marqués de Astorga (thought to be Pedro Álvarez de Osorio, 1459–circa 1515).

So many of its highlights are larger-than-life developments of trends already in place that one is tempted to regard the *Cancionero general* as the apotheosis of all that went before. It is witness to the demise of *arte mayor,* the triumph of the *copla manriqueña,* and the flowering of the poetic gloss. Modern scholarly interest in genres that Castillo elevated to special prominence, such as the *canción* and the *invención,* acknowledges that the closing decades of the fifteenth century were a fertile period for poetic endeavor. The contents of the *Cancionero general,* however, are no more uniform in provenance or date than those of its manuscript predecessors. Castillo's reorganization obscures and collapses changes that had occurred during the forty years before 1511, for which manuscript and printed records are few. It is effectively impossible to distinguish between authors for whom the *Cancionero general* was just the beginning from those for whom it was the end of the road. In principle, establishing an historical background for these latest *cancionero* poets should be far easier than

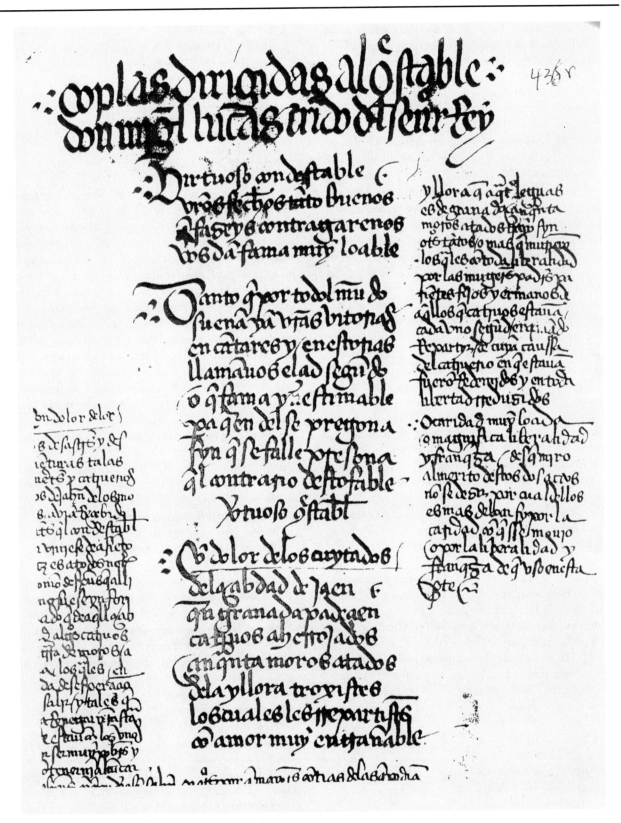

*Folio 436r from the manuscript for the* Cancionero de Oñate-Castañeda, *compiled and copied circa 1485. It comprises more than ninety works by sixteen poets (Houghton Library, Harvard University; courtesy of Jane Whetnall).*

for the earlier ones; but such is not the case, because Castillo is remiss in the matter of naming. Many of the best-represented poets are identified by surname only–Quirós, Soria, and Tapia–or share a common surname. Thanks to pioneering research by Juan Bautista Avalle-Arce, skeleton biographies have been constructed for Alonso Pérez de Vivero, second Vizconde de Altamira; Luis de Vivero, his brother, and Pedro de Cartagena (1456–1486), but many others still await formal identification.

The *Cancionero general* is the main source for the poems of Guevara, who has in the past been confused with one or the other of his older namesakes, the occasional poets Fernando de Guevara (a cousin of Santillana) and Carlos de Guevara. A contemporary of Álvarez Gato, he is probably to be identified as Comendador Nicolás de Guevara, who was active in the service of the Catholic Monarchs, Fernando and Isabel. Among the forty-two poems that have been ascribed to him are *pregunta* and *respuesta* exchanges with Gómez and Jorge Manrique, a *serrana*, an *infierno de amores,* and a quoting poem, "Recontar si mal sentí" (To say if I felt sad). His *Sepultura de amor,* which is not included in the *Cancionero general,* triggered a heated polemic with Juan Barba; Castillo includes the tail end of the debate. Three of Guevara's poems in particular have received critical attention from modern scholars. His *Esparsa a su amiga estando con ella en la cama* (To his mistress, on being in bed with her), "Qué noche tan mal dormida" (Such a sleepless night) was one of the lynchpins of Keith Whinnom's arguments in 1967 and 1981 for the nonplatonic nature of the fifteenth-century versions of courtly love. Rafael Lapesa saw evidence in 1962 of an incipient Petrarchism in Guevara's melancholy delight in nostalgia in "O desastrada ventura" (O ill-starred destiny). Francisco Rico confirmed the link in 1978 by citing close verbal parallels between Petrarch's *Rime* and *Llanto que hizo en Guadalupe* (Lament Composed in Guadalupe) in which Guevara revisits the spots where he first met his beloved. His most anthologized poem paints a vignette of springtime that is reminiscent of the traditional ballads *Fonte frida* (Cold Spring) and *Romance del prisionero* (Ballad of the Prisoner):

> Las aves andan volando,
> cantando canciones ledas,
> las verdes hojas temblando,
> las aguas dulces sonando,
> los pavos hacen sus ruedas;
> yo, sin ventura amador,
> contemplando mi tristura,
> deshago por mi dolor
> la gentil rueda de amor
> que hice por mi ventura.

> (Birds on the wing
> are merrily singing,
> green leaves are trembling,
> sweet waters tinkling;
> peacocks are spreading their tails;
> I, hapless lover,
> brooding on my sorrow,
> dismantle in pain
> the pretty wheel of love
> I devised for my happiness.)

Cartagena's early death fighting on the frontier makes his love poetry datable to within ten or twelve years. It also helps to explain why he was one of the most highly regarded poets of his generation. Sixty-three compositions are reliably attributed to him in a variety of manuscript and printed sources. His crowning achievement seems to have been a breathless tongue twister, "La fuerça del fuego que alumbra, que ciega" (The strength of that fire that dazzles, that blinds), which defines love in terms not far from Petrarchan and may have been conceived as a pretext for his own *arte mayor* gloss. He revisits the definition of love in several shorter lyrics, and these witty *esparsas* and *canciones* ensured him a place in the pantheon of fifteenth-century classics. Lyrics such as "Donde Amor su nombre escribe" (Where Love writes his name), "No sé para qué nascí" (I know not why I was born), and "Nunca pudo la passión" (Never could suffering) are repeatedly quoted or glossed in the pages of the *Cancionero general.* Outside of it, four of his *canciones* are quoted by Pietro Bembo in correspondence with Lucrezia Borgia, and three are quoted by Baltasar Gracián in the *Agudeza y arte de ingenio* (Anatomy of Wit and the Art of Conceits, 1642).

Records of the work of Garci Sánchez de Badajoz (circa 1460–circa 1535) are more plentiful; his corpus of sixty-five poems is preserved in at least fifteen manuscripts, including a nineteenth-century copy of an individual *cancionero* and ten early printings. He is one of the most dynamic and enduring of *cancionero* poets, whose *canciones, esparsas,* and *villancicos,* many of which were set to music ("Lo que queda es lo seguro" [That which remains is tried and true], "O dulce contemplación" [O sweet contemplation], "Secaronme los pesares" [My sorrows have drained], "Ve do vas, mi pensamiento" [Go your way my thought]), still speak to readers today. His *Infierno de amadores* "Caminando en las honduras" (Traveling in the depths) is a tour de force: Garci Sánchez's innovation was to amalgamate the two formats of the *infierno* and the quoting poem and to populate his erotic hell with contemporary, as well as historical, figures. It was expanded in later versions, apparently in response to the poet's invitation to readers to contribute extra stanzas. Two of his poems take *hipérbole sagrada* to the logical limit by using sacred texts as a source for lyric renewal. His blasphemous adaptation of the Office of the Dead, *Liciones de Job* (Lessons of Job), was notorious and frequently censored. The later *Lamentaciones,* "Ansias y pasiones mías" (My anguish and suffering), on the other hand, owes as much to Costana's *Conjuros que fizo Costana a su amiga* as it does to Jeremiah. According to Patrick Gallagher, this poem was his most influential work and spawned a whole subgenre of imitations. In the closing stanzas, having run through the gamut of bird exemplars, he chooses the phoenix as the ultimate emblem of the poet-lover:

> Ave fenix que sin par
> tú te quemas y deshazes
> en el fuego,
> y otra nueva sin dudar
> a la ceniza que hazes
> naces luego;
> Ansí yo, triste mezquino,
> me muero por quien no espero
> galardón;
> doyme la muerte contino
> y buelvo como primero
> a mi pasión.

> (O matchless, mateless Phoenix, who
> are consumed and unmade
> in fire,
> and unfailingly
> from the ashes of yourself
> are born anew;
> So too must I, poor wretch,
> die for her sake from whom I know
> no reward is due;
> I die continually;
> and continually return
> to my life of suffering.)

As with Macías and Rodríguez del Padrón, Garci Sánchez's life became the stuff of legend. A letter to his sister and a series of literary anecdotes give substance to stories of incest, insanity, and suicide. His poetic reputation was buoyant long after the *cancionero* style had been superseded by the fashion for Italian forms. José J. Labrador Herraiz and Ralph A. DiFranco, in their register of two hundred *cancionero* poems in later sources (in *Nunca Fue Pena Mayor*) discover Garci Sánchez to be by far the most popular fifteenth-century poet, with a dozen lyrics cited and reproduced continuously throughout the sixteenth century.

The *Cancionero general* was an instant commercial success. The initial print run of a thousand copies evidently fell short of demand, and a revised edition, with deletions and additions, appeared in 1514. It continued through seven further editions or printings up to 1573. According to F. J. Norton, "This great collection of poems by numerous fifteenth-century and contemporary authors, compiled by Fernando del Castillo, is not only of outstanding literary importance but is of peculiar interest for the influence which it was very rapidly to exercise on the whole Spanish book trade. For a good many years it formed a quarry from which the editors of poetical chapbooks drew much of their material." It also served as inspiration to Garcia de Resende to produce an equivalent anthology for Portugal, the *Cancioneiro Geral,* in 1516.

The printing revolution did not bring about a wholesale replacement of manuscript by print culture. The two formats coexisted for many decades, and late-medieval poetry continued to be collected and copied by hand well into the seventeenth century. The most important late manuscript *cancionero* is the *Cancionero de de la British Library* (formerly the *Cancionero del British Museum*), also known as the *Cancionero de Londres* (London) or the *Cancionero de Rennert* because of the 1899 description by Hugo Albert Rennert. Its relationship to the first two editions of the *Cancionero general* has been the subject of debate, but no clear dependence either way has emerged, and suggested dates range between 1495 and 1520. The similarities between the two collections are marked. Like the *Cancionero general,* the *Cancionero de la British Library* favors recreational genres—love poetry, *invenciones,* and *glosas*—and most of the major poets of the last quarter of the fifteenth century are given individual sections: Altamira, Cartagena, Costana, Sánchez de Badajoz, Guevara, López de Haro, Nuñez, Pinar, and Tapia. But it is not just a scaled-down version of the *Cancionero general.* Despite the considerable overlap in content—two-fifths of the 470 texts—the coverage is more consistently contemporary than Castillo's, with a much diminished Valencian presence, and it preserves 166 compositions that are not found elsewhere. The *Cancionero de la British Library* also has a higher proportion of folk-song material, including three *romances viejos* (traditional ballads) that, until Miguel Ángel Pérez Priego's "Los romances atribuidos a Juan Rodríguez del Padrón "(1995), critics had attributed with questionable confidence to Rodríguez del Padrón.

The manuscript presents a physical profile quite unlike that of any other late medieval *cancionero* in that it approximates to the compiler-copyist model often assumed—anachronistically—for early collections. It is a small quarto volume of 120 leaves, copied by a single hand. A block of four leaves has been lost, probably to censorship, but otherwise the collection is intact. It has built-in scribal parameters: a title for the collection on folio 1r and a colophon in the form of a verse prayer on folio 120v. Toward the end of the manuscript a few lyrics by Encina are ascribed to "el autor de este libro"

Otras de maſtre juan el trepador porque
vn cauallero q̃ paſſados ya los .xl. años
ſallo veſtido de carmeſi el ſayo y bonete y
el jubon de otra color ſeyendo cerca de na
uida fo.                                        ccxxx

Otra de anton de montoro al corrigidor
por que no hallo enla carneceria carnero
y ouo de comprar puerco fo.          ccxxx

Otra ſuya aun prior fo.                 ccxxx

Otra ſuya /al condeſtable por vn ſaualo
fo.                                             ccxxx

Otra del hijo del ropero a ſu padre y la re
ſpueſta fo.                                   ccxxx

Otra dl ropero a dos mugeres la vna pu
ta la otra beuda fo.                       ccxxx

Otra ſuya /a vn bebrero q̃ llouia mucho
fo.                                             ccxxx

Otra ſuya al duq̃ de medina ſidonia por
vn jubon de brocado q̃ traya fo.      ccxxx

Otra ſuya/a vn portogues q̃ vido veſti
do de colores fo.                           ccxxx

Pregunta de vn cauallero a vno q̃ ſe de
zia garcia de huete por vna cuchillada q̃
tenia enla cara fo.                          ccxxx

Otras de gõçalo dauilla eſtãdo enla gue
rra de nauarra fo.                          ccxxxj

Un atauio de vn eſcudero/y de ſu amiga
fo.                                             ccxxxj

Otra del ropero a juan marmolejo
fo.                                             ccxxxij

Otras coplas de juan agraz a juan mar
molejo y la reſpueſta fo.                 ccxxxij

Coplas de don jorge manrrique /a vna
muger /q̃ tenia empeñado en la tauerna
ſu brial fo.                                   ccxxxiij

Otra ſola de vn galan a juã poeta embia
dole vn ſayo de ſeda cõ vn judio
fo.                                             ccxxxiiij

Otra del adelantado de murcia a vn tro
bador mal veſtido fo.                     ccxxxiiij

Otra de vn cauallero a juã poeta porque
alegre el truban venia ala corte do el eſta
ua fo.                                         ccxxxiiij

Otra de vn cauallero al miſmo por q̃ eſta
do jugando le demãdo/y el diole vna do
bla quebrada fo.                           ccxxxiiij

Otra dl ropero a vn moça llamada cata
lina fo.                                        ccxxxiiij

¶ Los autores cuyas obras van eneſte cãcionero/ ſon los ſiguientes.

| | | |
|---|---|---|
| El maeſtre de calatraua | El marques de ſantillana | El conde de oliua |
| El duque de medina ſidonia | El marques de aſtorga | El conde de benauẽte |
| El duque de alua | El marques de villena | El conde de baro |
| El duque de alburquerque | El marques de villa frãca | El conde de ribadeo |
| | | El conde de curuña |

*Pages from the table of contents and list of authors in the* Cancionero general *(1511), compiled by Hernando del Castillo
(Real Academia Española, Madrid; courtesy of Jane Whetnall)*

El conde de castro
El conde de feria
El conde de vreña
El conde de paredes
El conde de ribagorça
El vizconde daltamira

Ellalmiráte de castilla
Eladelantado de murcia
El mariscar saya vedra
Fernan perez de guzmã
Gomez manrrique
Lope destuñiga

Don enrrique enrriquez
Don diego lopez de haro
Don jorge manrrique
Don juan manuel
Don yñigo de velasco
Don luys de biuero
Don antonio de velasco
Don diego de mēdoça
Don alonso de silua
Don rodrigo mãrrique
Don juã de meneses
Don carlos de gueuara
Don pedro dacuña
Don aluaro de luna
Don esteuã de guzmã
Don luys de torres
Don bernãdo dacuña
Don aluaro de daça
Don bernãdo de vega
Don alonso carrillo
Don juã de mēdoça
Don gõçalo chacõ
Don alonso de cardona
Don juã de cardona
Don frãces carroz
Don luys de casteluj
Don frãcisco de mõpalao
Don frãcisco fenollete

Juã de mena

El ropero
Juã rodriguez õl padrõ
El bachiller dela torre
Juã aluarez gato
Gueuara
Juã destuñiga
Rodrigo cota
Pedro torrellas
Rodrigo daualos
Barua
Hernã metia
Fray yñigo de mēdoça
Diego de burgos
Cartagena
Garci sanches
Tapia
Diego de san pedro
Juã del enzina
Diego de quiñones
El comēdador romã
Juã fernãdez deredia
Mossen cabañillas
Enrrique de mõtagudo
Juan de vlloa
Lope de sosa
Aluaro de mēdoça
Mossen crespi
Mossen viñoles
Mossen gaçul
Geronimo de artes
Puerto carrero
Hernãdo de silueyra
Antonio frãco
Frãcisco vaca
Costana
Suarez
El comēdador estuñiga
Tristan destuñiga
Juã de lepua
Aluaro destuñiga
El comēdador de triana
Juã de lezcano
Arellano
Mossen tallante

Gines de cañizares
El bachiller alonso de proaza
El bachiller ximenez
El comēdador auila
Pero guillen de segouia
Niculas nuñez
Sancho de rojas
Gonçalo carrillo
Luys de touar
Ribera
Llanos
Vendaño
Peralta
Romero
Pedro de mirãda
Diego nuñez
Garcia destorga
Vargas
Erãcisco dela fuēte
Diego de castro
Francisco de leon
Diego de çamora
Durango
Frãcisco de cumillas
Losada
Pardo
Serrano
Gabriel el musico
Gamez
Vazquez de palencia
Soria
Geronimo de pinar
Florēcia pinar
Peraluarez de ayllon
Badajoz el musico
Quiros
Frãcisco hernãdez coronel
Juã poeta
Juã agraz
Mastre juã el trepador

¶ Y mas algunos q por no sa
ber sus nõbres no vã aqui nõ
brados.

(the author of this book). Some eight other compositions with links to Encina led R. O. Jones to surmise in 1961 that the material had been collected by Encina but that a scribe was responsible for the copy. Giuseppe Di Stefano's arguments for thematic continuity in the recurrence of ballad texts and themes in "Romances en el *Cancionero de la British Library,*" included in Menéndez Collera and Roncero López's *Nunca fue pena mayor,* tend to support the Encina connection. The generally poor and confused quality of the copy, however, makes it unlikely that he was involved in the confection of the manuscript: lines and stanzas are missing; texts are conflated, truncated, or lacking heads; misattributions are frequent; and at least three of the individual sections are disrupted by poems or parts of poems by someone else.

Notwithstanding its manifest defects, the *Cancionero de la British Library* is valuable for the way it corroborates and supplements Castillo's account of poetic trends at the Isabelline court and for its very transparency. This manuscript, albeit at one remove, provides some idea of what Castillo may have had to contend with among the sources he had collected for the *Cancionero general.*

The *Cancionero de la British Library* signals the shape of things to come. Manuscript anthologies continued to be made by individual enthusiasts, who collected and copied favorite pieces into notebooks known as *cartapacios.* These sixteenth-century collections not only testify to the strength of interest in particular authors or poems but also preserve otherwise unknown fifteenth-century texts and evidence of the artifacts from which they were copied, which sometimes hold the key to earlier networks of transmission.

## Bibliographies:

Eugenio de Ochoa, *Catálogo razonado de los libros españoles existentes en la Biblioteca Real de París* (Paris: Biblioteca Real, 1844), pp. 378–525;

Adolfo Mussafia, "Per la bibliografia dei *cancioneros* spagnuoli," *Denkschriften der kaiserlichen Akademie der Wissenschaften in Wien,* Philosophisch-Historische Classe, 47, part 2 (1902): 1–24;

Charles V. Aubrun, "Inventaire des sources pour l'étude de la poésie castillane au XV<sup>e</sup> siècle," in *Estudios dedicados a Menéndez Pidal,* volume 4 (Madrid: CSIC, 1953), pp. 297–330;

Jacqueline Steunou and Lothar Knapp, *Bibliografía de los cancioneros castellanos del siglo XV y repertorio de sus géneros poéticos,* 2 volumes (Paris: Centre National de la Récherche Scientifique, 1975, 1978);

Joaquín González Cuenca, "Cancioneros manuscritos del Prerrenacimiento," *Revista de Literatura,* 40 (1978): 177–215;

Brian Dutton, Stephen Fleming, Jineen Krogstad, Francisco Santoyo Vásquez, and Joaquín González Cuenca, *Catálogo-índice de la poesía cancioneril del siglo XV,* Bibliographic Series, no. 3 (Madison, Wis.: Hispanic Seminar of Medieval Studies, 1982);

Dutton, Charles B. Faulhaber, Ángel Gómez Moreno, David Mackenzie, and John Nitti, *Bibliography of Old Spanish Texts* (Madison, Wis.: Hispanic Seminary of Medieval Studies, 1984) with now definitive edition on the Internet at http://sunsite.berkeley.edu/Philobiblon;

Dutton and Jineen Krogstad, eds., *El cancionero del siglo XV, c. 1360–1520,* 7 volumes, Biblioteca Española del Siglo XV, Serie Maior, nos. 1–7 (Salamanca: Biblioteca Española del Siglo XV & Universidad de Salamanca, 1990–1991).

## References:

José María Aguirre, "Reflexiones para la construcción de un modelo de la poesía castellana del amor cortés," *Romanische Forschungen,* 93 (1981): 55–81;

Álvaro Alonso, *Poesía amorosa y realidad cotidiana: Del Cancionero general a la lírica italianista,* Papers of the Medieval Hispanic Research Seminar, no. 32 (London: Department of Hispanic Studies, Queen Mary, University of London, 2001);

Carlos Alvar, "LB1 y otros cancioneros castellanos," in *Lyrique romane médiévale: La tradition des chansonniers. Actes du Colloque de Liège, 1989,* edited by Madeleine Tyssens (Liège: Bibliothèque de la Faculté de Philosophie et Lettres, 1991), pp. 469–500;

Juan Bautista Avalle-Arce, *El cronista Pedro de Escavias: Una vida del siglo XV,* University of North Carolina Studies in Romance Languages and Literatures, no. 127 (Chapel Hill: University of North Carolina Press, 1972);

Avalle-Arce, "Tres poetas del *Cancionero general,* (i) Cartagena; (ii) El vizconde de Altamira; (iii) Perálvarez de Ayllón," in his *Temas hispánicos medievales,* Biblioteca Románica Hispánica, Estudios y Ensayos, no. 203 (Madrid: Gredos, 1974), pp. 280–367;

José María Azáceta, "El *Pequeño cancionero,*" in *Estudios dedicados a Menéndez Pidal,* volume 7 (Madrid: Consejo Superior de Investigaciones Científicas, 1957), pp. 83–112;

Gonzalo de Baeza, *Cuentas de Gonzalo de Baeza, tesorero de Isabel la Católica,* 2 volumes, edited by Antonio de la Torre and E. A. de la Torre (Madrid: Consejo Superior de Investigaciones Científicas, 1955, 1956);

Ingrid Bahler, *Alfonso Álvarez de Villasandino: Poesía de petición,* Colección Maisal de Literatura Hispánica, no. 3 (Madrid: Maisal, 1975);

Bahler and Katherine G. Gatto, *Of Kings and Poets:* Cancionero *Poetry of the Trastámara Courts* (New York: Peter Lang, 1992);

Jeanne Battesti-Pélégrin, "Lire autrement la poésie médiévale: Codes amoureux, codes poétiques dans la lyrique du XV^ème siècle," *Langues Néo-Latines,* 252 (1985): 59–79;

Vicenç Beltran, *La canción de amor en el otoño de la Edad Media,* Estudios Literarios, no. 1 (Barcelona: PPU, 1988);

Beltran, "La reina, los poetas y el limosnero: La corte literaria de Isabel la Católica," in *Actas del VIII Congreso Internacional de la Asociación Hispánica de Literatura Medieval, Santander, 22–26 de septiembre de 1999,* 2 volumes (Santander: Consejería de Cultura del Gobierno de Cantabria & Asociación Hispánica de Literatura Medieval, 2000), I: 353–364;

Beltran, "Tipología y génesis de los cancioneros: El caso de Jorge Manrique," in *Historia y ficciones: Coloquio sobre la literatura del siglo XV,* edited by Rafael Beltrán, José Luis Canet, and Josep Lluís Sirera (Valencia: Universitat de València, 1992), pp. 165–188;

Beltran, "Tipología y génesis de los cancioneros: Los cancioneros de autor," *Revista de Filología Española,* 78 (1998): 49–101;

Beltran, "Tipología y génesis de los cancioneros: Las grandes compilaciones y los sistemas de clasificación," *Cultura Neolatina,* 55 (1995): 233–265;

Eloy Benito Ruano, "Lope de Stúñiga, vida y cancionero," *Revista de Filología Española,* 51 (1968): 17–109;

Robert G. Black, "Poetic Taste at the Aragonese Court in Naples," in *Florilegium Hispanicum: Medieval and Golden Age Studies Presented to Dorothy Clotelle Clarke,* edited by John S. Geary, Charles B. Faulhaber, and Dwayne E. Carpenter (Madison, Wis.: Hispanic Seminary of Medieval Studies, 1983), pp. 165–178;

Alberto Blecua, "'Perdióse un quaderno . . .': Sobre los cancioneros de Baena," *Anuario de Estudios Medievales,* 9 (1974–1979): 229–266;

Roger Boase, *The Troubadour Revival: A Study of Social Change and Traditionalism in Late Medieval Spain* (London: Routledge & Kegan Paul, 1978);

Patrizia Botta, Carmen Parrilla, and Ignacio Pérez Pascual, eds., *Canzonieri iberici,* 2 volumes, Biblioteca Filológica, nos. 7, 8 (Noia: Toxosoutos, Università di Padova, Universidade da Coruña, 2001).

Giovanni Caravaggi, Monika von Wunster, Giuseppe Mazzocchi, and Sara Toninelli, eds., *Poeti "can-cioneriles" del sec. XV,* Romanica Vulgaria, no. 7 (L'Aquila: Japadre, 1986);

Caravaggi, "I *sonetos* di Juan de Villalpando," in *Symbolae Pisanae: Studi in onore di Guido Mancini,* 2 volumes, edited by Blanca Periñán and Francesco Guazzelli (Pisa: Giardini, 1989), I: 99–111;

Caravaggi, "Villasandino et les derniers troubadours de Castille," in *Mélanges offerts à Rita Lejeune, professeur à l'Université de Liège,* volume 1 (Gembloux: Duculot, 1969), pp. 395–421;

Pedro de Cartagena, *Poesía,* edited by Ana María Rodado Ruiz, Clásica, no. 1 (Cuenca: Universidad de Alcalá & Universidad de Castilla-La Mancha, 2000);

Carvajal, *Poesie,* edited by Emma Scoles, Officina Romanica, no. 9 (Rome: Ateneo, 1967);

Juan Casas Rigall, *Agudeza y retórica en la poesía amorosa de cancionero,* Monografias da Universidade de Santiago de Compostela, no. 185 (Santiago de Compostela: Universidade, 1995);

Pedro M. Cátedra, *Amor y pedagogía en la Edad Media (Estudios de doctrina amorosa y práctica literaria),* Acta Salmanticensia, Estudios Filológicos, no. 212 (Salamanca: Universidad de Salamanca, 1989);

Antonio Chas Aguión, *Amor y corte: La materia sentimental en las cuestiones poéticas del siglo XV,* Biblioteca Filológica, no. 5 (Noia: Toxosoutos, 2000);

Chas Aguión, *Preguntas y respuestas en la poesía cancioneril castellana,* Serie L (Literatura), no. 12 (Madrid: Fundación Universitaria Española, 2002);

Marcella Ciceri, "Il canzoniere spagnolo della Biblioteca Estense di Modena," *Rassegna Iberistica,* 46 (1993): 17–28;

Dorothy Clotelle Clarke, *Morphology of Fifteenth-Century Castilian Verse* (Pittsburgh: Duquesne University Press / Louvain: Neuwelaerts, 1963);

Francisco Crosas López, *La materia clásica en la poesía de cancionero* (Kassel: Reichenberger, 1995);

John G. Cummins, "Methods and Conventions in the 15th-Century Poetic Debate," *Hispanic Review,* 31 (1963): 307–323;

Cummins, "Pero Guillén de Segovia y el ms. 4.114," *Hispanic Review,* 41 (1973): 6–32;

Cummins, "The Survival in the Spanish *Cancioneros* of the Forms and Themes of Provençal and Old French Poetic Debates," *Bulletin of Hispanic Studies,* 42 (1965): 9–17;

Alan Deyermond, "Baena, Santillana, Resende and the Silent Century of Portuguese Court Poetry," *Bulletin of Hispanic Studies,* 59 (1982): 198–210;

Aida Fernanda Dias, *O* Cancioneiro geral *e a poesia peninsular de quatrocentos: Contactos e sobrevivência* (Coimbra: Almedina, 1978);

Juan de Dueñas, "La *Misa de amores* de Juan de Dueñas," edited by Jules Piccus, *Nueva Revista de Filología Hispánica,* 14 (1960): 322–325;

Dueñas, *La nao de amor; Misa de amores,* edited by Marco Presotto, Agua y Peña, no. 4 (Lucca: Mauro Baroni, 1997);

Brian Dutton, "El desarrollo del *Cancionero general* de 1511," in *Actas del Congreso Romancero-Cancionero, UCLA (1984),* volume 1 (Madrid: Porrúa Turanzas, 1990), pp. 81–96;

Dutton, "Spanish Fifteenth-Century *Cancioneros:* A General Survey to 1465," *Kentucky Romance Quarterly,* 26 (1979): 445–460;

Juan del Encina, *Poesía lírica y cancionero musical,* edited by R. O. Jones and Carolyn R. Lee, Clásicos Castalia, no. 62 (Madrid: Castalia, 1975);

Anon., attributed to Pedro de Escavias, *Hechos del Condestable don Miguel Lucas de Iranzo,* edited by Juan de Mata Carriazo (Madrid: Espasa-Calpe, 1940);

de Escavias, *Repertorio de príncipes de España y obra poética del alcaide Pedro de Escavias,* edited by Michel Garcia (Jaén: Instituto de Estudios Jiennenses del Consejo Superior de Investigaciones Científicas, 1972);

David Fallows, "A Glimpse of the Lost Years: Spanish Polyphonic Song, 1450–70," in *New Perspectives in Music: Essays in Honor of Eileen Southern,* edited by Josephine Wright and Samuel A. Floyd Jr., Detroit Monographs in Musicology / Studies in Music, no. 11 (Warren, Mich.: Harmonie Park Press, 1992), pp. 19–36;

Charles F. Fraker, *Studies on the* Cancionero de Baena, University of North Carolina Studies in Romance Languages and Literatures, no. 61 (Chapel Hill: University of North Carolina Press, 1966);

Fraker, "The Theme of Predestination in the *Cancionero de Baena,*" *Bulletin of Hispanic Studies,* 51 (1974): 228–243;

Margit Frenk Alatorre, "¿Santillana o Suero de Ribera?" *Nueva Revista de Filología Hispánica,* 16 (1962): 437;

Patrick Gallagher, *The Life and Works of Garci Sánchez de Badajoz* (London: Tamesis, 1968);

Montserrat Ganges Garriga, "Poetes bilingües (català-castellà) del segle XV," *Boletín bibliográfico de la Asociación Hispánica de Literatura Medieval,* 6, no. 1 (1992): 57–231;

M. García Viñó, "Los poetas sevillanos en el *Cancionero de Baena,*" *Archivo Hispalense,* segunda época, 32 (1960): 117–143;

E. Michael Gerli, "La 'religión del amor' y el antifeminismo en las letras castellanas del siglo XV," *Hispanic Review,* 49 (1981): 65–86;

Gerli and Julian Weiss, eds., *Poetry at Court in Trastamaran Spain: From the* Cancionero de Baena *to the* Cancionero general, Medieval & Renaissance Texts & Studies, no. 181 (Tempe, Ariz.: Medieval & Renaissance Texts & Studies, 1998);

Ana M. Gómez-Bravo, *Repertorio métrico de la poesía cancioneril del siglo XV (basado en los textos del "Cancionero del siglo XV" de Brian Dutton)* (Alcalá de Henares & Madrid: Universidad de Alcalá, 1998);

John Gornall, "Right Author but Wrong Text? Towards a Critical Edition of Suero de Ribera's 'En una linda floresta,'" *Hispanic Research Journal,* 2, no. 1 (2001): 3–13;

Baltasar Gracián, *Agudeza y arte de ingenio,* edited by Evaristo Correa Calderón, Clásicos Castalia, nos. 14 and 15 (Madrid: Castalia, 1969);

Otis H. Green, "Courtly Love in the Spanish *Cancioneros,*" *PMLA,* 64 (1949): 247–301;

Guevara, *Poesie,* edited by Maria D'Agostino, Romanica Neapolitana, no. 33 (Naples: Liguori, 2002);

Pero Guillén de Segovia, *Obra poética,* edited by Carlos Moreno Hernández (Madrid: Fundación Universitaria Española, 1989);

Barry Ife, "Dutton LB1 and the Sources of Garci Sánchez de Badajoz," in *Spanish Poetry of the Golden Age: Papers of a Colloquium held at University College Cork,* edited by Stephen Boyd and Jo Richardson, Manchester Spanish and Portuguese Studies, 12 (Manchester: University of Manchester, 2002);

Micer Francisco Imperial, *"El dezir a las syete virtudes" y otros poemas,* edited by Colbert I. Nepaulsingh, Clásicos Castellanos, no. 221 (Madrid: Espasa-Calpe, 1977);

R. O. Jones, "Encina y el *Cancionero del British Museum,*" *Hispanófila,* 11 (1961): 1–21;

Jones, "Isabel la Católica y el amor cortés," *Revista de Literatura,* 21 (1962): 55–64;

Tess Knighton, "Spaces and Contexts for Listening in 15th-Century Castile: The Case of the Constable's Palace in Jaén," *Early Music,* 25 (1997): 661–677;

Rafael Lapesa, "La lengua de la poesía lírica desde Macías hasta Villasandino," in his *Estudios de historia lingüística española* (Madrid: Paraninfo, 1985), pp. 239–248;

Lapesa, "Notas sobre Micer Francisco Imperial," in his *De la Edad Media a nuestros días: Estudios de historia literaria,* Biblioteca Románica Hispánica, Estudios y Ensayos, no. 104 (Madrid: Gredos, 1971), pp. 76–94;

Lapesa, "Poesía de cancionero y poesía italianizante," in *Strenae: Estudios de filología e historia dedicatos al Profesor Manuel García Blanco,* Acta Salmanticensia,

Filosofía y Letras, no. 16 (Salamanca: Universidad de Salamanca, 1962), pp. 259–280;

J. N. H. Lawrance, "The Spread of Lay Literacy in Late Medieval Castile," *Bulletin of Hispanic Studies,* 62 (1985): 79–94;

Pierre Le Gentil, *La Poésie lyrique espagnole et portugaise à la fin du Moyen Age,* 2 volumes (Rennes: Plihon, 1949, 1953);

María Rosa Lida de Malkiel, "La hipérbole sagrada en la poesía castellana del siglo XV," in her *Estudios sobre la literatura española del siglo XV* (Madrid: Porrúa Turanzas, 1978), pp. 291–309;

Francisco López Estrada, ed., *Las poéticas castellanas de la Edad Media,* Temas de España, no. 158 (Madrid: Taurus, 1985);

Ian Macpherson, *The* Invenciones y Letras *of the* Cancionero general, Papers of the Medieval Hispanic Research Seminar, no. 9 (London: Department of Hispanic Studies, Queen Mary and Westfield College, 1998);

Nancy F. Marino, *La serranilla española: Notas para su historia e interpretación,* Scripta Humanistica, no. 40 (Potomac, Md.: Scripta Humanistica, 1987);

Francisco Márquez Villanueva, *Investigaciones sobre Juan Álvarez Gato: Contribución al conocimiento de la literatura castellana del siglo XV,* enlarged edition (Madrid: Real Academia Española, 1974);

Ana Menéndez Collera and Victoriano Roncero López, eds., *Nunca fue pena mayor: Estudios de literatura española en homenaje a Brian Dutton* (Cuenca: Universidad de Castilla–La Mancha, 1996)–includes Giuseppe Di Stefano, "Romances en el *Cancionero de la British Library,*" pp. 239–253, José J. Labrador Herraiz and Ralph A. DiFranco, "Del XV al XVII: Doscientos poemas," pp. 367–418, and Emma Scoles and Ines Ravasini, "Intertestualità e interpretazione nel genere lirico della glosa," pp. 615–631;

Ramón Menéndez Pidal, *Poesía juglaresca y orígenes de las literaturas románicas: Problemas de historia literaria y cultural,* sixth edition (Madrid: Instituto de Estudios Políticos, 1957);

Antón de Montoro, *Poesía completa,* edited by Marithelma Costa (Cleveland: Cleveland State University, 1990);

Manuel Moreno, "La autoría como problema en la edición de la obra poética de Nicolás Núñez, poeta del *Cancionero general* (Valencia 1511)," in *Edición y anotación de textos: Actas del I Congreso de Jóvenes Filólogos (A Coruña, 25–28 de septiembre de 1996),* Colección Cursos, Congresos e Simposios, no. 49, 2 volumes (Corunna: Universidade da Coruña, 1998), II: 463–478;

Moreno, "Sobre la relación de LB1 con 11CG y 14CG," in *Actas del VI Congreso Internacional de la Asociación Hispánica de Literatura Medieval (Alcalá de Henares, 12–16 de septiembre de 1995),* 2 volumes, edited by José Manuel Lucía Megías (Alcalá de Henares: Universidad de Alcalá, 1997), II: 1069–1083;

Margherita Morreale, "El *Dezir a las siete virtudes* de Francisco Imperial: Lectura e imitación prerrenacentista de la *Divina Commedia,*" in *Lengua, literatura, folklore: Estudios dedicados a Rodolfo Oroz,* edited by Gaston Carrillo Herrera (Santiago: Universidad de Chile, 1967), pp. 307–377;

Carlos Mota Placencia, "La obra poética de Alfonso Álvarez de Villasandino," 2 volumes, dissertation, Universitat Autónoma, Facultat de Filosofia i Lletres, 1990;

Tomás Navarro Tomás, *Métrica española: Reseña histórica y descriptiva* (Syracuse, N.Y.: Syracuse University Press, 1956);

Manuel Nieto Cumplido, "Aportación histórica al *Cancionero de Baena,*" *Historia, Instituciones, Documentos,* 6 (1979): 197–218;

Nieto Cumplido, "Juan Alfonso de Baena y su *Cancionero:* nueva aportación histórica," *Boletín de la Real Academia de Córdoba,* 52 (1982): 35–57;

F. J. Norton, *Printing in Spain, 1501–1520* (Cambridge: Cambridge University Press, 1966);

Juan Paredes Núñez, ed., *Medioevo y literatura: Actas del V Congreso de la Asociación Hispánica de Literatura Medieval,* 4 volumes (Granada: Universidad de Granada, 1995);

Alexander A. Parker, *The Philosophy of Love in Spanish Literature, 1480–1680,* edited by Terence O'Reilly (Edinburgh: Edinburgh University Press, 1985);

Carmen Parrilla and Ignacio Pérez Pascual, eds., *Estudios sobre poesía de cancionero,* Biblioteca Filológica, no. 1 (Noia: Toxosoutos, 1999);

Miguel Ángel Pérez Priego, "Los romances atribuidos a Juan Rodríguez del Padrón," in *Medioevo y literatura,* volume 4, pp. 35–49;

Pérez Priego, ed., *Poesía femenina en los cancioneros,* Biblioteca de Escritoras, no. 13 (Madrid: Castalia & Instituto de la Mujer, 1990);

Paolo Pintacuda, "Un poeta cancioneril del XV secolo: Alfonso Enríquez," *Rivista di Filologia e Letteratura Ispaniche,* 2 (1999): 9–45;

Ricardo Polín, *Cancioneiro Galego-Castelán (1350–1450): "Corpus" lírico da decadencia,* Publicacións do Seminario de Estudos Galegos, no. 3 (Sada, Corunna: O Castro, 1997);

Isabel Pope, "La Musique espagnole à la cour de Naples dans la seconde moitié du XVᵉ siècle," in *Musique et poésie au XVIᵉ siècle,* edited by Jean Jacquot (Paris: Centre National de Recherche Scientifique, 1954), pp. 35–61;

Claudine Potvin, *Illusion et pouvoir: La poétique du* Cancionero de Baena, Cahiers d'Etudes Médiévales, no. 9 (Montreal: Bellarmin / Paris: Vrin, 1989);

Hugo Albert Rennert, *Macias o Namorado, a Galician Trobador* (Philadelphia: Privately printed, 1900);

Suero de Ribera, "Las poesías de Suero de Ribera: Estudio y edición crítica anotada de los textos," edited by Blanca Periñán, in *Miscellanea di Studi Ispanici,* Istituto di Letteratura Spagnola e Ispano-Americana, no. 16 (Pisa: Università di Pisa, 1968), pp. 5–138;

Francisco Rico, "De Garcilaso y otros petrarquismos," *Revue de Littérature Comparée,* 52 (1978): 325–338;

Rico, "'Un penacho de penas': Sobre tres invenciones del *Cancionero general,*" *Romanistisches Jahrbuch,* 17 (1966): 274–284; revised and enlarged as "Un penacho de penas: De algunas invenciones y letras de caballeros," in his *Textos y contextos: estudios sobre la poesía española del siglo XV* (Barcelona: Crítica, 1990), pp. 189–230;

Martín de Riquer, "Alfonso el Magnánimo visto por sus poetas," in *Estudios sobre Alfonso el Magnánimo con motivo del quinto centenario de su muerte* (Barcelona: Universidad de Barcelona, 1960), pp. 175–196;

Riquer, *Caballeros andantes españoles,* Colección Austral, no. 1397 (Madrid: Espasa-Calpe, 1967);

Pero Rodríguez de Lena, *El Passo Honroso de Suero de Quiñones,* edited by Amancio Labandeira Fernández (Madrid: Fundación Universitaria Española, 1977);

Antonio Rodríguez-Moñino, *Poesía y cancioneros (siglo XVI),* Discurso leído ante la Real Academia Española (Madrid: Real Academia Española, 1968);

Nicholas G. Round, "Garci Sánchez de Badajoz and the Revaluation of *Cancionero* Poetry," *Forum for Modern Language Studies,* 6 (1970): 178–187;

Juan Carlos Rovira, "Los poemas al amor de Lucrezia d'Alagno y Alfonso de Aragón," *Boletín de la Real Academia Española,* 67 (1987): 77–107;

Concepción Salas Espinosa, *Poesía y prosa didáctica en el siglo XV: La obra del bachiller Alfonso de la Torre,* Humanidades, no. 30 (Saragossa: Prensas Universitarias de Zaragoza, 1997);

Nicasio Salvador Miguel, *La poesía cancioneril: El* Cancionero de Estúñiga (Madrid: Alhambra, 1977);

Garci Sánchez de Badajoz, *Cancionero,* edited by Julia Castillo, Biblioteca de la Literatura y el Pensamiento Hispánicos, 43 (Madrid: Editora Nacional, 1980);

Guillermo Serés, *La transformación de los amantes: Imágenes del amor de la antigüedad al Siglo de Oro* (Barcelona: Crítica, 1996);

Jesús L. Serrano Reyes and Juan Fernández Jiménez, eds., *Juan Alfonso de Baena y su cancionero: Actas del I Congreso Internacional sobre el* Cancionero de Baena *(Baena, del 16 al 20 de febrero de 1999),* Colección Biblioteca Baenense, no. 2 (Baena: Ayuntamiento de Baena & Diputación de Córdoba, 2001);

Josep Lluís Sirera, "Diálogos de cancionero y teatralidad," in *Historia y ficciones,* pp. 351–63;

Robert Stevenson, *Spanish Music in the Age of Columbus* (The Hague: Nijhoff, 1960);

Lope de Stúñiga, *Poesías,* edited by Jeanne Battesti-Pélégrin, Études Hispaniques, no. 4 (Aix-en-Provence: Université de Provence, 1982);

Stúñiga, *Poesie,* edited by Lia Vozzo Mendia, Romanica Neapolitana, no. 25 (Naples: Liguori, 1989)

Cleofé Tato, *Vida y obra de Pedro de Santa Fe,* Biblioteca Filológica, no. 4 (Noia: Toxosoutos, 1999);

Jane Yvonne Tillier, "The Devout Lover in the *Cancionero de Herberay,*" *La corónica,* 12 (Spring 1984): 265–274;

Barclay Tittmann, "A Contribution to the Study of the *Cancionero de Baena* Manuscript," *Aquila,* 1 (1968): 190–203;

Isabella Tomassetti, "Sobre la tradición ibérica de los decires con citas: Apuntes para un estudio tipológico," in *Actas del VIII Congreso Internacional de la Asociación Hispánica de Literatura Medieval, Santander, 22–26 de septiembre de 1999,* 2 volumes (Santander: Consejería de Cultura del Gobierno de Cantabria & Asociación Hispánica de Literatura Medieval, 2000), II: 1707–1724;

María Isabel Toro Pascua, "Algunas notas para la edición de la poesía de Guevara," in *Medioevo y literatura,* volume 4, pp. 389–403;

Pedro Torrellas, *The Works of Pere Torroella, a Catalan riter of the Fifteenth Century,* edited by Pedro Bach y Rita (New York: Instituto de Las Españas, 1930);

Juan de Valdés, *Diálogo de la lengua,* Clásicos Castellanos, no. 86 (Madrid: Espasa-Calpe, 1946);

Kenneth Hale Vanderford, "Macías in Legend and Literature," *Modern Philology,* 31 (1933–1934): 35–63;

Alberto Vàrvaro, *Premesse ad un' edizione critica delle poesie minori di Juan de Mena* (Naples: Liguori, 1964);

Francisca Vendrell, "La corte literaria de Alfonso V de Aragón y tres poetas de la misma," *Boletín de la Real Academia Española,* 19 (1932): 85–100, 388–405, 468–484, 584–607, 733–747; 20 (1933): 69–92;

Lia Vozzo Mendia, "La lírica spagnola alla corte napoletana di Alfonso d'Aragona: Note su alcune tradizioni testuali," *Revista de Literatura Medieval,* 7 (1995): 173–186;

Julian Weiss, *The Poet's Art: Literary Theory in Castile, c. 1400-60,* Medium Aevum Monographs, new series 14 (Oxford: Society for the Study of Mediaeval Languages and Literature, 1990);

Jane Whetnall, "Isabel González of the *Cancionero de Baena* and Other Lost Voices," *La Corónica,* 21 (Fall 1992): 59–72;

Whetnall, "*Lírica femenina* in the Early Manuscript *Cancioneros,*" in *What's Past Is Prologue: A Collection of Essays in Honour of L. J. Woodward,* edited by Salvador Bacarisse and others (Edinburgh: Scottish Academic Press, 1984), pp. 138–150, 171–175;

Whetnall, "Unmasking the Devout Lover: Hugo de Urriés in the *Cancionero de Herberay,*" *Bulletin of Hispanic Studies* (Liverpool), 74 (1997): 275–298;

Keith Whinnom, *La poesía amatoria de la época de los Reyes Católicos,* Durham Modern Languages Series, Hispanic Monographs, no. 2 (Durham: University of Durham, 1981);

Whinnom, *Spanish Literary Historiography: Three Forms of Distortion. An Inaugural Lecture Delivered in the University of Exeter on 8 December 1967* (Exeter: University of Exeter, 1967);

Whinnom, "Toward the Interpretation and Appreciation of the *Canciones* of the *Cancionero General* of 1511," in his *Medieval and Renaissance Spanish Literatures: Selected Essays,* edited by Alan Deyermond, W. F. Hunter, and Joseph T. Snow (Exeter: University of Exeter Press and Journal of Hispanic Philology, 1994), pp. 114–132.

# Late-Medieval Castilian Theater

Karoline J. Manny
*Seminole Community College at Oviedo*

WORKS: *Auto de la huida a Egipto* (ca. 1475–1490)

**Manuscript:** Madrid, Biblioteca Nacional R 31133; bound with devotional poetry for the nuns of the convent of Santa María de la Bretonera in Burgos.

**Modern edition:** José Amícola, "El *Auto de la huida a Egipto,* drama anónimo del siglo XV," *Filología,* 15 (1971): 1–29.

Alonso de Campo, *Auto de la Pasión* (ca. 1486–1499)

**Manuscript:** Biblioteca de la Catedral de Toledo 94, late fifteenth century.

**Modern edition:** Carmen Torroja Menéndez and María Rivas Palá, *Teatro en Toledo en el siglo XV: "Auto de la Pasión" de Alonso del Campo* (Madrid: Real Academia Española, 1977).

Francisco de Madrid, *Egloga* (1495)

**Manuscripts:** Santander, Biblioteca Menéndez Pelayo MS. 183, no. 63, transcription by Manuel Cañete (Joseph Gillet bases his modern edition on this copy); Madrid, Biblioteca del Palacio II-617, from a *cancionero* (songbook or anthology), circa 1568–1571 (Alberto Blecua bases his edition on this copy).

**Modern editions:** Gillet, "Égloga hecha por Francisco de Madrid," *Hispanic Review,* 11 (1943): 275–303; Blecua, "La Égloga de Francisco de Madrid en un nuevo manuscrito del siglo XVI," in *Serta Philologica F. Lázaro Carreter natalem diem sexagesimum celebranti dicata,* edited by Emilio Alarcos Llorach and others, volume 2: *Estudios de literatura y crítica textual* (Madrid: Cátedra, 1983), pp. 39–66.

Juan del Encina, *Egloga representada en la noche de la Natividad de Nuestro Salvador; Egloga representada en la mesma noche; Representación de la muy bendita pasión y muerte de Nuestro Precioso Redentor; Representación a la santíssima resurrección de Cristo; Egloga representada en la noche postrera de Carnal; Egloga representada en la mesma noche de Antruejo; Egloga representada en requesta de unos amores; Egloga representada por las mesmas personas; Egloga sobre los infortunios de las grandes lluvias; Representación ante el muy esclarecido y muy ilus-*tre *príncipe don Juan sobre el poder del Amor; Egloga de Cristino y Febea; Egloga de Fileno, Zambardo y Cardonio; Aucto del Repelón;* and *Egloga de Plácida y Victoriano*

**Manuscripts:** *Egloga de Plácida y Victoriano,* Madrid, Biblioteca Nacional R-4888; Paris, Bibliothèque de l'Arsenal 12261.

**Early editions:** *Cancionero* (Salamanca, 1496; Seville, 1501; Burgos, 1505)—includes *Egloga representada en la noche de la Natividad de Nuestro Salvador, Egloga representada en la mesma noche, Representación de la muy bendita pasión y muerte de Nuestro Precioso Redentor, Representación a la santíssima resurrección de Cristo, Egloga representada en la noche postrera de Carnal, Egloga representada en la mesma noche de Antruejo, Egloga representada en requesta de unos amores,* and *Egloga representada por las mesmas personas;* enlarged to include *Egloga sobre los infortunios de las grandes lluvias* and *Representación ante el muy esclarecido y muy ilustre príncipe don Juan sobre el poder del Amor* (Salamanca, 1507); 1507 edition enlarged to include *Egloga de Fileno, Zambardo y Cardonio* and *Aucto del Repelón* (Salamanca, 1509); *Egloga de Cristino y Febea* (Santander, n.d.).

**Modern editions:** *Teatro completo,* edited by Miguel Angel Pérez Priego (Madrid: Cátedra, 1991); *Obra Completa,* edited by Pérez Priego (Madrid: Fundación José Antonio de Castro, 1996).

Lucas Fernández, *Comedia* (1496), *Diálogo para cantar* (1497), *Farsa o cuasicomedia de la Doncella* (1497), *Egloga o farsa del Nacimiento de Nuestro Redentor Jesucristo* (1500), *Auto o farsa del Nacimiento de Nuestro Señor Jesucristo* (ca. 1500–1502), *Farsa de Prabos* (1503), and *Auto de la Pasión* (1503)

**First publication:** *Farsas y eglogas al modo y estilo pastoril y castellano* (Salamanca, 1514).

**Modern editions:** *Farsas y eglogas al modo y estilo pastoril y castellano,* facsimile of the 1514 edition, edited by Manuel Cañete (Madrid: Real Academia Española, 1867); *Farsas y églogas,* edited by Emilio Cotarelo y Mori (Madrid: Real Academia

Española, 1929); *Farsas y églogas,* edited by John Lihani (New York: Las Américas, 1969); *Farsas y Eglogas,* edited by María Josefa Canellada (Madrid: Castalia, 1976); *Farsas y églogas,* edited by Juan Miguel Valero Moreno (Salamanca: Ediciones Universidad de Salamanca, 2002).

Gil Vicente, *Copilacam* [sic] *de toda las obras de Gil Vicente Empremiose em a muy nobre e sempre leal cidade de Lixboa em casa de Ioam Alvarez impresor del Rey nosso senhor Anno de M.D.L.XII* (N.p., 1562).

**Modern editions:** *Obras completas,* edited by Alvaro Julio da Costa Pimpão (Barcelos, Portugal: Companhia Editora do Minho, 1946; revised, Porto, Portugal: Livraria Civilização, 1962); *Obras dramáticas castellanas,* edited by Thomas R. Hart (Madrid: Espasa-Calpe, 1968); *Copilaçam de toda las obras de Gil Vicente,* 2 volumes, edited by Maria Leonor Carvalhão Buescu (Lisbon: Imprensa Nacional-Casa da Moeda, 1983).

Preserved dramatic texts are rare for the late-medieval Castilian period, a situation that could lead one to think that courtly and popular theater were uncommon. Extensive archival work by Charlotte Stern, however, has uncovered a wealth of evidence in the form of play schedules, reports of street performances, bills for costumes and outdoor-stage carts, and incidental reports of ethnic or religious violence during shows—all of which testify to both popular and elite forms of dramatic production, at least for special celebrations and during public festivals, such as Holy Week and Corpus Christi. When the texts were composed mostly of songs, the verses were simply taught by rote to illiterate vocalists, a theatrical constant from classical Greek tragedy through the time of Lope de Vega and William Shakespeare. The late-medieval festival included playlets. These compositions were unlikely to be preserved in written form, especially when the authors were not noblemen and thus did not have regular access to the mechanisms of textual exchange, such as church offices, royal scriptoria, and established educational institutions. The authors of the surviving texts, however, all belonged to that privileged and therefore somewhat uncharacteristic group.

Several theatrical pieces were produced and transcribed in late-fifteenth-century Spain. Gómez Manrique's *Representación del Nascimiento de Nuestro Señor* (Play of the Birth of Our Lord) and *Coplas fechas para Semana Santa* (Verses Written for Holy Week) appeared in the middle part of the century. The anonymous *Auto de la huida a Egipto* (Play of the Flight from Egypt) was written some time between 1475 and 1490. *Auto de la Pasión* (Play of the Passion), attributed to Alonso de Campo, was created some time between 1486 and 1499. A dra-

matic *Egloga* (Eclogue), written by Francisco de Madrid, appeared in 1495. The three most important dramatic authors of this period—Juan del Encina, Lucas Fernández, and Gil Vicente—wrote multiple pieces.

The 354-line manuscript of *Auto de la huida a Egipto* was found in the monastery of Santa María de la Bretonera, near Burgos. The play opens with an angel speaking to Joseph and commanding him to flee with his family because of the threat to Jesus posed by King Herod. Joseph tells Mary they must leave, and she promptly agrees, saying they must obey God's will. They begin their journey as Joseph asks for God's guidance, but soon three thieves approach and rob them. Seeing that Jesus is the Messiah, they kneel before Mary to repent and return what they have stolen. John the Baptist appears next, stating that he wants to leave home to look for the Messiah. St. Zechariah and St. Isabel tell him that Joseph and Mary are coming to Judea, a report confirmed by a passing pilgrim who saw them on the road. John sends the pilgrim back to find them; when he finds them, Mary tells him to return to console John and tell him that they will soon arrive. The pilgrim affirms to John that the Messiah is coming and that he now believes in him, asking John to go with him to a cave in order to escape the devil's temptations. In a prophetic reply Christ's precursor reminds him that Jesus will suffer even greater temptation in the desert and die for people's sins. The play ends with the angel telling Joseph and Mary that they can return home because the danger posed by Herod has passed.

The anonymous author of *Auto de la huida a Egipto* serves up one of the few liturgical plays with true action—Mary and Joseph's trip to Egypt, the robbery, and the shuttling back and forth of the pilgrim. He also develops conflict through the confrontation between the robbers and Joseph and Mary, in John's frustrated desire to travel to see Christ, and in the pilgrim's initial doubt and later conversion. The verse used in this play, though still irregular, is considered by scholars to be sophisticated. Especially noteworthy are the work's *villancicos* (folk carols), an element thought to have been introduced by Encina.

The next extant play from the Iberian Peninsula was *Auto de la Pasión,* attributed to Campo, who organized the Corpus Christi celebrations in Toledo between 1481 and 1499. The manuscript consists of eight scenes of irregular length: Christ's prayer in the garden, the arrest, Peter's denial, Pilate's sentence, the moment when St. John (the Evangelist) tells Mary that Jesus has died, and the laments of Peter, John, and Mary. Critics praise the sophistication and lyricism of the verse in *Auto de la Pasión.*

An additional play, probably produced before those of Encina, is the *Egloga* by Madrid, the first extant

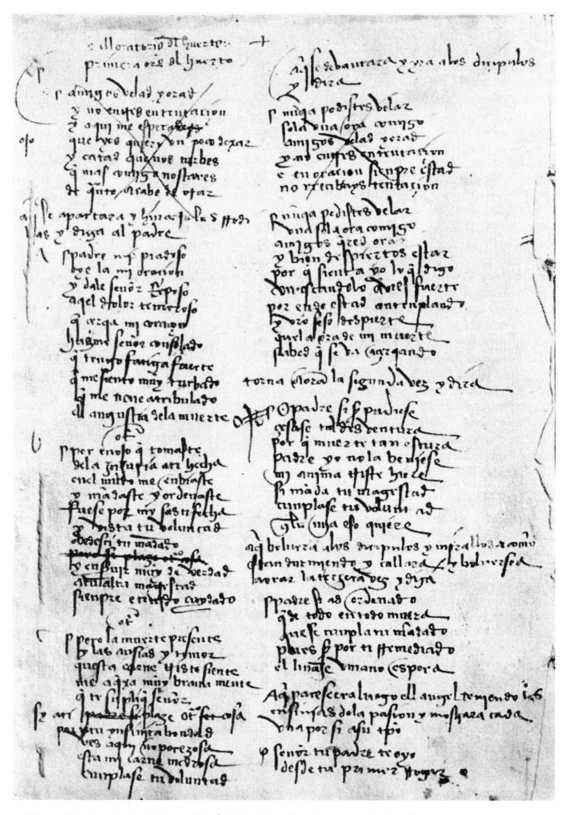

*Folio 8v of the manuscript in the library of the Toledo Cathedral for the* Auto de la Pasión *(Passion Play, circa 1486–1489),*
*attributed to Alonso de Campo (from Carmen Torroja Menéndez and María Rivas Palá,* Teatro en
Toledo en el siglo XV: "Auto de la Pasión" de Alonso del Campo, *1977;*
*Thomas Cooper Library, University of South Carolina)*

nonreligious play from the Iberian Peninsula. It features three shepherds called Evandro; Peligro, an allegorical representation of King Charles VIII of France; and Fortunado, representing King Fernando (Ferdinand) of Castile. Evandro tries to convince Peligro to mind his flock and not enter the lands of others. Despite the efforts of Evandro, Peligro embarks on a campaign to pillage surrounding territories. Fortunado informs Evandro of his intention to stop Peligro since he has already grazed his flock in the territories of Panteón (the Pope) and other allies. The play ends with a prayer for peace. The use of shepherds grazing their flocks in someone else's pasture to represent kings invading the sovereign territories of their peers is an interesting adaptation of a common allegorical device. There is, however, little action in the play, and the characters are rather flat, clearly drawn to please the royal house, for whom the play was undoubtedly written.

Of all the extant works of late-medieval Castilian drama with identified authors, those of Encina, Fernández, and Vicente are the most widely known. Encina, known as the father of Spanish drama, composed fourteen plays titled "eclogues." He was born Juan de Formoselle in Salamanca, the son of a shoemaker, and had at least five brothers and one sister. Despite their humble beginnings, three of his brothers, Antonio, Miguel, and Diego, became a lawyer, a priest, and a musician, respectively. Juan was named choirboy in the cathedral of Salamanca in 1484 and studied law at the University of Salamanca. In 1490 he was named *capellán de coro* (chorister) of the cathedral and changed his name to Juan del Encina. In 1492 or 1495 his first dramatic eclogue was performed in the palace of the duke of Alba. In 1496 the first edition of Encina's *Cancionero,* a collection of eight eclogues, was published in Salamanca. It was probably edited by Encina himself and included two *églogas de Navidad* (Christmas eclogues), two *representaciones de la Pasión y Resurrección* (pageants of the Passion and Resurrection), two *églogas de Carnaval* (eclogues for Shrovetide), and two *églogas en requesta de unos amores* (eclogues on taking the measure of love). These same works appeared in two subsequent editions, one from Seville in 1501 and another from Burgos in 1505.

In 1498 Encina competed unsuccessfully for the position of choirmaster of the cathedral of Salamanca, a position given to his rival and fellow dramatist Fernández. Two years later Encina made his first journey to Rome, where he was to stay until 1509. While in Rome he was a favorite of Pope Alexander VI, from whom he received a benefice in Salamanca, the chaplaincies in San Julián de Luisáñez and Santa María de Villarino, and a papal bull granting him the appointment as choirmaster of the cathedral of Salamanca. Unsurprisingly, Fernández appealed the papal bull, and the two rivals spent years in litigation over this position. In 1507 the second edition of Encina's *Cancionero* was published, with two additional eclogues, *Egloga sobre los infortunios de las grandes lluvias* (Eclogue on the Misfortunes of the Great Rains) and *Representación ante el muy esclarecido y muy ilustre príncipe don Juan sobre el poder del Amor* (Pageant Presented to the Distinguished and Illustrious Prince don Juan on the Power of Love). When Alexander VI was succeeded by Pope Julius II, Encina received a papal bull granting him the archdeaconry of Málaga in 1508.

In 1509 Encina assumed the responsibilities of the archdeaconry and published still another edition of the *Cancionero* that included the already published ten eclogues as well as two new works, *Egloga de Fileno, Zambardo y Cardonio* (Eclogue of Fileno, Zambardo and Cardonio) and *Aucto del Repelón* (The Hair-Pulling Farce). Sometime before this date Encina also published *Egloga de Cristino y Febea* (Eclogue of Cristino and Febea) as an individual work rather than as part of a collection. Many critics also attribute to Encina a second *obra suelta* (incidental work) from this period titled *Egloga interlocutoria* (Interlocutory Eclogue).

Encina made a second and much shorter trip to Rome in 1512. While there, he established ties with the new Pope, Leo X. Encina's masterpiece, *Egloga de Plácida y Victoriano* (Eclogue of Plácida and Victoriano), was written on the eve of Epiphany in 1513 for a private performance during this trip. Encina returned to Málaga by midyear in 1513 but petitioned to make another trip to Rome in 1514. This third trip to Rome lasted until 1516, and he made a fourth and final trip in 1517, staying until 1519. The year 1519 was busy for Encina: he was appointed prior of León, made a pilgrimage to the Holy Land, was ordained a priest, and celebrated his first mass in Jerusalem. In 1523 Encina returned to León to assume the responsibilities of prior, an office he retained until his death in 1529 or 1530.

Encina's first eight eclogues, all performed for the duke and duchess of Alba, were written to be staged in pairs. The first two, *Egloga representada en la noche de la Natividad de Nuestro Salvador* (Eclogue Presented on the Night of the Birth of Our Savior) and *Egloga representada en la mesma noche* (Eclogue Presented on the Same Night), are 180 and 260 lines long, respectively, and both are written in octosyllabic *novenas* (nine-verse stanzas). The first eclogue features two shepherds and the second, four. In both instances the characters speak in *sayagués,* a term used by modern scholars to refer to rustic, peasant speech usually employed for comic effect in Spanish drama. The name derives from Sayago, a region northwest of Salamanca and close to the Portuguese border. There is some controversy among scholars as to whether this "dialect" ever actually existed or was simply a literary convention created by dramatists such as Encina and Fernández and then copied by later Renaissance writers. The term is sometimes erroneously used interchangeably with the word *charro,* the proper name of the local Salamanca dialect. Encina is credited with being the first dramatist to use *sayagués* in his works. In *Egloga representada en la noche de la Natividad de Nuestro Salvador* the first shepherd, Juan, begins by praising the duke and duchess of Alba, while the second, Mateo, criticizes Juan, who replies that his upcoming publication will show him to be a capable writer.

The second of these paired works tells the Christmas story. The Evangelists–John, Matthew, Luke, and Mark–are represented by four shepherds. At the beginning of the play Luke reveals that Christ has been born of a virgin, after which the shepherds discuss how this birth fulfills the prophecies of the Old Testament. Finally, they decide to visit the Christ child, and the play ends in a *villancico* (carol). The *villancico* is traditionally sung by four shepherds. Despite its short length, it often took several minutes to perform since it was accompanied by music and dance. Encina is credited with the introduction of the *villancico* in Spanish theater.

Even these earliest plays demonstrate several of Encina's recurring stylistic devices, such as the inclusion of the playwright himself in the play: the character Juan in the first eclogue is clearly based on Encina. The author again interjects himself as a character in *Egloga representada en la noche postrera de Carnal* (Eclogue Presented on the Last Night of Carnival) and *Egloga sobre los infortunios de las grandes lluvias* to praise the duke and duchess and bemoan his lack of recognition as an artist.

Encina's religious plays all include references to external historical events. In the first eclogue Juan refers to the imminent publication of his 1496 *Cancionero.* This emphasis on popular life is a staple of Spanish religious drama and later Renaissance theater. Another stylistic feature is Encina's use of anachronisms. Juan and Mateo are modern-day shepherds in the first of the paired plays, but in the second they are transformed into two of the Evangelists. This conversion of contemporary figures into biblical characters is fairly common in early Spanish drama. Some scholars theorize that this device served to bring the contemporary audience closer to incidents from the Bible. Despite such anachronisms, the characters in Encina's plays are faithful to the religious characters they represent. In this case, Matthew focuses on the genealogy of Christ in the play, Mark is the expert on the prophecies of Isaiah, and John explains the theological implications of the birth of Christ.

Encina introduces apocryphal characters with regularity in his religious works. In the first two eclogues the shepherds mention the name of the Virgin Mary's mother, information unrecorded in any sacred text. The introduction of extrabiblical characters was a standard and apparently accepted device in late-medieval drama of the Iberian Peninsula.

Encina's second pair of eclogues–*Representación de la muy bendita pasión y muerte de Nuestro Precioso Redentor* (Play of the Very Blessed Passion and Death of Our Precious Redeemer) and *Representación a la santíssima resurrección de Cristo* (Play of the Most Holy Resurrection of Christ)–deal with the final events of the Passion. These plays are 368 lines and 198 lines long, respectively, and are composed of octosyllabic *coplas de pie quebrado* (stanzas that mix full lines with half lines). As befits the more serious topic of the Passion and Resurrection of Christ, the characters in these plays speak in standard, correct Spanish. The first play features two hermits, a father and son who have heard of the Crucifixion and are going to see the tomb. They encounter Veronica, who describes Christ's Passion. In response to their prayers, an angel appears to explain the Resurrection, and the play concludes on a joyful note.

In the second play Joseph of Arimathea is at the empty tomb. Mary Magdalene joins him and tells him Christ has appeared to her, and then Luke and Cleopas (a disciple who saw Christ on the road to Emmaus in Luke 24:13–35) enter and make the same claim. They all discuss the importance of the Resurrection, and the play ends with the appearance of an angel who wishes them peace and happiness. The concluding *villancico* expresses joy that Christ is risen.

These plays are typical of Encina's early religious works in that the characters have close ties to their New Testament inspiration, despite the introduction of an apocryphal character, Veronica, who enjoyed long popularity in Christian legend. The imagery surrounding Christ is secular and anachronistic; he is described as a conquering captain, and the Resurrection is referred to as a target at which to aim shots.

Scholars agree that although Encina's first four plays made important contributions to Spanish theater in their use of *sayagués* and the *villancico,* they were rather primitive. The two central aspects of drama, action and conflict, are practically nonexistent, the dialogue is simple, and the characters are flat.

The remaining plays in the original *Cancionero* show improvement in these areas. The first pair consists of *Egloga representada en la noche postrera de Carnal* and *Egloga representada en la mesma noche de Antruejo* (Eclogue Presented on the Same Night of Carnival). These plays are 264 lines and 231 lines long, respectively, and are written in octosyllabic *coplas de pie quebrado,* both featuring four shepherds who speak in *sayagués.* In the first, Beneyto (representing Encina) is grieving because his master must depart soon for the wars with France. Bras attempts to console him, but to no avail, and they resolve to pray for Beneyto's lord, the duke. Another

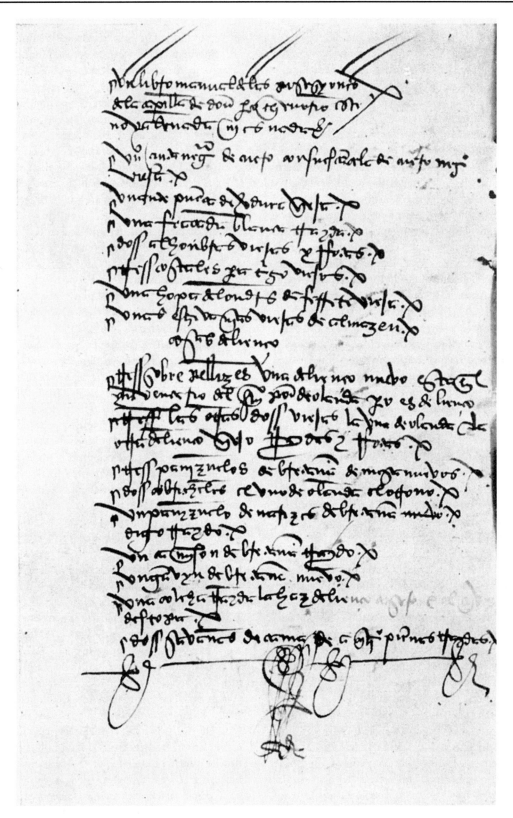

*Page from an inventory of Campo's property. The first book listed includes his* Auto de la Pasión *(from Carmen Torroja Menéndez and María Rivas Palá,* Teatro en Toledo en el siglo XV: "Auto de la Pasión" de Alonso del Campo, *1977; Thomas Cooper Library, University of South Carolina).*

shepherd, Pedruelo, returns with news from the market. He tells them he sold some cocks and chickens and bought some leeks and sardines for the upcoming Lenten season. He also says he has heard that Castile and France are not going to war, so they praise God. Lloriente arrives and, in a *villancico*, the shepherds pray for peace and victory if war comes.

In the companion piece Beneyto tells Bras to fill up in preparation for Lent. They eat a ham together, but Bras says that Lent will still be difficult for them. They relate a hilarious version of the well-known story of the battle between Lent and Carnival. Pedruelo and Lloriente enter, and they drink milk together. The scene degenerates into an argument over the virtues of cow's milk versus goat's milk. The characters wrap up their interlude with a song. Scholars agree that this play is more interesting because the characters actually interact. In *Egloga representada en la noche postrera de Carnal* Beneyto's grief and Bras's attempts to help and, in *Egloga representada en la mesma noche de Antruejo*, the argument over milk are the best examples of interaction between characters seen in Encina's works thus far.

Encina's first secular plays, *Egloga representada en requesta de unos amores* (Eclogue Acted in a Dispute over Love) and *Egloga representada por las mesmas personas* (Eclogue Presented by the Same People), also show marked progress in dramatic craftsmanship. These works are based on the *pastorela* (shepherd's song), a medieval convention in which a knight encounters a shepherdess. The first is composed of 253 lines and the second of 557. Both plays are written in octosyllabic *redondillas dobles* (double 4-line stanzas). They feature Pascuala, a shepherdess; Mingo, a shepherd; and Gil, a squire. Pascuala and Mingo speak *sayagués* while Gil speaks standard Spanish until his voluntary surrender of status. In the first play, Mingo, although married, is pining for Pascuala. He praises her beauty and offers her a flower. At that moment the squire enters, falls immediately in love with her, and promises her wealth if she will love him. Mingo and Gil have a verbal altercation, which ends when Mingo insists that Pascuala choose between them. She decides that if the squire will become a shepherd, she will love him.

The second play is divided into two parts. In the first part Mingo, encouraged by Gil, timidly presents the duke and duchess a gift, Encina's own *Cancionero* of 1496. Gil then asks Mingo to help him write some verses to celebrate his first anniversary with Pascuala. At first Mingo is upset, since Gil stole Pascuala from him, but he finally concedes. They call in Pascuala and Menga, and they sing a song together. In the second part Gil complains that he is tired of the peasant life and asks Pascuala to join him in upper-class society. She dresses up in fine clothes, and everyone is amazed by her beauty, which they attribute to a transformation owing to love. They try to convince Mingo and Menga to join them. At first they resist, but they eventually capitulate, dress in fine clothes, and sing a song.

This pair of plays is noteworthy because in addition to maintaining several traditional aspects of Encina's plays, such as inclusion of the playwright as a character and the appropriate use of *sayagués* and Castilian speech, it also introduces several sophisticated elements. First, the second play is divided into two scenes, the first such division seen in Encina's plays. Second, the characters exhibit a wide range of emotions—timidity, jealousy, love, aggression, and coquettishness. Encina displays considerable skill in creating conflict in the scenes involving Mengo and Gil. In addition to the use of *sayagués* and the *villancico*, Encina's mixture of religious, secular, popular, and comic elements is a device that resurfaces repeatedly in later Spanish drama. He is also credited with setting the standards for poetic skill and lyricism in the verse of his plays.

Encina's *Egloga sobre los infortunios de las grandes lluvias* and *Representación ante el muy esclarecido y muy ilustre príncipe don Juan sobre el poder del Amor* both appear in the 1507 edition of the *Cancionero*. The first is a semireligious play of 256 lines written in octosyllabic verses of *coplas de pie quebrado*. It features four shepherds who speak *sayagués* and an angel that speaks standard Castilian. Juan and Miguellejo summon their friends Antón and Rodrigacho to shelter themselves from a storm. The four complain about the terrible weather and the damage it has done to bridges and dams near Salamanca. They also mention the death of the *cantor* (choirmaster) in the cathedral, which leads to a lengthy digression on Encina's musical career and aspirations to be *cantor*. Finally, they ask Juan what he brought from town, divide it up, and begin gambling. Miguellejo loses several times and begins to curse. An angel appears and announces the birth of Christ. The shepherds depart to visit him, listing the gifts they will bring him.

In *Egloga sobre los infortunios de las grandes lluvias* Encina combines his traditional conventions with a more sophisticated style. Anachronism is evident in the switch between Salamanca and Bethlehem, and Encina mixes secular elements (a discussion of bad weather) with the religious story. He interjects himself and his career into the story. In this play, however, he has also drawn quite human shepherds, as is indicated by their bickering and gambling.

*Representación ante el muy esclarecido y muy ilustre príncipe don Juan sobre el poder del Amor* is the first play in which Encina focuses on the power of love. This theme was hinted at through Pascuala's conversion to a great beauty by love in *Egloga representada en requesta de unos amores,* but the later plays do not portray love in a happy light. *Representación ante el muy esclarecido y muy ilustre príncipe don Juan sobre el poder del Amor* is a 450-line play written in *coplas de pie quebrado*. It features three shepherds, who speak *sayagués,* and a squire and Cupid, who speak Castilian. Cupid opens the play with a monologue on the power of love. Pelayo enters and tells Cupid that he has no right to hunt on that land. Cupid warns him not to be rash, but Pelayo ignores him, and Cupid shoots him with one of his arrows. Another shepherd, Bras, enters to find Pelayo conscious but prostrate on the ground. Pelayo finally confesses what his trouble is and passes out. Bras calls in Juanillo, and the two debate the question of whether they need a priest for Pelayo's last rites. The squire encounters them on the road and wonders if peasant folk feel the pangs of love as keenly as the noble class. They see Marinilla, the cause of Pelayo's affliction, and Pelayo awakens at the sound of her name. They discuss the differences between how noblemen and peasants love, and the play ends in a song.

Love in Encina's plays is based on the tradition of courtly love, which requires the man to be an obedient slave to a disdainful, unobtainable lady while he suffers the physical symptoms of the disease of love. Courtly love is no stranger to the Spanish *cancionero* and sentimental romance novels, and Encina might have been familiar with Fernando de Rojas's *La tragicomedia de Calisto y Melibea* (The Tragicomedy of Calisto and Melibea, 1499–1501), also known by the name of its most colorful character, *Celestina*. Encina, however, focuses on the hopelessness and complete despair of the lover, taking his misery to extremes seldom seen in works by other writers.

Another facet of *Representación ante el muy esclarecido y muy ilustre príncipe don Juan sobre el poder del Amor* worth noting is the division into scenes: Cupid's monologue, the fight between Cupid and Pelayo, Bras and Juanillo's questioning of Pelayo, and the debate on love with the squire. Encina's love plays have an increasingly sophisticated structure, beginning, as in this play, with vague divisions and culminating in the full two-act structure of *Egloga de Plácida y Victoriano.*

Between the publication of the 1507 and the 1509 editions of the *Cancionero,* the *Egloga interlocutoria* was published separately. Scholars debate the authorship of this work, but it is said to have been bundled with four other plays written by Encina, of which only the *Egloga interlocutoria* is extant. Unfortunately, neither the place of publication nor the titles of those other plays were recorded. The play does open with references to the ducal palace and to private affairs concerning Encina, lending credence to the theory of his authorship. Other scholars contest the attribution of this play to Encina, arguing that it employs mixed verses and *quintillas* (five-

line stanzas), which are not found in any of his known works. The play is a mixture of *quintillas* and *coplas de arte mayor* (lines of nine or more syllables). Other scholars respond that there is little reason to deny Encina's authorship, countering that he did use *novenas* (nine-line stanzas), which consist of *quintillas* and *redondillas* (four-line stanzas).

*Egloga interlocutoria* is a Nativity play in which Pascual announces the birth of Christ and predicts the perdition of the Jews and Muslims. Pascual wishes to go to the ducal palace but is criticized by Benito. Two other shepherds arrive and confirm that Jesus is born. They describe the gifts they have given him. Pascual wants to keep his possessions for himself, which provokes an argument between him and Gil Verto. Benito intervenes; they decide to gamble and end up praising their masters. The use of anachronisms such as the transformation from Salamanca to Bethlehem is typical of Encina, and Benito's criticism of Pascual and the gambling shepherds also remind the reader of previous plays by Encina.

Encina's *Egloga de Cristino y Febea,* published sometime between the 1507 and the 1509 editions of the *Cancionero,* consists of 631 lines composed in *coplas de pie quebrado.* It survives in a single undated copy in Santander. The theme of the play is the sacrilegious triumph of the pagan forces of love over godliness. Cristino complains to an older friend that he is tired of life and is ready to become a hermit. Justino advises against it, but Cristino is determined and leaves to become a hermit. Cupid enters and is furious that he has been scorned by Cristino. Cupid calls upon Febea, a nymph, to seduce Cristino, and although the novice hermit tries to resist, he is overcome by temptation and curses Cupid for his pains. Cupid replies that if Cristino is in pain, it is his own fault, but he does grant him Febea's love. Cristino relates his misadventures to Justino, despite his shame for his weakness and the damage it will do to his reputation, and he joins the others in the concluding song.

In *Egloga de Cristino y Febea* scholars note the continuing emphasis on the pain caused by love. As in *Representación ante el muy esclarecido y muy ilustre príncipe don Juan sobre el poder del Amor,* love is embodied by Cupid, who vindictively pursues his powerless male victim. Even godly pursuits are defeated by love. Also noteworthy is the still clearer division into scenes: the conversation between Cristino and Justino, Justino's monologue, Cupid's conversation with Justino and Febea, the temptation, Cristino's monologue, the pact between Cupid and Cristino, and the final scene between Cristino and Justino.

This increasingly sophisticated structure is accompanied by improvements in the use of dramatic

The villancico (folk carol) "Mi libertad en sosiego," by Juan del Encina, who is thought to have originated the use
of carols in Castilian drama (from Henry W. Sullivan, Juan del Encina, 1976;
Thomas Cooper Library, University of South Carolina)

conflict and action. The play has a fully developed internal and external conflict in the character of Cristino, who is torn psychologically by his exhaustion with life and his desire to repent for his sins. Tempted by physical desire for Febea, Cristino's fatal flaws are his pride and confidence that he is fit for a religious life. He should have listened to his wiser friend's advice and not invoked the wrath of Cupid. Rather than being a static character, Cristino evolves somewhat, recognizing his error and paying for it.

Encina's last three plays were all written to some degree under the influences he experienced while living in Rome. The first two of these plays were published in the 1509 *Cancionero*. The *Egloga de Fileno, Zambardo y Cardonio,* in 704 lines of *coplas de arte mayor,* is one of Encina's most extreme expressions of the despair caused by love. Fileno bewails his fate as the rejected suitor of Zefira and seeks consolation from Zambardo. Fileno bitterly complains of his attempt to love Zefira, but Zambardo is exhausted from defending his flock from a wolf and keeps falling asleep. After calling in Cardonio, Fileno condemns all women, but Cardonio criticizes him for blaming all women for the cruelty of a single mistress and defends the virtues of good women. Debating the evils and virtues of women, Cardonio makes Fileno promise not to do anything desperate and leaves to do his work. Fileno, however, kills himself with his knife. Finding Fileno dead, Cardonio awakens Zambardo, and they bury him.

Italian influences are clearly evident in this play. First, the names Encina chooses for his shepherds are reminiscent of Phylenio and Saphyra, used in the Italian eclogue tradition. The use of *arte mayor,* traditionally considered a "high-style" form of verse because of the length of the lines, is also evidence of his attempt to write with more sophistication.

Encina's exploration of the theme of love is brought to a climax in the *Egloga de Fileno, Zambardo y Cardonio.* Fileno's diatribe against women goes beyond the courtly-love tradition into the territory of Alfonso Martínez de Toledo's *El arcipreste de Talavera* (The Archpriest of Talavera, 1466; also known as *El Corbacho,* or The Whip), which Fileno cites. His belief that all women are evil drives him to the ultimate fate of the suffering lover, a self-inflicted death. Rather than merely pining away, Fileno literally kills himself for love, but his is one of the few true suicides in Spanish theater.

The second play in the 1509 *Cancionero* is Encina's only farce and one of the earliest extant in Spanish theater. *Aucto del Repelón* consists of 441 lines of *redondillas dobles.* The characters speak the most highly dialectical example of *sayagués* in any of Encina's plays. The play describes the misadventures of Pienicurto and Johan Paramas, two shepherds who, when trying to sell their goods in town, are attacked by mischievous students. They flee to a nobleman's house to beg protection, lamenting the loss of their goods and the probable need to repay their master for their loss. Puernicurto falsely brags that he received no beating and ran to the nobleman's house only out of concern for his friend, but he soon admits that he is lying. A student then enters the house and, feigning ignorance, tries to engage the peasants in conversation. They try to avoid speaking, but Johan finally tells of the beating he received. Puernicurto again tries to deny that he was beaten, and an argument ensues that is interrupted when the student pulls Puernicurto's hair. The shepherds team up to avenge themselves on the student, and the play ends with a *villancico* in which the shepherds thank God that they were not born academics.

This farce is generally praised by scholars for its lively characters and humorous language and situations. The use of *sayagués* is extremely exaggerated, as befits the tone of the play. The theme of student pranksters is a standard in medieval literature and a repeated comedic element in much later Spanish literature.

The last extant example of Encina's drama, *Egloga de Plácida y Victoriano,* is also considered his masterpiece. The play survives in two manuscripts, one at the Biblioteca Nacional in Madrid and one at the Bibliothèque de l'Arsenal, Paris. It consists of two formally divided *actos,* with 2,577 lines of primarily *coplas de pie quebrado.* In the first scene of act 1 Plácida laments the loss of her lover, Victoriano, after a quarrel, while in the second scene Victoriano enters, complaining of his sadness and inability to stop loving Plácida. He seeks advice from Suplicio, who tells him to find comfort in the arms of another woman. In the third scene Victoriano halfheartedly woos Fulgencia but finally decides that he cannot forget Plácida and goes to look for her. He learns from Pascual that she is distraught over his unfaithfulness. While Suplicio and Pascual talk, Victoriano leaves. There follows a comic interlude between the shepherds, which ends in a *villancico.* Act 2 begins with Plácida longing for death until she takes Victoriano's dagger and plunges it into her breast. In the second scene Victoriano enters, still bemoaning his lover's absence, and stumbles over her corpse. When he sees that she killed herself with his own weapon, he is restrained from committing suicide himself only by Suplicio's reminder of eternal damnation. Scene 3 of act 2 consists of a series of prayers for the dead invoking the name of Cupid. Afterward, Suplicio tries to persuade the other shepherds to help bury Plácida, but they want to take a nap. Meanwhile, Victoriano is about to kill himself when Venus intervenes and tells him that Plácida is not dead. She summons Mercury to restore her soul, and Plácida awakens. When the shepherds come to bury her, neither lover can explain Venus's gift, but Victoriano states that he is free, alive, and well. The play ends in a song.

With regard to structure, *Egloga de Plácida y Victoriano* is the most complex drama attempted by Encina. The play consists of a *loa* (an introductory piece) followed by two acts, each with clearly divided scenes written in a variety of verse forms. The play is also Encina's most complex attempt at dealing with the theme of love. Victoriano, like Cristino and Fileno, is driven to desperation by love. He is the epitome of the courtly lover until the resurrection of Plácida, when he becomes its antithesis—free, alive, and well.

Despite the fact that *Egloga de Plácida y Victoriano* is Encina's most outwardly sophisticated play, scholars generally agree that it is not a complete success. The action of the play is not unified, and the ending is contrived and abrupt, though intervention of a deity was not unheard of in medieval and Renaissance works. Finally, although the play is longer than Encina's earlier works, allowing more room for character development, the characters are not as powerfully delineated as some of his other figures.

Encina's greatest professional rival was Fernández, born Lucas González in 1474. His father, Alonso González, was a carpenter and wood-carver; his mother was María Sánchez de Cantalapiedra. Both of Lucas's parents died in 1489, probably of the plague that was then raging in Salamanca. Lucas and his brothers became wards of a maternal uncle, Alonso González de Cantalapiedra. By 1490 Fernández was a choirboy in the choir of the cathedral of Santa María. He began studies at the University of Salamanca, receiving a degree probably around 1495. In 1496 he was in residence in the palace of the duke of Alba, where he probably performed in the early plays of Encina and where he wrote his first play, titled simply *Comedia*. In 1497 Fernández presented *Diálogo para cantar* (Dialogue to Be Sung) and *Farsa o cuasicomedia de la Doncella* (The Farce or Quasi-comedy of the Young Lady), also known as *Farsa o cuasicomedia del Caballero* (The Farce or Quasi-comedy of the Gentleman). He obtained the position of choirmaster at the cathedral of Salamanca in 1498. He initially shared this position with two other gentlemen, but by 1502, when Encina tried to assume the post with the support of a papal bull, Fernández had sole responsibility for this position. Fernández appealed the papal grant, and the litigation that ensued was drawn out.

In 1500 Fernández wrote *Egloga o farsa del nacimiento de Nuestro Redentor Jesucristo* (Eclogue or Farce of the Birth of Our Savior Jesus Christ). Sometime between 1500 and 1502 he wrote a second Nativity play, titled *Auto o farsa del nacimiento de Nuestro Señor Jesucristo* (Play or Farce of the Birth of Our Lord Jesus Christ). In 1502 Fernández received a benefice in Alaraz upon the death of his uncle. Fernández presented *Farsa de Prabos* (Farce of Prabos) in 1503 during the Corpus Christi celebrations. Scholars also generally agree that he had composed *Auto de la Pasión* (Play of the Passion) by 1503. In 1507 he is described for the first time as a cleric, and church records indicate that he was no longer the choirmaster at the cathedral of Salamanca. Court records reveal that by 1513 he had been sued by Alaraz for neglecting his duties to the parish. Fernández received his second benefice, from the parish of Santo Tomás Cantuariense, in 1514. Despite the burdens of two benefices, he managed to compile the dramas he had written for publication in Salamanca the same year as *Farsas y eglogas al modo y estilo pastoril y castellano* (Farces and Eclogues in the Pastoral and Castilian Manner). Fernández might have continued to write, but there are no other surviving texts to attest to this. He devoted the rest of his life to parish duties and in 1520 was appointed abbot of the clergy at the cathedral of Salamanca. In 1522 he became a professor of music at the University of Salamanca and in 1526 earned a master's degree in music, which entitled him to receive the salary of chair of music at the university. Fernández died in 1542 and was buried in the old cathedral of Salamanca.

Like Encina, Fernández began his career with short theatrical pieces. Unlike his rival, Fernández focused on secular plays with the theme of unrequited love. Of his seven pieces, four are secular, two are semi-religious, and one, his masterpiece, is fully religious.

Fernández's first play, *Comedia*, opens with Bras Gil, a shepherd, describing the symptoms of his pain at being in love. The object of his affection, Beringuella, appears; he declares his love for her and describes his anguish, for which she merely recommends medicines. Bras Gil gives her a gift, which changes her attitude, and she reciprocates by giving him a favor—a piece of cloth. They sing a *villancico* but are interrupted by Juan Benito, Beringuella's grandfather and Bras Gil's master. He is angry that the shepherd is courting his granddaughter since he is below her station, and the two men soon exchange insults, with Juan Benito falsely accusing Bras Gil of deflowering his granddaughter. A wise fellow shepherd intervenes, stating that the best recourse would be to allow the lovers to marry. Juan Benito resists until he realizes that he knows Bras Gil's grandmother well and then consents. The youths promise to marry with an oath as binding as the marriage ceremony itself, and the play ends in a song.

This first attempt by Fernández shows a relatively high level of sophistication compared to Encina's plays of the same period. *Comedia* shows Encina's influence in Fernández's use of rustic *sayagués* speech and the *villan-*

*cico.* The characters are the types one expects for a play on courtly love, but they are not flat characters. Their dialogue in bandying homespun animal comparisons is realistic for their social status and at the same time projects strong images. Bras Gil's emotions are engaging, and the insult battle between him and Juan Benito is both humorous and deftly written. The use of false accusations to heighten the conflict in the play was a device Fernández repeated in later plays. Finally, the characters evolve during the play—Beringuella converting from disdain to affection and Juan Benito moving from anger to consent—although their evolution is rather abrupt.

*Diálogo para cantar,* the second play in Fernández's *Farsas y eglogas al modo y estilo pastoril y castellano,* follows the traditional structure for this type of work. It consists of twenty-two strophes of seven octosyllabic lines. Juan, the protagonist, was formerly a happy man, but his personality has changed so abruptly that members of his village do not recognize him. This shift in character was precipitated by the loss of his love. His friend Bras encourages him to be strong, but Juan replies that his pain will be eternal and is so intense that he cannot even stand. He is about to reveal the name of the woman causing his distress when the play comes to a sudden end.

Because of this unexpected conclusion, the modern reader is left to believe that *Diálogo para cantar* must have had a second part no longer extant. This piece is not much esteemed in Fernández's repertoire, but it provides an interesting example of formulaic dialogue in song.

With *Farsa o cuasicomedia de la Doncella* Fernández continues with the theme of love. The play opens with Doncella searching for her lover, Caballero. On the road she encounters a pastor, who immediately falls in love with her and woos her, but she replies that his words only make her long for the caballero. Pastor tries to distract her by singing and playing music, but this inspires her to philosophize on love. As Pastor begins to lament his unrequited love for her, Doncella prepares to leave; to detain her, the pastor offers her gifts if she will accompany him to his house. At this climactic moment—the audience of course knows exactly what will happen if she agrees—the caballero arrives. Pastor and Caballero argue over Doncella but eventually reconcile since Pastor realizes that Doncella and Caballero have been together for a long time. The play ends amicably in a song.

Like Encina's *Egloga representada en requesta de unos amores,* this play is based on the *pastourelle* tradition of a knight who encounters and tries to press his affections on a shepherdess, but Fernández's example is superior to Encina's. The characters are more thoroughly delineated through dialogue, and the language is more advanced. The plot, too, is more suspenseful, for the

Title page for the collection of Gil Vicente's works that was compiled by his son Luis (from Copilaçam de toda las obras de Gil Vicente, edited by Maria Leonor Carvalhão Buescu, 1983; William T. Young Library, University of Kentucky)

suggestion that Doncella accompany Pastor to his house is not resolved until the end.

Fernández's fourth work was his only attempt to write a true farce. In *Farsa de Prabos* the title character, a shepherd, begins the play complaining about being in love, a state that is again portrayed as a physical sickness. Prabos claims to be half-dead and lost when a soldier appears on the scene and asks him about his ailment. He promises to help Prabos, but another shepherd, Pascual, tells Prabos not to trust a soldier. Pascual and the soldier argue, exchanging exaggerated threats and comical misunderstandings, until the object of Prabos's affection, Antona, enters. At first she rejects Prabos's love, calling him a trickster, until the others finally convince her that Prabos wants to marry her, and the play ends happily.

Fernández's attitude toward love as presented in *Farsa de Prabos* is considerably different from that in some of Encina's works, in which male characters are destroyed by love to the point of literally dying for it. Conversely, Fernández's farce ends with the statement "Quien sirve al amor / con firme esperanza / su fe siempre alcanza . . ." (He who serves Love / with firm hope / will always achieve his goal . . .). The spectator sees that love naturally causes the lover extreme pain and suffering–it is bitter, bad for the digestion, and leaves the body poisoned–but it eventually unites the lovers as one. Fernández shows great familiarity with his rival's works, referring in *Farsa de Prabos* to Encina's *Egloga representada en requesta de unos amores, Egloga de Cristino y Febea,* and *Egloga de Fileno, Zambardo y Cardonio.* Fernández's opposing view of love in *Farsa de Prabos* is considered by many critics to be a direct answer to Encina's exploration of the same theme.

*Farsa de Prabos* is also considered valuable because of the inclusion of the character of the *miles gloriosus* (boastful soldier). In classical and classically influenced literature from Plautus to Rojas, the swaggering soldier brags of his bravery in battle but later is shown to be a coward. In his confrontation with Pascual, Fernández's soldier proves himself to be a braggart but not a coward–on the contrary, his is a voice of wisdom. In standard Spanish he delivers steady reason, encouraging Prabos and Antona to marry.

Scholars note Fernández's stylistic sophistication in *Farsa de Prabos;* he again makes use of a false accusation (Pascual's generalization that all soldiers are not to be trusted) to heighten the conflict in the play. Even more interesting is his linguistic cleverness. Rather than using the traditional physical humor of slapstick comedy seen in the farces, the comedy is based on puns, such as a play between the words *alabarda* (halberd–a soldier's weapon) and *albarada* (a packsaddle) during the insult battle between the shepherd and soldier.

Fernández's last three plays are religious or semi-religious, including two Christmas plays. *Egloga o farsa del Nacimiento de Nuestro Redentor Jesucristo* features three shepherds, Bonifacio, Gil, and Marcel, who all speak *sayagués,* and a hermit, Macario, who speaks good Castilian. At the opening of the play Bonifacio is bragging about himself, and then Gil enters and scoffs at him. They launch into a bragging contest, which ends with a humorous narration of their lineages. Gil is bored to sleep; to keep him awake, Bonifacio reminds him of biblical figures who suffered disaster upon nodding off. Macario stumbles upon the shepherds while looking for the road. They question him, and another conflict arises. The hermit replies that the shepherds should leave him alone since Christ is soon to be born, bringing peace to the world. The shepherds are curious

about Christ, so Macario tells them the prophecies. They express doubt over the Virgin Birth but eventually give way and decide to take gifts to the Christ child.

*Egloga o farsa del Nacimiento de Nuestro Redentor Jesucristo* shows some similarities to Encina's plays, particularly in the anachronism of the plot. The shepherds mention the Pope at one point and later state their intent to visit the Christ child. More prevalent, however, are the differences between Encina's and Fernández's approach, for the latter places far more emphasis on mixing religious themes and humor, and his shepherds openly doubt a key religious doctrine, the Virgin Birth.

These differences are also seen in Fernández's second Christmas play, *Auto o farsa del Nacimiento de Nuestro Señor Jesucristo,* which opens with Pascual complaining about the cold, wet morning. He awakens a friend, Lloreynte, to keep him company, and they fall to playing games to warm up. They are interrupted by Juan, who announces to them the birth of Christ. Initially, they doubt him, so he explains the prophecies to them, and they are convinced. Another shepherd, Pedro, appears and tells them that he has seen angels who informed him that Christ was born. Deciding to go and adore Jesus, they discuss what gifts to bring him. They prepare to sing a song, but they need a fourth singer. Lloreynte cannot join them because he is too stuffed with garlic, so they call in a fourth singer, and the play ends with the song.

Again, Fernández's characters express doubt about a core religious tenet, that Christ has been born. Scholars also call attention to the humor of the piece; even the conclusion, which should focus on the momentous event of the Savior's birth, is marred by Lloreynte's garlic belches.

The open humor of these two religious plays is completely absent in Fernández's masterpiece, the *Auto de la Pasión,* which features Peter, Matthew, the three Marys, Jeremiah, and a figure called Dionysius of Athens. In the prologue Peter grieves over having denied Christ three times; Dionysius enters, and Peter goes on to describe the closing events of Christ's life–his betrayal and his suffering. Matthew enters and contributes to the story. The three Marys then appear, sing an *endecha* (funeral song), and express their grief. An *Ecce homo* (behold the man; a representation of the suffering Christ) is shown, inspiring another song. Matthew further describes Christ's Passion, particularly the *planctus Mariae* (Mary's lament). The climactic moment of the play is Matthew's description of the Crucifixion. A cross is brought onto the stage, and the actors kneel and sing yet another hymn. Afterward, the prophet Jeremiah, bearing a flag with five stains representing the wounds of Christ, arrives and repeats his prediction of the destruction of Jerusalem. Matthew recites the Latin poem known as *Planctus Mariae*. The emotion of the moment inspires Dionysius to express his desire to see the tomb of Christ since he never saw Christ in life. The others tell him that he can see a receptacle in the tabernacle that contains the Sacred Host. Mary Magdalene leads Dionysius to it, and they fall to their knees in adoration, singing a final song, which recounts Christ's life.

Two anachronisms are present in Fernández's masterpiece. The first is the appearance of Dionysius of Athens, a convert of Paul who was not present at the Crucifixion. The second is the appearance of the Old Testament figure Jeremiah in dialogue with companions of Christ.

Nevertheless, the innovations in *Auto de la Pasión*—intensity of emotion, imagery, and language—make it truly notable. The three Marys are almost interchangeable—in fact, their lines are preceded only by the letter M. Despite this fact, their emotions reach an intensity that is unprecedented in Spanish theater, making them unforgettable characters. The spectator's own emotions are further wrenched by the violent imagery in the play. Verbs of emotion and violence predominate—*llorar, gemir, repelar* (to cry, to moan, to tear at one's hair); *llagar, arrancar, herir* (to pierce, to yank out, to wound). Christ's body is described as *desgarrado* (torn apart) and *descoyuntado* (disjointed), his face is *ensangrentada* (bloodied), and his veins are *rompidas* (slashed). Scholars have noted that these participial verb forms used as adjectives churn with violent memory as shared dramatic experience.

Fernández and Encina were rivals, but the former profited from his early exposure to Encina's plays. Although he did not write as many plays as Encina, and Fernández never attempted a play of the length or heightened style of *Egloga de Plácida y Victoriano,* his works clearly took the best of Encina's example and expanded on it, continuing the use of lower-class *sayagués* patois, pastoral characters, popular-stage business, and (in the religious plays) anachronistic characters. Fernández also experimented with the nature of love in four of his plays. On the whole, his works have more action and conflict than Encina's, the action is more unified, and the characters are often more developed. Finally, some scholars assert that Fernández's verse is more sophisticated and lyrical than Encina's.

Just as Encina is known as the father of Spanish drama, the bilingual Vicente was the father of Portuguese drama. Little is known of his life. He was probably born around 1470 and was attached to the courts of the Portuguese kings Manuel I and John II. His first staged work, *Auto de la visitación* (Play of the Visitation), appeared in 1502 to celebrate the birth of the prince who later became King Juan III of Portugal. Vicente's last staged work, *Floresta de enganos* (Grove of Deceits), was performed in 1536. Vicente is referred to as dead in a document dated 16 April 1540.

The majority of Vicente's works were gathered into one edition, *Copilaçam* (Compilation), by his son Luis and published in 1562. Vicente wrote at least forty-four plays, eleven of which are in Spanish, fifteen in Portuguese, and the rest in a mix of both languages. Scholars have debated why Vicente chose to write using this combination of languages. One possible reason is that he wrote in Spanish—or, more specifically, in *sayagués*—in order to imitate the styles of Encina and Fernández. Another possibility is that because many courtiers were also functionally bilingual, the alternation of languages lent authenticity to his works. Finally, for his Portuguese audiences, Spanish was a prestige tongue at the time.

When he published his father's works, Luis Vicente divided the collection into five sections—devotions, comedies, tragicomedies, farces, and other various works. This organizational plan leads to the second controversy surrounding Gil Vicente's plays, since scholars doubt that the dramatist, dead for possibly fifteen years by the time *Copilaçam* was published, had any input into these divisions. In the prologue to *Tragicomedia de Don Duardos* (Tragicomedy of Don Duardos) Vicente does classify his works, saying they are "comedias, farsas y moralidades que he compuesto" (comedies, farces and morality plays that I have composed). Regardless, scholars have dedicated much effort to assigning Vicente's works to neat categories, and the argument cannot be settled here.

The first of Vicente's dramatic works are religious, such as the early, short dramatic pieces *Monólogo de la Visitación* (Monologue of the Visitation), *Auto pastoril castellano* (Spanish Pastoral Play), and *Auto de los Reyes Magos* (Play of the Three Kings). He found his inspiration for these works not in the religious tropes of the early Middle Ages but rather in the pastoral religious plays of Encina and Fernández. Simple in style and structure, these plays also employ *sayagués,* but many critics affirm that Vicente's works are superior to those of his predecessors in their lyricism.

Vicente quickly advanced to more-complex religious works, the most noteworthy being *Auto de la Sibila Casandra* (Play of Sibyl Casandra) and the trilogy consisting of *Barca do Inferno* (Ship of Hell), *Barca do Purgatorio* (Ship of Purgatory), and *Barca de la Gloria* (Ship of Glory). In *Auto de la Sibila Casandra* the protagonist, Casandra, refuses to marry, stating that marriage is a prison and painful because men are lazy, abusive, and so jealous that they can destroy a marriage. She prefers to remain a virgin, rejecting Salomon, who wants her for his wife. He turns to her aunts—Erutea, Peresica, and

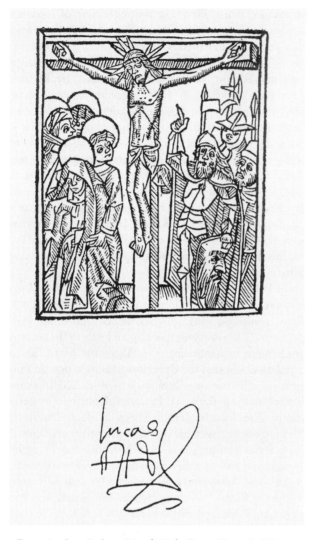

*Engraving from the first edition (1514) of Lucas Fernández's* Farsas
y eglogas al modo y estilo pastoril y castellano *(from
Fernández,* Farsas y Eglogas, *edited by María Josefa
Canellada, 1976; Central Library, Joint University
Libraries, Nashville, Tennessee)*

and Christian elements. Casandra's aunts are pagan
seers, while her uncles are Christian prophets. Vicente
uses this device repeatedly–likening Jupiter and Christ
in *Auto de los Cuatro Tiempos* (Play of the Four Seasons),
for example. These plays have a symbolic richness
unprecedented in medieval theater, making their allegories precursors to the elaborate *autos sacramentales* (sacra-
mental plays) of Pedro Calderón de la Barca.

The characters in Vicente's mature religious plays
are vividly drawn. *Auto de la Sibila Casandra* revolves
around the theme of haughtiness versus humility.
Casandra embodies haughtiness, presumptuously refusing to marry because she believes herself destined to
become the mother of God. Salomon, on the other
hand, is a Christ-like character, a simple man, honest
and hardworking. When Casandra rejects him, she represents the pagan world rejecting Christian humility.
This rejection is summarized at the end of the play by
the prophets, who predict that arrogance will be the
downfall of the world.

During the next stage of his literary development,
Vicente, now secure in his position of court playwright,
focused on secular plays. His best include *Tragicomedia
de Don Duardos, Comedia del viudo* (Comedy of the Wid-
ower), and a dramatic version of the medieval chivalric
romance *Amadís de Gaula*. The *Tragicomedia de Don Duardos* is considered by many critics to be Vicente's masterpiece. It tells the story of Prince Duardos of England,
who falls in love with the Princess Flérida, daughter of
the emperor of Constantinople. Advised that to win her
love in return he should pretend to be a gardener in her
household, he accedes, hoping to be near her and gain
her notice. Posing as the son of a rustic couple, Juan
and Constanza, Duardos soon gains Flérida's love, but
it torments her because she must choose between her
heart and a social law that forbids her to associate with
a man of such apparently low stature. Finally, she capit-
ulates to her feeling, Duardos reveals his true identity,
and they sail off to England together. Alongside this
love story Vicente presents two other romantic pairs.
Camilote and Maimonda are buffoonish lovers, Maimonda a truly unattractive girl, and Camilote so besot-
ted that he proclaims her to be stunning. Juan and
Constanza represent tender attachments among the
lower classes: although long married they still call each
other by endearing pet names, such as "mi amor" (my
love) and "mi alma" (my soul).

*Tragicomedia de Don Duardos* shows impressive
advancement in at least five fields. First, the verse is
beautifully delicate and lyrical: the poetry describing
the garden and the lovers in it is exquisite and refined.
Second, the dramatic tension created by Flérida's
dilemma and Duardos's unrequited desire must have
moved the noble audience for whom this play was

Cimeria–for help, but when they cannot, he seeks out
her uncles, Moses, Abraham, and Isaiah, who also fail to
convince her to marry. When they foretell the birth of
Christ, the true reason Casandra does not want to
marry is revealed–she wants to remain a virgin because
she believes she is destined to be the mother of God.
Her aunts and uncles are scandalized and prophesy the
end of a world full of arrogance that is too interested in
building palaces. At this point a curtain opens, and the
spectators see the birth of the true Christ to a true virgin. All the characters fall on their knees to adore him.

This innovative approach to the Nativity theme is
a valuable example of Vicente's style in his mature religious dramas. *Auto de la Sibila Casandra* is typical of
Vicente's works because it skillfully interweaves pagan

intended and led them to sympathize as Flérida slowly falls in love with someone she believes to be unsuitable as a marriage partner. Duardos suffers immensely as well, waiting to see if the woman he desperately loves will return his affection, all the while knowing that everything rides on his deception, his only means of getting close to her. Third is the beauty of the imagery of the garden, an avatar of the classic *locus amoenus* (pleasant place) that implies both the intensity of feeling and the obligatory chastity that crackles around the lovers. Fourth, the complexity of the plot anticipates later Spanish drama of the Golden Age in the juggling of subplots and secondary characters, a practice rarely attempted by late-medieval dramatists. This tragicomedy focuses on a love between nobles, but it interweaves and contrasts their love with comical and admirable, albeit rustic, examples. Finally, the *Tragicomedia de Don Duardos* is praised for the dramatic rhythm of its dialogue and the economy of its action.

Finally, one aspect of Vicente's plays that all critics note is the range of characters and themes seen in his secular pieces. The spectator sees a whole procession of social types, customs, and beliefs, with Jews, Christians, disguised princes, peasants, simpletons, doctors, gypsies, and squires. One of the most valuable aspects of these plays is that, together, they present a cross section of social identities during Vicente's day.

Vicente's works represent a mature theatrical style. The lyricism of his verse has led critics to praise him as the best poet in Portugal, second only to Luis de Camões. The complexity of Vicente's works, with regard to character development, structure, and plot development, is the closest approximation in late-medieval Spain to the sophistication of Renaissance theater. Furthermore, the far greater number of plays that he wrote allowed him to explore far more character types and themes than Encina or Fernández. Of all the members of the "Salamancan school" of dramatists, Vicente wrote the most fully developed and modern works.

The last half of fifteenth-century Spain was a time of extraordinary progress in the evolution of drama. From a country with almost no previous examples of extant drama, it became a leader of dramatic production in Europe. Encina's plays brought to the stage popular everyday life and achieved their characterization through language and the use of a stylized *sayagués* dialect and the creation or recycling of colorful *villancicos*. Other great playwrights, such as Fernández and Vicente, learned from Encina's example and created increasingly complex dramatic characters, situations, and structures. By the early 1500s the foundations for the works of Vega and Calderón de la Barca had been firmly established by these early dramatists.

**References:**

José Amícola, "El Auto de la huida a Egipto, drama anónimo del siglo XV," *Filología*, 15 (1971): 1–29;

Amícola, "El siglo XV y el teatro castellano," *Filología*, 14 (1970): 145–169;

Alberto Blecua, "La Egloga de Francisco de Madrid en un nuevo manuscrito del siglo XVI," in *Serta Philogica F. Lázaro Carreter: Natalem diem sexagesimum celebranti dicata*, 2 volumes, edited by Emilio Alarcos Llorach and others (Madrid: Cátedra, 1983), II: 39–66;

Manuel Cañete, *Teatro español del siglo XVI: Estudios histórico literarios* (Madrid: M. Tello, 1885);

Joseph E. Gillet, "Egloga hecha por Francisco de Madrid (1495?)," *Hispanic Review*, 11 (1943): 275–303;

John Lihani, *Lucas Fernández* (New York: Twayne, 1973);

Miguel Angel Pérez Priego, "El teatro castellano del siglo XV," *Insula*, 537 (1990): 14–15, 17;

Francisco Ruiz Ramón, *Historia del teatro español*, volume 1: *Desde los orígenes hasta 1900* (Madrid: Alianza, 1967);

Charlotte Stern, "The Early Spanish Drama: From Medieval Ritual to Renaissance Art," *Renaissance Drama*, new series 6 (1973): 177–201;

Stern, "The Genesis of the Spanish Pastoral: From Lyric to Drama," *Kentucky Romance Quarterly*, 25 (1978): 414–434;

Stern, "Juan del Encina's Carnival Eclogues and the Spanish Drama of the Renaissance," *Renaissance Drama*, 8 (1965): 181–195;

Stern, *The Medieval Theater in Castile* (Binghamton, N.Y.: Medieval & Renaissance Texts & Studies, 1996);

Henry W. Sullivan, *Juan del Encina* (Boston: Twayne, 1976);

Ronald E. Surtz, *The Birth of a Theater: Dramatic Convention in the Spanish Theater from Juan del Encina to Lope de Vega* (Princeton: Department of Romance Languages and Literatures, Princeton University / Madrid: Castalia, 1979);

Angel Valbuena Prat, *Historia del teatro español* (Barcelona: Noguer, 1956);

Gil Vicente, *Lírica*, edited by Armando López Castro (Madrid: Cátedra, 1993);

Karl Young, *The Drama of the Medieval Church*, 2 volumes (Oxford: Clarendon Press, 1933).

# Protest Poetry in Castile

(*circa 1445 – circa 1506*)

Barbara F. Weissberger
*University of Minnesota–Twin Cities*

**WORKS:** *Coplas de la panadera* [*Coplas de "Ay, panadera"* or *Coplas de "Di, panadera"*], attributed to Rodrigo de Cota, Juan de Mena, or Iñigo Ortiz de Estúñiga (after 1445)

**Manuscripts:** Of the several known manuscripts, the oldest are Madrid, Biblioteca Nacional MS. 10475; Santander, Biblioteca Menéndez Pelayo MS 71.

**First publication:** In Liciniano Sáez, *Demostración histórica del verdadero valor de todas las monedas que corrían en Castilla durante el reynado del Señor don Enrique IV* (Madrid: Imprenta de Sancha, 1805).

**Standard edition:** *Coplas de la panadera,* edited by Paola Elia (Verona: Universita degli Studi di Verona, 1982), based on Santander, Biblioteca Menéndez Pelayo MS. 71.

*Coplas de Mingo Revulgo* (1464), attributed to Fray Íñigo López de Mendoza and Juan de Mena

**Manuscripts:** There are several known manuscripts. Santander, Biblioteca Menéndez Pelayo MS. 78, includes a thirty-two-stanza version with a prose gloss by Fernando del Pulgar and appears to be a copy of the incunabulum of 1485; London, British Library, Egerton 939, no. 18, records a thirty-five-stanza variant; Madrid, Biblioteca Nacional, Vitr. 26-13, includes thirty-five stanzas, thirty-five rhymed "responses," and an anonymous prose gloss.

**First publication:** *Coplas de Mingo Revulgo* (Burgos: Fadrique de Basilea, 1485).

**Standard edition:** *Las Coplas de Mingo Revulgo,* edited by Viviana Brodey (Madison, Wis.: Hispanic Seminary of Medieval Studies, 1986).

*Coplas del provincial* (1465–1466), attributed to Alonso de Palencia, Rodrigo de Cota, Antón de Montoro, and Juan Hurtado de Mendoza

**Manuscripts:** Various; one is included in *Miscelánea genealógica,* Biblioteca de Vicente Salvá; another, copied by Vicente Joaquín Noguera in 1797, is housed in Madrid Real Academia de la Historia Est. 20, gr. 7, no. 92.

**First publication:** *Las coplas del provincial,* Raymond Foulché-Delbosc, *Revue Hispanique,* 5 (1898): 255–266, based on the Salvá MS.

**Standard edition:** *Las coplas del provincial,* edited by Marcella Ciceri, *Cultura neolatina,* 35 (1975): 39–210.

*Carajicomedia* (1502–1503?), attributed to Ambrosio Montesino and Hernando del Castillo

**Manuscripts:** Unknown.

**First publication:** *Cancionero general,* edited by Castillo (Valencia, 1519).

**Modern edition:** In *Cancionero de obras de burlas provocantes a risa,* edited by Frank Domínguez (Valencia: Albatros Hispanófila, 1978), pp. 139–184.

**Standard edition:** *Carajicomedia,* edited by Carlos Varo (Madrid: Playor, 1981).

**Edition in English:** *A Cock-eyed Comedy: Starring Friar Bugeo Montesino and Other Faeries of Motley Feather and Fortune,* edited by Juan Goytisolo, translated by Peter Bush (London: Serpent's Tail, 2002).

Satirical vernacular verse targeting contemporary social and political ills—what would now be called protest poetry—has a long tradition in Iberia. The Galician-Portuguese lyrics known as *cantigas d'escarnho y maldezir* (songs of ribaldry and ill repute) flourished in the courts of Portugal and Spain between the late twelfth century and the early fourteenth. The best-known poet and patron of the *cantigas* is Alfonso X, the Learned King (reigned 1252–1284), whose targets range from the Pope to María Balteira, a well-known prostitute who frequented the royal court. The latter class of women is one of the most frequent objects of mockery and insult in the *cantigas.* Most often called *soldadera,* her name points both to the money (*soldada* = pay; *soldo* = a type of coin) that she received for sex and to a venue she apparently frequented (*soldados* = soldiers). There is persistent overlap between the figures of the *soldadera* and the *panadera* (baker girl). The *panadera* early on becomes something of a stock comic character, especially in sacrilegious texts (for example, the "Cruz, cruzada" episode in *Libro de Buen Amor* by Juan Ruiz), because of the obvious relationship between the bread she sells and the bread of holy communion.

The language of the *cantigas d'escarnho y maldezir* and the body politic associated with the *soldaderas,* who are principal targets of jest, link these early lyrics with the narrative satirical poetry written in Castilian during the second half of the fifteenth century. The best-known examples of this genre, in roughly chronological order, are *Coplas de la panadera* (Stanzas of the Baker Girl, after 1445; also called *Coplas de "Di, panadera"*: or *Coplas de "Ay panadera"*), *Coplas del provincial* (Stanzas of the Provincial, 1465–1466), *Coplas de Mingo Revulgo* (Stanzas of Mingo Revulgo, 1464), and the longer and more ambitious *Carajicomedia* (1502–1503?; translated as *A Cock-eyed Comedy: Starring Friar Bugeo Montesino and Other Faeries of Motley Feather and Fortune,* 2002). The fact that all of these works have survived without indication of authorship is understandable, for they not only assail the decadent character and shameful behavior of named nobles and monarchs, but they do so using explicitly scatological and pornographic language.

Exact dates of composition have not been determined for these later individual poems, but all were most likely composed during the reigns of Enrique IV (1454–1474) and Isabel I of Castile (Isabella the Catholic, 1474–1504). The view from below they adopt serves as a useful corrective to the triumphalism and adulation of much of the literature commissioned by or addressed to those monarchs, such as Juan de Mena's *Laberinto de Fortuna* (Labyrinth of Fortune, 1445; Mena has been suggested as author of *Coplas de Mingo Revulgo*) or the official chronicles of the reign of Isabel written by Fernando del Pulgar (who composed a gloss to the *Coplas de Mingo Revulgo*).

Up until the second half of the twentieth century the graphic nature of the discourse employed in these texts inhibited their due critical consideration. Eduardo Rincón, the editor of the widely used 1968 anthology *Coplas satíricas y dramáticas de la Edad Media* (Satirical and Dramatic Stanzas of the Middle Ages), omitted *Coplas del provincial* because of "su lenguaje excesivamente procaz y obsceno" (their excessively lewd and obscene language). Until the last quarter of the twentieth century, scholarship on these works focused primarily on identifying the authors and subjects of the poems; the latter have been somewhat easier to determine.

*Coplas de la panadera* consists of forty-seven *redondillas,* eight-line stanzas of octosyllabic verse with the rhyme scheme *abba acca.* Some versions begin with a stanza addressed directly to a *panadera* or *soldadera* who is

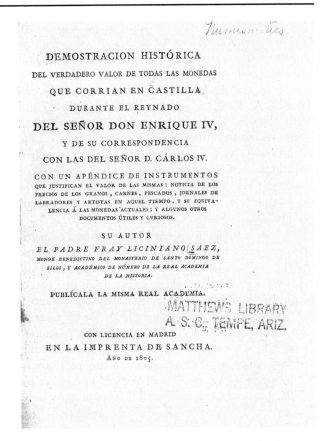

*Title page for the financial treatise in which the ribald fifteenth-century satire* Coplas de la panadera *was first published (Matthews Library, Arizona State University)*

presumed to have been present at the Battle of Olmedo. This witness-addressee continues to be invoked by the refrain "Di, panadera" (in one version, "Ay, panadera"), which recurs after some of the stanzas. The refrain rhymes with lines 1, 4, 5, and 8 of the *redondillas.*

The date of composition for the poem is unknown, but its terminus a quo is necessarily the date of the battle that is its subject. The armed conflict that took place near Olmedo on 19 May 1445 must be seen in the context of the repeated attempts by the Aragonese branch of the Trastámara dynasty to secure its claims in Castile and of the constant struggle between rival noble factions within fifteenth-century Castile. A key figure in both struggles and in the poem is Álvaro de Luna, King Juan II's powerful favorite, who was appointed *privado,* or royal adviser, in 1419. Luna was despised by much of Castile's high aristocracy and clergy, for whom he represented the rapid social and political ascent of Castile's *conversos* (Jews whose ancestors had converted to Christianity), though not a *converso* himself. Luna's rapid rise to wealth and power and subsequent precipitous fall from favor (Juan II ordered his execution in 1453) stirred the imagination of fifteenth-century writers in a way that must be partially attributed to his embodiment of the capriciousness of fortune but also to the anxieties stirred by decades of political and social instability in Castile and by the ambitions in Castile of the Aragonese branch of the Trastámara dynasty. At the Battle of Olmedo the royal forces and noble allies led by Luna defeated the Castilian noblemen who had rallied around Juan and Enrique, the infantes of Aragon, thereby blocking Aragonese pretensions in Spain for three decades, until the marriage of Isabel and Fernando II (Ferdinand) of Aragon, son of the infante Juan who appears in the poem as king of Navarra.

The anonymous satirist has no political or patriotic allegiance, however. The poem expresses not so much a militaristic protonationalism as a war-weary cynicism toward the nobles engaged in the battle. Stanza by stanza, the poet savages forty-five highborn noblemen and clerics who fought in the battle, naming names and accusing each one of cowardice, ridiculous dress, drunkenness, avarice, excessive pride, and a sullied bloodline. A personage of the status of Rodrigo Manrique (who was solemnly eulogized years later by his son Jorge in the poem *Coplas a la muerte de su padre* [Stanzas on the Death of His Father], circa 1476–1479) is here described as having a "coraçón de alfeñique" (sugar-paste heart) and fleeing the battle on a swift horse. Similarly, Alonso Carrillo, who became archbishop of Toledo, is so fearful "que a los sus paños menores / fue menester labrandera" (he required a laundress for his underwear).

A curious framing device unites the individual portraits in *Coplas de la panadera,* reinforcing the poet's critique of Castilian and Aragonese manhood. The poem is presented as a kind of interview between the poetic persona and a *soldadera,* who has presumably recently witnessed the battle. The introductory stanza addresses the unusual wartime correspondent as follows: "Panadera soldadera, / que bendes pan de barato, / qüentanos algún rebato / que te aconteció en la vera" (Baker-girl, troop-follower, / you who sell your bread cheap, / tell us about the surprise attack / you witnessed on the plain). The prostitute troop-follower, who sells her bread–and body–to the soldiers, is implicitly constituted as an appropriately degraded eyewitness reporter for a shameful conflict. The warrior ideology dominant in Reconquest Spain, but weakened in the reign of Juan II and Enrique IV, is thereby casually and caustically turned upside down.

Scholars have suggested three fifteenth-century poets as possible authors of *Coplas de la panadera:* Rodrigo de Cota, Iñigo Ortíz de Estúñiga, and Juan de Mena, the most admired poet of the fifteenth century. Within the *Coplas de la panadera* the latter two trade insults in a brief poetic polemic (two, and in some versions three, *redondillas*) appended to one of the recensions of the work. In the first stanza, Mena accuses Ortiz de Estúñiga of slandering the soldiers at Olmedo without being a participant himself; the latter counters by calling Mena a Jew. The fact that Juan II and Luna are among the few subjects to escape the poet's satirical scalpel favors Mena's authorship, since he was both royal secretary to Juan II and a fervent supporter of Luna. There is also critical support for the notion that the poet was a *converso* (like Cota and perhaps Mena as well) who had the perspective to ridicule both sides of the conflict. A similar argument is advanced by Nilda Guglielmi, who considers the author to have been an intellectual, perhaps a court poet who coexisted with the nobles he portrayed but who was not one of them. The poem enjoyed success outside of Castile, as evidenced by three anonymous Catalan invectives that make use of the one-line refrain.

The bucolic satire *Coplas de Mingo Revulgo* exists in various versions consisting of from thirty to thirty-five strophes of nine octosyllabic lines (four lines rhyming *abba* or *abab* followed by five lines rhyming *ccddc*). Many editions (twenty-four in the sixteenth century alone), at least one imitation, and several extant verse and prose glosses from the fifteenth and sixteenth centuries attest to the popularity of the anonymous poem, attributed to Íñigo López de Mendoza by Julio Rodríguez-Puértolas. The most admired of the glosses, by the learned court historian and biographer Pulgar, accompanies most printed editions of *Coplas de Mingo Revulgo* since the initial one (1485). As in the case of Mena's political allegory *Laberinto de Fortuna* (Labyrinth of Fortune, 1444) and the learned prose gloss composed by Hernán Núñez for its 1499 edition, the editorial practice that paired *Coplas de Mingo Revulgo* and Pulgar's erudite gloss enhanced the cultural prestige of the work. Its status in the sixteenth century is demonstrated in its frequent pairing with such respected poems as the *Proverbios* of the marqués de Santillana and the *Coplas* of Jorge Manrique.

*Coplas de Mingo Revulgo* is a political allegory that takes the form of a dialogue between two shepherds, the prophetic Gil Arribato (whose name Pulgar derives from the Latin *ariolor* and *vaticinior*) and the disgruntled Mingo Revulgo. According to Pulgar, the latter stands for "el pueblo" (the intensifying prefix "re-" indicating a rustic background), the subjects of Enrique IV. At the beginning of the poem, Gil questions Mingo about his dejected, disheveled appearance. Mingo attributes his misfortunes to the indifference and dissoluteness of the chief shepherd, Candaulo (King Enrique), who leaves his flock unattended while he disports himself with the shepherd's helpers (his advisers, especially the maligned *privado* Beltrán de la Cueva). The neglect of

*Page from Santander, Biblioteca Mendéndez Pelayo MS. 78 of* Coplas de Mingo Revulgo *(1464), attributed by some scholars to Fray Íñigo López de Mendoza and by others to Juan de Mena (from* Las Coplas de Mingo Revulgo, *edited by Viviana Brodey, 1986; Thomas Cooper Library, University of South Carolina)*

the flock by the head shepherd and his guard dogs (the four cardinal virtues) has made them easy prey for the wolves (rebellious nobles). Gil rejects Mingo's assignment of blame, insisting that he himself is to blame for losing the three theological virtues: "verías que por tu ruindad / has avido mal pastor" (you would see that your own sins / have merited this bad shepherd). Prayer, confession, and penance are necessary for his fortunes to change, either by a change in his present leader's behavior or by God granting him another, worthier leader (Pulgar's commentary, written during the reign of Isabel the Catholic and addressed to the count of Haro, identifies her as the monarch in question). Gil then prophesies apocalyptically that if proper contrition and penance do not occur, three rabid wolves (war, hunger, and pestilence) will destroy the flock.

The elevated, apocalyptic tone of *Coplas de Mingo Revulgo* contrasts with the bawdiness of the other satirical poems produced during the same tumultuous era. The invocation of the four cardinal and three theological virtues and the preoccupation with confession, contrition, and penance give it a religious fervor that is more common in the reign of Enrique IV's half sister and successor, Isabel.

*Coplas de Mingo Revulgo* has received more critical attention than most other satirical poems of the time. Its importance to literary historians derives first from its apparent indebtedness to Virgil's eclogues and to pastoral imagery of the New Testament (particularly Christ as the Good Shepherd and the parable of the lost sheep), and second, from the influence of its rustic characters and speech on the development of drama in late-fifteenth- and sixteenth-century Spain, as Charlotte Stern demonstrated in her 1976 essay "The *Coplas de Mingo Revulgo* and the Early Spanish Drama." Some scholars believe that Juan del Encina, the "father of Spanish drama," adopted the names of Mingo and Gil for two of the stock characters in his dramatic eclogues precisely because of the ironic resonance they had for a public familiar with the political satire. More attention has been devoted to the distinctive speech from the region of Mingo and Gil, loosely based on rustic speech around Salamanca and Zamora. This dialect, which came to be known as *sayagués*, was adopted by Encina, Torres Naharro, Lucas Fernández, Sánchez de Badajoz, and other sixteenth-century dramatists up to and including Lope de Vega.

*Coplas de Mingo Revulgo* has been attributed to various authors, notably its commentator, Pulgar, but also to Cota, Alonso de Palencia (who wrote the allegorical *Batalla campal de los perros contra los lobos* [The Pitched Battle of the Dogs against the Wolves, 1457], which bears some similarity to the poem), and Fernán Pérez de Guzmán. A strong argument was made by Rodríguez-

Puértolas in 1972 for authorship by Mendoza, whose lengthy *Vita Christi* (Life of Christ), also composed in the reign of Enrique IV, paraphrases five stanzas from *Coplas de Mingo Revulgo* and alludes to some "coplas aldeanas" (village stanzas) in a passage satirizing the moral laxity of Enrique's court.

Judging from the extensive manuscript tradition, the many versions and contaminations, as well as at least two prose commentaries and a continuation written in the sixteenth century, the aggressive satire *Coplas del provincial* was immensely popular. The extant versions of the poem vary between 104 and 306 stanzas, with a core version of 149 stanzas. This range, along with the existence of a *Segundo Provincial* (Second Provincial), a continuation written during the reign of Carlos V (from 1517 to 1556), suggests that the work circulated widely and invited emendation.

Like *Coplas de Mingo Revulgo,* although in more rudimentary fashion, *Coplas del provincial* uses an allegorical structure. A father provincial (the head of a province of a religious order) arrives for an inspection visit at one of his monasteries, identified in the second verse of the poem as "aquesta corte real" (this royal court). The provincial questions first the male and then the female inhabitants of the monastery about their debauched behavior or despised ancestry. Every stanza levels accusations of sodomy, incest, adultery, and prostitution and of possessing Jewish or Moorish lineage at named and unnamed aristocratic persons from the "capellán mayor" (main chaplain), King Enrique IV, on down. Many of the nobles savaged by the author of *Coplas del provincial* were previously attacked in the contemporary *Coplas de la panadera* for cowardice and greed. The parallels led some to posit an influence of *Coplas de la panadera* on *Coplas del provincial,* but the latter's slanderous discourse is more virulent and prurient, obsessed with exposing the most contaminated parts of the body politic: sodomites and converted Jews.

It is likely that *Coplas del provincial* simply codifies slander that had been circulating orally since early in Enrique IV's reign. As Raymond Foulché-Delbosc observes in his "Notes sur las *Coplas del provincial*" from an 1899 issue of *Revue Hispanique,* the anonymous sixteenth- or seventeenth-century commentator of *Coplas del provincial* claims that the slanderous verses had been both used by the Inquisition in its proceedings against some of the families mentioned and later censored by the same institution. Although the assertion is undocumented, it gives some idea of the power of such defamatory discourse in a society as preoccupied with questions of bloodline and honor as early modern Spain. Less than a decade after *Coplas del provincial* circulated, some of its calumny, in particular its allusions to Enrique IV's various adulterous and sodomitical relationships, was institutionalized by Isabel and

Page from British Library MS. Egerton 939 of Coplas de Mingo Revulgo (*from* Las Coplas de Mingo Revulgo, *edited by Viviana Brodey, 1986; Thomas Cooper Library, University of South Carolina*)

*Title page for the 1519 collection of bawdy songs that includes the parodic* Carajicomedia *(Doe Library, University of California, Berkeley)*

Fernando's court chroniclers as part of a comprehensive propaganda campaign against Enrique and his putatively illegitimate heir, Juana de Castilla. The accusations have remained a part of the historiographical record.

The authorship of *Coplas del provincial* has been much debated. Some scholars, basing their judgments on stylistic shifts within the poem, believe it is the work of multiple authors. Others propose a single *converso* author, variously Pulgar, Palencia, Cota, or Antón de Montoro. Others have argued that the virulence toward those with Jewish ancestry expressed in the poem makes it unlikely that it was composed by a *converso*.

*Carajicomedia,* one of the most ambitious protest poems of the time, was probably written at the end of Isabel's long reign or shortly after her death. The textual reference to the work of Fray Ambrosio Montesino, whose translation of Ludolph of Saxony's *Vita Christi* appeared in 1502–1503, offers a terminus ad quem. *Carajicomedia* and its accompanying prose gloss first appeared in the final section of the 1519 edition of Hernando del Castillo's massive songbook, *Cancionero*

*general,* first published in 1511. It was the centerpiece of the *Cancionero de obras de burlas provocantes a risa* (Songbook of Mirth-Provoking Burlesque Works, 1519), a collection of bawdy satiric poems, most of them brief occasional works bandied about by well-known court poets such as Montoro and Juan de Valladolid. *Carajicomedia* stands out among its congeners for its intertextuality: it is an accomplished stanza-by-stanza parody of the most admired poem of the fifteenth century, Mena's *Laberinto de Fortuna.*

*Laberinto de Fortuna* recounts the poetic persona's dream vision of Fortune and her three wheels, which represent past, present, and future time. His guide, Providence, explains the significance of each of the seven astrological circles contained in the wheel of the past and the present and introduces the exemplary individuals from ancient and modern times who inhabit them. Throughout the poem Mena repeatedly exhorts his addressee, Juan II, to rule firmly and wisely and to control feuding and adultery among the aristocracy, directing its energy toward the fulfillment of Castile's providential mission: the completion of the Reconquest of the kingdom of Granada from the Moors.

The sarcastic author of *Carajicomedia* turns Mena's militant and virile monarchism upside down in classic carnivalesque fashion. The poem narrates the "heroic" quest of Diego Fajardo to find a cure for his age-induced impotence. Both the hero and the "author" of *Carajicomedia* allude to historical persons. Fajardo was the son of a hero of the Reconquest who served under Isabel, and "Fray Bugeo Montesino" alludes to Fray Ambrosio Montesino, the queen's confessor and close adviser and the translator of *Vita Christi.* Fajardo's guide in his quest is an old go-between (a character explicitly indebted to Celestina from Fernando de Rojas's *Tragicomedia de Calisto y Melibea,* first published in 1502, the title of which the author of *Carajicomedia* most certainly parodies). Fajardo is transported to a brothel where the most famous prostitutes in Spain, grouped by geographical region, have congregated. The old *alcahueta* (madam) introduces each of these exemplary women and praises their accomplishments.

An accompanying prose commentary, presumably written by the translator of the poem, fleshes out the erotic biographies of each of the prostitutes in graphic detail, citing burlesque theological sources with outrageous irreverence. The poem ends with a material battle of the sexes, in which Fajardo's penis loses to a battalion of female genitalia. The ignominious demise of the hero of *Carajicomedia* is a travesty of the heroic death of the count of Niebla during a siege of Gibraltar, as recounted in *Laberinto de Fortuna* by Mena.

The author of *Carajicomedia* remains unknown. One of the earliest editors of the work, the nineteenth-century anticlerical writer Luis Usoz y Río, believed that its licentious tone and sacrilegious humor could only have come from the pen of a cleric. More recent attributions include Montesino and the work's first editor, Castillo. As for a date of composition, the structural similarity of the work to Hernán Núñez's 1499 glossed edition of *Laberinto de Fortuna,* its allusions to *Celestina,* and its mockery of persons closely associated with the court of Queen Isabel suggest that the poem was composed toward the end of her life or shortly after her death in 1504. Internal reference to the bishop of Osma led Frank Domínguez, in his 1978 edition of the *Cancionero de obras de burlas provocantes a risa,* to affirm a terminus ad quem of 1506.

The fact that some of the prostitutes in *Carajicomedia* are named Isabel and appear to refer to several of the queen's official titles is also telling. The first modern editors of the work saw it as a libertarian defense of pleasure and a critique of political and moral repression during the reign of Isabel and Fernando. In the late twentieth century, scholars such as Luis Montañés, Linde Brocato, and Barbara F. Weissberger have pointed out the *ad feminam* (misogynist) and specifically anti-Isabelline nature of the invective in *Carajicomedia.* Whereas Mena's goal was to goad King Juan II into action so as to restore vigor to an ailing patriarchal state—a goal similar to that sought by the authors of *Coplas del provincial* and *Coplas de Mingo Revulgo* for Juan's successor, Enrique IV—the author of *Carajicomedia* is critical of the fulfillment of that masculinist goal by a female sovereign. The bitter carnivalesque discourse of *Carajicomedia* expresses anxieties of emasculation produced by the presence on the throne of a powerful woman, and in particular, a powerful woman with an authoritarian and repressive patriarchal political agenda.

Many of the protest poems of the second half of the fifteenth century critique the abuses of monarchic power. In *Coplas del provincial, Coplas de Mingo Revulgo,* and *Carajicomedia,* power is constructed primarily in terms of gender and sexuality: in *Coplas del provincial* and *Coplas de Mingo Revulgo* the target is the purported effeminacy of Enrique IV, known to history as "el Impotente" (the Impotent); in *Carajicomedia* the target is the perceived anomalous masculinity of the virago Isabel. The satiric aim of *Coplas de la panadera* is more generalized, but its use of a sexually promiscuous "witness" to authoritatively report on the cowardice of the male combatants at Olmedo implies that it too related Castile's political problems to a breakdown in the traditional sex-gender system.

### References:

Carlos Alvar, "Poesía y política en la corte alfonsí," *Cuadernos hispanoamericanos,* 410 (1984): 5–20;

Linde Brocato, "'Tened por espejo su fin': Mapping Gender and Sex in Fifteenth- and Sixteenth-Century Spain," in *Queer Iberia: Sexualities, Cultures, and Crossings from the Middle Ages to the Renaissance,* edited by Josiah Blackmore and Gregory S. Hutcheson (Durham, N.C. & London: Duke University Press, 1999), pp. 325–365;

Manuel Ferrer-Chivite, "Las *Coplas del provincial:* Sus conversos y algunos que no lo son," *La corónica,* 10, no. 2 (1982): 156–178;

Raymond Foulché-Delbosc, "Notes sur las *Coplas del provincial,*" *Revue Hispanique,* 6 (1899): 417–446;

Juan Goytisolo, "Protesta, linajes y loco amor en '*El Cancionero de obras de burla,*'" in his *Cogitus interruptus* (Barcelona: Seix Barral, 1999), pp. 123–142;

Nilda Guglielmi, "Los elementos satíricos en las *Coplas de la Panadera,*" *Filología,* 14 (1970): 49–104;

Celestino López Alvarez and Francisco Torrecilla del Olmo, "El autor, sus pretensiones y otros aspectos de las *Coplas del provincial,*" *Bulletin Hispanique,* 83, nos. 3–4 (1981): 237–262;

Luis Montañés, "La *Carajicomedia:* Avatares bibliográficos de un texto maldito," *Cuadernos de bibliofilia,* 9 (1982): 35–51;

Fernando del Pulgar, *Letras. Glosa a las Coplas de Mingo Revulgo,* edited by J. Domínguez Bordona (N.p., 1929; reprint, Madrid: Espasa-Calpe, 1958);

Julio Rodríguez-Puértolas, "Poesía satírica medieval: *Coplas de la Panadera,*" in *El comentario de textos, IV: La poesía medieval,* edited by Manuel Alvar (Madrid: Castalia, 1983), pp. 383–404;

Rodríguez-Puértolas, "Sobre el autor de las *Coplas de Mingo Revulgo,*" in his *De la edad media a la edad conflictiva: Estudios de literatura española* (Madrid: Gredos, 1972), pp. 121–136;

Kenneth R. Scholberg, *Sátira e invectiva en la España medieval* (Madrid: Gredos, 1971), pp. 242–338;

Bernhardt Roland Schultz, "Las *Coplas de Mingo Revulgo:* Más allá de la crítica al rey," *Explicación de textos literarios,* 18, no. 1 (1989–1990): 109–118;

Charlotte Stern, "The *Coplas de Mingo Revulgo* and the Early Spanish Drama," *Hispanic Review,* 44 (1976): 311–332;

Barbara F. Weissberger, "Male Sexual Anxieties in *Carajicomedia:* A Response to Female Sovereignty," in *Poetry at Court in Trastamaran Spain: From the "Cancionero de Baena" to the "Cancionero General,"* edited by E. Michael Gerli and Julian Weiss (Tempe, Ariz.: Medieval and Renaissance Texts and Studies, 1998), pp. 221–234.

# Spanish Travel Writers of the Late Middle Ages

## Michael Harney
### *University of Texas at Austin*

WORKS: Anonymous, *Libro del conoscimiento de todos los reinos* (late fourteenth century)

**Manuscripts:** Madrid, Biblioteca Nacional MS. 1997 (manuscript S); Madrid, Biblioteca Nacional MS. 9055 (manuscript N); University of Salamanca MS. 1890 (manuscript R); Munich, Bayerische Staatsbibliothek Cod. hisp. 150 (manuscript Z).

**Editions:** *Libro del conosçimiento de todos los reynos tierras señoríos que son por e mundo de las señales armas que han cada tierra señorío por sy de los reyes señores que los proueen, escrito por un fransicano español á mediados del siglo XIV,* edited by Marcos Jiménez de la Espada (Madrid: Fortanet, 1877; facsimile reprint, with prologue by Francisco López Estrada, Barcelona: El Albir, 1980); *Text and Concordance of Libro del conosçimiento, BNM MSS 1997, 9055, Salamanca MS 1890,* edited by Nancy F. Marino, Spanish Series, no. 85 (Madison, Wis.: Hispanic Seminary of Medieval Studies, 1993), microfiche.

**Standard editions:** *El Libro del conoscimiento de todos los reinos (The Book of Knowledge of All Kingdoms),* edited, translated, and with a study by Marino (Tempe: Arizona Center for Medieval and Renaissance Studies, 1999); *Libro del conosçimiento de todos los rregnos et tierras et señorios que son por el mundo, et de las señales et armas que han: Edición facsimilar del manuscrito Z (Múnich, Bayerische Staatsbibliothek, Cod. hisp. 150),* edited by María Jesús Lacarra, María del Carmen Lacarra Ducay, and Alberto Montaner (Saragossa: Institución "Fernando el Católico," 1999).

**Editions in English:** *Book of the Knowledge of All the Kingdoms, Lands, and Lordships That Are in the World, and the Arms and Devices of Each Land and Lordship, or of the Kings and Lords Who Possess Them, Written by a Spanish Franciscan in the Middle of the XIV Century,* edited by Jiménez de la Espada, translated by Clements R. Markham, Hakluyt Society, second series, no. 29 (London: Hakluyt Society, 1912); *El Libro delconoscimiento de todos los reinos (The Book of Knowledge of All Kingdoms),* edited, translated, and with a study by Nancy F. Marino (Tempe: Arizona Center for Medieval and Renaissance Studies, 1999).

Ruy González de Clavijo (1356–1412), *Embajada a Tamorlán* (early fifteenth century)

**Manuscripts:** Madrid, Biblioteca Nacional MSS. 9218 and 18050; Madrid, Biblioteca de Palacio MS. II/2527; British Library MS. Add. 16613.

**Editions:** *Historia del Gran Tamorlán e Itinerario y Enarración del viage, y relacion de la embaxada que Ruy Gonçalez de Clavijo le hizo por mandado del muy poderoso Señor Rey Don Henrique el Tercero de Castilla,* edited by Gonzalo Argote de Molina (Seville: printed by Andrea Pescioni, 1582); *Embajada a Tamorlán: Estudio y edición de un manuscrito del siglo XV,* edited by Francisco López Estrada (Madrid: Consejo Superior de Investigaciones Científicas, Instituto Nicolás Antonio, 1943); *Text and Concordances of Biblioteca Nacional Manuscript 9218: Historia del gran Tamerlán,* edited by Juan Luis Rodríguez Bravo and María del Mar Martínez Rodríguez, Dialect Series, no. 7, Spanish Series (Hispanic Seminary of Medieval Studies), no. 20 (Madison, Wis.: Hispanic Seminary of Medieval Studies, 1986).

**Standard edition:** *Embajada a Tamorlán,* edited by López Estrada, Clásicos Castalia, no. 242 (Madrid: Castalia, 1999).

**Editions in English:** *Narrative of the Embassy of Ruy González de Clavijo to the Court of Timour at Samarcand, A.D. 1403–6,* edited and translated by Clements R. Markham, Works Issued by the Hakluyt Society, no. 26 (London: Printed for the Hakluyt Society, 1859; New York: Burt Franklin, 1963); *Embassy to Tamerlane, 1403–1406,* translated by Guy Le Strange (New York: Harper, 1928; London: Routledge, 1928).

Pero Tafur (ca. 1405–ca. 1480), *Andanças e viajes de Pero Tafur por diversas partes del mundo avidos* (late fifteenth century)

**Manuscript:** The only known manuscript of this work is an eighteenth-century copy in the University Library of Salamanca MS. 1985.

**Standard edition:** *Andanças e viajes de un hidalgo español, Pero Tafur (1435–1439),* edited by Marcos Jiménez de la Espada, reedited by Francisco López Estrada, introduction by José Vives Gatell (Barcelona: El Albir, 1982).

**Edition in English:** *Pero Tafur: Travels and Adventures, 1435–1439,* edited and translated by Malcolm Henry Ilkin Letts (New York: Harper, 1926; London: Routledge, 1926).

Travel literature must be distinguished from several other types of literature that have influenced it or been influenced by it but that have significantly different subject matters. First, it is distinct from the literature of navigation, exploration, and conquest, such as the accounts of the voyages of the Portuguese navigators and of Christopher Columbus. Second, travel literature departs, at least to a degree, from the medieval tradition of fanciful or speculative geography that characterizes Prester John's *Letter, The Travels of Sir John of Mandeville* (circa 1350), or the late-fifteenth-century *Libro del Infante don Pedro* (Book of the Royal Prince Don Pedro). These and innumerable other medieval works represent a world whose geography and ethnography are recycled variations, written by armchair travelers, of the formulaic pseudogeography of Pliny, Caius Julius Solinus in the third century, Paulus Orosius in the early fifth century, St. Isidore of Seville in the seventh century, the Alexander romances, and the *Imago Mundi* in the early twelfth century attributed to Honorius Augustodunensis (Honorious of Autun). The French historian Jacques Le Goff describes the persistent credulity that informed the perceptions even of missionaries and merchants who went on authenticated journeys: theirs, he says, was the perspective of "men did not know how to look but were always ready to listen and believe all that they were told." Travelers who "carried their mirages with them," they absorbed many fantastic tales during their journeys and "believed that they had seen what they learned, on location no doubt, but nonetheless by hearsay." Third, travel literature may be further differentiated from texts that deal with voyages, wanderings, and sojourns in foreign lands as a secondary rather than a central theme. For example, the voluminous category of texts devoted to religious pilgrimage must be regarded as a related but separate category, although accounts of travel to shrines may be considered an informative predecessor and significant contemporary of travel narratives. Another related type is represented by accounts of missionary exploits, such as those of Francis Xavier in the early sixteenth century or of David Livingstone in the mid nineteenth century. These works are not travel literature insofar as they concentrate on the mission carried out in the lands traversed or resided in, rather than

on the outward-bound and return trip. Other related but distinct modes and forms include the literature of exile and emigration, biographies and autobiographies that treat their subjects' travels, diaries and epistolary exchanges containing descriptions of travel, annals of trade organizations, journals of scientific expeditions, records of overseas bureaucracies, and reportage of foreign correspondents.

Before the age of recreational tourism and specialized travel, travel writing was a perceptible mode or occasional topic, rather than a genre, of literature. Narratives of journeys undertaken for practical purposes, however, often express an ancillary curiosity concerning the peoples and places visited. This curiosity led late-medieval travel writers to begin to cross the threshold between perfunctory descriptions and meticulous accounts of particular journeys. The travel chronicle became the framework to which were appended digressions from the mere linear record of voyages and routes. These digressions, taking the form of trivia, anecdotes, observations, and vignettes, conveyed not only the narrator's experiences but also his opinions about them and about impressionistically associated subjects.

Whereas pseudogeography consists of little but paraphrased variations on the ancient commonplaces, later medieval travel literature began to insert its inherited formulaic content into the framework of an alleged or authentic itinerary. It began to disengage from the pseudogeographical tradition characterized by the historian of geography Leonardo Olschki in his *Marco Polo's Asia* (1960):

> Geography evidently did not form part of the interests of those centuries, in which other fields of human knowledge and activity, for example medicine and astrology, were preëminent in the intellectual activity of the West. Hence, all that existed beyond the limits of the Christian world entered the kingdom of fancy; even the goods that came from these inaccessible lands were from regions beyond belief.

It would be wrong, Olschki says, to assume that commercial exchange presupposes "an exchange of culture and ideas." While Arab geographers' accounts overflow with information, both accurate and inaccurate, on India, central Asia, and the Far East, earlier medieval European literature offers no "empirical contribution to the mass of traditional, erudite, and literary information in which it abounded." This discrepancy of perspectives between European geographers and their Islamic counterparts is nowhere more evident than in the nonreception by Europeans of the voluminous Arabic tradition in geographical literature. In virtually all other fields of knowledge, including mathematics, astronomy,

*Frontispiece for a late-fifteenth-century edition in the British Museum of an Italian poem by Giuliano Dati about the mythic figure Prester John,
who is mentioned in the anonymous late-fourteenth-century travel narrative* Libro del conoscimiento de todos los reinos
(*from Arthur Percival Newton, ed.,* Travel and Travelers of the Middle Ages,
*1926; Thomas Cooper Library, University of South Carolina)*

agronomy, biology, philosophy, and political science, the works of Arab writers—either original ones or translations of, or commentaries on, Greek texts—were translated and disseminated in the West. Only in the area of geography was the Arab tradition neglected. Weighed down by their didactic and stereotypical baggage, medieval European geographers thought that they already knew all the answers.

*Travel* implies the intention of returning home. The traveler is not an immigrant but a visitor whose sightseeing has been expedited by others who came

before. Travel literature exists, that is, where travel itself is facilitated by economic and geopolitical conditions. The traveler goes to lands of which he or she has heard and, while accepting some discomfort and even the risk of injury or death, has a reasonable expectation of surviving the trip. He or she makes side trips and may sojourn for various lengths of time in this or that locale, but the end result is the completion of a circuit.

Travel requires a travel industry to support it. The traveler, whether tourist, merchant, or diplomat, requires transportation networks on land and sea, inns, travelers' aid stations, physicians, chaplains, market-places, monetary exchange, and some degree of political stability and law enforcement–however intermittent or precarious, and even if it is only imposed by local chieftains or functionaries extorting tribute–in the territories through which he or she passes.

Borders and customs, and the polities they imply, are, therefore, commonplaces of travel literature. J. K. Hyde points out that the advent of the Mongol Empire, extending from southern China to eastern Europe, "allowed western missionaries, merchants and craftsmen, with little more than the inevitable discomforts and dangers, to travel more freely on the Eurasian continent than ever before." At the same time, Hyde notes, the *portolan* navigational chart gradually came to be consulted not only by mariners and merchants but also by the learned, transforming "descriptive geography from an exercise in literary compilation into one in which the traditional lists of natural features, towns and provinces, had to be fitted convincingly into pre-existent spaces."

Marco Polo's narrative of his journey from Venice to Asia and back, which lasted from 1271 to 1295, is the preeminent text in the maturation of modern travel literature. It is significant not so much for its geographical accuracy as for its author's freedom from traditional geographical erudition: not knowing any better, he tended to tell what he had actually seen and heard. Even his hearsay is more scientific than that of the medieval encyclopedists. Polo personifies what Michael Nerlich has called the mercantile aspect of the ideology of adventure. According to this outlook, the knowledge and skills of the traveling entrepreneur are placed in the service of acquiring wealth, which, in turn, is used to satisfy the merchant's curiosity about the world and its inhabitants. Expanding trade propels the merchant into the world in search of riches at the same time that mercantile activity requires the traveler to learn languages, to acquire geographical knowledge, and to become familiar with the ways of many nations. Unbridled random curiosity, according to this mentality, is practical: one learns everything, because one never knows what might turn out to be useful.

Polo achieved a broad readership that, Hyde observes, was "predominantly lay" and did not have "a mastery of Latin." This reading public was "avid for knowledge in palatable form; information combined with entertainment." The thirteenth and fourteenth centuries, therefore, fostered the rise of travel literature by nurturing both traffic through many lands and a reading public eager to consume tales about that travel. The existence of a widespread audience for accounts of real and imaginary travel, as well as the existence of many specimens of the genre, in the fourteenth century may

be deduced from Giovanni Boccaccio's parodies of travel narratives.

Readers of travel literature are interested not only in the itinerary followed by the author but also in the day-to-day ordeals and incidents and varying conditions that the traveler undergoes en route. Hence, the many references to the adversities endured–heat and cold, problems with transportation, obstacles and setbacks, and fatigue and illness. Likewise of great interest in travel literature are the traveler's accommodations, as well as the exotic variety and uneven quality of the food consumed. Hunger and thirst and such hazards of the road as bandits and poor treatment at the hands of locals are recurrent subjects for the travel narrator. In short, geography and topography are the setting for what really interests the narrator and, presumably, his or her readership: what Nancy F. Marino, in the introduction to her 1993 edition of the late-fourteenth-century *Libro del conoscimiento de todos los reinos* (Book of Knowledge of All the Kingdoms; translated as *Book of the Knowledge of All the Kingdoms, Lands, and Lordships That Are in the World, and the Arms and Devices of Each Land and Lordship, or of the Kings and Lords Who Possess Them, Written by a Spanish Franciscan in the Middle of the XIV Century*, 1912), calls "the human element," consisting of "the personal anecdote, the adventure."

Within travel literature one may distinguish whole works devoted to travel themes from incidental or intermittent passages occurring in works of other genres, such as chronicles, biographies, and even some fictional works that show a concern for geographic precision–for example, the several realistic and accurate geographical interludes in the early-fourteenth-century *Libro del caballero Zifar* (Book of the Knight Zifar). Significant travel sections are found in *El Victorial*, the biography by Gutierre Díaz de Games of the fifteenth-century soldier and diplomat Pero Niño. Many adventures recounted in this biography take place "throughout the seas of East and West." Several passages in the work can be considered specimens of travel literature because they show a concern for incidental details and a tendency to digress into matters having little to do with the mission. The book begins with Niño being ordered by the king to outfit a fleet in Seville and set out in pursuit of pirates who are raiding Castilian and foreign shipping off the eastern coast of the Iberian Peninsula. The expedition's outfitting and financing are described with that fixation on detail that marks the travel writer and his or her audience. The best navigators, sailors, rowers, shipwrights, armorers, and crossbowmen are recruited; gold and silver are lavished; a feast in honor of the expedition treats the men to many delicacies, while musicians play songs of love and war. At Gibraltar, as they sail into the Mediterranean, they receive *adi-*

*afa* (tribute in kind) of cattle, sheep, chickens, bread, couscous, and other foods under the terms of a treaty between the Moorish rulers of that part of Spain and the Castilian monarchy.

The description of the fleet's approach to the city of Málaga typifies the author's travelogue mode. The surrounding land and water and the layout of the town are described. Then the author excitedly relates how a sudden fog arises, even though it is mid May, as the ships approach the port. This unexpected condition, attributed to the malignant sorcery of the Moors, prevents the ships from seeing each other or the coastline. When the fog lifts, the narrator recounts the details of another instance of *adiafa* and its attendant ceremonies.

Later, a storm and the crew's response to it are described with precision. This passage typifies the author's preference for delineating the processes and technicalities of travel. The reader also gains a glimpse of maritime professionalism and of the specialized division of labor aboard ship. Preparing to cross over to England, the mariners arrange their equipment while scanning the skies. The position of the sun and the moon are mentioned; course is set for the northeast; the rise and fall of the wind is noted. On the afternoon of the day following departure, a gale comes up; the sailors steady the rudders; the pilot, reading the weather signs as bad, pales as he inspects his compass and his charts. The captain demands to know what is happening; the pilot replies that the captain does not need to know and should leave his men to their work. When the captain insists, the pilot informs him that the wind is blowing toward the west-southwest; they must turn back for safety's sake. The captain, however, decides to stay on course. The winds grow stronger; the waves are "as high as mountains"; the ships of the flotilla disperse; and Niño's ship has to run before the wind. The waves pound the vessel, flooding the decks; as the crew bails, all aboard cry out for God's mercy, despairing of their lives. The storm lasts all night; the driving rain, notes the narrator, is a particular torment to the sailors.

Miraculously surviving the tempest, the ship arrives in England. Here the narrator regales the reader with pseudohistorical and pseudoethnographic detail, beginning with the folk etymology of the meaning of the name *Angliaterra* as "land of marvels." He tells of the aboriginal inhabitants' barbaric dress: they are "covered with furs, like animals." The island had been the abode of serpents and dragons; even now, the narrator assures the reader, there are rumored to exist bizarre birds born from pods growing on trees. Skeptical, he investigates this phenomenon by consulting a native from whom he learns of the breeding habits of various kinds of birds that appear to be the origin of the legend. The details provided may not be strictly accurate as

ornithology, but their insertion into the account and the very fact of the conference with a native informant bespeak the observational outlook and inquisitive disposition of the modern travel narrator.

In the domain of complete works devoted to travel themes, the stylistic and thematic paradigm for later medieval travel literature was set by Polo's book, originally titled *Divisament dou Monde* (Description of the World) but conventionally known as *Il milione* (The Million), which appeared in the first quarter of the fourteenth century. The Aragonese translation completed under the sponsorship and supervision of Juan Fernández de Heredia in the last third of the century marks a significant moment in the history of Peninsular travel literature. Although it is a considerable abbreviation of the original, the Aragonese text reveals Polo's characteristic presentation of the world as a series of provinces, cities, and kingdoms, to each of which is appended a sketch recounting information of various kinds: historical, ethnographic, religious, political, economic, and so on. Polo's account is the model for three complete works of travel literature that may be taken as representative of the genre: the *Libro del conoscimiento de todos los reinos;* the *Embajada a Tamorlán* (Embassy to Tamurlane; translated as *Narrative of the Embassy of Ruy Gonzalez De Clavijo to the Court of Timour at Samarcand, A.D. 1403–6,* 1859), attributed to Ruy González de Clavijo, from the first decade of the fifteenth century; and the *Andanças e viajes de Pero Tafur por diversas partes del mundo avidos* (Travels and Voyages Undertaken by Pero Tafur through Diverse Parts of the World; translated as *Pero Tafur: Travels and Adventures, 1435–1439,* 1926), composed toward the middle of the fifteenth century.

The *Libro del conoscimiento de todos los reinos,* once thought to date from the middle of the fourteenth century, is more likely to have been written after 1375. Factors supporting this date are the apparent reference in the book to the Catalan Atlas, which appeared that year; the depiction of the French coat of arms as bearing a fleur-de-lis, a device that appeared on the French flag only after 1376; and the allusion to Avignon as "una çibdat do mora el Papa de Roma" (a city where the Roman Pope lives)—Clement VII moved his court to that city in 1378.

Additional evidence for the notion of a later terminus a quo for the *Libro del conoscimiento de todos los reinos* is the perspective on Prester John taken in the work. The legend of a fabulous Christian priest-king of a realm located in an unspecified "India" beyond the Muslim kingdoms arose in the eleventh and twelfth centuries and was probably fostered as Christian propaganda in the age of the Crusades. Thirteenth- and fourteenth-century missionaries and lay travelers such as Giovanni da Pian del Carpini, Giovanni da Montecorvino, and Polo all sought the kingdom of Prester John in the course of their journeys.

When it was reported that Prester John's kingdom was not to be found in the "Indies" visited by the travelers or investigated by them in the course of their journeys through neighboring lands, the legend migrated to other regions. Olschki distinguishes three phases in this relocation. The first, or "Western," phase comprises a broad acceptance and complex literary development of the myth in Europe. The second, or "Asiatic," phase results from the correlation of European travelers' accounts with independent Asian traditions and leads to the rise of regional variations on the theme. Polo's is perhaps the most significant and influential expression of this phase. He identifies a Tartar ruler, "Unc Kan," as "a mighty monarch . . . which in the French language we call Prestre Johan." This personage, Polo assures his readers, is the legendary priest-king "of whose great power the whole world speaks." The final stage in the evolution of the Prester John legend in Europe may be called the "African" phase. It apparently originated with the missionaries Jordanus of Sévérac, whose account circulated after 1340 and, somewhat later, Friar Giovanni de Marignoli, who identified Prester John with the *negus* (emperor) of Ethiopia. Ethiopia, considered throughout the early middle ages as one of the three Indies—"Hither," as opposed to "Middle" and "Further" India—was conventionally identified as the land where St. Bartholomew preached the gospel; the *Libro del caballero Zifar* describes the country in these terms. The earliest map situating Prester John in northeast Africa dates from 1339. The notion of an Ethiopian Prester John was further promulgated by Portuguese chroniclers of the later Middle Ages, and an important objective of much Portuguese exploration along the African coast was the establishment of contact with the legendary monarch. The reference in the *Libro del conoscimiento de todos los reinos* to Prester John as the patriarch of Nubia and Ethiopia is significant in an author who reveals in so many other places in his work a continuing attachment to traditional geographical notions. Given the slowness of dissemination and assimilation of new geographical information at the time, the explicit and unequivocal statement of the newer Ethiopian view of Prester John substantiates the theory that the *Libro del conoscimiento de todos los reinos* was composed a considerable time after the mid fourteenth century.

Another indicator of a later date is the author's understanding of Ethiopia and India as separate places—unlike the *Libro del caballero Zifar* earlier in the same century, which still viewed Ethiopia as one of the three Indies. Not until well into the fourteenth century did the old notions of a land bridge joining Ethiopia to the "other Indies" and of the separateness of the African

kingdom from India begin to be widely understood. Hyde remarks on the author's apparently genuine knowledge of the Western Sahara, Dongola, and Nubia and notes that the book clearly conveys the feasibility of circumnavigating Africa.

The virtual absence of the personal element distinguishes the *Libro del conoscimiento de todos los reinos* from much other travel literature of the late Middle Ages. There is no allusion to the problems of lodging and meals, to meteorological or travel conditions, to illness, or to dangers or mishaps along the way. This lack of detail, along with an apparent ignorance of the time required to travel between the points covered in his itinerary, raises the possibility that the author was an armchair traveler rather than an actual one. Whatever the source of his information, the work is one of the earliest medieval European books on geography and can be considered travel literature because it presents itself as an itinerary of places visited. Clements R. Markham, who translated it into English, argues in his introduction that the author "was probably a great traveler" who "diligently collected all the geographical information he could obtain, in the various places . . . his wanderings took him." Naturally, "what he actually saw cannot always be separated from what he heard." Hyde asserts that despite the possibly imaginary character of much of its itinerary, the book reflects a detailed consultation of maps. While much of the geographical information in the *Libro del conoscimiento de todos los reinos* is erroneous, muddled, or fictional (for example, the account of the eastern Mediterranean), the work is, nonetheless, frequently accurate or, as in the descriptions of the Baltic Sea, tantalizingly sophisticated. The author reveals the lingering influence of antiquity's formulaic notions of the East but departs from traditional erudite geography in many of his references to authentic places and peoples; and this very inconsistency makes him modern. He does not neglect the new information about the East that has come to him from the accounts of missionaries and merchants. He is aware, for example, that China, rather than the mouth of the Ganges, is the easternmost region of the Asian landmass. Hyde concludes that the author, "drawing together . . . the world of merchants and missionaries," bases his account "almost entirely on up-to-date information and maps." The book, therefore, presents a journey that is "credible rather than merely conventional or fantastic." Taking relative skepticism as an indicator of emerging modernity in geographical sensibility, one may characterize the *Libro del conoscimiento de todos los reinos* as still medieval but with adumbrations of geographical sophistication. The spare descriptive style and linear presentation make it sound prosaically instructional.

ANDANÇAS É VIAJES

DE

POR DIVERSAS PARTES DEL MUNDO AVIDOS.

(1435-1439.)

IMPRENTA DE MIGUEL GINESTA
calle de Campomanes, núm. 8.
—
1874.

*Title page for a nineteenth-century edition of the early-fifteenth-century travel narrative by Pero Tafur, a native of Cordova who journeyed throughout Europe and the Middle East (from Tafur,* Andanças e viajes de un hidalgo español, Pero Tafur [1435–1439], *edited by Marcos Jiménez de la Espada, reedited by Francisco López Estrada, 1982; Harold B. Lee Library, Brigham Young University)*

The work consists of a long series of descriptions of kingdoms and lands that the narrator claims to have visited. He begins with the kingdom of Castile, which he divides into the archbishoprics of Seville, Toledo, and Compostela and twenty-five bishoprics. He enumerates Castile's twenty-eight chief cities, names and briefly describes and locates its mountain ranges, and mentions certain of its principal rivers, including the Guadalquivir, the Tagus, and the Duero. Few topographical details, other than the lands through which the rivers flow, are provided. At the conclusion of the account of Castile a brief description of the kingdom's coat of arms is given; the effect is akin to that produced in modern gazetteers and almanacs that include pictures of the flags and national emblems of the countries catalogued.

The pattern is repeated for the rest of the narrative: a kingdom, country, or lordship is named; its cities, mountains, coastlines, lakes, or rivers are cursorily reported; neighboring domains and seas are mentioned; and the coat of arms is described. Occasionally, the author briefly digresses to remark on historical, religious, or folkloric themes or to convey some bit of local color: Cologne is the burial place of the Magi; Norway is the land where day and night each lasts six months and where "ay unas gentes que an las cabeças fixas en los pechos, que non an cuellos ninguno" (there are some people whose heads are attached to their shoulders, who do not have necks at all); "Ibernia" (Iceland) has trees the fruit of which are fat birds, "muy sabrosas de comer, quyer cozidas quier asadas" (delicious to eat, whether boiled or roasted), and men more than two hundred years old who "non pueden morir demientra que estan en la ysla" (cannot die as long as they are on the island); on the banks of Guinea's River of Gold the precious mineral is collected from anthills made by ants as big as cats (an ancient belief mentioned by Megasthenes and Arrian); the River of Gold originates in the Nile, which, in turn, flows from the "altas sierras del polo Antartico do dizen que es el Paraisso Terrenal" (high sierras of the Antarctic Pole where they say Earthly Paradise is). From the mountain where the Earthly Paradise is located flow the four rivers of Paradise: the Tigris, the Euphrates, the Gion, and the Ficxion, whose cataracts can be heard from two days away. On top of this mountain "nunca faze noche, nin tiniebra, nin faze frio, nin calentura, nin sequedat, nin umidat, mas mucho egual tenplamiento" (it is never night, nor dark, nor cold, nor hot, nor dry nor wet, but a great even temperature). In this special space no living thing can ever decay or die.

In Mesopotamia, the narrator says, he passed near the site of the ruined city of Nineveh, "que fue destruyda por el pecado de Sodomia que fazian los omes" (which was destroyed for the sin of sodomy that men committed). Shortly thereafter, sojourning in Arabia, he visits Mecca, "donde esta la ley et el testamento de Mahomat" (where the law and testament of Muhammad is found); it is stored "en una arca de fierro en una casa de piedra calamita" (in an iron chest in a house of lodestone) that floats in the air, neither ascending nor descending. Far south of the "Mar de India" (Sea of India), in the vast land of "Trapovana" that stretches toward the Antarctic Pole and "es la deçima parte de la faz de la tierra" (is one tenth of the face of the earth), live the Antipodeans, "gentes negras quemadas de la grand calentura del sol" (black people, burned from the great heat of the sun). In this land, famous for its pepper and other spices, live "grandes grifos et las grandes cocatrizes" (large griffins and crocodiles).

The "Trapovana" mentioned in the *Libro del conocimiento de todos los reinos* is Taprobane, the ancient Greek and Latin name for what was later known as Ceylon and today is Sri Lanka. It appears in the writings of Megasthenes, the most influential ancient authority on India, who flourished in the early third century B.C. Megasthenes describes Taprobane as a long and mountainous island 7,000 stadia in length and 5,000 stadia in breadth—much larger than the real Sri Lanka. It has no cities but many villages; the surrounding seas, Megasthenes says, breed tortoises so huge that their shells are used to make roofs for the inhabitants' houses. Realistic descriptions of palm-tree cultivation and elephant hunting are followed by references to sea monsters resembling lions, panthers, rams, satyrs, and women with prickly hair. Taprobane persisted as the name for the large island south of India well into the thirteenth century; it is still used in Brunetto Latini's widely read *Livres dou trésor* (The Book of the Treasure), compiled around 1260. Polo, who actually visited Ceylon and Sumatra, does not use the name Taprobane; he refers to the island as "Seilan" and differentiates it from the islands of Java and "Samatra." Reporting from sailors' descriptions, he calls Java "es muy grand ysla que ha en luengo quarenta jornadas" (the largest island in the world, having a compass of quite 3,000 miles). His description is echoed by Friar Oderic, who traveled in southern India and adjacent lands and islands in the 1320s: despite having visited the place he calls Java, he, too, reports the exaggerated circumference of 3,000 miles. Olschki attests that the Greater Java referred to by Polo has not been definitely identified, while the smaller island he calls "Java the Lesser" is probably Sumatra.

The "Trapovana" in the *Libro del conocimiento de todos los reinos* departs both from traditional pseudogeography and from the more accurate notions of Polo and is not clearly identifiable with any known place. Marcos Jiménez de la Espada, noting the extremely large dimensions of the land described, thinks that the author may be referring to Australia—an unlikely surmise, however, since that continent was unknown, even to Chinese and Southeast Asian peoples, until the early modern era. Markham conjectures that the name refers to Sumatra, as does Edward Farley Oaten in a study that appeared three years before Markham's 1912 translation. Markham and Oaten base their inference on an account by the Venetian Nicolò Conti that is translated in R. H. Major's *India in the Fifteenth Century: Being a Collection of Narratives of Voyages to India in the Century Preceding the Portuguese Discovery of the Cape of Good Hope, from Latin, Persian, Russian, and Italian Sources* (1857). Conti assigns a 3,000-mile circumference not to Java but to Ceylon, while identifying Taprobane with Sumatra. Arab and Chinese authors refer to a southern land but with no greater accuracy than that shown by European speculations, going back to antiquity, concerning a *terra australis incognita*. A landmass referred to in some medieval geographies and maps as "Java la Grande" has led some scholars to conjecture a Portuguese discovery of the Australian continent sometime in the early sixteenth century.

The "Trapovana" mentioned in the *Libro del conocimiento de todos los reinos* reflects the continued influence of Megasthenes in the use of the ancient name itself, in the exaggerated dimensions of the island, and in its vaguely defined location in the seas to the south of India. But the reference to Java, a place-name unknown to Megasthenes, might indicate that the author is attempting to combine traditional lore and names with some elements known to him from more-recent accounts. The *Libro del conocimiento de todos los reinos,* mentioning two islands, Taprobane and the neighboring Java, is, therefore, ambiguous but not entirely formulaic. It reflects the same shuffling of real names and places, the same uncertain and inconsistent retention and attribution of old names to newly discovered or reported places, shown by the other travel narratives from Polo's era onward. This mixture of handed-down notional toponymy and newly known place-names marks the *Libro del conocimiento de todos los reinos* as a text moving in the direction of modern descriptive geography.

After descriptions of several more regions and countries, the reader arrives at another commonplace ingredient of European accounts of the East: the land of Gog and Magog at the entrance to "la Tartaria çercada" (encircled Tartaria), a region occupying "la quarta parte de la faz de toda la tierra" (one fourth of the face of the earth) whose chief inhabitants are called "mogoles" (Mogols). The narrator says that he reached the "Montes Caspios (Caspios Mountains) and the twin castles of "Got et Magot" by traveling sixty-five days north of Cathay. This account, like his references to Prester John, is further evidence of a later date of composition for the *Libro del conocimiento de todos los reinos* than earlier editors had assumed: maps began to locate Gog and Magog in the far east beyond China in the early fourteenth century. In some maps of the last decades of that century, including the *Carta Catalana* (Catalan Map) of 1375, not only Gog and Magog but the Monte de Caspis (Caspian Mountain) as well have been transported to the far northeast of Asia.

The account of Gog and Magog and enclosed Tartaria is followed by yet another fantastic reference: on the northern borders of this region live the notorious *cynocephali,* men who eat raw meat and fish and have long faces like dogs but are white and do everything they see done. This species is an example of what John Block Friedman has called the "Plinian Races." *Cynoceph-*

*alic* peoples are met again in the *Libro del conoscimiento de todos los reinos* in the Caspian region. Other specimens from the fabulous Plinian menagerie are encountered, still later, in Yrcania: men with "las cabeças pegadas sobre los ombros, que non han cuellos ningunos" (their heads attached to their shoulders, who have no necks).

The first mention of the *cynocephali* is followed by a utopian description of the kingdom of Trimit in "Upper India." The narrator here entertains the reader with hyperbolic details that prefigure Shangri-La in James Hilton's novel *Lost Horizon* (1933). Trimit, "todo çercado de montes" (totally surrounded by mountains), is a "tierra muy templada et muy egualada" (very temperate and healthy land) whose inhabitants "biven mas de dozientos años" (live more than 200 years) and are "omes de buen entendimientos, et sanas memorias" (men of good understanding and healthy memory)," "han profundas sçiençias" (very learned in science), and "biven por ley" (live by the law of religion), doing harm to none.

According to Jiménez de la Espada and Markham, Trimit may be Tibet; but it has little resemblance to the "devastated province" of "Tebet" pictured by Polo. The Venetian relates the dangers facing the traveler from wild beasts and the hardships owing to lack of supplies and hostelries and describes the natives' bizarre marriage customs, idolatry, and penchant for brigandage. Some twenty years after Polo, Oderic described in more positive terms a kingdom subjected to the authority of the Great Khan, where the people live mostly in tents of black felt, the capital is surrounded by beautiful walls, and the roads are well paved. The people, through religious conviction, refrain from shedding blood, whether human or animal. The only details in this realistic description that strike the modern reader as somewhat exaggerated are, perhaps, explicable as misunderstood secondhand reporting or even faintly delusional firsthand observation: the women's hair is "plaited in over a hundred tresses," and their canine teeth are "as long as the tusks of a boar." Oderic's description of funeral rites, in which the body of the deceased is butchered and left for vultures to consume, is macabre but not beyond the bounds of ethnographic possibility.

Different from the *Libro del conoscimiento de todos los reinos* in style and outlook is the *Embajada a Tamorlán,* the account of the diplomatic mission to Asia in which Clavijo was a participant. Patricia E. Mason notes that although it takes the form of a private travel diary, it is clearly written "with the intention that it be read by others." Little is known about the supposed author of the text. The *Treatise on Lineages,* attributed to Pero López de Ayala, mentions Clavijo's celebrated journey but otherwise says only that his family was from Madrid and that

its coat of arms consisted of a shield quartered, with two quarters containing a white moon on a red field and with the other two containing three vermilion bars on a yellow field. Other texts describe Clavijo as a hidalgo and a "noble orator," one of the best of his day, who, by virtue of his breeding, talents, and refined character, was named chamberlain and then ambassador by Enrique III. In 1405, a year after his return from the voyage, he was present at Enrique III's death; he was subsequently named chamberlain under Enrique's son and successor, Juan II. Clavijo died in 1412; his journey as ambassador to Tamurlane is mentioned on his tombstone.

Clavijo's place in history is based not on his lineage or on his career as a courtier and statesman before and after his journey but on the three-year journey itself and the account of it in the *Embajada a Tamorlán.* Authorship of the account has traditionally been attributed to him, perhaps chiefly by virtue of his having been a man of letters and the senior diplomat of the expedition. This attribution, made by Gonzalo Argote de Molina in the earliest edition of the work (1582), which circulated widely, has become conventional in the scholarship devoted to the *Embajada a Tamorlán.*

Clavijo's authorship can be questioned, however. The ambassadors sent forth by Enrique III, the prologue informs the reader, were Friar Alfonso Páez de Santa María, a doctor in theology; Ruy González de Clavijo, the king's *criado* (page) and chamberlain; and Gómez de Salazar, a royal guard. Francisco López Estrada, citing Sebastián Cirac Estopiñán, suggests that the friar's probable background in languages and other disciplines would have made him the most likely to deal directly with the people encountered on the journey and the best suited to report the varied and copious information accumulated by the ambassadors. Mason summarizes a position maintained by several scholars that the traditional attribution to Clavijo is rendered suspect by the narrative's frequent use of the third person; further complications are the recurrent appearance of an unnamed first-person narrator who is not readily identifiable as Clavijo and the narrative's repeated lapses into the first-person plural. Mason, however, argues that this apparent inconsistency of viewpoint does not disprove Clavijo's authorship. She cites many historical and biographical narratives that reveal a similar variability of perspective, among them Julius Caesar's *Gallic Wars* and the works of Thomas Babington Macaulay, Edward Gibbon, and Alexis de Tocqueville. More tellingly, she demonstrates a pattern in the use of viewpoint in the *Embajada a Tamorlán:* the third person tends to appear in contexts calling for a stance of impersonal objectivity or detachment; the first-person plural distinguishes the narrator and the Spanish readership of the work from the many other nations mentioned; and the first-person singular is used to "maintain a formal separation between [the] dual functions of author/narrator on the one hand, and protagonist on the other."

Although the profile of the narrator that can be deduced from the work matches both the secular diplomat Clavijo and the senior churchman Páez de Santa María—who was, presumably, also a man of the world—who are the most plausible candidates for authorship of the *Embajada a Tamorlán,* the narrator's point of view certainly suggests a man of Clavijo's background and outlook. Rather than that of a clergyman sent forth to defend the Church's interests, the perspective seems to be that of a Castilian courtier and Catholic nobleman of the late fourteenth century—devoted to his religion, to be sure, but also to king and country and to family and friends. Relatively little attention is paid to religious issues or agendas; that the expedition's mission is diplomatic and secular is clear throughout the narrative. The erudition revealed, moreover, is not beyond the education of a man of Clavijo's class and background; at the same time, there is little evidence of the traditional learning typical of churchmen's geography. The narrator writes more about what he sees than about what he heard before his departure. Margaret Wade LaBarge points to the high degree of observational acuity shown by the narrator of the *Embajada a Tamorlán:* he accurately describes a giraffe, for instance, with no reference to the extensive pseudobiological lore concerning it or similar animals. The point of view is that of a man intent on seeing things for himself, one who is "unwilling to put much trust in . . . rumours and secondhand tales," LaBarge notes. The narrator's consistently perceptive accounts of the persons, locales, buildings, races, and customs he sees are suggestive of a more worldly perspective than that of a clergyman. The narrator's interest is that of a sightseer, rather than of a pilgrim or a church emissary, when the narrative lingers to describe the size and wealth of cities such as Tabriz, Tehran, and Samarqand. The narrator's admiration of the Mongol postal network, with its speedy riders and many relay stations; his evident appreciation of the highly efficient ferrying system at the river Oxus; his description of Samarqand's streets, bazaars, fountains, gardens, noble houses, and fertile hinterland; his precise depiction of the meeting with Timur, which includes details of protocol and ceremony, the splendid jewels and finery, and the onlooking elephants decorated with banners—all of these factors point to the practical courtier and worldly eyewitness.

The author, whoever he was, is curious about the world. Where the *Libro del conoscimiento de todos los reinos* is repetitious and impersonal, the *Embajada a Tamorlán* is lively, candid, and detailed. Most of the aspects mentioned by Marino as typical of travel literature are con-

spicuously lacking in the *Libro del conoscimiento de todos los reinos* but are present in this narrative of a journey undertaken in the context of the geopolitical realities of the turn of the fifteenth century.

Timur, known in English as Tamerlane or Tamburlaine, was born in 1336 near Samarqand, Transoxania (today Uzbekistan), and died in 1405. The last of the great nomadic conquerors of central Asia, he inspired admiration and awe after rising from leadership of a small nomadic band to imperial supremacy through cunning, valor, and strategic genius. Always capitalizing on the mistakes and vulnerabilities of his adversaries, Timur pursued his conquests by means of an ingenious combination of alliance, machination, and betrayal that foreshadows Niccolò Machiavelli's recommendations to rulers in *Il principe* (The Prince, 1513).

As subtle in diplomacy as he was in warfare, Timur maintained intricate negotiations with countries both neighboring and remote. His outlook was nourished by personal ambition and vision; by the central location of his native domain, the Chaghatay Khanate; and by what Beatrice Forbes Manz calls "recognition of Mongol traditions and a habit of nomad rule." It was, perhaps, this imperial and universalist viewpoint that made him receptive to embassies from many lands far beyond his borders, including that of Clavijo.

Although his capital of Samarqand became proverbial for its size, prosperity, architecture, and distinction as an emporium, Timur himself never settled there. Personally conducting his many campaigns and enduring the same conditions as his men, he typified that combination of ambition and asceticism that so endeared Cyrus and Alexander the Great to medieval and Renaissance Europeans. European Christians, moreover, probably perceived Timur as a figure analogous to the legendary Prester John. They were intrigued by the possibility that out in the East, beyond the enemy infidel, was an enemy of their enemy—a possible collaborator against the common foe. For, although he was himself a Muslim, Timur was the scourge of the Muslims in Egypt, the Holy Land, and Turkey, who had long been seen as the archenemies of European Christendom.

Following the calamitous regime of his father, Juan I, Enrique III's short reign began in 1390 and ended with his death in 1406. In that time, despite the ill health that caused him to be known as *El Doliente* (The Ailing), he attempted with some success to revive the centralizing policies of Alfonso XI, who reigned from 1312 to 1350, and Pedro I, who ruled from 1350 to 1369. Seeking, like those predecessors, to ease internal strife and control unruly magnates, Enrique suppressed rebellions and imposed peace on warring factions; he also attempted legal, monetary, parliamentary, administrative, and budgetary reforms. In 1402 he began the occupation and col-

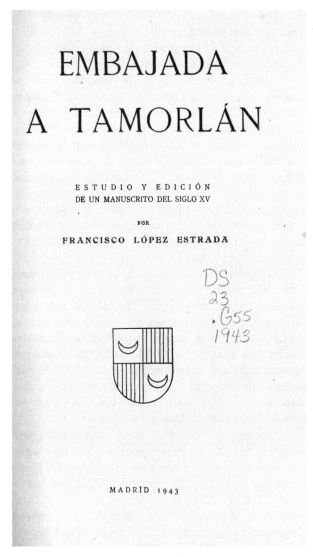

# EMBAJADA

# A TAMORLÁN

ESTUDIO Y EDICIÓN
DE UN MANUSCRITO DEL SIGLO XV

POR

FRANCISCO LÓPEZ ESTRADA

MADRID 1943

*Title page for a modern edition of the early-fifteenth-century travel narrative attributed to Ruy González de Clavijo, a member of the diplomatic mission to the court of Tamerlane (Thomas Cooper Library, University of South Carolina)*

onization of the Canary Islands. To fortify Spain's role in the geopolitical arena Enrique sent emissaries to many foreign powers, including kingdoms in North Africa and the Near East. A particular concern of his foreign policy was to monitor and counter the activities of the Grand Turk, Bayazid. Enrique's kingship, in other words, confronted all the social, economic, and political problems of the emergent nation-state, including the maintenance of public order, the advancement of economic and monetary stability, the cultivation of useful alliances, the enhancement of territorial sovereignty, and cultural expansionism. The *Embajada a Tamorlán* shows a partiality toward the strategic and centralizing viewpoint

implied by these nationalistic concerns in its tacit aversion to such customs as the extortion of tribute by petty chieftains along the road and in the curious tolerance, even implicit approval, with which it recounts some of Timur's more excessive actions and policies.

Having heard of the many conquests of the great Timur, King Enrique III of Castile—the introduction to the *Embajada a Tamorlán* tells the reader—saw fit to send two emissaries, Pelayo de Sotomayor and Fernando de Palazuelos, to determine the might and extent of that potentate's empire. The two ambassadors found themselves present at the great battle between the Turks and Timur that was resoundingly won by the latter. The great monarch welcomed these emissaries honorably, entertaining them with feasts and giving them impressive gifts. Hearing of the authority and prestige of the Castilian king and of his prominence among Christian monarchs, Timur sent to Spain an ambassador of his own, Muhammad Alcagi, with gifts that included Timur's customary offering of jewels and women. After receiving Timur's ambassador and the gifts, Enrique III decided to answer these courtesies with another embassy of his own, "so that the love between the two kings would grow yet greater."

The *Embajada a Tamorlán* reads from the beginning like a somewhat effusive ship's log. Making frequent note of the precise day, month, and year in which the many events of the trip take place, it is always careful to coordinate the temporal and the geographical. Mention of the date usually begins each section. The departure, for example, takes place on Tuesday, 22 May 1403, from the port of Santa María. Passing Corsica and Sicily, the travelers come to the Greek islands. In Rhodes they are received by the absent Grand Master's lieutenant. Returning to the city of Pera (today Beyoğlu, Turkey), after a shipwreck on the shores of the Black Sea, they wait out the winter, resuming their journey on Thursday, 20 March 1404.

Places and peoples are rendered in detail. On Rhodes, for example, the travelers see the walls and fortress of the principal city, together with the wharves and jetties and diverse shipping of the busy port. At Mytilene they view the ruins of the city and palace toppled by an earthquake some twenty years before, a disaster from which the present ruler, at that time an infant, miraculously escaped when his cradle was thrown clear of the rubble. Near the site of Troy the narrator reports good hunting of partridges and rabbits; shortly afterward he tells of an island left devastated and depopulated by a war between the Venetians and the Genovese. At Gallipoli the Turkish fleet is anchored, always ready to beleaguer the neighboring Byzantines.

Folklore and the folkways of the peoples visited are frequently discussed. The narrator recounts a tale concerning Antioch in pagan times: every year a victim was chosen by lot and sacrificed to a dragon. When a well-to-do burgher's daughter was chosen, the anguished father went to a monastery devoted to St. John, declaring his intention to convert and begging the monks to pray for a miracle. Having secretly bitten off a finger from the mummified arm of the saint, the father threw the digit into the dragon's mouth as it was about to devour the girl. When the creature burst, the father—and, presumably, his family—converted to Christianity.

Zulmarin, Armenia, is described as "the first city that was made in the world after the deluge, and was settled by the descendants of Noah." Near there, on the slopes of the mountain of Noah's Ark, lies the castle Izidu, once the stronghold of thieves and highwaymen but now, having been stormed by Timur, it is purged of its thievish occupants, stripped of all its doors, and governed by the widow of its erstwhile warlord.

The Greeks are portrayed as devout Christians, although they practice many "errors of faith," beginning with their use of leavened bread in the Eucharist. The narrator remarks that the priest who says their mass is unseen by the congregation as he consecrates the Host; then, as he steps forth before the people, they prostrate themselves before him, crying out their unworthiness. Clergymen among them are allowed to marry but not to remarry if widowed; Wednesday is a holy day on which they eat no meat.

Details concerning accommodations and food, including regional and ethnic peculiarities, are frequently discussed in the *Embajada a Tamorlán*. For example, in Arzinga, which is tributary to Timur, the lord of the city treats the ambassadors to a banquet of many dishes and courses. A hundred iron plates, deep and round like basins, are placed before them. On these plates are beef, lamb, meatballs and rice, and dishes of many other ingredients; on each plate is a small, thin loaf of bread. A length of silk cloth is placed before each diner.

At the court of Timur a banquet follows the ambassadors' initial reception. Lamb, boiled or roasted, is served, along with roasted horse meat; the plates are brought forth on large round quilts of fine soft leather carried by many attendants. Carvers slice off great slabs of meat and serve it on platters of gold, silver, and porcelain. At a later banquet the ambassadors are served various sugary confections, raisins, almonds, and meatballs. At yet another feast, as the guests of Timur's daughter-in-law, the Spaniards behold the ritualistic spectacle of heavy drinking that is customary among the great ruler's courtiers. The "fortyish, white-skinned, and stocky" princess is served many jars of wine and of fermented, sweetened mare's milk. Observing a complex ritual, the hostess and her guests, including Timur's principal wife, drink so much over the next several

hours that the men finally have to be dragged in a stupor from the lady's presence.

Mountain ranges, coastlines and entrances to harbors, and the position and design of castles are described with some frequency. As the expedition leaves behind the northern Turkish coast and adjacent highlands and starts out for the interior of Asia, the road and its surroundings are depicted in harsh detail. The way is difficult, owing to deep snow and excessive runoff as it melts. Approaching a castle, they find themselves between a rushing river and a high, deforested, impassable mountain range. The only negotiable route requires the men and horses to proceed in a single-file column. As frequently occurs, from the castle issue men who demand tribute to allow the travelers to continue their journey. Shortly thereafter, they encounter another toll stop. The passage is a vivid example of a familiar scene in travel literature. Messengers from a tower overlooking the road inform the travelers that they must halt; the Spaniards send ahead an interpreter to inform the local lord of their mission; an agent of the lord rides down to meet them; their goods and equipment are inventoried and taken to a nearby temple; and the herald tells them that a certain monetary fee is expected of wayfarers, as well as a portion of whatever they bring with them. The agent explains that his lord, Cabasica, lives on such exactions and from plunder taken from the Turks, needing both the tribute and the loot to sustain his war against the perpetual adversary.

The Spaniards ask to meet this chieftain, who comes down the following day accompanied by thirty mounted men with bows and arrows. Cabasica explains that without the payments he and his men would starve. The ambassadors reply that they are not merchants but emissaries of the king of Spain, who is sending gifts to Timur. Timur's ambassador, who is traveling back to his lord with the Spanish party, reminds Cabasica that the overlord of his territory is the emperor of Trebizond, a vassal of Timur; since the property they carry is destined for the latter, they are exempt from tolls. Cabasica admits that such is the case but repeats that he lives only from tribute; lacking such payments, he would be obliged to plunder the territory of his own lord. Seeing his resolution, the ambassadors give him a length of scarlet cloth and a silver cup; Timur's ambassador contributes an item of crimson finery, made in Florence, as well as a piece of fine linen. Cabasica responds that all pleas are futile. To supplement their gifts, the ambassadors are obliged to purchase a length of fine cloth from a passing merchant. Appeased at last, although grudgingly, Cabasica grants them passage and even offers to escort them to the next city.

Architecture is frequently described, sometimes extensively, as in the case of the Church of St. John in

Constantinople with its high-ceilinged chapel and lofty pillars surmounting the entrance, the whole adorned with elaborate sculptures and decorated with mosaics of gold and multicolored enamel pieces. No less detailed is the description immediately following of the Church of St. Mary, which is abundantly adorned with pictures embellished with gold and many shades of blue and with statues enhanced by pictures of cities and castles. The narrator also presents a lengthy description of the arena in Constantinople where jousting tournaments take place. He delineates the thickness and height of the marble walls surrounding the field, the dimensions of the many pillars and their plinths, the composition and design of the arches they support, the disposition and gradations of the stands, and many other details. Equally meticulous is the depiction of the church of Hagia Sofia with its massive doors, ornate ceilings and intricately decorated floors, marble pillars and walls, magnificent statues of the Emperor Justinian and many saints, and its exquisite chapels and alcoves. Constantinople is clearly perceived by the narrator as the gateway to the East and, therefore, as itself exotic and strange, and he describes its other principal buildings, walls, towers, and streets with much attention to architectural detail.

Similarly intricate descriptions are given of mosques and palaces in Timur's capital, Samarqand, and of Timur's great pavilion, one hundred feet wide and twenty feet high, with a ceiling that is round like a dome and painted gold, blue, and other colors and held up by a dozen tent poles, each as big around as a man's torso. From the tops of these poles gorgeous silken hangings are suspended, forming arches between the poles. The floor of the pavilion is covered by a vermilion rug with complex designs embroidered in gold thread. In the ceiling is set the most splendid decoration of all, a device of four eagles with spread wings. On top of the pavilion is a high mast surmounted by a copper apple and crowned by the figure of a moon. The great pavilion is so tall that from afar it could be taken for a castle.

Clothing and furniture are never beneath the notice of the author. On their visit to the emperor of Constantinople, for example, he observes that the monarch is seated on a dais that is rather more elevated than is the norm; the dais is equipped with small rugs, as well as a tawny lion skin; and the emperor makes use of a pillow with gold lacings. Later, an audience with the emperor of Trebizond and his son prompts a description of the raiment of this imperial duo: both wear high hats reinforced by golden rods, adorned with crane feathers, and topped by marten fur.

Obstacles, hardships, vicissitudes, and perils are frequently mentioned. As they are about to continue their journey east, inclement November weather prevents them from sailing. They are obliged to charter a Genovese galley commanded by a man named Micer Nicoloso Taco; but they are delayed again, this time owing to a shortage of galley slaves. The hardships of travel are nowhere more apparent than in the episode on the waterless steppes in which Salazar, one of the three leaders of the delegation, is rendered unable to walk by a protracted illness. He is carried on a travois to the city of Nishapur but expires before physicians can attend him.

The *Libro del conoscimiento de todos los reinos* often mentions regional climates but never describes the specific conditions its voyager-narrator encounters; in contrast, whenever travel is affected by weather, either favorably or adversely, the *Embajada a Tamorlán* is careful to inform the reader of the particulars. A storm off Sicily is vividly pictured, with descriptions of high winds and waves, lightning and thunder, the mast stripped of sail, and a fearful captain ordering the singing of the litany. Contrary winds off the coast of Turkey delay their sailing, while shortly thereafter a favorable wind brings them to the mouth of the Dardanelles—only to fail and leave them becalmed until the following day. Later, heading out from Constantinople into the Black Sea, the travelers face another storm; the mariners maneuver between rocks and other ships, cast out anchors, strike sail, and bail for dear life, but the vessel is beached. At some risk to the crew, the ambassadors' luggage and accoutrements are carefully unloaded from the crippled vessel. In a new ship the expedition is again beset by adverse weather in the form of dense fog, high winds, and waves.

The narrator pays close attention to the various transportation technologies and systems observed along the way. He notes that the league, as defined under Timur and called a "Mongolian league," is twice the length of the Castilian unit; that the emperor's couriers—"estos malditos" (these devils)—customarily travel fifteen or even twenty of these units in a twenty-four-hour period, riding day and night; that the couriers' journeys are admirably speeded by a system of milestone markers and relay posts and by a supply of fresh horses that allows them to push their mounts without mercy. The number of horse carcasses along the side of the road, records the narrator, is a veritable marvel.

In the markets of Tabriz, Sultaniyah, Kaffa, and Tehran the ambassadors observe the myriad activities of a flourishing overland commerce. The buying and selling of immense quantities of fabrics, including silk, cotton, and taffeta; a vast trade in Eastern spices such as nutmeg, cloves, and cinnamon; the thriving traffic in pearls and jewels; and the many bazaars and caravansaries in each city are described with awareness of the far-flung network of markets and towns nurtured by Timur's overarching authority.

The *Embajada a Tamorlán* is a quest story. The reader does not meet the great Timur until two-thirds of the way through the account. Along the way, anecdotes are recounted to illustrate the character, fortitude, and puissance of the ruler, building suspense leading up to the moment of the expedition's reception at Timur's court. Ever on the move, the mighty khan, as if to taunt the Europeans, keeps retreating before them, obliging them to hasten after him toward Samarqand. The people of the country flee at the ambassadors' approach, reminding the narrator and the rest of the party of Timur's habitual despoiling of villages for the benefit of his emissaries. In Kara-Kum, the region of the black sands, they encounter Timur's own people: the nomadic Chagatai Tartars, formidable riders and prodigious archers who are possessed of endurance beyond that of other men. At last, passing through the fertile, well-watered lands of Quex (Kesh), they reach Samarqand. On Monday, 8 September 1404, they are finally commanded to appear before the mighty Timur.

Throughout the work the narrator is awed by the formidable order implemented by the lord Timur and, at the same time, by the terrible violence of his rule. At one moment the *Embajada a Tamorlán* admires some policy or achievement, such as the efficacy of the courier system or Timur's farsighted resettlement of thousands of artisans and merchants in Samarqand, thus securing the capital's prosperity. At another, the reader senses the narrator's dread in reporting such sights as the twin towers made of the skulls of Timur's defeated enemies or such episodes as that in which the haughty Turkish sultan foolishly scorns Timur's diplomatic overtures: enraged at the effrontery of this obscure nomadic upstart, the reckless sultan vows to seek the Tarter chieftain out wherever he may be, take him prisoner, and lie with his principal wife before his very eyes. Timur, "being of stout heart and resolute nature," decides to make an example of this insolent despot. Laying siege to the town of Samastria before a Turkish relief force of two hundred thousand men can arrive, Timur takes the city by means of a ruse: the inhabitants seek a truce, offering a tribute of gold and silver and asking that Timur give his word not to shed the blood of those who came out; when a delegation of the town leaders ventures forth at Timur's invitation, reassured by the terms of the safe conduct, he has them buried alive in trenches dug for the purpose, pointing out that he had promised only not to shed their blood. Thereupon he unleashes his horde on the city, ordering them to loot it thoroughly, while burying alive any other inhabitants who come out. Afterward the depopulated city is destroyed.

The *Embajada a Tamorlán* is eloquent in its description of Timur's palace and court, describing the monarch's silken robes, his tiara, and the six elephants that defend the approach to the emperor. Almost blind in his old age, Timur blesses these representatives of "his son and friend, the King of Spain, the greatest sovereign there is among the Franks, who live at the end of the world, and are a great people." Some days after this stately reception, they witness Timur's implacable justice. The mayor of Samarqand, accused of malfeasance, is summarily hanged, and all his possessions are confiscated. The punishment is the more shocking to the onlookers for being carried out on a man known to have been Timur's trusted confidant. A friend who testifies on the mayor's behalf is also hanged. Another erstwhile favorite among the accused offers a large sum in silver if Timur will pardon him; the great lord agrees, after which, the sum in hand, he orders the man tortured until he surrenders still more of his wealth. When no more can be found, he is hung upside down until he dies.

The *Embajada a Tamorlán* contrasts in many respects with the *Libro del conoscimiento de todos los reinos,* and the *Andanças e viajes de Pero Tafur por diversas partes del mundo avidos* presents a striking contrast to both. Born around 1405 into an established hidalgo family in Cordova, Tafur might have become acquainted with some of the Genovese and Venetian merchants who were residing in the city. He must have been familiar with Seville, as well, because he frequently compares the two Spanish cities to the various towns he visits on his travels. After his voyage, which began in November 1435 and ended in April 1439, he married, fathered children, and participated in public life, serving as an alderman in Cordova in 1479. His wife's will, dated 1490, indicates that he died in the early 1480s.

Tafur is sophisticated about the international banking and finance system of his day, as can be seen from his use of bills of exchange on several occasions. That he was familiar with such procedures and had the means to travel extensively confirms his affluence. His narrative provides other hints as to his social background and outlook. Neither dryly descriptive nor excessively businesslike, it is the only one of the three texts to refer to travel as an activity that one might undertake for sheer adventure. Although, as Sofía M. Carrizo Rueda points out, political, religious, or perhaps even mercantile motives may be construed from a reading of the text, the narrative seems to be inspired by its author's preoccupation with the ethics, obligations, and lifestyle of knighthood.

The importance of travel for its own sake among the European and Spanish gentry has been demonstrated by Antonio Antelo Iglesias. For members of what could be

*Illustration from a fifteenth-century manuscript in the Bibliothèque Nationale, Paris, depicting Jerusalem, one of the places Tafur
visited in the travels described in* Andanças e viajes de un hidalgo español *(from Margaret Wade Labarge,* Medieval
Travellers: The Rich and the Restless, *1982; Thomas Cooper Library, University of South Carolina)*

called the chivalric class—those who enjoyed or aspired to knightly status—travel was motivated by a curiosity to see exotic sights, by a yearning for adventure in foreign locales, and by a desire to prove oneself through valorous exploits. Real-life knights, who read chivalric literature and the biographies of great men of their day and of the past, were affected by what the French historian Georges Duby has called the "refus du séjour" (refusal to stay put). This wanderlust is, perhaps, what most characterizes the knight. It is prompted by a malaise, a restlessness expressed as a set of expectations and dissatisfactions: one must set forth to make one's fortune; a man cannot stay at home if he expects to make his mark; time is short, and so forth. Maurice Keen refers to an obsession in chivalric biographies with *lointains voyages* (far-ranging journeys). The knight, he says, must be cosmopolitan, "a man who has been at jousts and tournaments and at war in other lands besides his own, who has served his lord in arms and has crossed the sea in quest of adventures and fame."

Although he never participates in a joust or becomes involved in a duel, Tafur nonetheless boasts of dubbing two Germans and a Frenchman as knights while visiting the Holy Sepulchre, and he constantly betrays both a mania for the chivalric and a yearning for sophistication. This orientation is seen also, as Carrizo Rueda points out, in certain narrative techniques that disclose the influence of the chivalric romances: for example, the theme of the unknown knight whose true status is revealed. This chivalric commonplace is at the core of an episode in which the narrator is mistaken for an ordinary pilgrim by several Italian gentlemen; afterward, when his true standing is revealed, he is treated to effusive hospitality and extravagant gifts. Similarly, the narrator, like the protagonist of a chivalric romance, discovers that his actual genealogy is more illustrious than he had thought. In Constantinople he learns that he is the legitimate descendant of a Byzantine emperor, the direct ancestor of the ruler who welcomes him so effusively. While he is still at the emperor's court, he is offered the companionship of a Byzantine gentleman's beautiful sister; Tafur senses that he is being asked to remain and establish his family there but decides, like so many literary knights-errant who resist similar offers, to continue his travels. These scenes, Carrizo Rueda demonstrates, are frequently punctuated with examples of the narrator's bravery and piety. This amalgamation of godliness and chivalry is fundamental to the medieval European chivalric ethos. It is expressed in many places in the *Andanças e viajes de Pero Tafur;* noteworthy among them are the passages that describe the Christian fervor and militant chivalry of the renowned Luis de Guzmán and those that discuss the nobility and devotion of the Knights Hospitaller of Rhodes.

In his prologue Tafur emphasizes travel as a necessary component of a chivalric education. From voyages abroad, he avers, a man acquires the mental and spiritual means of practicing the noble virtues of knighthood. Hidalgos who journey to many lands learn fortitude from coping with adversities and dangers; they are obliged to live up to the memory of their forebears and to earn a reputation among strangers by their own deeds. The knowledge they acquire concerning various forms of government and the diverse ways of life practiced in other countries fosters their ability to promote the common good on returning to their homeland. In this respect Tafur resembles Amadís of Gaul, the most famous of all knights-errant, whose adventures also take place in many lands. Amadís is a wanderer who acquires several languages, including German and Greek, in the course of his travels. The knowledge gained in these journeys prepares him, the story makes clear, to be the eventual ruler of his own utopian realm, the celebrated Ínsula Firme (Firm Island).

Further evidence of Tafur's idealistic chivalry is his account of the adventure of Mosen Suárez at the court of the sultan of Egypt. Suárez is portrayed as a knight-errant who by his prowess, achievements, and personal integrity comes to be treated as the admired equal of the great. When Suárez accompanies the captured king of Cyprus into the presence of the sultan, the latter honors him equally with the royal captive. Later, after negotiating the ransom of the Cypriot monarch, Suárez is treated by the sultan as if he were the sultan's own son. Back in Cyprus, the grateful king seats Suárez at his side, betroths the knight to one of his illegitimate daughters, and makes Suárez his admiral and heir. The episode is reminiscent of those in *Amadís de Gaula* and in the late-fifteenth-century Catalan romance *Tirant lo blanch* (Tirant the White), in which the wandering heroes are virtually adopted by grateful Greek emperors.

Tafur's experiences and the adventures of others that he recounts illustrate what Nerlich calls "the chivalric adventure." The chivalric romances constituted a polemical literature, vastly popular throughout Europe, that saw adventure in terms not of material and intellectual enrichment—the perspective of the mercantile voyager—but, rather, in terms of status affirmation. The ideal knight-adventurer is a man of letters as well as a warrior, a lover, and, above all, a wanderer. His regard for the variety of lands and peoples, languages and ways of life that he experiences bespeaks a reverence for the cosmopolitan viewpoint. But his idealized sophistication does not enhance his ability to acquire more wealth or more knowledge. Tafur's statement concerning the social utility of travel finds no counterpart in Polo, whose narrative takes as axiomatic the absolute value of knowledge. For Tafur, to be sure, knowledge is attained through travel, and curiosity must be gratified. The journey, however, chiefly serves not as a source of knowledge for its own sake but as a rite of passage, a training phase that prepares the noble traveler for his real mission back home.

The *Andanças e viajes de Pero Tafur* more closely approximates pure travel literature than does the *Libro del conoscimiento de todos los reinos* or the *Embajada a Tamorlán.* Tafur's social motives correspond to the status-centered impetus of modern tourists, for whom luggage stickers, photograph albums, and souvenirs are symbols of a status-affirming adventure. It is, perhaps, significant that Tafur's journeys, although far-ranging, stay within the confines of countries and regions well known to European travelers and pilgrims: Italy, the Holy Land, the eastern Mediterranean, Egypt, Mount Sinai, Constantinople, the Black Sea, Germany, Belgium, and Poland. As López Estrada points out in his article "Viajeros castellanos a Oriente en el siglo XV" (Spanish Travelers to the Orient in the Fifteenth Century, 1997), Tafur follows the established routes "like an obedient tourist." When he arrives at the boundary of the Mediterranean world and considers the possibility of continuing on to "Tartaria," he turns back, taking the advice of those who—like Conti, whom he encounters on the shore of the Red Sea—remind him of the unreasonable risks involved: "I was counseled against it, as it would be unsafe to dare to foray amongst heathens who know not the restraints of law, nor the command of any ruler." Commenting on Tafur's modernity of mind in making this prudent decision, López Estrada remarks that he is a traveler who takes stock of his capabilities and weighs his chances.

That tourism is on Tafur's mind can be seen from a comparison of two passages in his account. In a chapter on Rome he describes how Gregory the Great, seeing Christian pilgrims distracted from their spiritual objectives by the magnificence of the city's ancient monuments, ordered the destruction of the majority of surviving antiquities. Later, in a chapter recounting his visit to the Holy Land, Tafur describes his surreptitious visit, disguised as a Muslim and with the help of a Portuguese renegade whom he pays two ducats, to the so-called Temple of Solomon, a mosque to which infidels are forbidden entrance. This illicit visitation, clearly the highlight of his sojourn in Jerusalem, is conveyed with abundant detail: the reader is told of the temple's elaborate gold mosaics, its floors and walls of beautiful white stone, and its dazzling profusion of lamps. The particulars of the setting are pruriently commodified by the taboo nature of the intrusion: if he had been caught, he would have been executed immediately. Although the risks to which he was exposed were greater, perhaps, than those of modern tourists who similarly trespass, willfully or inadvertently, in forbidden places, his account reveals the wayward curiosity that inspires many a foreign sightseer to invade temples, churches, shrines, or sanctuaries where the outsider's inquisitive gaze, and even his or her very presence, are regarded by the locals as sacrilegious.

The tourist's gaze is likewise evident in Tafur's depiction of elephants in Cairo (the same chapter includes graphic descriptions of giraffes, crocodiles, and hippopotamuses). The passage typifies the occasional combination in the book of realism laced with folkloric balderdash. Black in color, "bigger than camels," with forelegs and hind limbs so massive as to seem "made of marble," the creatures' feet are round and equipped with a "very strong hoof." The legs, although jointed, have no marrow. The eyes of the beasts are as small and red as copper farthings; the tails are short like a bear's; the ears are like shields; the heads are like great jars; the tusks are four spans, the trunk fully six palms in length. The prehensility of the trunk is described with precision: the animals can grasp any object with it, including food, which they convey to their tiny mouths; they use

the same organ to drink. Elephants, Tafur informs the reader, are both intelligent and playful, showing an aptitude for throwing and catching things, as well as for squirting water on anyone they please. When wounded, the beasts are cured by exposure to moonlight.

Tafur portrays the marketplace of Cairo with an eye for detail worthy of a nineteenth-century novelist. Among the goods sold there are pearls and jewels; spices, perfumes, and fragrances of all kinds; and silks and choice linens. Barbers equipped with mirrors circulate among the crowds; black youths scurry about advertising a shaving and bathing service for women; peddlers, dealers, tradesmen, and hirelings, vending all manner of wares and services, swarm the streets and squares. Cooks roam about, carrying braziers and little stew pots; others tote plates of fruit; still others sell water from casks hauled by camels or donkeys or on the vendors' own backs. No less vivid is a later description of the slave market in the Crimean port city of Kaffa, the biggest such market, Tafur tells the reader, in the entire world. There he purchases two females and a male, who, he says, remain with him as he writes his account at his home in Cordova.

Tafur is both shrewdly observant and quaintly credulous. His shrewdness is nowhere more evident than in his bleak description of Constantinople and the living conditions of the populace and the imperial household. His account may be contrasted with the glamorous portraits of Byzantine magnificence in *Amadís de Gaula* and *Tirant lo blanch*. Unimpressed by the glories of the imperial past, Tafur notes that the emperor's palace must once have been splendid but now suffers from decay and neglect. The interior is badly maintained, save for the areas in which the imperial family resides—and even there, he notes, conditions are crowded. Although the emperor's attire and the ceremonies of state remain elaborate, he is "like a bishop without a diocese." Although he goes abroad with all the traditional pomp and formality, the emperor's capital, under perpetual siege, is sparsely populated. Such inhabitants as may be seen are shabbily clad, impoverished, and cheerless.

Credulity, by contrast, is manifested in the segment in which Tafur tells the tale of the sea monster, "fish from the waist down, human-shaped with bat's wings from the waist up," who abducts a girl, and again when he relates his meeting with Conti. The Italian urges Tafur to desist from traveling on to India and tells of how he had set out, having squandered his fortune, to visit the court of Timur. From that point, it would seem, Conti spins for his listener a tall tale—at any rate, one that differs considerably from his own published narrative. He says that in India he met Prester John, who performed the ceremony when Conti married. After forty years in India, Conti returned to the West, passing through Mecca, where he and his family were forced under threat of death to renounce Christianity. The way east, he declares, is long, hard, and dangerous, with countries inhabited by strange and savage peoples. There is no law, since no king or ruler can consistently enforce one's safe conduct. The food is alien, and the people who possess the gold and jewels one sees, and might well covet, are barbarians and heathens; intercourse with them is worth neither the risk nor the defilement of associating with them.

Tafur learns of various marvels from Conti. In India there is a mountain so high that in ancient times those dwelling on its lower slopes knew nothing of those living higher up. On a seacoast there are crabs that turn to stone on reaching land and dry air. Asked about the monsters of the East, Conti answers that he has not seen the famous ones with his own eyes; but he did see an enormous albino elephant, bound by golden chains and worshiped as a god; a many-colored ass; and many unicorns. The people of the East, Conti attests, are masters of the black arts and often consult with demons. In reference to another kind of magic, Conti tells of certain Indians who carry with them pellets of earth dug from around the tomb of the Apostle Thomas; if one cannot take communion at the moment of death, it is sufficient to swallow one of these pellets. Conti gives Tafur five or six of the mystical pellets, and Tafur, back in Cordova writing his narrative, declares that he still has them.

Alicia Martínez Crespo asserts that a pronounced similarity exists between the array of cultural and geographical themes that preoccupy travel accounts such as the *Libro del conoscimiento de todos los reinos,* the *Embajada a Tamorlán,* and the *Andanças e viajes de Pero Tafur,* on the one hand, and the chronicles—indeed, even the handbooks, methodologies, and protocols—of early colonial diplomacy and bureaucracy, on the other hand. The travel narratives of the fifteenth century, she suggests, established the elements of a diplomatic grammar—of a system for understanding strange lands and for encountering and interacting with exotic peoples. This characterization is particularly true of the *Embajada a Tamorlán,* the most officially defined of the three works and one that precisely enunciates its own purpose. However arduous the expedition, declares the *Embajada a Tamorlán,* and however faraway the lands traversed, it is necessary to record all the locations and countries visited by the ambassadors and all the things that happened to them, so that these things may not be forgotten but may be, on the contrary, more readily recounted and made known.

Martínez Crespo points out the parallel between the author's statement of the mission of the *Embajada a Tamorlán* and Columbus's declaration in the diary of his first voyage that the purpose of both the voyage and his report concerning it is to seek out and arrive at the Indies and "dar la embaxada de Vuestras Altezas" (establish diplomatic relations on behalf of their Catholic Majesties) Fernando and Isabel (Ferdinand and Isabella) with the princes of those lands. For this reason, he affirms, he has determined to write down punctually, day after day, everything that he does or sees and everything that happens. He furthermore intends to make a "carta nueva de navegar" (new navigation map) of the Ocean Sea and its adjacent lands, with precise coordinates for all locales. It behooves him, in short, to compose a book, forgoing sleep, in order to capture the whole truth of his exploits. His determination to reach the Indies and make contact with the Great Khan is confirmed in a log entry for 3 October 1492 on the first voyage. He declares that, despite evidence of islands on either side of their route, he is determined to continue directly on to the Indies, rather than swerve from his course in search of unknown lands.

Although the literature of exploration and discovery is to be distinguished from that of travel, it is worth noting that Columbus, the most famous discoverer of them all, worked for years in a literary and cultural environment in which travel narratives contributed prominently to the formulation of geographical thought. Inspired by Polo and many other travelers, by Portuguese navigators and Catalonian cartographers, as well as by theoretical or speculative geography that is now known to be wrong, Columbus consciously sought to expand the travel circuit. His confident expectation of returning to home base, his firm belief in the theory of a "narrow Atlantic," and his intention of setting out for renowned Eastern lands rather than for countries previously unknown all mark him less as an explorer than as a traveler in the sense exemplified by the *Libro del conoscimiento de todos los reinos,* the *Embajada a Tamorlán,* and the *Andanças e viajes de Pero Tafur.* Although he did not live to see the new circuit completed or come to comprehend the magnitude or full implications of his discoveries, his efforts furnished the points of reference for the enlarged sphere of travel, commerce, and diplomacy of the Spanish overseas empire and of the modern world in all its interconnected complexity.

**References:**

A. R. Anderson, *Alexander's Gate, Gog and Magog, and the Inclosed Nations* (Cambridge, Mass.: Harvard University Press, 1932);

Antonio Antelo Iglesias, "Estado de las cuestiones sobre algunos viajes y relatos de viajes por la Península Ibérica en el siglo XV: Caballeros y burgueses," in *Viajes y viajeros en la España medieval: Actas del V Curso de Cultura Medieval, celebrado en Aguilar de*

*Campoo (Palencia) del 20 al 23 de Septiembre de 1993*, edited by Miguel Ángel García Guinea (Aguilar de Campóo, Madrid: Fundación Sta. María La Real, Centro de Estudios del Románico, 1997), pp. 37–57;

C. F. Beckingham, "The Quest for Prester John," *Bulletin of the John Rylands Library*, 62 (80): 290–304;

Benjamin of Tudela, *The Itinerary of Benjamin of Tudela. Travels in the Middle Ages. Introductions by Michael A. Signer, 1983, Marcus Nathan Adler, 1908, A. Asher, 1840* (Malibu, Cal.: Joseph Simon/Pangloss Press, 1983).

Sofía M. Carrizo Rueda, "Hacia una poética de los relatos dc viajes: Λ propósito dc Pero Tafur," *Incipit*, 14 (1994): 103–144;

Carrizo Rueda, "La selección de elementos descriptivos y los alcances de códigos diversos en el discurso de Tafur," in *Studia Hispánica Medievalia*, volume 3, edited by Rosa E. Penna and Maria A. Rosarossa (Buenos Aires: Facultad de Filosofía y Letras, Universidad Católica Argentina, 1995), pp. 15–20;

Carrizo Rueda, "El viaje y las crisis del mundo caballeresco en el relato de Pero Tafur," in *Literatura hispánica, reyes católicos y descubrimiento: Actas del Congreso Internacional sobre Literatura Hispánica en la Época de los Reyes Católicos y el Descubrimiento,* edited by Manuel Criado de Val (Barcelona: PPU, 1989), pp. 417–422;

Sebastián Cirac Estupiñán, "Tres monasterios de Constantinopla visitados por españoles en el año 1403," *Revue des Etudes Byzantines,* 19 (1961): 358–381;

Gutierre Díaz de Gámez, *El victorial; crónica de don Pero Niño, conde de Buelna, por su alférez Gutierre Díez de Games,* edited by Juan de Mata Carriazo (Madrid: Espasa-Calpe, 1940);

Rolf Eberenz, "Ruy González de Clavijo et Pero Tafur: L'Image de la ville," *Etudes de Lettres,* 3 (1992): 29–51;

Felipe Fernández Armesto, *Before Columbus: Exploration and Civilization from the Mediterranean to the Atlantic, 1229–1492* (Philadelphia: University of Pennsylvania Press, 1987);

Barbara W. Fick, *El libro de viajes en la Espana medieval* (Santiago, Chile: Editoría Universitaria, 1976);

John Block Friedman, *The Monstrous Races in Medieval Art and Thought* (Cambridge, Mass.: Harvard University Press, 1981);

Michael Harney, "The Geography of the *Libro del Caballero Zifar,*" *La corónica,* 11 (1983): 208–219;

Harney, "The Literary Geography of the *Libro del Cauallero Zifar,*" dissertation, University of California, Berkeley, 1983;

Harney, "More on the Geography of the *Libro del Caballero Zifar,*" *La corónica,* 16 (1988): 76–85;

Hilda Hookham, *Tamburlaine, the Conqueror* (London: Hodder & Stoughton, 1962);

J. K. Hyde, "Real and Imaginary Journeys in the Later Middle Ages," *Bulletin of the John Rylands Library,* 65, no. 1 (1982): 125–147;

Margaret Wade Labarge, *Medieval Travellers: The Rich and the Restless* (London: Hamilton, 1982);

Labarge, "Pero Tafur: A Fifteenth-Century Spaniard," *Florilegium: Carleton University Papers on Late Antiquity & the Middle Ages,* 5 (1983): 237–247;

Angel Lasso de la Vega, "Viajeros españoles de la Edad Mcdia," *Boletín de la Sociedad Geográfica de Madrid,* 12 (1882): 227–257;

Francisco López Estrada, "La 'Embajada a Tamorlán' castellana como libro de relación entre occidente y oriente en la edad media," in *Melanges Maria Soledad Carrasco Urgoiti/Tahiyyat taqdir lil-dukturah Maria Soledad Carrasco Urgoiti,* 2 volumes, edited by 'Abd al-Jelil al-Tamimi (Zaghouan, Tunisia: Fondation Temimi pour la Recherche Scientifique et l'Information, 1999), I: 73–80;

López Estrada, "La Relation de l'ambassade d'Henri III au Grand Tamerlan," *Etudes de Lettres,* 3 (1992): 5–28;

López Estrada, "Viajeros castellanos a Oriente en el siglo XV," in *Viajes y viajeros en la España medieval,* edited by García Guinea (Aguilar de Campóo, Madrid: Fundación Sta. María La Real, Centro de Estudios del Románico, 1997), pp. 59–81;

Beatrice Forbes Manz, *The Rise and Rule of Tamerlane* (Cambridge: Cambridge University Press, 1989);

Alicia Martínez Crespo, "Los libros de viajes del siglo XV y las primeras crónicas de Indias," in *Literatura hispánica, reyes católicos,* edited by Criado de Val (Barcelona: PPU, 1989), pp. 423–430;

Patricia E. Mason, "The *Embajada a Tamorlán:* Self-Reference and the Question of Authorship," *Neophilologus,* 78, no. 1 (1994): 79–87;

Franco Meregalli, *Cronisti e viaggiatori castigliani del quattrocento* (Milan: Istituto Editoriale Cisalpino, 1957);

Arthur Percival Newton, "The Conception of the World in the Middle Ages," in *Travel and Travelers of the Middle Ages,* edited by Newton (New York: Knopf, 1926), pp. 1–18;

C. E. Nowell, "The Historical Prester John," *Speculum,* 28 (1953): 435–445;

Edward Farley Oaten, *European Travellers in India during the Fifteenth, Sixteenth, and Seventeenth Centuries: The Evidence Afforded by Them with Respect to Indian Social Institutions, and the Nature & Influence of Indian Governments* (London: Kegan Paul, Trench, Trübner, 1909);

Leonardo Olschki, "Der Brief des Presbyters Johannes," *Historische Zeitschrift,* 144 (1931): 1–14;

Olschki, *Marco Polo's Asia,* translated by John A. Scott (Berkeley: University of California Press, 1960);

Boies Penrose, *Travel and Discovery in the Renaissance, 1420–1620* (New York: Atheneum, 1962);

Rafael Ramírez de Arellano, "Noticias acerca de Pero Tafur," *Boletín de la Real Academia de la Historia,* 41 (1902): 273–293;

Francis M. Rogers, *The Travels of the Infante D. Pedro of Portugal* (Cambridge, Mass.: Harvard University Press, 1961);

E. Denison Ross, "Prester John and the Empire of Ethiopia," in *Travel and Travelers of the Middle Ages,* edited by Newton (New York: Knopf, 1926), pp. 174–194;

Joaquín Rubio Tovar, "Viajes, mapas y literatura en la España medieval," in *Viajes y viajeros en la España medieval,* edited by García Guinea, pp. 9–35;

J. E. Ruiz-Domènec, "El viaje y sus modos: peregrinación, errancia, paseo," in *Viajes y viajeros en la España medieval,* edited by García Guinea, pp. 83–94;

Vsevolod Slessarev, *Prester John: The Letter and the Legend* (Minneapolis: University of Minnesota Press, 1959);

Luis Suárez Fernández, "Algunos datos sobre la política exterior de Enrique III," *Hispania,* 10 (1950): 539–593;

Barry Taylor, "Los libros de viajes de la Edad Media Hispana: Bibliografía y recepción," in *Actas. IV Congresso da Asociação Hispânica de Literatura Medieval,* volume 1 (Lisbon: Cosmos, 1991), pp. 57–70;

A. A. Vasiliev, "Pero Tafur: A Spanish Traveler of the Fifteenth Century, and His Visit to Constantinople, Trebizond, and Italy," *Byzantion,* 7 (1932): 74–122;

José Vives Gatell, "Andanças e viajes de un hidalgo español (Pero Tafur, 1436–1439), con una descripción de Roma," *Spanische Forschungen der Garresgesellschaft,* 7 (1938): 127–207;

John Kirtland Wright, *The Geographical Lore of the Time of the Crusades,* 2 volumes (New York: American Geographical Society, 1925).

# Vernacular Translations in the Crowns of Castile and Aragon (1352–1515)

Roxana Recio
*Creighton University*

WORKS: Bernat Metge (1340 or 1346–1413), *Valter e Griselda* (1388)

**Manuscripts:** Barcelona, Universitària MS. 89; Paris, Nationale-Richelieu MS. 305; Barcelona, Catalunya MS. 12; Barcelona, Universitària MS. 17.

**Editions:** *Les obres d'en Bernat Metge,* edited by Ramón Miquel i Planas (Barcelona: Nova Biblioteca Catalana, 1910); *Obras de Bernat Metge,* edited by Martín de Riquer (Barcelona: Universidad de Barcelona, Facultad de Filosofía y Letras, 1959), pp. 117–153.

Pero López de Ayala (1332–1407), *Flores de los Morales de Job* (ca. 1390)

**Manuscript:** San Lorenzo de El Escorial, Monasterio MS. b.II.7.

**Edition:** *Las Flores de los "Morales de Job,"* edited by Francesco Branciforti (Florence: Le Monnier, 1963).

Antoni Canals (1352–1419), *Dictorum factorumque memorabilium de Valerio Maximo* (1395)

**Manuscripts:** New York, Columbia University (Butler) MS. Lodge 13; San Lorenzo de El Escorial, Monasterio MS. r.I.11.

**Edition:** *Llibre anomenat Valeri Màximo dels dits i fets memorables; traducció per frare Antoni Canals,* 2 volumes, edited by Ramón Miquel i Planas (Barcelona: Biblioteca Catalana, 1914).

Francesch Eiximenis (1327–1409), *Vita Christi* (ca. 1397)

**Manuscripts:** Madrid, Biblioteca Nacional MSS. 4236, 6176; Paris, Arsenal MS. 8321.

**Edition:** Portion included in "La *Vita Christi* de Fr. Françesc Eiximenis, OFM y la tradición de las Vitae Christi medievales," 2 volumes, edited by Albert Hauf Valls, dissertation, Universidad de Barcelona, 1976.

Canals, *Scipió e Anibal* (ca. 1399)

**Manuscripts:** Barcelona, Universitària MSS. 17, 101, 472; Barcelona, Catalunya MSS. 352, 991; Paris, Nationale-Richelieu MS. Esp. 55.

**Edition:** *Scipió e Anibal,* edited by Martín de Riquer (Barcelona: Barcino, 1935).

Alfonso de Cartagena (ca. 1384–1456), *Rethórica* (1422)

**Manuscript:** San Lorenzo de El Escorial, Monasterio MS. T.II.12.

**Edition:** *La Rethórica de Marco Tullio Cicerón,* edited by Rosalba Mascagna (Naples: Liguori, 1969).

Cartagena, *De los oficios* (1422)

**Manuscript:** British Library MS. Harl. 4796.

**Edition:** *Libros de Tulio: De senectute, De los oficios,* edited by María Morrás (Alcalá de Henares: Universidad de Alcalá, 1996), pp. 201–362.

Cartagena, *De senectute* (1422)

**Manuscript:** British Library MS. Harl. 4796.

**Edition:** *Libros de Tulio: De senectute, De los oficios,* edited by María Morrás (Alcalá de Henares: Universidad de Alcalá, 1996), pp. 153–197.

Enrique de Villena (ca. 1384–1434), *Divina Commedia* (ca. 1427)

**Manuscript:** Madrid, Biblioteca Nacional MS. 10186.

**Edition:** *La traducción de la Divina Commedia atribuida a D. Enrique de Aragón: Estudio y edición del Infierno,* edited by José A. Pascual (Salamanca: Universidad de Salamanca, 1974).

Villena, *Eneida* (ca. 1427)

**Manuscripts:** Madrid, Biblioteca Nacional MS. 17975; Paris, Bibliothèque Nationale MS. Esp. 207; Santander, Biblioteca Menéndez y Pelayo MS. M/102; Seville, Colombina MS. 82-1-1.

**Editions:** *La primera versión castellana de "La Eneida" de Virgilio: Los libros I–III traducidos y comentados por Enrique de Villena (1384–1434),* edited by Ramón Santiago Lacuesta, Anejos del BRAE, no. 38 (Madrid: Real Academia Española, 1979); *Obras completas,* 3 volumes, edited by Pedro M. Cátedra (Madrid: Turner, 1994), II: 5–889.

Villena, *Los doze trabajos de Hércules* (ca. 1427–1428)

**Manuscript:** San Lorenzo de El Escorial, Monasterio MS. Q.I.20.

**Editions:** *Los doze trabajos de Hércules,* edited by Margherita Morreale, Biblioteca Selecta de Clásicos Españoles, no. 20 (Madrid: Biblioteca de la Real Academia Española, 1958); *Obras completas,* 3 volumes, edited by Pedro M. Cátedra (Madrid: Turner, 1994), I: 1–111.

Andreu Febrer (1375–1444), *Commedia* (1429)

**Manuscript:** San Lorenzo de El Escorial, Monasterio MS. L.II.18.

**Edition:** *Divina Comèdia,* 6 volumes, edited by Anna Maria Gallina (Barcelona: Barcino, 1974).

Juan Rodríguez del Padrón (or de la Cámara) (ca. 1390–1450), *Bursario, o Heroidas de Ovidio* (ca. 1440)

**Manuscripts:** Madrid, Biblioteca de Palacio MS. II / 2790; Seville, Colombina MS. 5-5-16; Madrid, Biblioteca Nacional MS. 6052.

**Edition:** *Bursario o Heroidas de Ovidio,* edited by Pilar Saquero Suárez-Somonte and Tomás González Rolán (Madrid: Universidad Complutense, 1984).

Juan de Mena (1411–1456), *La Ylíada en romance* (1442)

**Manuscripts:** Santander, Biblioteca Menéndez y Pelayo MS. M-96 (= 36); Madrid, Biblioteca Nacional MS. R 6944.

**Editions:** *La Ylíada en romance,* edited by Martín de Riquer (Barcelona: Selecciones Bibliófilas, 1949); *Obras completas,* edited by Miguel Ángel Pérez Priego, Clásicos Universales, no. 175 (Barcelona: Planeta, 1989), pp. 332–378.

Alfonso de Madrigal (ca. 1405–1455), *Tostado sobre el Eusebio* (ca. 1450)

**Manuscripts:** Lisbon, Nacional MS. 117–121; Madrid, Biblioteca Nacional MSS. 10808–10812.

**Edition:** *Tostado sobre el Eusebio,* 5 volumes (Salamanca: Hans Gysser, 1506–1507).

Ferran Valentí (ca. 1400–1476), *Les Paradoxes de Ciceró* (ca. 1450)

**Manuscript:** Barcelona, Catalunya MSS. 296, 1029.

**Edition:** *Traducció de les Paradoxa de Ciceró,* edited by Josep Maria Morató i Thomàs (Barcelona: Biblioteca Catalana d'Obres Antigues, 1959).

Pero Díaz de Toledo (ca. 1415–1499), *Fedón* (1455)

**Manuscripts:** Salamanca, Universitaria MS. 2614; Santander, Biblioteca Menéndez y Pelayo MS. M-96 (= 36); Madrid, Biblioteca Nacional MS. Vitrina 17-4.

**Edition:** *Libro llamado "Fedrón": Plato's "Phaedro"* translated by Pero Díaz de Toledo (ms. Madrid, B.N., Vitr. 17,4), edited by Nicholas Round (London: Tamesis, 1993).

Alfonso de Palencia (1424–1492), *Batalla campal que los lobos y los perros ovieron* (1457)

**Manuscript:** Madrid, Biblioteca de Palacio MS. I-1390.

**Edition:** *La guerra & batalla campal entre los perros & los lobos avida* (Seville: Cuatro compañeros alemanes, ca. 1490).

Joan Roís de Corella (1433–1497), *El Psalteri* (1480)

**Manuscript:** Barcelona, Catalunya MS. Esp 8 8au.

**Edition:** *Psalteri,* edited by J. Barrera (Gerona: Viader, 1928).

Bernardí Vallmanya, *Lo Càrcer d'Amor* (1493)

**Manuscript:** British Library MS. IA.52542.

**Editions:** *Lo Càrcer d'Amor (Barcelona, 1493),* edited by Ramón Miquel i Planas, Novelari Català, no. 3 (Barcelona, 1912); *Càrcer d'Amor, Carcer d'Amore: Due traduzioni della "novela" di Diego de San Pedro,* edited by Vincenzo Minervini and Maria Luisa Indini (Bari: Schena, 1986), pp. 35–131.

Isabel de Villena (1430–1490), *Vita Christi* (1497)

**Manuscript:** Barcelona, Universitària MS. ROSS.I.90.

**Editions:** *Llibre anomenat Vita Christi compost per sor Isabel de Villena,* 3 volumes, edited by Ramón Miquel i Planas (Barcelona: Biblioteca Catalana, 1916); *Vita Christi,* 2 volumes, edited by Josep Almiñana Vallés (Valencia: Ajuntament, 1992).

Álvar Gómez de Ciudad Real (or de Guadalajara) (ca. 1488–1538), *Triumpho de Amor* (ca. 1510)

**Manuscripts:** Madrid, Biblioteca Nacional MSS. 2882, 3993.

**Editions:** "Der Cancionero Gayangos," edited by Karl Vollmöller, *Romanische Studien,* 4 (1879–1880): 197–228; *Ensayo de una biblioteca de libros raros y curiosos,* 4 volumes, edited by Bartolomé José Gallardo (Madrid: Gredos, 1968), I: 618–638; *Cancionero de Juan Fernández de Ixar,* 2 volumes, edited by José María Azáceta (Madrid: Consejo Superior de Investigaciones Científicas, 1956), II: 819–862; *El Cancionero de Gallardo,* edited by Azáceta (Madrid: Consejo Superior de Investigaciones Científicas, 1962), pp. 98–151; *El "Triumpho de Amor" de Petrarca traduzido por Álvar Gómez,* edited by Roxana Recio (Barcelona: PPU, 1998).

Francisco de Madrid, Arcediano de Alcor, *De los remedios contra próspera y adversa fortuna* (1510)

**Manuscript:** Madrid, Biblioteca Nacional MS. R 11750.

**Edition:** *Delos remedios contra próspera y adversa fortuna* (Valladolid: Diego de Gumiel, 1510).

Antonio de Obregón, *Francisco Petrarca, con los seys triunfos de toscano sacado en castellano con el comento que sobrellos se hizo* (1512)

**Manuscript:** Madrid, Biblioteca Nacional MS. R 2540.
**Edition:** *Francisco Petrarca, con los seys triunfos de toscano sacado en castellano con el comento que sobrellos se hizo* (Logroño: Arnao Guillén de Brocar, 1512).

Pero Fernández de Villegas, *La traducción del Dante de la lengua toscana en nuestro romance castellano* (1515)
**Manuscript:** New York Hispanic Society MS. B:2813.
**Edition:** *La traducción del Dante de la lengua toscana en nuestro romance castellano* (Burgos, 1515); *La Divina Comedia de Dante,* edited by Juan Eugenio Hartzenbusch (Madrid: Tomás Rey, 1868).

During the thirteenth century, translations in the Iberian Peninsula were frequently collective works from "translation schools" that depended on the patronage of the king or the nobility. The most representative examples are those schools of Toledo and Tarazona. The utilitarian nature of these translations seems to explain the absence of any reflections on the part of translators about their craft, such as translation goals, guidelines, or obstacles, as José Francisco Ruiz Casanova observes in his *Aproximación a una historia de la traducción en España* (2000). Throughout the thirteenth century, Latin maintained its privileged position as the language of cultural exchange, but in the fourteenth century there were several changes in the practice of translation, as Julio César Santoyo noted in his essay "El siglo XIV: traducciones y reflexiones sobre la traducción" (1985): the number of vernacular renderings from Latin originals increased dramatically and evidenced a lack of classical training on the part of their potential readers; translation practice became an individual activity not centered around a court or a group of translators; and, finally, with individual investment in these translations, reflections and criticism on the process begin to appear toward the end of the century. The growing role played by vernacular languages also shows in the increasing number of translations from other Romance languages and a parallel evolution or revolution in the translator's craft.

At the end of the fourteenth century most readers of the classics believed that good translations from Latin to contemporary languages were impossible because the latter did not have the terms for many Latin concepts. Those scholars who tried vernacular translations followed the source text in a word-by-word rendering as exactly as possible, even if it was not totally intelligible to their readers, in order to preserve the stylistics (and therefore content) of the original.

The scribes who took this position were in favor of literal translations because of their respect for the rhetorical constructions of ancient classical works. In attempting to preserve these qualities, they did not mind the difficulty their versions presented to their readers, believing that the author's meaning and style needed to be reflected in the translation, even if that meant the use of obscure words or twisted grammar. Among these translators, the best known are Pero López de Ayala, Alfonso de Cartagena, and Alfonso de Palencia, but, as late as 1513, authors such as Diego López de Cortégana were still arguing for the supremacy of Latin over Castilian.

That superiority was challenged quite differently in Castile and in the Crown of Aragon. Translators into Catalan tended to be more flexible and allowed for two types of translation, either following the source with close parallels of wording or allowing for certain modifications for sense. These norms were able to coexist because Latinists did not dominate Catalan intellectual life as they did in Castile, where scholars seemed less flexible and more adamant about the supposed superiority of Latin, with all that that opinion implied.

Despite these broad differences, earlier translators into Catalan had also believed in the superiority of Latin and the need for extremely literal translations. Fourteenth-century writers such as Nicolau Quilis, Guillem Nicolau, Jaume Conesa, and Ferrer Sayol were essentially Latinists whose translations were promoted by the Crown, an authority doggedly concerned about cultural matters. Other literary figures also translated earlier works, such as Bernat Metge, who reworked the Griseldis episode from Petrarch's *Rerum senilium* (Letters of Old Age, 1361–1374) into Catalan as *Valter e Griselda* (1388).

A different approach to translation is that of Antoni Canals, at the end of the fourteenth century, who took some liberty with his texts: he added geographical details, omitted historical characters (as Francesch Eiximenis did before him), and sometimes inserted passages meticulously copied from other works. The prologue to his *Scipió e Aníbal* (Scipio and Hannibal, circa 1399) declares:

> Per lo gran plaer que vostra senyoría trobava en aver lo parlament de Scipió e de Aníbal, e la batayla saguent, en la qual lo dit Scipió Affricha fou vençedor, volent servir a la dita vostra senyoria, som estudiat de traura lo dit parlament, axí planariement com miylor he pogut. Per que, ligint de una part Tito Livio, qui'l posa assatz largament, e d'altra Francesch petrarcha, qui en lo seu libra appelat Affricha trecta fort belament e diffusa, he aromansat lo dit parlament sagons mon petit enginy.

> (For the great pleasure that your lordship found in receiving the speech by Scipio and Hannibal, and the subsequent battle in which this Scipio Africanus was the victor, wishing to serve your lordship, I strove to play out such speech as completely as I could. On account of that, reading on the one hand Titus Livius, who puts it quite broadly, and on the other Francis Petrarch, who treats it very beautifully and extensively

*Page from a manuscript at Universitat de Barcelona of Bernat Metge's* Valter e Griselda *(1388), a Catalan translation of an episode from Petrarch's* Rerum senilium *( from Martín de Riquer, ed.,* Obras de Bernat Metge, *1959; John Williard Brister Library, Memphis State University)*

in his book named Africa, I have rendered this speech into Romance in accordance to my small talent.)

Canals clearly cast doubt on the classical distinction between translations *ad verbum* (word by word) and *ad sensum* (sense for sense).

The Majorcan Ferran Valentí went a step farther. He wanted to make his translations more accessible to the reader, no matter what he was translating. Valentí declared that he changed the words when necessary but not their meaning:

Jo Ferrando Valentí, inerudit e dexeble dels dexebles, he posada e transferida aquesta petita obreta de Tulli, gran en sentencia, de latí en vulgar materno e malorquí segons la ciutat de on só nat e criat e nodrit, alcunes paraulas e a les voltes tolent de la textura literal de aquella, no pero tocant en sentencia alcuna, ans per retre aquella clara e perceptible, e alcuna volta transferint de mot per no mudar sentencia en aquella.

(I, Ferrando Valentí, unlearned and disciple of disciples, have rendered and transferred this small work by Cicero, great in wisdom, from Latin into the Majorcan vernacular according to the city where I was born and raised and nurtured, taking out some words from their literal context, not altering any of the sense, but in order to render them clear and perceptible, and sometimes translating word-by-word in order not to change the meaning.)

With respect to Catalan and other Valencian translators who recomposed texts from other vernacular languages, there were two groups developing at the same time from the end of the fourteenth century through the end of the fifteenth. The first band produced rather literal translations, remaining strictly dutiful to their sources, such as the anonymous translation of Giovanni Boccaccio's Italian *Fiammetta* and Bernardí Vallmanya's 1493 rendition of Diego de San Pedro's Castilian *Cárcel de Amor* (1492). In both cases the literalness of the translation is favored by the proximity of the languages. Other translations, however, introduce important changes in the text despite proximity between neighboring tongues. This second group of translators openly took major liberties with respect to their sources, such as the anonymous Catalan translation of Boccaccio's *Decameron* and Ferrer de Blanes's paraphrase version of Dante's *Commedia*. The latter wrote extensive glosses on several passages of the *Commedia* in order to emphasize Christian ideology. These glosses became the most important part of the text.

The changes introduced by these translators are usually aimed at rendering a more familiar translation to the readers. Some of Blanes's additions to the *Commedia*, for example, have regionalist features:

Lo qual fugint de las reals grans honors y delicat viure vist y conegut lo jouvenet lo gran perill de tal estament deixadas las suas ricas vestiduras ab pobre abit de hun simple pelegri pres son cami y per divina providentia peruingue en Cathalunya en lo vescontat de Cabrera y en la mes alta muntanya anomenada Monseny en la mes aspra y solitaria part de aquella en vna i[s]treta coua feu una xica cella en la qual contemplant los grans actes de la santissima redemptio nostra apres molts anys de la sua gloriosa y molt aspra vida fini los seus benaventurats dies.

(Fleeing from the great royal honors and refined living, after having seen and known as a young man the great danger of such an estate, and having doffed his rich clothes, he departed with the poor habit of a simple pilgrim and through divine providence he wandered through Catalonia, to the viscountship of Cabrera, and in the highest mountain, named Montseny, in the roughest and most desolate part of it, he made, in a narrow cove, a small cell where, contemplating the great history of our most holy redemption, he ended his blessed days after many years of his glorious and very harsh life.)

Blanes's purpose is to make his readers familiar not only with Dante's work but also with Dante himself. This kind of freer translation has a long tradition in Catalonia, probably beginning with popular preachers and extending to the translations of historians such as Canals and writers of literary works such as Isabel de Villena. Her explications of Christ's life rely on amplifications, glosses, Latin within a Romance text, or a familiar dialect to identify with a specific group.

In Castile, however, the authority of Latinists was more prevalent, which made the translation norms initially more rigid. Castilian, as the other Romance languages, was considered ill suited to express concepts that were easily communicated in Latin. This assumption forced the translators to include long explanations of vernacular terms, because otherwise they would not be understood by their readers. This approach was followed by Latinists such as Cartagena and Palencia, but it can also be found in the best-known Castilian poets of the time, such as Íñigo López de Mendoza (the Marqués de Santillana) and Juan de Mena. For example, after pointing out that Homer's Greek masterpiece was first translated into Latin and that he translates from this derived version, Mena says in his prologue to his version of the *Iliad, La Ylíada en romance* (1442):

La qual obra apenas pudo toda la gramática y aún eloquencia latina conprenhender, y en sí rescebir los eroicos cantares del vaticinante poeta Omero; pues, quánto más fará el rudo y desierto romance! Acaescerá por esta cabsa en la omérica *Ylíada* como a las dulces y sabrosas frutas en la fin del verano, que a la primera agua se dañan y a la segunda se pierden. E así esta obra rescibirá dos agravios: el uso en la traslación latina y, el más dañoso y mayor, en la interpretación del romance que presumo y tiento le dar.

(The sum of all Latin grammar and eloquence could barely contain this work and bear in itself the heroic songs of the poet-seer Homer; therefore, how much worse will the unpolished and desolated Romance serve! For this reason the same will happen to the Homeric *Iliad* as happens to the sweet and juicy fruits at the end of the summer, that they are harmed with the first rain and ruined with the second. And so Homer's work will receive two injuries: rough handling in the Latin translation and, the worst and most damaging, in the conversion into Romance that I presume and attempt to give it.)

Mena makes his deference to Latin still more explicit when he explains the nature of what he translated and accepts the loss of the "sweetness" of style of the original language:

E por esta razón, muy prepotente señor, dispuse de no interpretar de veinte y quatro libros, que son en el volumen de la *Ylíada,* salvo las sumas brevemente de ellos. . . . Y aun dexélo de fazer por non dañar nin ofender del todo su alta obra, trayéndogela en la umilde y baxa lengua del romance.

(And for this reason [the imperfection of Castilian], my most powerful lord, I decided to translate, out of twenty-four books that make up the volume of the *Iliad,* only their brief summaries. . . . And I even stopped doing it so as not to totally harm nor offend its preeminence by bringing it down to the level of the humble and lowly romance.)

Mena echoes Cartagena's *Rethórica* (1422) in accepting the loss of the Latin "sweetness." Santillana takes an identical position in his *Prohemio e carta al Condestable de Portugal* (Proem and Letter to the Constable of Portugal, 1449) when he admits his lack of knowledge of Latin and the poverty of vocabulary of the Romance vernaculars:

Bien sé yo agora que, según que ya otras vezes con vos y con otros me ha acaescido, diredes que la mayor parte o quasi toda de la dulçura o graçiosidad quedan y retienen en sí las palabras y vocablos latinos. . . . Ca difíçil cosa sería agora que, después de assaz años e no menos travajos, yo quisiese o me despusiesse a porfiar con la lengua latina, como quiera que Tulio afirma Catón–creo Uticense–en hedad de ochenta años aprendiesse las letras griegas; pero solo e singular fue Catón del linage humano en esto y en otras muchas cosas. E pues no podemos aver aquello que queremos, queramos aquello que podemos. E si careçemos de las formas, seamos contentos de las materias

(I know well that, as has already happened to me with you and others, you will say that my words preserve and retain in themselves most or almost all of their Latin sweetness and grace. . . . For it would be difficult now that, after so many years filled with countless struggles, I should strive or presume to master the Latin language, in spite of the fact that Cicero claims that Cato–from Utica, I think–learned Greek letters when he was eighty; but Cato was unique and singular among those of the human race in this and many other things. And since we cannot have what we want, let us want what we can have. And if we lack the forms, let us be content with the substance).

Santillana refers to an important element in translations: the superficiality of the readers' knowledge of Latin, and even of the translators'. Obscure translations that attempted to preserve the Latin "forms" required an additional explanation for most readers, as several testimonies indicate. An example is Fernán Pérez de Guzmán's letter to Gonzalo de Ocaña:

Es así que yo leí algunas veces aquel libro que compuso el sanctísimo papa e glorioso doctor sant Gregorio, que es dicho Diálogos, el cual como es en latín e yo, por alguna escuridad de vocablos y alteza de estilo que en él es, no le podía así claramente entender para que dél cogiese el fruto que deseo

(The fact is that several times I read over the book called the *Dialogues* written by the very holy Pope and glorious doctor Saint Gregory, and because it is written in Latin and because of its obscure words and high style, I could not understand it clearly so that I could gather all the fruit that I want from it).

Pero Guillén de Segovia indicates with respect to the *Gaya Ciencia:* "La pusieron en el latyn y en estilo tanto elevado que pocos de los lectores pueden sacar verdaderas sentencias de sus dychos" (It was written in Latin and in a style so elevated that few readers can extract reliable truths from its sayings).

To present a difficult text to readers was common among Latinists, who believed in the value of hard work. López de Ayala, in his introduction to *Flores de los Morales de Job* (circa 1390), calls Latinists "wise men":

dificultaron sus escrituras y las posieron en palabras dificiles y aun obscuras, porque las leyesen los hombres muchas veces y mejor las retoviesen y mas las preciasen, quanto en ellas mas trabajo tomasen; ca lo que con mayor trabajo se gana, con mayor prescio se guarda

(They made their writings difficult and they put them in difficult and even obscure words, so that men would read them many times, and be able to retain their readings better, and value them more, the harder they

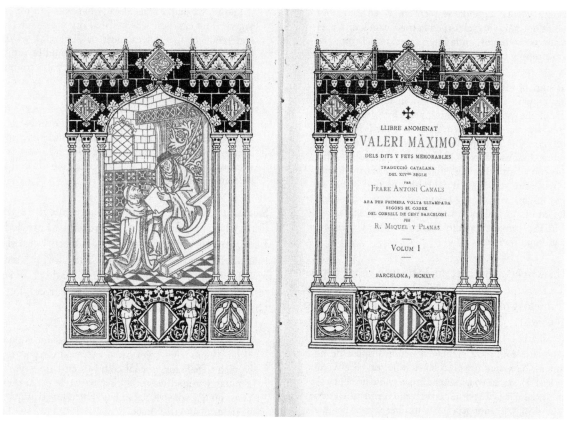

*Frontispiece and title page for the standard modern edition of Antoni Canals's 1395 Catalan translation of the Roman historian Valerius Maximus (University of California at Los Angeles Library)*

worked on them; because what is gained with hard work, is valued more).

López de Ayala, Cartagena, and Palencia are among those who followed in their translations the outlines established by these predecessors, as Santoyo details in his *Teoría y crítica de la traducción: Antología* (1987). Nonetheless, the translator often contradicts the approach he claims to defend in his actual translation practices, so it is not surprising that some translators began to value the vernacular, even to the point of seeing Latin as just another tongue, and so their work took a new turn.

The approach of these translators was based on writings from Cicero and Horace, but especially from Jerome. Margherita Morreale sees Jerome as the patron of this more liberal tendency, since his concept of *sensum exprimere de senso* (to extract sense from sense) lay at the base of their ideas. The real translator, according to Jerome, is capable of rendering the true meaning of the translated text in his own language. With the advance of the sixteenth century, attempts to make translations more accessible to readers reintensified. In this context some of the statements made by Enrique de Villena take on a new meaning. For Villena a translation

should be readily understandable and in the language closest to the reader's that still displays an interest in good style:

Que en la presente traslación tove tal manera que non de palabra ha palabra, ne por la orden de palabras que está en el original latino, mas de palabra a palabra segúnd el entendimiento e por la orden que mejor suena, siquiere paresce, en la vulgar lengua. En tal guisa que alguna cosa non es dexada ho pospuesta, siquiere obmetida, de lo contenido en su original, antes aquí es mejor declarada e será mejor entendido por algunas expresiones que pongo, acullá subintellectas, siquiere impriçitas ho escuro puestas, segúnd claramente verá el que ambas las lenguas latina e vulgar sopiere e viere el original con esta traslaçion comparado.

(For in the present translation I followed the principle of not word-for-word, nor according to the word order of the original Latin text, but word-for-word according to what is the sense and what sounds best, or seems to, in the vulgar tongue. In such manner that nothing of the original content is left out or repositioned or omitted, rather it is here better stated and will be better understood through various expressions I employ, and there again they are assumed, implicit or obscurely

stated, as will be clear to him who knows both languages, Latin and vernacular, and who is able to see
the original compared to this translation.)

Villena attempts to substitute the lack of "sweetness
and grace" of Latin eloquence in his translations with a
discourse that is eloquent in the target language. The
new goal was to reach a reader who might not be familiar with the original text in his own language by adapting to his mentality.

Essential to this movement are the works of
Alfonso de Madrigal, also known as "El Tostado," and
the cultural atmosphere in Salamanca and its university
during the first half of the fifteenth century, which distinguished between *interpretación* (word-by-word translation) and *glosa* (allowing changes, additions, and
suppressions), as Madrigal explained in his *Comento o
exposición de Eusebio* (1450–1451):

La primera es de mas autoridad. La segunda es mas
clara para los menores ingenios. En la primera non se
añade et, por ende, siempre es de aquel que la primero
fabrico. En la segunda se fazen muchas adiciones e
mudamientos, por lo qual non es obra del autor mas
del glosador.

(The first one has more authority. The second is
clearer for lesser minds. In the first one nothing is
added and thus it always pertains to the one who first
composed it. In the second many additions and
changes are made, and is therefore not so much the
author's work as the glossator's.)

This distinction is little more than a gesture of respect
toward the Latinists' theories of fidelity, however.
Unlike Cartagena's, Madrigal's aim was a *hermosa* (beautiful) translation in the target language, meaning that he
adapted his work to the target language and culture. In
addition to knowing well the work to be translated and
its author, translators should also show their mastery of
the subject matter being dealt with and of the cultural
worlds to which both the old and the new work would
belong, the "lineage of knowledge" in Madrigal's terms.
For him the new product, the translation, lives in a separate world from the source. The translation should be
adapted to a new code of language that is different from
the original. For this reason it is necessary to introduce
changes through amplifications and explanations, as an
integral part of the translation.

Jerome's ideas as recast by Villena and Madrigal
came to be accepted by more translators in Castile and,
as the fifteenth century advanced, even by those who
prized the merits of Latin. Carlos of Aragon, Prince of
Viana, for example, mentions Jerome to defend his
translation of Aristotle's *Ethics,* which was based not on
the original but on Bruni's Latin version, as Peter Rus-

sell indicates in his *Traducciones y traductores en la Península
Ibérica, 1400–1550* (1985). The acceptance of Jerome's
ideas can be traced through the study of how glosses
and amplifications were used by translators. These
additions tended to be transformed from long explanations formatted separately to becoming incorporated in
the running text.

In Villena's version of the *Aeneid, Eneida* (circa
1427), for example, he uses a separate gloss to clarify
his translation:

*E si requieres los fados, etc.* Queriendo dezir: "Si tú, reina,
dexado de preguntar las otras seguidas cosas e quieres
saber prinçipalmente lo que a Príamo acaesçió en el
extremo de su desventura e cómo se ovo en aquel paso
en do cumplía mostrar la mayor virtud." Esto dizía
Eneas dignamente, presumiendo que la entendida reina
más quería saber este acto de Príamo que todas las
otras cosas ende contesçidas. E aquella palabra *fados* se
entiende por los acarreos que su costillaçión le troxo a
tal salida e fin. E como aquel que bien a ello paró
mientes, dize que le çertifica, ansí como çierto d'ello por
occulada fe, el dicho Príamo, visto aquel decaimiento,
vencida e tomada Troya de los enemigos e derribados
sus hedificios solempnes e su alcáçar apoderado de los
enemigos irrecuperablemente, como quien ya non espe-
rava sinon captividat ho muerte, quiso mostrar su virtud, non obstándole la vejez e debilitaçión de fuerças;
que ya pasava de ochenta e nueve años, segúnd collegir
se puede de los istoriales que d'él fablan.

(*And if you inquire about Priam's fate, etc.* Meaning: "If you,
Queen, after asking the other things that followed,
want to know mainly what happened to Priam at the
nadir of his misfortune, how he behaved in that predicament when it behooved him to show his greatest courage." Aeneas said this with dignity, assuming that the
well-informed queen preferred to know this final act of
Priam over all the other things that happened later.
And that word *fate* is understood as the events brought
to him by his stars for that end and outcome. And as
one who really thought about it, he says that he bears
witness, and is also certain about it as an eyewitness to
the aforementioned Priam, having seen his enfeeble-
ment, Troy conquered and seized by its enemies, its
monumental buildings and its stronghold captured irrevocably by enemies, as one who did not expect anything else but captivity or death, resolved to show his
courage, despite his old age and weakness; for he was
more than eighty-nine years old, as we can infer from
the histories that mention him.)

Villena's explanations are part of his translation. He
uses the commentary to clarify not only cultural aspects
but also translation difficulties. Lengthy explanations
are necessary to complement a more literal rendering of
the text. The work may be compared to the anonymous
Catalan translation of Petrarch's *Trionfi,* in which the
Italian verses are maintained in that language while the

*Page from MS. L.II.18 at San Lorenzo de El Escorial Monasterio of Andreu Febrer's 1429 Catalan translation of Dante's* Divina Commedia *(from Joan Ruiz I Calonja,* Historia de la Literatura Catalana, *1954; Thomas Cooper Library, University of South Carolina)*

text of the commentary is a translation of Illicino's. Both parts, text and commentary, are completely separate from each other. Villena, on the other hand, conceives of both as a unit, one complementing the other.

As Latin lost its aura of superiority, the purpose of additions was meant less to convey the superior values of Latin and more to correct the obscurity of literalist translations. The call for explanations could then become an argument in favor of clearer translations. As the fifteenth century advanced, glosses acquired an explanatory function, while amplifications were seen as explanatory and embellishing. For example, the Castilian translation of Boccaccio's *Decameron* at the end of the fifteenth century adds a Castilian song and several episodes, while Italian songs are eliminated. Amplifications are also so frequent that modern editors of this translation have "corrected" the text with the help of the original.

Francisco de Madrid, in his *De los remedios contra próspera y adversa fortuna* (1510), provides a clear example of how translators approached their texts with respect to amplifications:

Que no tiene menos necesidad de templança el prospero que de paciencia el abatido y en la traslacion del quise me aprovechar de la dotrina del bienaventurado Doctor San Hieronimo: trasladando en algunas partes que lo requerian mas la sentencia que la letra y en otros, por algun rodeo, trayendo la escuridad de su latin a la claridad de nuestro romance, dexando algunas vezes algunos vocablos perdidos que sirven mas a la abundancia de la lengua que a la claridad de la sentencia, y otras añadiendo algo necesario para que las sentencias vayan encadenadas, porque quien quisiese trasladar este libro, (segun su escuridad) letra por letra, como en el latin, ésta seria una cosa tan desabrida y tan escura que ni se podria leer ni, ya que se leyese, se podria entender.

(Because the prosperous do not have less need for temperance than the unfortunate have of patience, in this translation I wanted to take advantage of the doctrine by the blessed doctor Saint Jerome, translating more the sense than the letter in some parts where it was required, and in others, through some circumlocution, bringing the obscurity of its Latin to the clarity of our Romance, leaving out sometimes some isolated words that contribute more to the abundance of the language than to the clarity of the sense, and other times adding something necessary to link the sentences together, for whoever wanted to translate this book [because of its obscurity] letter-by-letter, as it is in Latin, would end up with a thing so tasteless and obscure that no one could read it or, if it were read, could be understood.)

Madrid introduces amplifications, necessary explanations, and many other changes in his poetic translation, and the text itself is a gloss that the translator is free to modify when necessary. The important element is the vernacular, not the Latin. The translator's job is to clarify the obscurities of the original and to look out for the reader, composing a text that is accessible. This change in translators' attitudes is a fundamental aspect of Peninsular humanism.

Like Madrid, Pero Fernández de Villegas clearly states in his 1515 version of Dante's *Inferno* that on some occasions he has included in his verse translation the information that appears in the commentary in the original. He reduces the number of glosses in his translation, denies the value of a word-by-word translation, and claims that translators should pay more attention to sense than to words.

A later illustration of Jerome's acceptance in Castile is seen in the work of the *licenciado* Peña, translator of Petrarch's *De vita solitaria*. In his 1553 edition he maintains, as did Villegas, that the most important element for a translator must be the idea, the true content, of the work and not the mere words. By the time of his writing, however, the idea seemed so well established that he did not need to justify this type of translation, so it is not appropriate to use the same standards to compare Villena's *Divina Commedia* (circa 1427) with Juan Boscán's 1532 translation of *El Cortesano* (The Courtier), as some modern scholars have done.

It is important to distinguish three periods in the history of translation in Castile between the fifteenth century and the end of the first half of the sixteenth, although these divisions cannot be absolute. During the first period, between 1400 and 1492, most translations considered the vernacular as inferior and insufficient. Cartagena, López de Ayala, and Palencia are representative practitioners of this "subservient craft." By 1492, the year of Palencia's death, the tendency to produce translations eloquent in the vernacular language predominated.

*Illustration from the 1513 Valencia edition in the Biblioteca Nacional in Madrid of Isabel de Villena's* Vita Christi, *composed in 1497 (from Joan Ruiz I Calonja,* Historia de la Literatura Catalana, *1954; Thomas Cooper Library, University of South Carolina)*

Translators during the second period, from 1493 to 1526, did not consider the vernacular inferior to Latin anymore. As a consequence, translations show a balance between *ad litteram* and *ad sensum* methods and propose a familiar, flexible text that is not far from the common tongue. Representatives of the period are Álvar Gómez de Ciudad Real, Fernández de Villegas, Antonio de Obregón, and Francisco de Madrid. The 1526 establishes the terminus as the publication date of Alfonso Fernández de Madrid's *El Enquiridión o Manual del caballero cristiano.*

The third period, between 1526 and 1564, belongs completely to the Renaissance, during which the style of the translation is as important as faithfulness to the source. By 1564, in his *Memorial de cosas notables,* the fourth duque del Infantado considers translations executed at the time of his ancestor Santillana to be out of date and completely useless compared to more-contemporary translations. In addition to Fernández de Madrid's aforementioned work, Boscán's *El Cortesano* is representative of this period.

In Aragon there was a different attitude. There the two translation methods that contested their merits in Castile coexisted. The choice between them seems to depend on the translator's taste rather than intellectual norms established by a dominant elite. Only through this process, with respect to the theory and practice of translation, can the changes, embellishments, and suppressions present in so many texts, as in the Catalan *Decameron,* be understood.

References:

R. Flora Amos, *Early Theories of Translation* (New York: Columbia University Press, 1920);

Nuria Belloso Martín, *Política y humanismo en el siglo XV* (Valladolid: Universidad de Valladolid, 1989);

Judith Berg Sobré, "Eiximenis, Isabel de Villena and Some Fifteenth Century Illustrations of Their Works," in *Estudis de Llengua, Literatura i Cultura Catalanes,* edited by Albert Porqueras-Mayo, Spurgeon Baldwin, and Jaume Martí-Olivella, Actes del Primer Colloqui d'Estudis Catalans a Nord-Amèrica (Montserrat: Publicacions de l'Abadia de Montserrat, 1979), pp. 303–313;

Rita Copeland, *Rhetoric, Hermeneutic and Translation in the Middle Ages* (Cambridge: Cambridge University Press, 1991);

José Luis Coy, "La génesis de las 'Flores de los *Morales sobre Job,*' de Pero López de Ayala," *Hispanófila,* 63 (1978): 39–57;

Georges Cuendet, "Cicéron et Saint Jerôme traducteurs," *Revue des Etudes Latines,* 5 (1933): 380–400;

Ottavio Di Camillo, "Humanism in Spain," in *Renaissance Humanism: Foundations, Form and Legacy,* 3 volumes, edited by Albert Rabil (Philadelphia: University of Philadelphia Press, 1988), II: 54–108;

Di Camillo, *El humanismo castellano del siglo XV* (Valencia: Doménech, 1976);

Iaume Ferrer de Blanes, *Sentencias catholicas del divi, poeta Dant florenti compilades per lo prudentissim mossen Iaume Ferrer de Blanes* (Barcelona, 1545);

Gianfranco Folena, "'Volgarizzare' e 'tradurre': idea e terminologia della traduzione del medio evo italiano e romanzo all'umanesimo europeo," in *La traduzione: Saggi e studi,* Centro per lo Studio dell'Insegnamento all'Estero dell'Italiano (Trieste: LINT, 1973), pp. 59–120;

Michel Garcia, "Las traducciones del canciller Ayala," in *Medieval and Renaissance Studies in Honour of Robert Brian Tate,* edited by Ian Michael and Richard Andrew Cardwell (Oxford: Dolphin, 1986), pp. 13–25;

Valentín García Yebra, "¿Cicerón y Horacio preceptistas de la traducción?" *Cuadernos de Filología Clásica,* 16 (1979–1980): 139–154;

García Yebra, *Teoría y práctica de la traducción* (Madrid: Gredos, 1982);

García Yebra, "La traducción en la cultura española," in his *En torno a la traducción (teoría, crítica, historia)* (Madrid: Gredos, 1983);

María Isabel Hernández González, *En la teoría y en la práctica de la traducción: La experiencia de los traductores castellanos a la luz de sus textos (Siglos XIV–XVI)* (Salamanca: Seminario de Estudios Medievales y Renacentistas, 1999);

R. G. Keightley, "Alfonso de Madrigal and the *Chronici Canones* of Eusebius," *Journal of Medieval and Renaissance Studies,* 7 (1977): 225–248;

Louis Kelly, *The True Interpreter: A History of Translation Theory and Practice in the West* (Oxford: Blackwell, 1979);

J. M. Lásperas, "La traduction et ses théories en Espagne au XVe et XVIe siècles," *Revue des Littératures Romanes,* 84 (1980): 81–92;

Jeremy Lawrance, "La autoridad de la letra: un aspecto de la lucha entre humanistas y escolásticos en la Castilla del siglo XV," *Atalaya,* 3 (1991): 85–107;

Lawrance, "Humanism in the Iberian Peninsula," in *The Impact of Humanism in Western Europe,* edited by A. E. Goodman and Angus Mackay (London: Longman, 1990), pp. 220–258;

Lawrance, "On Fifteenth-Century Spanish Vernacular Humanism," in *Medieval and Renaissance Studies in Honour of Robert Brian Tate,* pp. 63–70;

Lawrance, "The Spread of Lay Literacy in Late Medieval Castile," *Bulletin of Hispanic Studies,* 62 (1985): 82–90;

María Rosa Lida de Malkiel, *Juan de Mena, poeta del prerrenacimiento español* (Mexico City: Fondo de Cultura Económica, 1950);

Iñigo López de Mendoza, *Prohemios y cartas literarias,* edited by Miguel García-Gómez (Madrid: Editora Nacional, 1984);

J. E. Martínez Fernando, ed., *Estudios sobre Alfonso el Magnánimo con motivo del quinto centenario de su muerte: Curso de conferencias, mayo de 1959* (Barcelona: Universidad de Barcelona, 1960);

Tomás Martínez Romero and Roxana Recio, eds., *Essays on Medieval Translation in the Iberian Peninsula* (Barcelona: Universitat Jaume I / Creighton University, 2001);

Franco Meregalli, "Las relaciones literarias entre Italia y España en el Renacimiento," *Thesaurus,* 17 (1962): 606–624;

Jacques Monfrin, "Humanisme et traductions au Moyen Âge," in *L'Humanisme médiéval dans les littératures romanes du XIIe au XIVe siècle: Colloque organisé par le Centre de Philologie et de Littératures romanes de l'Université de Strasbourg du 29 Janvier au 2 Février 1962,* edited by Anthime Fourrier, Actes et Colloques, no. 3 (Paris: Klincksieck, 1964), pp. 217–246;

María Morrás, "Latinismo y literalidad en el origen del clasicismo vernáculo: las ideas de Alfonso de Cartagena (1384–1456)," in *La traducción en España (ss. XIV–XVI)*, edited by Roxana Recio (León: Universidad de León, 1985), pp. 35–58;

Margherita Morreale, "Apuntes para la historia de la traducción en la Edad Media," *Revista de Literatura*, 15 (1959): 3–10;

Morreale, "*Los doze trabajos de Hércules* de Enrique de Villena," *Revista de Literatura*, 5 (1954): 21–34;

Eric W. Naylor, "Pero López de Ayala: Protohumanist?" in *La traducción en España (ss. XIV–XVI)*, pp. 121–128;

Jaime Nicolopulos, "The Dilemma of the Iberian Proto-Humanist: Hermeneutic Translation as Presage of Necromantic Imitation," in *La traducción en España (ss. XIV–XVI)*, pp. 129–148;

Eugene A. Nida and Charles R. Taber, *The Theory and Practice of Translation* (Leiden: Brill, 1969);

Glynn P. Norton, "Humanist Foundations of Translation Theory (1400–1450): A Study in the Dynamics of the Word," *Canadian Review of Comparative Literature*, 8 (1981): 173–203;

S. Pannunzio, "Sobre la traducció catalana de la *Cárcel de Amor* de Diego de San Pedro," in *Miscellania Pere Bohigas*, 4 volumes, Estudis de Llengua i Literatura Catalanes, no. 4 (Montserrat: Abadia de Montserrat, 1982);

Juan Paredes and Eva Muñoz Raya, eds., *Traducir en la Edad Media: La traducción de la literatura medieval románica* (Granada: Universidad de Granada, 1999);

Roxana Recio, "Alfonso de Madrigal (El Tostado): La traducción como teoría entre lo medieval y lo renacentista," *La corónica*, 19, no. 2 (1992): 112–131;

Recio, "Las canciones intercaladas en la traducción del *Triunfo de Amor* de Petrarca por Alvar Gómez de Ciudad Real," *Hispanic Journal*, 12, no. 2 (1991): 247–265;

Recio, "El concepto de la belleza de Alfonso de Madrigal (El Tostado): La problemática de la traducción literal y libre," in *La traducción en España (ss. XIV–XVI)*, pp. 59–68;

Recio, "El concepto *intérprete tan fiel* de Antonio de Obregón," *Bulletin of Hispanic Studies*, 83 (1996): 225–237;

Recio, "Del latín al vernáculo: La difusión peninsular del *Decamerón*," *Livius*, 9 (1997): 109–119;

Recio, "Humanismo y exégesis medieval: El caso de Ferrer de Blanes," in *Actas del XII Congreso de la Asociación Internacional de Hispanistas: 21–26 de agosto de 1995, Birmingham*, 7 volumes, edited by Aengus M. Ward

(Birmingham: University of Birmingham Press, 1998), I: 293–301;

Recio, "Las interpolaciones latinas en la *Vita Christi* de Sor Isabel de Villena: ¿Traducciones, glosas o amplificaciones?" *Anuario Medieval*, 5 (1993): 126–140;

Recio, "La interrelación intelectual en la Península: Santillana y Ferrer de Blanes," *Anuario Medieval*, 6 (1994): 159–173;

Recio, "La literalidad y el caso de la *Cárcel de Amor*: El quehacer del traductor catalán y del traductor italiano," *Hispanic Journal*, 17, no. 2 (Fall 1996): 271–283;

Recio, *Petrarca y Alvar Gómez: La traducción del Triunfo de Amor* (New York: Peter Lang, 1996);

Recio, "'Por la orden que mejor suena': Traducción y Enrique de Villena," *La corónica*, 24 (Spring 1996): 140–153;

Recio, ed., *La traducción en España (ss. XIV–XVI)* (León: Universidad de León, 1995);

Riquer and Antoni Comas, *Historia de la literatura catalana*, corrected edition, 4 volumes (Barcelona: Ariel, 1980);

Jordi Rubió i Balaguer, *Estudis de literatura catalana* (Barcelona: Publicacions de l'Abadia de Montserrat, 1992);

Rubió i Balaguer, *Humanisme i Renaixement* (Barcelona: Abadia de Montserrat, 1990);

José Francisco Ruiz Casanova, *Aproximación a una historia de la traducción en España* (Madrid: Cátedra, 2000);

Joan Ruiz I Calonja, *Historia de la Literatura Catalana* (Barcelona: Editorial Teide, 1954);

Peter Russell, "Francisco de Madrid y su traducción del *De remediis* de Petrarca," in *Estudios sobre literatura y arte dedicados al profesor Emilio Orozco Díaz*, edited by Antonio Gallego Morell and others (Granada: Universidad de Granada, 1979), pp. 203–220;

Russell, *Traducciones y traductores en la Península Ibérica, 1400–1550* (Barcelona: Universidad Autónoma de Barcelona, 1985);

Julio César Santoyo, "El siglo XIV: traducciones y reflexiones sobre la traducción," in *La traducción en España (ss. XIV–XVI)*, pp. 17–34;

Santoyo, *Teoría y crítica de la traducción: Antología* (Bellaterra: Universitat Autonoma de Barcelona, 1987);

Mario Schiff, *La bibliothèque du Marquis de Santillana*, Bibliothèque de l'Ecole des Hautes Etudes, no. 153 (Paris: Bouillon, 1905);

Julian Weiss, *The Poet's Art: Literary Theory in Castile c. 1400–60*, Medium Aevum Monographs, new series 14 (Oxford: Society for Mediaeval Languages and Literature, 1990);

A. K. Zholkovski, "Sobre la amplificación," in *Teoría y práctica del estructuralismo soviético* (Madrid: Corazón, 1972), pp. 173–182.

# Checklist of Further Readings

Alborg, Juan Luis. *Historia de la literatura española,* 5 volumes. Madrid: Editorial Gredos, 1966.

Allen, Don Cameron. *Mysteriously Meant: The Rediscovery of Pagan Symbolism and Allegorical Interpretation in the Renaissance.* Baltimore: Johns Hopkins University Press, 1970.

Alonso, Dámaso. *De los siglos oscuros al de oro.* Madrid: Editorial Gredos, 1958.

Alvar, Carlos, and Angel Gómez Moreno. *La poesía lírica medieval.* Madrid: Taurus, 1987.

Alvar, Gómez Moreno, and Fernando Gómez Redondo. *La prosa y el teatro en la Edad Media.* Madrid: Taurus, 1991.

Alvar and José Manuel Lucía Megías, eds. *Diccionario filológico de literatura medieval española: Textos y transmission.* Madrid: Editorial Castalia, 2002.

Auerbach, Erich. *Literary Language and Its Public in Late Latin Antiquity and the Middle Ages,* translated by Ralph Manheim, foreword by J. M. Ziolokowski, Bollingen Series, no. 74. Princeton: Princeton University Press, 1993.

Beltrán Pepió, Vicente. *La canción de amor en el otoño de la Edad Media,* Colección Estudios Literarios, no. 1. Barcelona: PPU, 1988.

Blackmore, Josiah, and Gregory S. Hutcheson, eds. *Queer Iberia: Sexualities, Cultures, and Crossings from the Middle Ages to the Renaissance.* Durham, N.C. & London: Duke University Press, 1999.

Blanco Aguinaga, Carlos, Julio Rodríguez Puértolas, and Iris M. Zavala. *Historia social de la literatura española (en lengua castellana),* 3 volumes. Madrid: Editorial Castalia, 1978–1979.

Breisach, Ernst. *Historiography: Ancient, Medieval, and Modern.* Chicago: University of Chicago Press, 1983.

Bruyne, Edgar de. *The Esthetics of the Middle Ages,* translated by Eileen Hennesey. New York: Ungar, 1969.

Castro, Américo. *La realidad histórica de España.* Madrid: Editorial Porrúa, 1954.

Cátedra, Pedro M. *Amor y pedagogía en la Edad Media (Estudios de doctrina amorosa y práctica literaria),* Acta Salmanticensia, Estudios Filológicos, no. 212. Salamanca: Universidad de Salamanca, 1989.

Chejne, Anwar G. *Islam and the West: The Moriscos, a Cultural and Social History.* Albany: State University of New York Press, 1983.

Curtius, Ernst. *European Literature and the Latin Middle Ages,* translated by Willard R. Trask. New York: Pantheon, 1953.

Deyermond, Alan D. *A Literary History of Spain: The Middle Ages.* London: Benn / New York: Barnes & Noble, 1971.

Deyermond. *La literatura perdida de la Edad Media castellana: Catálogo y estudio,* 1 volume published. Salamanca: Universidad de Salamanca, 1995– .

Deyermond. *Tradiciones y puntos de vista en la ficción sentimental.* Mexico City: Universidad Nacional Autónoma de México, 1993.

Deyermond, ed. *Historical Literature in Medieval Iberia.* London: Department of Hispanic Studies, Queen Mary and Westfield College, 1996.

Deyermond and Ian Macpherson, eds. *The Age of the Catholic Monarchs, 1474–1516: Literary Studies in Memory of Keith Whinnom.* Liverpool: Liverpool University Press, 1989.

Di Camillo, Ottavio. *El humanismo castellano del siglo XV,* translated by Manuel Lloris. Valencia: Fernando Torres, 1976.

Díaz-Plaja, Guillermo. *A History of Spanish Literature,* translated and edited by Hugh A. Harter. New York: New York University Press, 1971.

Díez Echarri, Emiliano, and José María Roca Franquesa. *Historia de la literatura española e hispanoamericana.* Madrid: Aguilar, 1966.

Dutton, Brian, and Jineen Krogstad, eds. *El cancionero del siglo XV, c. 1360–1520,* 7 volumes, Biblioteca Española del Siglo XV, Serie Maior, nos. 1–7. Salamanca: Universidad de Salamanca, 1990–1991.

Fletcher, Angus. *Allegory: The Theory of a Symbolic Mode.* Ithaca, N.Y.: Cornell University Press, 1964.

García de la Concha, Victor, ed. *Nebrija y la introducción del Renacimiento en España: Actas de la III Academia Literaria Renacentista.* Salamanca: Academia Literaria Renacentista, Universidad de Salamanca, 1983.

García Guinea, Miguel Ángel, ed. *Viajes y viajeros en la España medieval: Actas del V Curso de Cultura Medieval, celebrado en Aguilar de Campóo (Palencia) del 20 al 23 de Septiembre de 1993.* Aguilar de Campóo & Madrid: Fundación Sta. María La Real, Centro de Estudios del Románico, 1997.

Gerli, E. Michael, ed. *Medieval Iberia: An Encyclopedia.* New York: Routledge, 2003.

Gerli and Joseph J. Gwara, eds. *Studies on the Spanish Sentimental Romance (1440–1550): Redefining a Genre.* London: Tamesis, 1997.

Gerli and Julian Weiss, eds. *Poetry at Court in Trastamaran Spain: From the* Cancionero de Baena *to the* Cancionero general, Medieval and Renaissance Texts and Studies, volume 181. Tempe, Ariz.: Medieval and Renaissance Texts and Studies, 1998.

Gil-Albarellos, Susana. Amadís de Gaula *y el género caballeresco en España.* Valladolid: Universidad de Valladolid, 1999.

Gimeno Casalduero, Joaquín. *La creación literaria de la Edad Media y del Renacimiento: Su forma y su significado.* Madrid: Porrúa Turanzas, 1975.

Gimeno Casalduero. *Estructura y diseño en la literatura castellana medieval.* Madrid: Porrúa Turanzas, 1975.

Gómez Redondo, Fernando. *Historia de la prosa medieval castellana,* 3 volumes. Madrid: Cátedra, 1998–2002.

González López, Emilio. *Historia de la literatura española: Edad Media y Siglo de Oro.* New York: Las Americas, 1962.

Green, Otis H. *Spain and the Western Tradition: The Castilian Mind in Literature from* El Cid *to Calderón,* 4 volumes. Madison: University of Wisconsin Press, 1963–1966.

Hardison, O. B. *Christian Rite and Christian Drama in the Middle Ages: Essays in the Origins and Early History of Modern Drama.* Baltimore: Johns Hopkins University Press, 1965.

Huizinga, Johan. *The Waning of the Middle Ages,* translated by Rodney J. Payton and Ulrich Mammitzsch. Chicago: University of Chicago Press, 1996.

Jayyusi, Salma Khadra, ed. *The Legacy of Muslim Spain,* 2 volumes. Leiden & New York: Brill, 1992.

Kamen, Henry Arthur Francis. *The Spanish Inquisition: A Historical Revision.* New Haven: Yale University Press, 1998.

Keen, Maurice. *Chivalry.* New Haven: Yale University Press, 1984.

Kristeller, Paul. *Renaissance Thought and Its Sources.* New York: Columbia University Press, 1979.

Lapesa, Rafael. *De la Edad Media a nuestros días: Estudios de historia literaria.* Madrid: Editorial Gredos, 1967.

Le Gentil, Pierre. *La poésie lyrique espagnole et portugaise á la fin du Moyen Age,* 2 volumes. Rennes: Plihon, 1949, 1953.

Lewis, C. S. *The Allegory of Love: A Study in Medieval Tradition,* corrected edition. London: Oxford University Press, 1953.

Lewis. *The Discarded Image.* Cambridge: Cambridge University Press, 1965.

Lida de Malkiel, María Rosa. *La idea de la fama en la Edad Media castellana.* Mexico City: Fondo de Cultura Económica, 1952.

López Morales, Humberto. *Historia de la literatura medieval española,* 1 volume published. Madrid: Hispanova, 1974– .

Menocal, María Rosa, Raymond P. Scheindlin, and Michael Sells, eds. *The Literature of Al-Andalus.* Cambridge: Cambridge University Press, 2000.

Mettmann, Walter. *La Littérature dans la Péninsule Ibérique aux XIVe et XVe siècles.* Heidelberg: Winter, 1985.

Meyerson, Mark D., and Edward D. English, eds. *Christians, Muslims, and Jews in Medieval and Early Modern Spain: Interaction and Cultural Change.* Notre Dame, Ind.: University of Notre Dame Press, 1999.

Murphy, James J. *Rhetoric in the Middle Ages: A History of Rhetorical Theory from St. Augustine to the Renaissance.* Berkeley: University of California Press, 1974.

Nader, Helen. *The Mendoza Family in the Spanish Renaissance, 1350–1550.* New Brunswick, N.J.: Rutgers University Press, 1979.

Netanyahu, B. *The Origins of the Inquisition in Fifteenth Century Spain.* New York: Random House, 1995.

Panofsky, Irwin. *Renaissance and Renascences in Western Art.* New York: Harper & Row, 1972.

Pieper, Josef. *Scholasticism: Personalities and Problems of Medieval Philosophy,* translated by Richard and Clara Winston. New York: Pantheon, 1960.

Post, Chandler Rathfon. *Mediaeval Spanish Allegory.* Cambridge, Mass.: Harvard University Press, 1915.

Rico, Francisco. *Historia y crítica de la literatura española: Primer suplemento,* 8 volumes published. Barcelona: Editorial Crítica, 1991– .

Rico, ed. *Historia y crítica de la literatura española,* 9 volumes. Barcelona: Editorial Crítica, 1980–1992.

Río, Angel del. *Historia de la literatura española.* New York: Holt, Rinehart & Winston, 1963.

Rodríguez Velasco, Jesús D. *El debate sobre la caballería en el siglo XV: La tratadística caballeresca castellana en su marco europeo.* Salamanca: Junta de Castilla y León, 1996.

Rohland de Langbehn, Regula. *La unidad genérica de la novela sentimental española de los siglos XV y XVI.* Papers of the Medieval Hispanic Research Seminar, no. 17. London: Department of Hispanic Studies, Queen Mary and Westfield College, 1999.

Rubio Tovar, Joaquín. *La prosa medieval.* Madrid: Playor, 1982.

Russell, Peter E. *Traducciones y traductores en la Península Ibérica (1400–1550).* Bellaterra: Universidad Autónoma de Barcelona, 1985.

Sánchez Albornoz, Claudio. *España: Un enigma histórico.* Madrid: Fundación Universitaria, 1975.

Scholberg, Kenneth R. *Sátira e invectiva en la España medieval.* Madrid: Editorial Gredos, 1971.

Seniff, Dennis P. *Literature and the Law in the Middle Ages: A Bibliography of Scholarship.* New York: Garland, 1984.

Seniff. *Noble Pursuits: Literature and the Hunt. Selected Articles,* edited by Diane M. Wright and Connie L. Scarborough. Newark, Del.: Juan de la Cuesta, 1992.

Solomon, Michael. *The Literature of Misogyny in Medieval Spain: The* Arcipreste de Talavera *and the* Spill, Cambridge Studies in Latin American and Iberian Literature, no. 10. Cambridge: Cambridge University Press, 1997.

Stern, Charlotte. *The Medieval Theater in Castile.* Binghamton, N.Y.: Medieval and Renaissance Texts and Studies, 1996.

Taylor, Barry. "Los libros de viajes de la Edad Media Hispana: bibliografía y recepción," in *Actas: IV Congreso da Asociação Hispânica de Literatura Medieval,* volume 1. Lisbon: Cosmos, 1991, pp. 57–70.

Ward, Philip, ed. *The Oxford Companion to Spanish Literature.* Oxford: Clarendon Press, 1978.

Weiss, Julian. *The Poet's Art: Literary Theory in Castile, c. 1400–60,* Medium Aevum Monographs, new series 14. Oxford: Society for the Study of Mediaeval Languages and Literature, 1990.

Whitbourn, Christine J. *The* Arcipreste de Talavera *and the Literature of Love,* Occasional Papers in Modern Languages, no. 7. Hull, U.K.: University of Hull, 1970.

Wright, John Kirtland. *The Geographical Lore of the Time of the Crusades,* 2 volumes. New York: American Geographical Society, 1925.

Zumthor, Paul. *Essai de poétique médiévale.* Paris: Editions du Seuil, 1972. Translated by Philip Bennett as *Toward a Medieval Poetics.* Minneapolis: University of Minnesota Press, 1992.

Zumthor. *Introduction à la poésie orale.* Paris: Editions du Seuil, 1983. Translated by Kathryn Murphy-Judy as *Oral Poetry: An Introduction,* foreword by Walter J. Ong. Minneapolis: University of Minnesota Press, 1990.

# Contributors

Michael Agnew . . . . . . . . . . . . . . . . . . . . . . . . . . . . . . . . . . . . . . . . . . . . . *Columbia University*

Vincent Barletta. . . . . . . . . . . . . . . . . . . . . . . . . . . . . . . *University of Colorado, Boulder*

Lucia Binotti . . . . . . . . . . . . . . . . . . . . . . . . . . . . *University of North Carolina at Chapel Hill*

Derek C. Carr . . . . . . . . . . . . . . . . . . . . . . . . . . . . . . . . . *University of British Columbia*

Frank A. Domínguez . . . . . . . . . . . . . . . . . . . . . *University of North Carolina at Chapel Hill*

Noel Fallows . . . . . . . . . . . . . . . . . . . . . . . . . . . . . . . . . . . . . . *University of Georgia*

Philip O. Gericke. . . . . . . . . . . . . . . . . . . . . . . . . . . *University of California, Riverside*

Michael Harney. . . . . . . . . . . . . . . . . . . . . . . . . . . . . *University of Texas at Austin*

Gregory B. Kaplan . . . . . . . . . . . . . . . . . . . . . . . . . . . . . . . . *University of Tennessee*

Hilary W. Landwehr. . . . . . . . . . . . . . . . . . . . . . . . . . . *Northern Kentucky University*

Regula Rohland de Langbehn . . . . . . . . . . . . . . . . . . . . . *Universidad de Buenos Aires*

Joseph Abraham Levi . . . . . . . . . . . . . . . . . . . . . . . . . . . . . . . *Rhode Island College*

William Thomas Little . . . . . . . . . . . . . . . . . . . . . *California Polytechnic State University*

Karoline J. Manny. . . . . . . . . . . . . . . . . . . . . . *Seminole Community College at Oviedo*

Nancy F. Marino . . . . . . . . . . . . . . . . . . . . . . . . . . . . . . . . *Michigan State University*

Sol Miguel-Prendes . . . . . . . . . . . . . . . . . . . . . . . . . . . . . . . *Wake Forest University*

Madeleine Pardo . . . . . . . . . . . . . . . . . . . . . . . . . . . . . *University of Paris–Nanterre*

Carmen Parrilla. . . . . . . . . . . . . . . . . . . . . . . . . . . . . . . . *University of La Coruña*

José Perona . . . . . . . . . . . . . . . . . . . . . . . . . . . . . . . . . . . *Universidad de Murcia*

Roxana Recio . . . . . . . . . . . . . . . . . . . . . . . . . . . . . . . . . . . . *Creighton University*

Dayle Seidenspinner-Núñez. . . . . . . . . . . . . . . . . . . . . . . *University of Notre Dame*

Joseph T. Snow . . . . . . . . . . . . . . . . . . . . . . . . . . . . . . . . *Michigan State University*

Lillian von der Walde Moheno . . . . . . . . . . . *Universidad Autónoma Metropolitana–Iztapalapa*

Barbara F. Weissberger . . . . . . . . . . . . . . . . . . . . . . . *University of Minnesota–Twin Cities*

Jane Whetnall . . . . . . . . . . . . . . . . . . . . . . . . . . . . . . *Queen Mary, University of London*

# Cumulative Index

*Dictionary of Literary Biography,* Volumes 1-286
*Dictionary of Literary Biography Yearbook,* 1980-2002
*Dictionary of Literary Biography Documentary Series,* Volumes 1-19
*Concise Dictionary of American Literary Biography,* Volumes 1-7
*Concise Dictionary of British Literary Biography,* Volumes 1-8
*Concise Dictionary of World Literary Biography,* Volumes 1-4

# Cumulative Index

**DLB** before number: *Dictionary of Literary Biography,* Volumes 1-286
**Y** before number: *Dictionary of Literary Biography Yearbook,* 1980-2002
**DS** before number: *Dictionary of Literary Biography Documentary Series,* Volumes 1-19
**CDALB** before number: *Concise Dictionary of American Literary Biography,* Volumes 1-7
**CDBLB** before number: *Concise Dictionary of British Literary Biography,* Volumes 1-8
**CDWLB** before number: *Concise Dictionary of World Literary Biography,* Volumes 1-4

# H

K

Kacew, Romain (see Gary, Romain)

Kafka, Franz 1883-1924 . . . . . DLB-81; CDWLB-2

Kahn, Gus 1886-1941 . . . . . . . . . . . . . . DLB-265

Kahn, Roger 1927- . . . . . . . . . . . . . . .DLB-171

Kaikō Takeshi 1939-1989 . . . . . . . . . . . . DLB-182

Kaiser, Georg 1878-1945 . . . DLB-124; CDWLB-2

*Kaiserchronik* circa 1147 . . . . . . . . . . . . . . DLB-148

Kaleb, Vjekoslav 1905- . . . . . . . . . . . . DLB-181

Kalechofsky, Roberta 1931- . . . . . . . . . . DLB-28

Kaler, James Otis 1848-1912 . . . . . . . . DLB-12, 42

Kalmar, Bert 1884-1947 . . . . . . . . . . . . DLB-265

ISBN 0-7876-6823-0